The Second Handbook of
Organization Development in Schools

The Second Handbook of Organization Development in Schools

PREPARED AT THE
CENTER FOR EDUCATIONAL POLICY
AND MANAGEMENT
UNIVERSITY OF OREGON

By
RICHARD A. SCHMUCK
PHILIP J. RUNKEL
JANE H. ARENDS
RICHARD I. ARENDS

 Mayfield Publishing Company

Most of the work that led to this book was performed under grant or contract with the United States Office of Education and the National Institute of Education, Department of Health, Education, and Welfare. The content does not necessarily reflect the position or policy of those agencies, however, and no official endorsement should be inferred.

Library of Congress Catalog Card Number:
77-089920
International Standard Book Number:
0-87484-392-8

Manufactured in the United States of America
Mayfield Publishing Company
285 Hamilton Avenue
Palo Alto, California 94301

This book was set in IBM Century by Libra Cold Type and was printed and bound by the George Banta Company. Sponsoring editor was J. Boyce Nute, Carole Norton supervised editing, and Barbara Pronin was manuscript editor. Michelle Hogan supervised production, the book was designed by Nancy Sears and the cover drawing was by Ireta Cooper.

Contents

Preface

During the summer of 1967, at the University of Oregon's Center for the Advanced Study of Educational Administration (now the Center for Educational Policy and Management), Philip Runkel and Richard Schmuck initiated a program of research and development entitled Strategies of Organizational Change. Between the summer of 1967 and the spring of 1968 we spent the equivalent of twelve days training the staff of a junior high school to build new organizational norms and procedures for describing its goals on a continuing basis, comparing its reactions with what it would accept as movement toward its goals, generating revised hypotheses about actions that would move the school closer to its goals, making decisions to carry out revised plans, and checking whether movement toward goals improved.

The training began with development of skills in interpersonal communication, moved through strengthening constructive norms in actual work groups, and culminated in establishing new structures for communication among the staff, students, and outside community. This project, which we labeled Organizational Training for a School Faculty, resulted in a first research monograph from our program (Schmuck and Runkel 1970) and won the Douglas McGregor Memorial Award, presented to us by the National Training Laboratories, for the best study in applied behavioral science in 1969.

The success of this project led us to attempt to raise the self-renewing capability of an entire school district. In the fall of 1967 we began negotiating with the various sectors of the district concerned and collecting diagnostic data. Active training of subsystems began in April 1968 and climaxed in the summer of 1969 with the training of a cadre of organizational specialists, recruited from various district jobs, who would eventually comprise a permanent collegial structure through which OD consultation could be offered to peers within the district. The results of this project have been reported by Runkel, Wyant, and Bell (1975).

While the massive amounts of quantitative data collected in that project were being processed, Richard Schmuck and Matthew Miles reviewed the available work on OD consultation for schools and edited a compilation summarizing all the summative evaluations done on the topic to mid-1970 (Schmuck and Miles 1971). At the same time, Philip Runkel and Richard Schmuck mounted a project to test the efficacy of OD for implementing team teaching. In that project, whose field work ran from the summer of 1970 to the spring of 1971, we compared the usefulness of two strategies of consultation for enabling six elementary schools to convert from traditional structure to a multiunit teaming arrangement. Schmuck, Murray, Smith, Schwartz, and M. Runkel (1975) describe what occurred as those six staffs attempted structural change, reporting both detailed case studies and quantitative comparisons of a systematic field experiment.

From 1971 to 1975 we studied the procedures required to establish a cadre of organizational specialists within a school district that had received only a small amount of OD consultation. Organizational specialists—including Jane and Richard Arends—were recruited among teachers, administrators, and supporting staff and were trained to diagnose organizational conditions, plan interventions, and consult with subsystems within their district to promote creative adaptation. The results of that work are reported in chapter 12 of this volume. In 1975 we undertook a collaborative project with the Center for New Schools in Chicago to study organizational problem solving at nine experimental sites and to deliver consultation in organizational problem solving at some additional sites. This Documentation and Technical Assistance Project is still in progress.

Thus our development and dissemination efforts over the past ten years have been aimed simultaneously at establishing networks of OD specialists within school districts and producing aids for consultants in the form of intervention designs, diagnostic and feedback instruments, learning games, skill exercises, group procedures, and an audio-tape slide presentation. These were first described in our *Handbook of Organization Development in Schools* (Schmuck, Runkel, Saturen, Martell, and Derr 1972) and in a booklet entitled *Organization Development: Building Human Systems in Schools* (Arends, Phelps, and Schmuck 1973). This decade of effort at research, development, dissemination, and evaluation reaches its epitome in the present volume, which is a guide to change in education written for those who wish to make schools more joyful places for working and learning.

While we have prepared this book primarily for organizational specialists in school districts, for those learning to become organizational specialists, and for their trainers, we address ourselves as well to school administrators, state, county, and local departments of education, students of educational administration and curricula, school counselors and school psychologists, classroom teachers and department heads, and organizational researchers in universities, research and development centers, and regional educational laboratories. Consultants and personnel psychologists will also find matter of interest here. Indeed, our widest audience comprises members of organizations generally.

Above all, however, we have designed this book as a tool kit for organizational specialists who have been trained to operate as members of a coordinated team and also to help administrators and teachers understand and act upon the organization of their school. For the most part, each chapter and major section has been organized so as to be understood and used independently from the rest of the book. In addition to a table of contents, annotated chapter bibliographies, and diverse readings, we have prepared a detailed index so that the materials will be easily accessible to a wide audience. Throughout the book we have tried to compensate for inevitable redundancy by providing different perspectives on the same phenomena. We have also tried to keep our examples non-sexist.

The second edition of this book is a more mature product than the first edition, offering a more systematic and concisely stated theory, a more completely tested technology, more exercises and procedures, more information about diagnosis and evaluation, and much more conceptualization and techniques for designing. It is intended not so much to streamline our schools as to help establish the organizational climates that nurture personal fulfillment and in that way to create organizational norms and structures through which new dimensions of personal freedom, understanding, responsibility, and social equity can boldly be sought.

This book has been built upon ten years of collaborative effort among more than one hundred people within our program and upon work with ten times that number of participating educators in public schools. In carrying out the work that culminated in this book, we have always valued joining others to create new, more adaptable and humanistic social relationships. Aside from what else work in schools and R & D teams might achieve, it can also gratify fundamental human needs. Our experiences have shown that almost everyone has something valuable to offer almost every work group and that organizations can be arranged to permit most of us to act both productively and humanistically most of the time. We have sought ways to draw out the abilities, knowledge, and other resources of every individual with whom we have worked. We trust that most of those have received many personal benefits in return.

We wish especially to acknowledge the contributions of Steven Saturen, Ronald Martell, and Brooklyn Derr, who were coauthors for

the first handbook, and Mitchell Schwartz and Spencer Wyant who
assisted respectively in the chapters on designing and preparing the
first draft of chapter 4. We are also indebted to those who used portions of either the first or second handbooks as guides to OD interventions in the field and gave us feedback about them: Warren Bell,
Ronald Bigelow, Ann Burr, Dick Diller, Dave Drummond, Robert
Dwight, Don Essig, Wayne Flynn, Richard Francisco, Daniel Lang-
meyer, Gordon Lindbloom, Paul Macbeth, Isabelle Moser, Don
Murray, Jack Nelson, Molly Newcomb, Scott Pengelly, Deborah
Pickens, Roy Poole, Kay Porter, Mary Ann Smith, Nina Steefel, Lem
Stepherson, Robert Talbott, and Errol Young.

To those who have served as coordinators of district cadres we
give special thanks: Charles Blondino, Dolores McGuiness, Monte
Lee, William Starling, and Neil White. We are grateful, too, for the
varieties of assistance received from the following consultants to our
program: David Berlew, Paul Buchanan, Robert Crosby, Robert Daw,
Colin Fox, Fred Fosmire, Rosalie Howard, Dale Lake, Len Lansky,
Fred Lighthall, Matt Miles, Michael Milstein, Donald Murray, Larry
Porter, Irwin Noparstak, Shirley Terreberry, Saul Toobert, John
Wallen, and Mary Jo Woodfin. Two consultants, Ruth Emory and
Rene Pino, were especially helpful in reading and responding to
earlier drafts of this manuscript.

We also wish to acknowledge colleagues from several school districts who have worked closely with us on our projects: Claudia
Thomas, Joe Wiseman, Martha Harris, Marie Fielder, John Favors,
and Levi Poe. Several colleagues in our center, though not members
of our program, have given special encouragement and intellectual
support: Max Abbott, W. W. Charters, Jr., Lloyd DuVall, and John
Packard. Their help spans the period before 1972, during which our
center was known as CASEA, and also the more recent period when
CASEA has been the research and development branch of CEPM. We
are grateful as well to the professional educators in the school districts of Beaverton, Oregon; Kent, Washington; Eugene, Oregon;
Berkeley, California; and Oakland, California, without whose willingness to merge their destinies for a time with ours we could not have
done our work.

We thank our colleagues, Carole Norton and Barbara Pronin of
Mayfield, who worked closely with us during the final stages of getting the manuscript ready for publication. Carole Norton gave us
useful suggestions for the organization of the book, while Barbara
Pronin's assiduous and very wise editing immeasurably improved the
readability of the text. We also thank our typists Patti Christen and
Pat Eysenbach for their care and perseverance. To Dorothy Van
Cleef, our "assistant for everything" during these ten years, who has
relentlessly required accuracy, helped in every emergency, socialized
new members, championed the support staff, acted as special liaison
to the rest of the center and to colleagues elsewhere in the nation,
and aided our efforts at every turn, our very special affection and
thanks.

1

Theory and Technology

WHAT IS ORGANIZATION DEVELOPMENT?

Every two weeks for the past three months Mike has been driving from the College of Education to the central office of a nearby school district where he consults with the district superintendent's cabinet. Before each visit he talks with whoever is convening the upcoming meeting, both to coach the convener in ways to run the meeting and to find out what has happened since his last visit. Sometimes he interviews all members of the cabinet individually on how well they think the group is working and what he can do to be helpful.

Once the meeting begins, Mike observes how cabinet members work together on their agenda and how well they relate as they work. From time to time he comments on such group processes as the distribution of participation, the clarity and ownership of decisions, or the ways in which the group is collecting information to solve its problems. Occasionally he offers a summary of interview data to support his observations or to encourage cabinet members to talk with one another about how the group is working. The members of this cabinet value Mike's input because he is helping them learn effective procedures for conducting their meetings and clarifying their decision-making procedures.

■ ■ ■

Paula chairs the English Department and Don is a counselor at a large urban senior high school. While on sabbaticals last year receiving training in organizational consultation from a nonprofit training organization, they became aware of their mutual frustration with low parent involvement in their school. Working together on this problem, they persuaded their principal to allocate a small amount of in-service money so that other faculty members could join them in planning a parent-involvement strategy, then addressed a faculty meeting to explain what they wanted to accomplish and to recruit volunteers to serve on a task force. During the following month Paula and Don organized and convened a three-day retreat at which task-force members developed a proposal that called for creating a seven-member representative group to be comprised of one administrator, three teachers, and three parents, all to be elected by their respective constituencies. The function of this ad hoc group was to plan and coordinate all activities in the school that already did, or could, involve parents.

The faculty adopted this proposal, and the principal agreed to try out the new organizational structure if Paula and Don would train the group in collaborative problem solving and joint decision making. After elections were held, Paula and Don carried out with the new group a two-hour training session that included practice in the skills of interpersonal communication, systematic problem solving, and the procedures of consensual decision making. Paula, Don, and the members of the group are optimistic that their efforts will open the door to greater parent participation in the school.

■   ■   ■

Pat (an elementary school principal), Lee (a junior high counselor), and Lynn (a senior high biology teacher) are members of the cadre of organizational specialists in their school district. As an ad hoc consulting team, they are working with an elementary school faculty—including the principal, teachers, counselor, reading specialist, three aides, and secretary—that agreed last year to try out team teaching. Pat, Lee, and Lynn volunteered to help faculty members move out of their self-contained classrooms and isolated positions and to facilitate their taking on new role relationships as team leaders and team members.

The specialists attend all team meetings at the school and frequently serve as third-party consultants when interpersonal or inter-team conflicts surface, and there is a lot of conflict this year as faculty members try to articulate their goals and negotiate the sharing of materials, space, and human resources. School meetings allow time for team leaders and team members alike to discuss how supervision of instruction should function in the school. The specialists help to organize these confrontations and role-clarification sessions so that the faculty can productively uncover differences and organize to work collaboratively on important instructional problems. With the help of Pat, Lee, and Lynn, the faculty is now beginning to take an active part in solving organizational problems and in forming its own unique agreements on how the school should be run.

■　　■　　■

Mike, Paula, Don, Pat, Lee, and Lynn know that the well-meaning professionals, service personnel, parents, and students who make up schools often form into ineffective and poorly coordinated groups, much as employees in the bureaucracies of industry and government become separated from one another. They understand, too, that people in schools typically do not make deliberate efforts to examine their communication patterns, their customary ways of working together in meetings, or the ways in which people are linked together to get their daily work done. To legitimize examining such important phenomena, these consultants bring to their clients both a conceptualization of, and a strategy for, organizational change. This is what is meant by organization development, or simply OD.

Organization Development Strategy

It is not formal rules or procedures but rather the quality of the human involvement, commitment, and understanding exercised by professionals, parents, students, and others that make a school effective in meeting the challenges of a pluralistic and changing society. Organization development is at once a conceptual framework and a strategy aimed at helping schools to become self-correcting, self-renewing systems of people who are receptive to evidence that change is required and able to respond with innovative, integrated programs and arrangements.

OD strategy rests on several assumptions, of which perhaps the most basic is that many of the problems confronting changing schools arise from the nature of the group or organization in which the change is occurring. It is the dynamics of the group, not the skills of its individual members, that is both the major source of problems and the primary determiner of the quality of solutions. Although group processes and procedures often obstruct the full use of human potential, they can, if coordinated smoothly, allow the release of latent energy needed for responsiveness and creativity.

Organization development attempts to facilitate that release of energy by helping school people learn productive ways of working on their problems, improving their organizational capabilities, achieving new ways of interacting despite frustration, and becoming confident in their own ability to understand themselves, assess their own circumstances, identify their goals, and perform the functions to which they have committed themselves. The OD consultant does not impose solutions but instead brings to bear his or her knowledge about human interaction and the processes of change for the purposes of helping a group to identify its own circumstances, determine its own goals, and select the innovations its own members wish to implement.

OD strategy assumes further that it is not always either necessary or effective for groups to rely on outside experts or imported innovations. Although initial help toward improving the organization may come at first from an outside consultant, those people most directly concerned with the school may themselves possess much of the knowledge and skill needed to create and implement new programs, especially when the innovation involves reorganizing the structure of the school or changing the ways in which people customarily work together. The long-range goal of OD consultation is to transmit necessary knowledge and skills to the group or organization itself. A group that has internalized such knowledge and skills and that is capable of providing consultation for itself can truly be regarded as self-renewing.

Other Strategies

Most school-improvement strategies aim at increasing flexibility in public education by training individuals to cope in new and better ways and particularly by helping educators to perform more competently as group leaders and team members. To this end, two individual-change strategies have been given great attention—one emphasizing *cognitive change*; the other, *affective change*. Examples of the former are college classes, informational workshops, and in-service training programs; prominent examples of the latter include sensitivity groups, encounter groups, and various personal-growth training sessions. Neither of these strategies, however, has by itself brought about much organizational improvement in schools.

Most cognitive strategies assume that knowledge about the administrative sciences and the social psychology of groups will stimulate changes in the behavior of individuals in groups and that these changes, in turn, will improve the functioning of the staff of which the individuals are members. But increasing individual knowledge does not necessarily lead to behavioral changes. When confronted by discrepancies between their ideal and actual performances, for example, educators, like anyone else, often feel anxious and defensive and cling all the more tenaciously to their old behavior. Further, the fact that individual changes do occur is no guarantee that structural changes in the organization of the school are likely to result. At best, strategies of cognitive change help educators to become more articulate about how they think the school should be run.

Affective-change strategies provide an arena in which participants can explore the effect of their behavior on others, see at firsthand how the group's levels of trust, openness, and cohesiveness develop, and experience the forces affecting the group's commitment to a decision. Members of such self-analytic groups can also experience action, achievement, affiliation, and power strivings firsthand, learn to express and deal with their feelings, try out new behavior, learn to appreciate and accept human differences, and explore their own assumptions and theories about human behavior. Thus sensitivity groups and personal-growth sessions can have gratifying effects, but studies by Campbell and Dunnette (1968), Friedlander (1968), and Lansky et al. (1969) have shown that experience in these groups cannot be relied upon to bring about increased efficiency, effectiveness, or team development in organizations.

Cognitive and affective-change strategies seldom penetrate the complexities of educational organization. The individuals who work together in tutoring pairs, classroom groups, committees, departmental units, cabinets, and boards learn to behave according to the traditional norms, rules, and procedures of those subsystems, which are, in turn, continually being influenced by one another and by the surrounding, encompassing systems of the school district and community. While OD consultation employs some aspects of cognitive and affective-change strategies, it offers at least three other features of critical importance: (1) training in interpersonal skills, (2) consulting with the school's subsystems as intact working groups rather than as individuals, and (3) intervening into the structural and normative features of the school or district organization.

The importance of introducing and practicing interpersonal skills, especially those of communicating and listening, cannot be overstated. Acquiring these skills is the foundation of improving meetings, clarifying supervision, dealing with emotions as problems, giving helpful information about interpersonal relations, and generally extending the amount of shared and accurate information. Educators sometimes assume either that they have already acquired the interpersonal skills needed to carry out their work or that such skills cannot be learned through systematic practice. OD consultation proposes to help educators, as well as parents and students, learn interpersonal skills in the context of the actual work groups with which they are dealing. The core content of this book consists of designs and techniques for combining interpersonal skills to make work groups and the total organization of the school more effective.

The typical OD project teaches, legitimizes, and makes normative a systematic but flexible technique of problem solving in intact groups or subsystems. The process typically begins by clarifying problem areas and desirable group goals, proceeds to analyzing the forces that prevent problems from reaching solution, sets priorities on the restraining forces to be attacked, makes plans for action, and, finally, evaluates the effects of the action taken. When sufficient interpersonal skill has been developed in exchanging information, conceiving problems as gaps between the present situation and an ideal state, and moving beyond good intentions to action, attention is focused on group problem solving of real school issues and on making appropriate changes in the school's organizational structure to assure that continued use is made of interpersonal skills so that the group can continue to grow more effective.

Consultation for organization development differs in several ways from the help offered by traditional management-consulting firms. Traditional consultants generally accept problems as they have been defined by the organization's administrators, gather information to ascertain the severity of the problem and the conditions that might bear upon it, and issue a report describing the steps they advise the client to take to overcome the problem. But a traditional consultant does not necessarily stay with an organization long enough to help it carry the recommendations into practice.

OD consultants, on the other hand, understand that organizational change requires retraining subsystems, not just individuals or the organization's structure. They help their clients explore their problems from the perspectives of all parts of the district, and they include relevant parties from within and outside the district in designing and implementing the change. Through frequent consultative sessions, they help school personnel learn interpersonal skills for carrying out the practices they themselves design. Before they exit, OD consultants also help clients institutionalize a new role or some other organizational structure to ensure an ability to solve new problems as they arise.

OD consultative sessions are also run very differently from sensitivity-group or personal-growth sessions. The targets of an OD effort are the membership as a whole and its subgroups in relation to their interdependent tasks. The goal is not to demand that individuals change their natures or behave differently with persons off the job but to change the functioning of work groups and the ways in which roles are carried out and work is accomplished.

Encounter or personal-growth sessions can loosen up participants, enabling them to join into group exercises with less anxiety, but they do not give intact work groups practice in functioning more skillfully as teams. It is the local, intact, here-and-now staff group that must learn new ways and norms, not individuals. If the school organization is to become more adaptive and the work groups more effective, staff members cannot be exempted from participation on the grounds that they have already "had that" elsewhere. The consultant facing a staff group that is missing one or two members must decide whether to go ahead with the plan as if all members were present and hope that the group can later absorb the remaining members without a consultant's help, or whether to redesign the consultation to bring in the missing staff members immediately. In general, we recommend the latter course. An ordinary college class or workshop with a few members absent is not a worry; a work group in a school that is trying to establish new group norms is often crippled when one or two staff members are missing.

Previous experience in sensitivity training can sometimes hinder effective participation in an OD effort. Many group laboratories that emphasize personal growth do little more than concentrate on freeing individuals from their fear of expressing emotion publicly. People who have had such an experience sometimes interpret serious attention to feelings in the group as a signal for them to enlarge on their own personal attitudes. But mere expression of feeling does not in itself lead to group growth. We encourage a discussion of feelings only when the feelings relate directly to the work of the group so that fellow group members can choose acts that are helpful to the aroused person and the group can proceed to larger problems.

In summary, many attempts at organizational improvement in schools fall short because they do not encompass procedures for changing interpersonal, group, and organizational levels at the same time. Change attempts should consider the cognitive and affective aspects of the individuals involved, the small work group through which individual staff members carry out organizational goals, features of the total school culture that encourage or impede change, and the larger extraorganizational and community environments. Any major effort to ameliorate organization structures, subsystem functioning, and individual satisfaction must include improvement of most of the school's components, all of its system levels, and the relationships of these levels to one another.

Types of Involvement in Change

At this point it is useful to place the theory and technology of organization development in perspective with other types of change that human beings undergo. The following descriptions are adapted from Harrison (1970). Their contrasting cognitive and affective emphases help to clarify the psychology of organization development in schools.

1. *Rational assignment of tasks.* This essentially cognitive strategy redistributes tasks, resources, and power among the jobs in the organization by proclamation and can be done without knowledge of who will occupy the various positions. Most private firms offering traditional consulting services to management employ this technique, which arises from the classic theories of bureaucracy and time-and-motion developed by Max Weber and Frederick W. Taylor.

2. *Direct influence on performance.* This strategy evaluates and directly manipulates the performance of individuals. Specific techniques include appraising employee skills, placing employees in appropriate jobs or transferring them, increasing or decreasing salary or wages, and, in general, using the techniques of management by objectives. The classic theory here is reinforcement psychology, and its main proponent is B. F. Skinner.

3. *Direct influence on the interpersonal interactions through which work is accomplished.* This strategy of interpersonal instrumental rearrangements combines the cognitive and affective emphases and is interested in the organizational member primarily as a doer of work. Specifically, it opens to negotiation those task-oriented acts that individuals direct toward others, such as delegating authority or reserving decision to oneself, communicating or withholding information, collaborating or competing with others on work-related issues. Much of McGregor's (1967) theorizing deals with this level of involvement in change.

4. *Interpersonal emotional rearrangements.* In this more affective type of involvement, in which T-group sensitivity training is a typical technique, the consultant deals with feelings, attitudes, and perceptions and with the quality of human relations. "Interventions

are directed toward helping clients to be more comfortable in being authentically themselves with one another, and the degree of mutual caring and concern is expected to increase," writes Harrison (1970). This type of intervention has been carried out in numerous industrial organizations and has also been used extensively in the school districts in which Carl Rogers has worked.

5. *Therapy.* This strategy focuses on the individual's relations with himself and on increasing the range of experiences he can bring to awareness and cope with. Although religious leaders have historically directed most of their efforts toward this type of change, this is traditionally the realm of psychological therapy whose patron saint is Sigmund Freud.

The authors believe that achieving improved instructional programs in schools requires, above all, changing the interpersonal instrumental relationships among staff members (type 3) and that interventions of other types—such as program-planning-budgeting systems (type 2) and sensitivity grouping (type 4)—will not have sustained payoff with respect to improving the school's culture unless they are accompanied by interventions to rearrange role definitions and work norms. In our view, the best way of helping staff members to learn new role definitions, interpersonal norms, and group skills is to intervene with techniques of type 3 and to branch out to other techniques as the intervention progresses. For their part, OD consultants must be aware of their own values, biases, understandings, and skills and of how these influence their work with clients. Consultant teams likewise must be aware of themselves as formal groups and of how their own interpersonal subsystems and organizational characteristics can make them more or less helpful to their client organizations.

All kinds of people and teams can provide OD consultation. To intervene in a school for the purpose of increasing organizational adaptability requires only two basic resources—information and skill concerning the task itself and special information and skill to facilitate the work of the people who will actually do the task. Managing group processes, in other words, is a job in its own right. We see organization development as a way of helping school organizations and organizational consultants develop greater competence in using group processes to accomplish tasks.

A THEORY FOR ORGANIZATION DEVELOPMENT IN SCHOOLS

In our view, an effective theory for organization development in schools should begin by regarding schools not as clusters of individuals working at separate tasks but as systems of people working interdependently at particular tasks and moving into coordination with other sets of people as they move from task to task. The system nature of a school organization lies in this coordinated interdependence of sets of persons who together carry out particular tasks. We use the term *subsystem* to denote a subgroup carrying forward a unitary task, although, to be sure, a mere collection of persons is not necessarily a functioning subsystem. Often, a new subsystem must be built out of disparate individuals if the work is to be carried out in a new way.

In short, if changes are to be made in a school, those proposing to design the change must understand how and why schools work as they do. OD consultants must be able to discern the presence or absence of existing subsystems. They must try to understand the nature of subsystems, however temporary they may be, because change takes place through them. Because work in a subsystem is carried out by the person-to-person interactions within it and holding it together, these interpersonal processes must be understood as well.

This view has led us to distinguish what happens in schools or districts on three levels: the interpersonal level, the subsystem level, and the level of the organization as a whole. On the first level, individuals interact more or less skillfully with one another. On the second level, work groups or subsystems gather recurrently to perform certain functions more or less effectively and compatibly with other subsystems. On the third level, the organization as a whole maintains routines and structures that support certain interpersonal and subsystem behaviors and restrain others. By emphasizing these three levels, we leave the processes and structures within individuals to the individuals themselves, their ministers, or their psychiatrists. We also avoid giving special attention to the way in which an organization meshes with others in its environment, since the principles of interorganizational arrangements are not substantively different from those of putting subsystems together within an organization; they are only more complex, cumbersome, and time-consuming.

The following pages begin by describing the organization as a whole and the characteristics that constitute organizational adaptability, move to a consideration of interpersonal skill, and conclude with a discussion of subsystem effectiveness. This sequence allows us to describe, first, the ultimate goals of consultation in organization development; second, the minute blocks from which organizational capability is constructed; and, finally, the level at which the consultant's work typically occurs. Our theory amalgamates ideas gleaned from reading about other theories, by studying patterns of data collected in our own projects and reported by others, and by trying repeatedly to express on paper how all these ideas fit together. The references at the back of the book record resources we have used.

Organizational Adaptability

The ultimate goal of OD is organizational adaptability, by which we mean planned and constructive adaptation to change, not merely adjusting or acquiescing to externally imposed change. By *adaptable*, we mean what Gardner (1963) means by *self-renewing*, what Buckley (1967) calls *morphogenetic*, what Williamson (1974) calls *inquiring*, and what Hedberg, Nystrom, and Starbuck (1976) call *self-diagnosing*. To measure an organization's adaptability, we use four criteria: (1) problem solving, (2) maintaining access to resources, (3) responsiveness, and (4) assessing movement.

An adaptable organization is continually and consciously solving problems that arise either because groups in the organization's environment are pressing for change or because new goals are being established within the organization itself. Problem solving means reaching out for, remaining open to, and filtering information from both the environment and the organization, examining this information over a period of time, becoming aware of changes that occur, and attempting to predict changes to come. It also means employing systematic procedures to create solutions, changing a normal mode of operation to free resources for new or anticipated problems, and continually rechecking to see whether movement toward goals improves.

Becoming aware of environmental problems is of great importance because school environments in contemporary society are incredibly complex and undergoing rapid change all the time. The school that was equipped to serve white, middle-class, college-bound students five years ago, for example, may now find itself with a large proportion of students having very different needs and values. Again, schools with teachers and curriculum materials well suited to teaching computational skills may find the world of computer technology placing a whole new set of demands on them.

Hence, consciousness, anticipation, and persistence characterize the kind of problem solving that leads to organizational adaptability. It is not enough for a teaching staff to meet once a year to decide how to move in new directions or to try to solve problems only when they have reached crisis dimensions. People in adaptable organizations meet regularly to solve problems, maintain access to resources, improve responsiveness, and assess movement toward goals.

Schools as systems are adaptable, too, only if they recognize the existence of internal and external resource pools that can be tapped to aid in solving problems, responding with action, and assessing progress toward goals. Buckley (1967) called this repertoire of usable resources the *variety pool*—a term that refers not only to individual skills and interests but also to the expectations, policies, and procedures that exist in the school. Although most schools possess a rich variety of potential resources, the adaptable school makes use of all that it has and establishes ways of continually uncovering new ones.

In a period marked by taxpayers' revolts and decreased federal funding, using all available resources is of vital importance. One way in which adaptable schools can meet this challenge is by dealing actively and purposefully with conflict. That is, more resources will be available if there is routine questioning of established patterns and support for creative risk taking, if it is expected that people will inevitably disagree from time to time, and if communication does not shut down whenever disagreements are expressed.

Adaptive schools are also alert to usable resources outside the organization. Willingly looking to others for ideas and linking up with people or groups that face similar problems are meaningful ways of acquiring new resources that can be adapted to fit the unique circumstances of the school organization.

An organization that maintains access to resources cannot, in the long run, employ any single organizational structure or procedure exclusively. Form must follow function. As people organize into groups to solve specific problems, both the structure of the organization and the methods used by the groups will change to suit the nature of the problem. A group with the goal of modifying curriculum, for example, might be highly structured, with a designated leader, a strict agenda, and a well-defined method of voting to reach decisions. A long-range planning department, on the other hand, might be quite loosely organized to allow time for planning, for experts to pool their points of view, and for final decisions to be made by involved community groups, parents, and students.

The adaptable organization is not characterized by incessant talk and chronic inaction but is proactive, able to move, and able to muster action in response to new inputs. Many organizations—libraries, for example—are skillful at taking in and storing information but ineffective in using what they have taken in. School organizations exhibit low responsiveness when brochures describing in-service workshops for teachers, which no one attends, are buried on bulletin boards or on staff-room coffee tables; when students drop out for want of vocational experience while the district neither initiates new programs nor permits students to receive credit for working or attending courses in other institutions; and when questions from parents go unanswered. Other examples include charges by militant minority groups that education in urban schools is irrelevant to their wants and needs, the polarization of career education and liberal education, and strife over the proper priorities of reading skill and self-actualization.

Low responsiveness is often a result of poor coordination of effort. A system can respond quickly and effectively only if its subsystems can respond in coordinated and self-correcting ways. Thus a school in which people are skilled only in competition, have low skill in collaboration, and frequently work at cross-purposes without awareness that they are doing so is not a school that is likely to act responsively.

Low responsiveness can also be a result of misdirected decision making. Above all, effective decision making requires the presence of adequate, accurate information on the part of those making decisions, while, all too often, those in positions of legitimate authority either lack such information or have it in distorted form. The responsive school seeks not mere authority but rather the best possible decision. Hence in an adaptable district, a group of students and parents might decide on dress codes; teachers and students might decide on classroom procedures; while some teachers, the principal, and the superintendent might decide whether to involve principals in in-service leadership training. Since decisions are required from work groups at all levels in the adaptive school district, the intent of organization development is not to restrict consultation in problem solving to certain parts of the district but to prepare groups at all levels to exercise this function.

Finally, schools as systems are essentially goal-directed organizations whose various statements of purpose, of objectives to be met, and of outcomes expected tend to depict a condition that is regarded as a desirable replacement for the current condition. An organization's ability to assess progress toward goals, however, is inseparable from its ability to state and agree on goals. It is not uncommon among schools to find goals stated so ambiguously that no one, using any method, can tell whether the school is headed in the right direction or not.

How many schools, for example, have advertised an aim to "prepare young people for productive adulthood in a complex, industrialized society"? In addition to lacking any behavioral definition, this and other widely published goals have long time-frames and lack precise definitions of intermediate enabling goals. Some would attribute this kind of vagueness to mindlessness; others recognize one cause to be defensiveness—that is, if you do not tell people where you are headed, they cannot judge you incompetent if you do not get there.

Adaptable organizations determine whether they are moving toward their goals by keeping track of what is happening over long periods of time, by assessing different impacts and effects (whether intended or not), and by calculating costs and benefits with energy and precision. Although organizations with complicated or long-term projects may choose to hire assessment experts to do sophisticated data collection and interpretation, in the adaptable organization everyone is aware of the need for continual reflection and analysis and willingly allows resources to be allocated for this purpose.

Interpersonal Skill

Consultation for organization development rests on an assumption that school organizations can become more adaptable and self-renewing than they are and that one key to their becoming more adaptable lies in the improvement of interpersonal skills. Indeed, understanding the interpersonal dynamics of a task-oriented body facilitates an understanding of how organization development occurs. To this end, the following section describes four important domains of human motivation and shows how an organization can provide people with the energy to move in satisfying directions of behavior. We then discuss three interpersonal skills—exchanging information, conceiving problems, and responding—that are primary to the effective functioning of systems and that may lead in turn to the further development of the organization.

In choosing ways to design and improve school organizations, the satisfaction of human needs cannot be disregarded. Most of us would agree that a strong, resilient school that is able to meet internal and external challenges with competence and vigor will be populated by staff and students who come to school in the morning eager and confident and who go home after school feeling good about the day—in short, by people who are satisfied with their lives as parts of the school.

Available evidence (see Argyris 1973) suggests that work can be satisfying even if it frequently is not; that many people continue to perceive greater opportunities for personal satisfaction in their work than they do elsewhere; and that when work is dull and passive, people usually do not choose leisure pursuits that answer needs for variety and vigorous activity but turn instead to activities that are as undernourishing as is their work. To ignore the satisfaction of human needs in the work place is inevitably to bring about two undesirable results: students and staff will in one way or another increasingly remove themselves from serious work, and they will drag through each additional unrewarding day with growing discouragement. Whether member satisfaction can be used as a measure of an organization's health and adaptability or whether it is simply a worthwhile end in itself, there is unquestionably a link between satisfaction with organizational life and the fulfillment of human needs.

A substantial body of research* has shown that people tend to invest emotion in at least four domains of personal motivation: activity, achievement, affiliation, and power. That is, individuals act so as to maximize their chances of taking initiative, being successful, experiencing friendship, and exercising influence over their own fate. They choose between behavior that requires more or less expenditure of energy, that produces greater or lesser achievements, that is helpful and expressive of love or obstructive and expressive of hatred, and that either yields mastery of their environment or requires acquiescence to the will of others. In addition, Maslow (1954) and Alderfer (1969) have postulated that human needs are hierarchical in character. In Maslow's view, people will not be aware of needing to belong, of gaining the respect of others, or of "actualizing" themselves until their own physiological and safety needs are met. In Alderfer's hierarchy, too, the needs of relatedness and growth do not become important until existence needs are met.

We believe that people are more likely to remain motivated, have available more paths to further satisfaction, and are likely to become more productive if their motives can be expressed and satisfied in their work. Although we have little direct documentary evidence from schools to support this proposition, studies of other kinds of organizations yield evidence that this is true.† Findings indicate that organizational structures that require a formalization of rules, feature strong specialization of tasks, and are run by an authoritarian style of management reduce opportunities for feelings of

---

*We draw especially on the work of McClelland (1958); Osgood and Suci (1955); and Berlew (1974).

†See Argyris (1973) for a review of thirty-eight studies published between 1963 and 1972.

individual competence, feelings of companionship among employees, and for a feeling of power over one's own fate. According to Argyris, the human cost of this condition is to be found in increased absenteeism, noninvolvement, aggression (including outright sabotage), and in demands for extrinsic rewards. Since many of these organizational conditions are becoming common in schools today, we should not be surprised by their corroborating reactions.

On the other hand, people who experience inertia, failure, alienation, and powerlessness in their work can learn to satisfy their needs in the company of others in their work group. They can learn to achieve great successes by trying first to achieve small successes, thereby finding rewards that encourage greater risk taking. They can learn to reciprocate affection from colleagues if their colleagues learn to expect such reciprocity and make their expectations known. They can learn to influence others as others are around to influence.

In brief, people who find satisfaction in their work do less hanging back, stalling, backbiting, and sabotage than do those who find little satisfaction in their work, and organizational resources that aid people in finding these satisfactions are wisely spent insofar as they buy productive energy that might otherwise be lacking. The ways in which tasks are approached and accomplished in groups can provide opportunities for personal satisfaction, just as the ways in which tasks are divided and coordinated within the organization can give subsystems opportunities to be effective.

There can be little question that support from the subsystem and from the organization as a whole will be reciprocated by greater productivity from individuals. By making opportunities for people to learn skills, paying them for the time they spend doing so, rewarding them for learning, and legitimizing those who can teach them the interpersonal skills they need, the school can set in motion the cycle through which interpersonal growth induces organizational growth. Once participants experience higher-level satisfactions, they will have more energy available to act in productively interdependent ways.

Three interpersonal skills—processing information, conceiving problems, and responding—are indispensable to the effective functioning of subsystems that leads to organizational growth. Processing information means that individuals must be able both to elicit and to share relevant information if subsystems are to have information that clarifies problem identification. Individuals in groups also need skill in locating and acknowledging the problems in their environment. Having located the problems, they must have the ability to respond with productive action.

Processing information—that is, sharing relevant information about oneself and eliciting relevant information from others—is one of the primary interpersonal skills by which organizational subsystems can create the common reality that is prerequisite to common action. But people do not always exchange relevant information, and individual opinions of what is relevant to a work context can be highly restrictive. Especially when emotions are high, as they often are when anxiety and disagreement surface, people tend to close off channels of communication that are ordinarily open when things are going smoothly. In addition, those who withhold information about their skills, ideas, preferences, acquaintances, and other personal resources may be depriving others of useful information and the subsystem of potential ways of solving problems. Communication about relevant restraints and resources is an important interpersonal skill that can and should be learned.

Locating problems in the environment entails searching for available information about what is known of the present situation and what goals are valued or preferred. Specifically, it requires locating a discrepancy between present aspects of a situation and an ideal state and then calling the gap between the two conditions a problem. Conceiving problems, acknowledging them, and accepting them as challenges requires time, energy, creativity, and discipline. Above all, it requires interpersonal skill in taking risks and encouraging others to take risks in the hope of uncovering problems heretofore unknown or ignored. While there is no best way for all people at all times to think of the steps, phases, and skills involved in conceiving problems, we believe that people benefit from being conscious of the method they are using.

Finally, some individuals and groups are notoriously all talk and no action. Good intentions are not enough; individuals must be able to act on their intentions and at the same time be aware of the effect of their actions on others. Most people can become more skillful at stating their commitments, carrying them through, and being aware that they are doing so. Insofar as the responsive actions of people are important bits of observable information that can be discussed objectively and then analyzed to conceive new problems, responding and acting are keys to the skills of information exchange and problem processing.

Subsystem Effectiveness

Schools are constituted of subsystems that perform various functions, from designing curricula to ordering supplies, and each subsystem includes certain people, supplies, space, and information. Subsystems are bounded by the informally understood limits of responsibility for making decisions about a particular set of tasks, by the invisible lines that define who is in or out, or at the point where someone is or is not accountable for doing the job.

Some subsystems have vague, easily penetrable boundaries. The subsystem of a school district that serves the function of socializing new teachers, for example, does not have a designated space in which to carry out this task, a budget, or a stable roster of members. Others have more definite boundaries, which make them easier to locate. For example, the group responsible for teaching students in one school is different from the group responsible for teaching children in another school. In some cases, legal arrangements, such as contracts and credentials, prevent outsiders from being part of a subsystem. Locating subsystems is a very important part of OD consultation.

Unless consultants can identify the group of people who must act interdependently in order to carry out their jobs, they cannot intervene to assure that the group's total output is greater than the sum of its individual contributions.

Because the functions of school organizations are carried out by the coordinated efforts of persons in subsystems, understanding what makes subsystems effective is crucial to understanding what makes organizations adaptable. Indeed, improving subsystem effectiveness, coupled with efforts to improve interpersonal skill, constitutes the core of our strategy of organization development.

Differentiation and Integration. Compared with organizations like the military, for instance, a school contains a relatively small number of positions; numerous functions are discharged within one position; and each function is shared by a comparatively large number of people. In the military, policing is done by MPs, teaching by the training officer, and requisitioning by the first sergeant. In schools, all teachers, administrators, counselors, and secretaries have responsibility to see that children learn, that safety rules are obeyed, and that equipment and supplies are ordered. Since the same persons may participate in many subsystems, the subsystems tend to be relatively undifferentiated functionally.

More rigid differentiations are also to be found in schools, however. High schools are typically organized into departments along subject-matter lines, while grade schools are frequently organized to serve children according to their age. One can also find relatively strict functional differentiation where administrative subsystems interact with the board of education more often than teaching teams do, or where teachers and counselors deal more directly with students than does the superintendent's cabinet.

Schools typically establish a functional division of labor among their more formal subsystems in the hope of increasing their adaptability to various segments of the environment. But pressures from the environment call for both integration and differentiation among school subsystems, because without combined, coordinated, collaborative action, the synergy that epitomizes adaptability will not be released. Thus, much of the work performed in any school organization is devoted to bringing subsystems together to achieve unified solutions to environmental problems.

Although subsystems are differentiated and integrated by the functions they perform, differentiation by task can create other differences among them. In their studies of industrial organizations, Lorsch and Lawrence (1970) found four kinds of difference that apply to school organizations as well. These differences are in structural formality, goal orientations, time orientation, and interpersonal orientation.

Differentiated subsystems differ in their need for tight formal procedures, rules, policies, and control. A subsystem such as a community relations department, which must be responsive to a highly uncertain segment of the environment—i.e., no one can predict who will call for information or what information will be needed—needs a loose structure, simple procedures, few rules and policies, and freedom from controls that stifle quick creative responses. On the other hand, a subsystem such as the department that arranges bus schedules deals with a highly certain and predictable segment of the environment and can therefore rely on procedural manuals, rewarding only that behavior that is congruent with those procedures.

In many organizations, subsystems exhibit clearly differing subgoals. In schools, this situation is difficult to diagnose because the overall goals may be vague or because subsystems are not functionally distinct enough to be viewed as the foci of particular subgoals. This is not to say that conflicts never arise between or within subsystems. A frequent clash of subgoals may occur, for example, between teachers who are pursuing policing or custodial subgoals and counselors who are pursuing nurturant subgoals. Other conflicts can occur between curriculum consultants who wish to experiment with innovative practices and teachers who are trying to maintain regular schedules.

Subsystems also differ in time orientation. Food preparation subsystems develop daily and weekly menus; teachers prepare lesson plans by the period and unit; the board may appropriate money for a two-year revision of physics curricula. Channels for communication about time perspectives may or may not exist between subsystems. Subsystems can differ, too, in their interpersonal orientation. While giving information about occupations, for example, counselors pay considerable attention to the quality of their emotional interactions with students. School purchasing agents or custodians, on the other hand, are more concerned about the kind of floor wax they have ordered than about any feeling the supplier might have toward them.

Differentiation and integration are complementary forces. Without differentiation, the efforts of one subsystem are likely to be duplicated unnecessarily by others. Without integrative channels and norms for communication and collaboration, differences in structural, goal, time, and interpersonal orientations can make some subsystems blind to the needs and movements of others. Effective subsystems and adaptable organizations continually seek a productive balance between these two forces.

Norms and Roles. Subsystems carry out their functions through the interaction of norms and roles. By *norm*, we mean the shared expectation that a certain range of behavior within a specific context will either be approved or disapproved; by *roles*, we mean the set of norms that specifies how a person in a particular position should behave. To illustrate the former, a norm supporting moderation in teacher-student interaction exists when teachers approve of moderate friendliness or moderate harshness toward students and disapprove of overfriendliness or overharshness toward them. Again, a norm that supports adjourning a meeting at a specified time, regardless of progress on the agenda, can be a powerful force even if no one talks about it, because faculty members share an expectation that they will not be reprimanded for leaving the meeting even though agenda items remain to be dealt with.

Norms vary in regard to their restrictiveness and salience. Restrictive norms specify that only a very narrow range of behavior will be tolerated. The norm that students should arrive at school at 9:00 would be restrictive if the doors were locked until 8:50 and an excuse was required after 9:05. Salient norms are those associated with high degrees of approval or disapproval. In many places, norms requiring students not to smoke in school are so salient that a single example of deviance is sufficient cause for expulsion.

Normative expectations, in turn, help to shape roles. Subsystem norms, which encompass work methods, interpersonal values, and social-emotional customs, reward approved discussion topics as well as certain manners of gesture, speech, and behavior. Thus, if teachers expect the principal to convene faculty meetings, the principal assumes this role or runs the risk of incurring faculty disapproval. In addition, role taking is a reciprocal activity that is always part of an interaction with other role takers. To say that some organizational members are performing their roles poorly means either that their interaction with their role reciprocators has produced a breakdown in the subsystem or that the subsystem is failing to integrate its efforts with those of other subsystems.

Because schools are relatively undifferentiated systems, many people may take multiple roles, and this can lead, in varying circumstances, to coordination, to conflict, or to a condition of self maintaining stasis. On some occasions, as when a teacher is both a curriculum developer and a classroom teacher, it can serve to coordinate related activities. In at least two other circumstances, however, it can lead to conflict. First, incompatible expectations from different role reciprocators can create stress for an individual, as when some parents say that teachers should discipline students while other parents say they should not. Second, stress can arise when an individual is acting in two incompatible roles at once, as when a counselor is expected to advocate students' rights but is also expected to discipline them for breaking school rules. Finally, multiple role-taking by teachers and principals tends to be a self-maintaining phenomenon. When teachers do the major part of their own planning, operating, and evaluating, they inhibit both the division of labor and the integration of their efforts. When principals work with teachers singly, interdependence among teachers is not only prevented from developing but may even be prevented from being perceived as an alternative.

Norms are important to an organization in several ways. First, they help to coordinate its social structure by causing behavior to be guided by common expectations, attitudes, and understandings. They are especially serviceable and tenacious when individuals perceive normative behavior to be instrumental in helping them to reach goals they value. Second, norms can facilitate both the organization's viability and the individual's sense of well-being. Norms concerning the legitimate authority of the school board and superintendent, for example, help to maintain integrated behavior across diverse subsystems. Third, norms can promote differentiation by specifying the appropriate behaviors for each functionally separate task. Norms governing what teachers should or should not wear in the English and PE departments, for example, may reinforce other commonly shared but very different expectations for members of these two subsystems. Finally, for the individual, norms provide a basis for social reality, especially when objective reality is ambiguous. Since measures of student achievement are too ambiguous to provide a single clear indication of the quality of a teacher's performance, other norms concerning the proper behavior of teachers may serve the interests of predictability and social control instead.

In essence, then, norms constitute the organization's climate, and their importance to the organization lies in their strength and persistence. Although they may powerfully resist organizational change, norms can be changed to bring about changes in roles and consequently in organizational differentiation and integration as well. They can be altered if role takers conjointly try out new ways of doing things until they know that their colleagues will accept new patterns of behavior in the school. This is especially important when the norms to be changed are closely related to the interpersonal competencies or skills of individuals. Some interpersonal patterns can be altered by making explicit formal agreements, but patterns of interaction characterized by deep ego involvement can be changed only through new one-to-one actions supported by other members of the subsystem and legitimized through the formation of new norms.

Stress is not uncommon during the period of transition from old to new, as people are unclear about "how we do things around here." Roles that take their shape from the daily expectations that people have of one another and from the way these expectations are fulfilled will be hard to pin down. Extra effort is required to ensure that everyone understands the difference between the old norms and those being newly proposed or tried out. This effort, if it is to ease the stress of norm changing, requires the presence of a norm supporting explicitness about selecting old norms for discard and new norms for adoption.

Capabilities of Effective Subsystems. Much of the information to be found in later chapters of this book is organized under headings that describe the skills we believe to be primary for subsystem effectiveness. This has been done, first, because effective subsystem functioning is a major objective of OD consultation, and, second, because the organization as a whole becomes more adaptable only when interpersonal skills and effective subsystems are both in place. The following list describes seven highly interdependent capabilities of an effective subsystem and assumes that improvement of one capability will determine the ease with which another can be improved.

1. *Clarifying communication.* Because skill in communication opens channels within the subsystem, as well as between it and

other subsystems or segments of the environment, clarity of communication is absolutely essential to subsystem effectiveness. By developing more precision in the transmission and reception of information at the subsystem level, ambiguity and conflict about norms and roles can be alleviated and interpersonal trust can be built, which can, in turn, reinforce a climate of openness and authenticity.

2. *Establishing goals.* Because educational goals tend to be diffuse and ambiguous, sharpening goal definitions can lead to exploring the differentiation and integration of effort needed to achieve them. Recognizing the pluralism of goals within the subsystem, organization, and environment can be a vital step toward acceptance of differences and greater ownership of common goals.

3. *Uncovering and working with conflict.* Just as clarifying communication and goals will lead to increased awareness of areas of conflict, so confronting conflict can help to clarify the norms and roles that will aid the organization in accomplishing its tasks. Norms for collaboration can replace norms for avoiding conflict. Individualized roles can satisfy diverse motivational patterns and capitalize on diverse abilities and value systems as well.

4. *Improving group procedures in meetings.* The face-to-face group meetings in which most organizational activity occurs need not be frustrating or unproductive. Procedures aimed at facilitating task productivity and group maintenance can make such meetings more satisfying. Meetings can serve as integrating devices if group members use problem-solving procedures to maximize the use of available human resources.

5. *Solving problems.* Adaptability implies continual active engagement in problem-solving cycles for identifying, analyzing, and acting on environmental contingencies. Subsystems that harness human resources to extract creative solutions are more successful at finding solutions than are those that merely extrapolate past practice. Improved collaborative skills can give people the confidence to take risks in trying out new ways of performing vital functions.

6. *Making decisions.* Effective subsystems, like adaptable organizations, must be capable of moving decisions into action, which can be done effectively only when people clearly understand a decision and are committed to it. Although it is not necessary for some to have less influence for others to have more, it is sometimes helpful to reduce authority if it is not based on knowledge and competence.

7. *Assessing changes.* Change for its own sake does not necessarily lead to adaptability. Schools must develop criteria for measuring and evaluating progress toward meeting short-range and long-range goals. For their part, subsystems should become more conscious and analytical of the content of changes and of the processes through which change occurs.

TYPES OF INTERVENTIONS

We distinguish four types of interventions for organization development—training, data feedback, confrontation, and process observation and feedback—each of which calls for unique behaviors on the part of the OD consultant. Essentially, however, these are labels of convenience and do not designate "pure" forms. Macrodesigns usually employ some combination of the types and draw most heavily on a common core of consultant behaviors that cuts across the four. With people in schools, we have often found it easiest to classify the types of interventions into just training and consulting and then to contrast the highly structured pedagogical formats of training with the more pragmatic features of data feedback, confrontation, and process observation and feedback.

Training is the type of OD intervention that has been carried out most often with school organizations. As trainer, the OD consultant determines the learning goals for a particular period of time, initiates structure, and directs activities. Thus, training involves highly planned teaching and experience-based learning in highly structured formats that often feature lecturettes and assigned readings. Whatever the kind of work in which a group of educators may be engaged and whatever condition the trainers may be trying to teach about, there are inevitably certain useful skills, exercises, and procedures that can be regarded as the building blocks of organizational training.

We use the term *skills* to denote ways in which interactions can be executed within a group. The skill may be one of communication, such as paraphrasing what another has said so that the other can verify that he or she has been understood; it may be one of guiding a group through an opinion survey; or it may involve writing interview schedules to obtain diagnostic information about a school. In any case, all these skills are put to work only in reciprocal relations among persons; no individual can make use of them in isolation. Paraphrasing, for example, can be done only in conversation with at least one other person and is not a complete act until the other has verified its accuracy.

The skill of a pair or of a group is often surprisingly independent of the skill of the individuals of which the pair or group is composed. Thus, the convener can be skillful in conducting a survey only if the members know their parts of the role relation. An interview schedule can be prepared effectively only if the interviewers using the schedule act within the same set of goals and values as the writer and only if the respondents join the communicative act in the way the writer and interviewers anticipate.

There are, to be sure, many skills useful in organizational life that organizational training typically does not touch upon. It ignores, for example, the skills of rhetoric, of making conference telephone calls, of using Robert's Rules of Order, of choosing what to include in the minutes of a meeting, and many others. This book discusses only those skills that we believe to be very useful for improving organizational processes and that cannot be gained from the educated person's ordinary experience.

An *exercise*, or simulation, is a structured, gamelike activity designed to make prominent certain types of interpersonal group processes that participants can easily conceptualize because they are related to their personal experience. Exercises have two important advantages: they can be designed to produce specifiable learning experiences, and they typically have content very different from that of an organization's ordinary day-to-day work. These advantages make possible highly specific learning goals (such as using more sources of information in decision making or encouraging more communication between faculty and administration) without the necessity of dealing with the kind of specific content that may impede achieving these goals in everyday organizational life. By enabling participants to learn the advantages of one form of behavior over another, an exercise helps them to make plans to establish more productive behaviors. Typical questions that trainers ask in debriefing an exercise are, How is the behavior exhibited in this exercise similar to, or dissimilar from, your behavior on the job? and What did you learn from this exercise that applies to your behavior on the job?

Unlike exercises, whose content is determined by the trainer, *procedures* are content-free and are used for the purpose of making work more effective toward whatever goal the group has chosen. Under most conditions, experiencing an exercise takes a group away from its primary tasks. Procedures, on the other hand, are introduced to facilitate accomplishing a task the group is already facing. As steps or routines by which a group's actual business can be moved forward, procedures are less gamelike and also less obtrusive to the group's normal functioning. A procedure can be used for a variety of tasks or purposes. Voting is one example; another would be the Fishbowl technique for sharing ideas and observations. Procedures such as taking surveys and doing systematic problem solving have been useful to schools, departments, and cabinets, and sometimes to teachers who have tried them in their classrooms to improve the learning environment (for the latter application, see Schmuck and Schmuck 1975).

One of the most important intervention modes for the OD consultant is *data feedback*, or the systematic collecting of information which is reported back to appropriate subsystems as a basis for diagnosis, problem solving, and planning. Three aspects of the data-feedback process constitute the keys to its success. First, the consultant must be adept at collecting valid relevant data and at putting the data into a feedback form that will be understandable and energizing to the participants. Second, the consultant must strive to elevate mundane data to a level of larger essential significance so that the data are worthy of notice by participants. Third, the consultant must find ways of incorporating data feedback into the natural ebb and flow of larger consultative designs.

A *confrontation* design aims at identifying the character of the social relationships between two or more role takers or groups, as well as at identifying the problems that are contributing to conflicts among them. The consultant brings two or more bodies together to interact and to share the perceptions that each has of the other; to identify areas where each is viewed as helpful or unhelpful to the other; to establish clear communication channels between the two groups; to introduce a problem-solving procedure that may facilitate collaborative inquiry into mutual problems; and finally to identify the common concerns that cut across all parties involved in the confrontation. Although confrontation is unlikely in itself to bring about a total resolution of existing differences, it can set the stage for further explorations into how to manage interrole and intergroup conflicts.

In carrying out *process observation and feedback*, the purpose of which is to help group members become more aware of how they are working together, the consultant sits with the client group during its work sessions, observes the ongoing processes, and occasionally offers personal comments or observations. This type of intervention aims to involve the participants in talking about their working relationships themselves and in making group agreements to modify the ways in which they will work together in the future.

Other types of OD interventions may be specified as well. In addition to training, data feedback, confrontation, and process observation and feedback, Schmuck and Miles (1971) include four other intervention modes that are especially applicable to large-scale OD efforts. These comprise a sequence of problem solving, plan making, establishment of an OD task force for continuing consultation, and some modification in the technostructural activities of the client system.

PROCESSES OF TRAINING AND CONSULTATION

Organizational problems may be said to arise from discrepancies between a present unsatisfactory state of affairs and a perceived ideal state of affairs. OD training and consultation strive to resolve such problems by creating norms and skills that will reduce these discrepancies on a continuing and institutionalized basis. Training, data feedback, confrontation, and process observation and feedback offer four alternative ways of helping clients to identify their organizational problems. In training, clients are taught skills that allow them to begin to communicate previously unshared data. In data feedback, data collected from the clients concerning how they perceive and feel about the organization are reported back so that the group can make constructive use of them. In confrontation, groups are helped to report their perceptions and feelings to one another. In process observation and feedback, the consultant's observations of how group members are working together are fed back to the group.

Although specific OD activities for solving problems are typically embedded in designs that are tailored in the process of interaction between and among consultants and clients, it is convenient to think of any OD intervention as following a sequence of stages In the first, contract-building stage, the consultant discusses the OD effort with a variety of clients, usually including top management gatekeepers, carries out brief demonstrations of one or more types of training or consultation, and begins to build an informal contract with clients about how the intervention will attempt to alleviate organizational problems.

When the contract is acceptable to all parties involved, a diagnostic stage begins. Working with the clients, the consultant collects data about the organization using interviews, questionnaires, and observations, which yield a joint diagnosis of points of malfunctioning within the organization and help to shape the initial macrodesign that the consultant will construct. *Macrodesigning* means scheduling a sequence of intervention events aimed at overcoming the problems indicated in the diagnosis. The initial designing stage is followed by one or more stages comprised of *microdesigning* for a specific training or consultative event, assessing and implementing the macrodesign, and monitoring progress. The OD effort concludes with a stage during which the consultant and clients jointly evaluate the outcomes of the macrodesign and institutionalize the client's capability to continue changing as needed.

Even though particular tasks may accrue more to some stages than to others, the stages of an OD effort are cyclical, with very similar developmental issues recurring again and again. For example, trust, rapport, legitimacy, credibility, and dependability, which are core themes during entry, will inevitably recur during diagnosis and again during training and consultation. Even though diagnosis properly takes center stage after contract building, the clever consultant will be diagnosing the relationships among clients from the first meeting. Likewise, plans for monitoring effects of implementing microdesigns, for evaluating outcomes of the consultation, and for ways of institutionalizing the OD capability can be discussed in the earliest conversations.

In other words, the OD consultant should be collecting diagnostic data while the contract is being built. At the same time, a large measure of "true entry," in terms of trust and acceptance, can occur during one-to-one interviewing within the formal diagnostic stage and can be increased (or shattered) during events for training, data feedback, confrontation, or process observation and feedback.

Dynamics of Entry

A school organization acknowledges a problem when some influential person or group within the organization conceives a state of affairs significantly more satisfactory than that which exists at present. Problems can arise from interpersonal demands within the district, from new ways of perceiving things, or from demands made by people outside the district, as when parents, legislators, or other outsiders try to persuade a district to undertake some innovation, such as bicultural education, career education, community school programs, or individualized programs.

In our view, productive change is not likely to occur unless the district personnel acknowledge a discrepancy between an ideal and actual state of affairs before an outsider arrives on the scene. That is, a sizable portion of the organization, and especially its more powerful members, should accept the problems as their problems and become reasonably committed to solving them instead of merely acquiescing to a project that originates on the initiative of the outside consultant. Consultants should make it a rule to enter into contract only with those educational subsystems that are reaching out for help and that exhibit other signs of readiness to profit from an OD effort.

Chapter 2 elaborates on these signs of readiness and also suggests ways of discerning their presence. Here it suffices to call attention to the importance of two additional signs. First, in addition to being able to identify a problem they wish to solve, clients should know how to reward each other for collaboration in problem solving. In other words, the organization should exhibit a norm that supports recognizing interdependencies and working together. Second, the organization should have a norm supporting the expression of differences in opinions, values, and feelings. If clients do not know how to bring their various resources to bear on the problem that plagues them, the prognosis for their profiting from an OD effort will be poor until this readiness is built.

Consultants should be aware that what happens during the first phase of OD can foreshadow much of what is to come and that, if the consultative effort is to be built on a solid base of support, it is necessary to gain at least a verbal commitment to the enterprise from all key groups that will be participating in it. To this end, the critical importance of establishing relaxed rapport, credibility, and legitimacy at the outset, and of arriving at clear statements about motives, competencies, and shared expectations, cannot be overstated. Consultants should be explicit about their role, their goals, the project's budget, and the time they are willing to devote to the project. At the same time, they should note the extent to which clients adopt a collaborative attitude, as well as the extent to which clients are ready to collaborate with one another in new ways.

Although a consultant may initially be contacted by an individual at any level of the organizational hierarchy, interactions are best begun between the consultant and key leaders, because these hold crucial gatekeeping power over later contacts with other members of the system and it is therefore helpful if they become allies rather than enemies. In districts, powerful parties typically include the school board, the superintendent and his cabinet, the principals, teachers' organizations, and, increasingly, students' groups. In individual school buildings, the powerful parties may be the teachers, department heads, counselors, principal, and, again, certain students' groups. (Particularly powerful in many schools are teachers—e.g., athletic coaches—whose work is seen as having unalterable routines, so that the schedules of other teachers must defer to theirs.)

Although gaining the approval and collaboration of key authorities is essential, this alone will not necessarily win commitment or even acquiescence from others in the client system. Consultants must keep in mind that they are working not just with individuals but with a system, and they will want to test the willingness of authorities to carry introductory discussions of the potential program to others. How the consultant is introduced to more subordinate personnel will naturally influence subsequent support and program effectiveness, and consultants should not be slow in moving their attention to less powerful groups.

During the first phases of entry, and at every subsequent stage as well, working with an entire client subsystem is vital, and less powerful participants should not be allowed to believe that they are of less importance to the consultant than are administrators or others in authority. If the project is district-wide, the consultant will want to gain acceptance for it from every significant subsystem or group within the district. If it is limited to a single school, it will be necessary before proceeding very far to get not only the powerful persons on the faculty but as many other staff members as possible to support the project.

The OD consultant should almost never accept a meeting with only "whoever can come." In considering the crucial questions of what is the problem and who are willing to commit themselves to the OD effort, potential participants must consider the likely answers of those with whom they work, will want to see and hear how others in the work group react to the OD goals, and will want to ascertain how far their colleagues commit themselves to these goals. This is one reason why consultants should deal with intact work groups within the district from the outset. Another reason is that people who work together will be consulted within their intact groups at the later stages of the intervention, and to begin by dealing with them in intact groups will introduce that principle early and facilitate conceptualization later.

Although discussions of organizational processes, consultative techniques, and timelines are important, sound consultant-client relationships are not forged by agreement about tasks alone. It should be kept in mind that the dynamics of entry and contract building can arouse intense feelings of suspicion and trust, dissatisfaction and well-being, investment and caution, and openness and reserve. Directly acknowledging these feelings is a prime requisite for valid contract making.

The consultant should realize, too, that any improvement of organizational processes will take time. Wyant (1974) indicates that less than twenty-five hours of staff training in communication skills and problem solving can have detrimental long-run effects. In contrast, staffs that receive more than thirty hours of such training typically show favorable gains. Insofar as possible, the ideas of organizational processes and of adequate time and follow-through should be presented through experiential activities supported by eye-catching materials on paper or through other media during demonstrations.

As we conduct it, OD is largely experiential, and experience is an individual thing. Although consultants should take a few minutes to describe what the training or consultation will be like, they should not expect their listeners to get an accurate picture from words alone. The best way of conveying this information is to present a demonstration of OD consultation, by which we mean participation in laboratory training activities that communicate experientially the nature of OD to those who have previously had little experience in it.

We have found two program products to be especially useful for introducing OD to school people. The first is an audio-slide presentation entitled *Organization Development: Building Human Systems in Schools* (Arends, et al. 1973); the second is a booklet (Arends, Phelps, and Schmuck 1973) that is tied into the slide show with common pictures and explanations. At the end of the demonstration, participants keep the booklet, which includes the types of information about OD that school personnel want as they consider their own desires to enter into an OD effort.

Within the context of a particular project, of course, the material on which the demonstration is built can be the frustrations and conflicts actually existing in the district. Such a demonstration can produce three important results: it can motivate the participants toward further work by giving them a foretaste of success in dealing with one or more of their problems; it can give them a more accurate and complete conception of OD; and it can make them into supporters for later events.

Diagnosing Present Functioning

OD consultants must have detailed scientific information on which to base their macrodesigns, and they must also communicate to staff members of the client school that particular data on this specific school will be necessary for designing a tailored consultation. While collecting relevant data on goal setting, conflicts between groups, processes at meetings, methods for solving problems, and procedures used for reaching decisions, consultants communicate the focus of OD, in this way training clients in a definition of the foci even as they are collecting data for building a macrodesign.

Communication, goal setting, the realization of conflicts between groups, the study of processes at meetings, problem-solving procedures, methods for reaching decisions—which should receive first attention? In our opinion, first attention should be given to the processes that seem most impeding to the proper functioning of other processes. In other words, break the log jams first, and then treat those impaired processes that people in the organization feel are most painful, as success with these processes will motivate further work.

Apart from these rules, there seems to us to be a natural order among the processes treated in chapters 3 through 8 of this book. Interpersonal communication (chap. 3) has to some degree been unclear and inefficient in every school district that we have encountered and is probably below optimum in more than 99 percent of human organizations everywhere. Since poor communication can block every other process, it is usually profitable to begin with this (first gathering careful diagnostic information to help in choosing particular communicative links with which to begin). Choosing goals (chap. 4) must be done before goal-directed work can have any meaning. Even group conflicts (chap. 5) can be dealt with more intelligently when they can be judged on the basis of their effect on goals.

Since more effective meeting procedures (chap. 6) can be chosen if the goals they are intended to facilitate are clarified, the process of selecting or clarifying goals should usually be undertaken before undertaking the processes of bringing conflicts into the open and improving meeting procedures. It sometimes becomes clear to the OD consultant that members of an organization are hiding strong conflict and distrust from themselves, or that members who are aware of conflicts suppose that others have resigned themselves to "working around them" rather than dealing with them directly. In such cases, the consultant may judge it useful to reveal the true nature of the conflicts before beginning work to clarify goals. Finally, after communication, goal setting, meetings, and conflict management processes have been reexamined and altered, the organization is in a strong position to improve its daily work in problem solving (chap. 7) and decision making (chap. 8).

Here it may be remarked that resistance to diagnosis is typical even when high interest is manifested in becoming involved in an OD effort. Nowadays, for example, many school personnel who have experienced diagnosis and consultation frequently in the past may regard these OD efforts as old hat. It is also true that although the innovative zeitgeist has reigned supreme in many school districts, promises of change have often not materialized. If this has been part of a school's history, the consultant must emphasize that diagnosis of where things stand now is still critical because there can be no rational intervention without an accurate picture of the here and now.

Diagnosis should occur with even the most sophisticated faculty. Indeed, pessimistic comments by faculty members are important data in themselves. Special care should be taken with cautious or cynical faculty members to assess the amount of resistance to OD in general and to the diagnosis in particular. The consultant should strive to discover the kinds of workshop events that occurred within the school before, the kinds of organizational problems that were worked on, and why, from the clients' point of view, previous problem-solving efforts were aborted. Problems that are attacked later in the consultation, such as ineffective meeting procedures, can take into account the frustrations of previous problem-solving efforts.

During the diagnostic period the consultant should make use of multiple methods, of which self-report questionnaires, interview schedules, and systems for observation are the most typical. In addition to these formal methods, organizational memos and letters, informal conversations with organizational members, and even observations made during casual visits with clients offer important information about the organization. Collecting formal data can strengthen organizational members' views of the validity and legitimacy of the OD consultation. Ideally, OD consultants will let their first impressions, however they are obtained, guide the selection of formal questionnaires, interviews, and observations, whose results will be augmented in turn by insights gained from further data informally collected.

Designing Training and Consultation

The concepts and skills of designing, which together constitute a basic part of an OD consultant's repertoire, require an understanding of intervention objectives, as well as insight into one's own motives, adequate diagnostic information, and knowledge about the probable effects of different training and consultative procedures.

OD designs can usefully be divided into macroaspects and microaspects—the former including the design's overall structure and outline, sequence of parts, and the general forms through which activities flow; the latter including the specific activities carried out during a limited period, such as a week, a day, or even an hour of consultation. Tailoring macroaspects and microaspects of designing for specific objectives and participants is a major challenge for the OD consultant, who must be able to differentiate between what is most effective for particular clients and what the consultant personally is most comfortable doing.

Different diagnoses require different entry and diagnostic procedures and often call for different emphases in macrodesigns as well. Thus, while consultants should try to deal early with actual organizational problems among sophisticated staffs, among unsophisticated staffs they may offer more simulated skill training in the beginning phases of consultation. Moreover, particular diagnoses will lead to different decisions in designing. A lack of goal clarity, for example, may lead the consultant to begin with an agenda-building activity that will enable participants to deal with very short-term goals as a prelude to dealing with those of longer term. If decision making is the problem, the consultant may choose to present two or more designs, encouraging participants to decide which fits them better, and then offer observations and feedback that may help to illuminate their decision-making difficulties.

When designing, the consultant always does some detailed, rational planning in advance. We have often found it useful during initial meetings to attempt to describe the total OD effort or to post agenda and plans at the beginning of an event to invite clarification from clients. But even the best-laid plans must allow a certain amount of free time to accommodate the unanticipated. This slack allows for the unexpected event that can turn a highly task-oriented and unexciting consultative session into one in which clients can arrive at their own learnings, invent creative solutions to their problems, and find the confidence and zeal to go on. However self-confident the consultant may be and however willing to stick to the design in spite of short-term dissatisfaction on the part of the clients, the design should allow time for clients to analyze and criticize both the consultant's behavior and the design itself. Without this opportunity, the consultant-client relationship cannot grow steadily more collaborative and mutually helpful.

An effective OD effort must meet the challenges of improving interpersonal and group skills, changing subsystem norms, and changing organizational structure. Although none of these challenges is exclusive of the other two, they are usually approached in the following sequence.

Stage one typically involves building increased openness and ease of interpersonal communication by training members of the client organization in such skills as paraphrasing, describing behavior, describing their own feelings, and confirming their impressions of others' feelings. In addition, the consultant tries to build skills in conceiving problems and in responding, until clients are able to exhibit constructive openness and confidence that communication with colleagues can be worthwhile. Stage one can be achieved if the design continually confronts frustrations and mobilizes emotional states for productive ends, if the consultant exercises charismatic leadership, and if organizational norms are made explicit.

At this and every other stage of the design, consultants should help clients to clarify and achieve goals that are valuable both to the group and to its individual members by harnessing the need for affiliation, promoting interpersonal contact, and developing norms for the exchange of warmth and support. Training in the use of power and assertiveness, too, can be very useful for increasing feelings of potency, while increasing the sense of influence and control over problems can release much potential energy. It has been demonstrated that feelings of being influential can be expanded without necessarily increasing the incidence of dominance of some people by others.

Social psychologist David Berlew (1974) believes that charismatic leaders have the ability to help group members perceive the connection between their goals and the values they cherish, to help them feel strong enough to reach these goals, and to impart a sense of urgency in achieving goals. Consultants with these qualities are able to help participants define organizational goals that are compatible with personal interests, help them to achieve a sense of personal power and effectiveness, build confidence among them that they can solve their own problems effectively, and cause them to see that steps toward improvement can be taken immediately.

By pointing out the norms that appear to be guiding behavior, consultants can build awareness of discrepancies between what is being approved and what everyone wants to approve. By giving members a chance to applaud one another for moving plans into action, for example, consultants can evoke pressures to "put up or shut up" that create new norms in support of responsiveness. In addition, consultants can show how deviations from norms help to identify problems and resources in the school. A teacher who is approved for expressing rage during a faculty meeting may thereby signal the existence of stresses that might otherwise have remained hidden. Likewise, students who violate dress norms may be indicating the presence among students of expectations of which the faculty had previously been unaware. Helping people in a school to see that deviation from norms is a resource rather than a threat can move the school a long way toward organizational adaptation.

Although certain norms are changed in the course of improving interpersonal and group skills, in *stage two* of designing the consultant must still build new subsystem norms that will support helpfulness among client members in their day-to-day work. This, too, can be done in a number of ways.

As a lever for changing work norms, the consultant can attempt to ameliorate actual problems by asking professional personnel to state some of the frustrations they are encountering in their jobs and then to practice a sequence of cooperative problem-solving steps to reduce them. Cooperative problem solving not only reduces frustrations but also yields the satisfaction of knowing that one's contribution toward reaching a solution is valued by others. When staff members behave in new ways in their work groups, thereby enabling their colleagues to observe the new patterns of behavior in the school setting, changes are more likely to occur in organizational norms of openness and candor.

The consultant opens subsystems to greater communication with others than has previously been customary because in this way subsystems can plan more effectively for improvement. The budgeting department, for example, can better monitor the district's financial situation if school subsystems are more accurate and efficient in reporting the resources they acquire and use; conversely, school staffs can plan to prevent running out of funds if they are more open to feedback from the budgeting department. Consultation must help the subsystem examine not only how successfully it is performing its own function but also how far its effectiveness might be enhanced by allowing others "inside."

Because the total organization achieves its characteristic structure as a system from the ways in which functional subsystems relate their efforts to one another, increasing contact and cooperation among subsystems should help an entire system to respond more adaptively. OD consultation can clarify the functional subsystems in a school or district by calling attention to discrepancies between needed and actual differentiation and integration and also by helping subsystems uncover conflicts in their relationships with groups in the environment. When discussing the subsystems that should be represented on a district task force to redesign graduation requirements, for example, a staff should explore the subsystems that currently interact most often with people in other schools as well as those that ought to establish closer linkages with that segment of the environment.

Finally, changing organizational structure—*stage three*—means building new functions, roles, procedures, policies, or subsystems and making them formal and institutionalized, with budgetary support, so that these new structures become part of the basic fabric of the school.

Assessing Designs and Monitoring Progress

OD designs must be tailored to fit the characteristics of the client groups and consultants who will be using them. Tailoring means assessing design components to predict their feasibility and utility and monitoring the progress made during one consultative event so that the next event can fit new organizational characteristics. Since the next chapter discusses techniques for assessing designs and monitoring progress in detail, it suffices at this point to list five principles to guide formal data collecting of any kind.

First, the consultant should attempt to establish rapport and understanding by interviewing clients before collecting data via questionnaires. Second, it is very important during the interview for the consultant to employ the communication skills of paraphrasing, describing behaviors objectively, checking impressions of the clients' feelings, and describing one's own feelings, when appropriate. Such modeling can facilitate the introduction of these skills during later consultative sessions. More important, urging clients to describe behavior wherever possible will support the conception of the OD process as objective and constructive.

Third, when using questionnaires, the consultant should collect some data that can easily be quantified and other data that can yield quotable phrases. Ideally, the numbers and phrases will support similar themes and be useful rubrics of information for data feedback during later sessions. Fourth, over the full term of a sustained OD effort, the consultant should employ the same open-ended questionnaire item several times to engage participants in discussions of how things are changing within the organization. Finally, during feedback sessions, the consultant should observe the client group while it discusses meanings of the data and use these observations to encourage a process analysis of the client's interactions in the here and now. Thus, the diagnosis can lead directly into consultation processes and vice versa.

Evaluating Outcomes and Institutionalizing OD Capability

Because a certain dependency is inevitably established between consultant and clients, OD consultants should prepare clients for their eventual withdrawal by giving repeated advance notice of their date of leaving and then sticking firmly to that date. The macrodesign must move toward increasingly greater client control over the course of the OD project, with the consultant giving participants ample practice in taking over the OD functions before he leaves.

If the project is to be self-sustaining, the client organization should by this time have developed new structures and procedures to accommodate continual problem solving. Cognitive and affective change should have occurred; norms, roles, influence patterns, and communication networks should have become more receptive and responsive—indeed, the very culture of the school should have become different. Moreover, participants should realize that occasional consultation will continue to be necessary from year to year to maintain the new structures and procedures, and they should know where to find other helpful OD consultants. For a school organization, the most powerful support system for OD consultation is a cadre of OD specialists within the district. The final chapter of this book discusses how a district can go about institutionalizing a capacity for organization development.

READINGS

Review of Research Findings

Philip J. Runkel and Richard A. Schmuck

For ten years we have been conducting a series of interrelated research and development projects at the University of Oregon to investigate the usefulness of OD consultation for schools. The following review summarizes findings from our program on strategies of organizational change.

Philip J. Runkel and Richard A. Schmuck. "Organizational Development in Schools: A Review of Research Findings from Oregon." *Organization Development Journal*, in press.

Start-Up

It is of utmost importance to give adequate time for introducing what OD is and how it works to a potential client organization. An academic year is a reasonable period for a moderately large school staff to develop an understanding of what the OD effort will be like. When a clear understanding is followed by a staff vote that supports getting into an OD project, it is unlikely that time will have to be taken later to reconsider the decision. Indeed, our research evidence indicates that when participation in an OD project is reconsidered by a staff, the second decision is quite likely to be unfavorable. . . .

But, of course, introduction of OD to a potential client organization does not occur in a vacuum. Our evidence indicates that success of OD consultation in facilitating structural change is strongly influenced by the social-psychological readinesses of the client organization to change. Readiness is greatest where openness of communication is valued and communication skill is high, where there is a widespread desire for collaborative work, where the administration is supportive or at least not negative toward the intervention, where there is good agreement at the outset about the educational goals to be reached by restructuring, and where the staff does not have a history of one "innovation" after another that has failed to produce rewarding outcomes.

Before any consultation occurs, we recommend a thorough assessment of the levels of readiness throughout the potential client organization. Once the OD project is undertaken, moreover, the types of consultation and the designs for the work are based on detailed information about levels of readiness and the facilitating and debilitating dynamics within the organization. A continuing diagnosis of social-psychological readiness for OD and the gathering of systematic data during start-up focus on the following points.

Focus on subsystems. When there is more functional interdependence among a cluster of coworkers than between them and workers outside the cluster, we refer to those who are interdependent as a *subsystem.* When an intervention in one or two schools is followed by some desired outcomes, the evidence is sometimes too thin (because of having only one or two cases) or too complex (because of all the variables operating), or both, to give us great confidence that consulting solely with subsystems was necessary to the outcome. When we also find, however, that failure to work with subsystems in other schools is followed by aborted projects, the evidence for the necessity of focusing the intervention on subsystems becomes more pervasive. In several cases . . . where schools gave up the effort to achieve new organizational structures, we found evidence afterward that we had been mistaken about the subsystem character of the groups we had chosen for OD.

Support from administrators. Consultation in organization development will often have beneficial effects if administrators in the district office support the school becoming involved in an OD project, or at least are permissive toward it. [One study] described how the activities of a cadre of organizational specialists were affected by the superintendent's beliefs about their chief kind of usefulness. [Another] described how the dwindling support of the central office undermined an innovation in a senior high school. And [another showed] how crucial the building principal can be in supporting an OD effort.

It is the rare principal who can bring about altered organizational norms or new social structures without aid from others on the staff, but any principal can scuttle a project without help from others. If principals falter in their support of the project or vacillate in their efforts to learn the behavior that fits the new norms, the staff members will be more likely than otherwise to falter in their own efforts. This seems to be especially the case in OD projects. . . .

Variety pool. Consultation in organization development is more likely to have beneficial effects if most participants are willing to expose job-related disagreements (unusual and even strange ideas) to one another. To describe this type of organizational behavior, we use the technical language of "variety pool." . . . OD works best, in other words, with staffs that respect individual differences among staff and that have a high tolerance for an assortment of philosophical concepts and instructional behavior. . . .

Collaboration. While a variety of different ideas and instructional approaches are supportive of an OD effort, high degrees of collaboration and cooperation also are important. Consultation in OD is more likely to have beneficial effects in a school if the desire for collaborative work is widespread among staff members. . . .

Consensus on the innovation. OD is more likely to help a school achieve a significant structural change when the staff's decision to move into innovation is public and almost consensual . . . As a particular case, we have shown that OD consultation is more likely to help a school convert from a self-contained structure to team teaching, differential staffing, multiunit structure, or the like, when the staff has high agreement at the outset upon educational goals relevant to the new structure. . . .

Transition

An effort to bring about organizational change with OD consultation can be divided into a transition period during which new norms and structures are being built and a maintenance period during which the new organizational processes become institutionalized. These two phases are quite different; the former is replete with tension, anxiety, and mistakes while the latter includes more repetition, prodding, and less excitement. . . .

Amount of consultation required. Judging from outcomes in various client systems, a school showing appropriate conditions of readiness can expect to be able to make major changes in its structure and improve its ability to use its own resources to an important degree after a year during which about 160 hours of staff time are spent in direct OD work. Usually, this amount of time is best split into about 40 to 80 hours before a school opens and the remainder scattered over various occasions during the school year. Much of the work during the school year does double duty: accomplishing the actual work of the school and practicing OD methods. . . .

After studying a large number of faculties in several different studies that had received various amounts of OD consultation, we found that staffs receiving fewer than 24 hours of OD help actually declined in their communicative adequacy. Apparently, a mere two or three days of training in communication skills and problem solving, without follow-up work, can have detrimental effects.

Amount of time required from school staff. A staff involved in an important organizational change must expect to spend more time than usual in meetings during the transition. . . . Before the OD consultation, the staff in the school that successfully converted its structure spent an average of about 3¼ hours per week in meetings; during the transition year, this rose to 5½ hours. In the other school, the preexisting average of 2¼ hours per week stayed at the same level during the intervention year. These figures are means of estimates that all staff members gave of the time they spent in meetings.

Use of consultants. Consultation in OD is more likely to help a school modify its organizational structure when the staff makes frequent, knowledgeable, and proactive (not passive) use of the outside OD consultants. . . .

Problem solving. OD is more likely to help a school change its social structure when the steps of movement into the new structure are chosen to meet particular problems that have emerged in the school, in contrast to being chosen to follow a preconceived intervention sequence composed without regard to the school's particular problems. . . .

Choosing leaders. OD is more likely to help a school convert its organizational structure when new leaders, especially teacher-leaders, are chosen by equitable methods. . . . Conversion goes more smoothly, also, when the team leaders succeed in communicating up, down, and laterally with other members of the staff. . . .

Continuity of the principal. Consultation in OD progresses more effectively if the principal intends to stay with the organization until at least a year after the outside consultants leave. . . .

Conflict. A school that deals purposefully, actively, and confrontively with conflict during a transition to a new organizational structure is the more likely to achieve and stabilize the new structure. . . .

Pain. Significant effort toward organizational change will be experienced as painful to many of the participants, regardless of whether the change becomes stabilized or dissipates. With the risk-taking that is required to change comes anxiety and tension. . . .

Effects of OD

Our research and the analyses of others indicate that OD methods (properly chosen, sequenced, and applied) can increase a school's spontaneous production of innovative social structures to meet internal and external challenges, improve the relationship between teachers and students, improve the responsiveness and creativity of staff, heighten the influence of the principal without reducing the influence of the staff (and vice versa), expand the participation of teachers and students in the management of the school, and alter attitudes and other morale factors toward more harmonious and supportive expectations.

Structural outcomes. Structural innovation has often failed when *not* carried through the transition period by OD methods, and it has sometimes succeeded when OD methods *were* used. Nevertheless, it is hardly ever easy to understand in advance when a particular school will not need OD consultation to carry an organizational change through successfully, and it certainly is not easy to tell in advance the amount, kind, and sequencing of consultation that will be most efficient in a particular case. . . . Additional research is needed to elucidate the connections between levels and types of readiness, different designs for OD consultation, different sequences in installing the parts of a new organizational structure, and the various possible outcomes.

Schools that have received OD consultation quite often *devise new organizational substructures* to meet special needs. . . . Included . . . are accounts of a new sort of advisory committee for a junior high school principal, a way of reorganizing the first two weeks of the first grade to cope with differences in readiness among young students entering school for the first time, a specially tailored learning center for an elementary school, new substructures within a Parent-Teachers Association to improve speed and accuracy of information exchange between staff and parents, and others.

A school can learn to *marshal its resources* with sharper focus and greater commitment than is ordinary, thereby working more efficiently either to adopt a suitable innovation or to jettison an inappropriate one. If a school is to achieve this sort of capability, our research indicates that it must deal purposefully and actively with conflict during the transition to the new organizational structure. . . . In one district, an elementary school that received only about 46 hours of OD consultation has consistently outdistanced its fellow elementary schools in handling internal conflict, in stabilizing team teaching . . . and in exhibiting various indices of self-renewing capacity. . . . It turns out to be an exemplary case of a self-renewing, problem-solving school.

In another of our projects, six elementary schools received OD consultation designed to help them realize their expressed intention of converting from the traditional structure of the self-contained classroom to differentiated staffing with multiunit structure. . . . Three of the six succeeded (using criteria of success well beyond diagrams on paper or the pronouncements of officials) in stabilizing the innovative structure. Two withdrew from the intervention after about four months. The sixth school remained in the project and obtained some benefits, though it did not reach the structural criteria we required to call it a multiunit structure.

This rate of success—something over 50 percent—is worth noting, considering the large number of failures currently being reported in the literature. . . .

Our research experiences indicate that many school staffs do not benefit from many innovations and that a decision by a school to stop its efforts toward a structural change is not necessarily a "failure" of the change project. From the point of view of the school, the decision may actually be experienced as a success—a successful effort to ward off an unwanted change. Therefore, the two schools that discovered, in four months' time, that they really did not want differentiated staffing could be counted as cases where the schools succeeded in getting rid of outside pressures toward organizational change in a relatively short period instead of struggling to do so over a period of a year or two through the usual techniques of slowdown and deception. . . . However, reports on innovative attempts tend to concentrate on what the outside change agents want, and usually give too little information about the ability of a

38

staff to be clear about what *it* wants and to take steps toward *that*.
Correspondingly, and perhaps wrong-headedly, we have reported our
"success rate" as containing only those schools that did move past
the criteria we set for achieving the new structure, and have ignored
for present purposes the profitable aspects of the OD consultation
in the schools that withdrew. . . .

    Facilitating processes. Aside from helping to establish new
structures, OD consultation can also facilitate continuing efforts
and long-standing goals. For example . . . some evidence indicated
that schools that have received OD consultation, compared with
those that have not, are more likely to work out techniques for
reducing the adult-student ratio for certain kinds of instruction.
Moreover, OD consultation can improve the clarity of new norms
and hasten the development of trust in desegregating schools. . . .

    Research indicates that OD consultation given to a faculty
usually has spillover effects on the *relations between teachers and
students.* We have already mentioned the special arrangements a
single school worked out to welcome first graders. [One study]
reported a rise in student-initiated communication and improvement
in the expectations of helpfulness of students toward one another in
the classrooms of junior high schools. [Another] compared these
spillover effects with the effects of directly training teachers in
coding teacher-pupil interaction. . . . [Others] give evidence that
students are perceived by teachers as participating more in planning
their educational program after the school has received OD consultation. . . .

    Staffs of schools that receive OD consultation are likely to
increase their participation in *planning the school's curriculum.* . . .
Moreover, one school . . . that had received OD consultation succeeded in *eliminating the practice of grouping by ability,* while other
schools in the district did not. And our research indicates that training in collegial supervision (in which teachers observe one another,
give feedback, and engage in joint problem solving about teaching
methods) can enable teachers to give one another more help than
otherwise in improving their teaching. This mutual helpfulness is
strengthened when embedded in OD consultation for the faculty as
a whole. . . .

BIBLIOGRAPHY

Argyris, C., and Schön, D. A. 1975. *Theory in practice: increasing
professional effectiveness.* San Francisco: Jossey-Bass.

    This book tells what it means to be a competent professional
and how the education of professionals can be improved. The
authors say that competence is the ability to generate theories
that explain and predict behavior and the ability to interact
humanely and effectively with clients. The chapter on theories

that professionals actually use is especially helpful to consultants who wish to reflect on their own style.

Baldridge, J. V., and Deal, T. E., eds. 1975. *Managing change in educational organizations.* Berkeley, Calif.: McCutchan.

A useful compendium of studies and essays, this book demonstrates how educational research and development on organizational processes can help school administrators who must wrestle with school change. The book includes twenty-six carefully chosen contributions, more than half of which come from research and development work done at Stanford University and the University of Oregon.

Burke, W. W., and Hornstein, H. A., eds. 1972. *The social technology of organization development.* La Jolla, Calif.: University Associates.

This anthology provides a comprehensive conceptual overview of OD technology. The readings are primarily case studies and research reports that offer concise operationalization of OD and many examples of how OD principles are currently put into practice.

French, W. L., and Bell, D. H., Jr. 1973. *Organization development.* Englewood Cliffs, N.J.: Prentice-Hall.

This book introducing beginners to the fundamental concepts and techniques of organization development goes into the history of OD, its underlying assumptions and values, and relevant concepts and hypotheses, with a large part of the text devoted to such technological topics as team building, intergroup interventions, total organizational interventions, and third-party mediating.

Harvey, D. F., and Brown, D. R. 1976. *An experiential approach to organization development.* Englewood Cliffs, N.J.: Prentice-Hall.

Chapters include an overview of OD, role of the change agent, diagnosis, motivation, strategies of intervention, team building, intergroup techniques, and other topics, each chapter containing a brief theory section and several simulations or games. Although there is little material dealing directly with schools, almost all is easily transferable. Pages are perforated for removal and direct use in the simulations.

Havelock, R. G. 1973. *The change agent's guide to innovation in education.* Englewood Cliffs, N.J.: Educational Technology Publications.

Written primarily for those who attempt to bring about curriculum change, this book also has lessons for OD consultants. Of particular interest are descriptions of the benefits and difficulties of being inside or outside the target system. Also relevant are descriptions of the stages that educators go through in adopting, implementing, and stabilizing innovations and hints on how consultants can facilitate effective change at each stage.

Lawrence, P. R., and Lorsch, J. W. 1969. *Developing organizations: diagnosis and action.* Reading, Mass.: Addison-Wesley.

This book presents a coherent theory and technology of organization development. The theory revolves around three interfaces: (1) the organization environment, (2) relationships among groups, and (3) the individual organization. The authors present an elaborate and grounded theory of differentiation and integration that clarifies what an organization must be like to be effective. Their technology includes diagnosis, action planning, implementation, and formative evaluation.

Schmuck, R. A., and Miles, M. B., eds. 1971. *Organization development in schools.* La Jolla, Calif.: University Associates.

This book presents much of the theory and data-based research on organization development in schools. The readings cover in detail virtually all the important work before 1971; the 1976 printing contains an annotated bibliography covering research from 1971 to 1976. The material includes descriptions and evaluations of school interventions together with practical programs and suggestions for school districts with an interest in organization development.

2

Diagnosis

Diagnosing the conditions surrounding an OD project, assessing the project's design, and monitoring progress need not be highly technical or time-consuming processes. The underlying strategy is reasonably simple, and the methods employed—interviewing, questionnaires, direct observation, poring over documents, and others—need not be sophisticated if consultants persistently obtain enough of the right information to meet their purposes This chapter will discuss ways of gaining diagnostic information and, on the basis of later data, ways of checking the effects of steps taken. Information that other audiences, such as funders, taxpayers, and professors of education, might wish to use in judging whether an OD project was worth doing will receive extensive discussion in chapter 11.

INFORMATION GATHERING

Many purposes can be served by gathering information about a school or the people in it. A principal can seek information by which to judge whether teachers should be given a raise in salary. A superintendent might look for effects of a new curriculum on parental attitudes. Parents might want information on the degree of fear their children experience in the school. A government agency providing money for a special project could want information on project costs and benefits. A social scientist might find the school interesting as a site in which several abstract variables can be observed simultaneously. A teacher might want to know how many colleagues share her enthusiasm about a certain organizational change. Students might want to know whether a proposed curricular change will make it easier or harder for them to graduate.

When school people gather information for the purpose of taking timely action that will maximize the quality of a particular program, this information is called *formative*. It helps to form the project, and its audience consists of those carrying out the project and their consultants. When someone gathers information for the purpose of reaching a value judgment about a program, this information is called *summative*. It makes a summation of the project's value and is of use to many audiences.*

The purposes to be served by information gathering will understandably affect the client's reaction to a request for information. A situation in which a client is required to give information that may have a detrimental effect on his own welfare will typically arouse anxiety, distrust, reduced communication, and sometimes even hostility. Formally or informally, OD consultants will inevitably be collecting information and assessing actions, but they should stay out of positions that would give them any influence over pay, promotions, or accreditation. Consultants who allow themselves to be cast in the role of evaluator, or who are suspected of providing information or judgments that can be used by some people to the detriment of others, will soon find their effectiveness undone.

Even during the early, less risky stages of consultation and training, reticent participants should not be pushed to become freer in word and action. Skillful consultants wait for evidence of participants' trust before expecting to receive information that might be harmful if passed on to others. They should share their information freely with members of the school organization but at the same time should lean over backward to avoid betraying confidentiality.

In maintaining confidentiality, it sometimes happens that even anonymity is not enough. In a case described by Arends et al. (1976), one consulting team used a diagnostic questionnaire during entry to obtain a list of organizational problems perceived by clients. After summarizing the responses, they posted the list on a bulletin board, including a few examples from individual questionnaires but giving no names of respondents. To their surprise, several clients accused them of violating a trust, and many withdrew their support from the proposed project. In this case the consultants did not know that the first legitimizing memorandum from the administrator of the client group had aroused widespread resentment among clients who had interpreted the memorandum as imposing on them something they probably did not want. Posting the list of problems, even without names, suggested to already resentful clients that the consultants

---

* We borrow the terms *formative* and *summative* from Scriven (1967).

would carelessly make information public that they might wish to keep secret from their supervisors.

To avoid being perceived as collectors of potentially harmful information, OD consultants sometimes make it known at the outset that they will turn over the evaluation of outcomes to an independent person or agency. This ploy can shift the client's anxiety from the consultants to the independent evaluators; but the presence of distrust, to whomever it may be directed, and its effect on the early pretest data nevertheless remain to be dealt with. The consultants must still gain the clients' trust in their ability to keep confidential both the diagnostic information and the information obtained while monitoring progress. Least fraught with anxiety (although not always happy either) is the kind of situation in which clients diagnose their own condition and monitor their own changes. In this case clients are most likely to feel that the information is genuinely relevant to their work, worth their attention, and a good basis for action.

Developing the capacity for self-diagnosis is a common goal in organization development, and to this end OD consultants employ two important methods of diagnosis that have the added benefit of teaching clients how to do it themselves. In one method, consultants collect information about the clients from other persons and then feed it back to the clients, allowing plenty of time for clients to discuss possible interpretations of the data. In another method, they gather information about the clients from the clients themselves and then discuss the meaning of this information in the clients' presence. Both methods enable the clients to observe methods of information gathering, organizing, and interpreting as models.

At the opening of a consultative project, it is crucial that the OD consultant be clear with the client about several matters.

Who is the client? Who will have a claim on the consultant's time? Who is investing in the project such resources as money, person-hours, housing, supplies, etc.?

Who is the consultant? Who will have a claim on the client's time?

With whom is client or consultant interdependent? From whom might each require persmission at some point in the project?

To whom does client or consultant owe information about the project? What sort of information and how much? Whose permission will be necessary before giving it? Who will reach agreements with interested parties? What information now confidential might be released after a certain date?

All these questions are interlaced because roles and interdependencies are strengthened or weakened by the patterns of communication that are maintained among them, and communication is itself strengthened or weakened by the way roles and interdependencies are maintained. OD consultants should therefore clarify the possible demands on information to be produced by the project and discuss potential demands with persons who are potentially interdependent with those in the project. In this way they will reduce the likelihood of a sudden later demand for the release of information that is confidential or in some other way not properly public.

Finally, OD consultants should be able to accept the goals of the client school wholeheartedly or at least as a step in the right direction. If consultants think they know beforehand what is best for the school in that year, they should be cautious about undertaking the project. If consultants find the dominant values or goals of a school or district repugnant, they should refuse from the outset to act as consultants.

CONTEXT, DESIGN, PROGRESS, OUTCOME

The four major features of any change project—context, design, progress, and outcome—we borrow from Stufflebeam (1971) and Stufflebeam et al. (1971), although we have here changed the labels. We say *diagnosing the context* instead of *evaluating the context;* *assessing the design* instead of *evaluating the input; monitoring progress* instead of *evaluating process;* and *evaluating the outcome* instead of *evaluating the product.*

Organizational consultants should not waste time and money trying to bring about a state of affairs that already exists or to undertake a change that overstretches the resources and skills of either themselves or their clients. To avoid such elementary errors, the consultant should find out before beginning any significant intervention how the school organization functions within itself and the nature of its interchanges with its environment. To gain this kind of information is to *diagnose the context.* The information obtained is often called *base-line data,* and the task of collecting these data is often called a *pretest.*

Careful consultants build their intervention designs to match their diagnoses so that they can accurately predict the immediate effects of their design components as well as the cumulative effects of the sequenced components. At the same time, they invite colleagues to criticize their designs or to give them "dry runs," ceaselessly check as each component is carried through, and check immediately at its conclusion to be sure that the effect is satisfactorily close to that designed. This is what is meant by *assessing the design.*

Consultants want to know every few days—sometimes every few hours or even minutes—the effects of their work to that point and whether any changes have meanwhile occurred in the context or the environment. *Monitoring progress* means diagnosing the present functioning of the school or other client-unit and comparing that condition with plans for next steps. Consultants monitor progress to determine whether short-term and long-term goals are being met and whether the intervention is producing the knowledge, sensitivities, skills, or norms upon which further advances can be built.

Evaluating outcomes means assessing whether the intervention produced overall results that justified the time and expense, whether the products or effects are superior (in satisfying the needs of some audience) to the old products or effects, and whether the intervention has produced any unexpected or undesirable side effects. Training may produce a faculty with high agreement on goals, strong cohesiveness, and skill at working through any sort of problem, for example, but it may do so at the cost of forcing out a third of the original faculty. It is important to the success of future interventions to uncover all significant costs and benefits of a completed intervention.

These four types of information gathering are not mutually exclusive or neatly sequential; they are cyclic and overlapping, susceptible to assessment moment by moment, in episode, or in total. Each assessment of a small act is part of a feedback cycle that helps to shape a larger act, whose feedback helps to shape a still larger event, and so on.

In the smallest cycle, consultants can observe the effect of an act during the moments immediately following its initiation. Having asked a participant to describe helpful or unhelpful behavior on the part of others in the group, for example, they can note the participant's ability to respond directly to the request, the ways in which other participants help or fail to help, and signs of gratification or pain as these others learn the first participant's view of their behavior. The consultant takes in all this information to judge, as part of monitoring the progress, whether the relationships being brought to light will enable the group to attain the goals set for this part of the training. On the basis of that judgment, he or she then either encourages the discussion or suggests another direction.

In a larger cycle, while observing participants' reaction to such exercises, the consultant decides whether to proceed with a plan or to alter it. In a still larger cycle, he or she collects data on how an organization conducts its work in the months following a major intervention and, on the basis of those data, makes recommendations to the school board and superintendent concerning future programs in organizational development. The recommendations could be part of a summative evaluation.

Thus a single act that is at one point judged for itself may be judged at another point as a component of the episode or training event of which it is a part. The episode or training event may in turn come under scrutiny as part of the overall project design. The project can be judged for its contribution to the developmental policy of the year or the decade in that school organization, and so on. Observing the skill of participants in describing helpful or unhelpful behavior can at one time be part of monitoring progress and at another time part of diagnosing context, assessing design, or evaluating outcome. Indeed, at a single time, it can be context diagnosis in a segment of the school or district that the intervention has not yet touched; it can assess a design if the intervener has just instructed participants in how to do the exercise; and it can be a progress evaluation if the intervener gave the instructions a week ago.

Of course, the purposes of larger and smaller acts differ, and their manner of assessment must differ as well. Some judgments become very complex and can be made confidently only on the basis of a sophisticated design for evaluation. At bottom, however, diagnosis, assessment, or monitoring is the kind of how-am-I-doing activity that is a natural and recurring part of any human interaction.

Diagnosing the Context

Schools, like individuals, are best able to learn new skills when the right conditions of readiness exist within and around the organization. Some actions require the client to have a certain body of knowledge, a certain level of ability, a certain amount of encouragement from superiors, and the presence of other internal and external conditions if the action is to have a good chance of success. Ascertaining whether these necessary conditions of readiness exist is what is meant by diagnosis.

An organization acts within historical and environmental contexts. The historical context denotes the organization's condition at the present moment and the direction in which its history is moving it. The environmental context denotes the organization's relation to the environment from which it draws material and informational resources and to which it returns resources in other forms. An assessment of a school taken before its historical context is known as diagnosis of context; afterward, it is monitoring of progress.

To differentiate these two processes on the basis of environmental context is more difficult. Perhaps it is best to say that an environmental condition remains context until it must actively be dealt with as part of the intervention, at which point a monitoring of progress would normally begin. Existing parental opinions about sex education, for example, can be regarded as part of the context of the school. If, however, the project undertakes to change the relation of parents to the school or to change the curriculum for sex education, activities concerning the one, the other, or both would need to be monitored for progress.

For the consultant, diagnosis of context serves two purposes: it provides base-line or pretest information against which later outcome or posttest information can be compared, and it provides diagnostic information that the consultant can use in designing entry and first consulting steps. In any intervention, consultants will want to reconnoiter the condition of the school, district, or subpart that is closest to the client. The amount of present and past detail needed will vary, of course, with the size of the client organization and the scope and depth of the consultation.

General Information. It is often difficult to persuade clients to sit still for diagnosis. If a project is to run for only a week or a month, the consultant needs an abbreviated set of questions such as the very serviceable list that follows.*

1. Please describe what you do—your area of responsibility.
2. With whom does your work bring you into contact most often? Whom do you *need* in doing your work? Are there people in your school (department, etc.) whom you need to see more often?
3. How would you characterize the amount and type of confidence that the principal (department head, etc.) has in you? That the superintendent (the principal, etc.) has in him/her?
4. How much influence do you feel that you have over the goals and activities in your school (department, etc.)? How are goals set?
5. Characterize the principal's (the superintendent's, etc.) leadership.
6. How are budgets created?
7. How do you know when you are being productive? What are the criteria? Who notices? What makes you personally satisfied?
8. What is going very well currently in the school (department, etc.)?
9. In my brief meeting with your group at _____, certain issues came up that were called _____. Could you describe these for me briefly and tell me more about the nature of the issues?
10. If you were given the principal's (superintendent's) job for a month or a year, what would you change? How would you do that?
11. Is there anything you want to add that I haven't covered?
12. What specific things do we need to give attention at the next meeting (workshop, etc.)?
13. Now let's go back over the interview to give you a chance to strike out anything you don't want to be mentioned in the meeting (workshop, etc.) that's coming up.

For a project that will last over most of a school year or more, that will include a school or department of two dozen or more people, and that will make wrenching changes in roles and norms, more scope and depth will be required in the diagnosis. The following list of topics on which information might be collected is adapted from Levinson (1972, pp. 66-67), whose book offers useful guides to collecting organizational information of many kinds.

---

*We are grateful to Dale Lake, Paul Buchanan, and Matthew Miles for a handout containing these questions.

Identifying Information

Client's organizational type (committee, administrative team, department, entire nondepartmentalized school, departmentalized school, team-teaching school, etc.).

Chief connections to other segments of school district or community.

Size, departmentalization, decentralization, geographic spread, etc.

Nature of contract between consultant and client: consultative, research, mixed, ameliorative, change, self-renewal, confidentiality arrangements, etc.

Historical

Chief complaints or events leading to the initiation of contact with consultant.

Problems of the organization, short-term and long-term, as stated by managerial and other personnel.

Important developmental phases in the history of the client: experiences that significantly changed the direction, size, effectiveness, or strength of the group, as reported by members of the organization and as reported by outsiders.

Major crises experienced by the client group: loss of key personnel, employee alienation, financial emergencies, technological changes, severe community pressures, rapid growth or shrinkage of population, etc.

History of educational goals and emphases originating in school or community; successes and failures of educational programs.

In addition to information of this kind, the consultant will want information about current structure and process in the client's organization—topics that were the focus of the questions from Lake, Buchanan, and Miles. Further suggestions for obtaining useful information about process will be found in chapters 3 through 8 of this book and in Levinson (1972, chap. 6).

Readiness. During the course of an intervention, consultants diagnose the readiness of a principal to be confronted by staff, the readiness of a small group to attempt serious problem solving, the readiness of a school staff to join together in making decisions for the whole school, and so on. Readiness is an important principle at all stages of the work but is crucially important at the outset, when members of a school are asking themselves whether they want to undertake a serious project of change and whether they wish to accept a consultant's help. It is folly to begin even a small OD project if it calls for resources, skills, commitments, or values that are not there. If, however, the principal of a school asks an OD consultant's help in achieving some goal for which, after diagnosis, the consultant decides the school is not ready, the consultant need not simply walk away but can often think of ways to increase the school's readiness.

There is now a small but fairly solid body of research that points up the importance of certain beginning conditions to the success of a project of organizational change in schools. The following list of dimensions of readiness echoes the available literature reviewed by Runkel (1974), but it comes most directly from the research reports of Schmuck et al. (1975) and of Runkel, Wyant, and Bell (1975). This list has been written as if the project were being carried out with a school or district and as if the goal of the intervention were self-renewal or constructive adaptability. But an OD project can involve only a subsystem of a school or district, and its goal can have a much smaller scope than overall self-renewal. When diagnosing the conditions relevant to a small project, the consultant should scale down the points of readiness accordingly.

1. Participants should be ready to commit themselves to at least twenty-four hours of initial training to be distributed over three or four consecutive days (see Runkel, Wyant, and Bell, chap. 6).
2. A ponderable proportion of the participants should be able to see differences of philosophy or life-style among them not as reprehensible or shameful but as a source of strength (see Runkel, Wyant, and Bell, and Schmuck et al., p. 358).
3. Staff norms should support perseverance in group tasks. For example, meetings should run on past the usual quitting time when an agreement or decision seems within reach. When a promised job does not get done, someone should raise a question about it at a meeting of staff or committee (see Runkel, Wyant, and Bell, chap. 10, and Schmuck et al., pp. 357–58, for summary statements).
4. Staff norms should support openness and confrontation. At least a few members of the staff should exhibit the ability to continue to communicate about tasks while in a state of heightened emotion (see Runkel, Wyant, and Bell, chap. 5, and Schmuck et al., pp. 330, 357–58).

The kinds of readiness described in items 2, 3, and 4 are not independent but overlapping; if one is present, there is a fair chance that another will be present as well. If all three conditions are present, the school is all the more ready to profit from OD.

5. Staff members should know with some accuracy about the communication nets in which they are enmeshed. If asked to name people "with whom you talk seriously about things important to you, once a week or more," and then if asked to name persons *those* persons would name, the average staff member should be able to name at least one of those distal links correctly.
6. A ponderable proportion of the staff should have confidence in the organizational specialists, seeing them as competent, credible, legitimate, and not likely to depart prematurely.

7. The district administration should be willing and able to support the project participants as they pursue the project goals.

Items 6 and 7 are based simply on common sense, on our experience, and on the accounts we have had from other consultants. A narrative given by Runkel, Wyant, and Bell (chaps. 2 and 10) tells what happened when a superintendent who had high confidence in the district's organizational specialists was replaced by one with low confidence. Under the first superintendent, the OD specialists were conducting consultation with schools, central office groups, community groups connected with the schools, and others. They were replacing and retraining their own members and were becoming increasingly welcome in the district, despite the fact that a few years earlier the more conservative sector of the community had confused the OD activities with sensitivity training.

The new superintendent, unwilling to alienate the conservative sector, told the OD specialists that their past record meant nothing to him and that he would judge them on what usefulness they showed from now on. At his request, they facilitated a couple of meetings with parents and other community groups, and they did this so well that the superintendent commended them publicly in the district's newsletter. Nevertheless, although the OD specialists had some budgetary support during a couple of the following years, their budget was cut to nothing over the next five years, and the superintendent made no more public statements of support. After five years of dwindling and mostly absent support from the new superintendent, the OD cadre at last threw in the sponge.

8. The district administration should evince willingness and ability to reward participants in the project in some manner. Money is not the only effective reward (see Runkel, Wyant, and Bell, chap. 12 and chap. 14, p. 37, and Schmuck et al., p. 354).

9. School administrators should be ready to encourage and support changes in roles and norms that are necessary for changes in organizational structure, including any necessary changes in the cohesiveness of the administrative group itself. Changes in roles and norms often move toward greater collaboration among staff and greater participation in problem solving and decision making. Administrators should foresee changes of this sort (however dimly) and be able to visualize new and acceptable roles for themselves in the new structure.

   Administrators should anticipate, accept, and not fear the fact that heightened conflict is an ordinary concomitant of change. This assertion overlaps with the view that participants should be able to live with differences among themselves in philosophy and life-style. Here, however, the emphasis is on the administrator's function of leadership and on differences over time as well as among people at one time (see Flynn 1974; Simons 1974; Wacaster 1973; Runkel, Wyant, and Bell, chap. 12; and Schmuck et al., pp. 355-56).

10. Key administrators should expect to remain in their positions beyond the duration of the project (see Simons 1974; Wacaster 1973; and Runkel, Wyant, and Bell, chap. 14, p. 38).

11. Key staff members and most others should be willing to participate in the project at the outset. The school should review the decision periodically, trying for consensus as participants acquire skill in consensual decision making (see Runkel, Wyant, and Bell, chap. 12 and chap. 14, p. 37, and Schmuck et al., pp. 356–57).

Although an OD project may include only the professional staff of a school, or even a subpart of it, it may also reach out to nonprofessional staff, students, parents, community organizations, and so on. The remaining points of readiness become more important when more than one of these segments of the school-community is involved.

12. School administrators should be willing to arrange and participate in new structures that may arise among staff, students, and parents and to commit some resources toward this end (see Runkel, Wyant, and Bell, chap. 12, and Schmuck et al., p. 354).

13. At least some part of the professional staff should want to increase the effectiveness of their interaction with parents and students. They should believe that the pains of change and increased collaboration will purchase benefits for themselves and others.

14. Some of the staff should have attempted to work with parents and students in new ways in the past and should not believe that further efforts would be a waste of time.

15. There should be available some members of the community at large who have attempted to work with school staff in the past and who likewise do not believe that further effort would be a waste of time.

16. At least a few leaders should be appearing among students, staff, or parents who are pressing for orderly change. (For some experience behind items 13, 14, 15, and 16, see Arends 1975, Phelps and Arends 1973, and CNS 1975).

17. There should be visible signs of emerging interdependence among staff, students, or parents, as the case may be. As examples within staff, small clusters of teachers might be meeting before school, during lunch, or after school to discuss topics that imply collaboration, or a group might be trying to form a teaching team. If more than one segment of the school-community is involved in the project, one segment should not reject interaction with another (see Arends 1975; Runkel, Wyant, and Bell, chaps. 6, 7, 8, and 10; and most of Schmuck et al.).

18. The community at large should be willing to support, or at least be permissive toward, the changes in the school (see Arends 1975; CNS 1975; and Runkel, Wyant, and Bell, chap. 12).

19. If staff or staff-and-community are contemplating a project at

one level of need, they should show evidence that they are satis-fying lower levels of need as well. If students and teachers can-not achieve safety needs, for example—if they are being threat-ened every day by physical violence in the hallways, toilets, and even classrooms—they should not undertake a project to revise curriculum or institute team teaching; they should begin with their safety needs (see Arends 1975, and Runkel, Wyant, and Bell, chap. 2).

Indicators of Readiness. In seeking indicators of the nineteen points of readiness listed above, the reader should bear in mind that there is no one best way to get any particular piece of information. When we offer a questionnaire item, we do so only because we think it will serve well in many applications to get a certain kind of information. But some situations will weaken the usefulness of questionnaires, and then another method should be substituted. Moreover, to suggest a certain way of getting a certain kind of information is not to imply that that method can yield only the one kind of information. Even a single, specifically worded, tightly organized questionnaire item can become an indicator of two or more kinds of behavior or readiness. For a relatively uncomplicated example, consider the following.

- The principal of this school plays favorites.
     (   ) Often
     (   ) Sometimes
     (   ) Once in a while
     (   ) Never
     (   ) I don't know

On the one hand, this item can yield information about the direction toward which the bulk of faculty opinion leans. That is, among those respondents who check one of the first four answers, is the average closer to "often" or to "never"? On the other hand, this item can yield information about the proportion of people who are willing to give an opinion at all. That is, how many respondents did pick one of the first four choices in contrast to those who chose "I don't know" or skipped the item entirely?

For a more complex example, consider this one.

- The principal of this school maintains good relations with the central office.
     (   ) Agree
     (   ) Disagree
     (   ) I don't know

In one school, staff might feel that the central office is a potential source of benefits for the school and that the principal will be more successful in gaining those benefits if he stays on the good side of the people in the central office. In this school, respondents answering "agree" probably approve of the principal's behavior toward the central office, hoping that he will thereby wrest some benefits for the school. In another school, staff might feel embattled with the central office on some issue and would be sensitive to the principal's allegiance: Will the principal side with us or with the central office? In this situation, respondents answering "agree" might mean that they think the principal is siding with the central office against them and that they expect little benefit to come of it. In contrast to those in the first school, staff in this school who mark "agree" would be disapproving the principal's behavior toward the central office.

In sum, do not borrow methods or particular items from this book blindly. Consider the kind of information you want to get and the conditions existing where you must get it, and then select data gatherer, method, and situation accordingly. With this caution, we now offer some suggestions about indicators for several of the kinds of readiness described earlier. ·

1. *Commitment to training.* In attempting to determine client readiness for training and consultation, the OD consultant should always try to get decisions about next steps made in the groups that will be involved so that all concerned can see and hear one another's reactions. Although such enthusiasm is rare, imagine a meeting of a school staff at which several members propose four or five consecutive days in August when they want the consultant to begin training with them. One person asks, "How about two days now and two days then?" Others shout, "No, no, all together!" and "Solid! Solid!" and "We'd better be ready to work nights, too!" and "If we want this really to work, we have to bear down!" and so on. When the chairperson or consultant calls for objections, people say, "No objection," "I'm for the solid plan," and "Let's get on with it!"

If the principal and other key staff members joined in this enthusiasm, the consultant would have evidence of an enviable readiness to commit adequate time on consecutive days to initial training. The expressions of opinion would be publicly made, the commitment would be publicly heard, a large majority would have spoken, and the common commitment would be commonly understood. The only danger in this kind of enthusiasm is that a significant minority may have been outshouted or otherwise pushed into silence. Here, the consultant should demand a period of calm waiting during which people with objections can feel that their objections are being given honest attention.

When there are too many people in a group such as an entire school district to get together as a single body and hear everyone's degree of commitment to the proposed training, less satisfactory methods must inevitably be used.* Below are some other methods along with their disadvantages. All you can do is pick one or more methods whose weaknesses will hurt you the least.

---

*For an example, see Runkel, Wyant, and Bell (1975, chap. 2); for other relevant comments, see Derr (1972), and Derr and Demb (1974).

Should the consultant accept the principal's judgment that the staff is ready to commit a series of days to OD training? In practice, the consultant will seldom know at the outset how much confidence to place in the principal's judgment about this kind of matter. Frequently a principal who wants outside help is a poor judge of the staff's readiness to use it (see, for example, Arends 1975). Should the consultant conduct individual interviews with all the staff? Pass out a questionnaire? Interviewing everyone individually is costly, especially if respondents must be reached at home; in addition, these interviewees will not witness the responses of their colleagues. Questionnaires, too, offer certain disadvantages. If a questionnaire exhibits prewritten answer choices, information will be limited by the categories of response the consultant could imagine in advance and phrase clearly. If the questionnaire allows space for free write-ins, many respondents will be too hurried or unskilled in writing to answer intelligibly. Further, many respondents will simply skip items on a questionnaire.

Should the consultant examine records of participation in past in-service training? Query a reliable informant? Look in closets and basements for "murals" on newsprint, relics of past OD workshops? Even if there are existing records that show how people responded to past in-service training, it is likely that the previous training had been built to alter individual skills rather than the skills of staff, group, or team. While it is doubtful that prowling around the building's storage rooms will yield any profit, the consultant should seize upon the good luck if a participant should offer to lead him to some product of an earlier project that might contain useful information. Consultants will seldom have a ready, tested, and accurate informant during the entry stage, but they should certainly make use of any available informant who is known from previous experience to be accurate.

2. *Access to variety pool.* In the view of Saturen (1972), the ability of people to sustain communication while confronting anxiety-arousing alternatives to their present modes of working is a good indicator of a school's flexibility in summoning latent resources and applying them to nonroutine problems. Saturen also found the following four questionnaire items useful in assessing access to variety.*

- Suppose you are in a committee meeting when Teacher X and the other members begin to describe their personal feelings about what goes on in the school. Teacher X listens to them and tells his own feelings. How would you feel toward X?
   ( ) I would approve strongly.
   ( ) I would approve mildly or some.
   ( ) I wouldn't care one way or the other.

---

*Saturen's study is recounted in Runkel, Wyant, and Bell (1975, chap. 7). Another application of Saturen's items is described by Schmuck et al. (1975, pp. 169-74 and 310-14). These four items were originally adapted from items kindly supplied by Ray Jongeward and Michael Giammetteo of the Northwest Regional Educational Laboratory in Portland, Oregon.

(   ) I would disapprove mildly or some.
(   ) I would disapprove strongly.

- Suppose you are in a committee meeting with Teacher X and the other members begin to describe their personal feelings about what goes on in the school; Teacher X quickly suggests that the committee get back to the topic and keep the discussion objective and impersonal. How would you feel toward X?
  (   ) I would approve strongly.
  (   ) I would approve mildly or some.
  (   ) I wouldn't care one way or the other.
  (   ) I would disapprove mildly or some.
  (   ) I would disapprove strongly.

- Suppose Teacher X strongly disagrees with something B says at a staff meeting. In Teacher X's place, would most of the teachers you know in your school seek out B to discuss the disagreement?
  (   ) Yes, I think most would do this.
  (   ) Maybe about half would do this.
  (   ) No, most would *not.*
  (   ) I don't know.

- Suppose Teacher X strongly disagrees with something B says at a staff meeting. In Teacher X's place, would most of the teachers you know in your school keep it to themselves and say nothing about it?
  (   ) Yes, I think most would do this.
  (   ) Maybe about half would do this.
  (   ) No, most would *not.*
  (   ) I don't know.

Although some written items are too complex to be converted effectively to oral form, the queries in the above, as in most of the questionnaire items offered in this book, can also be made orally, in either a formal or informal interview schedule. Here are four additional question-items that can elicit information about the use of varieties of human resources in the school.

- Sometimes it is necessary for one person to tell another something or to raise a question that is difficult or embarrassing. Some people seem better able than others to open this kind of conversation in a spirit of helpfulness. Are there some people on the staff who clearly have this special ability?
- Do you think that carrying through with these embarrassing or difficult conversations ever results in anything beneficial to the school?
- Are there some people on the staff who seem especially confrontive, personal in a challenging way, or especially willing to open topics that raise anxiety?
- Does discussing these anxiety-raising topics ever result in anything helpful to the school?

3. *Perseverance in group tasks.* Some groups abandon a project at the first frustration; others keep working doggedly through thick and thin. But working doggedly at a lost cause is as foolish as yielding to the first obstacle. If the consultant can gain sufficient information about the school's past history in carrying projects through that will enable him or her to determine whether the staff applied its effort judiciously, his or her diagnosis will be that much stronger. Although we can offer no specific suggestions for getting information on long-term perseverance, the following may aid in ascertaining short-term perseverance in group tasks.

Describing six schools that undertook a project to adopt multiunit structure, Schmuck et al. (1975) say:

> We found that three of the four schools that became multiunit
> held meetings during which the task was given higher priority
> than the clock. In contrast, the two schools that did not con-
> tinue with the organizational change had an inflexible routine
> of leaving school at the same time every day. At Humboldt, for
> example, the lack of openness, combined with a norm of not
> putting in extra time at the school, kept the staff from dealing
> with the principal's attempts to transfer leadership to staff
> members. When staff members would not spend enough time
> together to take up the new responsibilities the principal was
> attempting to transfer, the principal became frustrated, inter-
> preted the situation as a "vacuum in leadership," and stepped
> in to stop the process of change (p. 358).

Smith (1972) used two questionnaire items to estimate the amount of time staff members spend in meetings.* The items can be phrased to ask about staff meetings, unit meetings, committee meetings, or whatever.

- How often does the staff meet in your school?
    - ( ) Usually meets oftener than once a week
    - ( ) About once a week
    - ( ) Twice a month or oftener, but not once a week
    - ( ) Once a month or oftener, but not twice a month
    - ( ) Less often than once a month
- How long does the typical meeting last?
    - ( ) About a quarter-hour
    - ( ) About half an hour
    - ( ) About three-quarters of an hour
    - ( ) About an hour
    - ( ) An hour and a quarter or an hour and a half
    - ( ) About two hours
    - ( ) About two and a half hours

---

*The first two items were adapted from Jongeward and Giammetteo; the third is original with us. These items appear as items 1, 5, and 7 in Runkel, Wyant, and Bell (1975, chap. 5).

( ) About three hours
( ) More than three hours

4. *Openness and confrontation.* In addition to Saturen's four
questionnaire items under "Access to Variety Pool," the following
three items can also be used as indicators of readiness for openness
and confrontation.*

- Suppose Teacher X is present when *two others* get into a hot
  argument about how the school is run. If teachers you know in
  your school were in Teacher X's place, what would most of
  them be likely to do? Would they try to help each one in the
  argument understand the viewpoint of the other?
  ( ) Yes, I think most would.
  ( ) Maybe about half would.
  ( ) No, most would *not* do this.
  ( ) I don't know.
- Suppose Teacher X feels hurt and "put down" by something
  another teacher has said to him. In Teacher X's place, would
  most of the teachers you know in your school be likely to tell
  the other teacher that they felt hurt and put down?
  ( ) Yes, I think most would.
  ( ) Maybe about half would.
  ( ) No, most would *not.*
  ( ) I don't know.
- Perhaps there are some people in your organization with whom
  you talk rather frequently about matters important to you.
  Please think of people with whom you talk *seriously about
  things important to you,* inside or outside formal meetings,
  once a week or more on the average. Write their names below.

In the study by Runkel, Wyant, and Bell (1975, app. 5-E), staff
members in elementary schools without OD consultation were found
to name, on the average, about three other persons in answer to this
item, while staff in schools that had received OD consultation named
closer to four.

Queries about school meetings can also be useful in ascertaining
tendencies toward openness and confrontation. The items below can
be used as questionnaire items with answer choices ranging from
"very typical" to "never," or they can be changed to questions and
asked from an interview schedule, or they can be asked informally.
For applications of these items, see Schmuck and Runkel (1970,

---

*Smith (p. 109) also explains how to put together a numerical estimate from these two
questions.

pp. 108-12); Schmuck et al. (1975, pp. 335-44); and Runkel, Wyant, and Bell (1975, app. 6-E).

- People are afraid to be openly critical or to make good objections.
- People hesitate to give their true feelings about problems that are discussed.
- People give their real feelings about what is happening during the meeting itself.

5. *Accuracy about communication.* To determine accuracy about communication links, Runkel, Wyant, and Bell (1975) used the following two-part questionnaire item.

- Perhaps there are some people in your organization with whom you talk rather frequently about matters important to you. Please think of people with whom you talk *seriously about things important to you,* inside or outside formal meetings, *once a week or more* on the average. Write their names below:

_____   _____
_____   _____
_____   _____

- Now look back at the above question. Each name is numbered. Listed below are all the pairs that can be made among six numbers. Perhaps you know whether some of the six people talk to *each other* about matters important to them. Please look at each pair of numbers below, look back to see what names they represent, and *circle* the pair of numbers if you have good reason to believe that the two people talk to each other *once a week or more* about matters important to them.

1-2	1-3	1-4	1-5	1-6
	2-3	2-4	2-5	2-6
		3-4	3-5	3-6
			4-5	4-6
				5-6

Runkel, Wyant, and Bell scored each respondent on the accuracy with which he or she indicated pairs who did or did not talk once a week, then examined the questionnaires of all the persons mentioned by any one respondent. If both members of a pair named each other in answer to the first item, and if the first respondent said that those two talked in answer to the second question, then that respondent was credited with one point of accuracy. If only one of a pair, or neither, named the other in answer to the first item and the first respondent refrained from circling that pair, (i.e., did *not* say they talked at least once a week), he or she was again credited with one point of accuracy. Points were cumulated for each respondent, and the mean was calculated for each school in the study. The results among fifteen elementary schools are shown in table 2-1.

TABLE 2-1   Accuracy Scores about Communication Links among
Fifteen Elementary Schools

	1968	1969	1970	1972
Highest school*	.80	1.56	1.38	2.77
Mean of trained schools	none	.73	.75	1.27
Mean of untrained schools	.20	-.06	.53	.46
Lowest school†	-.30	-1.24	-.10	-.33

*The highest school in every year was a trained school except in 1968, when
there was no trained school.
†The lowest school in every year was an untrained school.

The negative scores in the last line of the table tell us that in the
lowest-scoring schools (of which none had received OD training), the
average staff member was more often wrong than right in estimating
who talked to whom, even though these were persons with whom he
talked most about important matters. After OD training, the mean of
trained schools steadily increased, rising to 1.27 links correct in
1972; the highest scoring school (trained) reached a mean of 2.77. At
the same time, the untrained schools had a mean of only .46 in 1972,
and the lowest school (untrained) had a negative score: -.33. Clearly,
there is considerable room for improvement in most schools in accuracy about the communication linkage of which one is a part.

For the remainder of the 19 points of readiness, we have no particular data-gathering techniques to suggest. We do not advise asking
direct questions at the outset about point 6—the client's confidence
in the consultant. Clients almost always begin with doubts about the
consultant. If the consultant forces them to voice these doubts, they
may feel obligated to act with more reluctance than they actually
feel. Usually it is better to let clients express lack of confidence when
they feel it strongly enough and meanwhile to watch for indirectly
expressed reluctance, such as their frequently proposing alternatives
to the consultant's instructions and suggestions. When doubt about
the consultant arises after consultation or training has been under
way for some time, the consultant can use a more direct method,
such as administering an anonymous questionnaire, reading three or
four questions orally, or writing questions on newsprint and asking
participants to write carefully numbered answers on any handy
scratch paper.

Points 7 through 10 and 12, which are concerned primarily
with administrators and their chief assistants, can be evaluated most
directly by talking with the administrators and then observing
whether their actions match their words. The spirit of the remaining
points is that of catch-'em-where-you-can. One says, for example,
that "part of the professional staff" should want to increase the
effectiveness of their interaction with parents and students. Another

says that "some of the staff" should have attempted to work with parents and students in new ways in the past. The "part" and the "some" are acceptable sources of information wherever they may exhibit the desired characteristics. Since it is usually impossible to predict before entering the school where these special collections of persons will be found, certain problems arise in trying to find them for the purpose of evaluating their significance.

You can find any special group by making a blanket survey—whether by questionnaire, by interview, or by requesting over the school's public-address system that all persons with certain experience report to the office at 3:15—but these blanket methods have disadvantages. First, they arouse ill will by taking the time of many people for whom you are *not* hunting. Second, they waste time and money. If you try to get all the information you need in one shot, your questionnaire or interview schedule becomes far too complicated for the fish you are *not* trying to catch; and if you build the questionnaire or interview with all the necessary "ifs" to let through the unwanted fish, it becomes too complicated for the interviewer. You should use the blanket method only to capture likely fish, whom you must then interview in detail anyway.

Third, the blanket method may produce an undesired "reactive" effect on certain respondents. The points of readiness described here often require asking school people about actions that are not common in U.S. schools and not customarily specified in employment contracts—indeed, actions that would require special bargaining for time and salary allowances by teachers' organizations if they were to be included in contracts. They ask about the effectiveness of interaction with parents and students, about new ways of working with parents and students in the past, about parents and other community people who have become part of the life of the school and are willing to keep trying, about people pressing for change, and about groups wanting to work interdependently with one another.

In any school that is reaching out for the help of a consultant, there are some who will be panicked, or at least seriously worried, by such questions. If you begin with a blanket survey in a school where a ponderable proportion of the staff is fearful of change, merely asking these questions will cause participants to view you with alarm. In many schools, the best course will be to begin with your first contacts and ask them to tell you who would be likely to be doing, or to have done, the kinds of things mentioned in the points of readiness. When you talk to *those* people, ask them to tell you about others who have done similar things, and so on.

For purposes of diagnosis, it doesn't matter if you miss someone here and there. You want to know whether there is *enough* of a body of people with some readiness in these respects; and if you cannot easily find a fairly sizable group who know about one another, the answer is likely to be no. But don't take this statement as a rule any more than you took our previous statements in this section as rule. In the example that we gave earlier of the school staff that was adamant in demanding that the consultants mount a solid four days of initial training with them, you could distribute a four-page questionnaire about these points of readiness without fear of the questionnaire's reactivity. Such a staff would have stirred itself up before you got there.

Assessing the Design

In general, you assess a design by scrutinizing your plan and trying to think of what could go wrong before it does go wrong. First, you should scrutinize the macrodesign of your intervention, asking how it furthers overall goals and the goals of the client, how it fits into other planned interventions, and how it strengthens or draws strength from them. Attempting pilot runs of some of the instructions, exercises, and the like with which you have had little experience will strengthen the assessment further. Second, you should invite two or three colleague consultants, especially those who will be joining in the interventions, to examine and criticize the plan for possible slips and, for purposes of comparison, to devise alternative plans that they think might work as well or better.

Third, you should examine the microdesign of the team of consultants who will be carrying out the next intervention and check whether the plan is making good use of each of the team members, capitalizing on their strengths and not placing stress on their weaknesses. Using the principles set forth in chapter 10 and considering alternatives, let each person answer orally, so that all can hear, the questions, "Shall I feel sufficiently competent carrying out my part in this plan?" and "Shall I feel adequately supported by the rest of you?" If anyone feels an insecurity that might be debilitating, rearrange the plan.

A design can only be evaluated, of course, in the light of diagnostic information. During diagnosis of context, for example, consultants may discover that many of the potential clients, when contemplating the new communicative skills they might be called upon to learn, anticipate being required to reveal intimate facts or to engage in embarrassing exercises. A design that ignored this anticipation could run into trouble. After such a diagnosis, the consultants might decide to insert an early demonstration to alleviate the clients' fears, the demonstration to include exercises on communication that are nonthreatening but nevertheless rewarding and informative.

Finally, as each component of the microdesign is carried through, consultants should be alert to any unwanted side effects during the play of the component and in the first moments afterward. If some participants belittle the exercise or exhibit boredom, consultants should recognize that the exercise has failed to have the intended effect, at least with those individuals. With regard to desired main effects, if it was the one-way–two-way communication exercise, consultants might need to check whether alertness had increased sufficiently for the participants to use two-way communication on appropriate occasions. If the exercise was one in giving constructive feedback, consultants might have to see whether too many participants remained fearful of giving timely, direct, interpersonal feedback. If the exercise was relatively ineffective, consultants would need to redesign the remaining parts of the intervention.

As a general guide, consultants might ask themselves as an early component of training or consultation comes to an end, Have we now taken a sufficiently solid step toward meeting one of the goals described by the titles of chapters 3 through 8? When this is asked during the progress of the component or at the moment it ends, we call it assessing the design. When it is asked two hours, half a day, or a few days later, we call it monitoring progress.

Monitoring Progress

Organizational change is sequential and usually requires reeducating participants if the school organization is to move toward organizational adaptability. Especially during the period of active intervention by the consultant and active change by the client, it is vital for the consultant to make frequent formal or informal checks on progress to ascertain whether participants are actually using new skills and procedures, following through on problem-solving steps, monitoring their own commitments, and so on.

In chapter 1 we proposed three levels of skill, distinguished by the complexity of the social situation, that functioning groups must develop on the way to achieving organizational adaptability. We call a skill *interpersonal* if it can be exhibited and have its effect between only two persons. If certain minimal interpersonal skills in information exchange, problem conception, and responding are not absolutely prerequisite, they at least greatly facilitate learning, maintaining, and maximizing the skills necessary for a group to become a functioning subsystem.

The seven subsystem skills are necessary, we believe, or at least very facilitating, to organizational adaptability. We place a skill at the *subsystem* level if more than two persons are required for it to have a significant effect and if it can have its full effect without going beyond a face-to-face group. Each of the first seven subsystem skills has a chapter of its own among chapters 3 through 8 in this book, including a section on techniques for monitoring progress in the kind of skill described in that chapter. Evaluation of adaptability will be discussed in chapter 11.

We describe a skill of *adaptability* as one that can only be exhibited between groups or subsystems when not all members are face to face. An example is taking information into the school through one person (the principal, let's say) or one group and then distributing it promptly to all persons or groups who need it in their work. Groups find almost universally that collaborative skills of communication are never learned once and for all but must be recycled whenever groups take on a new kind of task, whenever they lose an old member or gain a new one, and whenever their relations with other subsystems change. For this reason, the consultant must constantly monitor the group's skill in adapting to changes in task, membership, and environment.

Just as any given piece of information obtained by any method can usually be used for diagnosing content, assessing design, monitoring progress, or evaluating outcomes, so a particular questionnaire item or an observation of a certain kind of behavior can, with minor modification, be used to ascertain more than one level of skill. If, for example, we observe frequency of paraphrasing between two persons in conversation, we are assessing interpersonal skill; but if we observe the *distribution* of frequency of paraphrasing throughout a discussion group, we are assessing subsystem skill. If we observe a group's skill at moving through the S-T-P method of group problem solving,* we are again assessing subsystem skill. But if we observe the instances in which a school responds to discrepancies between its ideals and its present state by selecting relevant groups in which to apply the S-T-P method, and if we note whether S-T-P is the appropriate choice of method, we are assessing organizational skill or adaptability. The reader should remember that assessment techniques can usually be adapted to another level of skill by changing the persons from whom the information is obtained, the period over which the information is collected, and the wording of the question.

Finally, consultation and training activities can double as opportunities for diagnosis or monitoring progress. Sometimes diagnostic information from an early training event can provide a good baseline against which to compare later assessment of design or later monitoring of progress.

In 1973, for example, we designed for key people in a school district a demonstration intended to yield prognostic information both to us and to them, and their reactions enabled us to go at least part of the way toward answering several questions of importance to us both: To what extent did the organization's members agree on the expectations that they placed on their various roles? Were there conflicting expectations? Did participants typically see their troubles as arising from other people, or did they include themselves as sources of trouble? Were they more concerned with finding out who was right or wrong or with getting problems solved? Were they aware of the productive aspects of conflict? Were the administrators hoping that an OD intervention would answer their own needs and alleviate their own problems, or were they hoping that seeming to approve the project would appease someone who might otherwise be a nuisance to them? How much were various members ready to invest in the project in terms of money, time, prerogatives, status, and other resources? What kinds of risks did people seem ready to take?

Sometimes, to be sure, the direction of an activity's usefulness changes in midstream. In the early 1970s we designed for a junior high school an initial training event that included the Planners and

---

*Situation-Target-Plan; for a detailed description of this procedure, see chapter 7

Operators exercise as a component.* Our purpose was to give the participants here-and-now evidence about their manner of working in groups but to elicit this evidence from a game that would arouse less anxiety than evidence taken from their performance in actual day-to-day work in the school. As it turned out, four of five groups failed to solve the Planners and Operators exercise even in forty minutes. The debriefing evinced very little discussion of interdependence, helpfulness or lack of helpfulness to others, explicit attention to influence processes, emotional reaction to personal experiences of release or frustration, or other organizational dynamics.

Instead, participants spent most of the time justifying their own behavior and castigating the trainers for having picked the wrong exercise, having given unclear instructions, and so on. The exercise was the wrong medium for the participants to learn about their own interaction during problem solving, but it provided excellent diagnostic information to the trainers concerning the participants' lack of readiness to examine their own interpersonal relations—a diagnosis that was amply verified by our experience with them during the subsequent year.

In sum, consultation and training are never entirely separate from diagnosis and monitoring progress. The skillful consultant uses occasions of assessing progress to provide clients with information they can use for their own diagnosis, to serve as examples of ways they can collect diagnostic or monitoring information for themselves, to enable them to become aware of how they react to having their performance evaluated, or to serve other purposes as the occasion permits. Conversely, the consultant often uses conferences, demonstrations, or training episodes as additional sources of diagnostic or monitoring information for his own purposes.

DIAGNOSTIC INFORMATION

Mapping Sentence

There are several methods by which data can be gathered, several roles to which data gathering can be added, and several kinds of circumstances within which the data gatherer can act. Figure 2-1 exhibits a "mapping sentence" that tells how several features of data gathering can be "mapped" onto the information that can be obtained about a school organization in its environment.† The idea is to compose a single sentence by taking one choice from under each of the five headings: Information Gatherer, Visibility, Source, Method, and Situation. (To clarify the term *invisible* as used in the mapping sentence, the consultant could become invisible by listening to the meeting by means of an electronic bug or by being introduced

---

*For a detailed description of this exercise, see the intergroup exercises in chapter 8.

†As far as we know, the mapping sentence was first given its name and laid out in the manner of figure 2-1 by Louis Guttman; see, for example, Guttman (1965a, b).

not as a consultant but as an applicant for a teaching position, although we do not recommend these or any other deceptions. The consultant could become partly invisible by staying away from the meeting and reading its minutes instead.)

FIGURE 2-1   Mapping Sentence for Information about Client-in-Environment

An information gatherer		*Visibility*	
Consultant	who is	visible	to the client collects *informa-*
Evaluator		invisible	*tion* about the client-in-
Researcher			environment
Client			

Source

from: client's self-report
a person or agency within the client's organization or in its environment who is observing or has observed the client and who is not a member of the staff of the information gatherer: an "informant"
behavior of the client directly observable now, such as manner of participating in meetings or manner of responding to demands from the environment
nonverbal traces of past behavior, such as glassless windows or murals by students
public document, such as a copy of a speech to the PTA
archives, such as attendance records

Method

by: questionnaire
interview of individual or group
spontaneous communication from client
existing documents
direct observation during consultation
direct observation of ordinary day-to-day work

Situation

in a situation that is: natural or spontaneously occurring.
convened or given structure by the data gatherer.
one of culling documents.

To form an opinion on whether the client is ready to begin actual training with a three-day workshop, for example, the consultant might think of getting information this way:

A consultant who is visible to the client collects self-report information via interview in a situation that is convened by the consultant.

A consultant might get information about how the faculty works together at meetings in this way:

> A consultant who is visible to the client collects information about the client by observing (method) a natural regular meeting (source and situation) of the faculty.

Sometimes a consultant asks trainees to participate in a game or simulation, the chief purpose of which is to enable the participants objectively to observe their own group dynamics. The mapping sentence for this kind of information gathering would be:

> A client group which is visible to itself collects information about itself from its members (source) who are present and observing (method) themselves as a group in a situation that has been given structure by the client's having agreed to participate in the game.

The debriefing after the game, when participants reveal to one another what they saw themselves and others doing, also gives the consultant information about the client's ability at self-diagnosis:

> A consultant who is visible to the client collects information about the client from behavior of the client directly observable now (the game and debriefing session) in a situation which the consultant has structured as a game.

And so on. The mapping sentence is a handy way of reminding ourselves of the many ways in which we can obtain information about clients and in which clients can obtain information about themselves. When planning diagnosis of context, assessment of design, monitoring progress, and evaluating outcomes, or when conferring with an outside evaluator, the consultant can use the mapping sentence as a check list from which to select appropriate data gatherers, visibility, sources, methods, and situations.

Reactivity

Some of the methods of data collecting are more likely than others to arouse a reaction in clients. When planning data collection, OD consultants should ask themselves how their method of gathering information will affect the clients' willingness and ability to give it, also how their gathering this information will affect the clients' readiness to participate in further consultative or training activities.

Communication can deal with matters distant or close. You can ask respondents for information about things they care little about (distant) or about things important to them (close). You can ask them about things that happened long ago and far away or about things that are happening here and now. You can ask them about abstractions or about things of direct concern to you both. You can ask them for intellectual opinions or about their emotional reactions, demand specific instances from their own experience or allow them to give vague generalities (these features of distance and closeness are diagrammed in figure 3-3 of chapter 3). Generally, and especially during the early stages of work with clients, communication about close matters is likely to raise more anxiety than communication about distant matters.

Heightened anxiety does not incapacitate the individual for action or reasoning, but it does cause the person to focus attention narrowly, to perceive only a few simple features of a situation and only a few alternatives for action. The ability to think creatively, to review alternatives, to withhold judgment, to try unusual or playful combinations—all decrease as anxiety rises, and anxiety is bound to rise when you are dealing with a problem that is threatening or full of uncertainties. Clients will not make a better decision by pretending the anxiety is not present, because it remains within them, narrowing their perspective. They will not make a better decision by waiting for the anxiety to go away, because this will not change the facts in the problem, and the anxiety will recur when their attention returns to the facts.

The client can compensate for narrowed vision, however, by continuing to communicate with the group in the meantime. Despite the presence of anxiety, each individual's narrowed vision will usually focus on a different aspect of the problem so that the group as a whole will still maintain a wider vision than would any one individual. Further, if the individuals admit their heightened anxiety to one another and so become aware of the danger, they can make an extra effort to bring out more facts and discuss a wider array of alternatives than any individual alone would feel inclined to do.

There is no simple rule that you can use to know when your method of data collection will or will not raise anxiety. What people feel is important differs from place to place and from time to time. The psychological distance of last year's events can be estimated only by knowing local history; the degree to which people feel that information about others is distant from them depends on how distant they feel the others are from them. The OD consultant should not purposefully add anxiety to that already occurring naturally in the school unless the anxiety-producing activity will bring more gain than loss to the client.

When a data gatherer is visible, clients confront the possibility that information about them is going to be conveyed to others. This happens even when one of their own group is taking notes that will later be given to the consultant. Information lying in nonpublic archives, in contrast, is often little affected by the desire of people to look good to outsiders. If early interviews between a school staff and a consultant turn too soon to serious interpersonal matters, they may turn into mere exercises in looking good by the interviewees.

Of course, the point at which it is no longer too soon to turn to close data differs with the client and the project's purpose, and ascertaining the right day, or even moment, challenges the consultant's skill. If people in a school feel that they have been dragooned into an OD project by a principal or superintendent, it may be longer before they are ready to talk about anxiety-raising problems and the people they believe to embody them. If participants have themselves joined together to invite a consultant's help, and particularly if they have had previous experience with the consultant, the time may be shorter.

If the data gathering is highly reactive—that is, if it causes some sort of relevant change within the clients—you will find yourself with data that tell you what the clients *were* like but what they are like no longer. Although this inconvenience should be avoided whenever possible, it is often worth using a reactive method if it gets a kind of information you need for effective consultation, even at the cost of having to recheck the client's condition before taking the action you based on your earlier diagnosis. You must make that timely check, no matter how informally, to be sure that your design for intervention matches the client's present condition and not a condition that no longer exists. If you do not check, you may pay the still higher price of having to redo that part of the intervention and suffer loss of confidence on the part of the clients. The recheck need not be as formal or extensive as the first assessment, of course; often a simple oral query will suffice.

Information is especially reactive when it is fed back to the client by the consultant; in fact, data feedback is very often a useful strategy for bringing about change.* Since it is natural for clients to consider whether the data show them as they wish to be seen, they may take the information as a prod to change.

Validity

How do you know, when you have collected information about your clients, whether your judgments about their condition, abilities, resourcefulness, and readiness correspond to fact? How can you know, when you act on your newly formed judgments, whether the clients will behave as your judgments lead you to expect? The only way you can know for sure is to design an action based on your new judgments, carry out the action, and note the clients' reactions. This seems the merest common sense; yet it is easy to forget that the judgments we make from data are only inferences subject to the errors of human logic, desire, impatience, and fatigue that are common to us all. It is important always to treat inferences from data as hypotheses and to check every hypothesis against relevant data for the purpose of confirming, revising, or further testing your conclusions.

If, for example, you deduce from questionnaires that teachers in a school show a low level of readiness for collaboration, the next

---

*For details of data feedback, see chapter 10. The pioneering standard text on nonreactive methods of data collection is that of Webb et al. (1966). A more recent book on the topic, and one more oriented toward schools, is that of Brandt (1972).

day at the school you could say to the first teacher you see: "I've sometimes worked on projects where the teachers took a year or two to build teaching teams and made them work pretty well. How would you react if one of your colleagues suggested an idea like that to you?" To the next teacher you might say: "Not long ago I visited a place where a half-dozen of the teachers figured out a way of scheduling classes so that they could include a two-week minicourse on about a week's notice and do it almost any time of the year. Do you know whether anyone here has tried anything like that or wanted to? If one of the other teachers told you tomorrow that three or four teachers were going to try to figure out how to do something like that, would you feel like joining in?" You might ask the next teacher: "Has anything been getting under way here to bring parents more into the life of the school? Have any teachers got together as a group to work out a place for parents? How would you react if another teacher asked you whether you wanted to join a group working on an idea like that?"

Questionnaire results that had suggested a low readiness for collaboration in the school would lead you to expect little enthusiasm in response to such questions. Your conclusion would be validated if you received answers like: "People never stick together on anything around here," or "I'd tell them that if they want to do it, they should go ahead on their own," or "That's not the way to get anything done. If the principal can do it, he should do it. If the principal can't do it, the teachers certainly can't." In this hypothetical example, you predicted a pessimistic answer and got it. Your conclusion from the questionnaires was given a further independent test, and, if the results gave you confirmation, your confidence in your conclusion would have increased. If, on the other hand, you had got answers more optimistic than you had expected, you would have to revise your conclusion and give the new conclusion still another test.

Consultants can increase their chances of learning whether they have designed well or poorly by giving a brief explanation at the start of each part of the training event that tells the clients how each item on the program is believed to fit into their goals. The consultants can then be alert to the amount of enthusiasm participants show as they move into the activities, the kinds of questions they ask as they go along, the features of the work to which they object, the speed with which they return from coffee breaks, and so on.

If the participants indicate that they find the training interesting and useful, the consultants know that they have designed well. If the participants drag their heels, suggest numerous changes that would make the work superficial or lead away from agreed goals, the consultants will have to reconsider their previous judgments about the clients. When a design for an intervention begins to go wrong, the remainder of the design should be reassessed immediately. When consultants are not confident in their judgments about revising the plan, it can sometimes be very effective to share these doubts with the participants and revise the plan jointly with them.

Anticipating the kind of reaction you are going to get to a certain kind of action, taking that action, and watching to see whether you get the anticipated response is called *hypothesis testing*. When you form your idea about the clients by examining data about them and then test your idea by gathering still more data, it is called *cross-validation.** When you get the second round of data by a different method, you are using the *multimethod strategy*. Many social scientists, it is true, try to collect their data in very simple situations instead of in complicated places like schools, so that they can have more confidence in their conclusions at the end of their data collection. But despite the differences between the laboratory and the natural setting, the basic logic of hypothesis testing, cross-validation, and multimethod strategy is the same in both places. The annotated bibliography at the end of this chapter will tell you where to read more about these techniques.

Multiple Methods.   When information gathered from one source or by one method agrees with information from another source or method, you are almost always justified in feeling more confidence in the validity of the information. Any method of data collecting is likely to have weaknesses, however, and information should never be discarded, no matter how unreliable its source, until you have clear evidence that it is faulty. Weak information does not weaken strong information. If it agrees with it, it may strengthen the strong information a bit; if it disagrees, it offers only a small challenge. Unless it has a noticeably spoiled odor, information of every sort should be added to your collection.

    At the early stages of entry, for example, no alternative method of getting information is likely to have greater validity than that which the consultant carefully infers from face-to-face conversations. Multiple-choice questionnaires may bring greater objectivity to the scorer than do records of conversations; but objectivity is no guarantee of validity, and questionnaires have shortcomings as well. Without adequate rapport between interveners and clients, questionnaires offer an easy occasion for carelessness and dissembling. Many teachers and administrators, especially those working near universities, have been badgered with questionnaires until they have become cynical about them. Many teachers, facing still another questionnaire, will be reminded of other occasions that were followed by no return of information, no action taken on the basis of information they gave, no demand that they stand responsible for their answers, and no evidence that their answers were kept confidential, whatever the investigator's promises.

    In these circumstances it is not surprising if disenchanted respondents write answers that are quick, noncommittal, or safe, or

---

*In the strict meaning of cross-validation, you would collect both rounds of data in a different school from the one in which you got your idea. The social scientists who invented the term were not interested in any particular bunch of people but in bunches of people in general. We are bending the concept only a little by using it in connection with OD practices, because the logic of double-checking is the same in both applications.

relieve their boredom by composing responses that they regard as humorous. Questions about interpersonal matters, especially, are likely to be resented and skipped. Even those who have had little previous contact with researchers, evaluators, or consultants may be suspicious about the use to be made of the data, so that they, too, give answers that will be safe even if they reach the superintendent. During the early days of acquaintance between client and consultant or evaluator, most of these weaknesses apply to interviews and direct observation as well.

This is not to say that any one method is generally better than another. Even in the early stages of a project, information can be strengthened by getting the same sort of information from two or more sources or methods. In discussing problems informally with teachers in a high school, for example, we noted that teachers in one department never hinted at any conflict with teachers in another department, even though we knew that both departments depended on the same school budget and must sometimes have been in competition for scarce resources. But we also knew that the schedule of classes and other duties prevented the department heads from having time for conferences and that the principal wrote each year's budget single-handedly.

We concluded that the department heads communicated very little, even outside school hours, that they knew very little about how the principal balanced demands on the budget, and that if they displayed very little overt conflict, it was because the schedule allowed them no occasion on which a first exchange of information could occur and because they had too little information about budgeting to express a sharp conflict, even if they had the occasion. To check our hypothesis, we arranged a meeting of five department heads, some pairs of which might have potentialities for conflict. The earlier conversations with teachers constituted one method and the meeting with department heads a second; the second method validated the first.

At the first meeting we said merely, "We asked the principal to make time in your schedules for this meeting specifically so that you could have time to discuss the question of whether there *is* anything that might be mutually profitable for you to discuss." After several questions about our own motivation (such as, "Are you getting a dissertation out of this?"), the department heads began to ask one another whether they had, in fact, any mutual concerns worth discussing. Before long, they decided that they wanted a regular time to meet together and wanted to know more about the school's budget. This lent further validity to our interpretation and also opened a point of entry for further work.

Another example of checking through different sources is the series of steps used by Wyant (1974) to ascertain whether schools had what he called "collaborative structure," by which he meant (1) a strong leadership team or "Improvement-of-Instruction committee," (2) a sharply differentiated position for leaders of teaching units, and (3) stable, well defined teaching teams to which all instructional personnel were assigned.* To make sure that a school met or failed to meet these criteria, Wyant first asked central office personnel, such as the director of elementary education, to name the schools in the district that satisfied these criteria and then asked the principals of the schools named whether their schools met the criteria. If the principal said yes, Wyant went to the leaders of the teaching units (if they existed) and asked once again about the criteria. Only those schools that passed the inquiry at all three steps were designated as having collaborative structure.

Testimonials. OD consultants are often tempted to accept complimentary remarks from their clients as a fair evaluation of their work. They are right in accepting compliments as part of the picture, but they are wrong if they leap to the conclusion that clients who did not speak felt the same as those who did. In one situation, those who are angry may be the more vocal; in another, the happier people may speak up. Testimonials can bring diagnostic information only if you give every sort of reaction an equal chance of reaching you. If you collect only the opinions of clients who initiate approaches to you, you are almost certainly allowing bias in one direction or another to affect the opinions you get.

The solution is to go after the data yourself, making sure to ask for opinions from every client or from a representative sample of them. At the end of a training day, for example, consultants can ask participants to form buzz groups and tell one another in what ways things are better or worse than they were yesterday or before the training. Recording all the remarks will usually bring information of reasonable validity, but the important point is how the remarks are selected. If the consultant or evaluator selects them in a way that allows each remark an equal chance to be heard, the evaluation will be a fair one.

Strictly random sampling gives everyone an equal chance to be heard and is less expensive than getting information from everyone. A strictly random sample is unbiased—that is, the error in the sample is no more likely to lie in one direction that in another—but every sample gives an estimate that is to some degree wrong. Strictly random sampling will give you small errors more often than large ones, but you never know whether your next random sample will be a really bad one. If you want to guarantee an accurate estimate of where a whole school stands, you must interview everyone in the school.†

Early Effects. At the outset of an intervention, things will often seem pleasant enough; but as the clients learn to speak more openly

---

*Wyant adapted these criteria from a list made by our CASEA colleagues Richard Carlson, W. W. Charters, Jr., and John Packard. For a more detailed list from the same source and another application of it, see Schmuck et al. (1975, p. 160).
† Sampling will be discussed again in chapter 11.

about their feelings and tell more about their disgruntlements with their working conditions, their colleagues may conclude that the consultants have upset them by stirring things up. The onlookers are here noting only an increase in expressed disgruntlement and are forgetting that the trainees may have been just as dissatisfied earlier but unwilling to talk about it. In our view, if a school staff does not increase its complaints soon after consultation starts, the consultants should conclude either that the training in openness of communication has been remarkably ineffective or that conditions in the school have remarkably improved very recently.

The famous "Hawthorne effect" is also susceptible to opposite interpretations. When an intervention in a school or other organization is followed by an increase in productivity or morale, some onlookers will remark that people almost always do better when they know they are being watched. This observation is only half-true. People usually act differently when they know they are being watched, but whether they will do better or worse depends on many other things. Indeed, workers who are subjected to an innovation by management sometimes show the "reverse Hawthorne effect"—they will slow down rather than speed up.

How people will react to attention is not a simple matter. When a classroom is visited by a principal, superintendent, or group of parents, for example, will the students want to be more or less obedient to the teacher than usual? Will they want to show more or less knowledge of the lessons? Will they want to recite with more or less clarity and enthusiasm? Whichever they choose to do, do they choose so as to gain self-approbation without regard to the opinions of others? Do they choose their acts in the hope of pleasing the teacher, other students, or someone not even present? Or do they choose their acts in the hope of displeasing teacher, fellow student, or someone else? If they choose a particular kind of act, are they capable of performing it or will their performance fall short in some way?

Similarly, if teachers are interviewed by central office persons after three or four months of OD training, how are they likely to perform during the interviews? Will they want to please or displease the interviewers, and are they correct about what will please or displease? Suppose the teachers are interviewed by their OD trainers, who want to monitor progress. Do the teachers want the consultants to feel good or bad, and do they know what will make them feel the one way or the other?

Arguments about the Hawthorne effect are further complicated by the view that this effect is somehow disreputable—that effects on a faculty, for example, are not due to the training but merely to the attention that faculty are getting from the consultants and from one another. This argument is difficult to refute rationally because it makes a false dichotomy. Communication, training, love, reward and punishment cannot be carried on without special attentiveness. In fact, one of the goals of OD training is to heighten the ability of participants to be more attentive to one another, to give routinely what now seems like special attention. From this point of view, the Hawthorne effect, however double-edged, becomes a tool, not necessarily a debility.

Summary. In sum, consultants, if they are to be effective, should extract information about context and progress from every source that is relevant and by every method that is appropriate. They must diagnose the conditions of context that exist at entry, carefully assess their intervention designs, continually monitor the progress of the change project, and assess the outcomes after intervention has ceased.

In large projects, diagnosis and evaluation can strongly influence participant reaction to the entire project. Consultants and evaluators, whether the same or different persons, will maintain more effective relations with clients if they allow clients to see that they can be trusted with potentially harmful information, if they avoid any role in which they could be perceived as influencing the fate of participants against their will, and if they teach participants how to gather and interpret information about themselves. Evaluators should also collect information under circumstances that permit participants' anxiety to be low and choose methods that do not stir participants to overmuch self-examination.

In initial diagnosis, consultants should ascertain the manner in which the client organization is functioning in its interpersonal communication, in its subsystems, as a whole organization, and in its interaction with its environment. Of great importance to the effectiveness of the project is the presence of certain conditions of client readiness. These include willingness to undergo a minimal amount of initial training; an attitude of receptiveness toward openness, confrontation, and the different philosophies and life-styles of colleagues; an ability to persevere in accomplishing tasks; reasonable accuracy about communication channels in the school; reasonable confidence in the interveners; and support from the district's administrators.

For their part, consultants' plans should not be regarded as exempt from critical examination but should be judged for their effectiveness by fellow consultants and compared with the principles and methods set forth throughout this book. Chapters 2 through 8 offer methods of monitoring the OD project while it is in process. Methods suggested for diagnosing context (chap. 2) and evaluating outcomes (chap. 11) can usually be modified to serve for monitoring progress as well. Similarly, methods suggested in this book for assessing one of the levels of interpersonal skill, subsystem skill, or organizational adaptability can usually be modified to be suitable at the two other levels. Multiple methods of collecting data on the same topic should be used whenever possible, and unfavorable testimonials should be given the same chance of access as favorable ones. Finally, consultants should always draw hypotheses rather than conclusions from their data and allow later data continually to test these hypotheses either for confirmation or revision.

READINGS

Interviews and Questionnaires

A. N. Oppenheim

The following excerpt offers a sound introduction to carrying out structured interviews or constructing questionnaires. In Oppenheim's view, questionnaires are used both to guide the formal interview and to obtain responses from respondents without benefit of an interviewer.

From Chapter 2 of *Questionnaire Design and Attitude Measurement* by A. N. Oppenheim, © 1966 by A. N. Oppenheim, Basic Books, Inc. Publishers, New York.

Before actually constructing the questionnaire, we would have formed a rough idea of the pattern that the inquiry is likely to follow. We would know approximate answers to such issues as how large will the sample be? Will we be dealing with children or with adults; with housewives, company directors, relatives of prisoners, or undergraduates; or with a representative sample of the population? Do we intend to approach the same respondents more than once? Are we concerned with seasonal fluctuations? Are we dealing with a short, factual inquiry or with analytic, attitudinal research? And so on. But we still have to make a number of decisions before we can begin to write our first question. These decisions fall into five groups: (1) Decisions concerning the main and auxiliary methods of data-collection, such as interviews, mail questionnaires, observational techniques, and study of documents; (2) The method of approach to the respondents, . . . including sponsorship, stated purpose of the research, confidentiality, and anonymity; (3) The build-up of question sequences and the order of questions and other techniques within the framework of the questionnaire; (4) For each variable, the *order* of questions within each question sequence, such as funneling, quintamensional design, and factual versus attitudinal opening; and (5) The use of precoded versus free-response questions. . . .

The greatest advantage of the *interview* in the hands of a skilled interviewer is its flexibility. The interviewer can make sure that the respondent has understood the question and the purpose of the research. We can ask the interviewers to probe further when particular responses are encountered; we can ask them to classify the answers on the spot (field coding); they can show the respondent cards, lists, or pictures, hand out product samples, or self-completion checklists, or diaries, and make ratings or assessments of attitudes, furnishings, dwelling areas, and so forth. Above all, they can build up and maintain rapport, that elusive motivating force that will keep the respondent interested and responsive to the end of the interview.

The interview situation is, however, fraught with possibilities of bias. The interviewer may give an inkling of her own opinion or expectations by her tone of voice, the way in which she reads the questions, or simply by her appearance, dress, and accent. She may unwittingly influence the respondent by pausing expectantly at certain points, by probing with leading questions, and by agreeing with the respondent in an effort to maintain rapport. Her own expectations and her selective understanding and recording of the answers may produce bias. An interviewer may misunderstand or fail to obey instructions; she may show surprise or boredom in tone of emphasis or in other ways unconsciously communicate her own attitudes and her expectations of the respondent's attitudes. Interviewers differ in age and sex, social background, skin color, dress, speech, and experience. Interviewers react differently to different respondents and carry out their probes with more or less care. Questions concerned with "delicate" issues raise special problems. Some of these biases can be largely eliminated by suitable selection and training and by careful checks and supervision; but other biases may remain and will influence the results to an unknown degree. . . .

The chief advantage of the *mail questionnaire* is cheapness. Since it does not require a trained staff of field workers, . . . virtually all that it requires is the cost of the planning and pilot work, printing or duplicating expenses, sampling, addressing, mailing, and providing stamped, self-addressed envelopes for the returns. The processing and analysis are usually also simpler and cheaper than in the case of interviews. . . .

By far the largest disadvantage of mail questionnaires, however, is the fact that they usually produce very poor response rates. For respondents who have no special interest in the subject matter of the questionnaire, figures of 40 per cent to 60 per cent are typical; even in studies of interested groups, 80 per cent is seldom exceeded. . . .

Question Sequence

The whole questionnaire will consist of a series of question sequences, and the order of question sequences must first be considered. We may wish to start with some factual questions, followed by attitudinal ones, or the other way around. We may wish to repeat the same questions in different contexts or by the use of different techniques. We must, however, avoid putting ideas into the respondent's mind early in the interview, if we need spontaneous responses on the same points later on. Last but not least, we must make the questionnaire attractive and interesting to the respondent. For instance, we ought to start off the interview with some easy, impersonal questions and not ask for details like age, family, occupation, and so forth until rapport has been well established. We must ask ourselves how this question sequence will strike the respondent. Is it too intimidating? Do the questions seem relevant to our explanation of the purpose of our research? Have we unwittingly made our own attitudes too obvious? Are the questions worded in a friendly way? We are not likely to produce a helpful attitude in the respondent if we start off the interview with some staccato questions such as: "Age," "Occupation," "Marital status," "Income." . . .

In what sequence can we best approach the relevant issue? The "funnel" approach, with various "filter" questions, is a well-known type of sequence. The funnel approach is so named because it starts off with a very broad question and then progressively narrows down the scope of the questions until it comes to some very specific points.

For instance, suppose we want to know whether some people avoid hard candies because they are said to be harmful to the teeth. It would not do to ask them a question such as, "Do you believe that hard candies are harmful to the teeth?" or, "Do you avoid eating hard candies because you feel that they harm the teeth?" These would be grossly leading questions, and, besides, the respondent may never eat hard candies, or he may avoid them for some other reason. Obviously, it would be valuable if we could get the respondent to say spontaneously that he avoids hard candies because they are damaging to his teeth, before we suggest it to him, and before he becomes aware what the questions are really about. Therefore, we may start off with some very broad questions, such as: "What is your opinion of hard candies?" "What do you think of people who eat hard candies?" Each question provides the respondent with an opportunity to mention the issue of dental decay spontaneously. Next, we might ask more restricted questions, such as: "Do you eat hard candies at all?" "Did you eat hard candies when you were a child?" "Do you allow your children to eat hard candies?" Each should be followed up with "Why?" if the reply is negative, thus providing further opportunities for the dental issue to emerge spontaneously. After that, we may narrow the questions still further: "Do you believe that hard candies can be harmful in any way?" "What would happen if you ate too many hard candies?" "What are some of the disadvantages of eating hard candies?" Note that the dental problem still has not been mentioned directly. Finally, we bring up the problem as nondirectively as possible: "Some people say that eating hard candies is bad for your teeth, but others say that it makes no difference. How do you feel about this?" Or, "Do you believe that eating hard candies is bad for your teeth, or do you think that most people's teeth will not be damaged by eating hard candies?" And so on. By proceeding in this way we not only increase our chances of obtaining what we are seeking through a spontaneous reply, we also place the whole issue of hard candies and tooth decay in the context of some of the other factors that determine the eating of hard candies. This context can be very important; it may well be that other reasons for not eating hard candies are mentioned far more frequently than the possible danger to the teeth.

A filter question is used to exclude a respondent from a particular question sequence if those questions are irrelevant to him. Thus, in the above example, we might wish to ask for some factual information about candy-buying behavior and hard-candy purchases. Obviously, if the respondent never buys these sweets then there is no point in asking him about frequency, weight, type of shop, type of container, color preferences, and so forth. Therefore, our illustrative question sequence will be preceded by a filter question, such as, "Do you buy hard candies from time to time?" or, "Have you bought any hard candies within the past two weeks?" If the answer is negative, the interviewer will be instructed to skip the next few questions and proceed to the beginning of the next question sequence.

Each survey produces its own problems of question order, which makes it difficult to offer general principles. We try, as much as possible, to avoid putting ideas into the respondent's mind or to suggest that he should have attitudes when he has none. Therefore, with regard to any issue, we will want to start with open questions and only introduce more structured or precoded questions at a later stage. . . .

Open and Closed Questions

Broadly speaking, all questions are either "open" or "closed." A closed question is one in which the respondent is offered a choice of alternative replies. He may be asked to check or underline his chosen answer(s) in a written questionnaire, or the alternatives may be read aloud or shown to him on a prompt card or a slide. Questions of this kind may offer simple alternatives, such as "Yes" and "No," or the names of five political parties in an election; or they can offer something more complex, such as a choice of ways of keeping order in a classroom or a choice of motives for smoking cigarettes.

Open or free-answer types of questions are not followed by any kind of choice, and the answers have to be recorded in full. In the case of a written questionnaire, the amount of space of the number of lines provided for the answer will help to determine the length and fullness of the responses we obtain. . . .

The chief advantage of the open question is the freedom that it gives to the respondent. Once he has understood the intent of the question, he can let his thoughts roam freely, unencumbered by a prepared set of replies. We obtain his ideas in his own language, expressed spontaneously, and this spontaneity is often extremely worthwhile as a basis for new hypotheses. In an interview, however, there is the risk that we will obtain, not so much a rounded and full account of the respondent's feelings, but rather just what happens to be uppermost in his mind at the time. If this is true, then we may still ask whether what comes first to the respondent's mind is not also most important for him and for us.

Free-response questions are often easy to ask, difficult to answer, and still more difficult to analyze. As a rule, we employ a classification process known as "coding," . . . which requires drawing up some system of categories, a coding frame. The composition of such coding frames and the actual coding operation require trained staff and are extremely time-consuming; for this reason survey workers have to curb their desire to have too many open questions.

Sometimes, if the first answer seems a little ambiguous or does not go far enough, we can instruct the interviewer to probe. This often takes the form of asking the respondent to explain further or to give his reasons for something stated earlier; at times, a particular issue may be brought into the discussion deliberately, if the respondent has not already mentioned it. Such probes should be as non-directive as possible, thus: "Could you say a little more about . . . ?" "Why did you say just now that . . . ?" "Now, what about the . . . ?" "And how do you feel about . . . ?" The risk of interviewer bias is probably at its highest whenever probes are employed. They are "safe" only in the hands of the most highly trained and experienced fieldworkers. . . .

Closed questions are easier and quicker to answer; they require no writing; and quantification is straightforward. This often means that more questions can be asked within a given length of time and that more can be accomplished with a given sum of money. Disadvantages of closed questions are the loss of spontaneity and expressiveness—we shall never know what the respondent said or thought of his own accord—and perhaps the introduction of bias by "forcing" him to choose between given alternatives and by making him think of alternatives that might not have occurred to him. Closed questions are often cruder and less subtle than open ones, although this is not necessarily so, and we do lose the opportunity to probe. There may also be some loss of rapport, if respondents become irritated because they feel that the choice of answers fails to do justice to their own ideas.

Sometimes, there may be good reasons for asking the same question both in open and closed form. For instance, if we ask, "What are some of the things that make a man move up in the world?" we shall get a pretty clear idea of the way in which the respondent thinks the social system works, and the relative importance to him of several avenues of mobility, such as education, hard work, money, luck. We get a free, spontaneous sketch in the respondent's own language and containing his own ideas. This is most valuable, but it makes it difficult to compare one group of respondents with another. Also, we cannot be sure that such an impromptu sketch really contains all the factors that are important to the respondent. A momentary lapse, a feeling of reticence, or the inability to put ideas into words can cause the omission of significant points. Therefore, later in the interview we may ask the same question again, but this time we will offer him a list that he may be asked to rate or rank . . . , or from which he may be asked to choose the three most important factors. Having already obtained the spontaneous responses, there can now be little harm in introducing a set of ideas, . . . even though some of these might not have occurred to our respondent. By using a "closed" approach we ensure that the results of several groups can readily be compared and that all respondents have considered the same universe of content before giving their replies.

Readiness, Training, and Responsiveness

Philip J. Runkel

If you do not pay attention to readiness during your diagnosis, you may not only fail in your goals but may actually do more harm than good. The following reading, prepared especially for this volume, gives evidence from an actual project of how some schools were helped by their readiness and how others were harmed by lack of it. The analysis of the data was complex because the relationships in the data were complex. Although consultants will seldom encounter such complexity in collecting and analyzing data, we believe it is useful to give an example of the subtle relations that sometimes arise among readiness, consultation, and outcomes.

Prepared especially for this volume.

Runkel, Wyant, and Bell (1975, chap. 5) selected four questionnaire items to yield diagnostic information about the existing willingness in a school to sustain communication about work-related matters during occasions of emotional arousal.* These four items, which we shall term a *Test of Communication,* do not ask for respondents' wishes or guesses about how they themselves would act; they ask for estimates of how others in the school would act. This ploy, we think, reduced the likelihood of distortion to which questions about self are prone and at the same time yielded a pooled estimate about the school as a whole instead of a mere nose count.

In another test, which we shall call the *Test of Responsiveness,* Runkel, Wyant, and Bell chose three items to indicate an expectation that other teachers would be helpful if they were asked for help to improve one's teaching. These items are more at the level of one-to-one interaction than at the level of intragroup coordination, but they indicate a necessary level of responsiveness, even if an elementary one.†

- Suppose Teacher X wants to improve his classroom effectiveness. If X asked another teacher to observe his teaching and then to have a conference about it afterward, how would you feel toward X?
  - ( ) I would approve strongly.
  - ( ) I would approve mildly or some.
  - ( ) I wouldn't care one way or the other.
  - ( ) I would disapprove mildly or some.
  - ( ) I would disapprove strongly.

---

* The four items are displayed earlier in this chapter under the heading "Indicators of Readiness." Two are the first and second items under the subheading "Access to Variety Pool"; the other two are the first and second items under "Openness and Confrontation."

† For a discussion of responsiveness, see chapter 1.

- Suppose Teacher X develops a particularly useful and effective method for teaching something. In Teacher X's place, would most of the teachers you know in your school describe it briefly at a faculty meeting and offer to meet with others who wanted to hear more about it?
  - ( ) Yes, I think most would do this.
  - ( ) Maybe about half would do this.
  - ( ) No, most would *not*.
  - ( ) I don't know.

- Suppose Teacher X wants to improve his classroom effectiveness. In Teacher X's place, would most of the teachers you know in your building ask another teacher to observe his teaching and then have a conference afterward?
  - ( ) Yes, I think most would do this.
  - ( ) Maybe about half would do this.
  - ( ) No, most would *not*.
  - ( ) I don't know.

The scores of respondents within schools were summed to yield a mean raw score for each school. Next, the raw scores were converted to "standard scores"—that is, the mean raw school-score for the year and district was subtracted from each school's score and that result was then divided by the standard deviation of the distribution of school scores. A positive standard score tells us that the school lay above the district's mean in that year; a negative standard score tells us that the school lay below the district's mean. Furthermore, even though schools are being compared on two different tests, a standard score of (say) 1.7* tells us that the school's score was high enough to exceed about 95 percent of other schools in that year and district, no matter which test the score came from and no matter what the mean and spread of *raw* scores happened to be. Standard scores make comparisons easier.

Runkel, Wyant, and Bell found that high and low skill in communication, as indicated by the Test of Communication, had helping and hindering effects respectively on work-related responsiveness—that is, on scores on the Test of Responsiveness. Table 2-2 shows the relevant mean scores and some other pertinent information. The table divides the elementary schools of the sample (which grew from twelve schools in 1969 to fifteen in 1972) into two clusters: the cluster at the left of the table contains those schools relatively high on the Test of Communication; the cluster on the right contains those relatively low. The separation is strong. Note that in every year, *both* means on communication in the left-hand cluster exceeded *either* mean in the right-hand cluster. In 1969, for example, both means 1.00 and 0.48 were higher than either mean -0.45 or -0.59.

When the schools were clustered according to their scores on the Test of Communication, it turned out that the means of the

---

*On the average, a school with a standard score of 1.00 exceeds 84 percent of schools in its year and district; a school with a standard score of 1.51 exceeds 93 percent.

TABLE 2-2   Mean Standard Scores of Groups of Elementary Schools: Tests of Respons ness and Communication

		Schools higher on the test of communication			
		Mean hours training	Mean on communication	Mean on responsiveness	Numl of schoo
1969	Trained	15	1.00	0.79	1
	Untrained	0	0.48	-0.05	5
	Difference			0.84	
1970	Trained	14	1.51	0.69	3
	Untrained	0	-0.09	-0.20	4
	Difference			0.89	
1972	Trained	25	1.01	0.82	4
	Untrained	0	0.04	-0.23	4
	Difference			1.05	

SOURCE: Adapted from tables 5-11 and 5-12 of Runkel, Wyant, and Bell (1975).

clusters on the Test of Responsiveness did not follow suit. It turned out, indeed, that level of communication made a great difference in the *relation* between training and responsiveness.

Looking first at the left-hand cluster, we see that in every year the means on responsiveness of the trained schools greatly exceeded those of the untrained schools. But the right-hand cluster shows that in every year the means of the trained schools fell *below* those of the untrained schools. Among trained schools, the score on communica- tion made a great difference in the score on responsiveness. This is easy to see in the most right-hand column of table 2-2. Moreover, training seemed to elevate responsiveness well above the district's mean when skill in communication during emotion was above average, but training *depressed* responsiveness when skill in com- munication was below average. Our conclusion is that too little readiness to communicate during emotion in the right-hand cluster of schools caused OD training in that cluster to do more harm than good to responsiveness among teachers when they asked one another for help in improving their teaching.*

---

* Runkel, Wyant, and Bell (1975) give evidence to rule out several alternative hypotheses.

ools lower on the test of communication

an ırs ning	Mean on communication	Mean on responsiveness	Number of schools	Difference between responsiveness means
6	-0.45	-0.50	1	1.29
0	-0.59	-0.00	5	-0.05
		-0.50		
6	-0.16	-0.30	1	0.99
0	-0.80	-0.20	5	0.00
		-0.10		
5	0.02	-0.77	3	1.59
0	-1.07	-0.01	4	-0.22
		-0.76		

BIBLIOGRAPHY

Brandt, R. M. 1972. *Studying behavior in natural settings.* New York: Holt, Rinehart & Winston.

Chapter 1 describes the place of naturalistic methods among other methods of research. Chapter 2 discusses ethics. Chapters 4 and 5 present many unobtrusive methods of collecting data in a variety of settings. Chapters 7 and 8 are devoted to data gathering in schools and their environments. Although it gives theory its due, this is a very practical book, a radical departure from standard texts on social-science method, and a landmark in its field.

Fox, R.; Luszki, M. B.; and Schmuck, R. A. 1966. *Diagnosing classroom learning environments.* Chicago: Science Research Associates.

Offering a rationale of diagnosis and an introduction to formative evaluation, this book is made up mostly of specific diagnostic instruments that can be used to measure features of classroom group life, such as climate, social relations, norms, student-teacher interactions, and self-esteem, and is filled with concrete practical suggestions.

Fox, R.; Schmuck, R. A.; Van Egmond, E.; Ritvo, M.; and Jung, C. 1973. *Diagnosing professional climates of schools.* La Jolla, Calif.: University Associates.

This book contains thirty field-tested instruments for diagnosing various aspects of school climates. Following some concepts about schools as social systems, diagnostic tools are presented for exploring organizational problem solving, staff responsibilities, staff behaviors, staff resources, and community involvement, with practical suggestions for using each of the diagnostic tools.

Kahn, R. L., and Cannell, C. F. 1957. *The dynamics of interviewing.* New York: Wiley.

This advanced text offers many helpful techniques for organizational diagnosis, includes information on how to design and construct questionnaires and interview schedules, and deals fully with the skills needed for effective interviewing, emphasizing ways of avoiding bias.

Oppenheim, A. N. 1966. *Questionnaire design and attitude measurement.* New York: Basic Books.

This text gives practical, do-it-yourself kinds of information about diagnosis. The contents include material on questionnaire design, question framing, rating scales, check lists, attitude formats, and methods of quantifying questionnaire data.

Simon, A., and Boyer, E. G., eds. 1967. *Mirrors for behavior.* Philadelphia: Research for Better Schools.

A compendium of observation instruments for diagnosing classroom dynamics, this anthology presents many instruments that can easily be adapted for use at faculty meetings and other adult gatherings.

Webb, E. J.; Campbell, D. T.; Schwartz, R. D.; and Sechrest, L. 1966. *Unobtrusive measures: nonreactive research in the social sciences.* Chicago: Rand McNally.

This book shows how interviews and questionnaires can be supplemented with unobtrusive (nonreactive) measures to enhance diagnostic accuracy. Unobtrusive measures do not alert the persons producing the information and therefore do not serve as input variables as questionnaires and interviews might. The book discusses accretion and erosion of data, archives and how to use them, and ways of using direct observations.

3

Clarifying Communication

Although many different activities, from ringing a school bell to reading a printed page, may be categorized as communication, this chapter will focus mainly on the kinds of face-to-face verbal and non-verbal interactions between people in subsystems by means of which educational functions are carried out. The first section explains what is meant by unilateral, directive, and transactional communication; the second section describes interpersonal communication; the third describes communication processes in subsystems; and the fourth considers communication in the organization as a whole. Instruments that the OD consultant can use to assess communication are enumerated in the fifth section. The sixth describes exercises and intervention designs that we have used to enhance clear communication in schools.

TYPES OF COMMUNICATION

In its simplest form, unilateral communication is a discrete event that is initiated by a speaker and terminated at a listener; examples in schools include reading the morning bulletins over the loudspeaker or making announcements at faculty meetings. But much unilateral communication involves a second step as well. In studying the mass media, for example, Katz (1957) found that information from the media reaches certain opinion leaders who in turn relay it, as they understand it, to others in face-to-face interactions. Although this second step involves two-way communication, the event remains unilateral because the original source of information is unable to clarify any misunderstandings that may have occurred during the transmission of the information. Indeed, any error in transmission is likely to be amplified during this second step.

In their study of the transmission of rumors, Allport and Postman (1945) describe three psychological processes that occur in the course of two-, three-, and four-step communications. In the first process, called *leveling*, the receiver tends to reduce contrasts between parts of a message—by omitting qualifying phrases, for example. In the second, the receiver *sharpens* certain parts of the information so that a few high points are remembered while most of the rest is forgotten. In the third, the receiver *assimilates* much of the message into his personal frame of reference, coloring his memories and interpretations of the message by his own thoughts and feelings. For all these reasons, unilateral communication is not an efficient way of transmitting information even when it is supplemented by a second step.

In directive communication, which occurs face-to-face, the exchange is complete when the receiver indicates to the sender that the message has been received and understood, as when a teacher gives an assignment and students indicate that they understand the assignment. The distinguishing feature of a directive communication is that the sender influences while the receiver merely complies, as when one student tells another to get out of his way and the second obliges. McGregor (1967) calls this kind of communication coercive because there is no provision for mutual influence and exchange. It is assumed that the source's position is correct. The listener is required only to understand the message; acceptance is implied.

As figure 3-1 demonstrates, transactional communication is a reciprocal process in which each participant initiates messages and attempts to understand the other. Information travels in both directions rather than in one direction only; each message has some impact on the next message; and the roles of source and receiver shift rapidly back and forth as communication takes place. Participants in transactional communication engage in active listening as

FIGURE 3-1   Transactional Communication

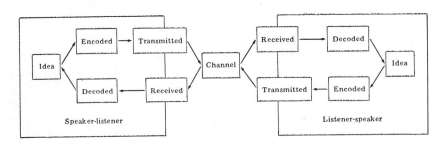

well. The listener attempts to grasp both the facts and feelings of a message, attempts to increase his understanding by discerning the speaker's point of view, and tests this understanding by advising the speaker of personal reactions to the message, thereby helping the speaker know whether the meaning was or was not communicated.

While many misunderstandings can be resolved through transactional communication, carrying out effective transactions takes a high degree of communicative skill. Participants must be able to state their thoughts and feelings clearly, ask each other for specific information, read the relevance of gestures, and make sure that the message was apprehended correctly. This mutual feedback and spirit of helpfulness between participants is of crucial importance.

INTERPERSONAL COMMUNICATION

People in schools communicate many different kinds of information to one another. They talk about the tasks they perform, the methods they use to get tasks accomplished, and sometimes, though rarely, about interpersonal dynamics they have experienced. The content of face-to-face conversations may also be viewed as belonging to one or another dimension of a problem statement—i.e., people talk about how things are (situations), how things ought to be (targets), or how to move from the situation to the target (proposals). This is known as the S-T-P model of problem analysis and will be explained in detail in chapter 7.

Features of Effective Interpersonal Communication

Openness, communication during emotion, eliciting personal resources, and trust are features that cut across the three levels of interpersonal skill, subsystem effectiveness, and organizational adaptability described in chapter 1 and are extremely important signs of a readiness to begin organization development. Their presence not only sets a context for interpersonal communication but also oils the way for improving the interpersonal skills and other subsystem processes on which improvements in organizational adaptability depend.

Openness. Luft (1969) depicts openness by means of the following useful illustration known formally as the Johari Awareness Model and informally as the Johari Window. In this model, a behavior, feeling, or motivation is assigned to one of four "quadrants" [sic] on the basis of who knows about it. Quadrant 1 refers to behavior, feelings, and motivation known both to oneself and to others (open); quadrant 2 refers to that which is known to others but not to oneself (blind); quadrant 3, to that which is known to oneself but not to others (hidden); and quadrant 4, to that which is known neither to oneself nor to others (unknown). Openness is the skill that increases the area of quadrant 1 in relation to other quadrants.

88

FIGURE 3-2   Johari Awareness Model

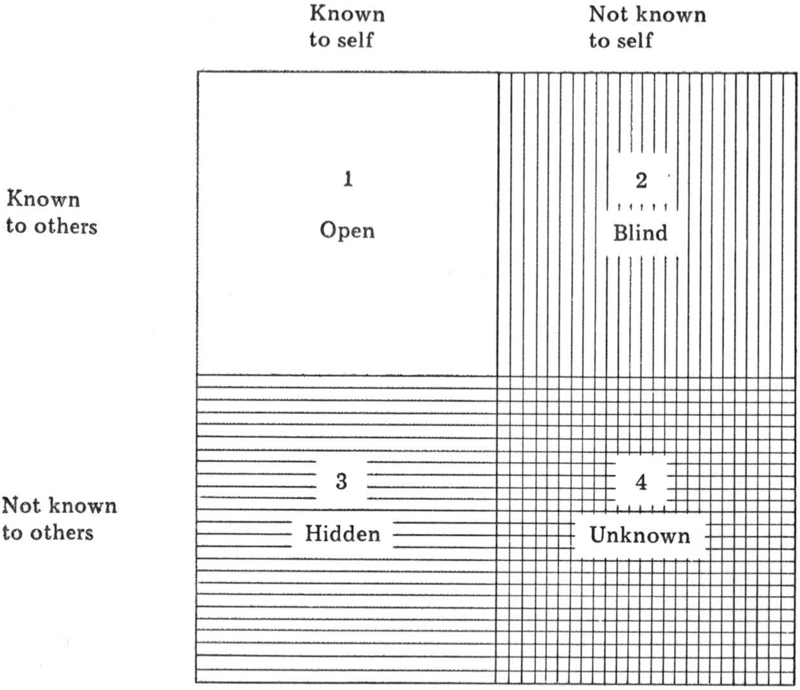

	Known to self	Not known to self
Known to others	1 Open	2 Blind
Not known to others	3 Hidden	4 Unknown

SOURCE: Luft (1969, p. 13).

Openness does not mean telling all, confiding indiscriminately, or giving information that is irrelevant to the work situation. It means giving information that both parties need in order to get work done or the feelings that are generated by people working together. By disclosing information that has heretofore been hidden and by attempting to understand their blind spots, people can increase the total amount of information in the open quadrant.

As figure 3-3 indicates, people communicate more or less openly depending upon the emotional closeness or distance they feel toward one another. In emotionally distant interactions, people know little about one another and view one another as objects that can either fulfill or frustrate their wishes and expectations. In emotionally close interactions, people recognize their interdependence with others, realizing that the other person's behavior simultaneously influences and is influenced by their own behavior.

Communication during Emotion.   It is extremely important to know how to communicate during emotion, whether it is you or another person who is hurt, angry, or embarrassed. Alberti and Emmons (1975) call this ability *assertiveness* and contrast it with nonassertive (acquiescent) and aggressive behavior. In their view, aggressive behavior enhances the sender's position at the receiver's expense; nonassertive behavior expresses the sender's self-denial and forces the receiver to make choices; assertive behavior allows the sender to be expressive and self-enhancing and to make his own choices. The following example illustrates the differences.

At the request of three teachers, the principal has agreed to order a set of books; but several weeks pass, and the teachers' irrita-

IGURE 3-3   Emotional Closeness and Distance

egree of
oseness
pends
on . . .

	CLOSE				DISTANT
hat TOPIC e are talk- g about	Concerns our rela- tion, you and me.	Concerns you or me.	Concerns people or things we both know directly.	Concerns people or things known to one of us directly.	Concerns people or things known directly to neither of us.
(ME rspective	*Now:* happening now or something that helps us understand what is happening now.			*Then:* past or future happening not related to what is happening now. *Or:* no time perspective, as in generalizations, jokes, etc.	
1PORTANCE ' topic	Important to *both* of us.		Important to *one* of us.	Important to *neither* of us.	
ow we use ır FEELINGS	Feelings seen as natural. Openly stating one's own feelings is viewed as helpful to both persons. Each accepts the other's feelings.			Feelings seen as unfortunate and disruptive. Openly stating one's own feelings is avoided, so feelings are indirectly reflected in intellectualizations and judgments about the external world, including the other.	
ow near DIRECT XPERIENCE the nversation	Specific, tangible reports of observations and examples from direct experience.			Abstract, vague generalizations without illustrative examples. No evidence is presented. The language is remote from any direct experience.	
ow much ERCION ters the teraction	Personal autonomy is respected. Because each knows that the other must lead his own life, make his own decisions, face his own consequences, he offers information but does not try to persuade him to follow a certain course of action.			One or both attempts to convince, persuade, coerce, or manipulate the other to be like him or to do what he thinks should be done.	

tion at not having the books increases along with their impression that nothing is being done about the matter. The nonassertive teacher grumbles to a friend but says "fine!" to the principal's inquiry of how things are going and feels guilty about having taken no action. In the middle of a faculty meeting, without preamble, the aggressive teacher angrily demands to discuss the matter, which embarrasses the principal and creates friction between them. In contrast to both the others, the assertive teacher one afternoon asks the principal if this is a good time to talk. Noting that the textbooks are long overdue, the teacher politely but firmly asks the principal to see to it that they are delivered or to arrange for borrowing some from another school until they arrive. The principal agrees, and both feel satisfied.

It should be added that assertiveness is equally necessary whether feelings are happy or unhappy. Although many persons have more difficulty in giving and receiving compliments than in exchanging criticism or standing up for themselves, showing others that you care about them helps to build the trust that enables communication during emotion to occur.

Many people refer to the teaching of communication skills as "trust and truth nonsense," believe that OD consultants should prepare participants for confrontation rather than collaboration, and would have them teach clients to know only what they want and how to demand it. Helping people to voice their wants and consulting with problem-solving groups that are trying to figure out how to get what they want are both responsible OD services, and it is true that people in schools should not shy away from the conflicts that often accompany differences in values. At the same time, however, in organizations where interdependence is high, we value skillful collaboration over confrontation and believe that collaborative goals can best be achieved through methods that emphasize trust building and open communication.

If parents want teachers to behave in new ways, they must work with teachers and not against them to make the necessary changes. If teachers want administrators to make fewer unilateral decisions, they must work together to change this condition. The systemlike nature of schools requires one part to change along with other parts if changes are to be sustained. Wresting power from an administrative subsystem and giving it to parent-controlled subsystems, for example, will not in itself produce important or lasting changes in education, although skillful collaboration between parents and administrators might.

Eliciting Personal Resources.   This third feature of effective interpersonal communication means being aware of the need for the resources of others, as well as offering one's own strengths, preferences, ideas, and feelings, in finding solutions to problems of mutual concern. But people are far more reticent about some of their personal resources than they are about others and frequently require strong encouragement to state their feelings.

Wallen (1972) suggests several reasons why this is so. First, many people have an unfavorable attitude toward emotion, often responding to someone else's expression of strong feelings with some variation of "please don't feel that way." Second, while actions and thoughts seem controllable, feelings seem to have a life of their own. Third, we too often think that others have more control over our feelings than we have ourselves. To believe that others can make one angry, for example, is to acknowledge a surrendering of some control over oneself. Feelings, in short, seem to threaten voluntary, planned control over one's own affairs.

Consultants must convince clients that feelings—whether of attraction, anxiety, interest, or resentment—provide important information that a group needs if work is to proceed efficiently and effectively and that to feel emotion toward another person is a sign of relatedness and interdependence. Acknowledging one's own feelings and the feelings of others eliminates unnecessary guesswork and releases energy that is otherwise spent in concealing emotions.

Trust. Being open, communicating during emotion, and offering one's personal resources involve taking risks, and risk taking depends in turn on the presence of interpersonal trust, which is in many ways the key to enhanced communication even where true differences exist. A fragile quality on which a single action can have profoundly destructive consequences, trust is built very slowly and in small increments, is established more by deeds than by words, and is sustained by openness in interpersonal relations. But it is very difficult to achieve this quality in interpersonal relations because being genuinely honest when an existing level of trust is low involves taking a very great risk. Perhaps this helps to explain why trust develops slowly and incrementally; if only small risks are taken, only small amounts of trust are built.

McGregor (1967) defines trust as the knowledge that the other person will not take unfair advantage of one, either deliberately or accidentally, consciously or unconsciously. Trust is built between people when each person is convinced that the other is both motivated and competent enough to sustain the relationship. Binding responses that diminish the other person's autonomy are likely to destroy trust; freeing responses that increase a sense of equality are likely to promote it. At the same time, however, the amount of gain or loss in trust depends on the amount that was present at the beginning; that is, a binding response is less binding and a freeing response less freeing when trust is low. Following is a list of interpersonal effects of various responses.

Freeing Responses
- listening attentively rather than merely remaining silent
- paraphrasing and checking your impressions of the other's inner state

- seeking information to understand the other
- offering information that is relevant to the other's concern
- describing observable behaviors that influence you
- directly reporting your own feelings
- offering your opinions or stating your value position

Binding Responses
- changing the subject without explanation
- interpreting the other's behavior by describing unchange-
  able experiences or qualities
- advising and persuading
- vigorously agreeing or obligating the other with "how
  could you?"
- approving the other for conforming to your standards
- claiming to know what motivates the other's behavior
- commanding the other or demanding to be commanded

Interpersonal Communication Skills

The four interpersonal skills described in the following four subsections* are neither new nor unique, but they must be used if openness, communication during emotion, and an exchange of personal
resources are to occur. Those who regard them as gimmicks and use
them perfunctorily should not be surprised when results are dis-
appointing. Merely becoming aware of communication skills will not
in itself improve the ability to communicate. The skills must be applied consciously and strategically if they are to help overcome some
of the problems inherent in the communication process, and they
must arise out of a genuine desire to understand the other person as
an individual.

Of these four skills, *paraphrasing* (checking your impression of
the other person's meaning) and *impression checking* (checking your
impression of the other person's feelings) are ways of helping you
understand the other person. *Describing the other's behavior* and
describing your own feelings aim at helping others to understand
you. As figure 3-4 illustrates, the four skills are so highly interdependent that it is virtually impossible to imagine a relationship of
trust in which all four are not used at one time or another. Public
information means that which should already be known to oneself
and to others; private information is similar in meaning to what Luft
has called *blind* or *hidden* in the Johari Awareness Model (see figure 3-2).

Every message and behavior has both a public and a private
component, and the listener, receiver, or observer always has five
choices: to say nothing, to describe the behavior, to paraphrase, to

---

*These subsections have been adapted from Jung et al. (1972).

FIGURE 3-4   Relationships among Four Basic Communication Skills

	When the information is public or visible	When the information is private and concerns inner states
To be candid	Tell what others did that affects you personally or as a group member by *describing behavior.*	Let others know as clearly and unambiguously as possible about your own inner state by *describing your feelings.*
To be receptive	Check to make sure you understand the ideas of the other person by *paraphrasing.*	Check to make sure how the other person feels by *impression checking.*

describe one's own feelings, or to check an impression of what the other is feeling. The best choice will depend largely upon the situation. Consider, for example, the question of whether it is normal to feel sad at the end of the school year. If a student asks this of a teacher on the last day of school, the teacher might wish to check an impression that the student is feeling sad. If a student teacher asks this in an introductory methods class, the professor might paraphrase to determine whether the student teacher is considering a research problem. If a friend sticks his head in your office for the fifth time one morning to ask this and if you are annoyed by the repeated interruptions, the best choice might be to describe your friend's behavior and your own feelings about it.

In gaining these skills, the key to success is practice. OD consultants should introduce them early and reinforce their use at every opportunity. With continuing practice clients will become more skillful, and increased clarity of understanding will result. There is no given point at which one finally becomes skilled at communication, however. Each new person, relationship, and situation calls for practicing the skills anew, and no one should be excused on the grounds that he has "had that" elsewhere.

Paraphrasing.   Many people mistakenly assume that they correctly understand what another person has meant to convey without troubling to check whether the remark means the same thing to both of them or giving the sender any evidence that the remark has in fact been understood. As it is used here, paraphrasing denotes any method of showing other people how you have apprehended their meaning. By testing your understanding against their intentions you show them that you want to understand and you invite them to clarify their meaning if you have not understood them correctly.

As the following example demonstrates, simply repeating another person's ideas in different words can result in a mere illusion of mutual understanding.

Sarah: Jim should never have become a teacher.
Fred: You mean teaching isn't the right job for him?
Sarah: Exactly! Teaching is not the right job for Jim.

Instead of trying to reword Sarah's statement, Fred should have asked himself, "What does this statement mean to me?" in which case the exchange might have gone:

Sarah: Jim should never have become a teacher.
Fred: You mean he is too harsh on the children? Maybe even cruel?
Sarah: No, I meant that he has such expensive tastes that he can't earn enough as a teacher.
Fred: Oh, I see. You think he should have gone into a field that would have ensured him a higher standard of living.
Sarah: Exactly! Teaching is not the right job for Jim.

A general statement may convey something specific to you.

Larry: I'd like to own this book.
You: Does it contain useful information?
Larry: I don't know about that. I meant that the binding is beautiful.

A very specific statement may convey a more general idea to you.

Ralph: Do you have twenty-five pencils I can borrow for my class?
You: Do you just want something for them to write with? I have about fifteen ball-point pens and ten or eleven pencils.
Ralph: Great. Anything that will write will do.

The comments of another person may possibly suggest an example to you.

Laura: This text has too many omissions; we shouldn't adopt it.
You: Do you mean, for example, that it contains nothing about the role of ethnic minorities in the development of America?
Laura: Yes, that's one example. It also lacks any discussion of the development of the arts in America.

Sometimes another person's idea will suggest its opposite to you.

Stan:	I don't want to go downtown today with all the crowds and the rain.
You:	Do you mean that you want to enjoy the privacy and warmth of your own home?
Stan.·	No, I was thinking of driving to the beach in the hope of catching some sun and a fish.

Skillful paraphrasing thus requires an ability to make generalizations, identify examples, and think of opposites. To develop these abilities requires trying out different ways and discovering what kinds of responses are most helpful to you.

Impression Checking. Inferences drawn from the words, tone, gestures, or facial expressions of another person are often inaccurate, not least because we may unconsciously attribute to that person our own feelings, attitudes, or desires. Impression checking involves describing what you perceive to be the other person's emotional state in order to determine whether you have accurately decoded his expressions of feeling. That is, you transform expressions of feeling into tentative descriptions, such as: "I get the impression that you're angry with me. Are you?" "Am I right that you're feeling disappointed because no one commented on your suggestion?" "I'm uncertain whether your expression means that my comment hurt your feelings, irritated you, or confused you. Can you help me?"

Skillful impression checking requires reading nonverbal clues, drawing tentative inferences from them, clearly describing the feeling that is inferred, and indicating that you recognize the inferential character of the impression. An impression check aims to convey the fact that you wish to understand the other person's feelings in order to avoid actions based on false assumptions about them; it does not express approval or disapproval of the feelings.

Describing Behavior. For most of us it is not easy to describe another person's behavior clearly enough for that person to understand which actions are affecting us. Indeed, instead of describing behavior, we usually discuss attitudes, motivations, and personality traits, often unaware that our conclusions are based less on observable evidence than on our own feelings of affection, insecurity, irritation, jealousy, or fear. Accusations that impute undesirable motives to another, for example, are usually not descriptions at all but expressions of the speaker's unpleasant feelings toward the other. Yet if we are to discuss the way we work together or what is occurring in our relationship, we must be able to talk about what each of us does that affects the other.

Behavior description means reporting specific observable actions of others without judging these actions as good or bad, right or wrong, or making generalizations or accusations about the other person's motives, attitudes, or personality traits. As the following examples illustrate, it also means describing the actions clearly and and specifically enough for others to know what you have observed.

To remind yourself to describe specific actions, it is helpful to begin your description with "I see that . . ." or "I noticed that . . ." or "I heard you say . . ."

> Example: "Jim, you've talked more than others on this topic. Several times you've cut off others before they had finished." (Not "Jim, you're too rude," which identifies a trait and gives no evidence, or "Jim, you always want to hog the center of attention," which imputes an undesirable motive or intention.)

> Example: "Bob, you've taken the opposite position on nearly everything that Harry has suggested today." (Not "Bob, you're just trying to show Harry up," which is an accusation of undesirable motivation, or "Bob, you're being stubborn," which is name calling.)

> Example: "Bob, earlier today, when I was worried about whether I could perform well, you told me about something you saw me do that you thought I did competently. That made me feel much better." (Not "Bob, you're really a nice guy," which tells Bob that you like him but does not tell him what you liked about his action. Not "Bob, you go out of your way to say comforting things to people," which attributes a particularized motive to Bob, whose primary intention may have been to help you keep in contact with evidence and the perceptions of the rest of the group.)

> Example: "Sam, you cut in before I had finished." (Not "Sam, you deliberately didn't let me finish," which implies that Sam knowingly and intentionally cut you off. All that anyone can observe is that he cut in before you had finished.)

To develop skill in describing behavior you must sharpen your observation of what actually occurred, pay attention to that which is observable, recognize when you are making inferences, and be able to couch them in language that reflects both their tentative nature and your desire to check them out.

Describing One's Own Feelings. Reporting one's own inner state provides more information that is necessary if two people are to understand and improve their relationship; certainly, others need to know how you feel if they are to take your feelings into account. Negative feelings should not be ignored because they signal that something may be going wrong in a relationship and that the two parties need to check for misunderstandings or faulty communication. The aim of describing your feelings is to open a dialogue that will improve a relationship; it should not be an effort to coerce the other into changing so that you won't feel as you do. Although the other person may behave differently on learning what distracts, bothers, or

FIGURE 3-5 How Emotional States Express Themselves

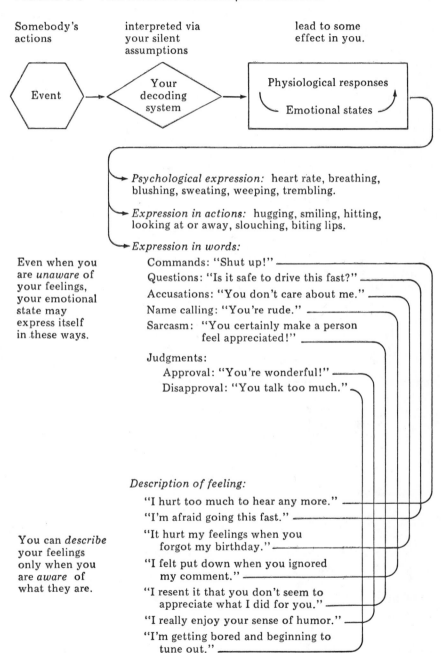

Somebody's actions — interpreted via your silent assumptions — lead to some effect in you.

Event → Your decoding system → Physiological responses / Emotional states

Even when you are *unaware* of your feelings, your emotional state may express itself in these ways.

Psychological expression: heart rate, breathing, blushing, sweating, weeping, trembling.

Expression in actions: hugging, smiling, hitting, looking at or away, slouching, biting lips.

Expression in words:

Commands: "Shut up!"
Questions: "Is it safe to drive this fast?"
Accusations: "You don't care about me."
Name calling: "You're rude."
Sarcasm: "You certainly make a person feel appreciated!"

Judgments:
Approval: "You're wonderful!"
Disapproval: "You talk too much."

You can *describe* your feelings only when you are *aware* of what they are.

Description of feeling:

"I hurt too much to hear any more."
"I'm afraid going this fast."
"It hurt my feelings when you forgot my birthday."
"I felt put down when you ignored my comment."
"I resent it that you don't seem to appreciate what I did for you."
"I really enjoy your sense of humor."
"I'm getting bored and beginning to tune out."

pleases you, you may also discover that your feelings were based on false perceptions and should themselves be changed.

To communicate your feelings accurately is very difficult because emotions can express themselves in bodily changes, actions, and words; because a specific expression of feeling can indicate a myriad of different feelings (as a blush may indicate pleasure, annoyance, embarrassment, or uneasiness); and because a specific feeling is not always expressed in the same way. The communication of feelings is often misleading as well. What may appear to be an expression of anger, for example, may turn out to result from hurt feelings or fear.

One way to describe a feeling is by naming it and by referring to *I*, *me*, or *my* to indicate that you own the feeling as: "I feel angry," "I feel embarrassed," or "I feel comfortable with you." Another way is to report the kind of action that the feeling urges you to take: "I feel like hugging you," "I'd like to slap you," or "I wish I could walk off and leave you." A feeling can also be specified by means of simile ("I feel like a tiny frog in a huge pond") or of metaphor ("I just swallowed a bushel of spring sunshine"). Finally, as the following examples demonstrate, any expression of feeling may represent quite different descriptions of feeling.

Expressions of Feeling	*Descriptions of Feeling*
Person blushes and says nothing.	"I feel embarrassed."
	"I feel pleased."
	"I feel annoyed."
Person suddenly becomes silent in the midst of a conversation.	"I feel angry."
	"I'm worried about this."
	"I feel as if I've been slapped."
"She's a wonderful person."	"I enjoy her sense of humor."
	"I respect her abilities."
	"I love her but feel I shouldn't say so."
"Shut up!"	"I hurt too much to hear any more."
	"I feel angry at myself."
	"I'm angry with you."
"You shouldn't have bought me such an expensive gift!"	"I really like your gift."
	"I feel obligated to you and resent it."
	"I feel inferior to you when I think of the cheap present I gave you."

Giving and Receiving Feedback. The concept of feedback originated in the field of cybernetics, the study of automatic control mechanisms in machines and living organisms. It refers to an error-correcting process in which information about a system's output is returned as input so that the system can control its own performance. Because of its circularity, the term *loop* is often used to describe the feedback process.

In human communication, feedback consists of information sent by the receiver back to the source of a message so that the original sender can gauge the effect of the message. By comparing this effect with his intention, the original sender can adjust his subsequent message, which can serve as the stimulus for further feedback, which in turn can be used to modify the succeeding message, and so on. Ideally, sender and receiver will continue to use this circular mode of interaction until the desired level of accuracy is achieved.

The feedback process is a two-way endeavor and should not be regarded primarily as a way for the listener to aid the speaker. Mutual feedback, a cardinal feature of transactional communication, is achieved when the person giving feedback is also given information that will help him gauge the effect of the feedback. Thus each communicator can help the other to become skillful in using feedback to the benefit of their mutual communication. To communicate transactionally with another person requires a great expenditure of time and energy, although limited evidence suggests that the need for great amounts of feedback diminishes with continued use (see, for example, Leavitt and Mueller 1951).

Without mutual feedback, miscommunications—discrepancies between messages that are intended and messages that are received—occur frequently, partly because certain behaviors are more difficult than others for some persons to perform, partly because of the confusion that arises from an effort to express oneself authentically while at the same time attempting to perform in ways meant to be attractive to others. To try to impress others is not necessarily to be phony; it is a natural phenomenon that enables people to cope more easily with superficial social events. But superficiality and self-concealment are often detrimental to effective transaction communication.

Whether it is given or received, feedback can best be carried out if the following guidelines are observed.

1. *Noncoercive.* Feedback should be given so that it does not require that the recipient change his behavior.
2. *Consideration.* Feedback should be given after a careful assessment has been made of the recipient's feelings. This does not mean, for example, that you should avoid showing anger to the other person; it means that the other should be ready to deal with it productively.
3. *Descriptive.* Feedback should involve a clear report of the facts rather than an explanation of why things happened as they did.
4. *Recency.* Feedback should be given close to the time of the events causing reaction. Gunny sacks of grievances are hard to carry and can burst at inopportune times.
5. *Changeability.* Feedback should be given about behavior that can be changed. It is not helpful, for example, to tell people that you are bothered by the color of their eyes.

Finally, mutual feedback must arise out of a true concern about, and interest in, the other person. Each participant should want to find ways of moving psychologically closer to the other and of help- ing that person to grow, for without such concern transactional com- munication will be hollow. Even when concern is keenly felt by all parties, however, the decision of whether to give feedback is not easy to make, perhaps because feedback seems to imply a desire to change the receiver.* To say, for example, "You've been quiet all through the meeting, and I feel anxious" is to imply that the receiver should speak up more often. To this, the receiver might reply, "I'm comfort- able speaking no more than I do. Why don't you learn to accept my quietness?" If the same feedback with its implied demand for change had been given many times before, an irritated receiver might snap, "Get off my back! I like being quiet!"

In such a case the sender must decide whether to pursue a re- quest for change or to accept the other person's behavior. If the sender considers his own values, explores the possibility of accepting the other, and still experiences the other's behavior as a violation of certain basic values, the receiver deserves to know that. If the sender can widen the band of behaviors that he finds acceptable, feedback can be withheld until something more important happens. The sender might also reexamine his own values to find reasons why the behav- ior initially appeared nonacceptable and thereby change himself instead of trying to change the receiver. In other words, feedback is not just a process of requesting another person to change but can often begin the process of changing oneself.

COMMUNICATION IN THE SUBSYSTEM

Although much of the work in schools is accomplished through com- munication exchanges between two persons, the work of people in groups—cabinets, departments, committees, and teams—is very im- portant as well. As groups increase in size, especially as they exceed three or four members, new issues and problems of communication arise. Since only one person can speak at a time and since speakers must follow one another serially, it is inevitable that some members will have more air time than others. Indeed, group norms develop that influence the amount of talking time that is considered appro- priate for each member of the group. When a norm supports speaking by the leader but by few others, for example, communication will be confined to a very small subgroup with the rest of the group partici- pating as a passive audience.

Group members who remain silent at formal meetings may nevertheless do a great deal of informal communicating with col- leagues based on such factors as shared responsibility, personal attraction, and the physical location of the work space. Although

---

*Many of the ideas here are adapted from Dyer (1969).

informal communication often serves a social function rather than the function of promoting work, at most schools communication at formal meetings is so poor that informal communication is necessary for tasks to be completed adequately.

Problems arise when informal communications run counter to formal communications. Most formal communication is followed by interactions in small informal groups that strive to achieve an adequate understanding of the original message. When the original message is distorted by these informal discussions, problems of coordination arise for the organization. When the most influential members of the informal networks disagree with the views and decisions of the formal leaders, the messages from the informal leaders often take precedence over the formal communications, a breakdown in authority occurs and norms about decision making become ambiguous, which leads to the development of distrust in a work situation, the more so when differences of opinion and belief are kept private.

OD consultants should gather data on both formal and informal communication networks to help group members become more aware of the effects of these patterns. Examining how communication structures affect small-group performance, Leavitt (1951) found that differences in degree of satisfaction, in accuracy, in time spent at problem solving, and in the emergence of a leader were all related to the type of network involved. The quality of performance in Leavitt's groups improved when they had one person or a subgroup with communicative contact with all other members of the group, and the satisfaction of members increased as each had some power through communication to influence the way the group performed.

The OD consultant also gives attention to the type of information that passes through communication channels and networks: the amount of time that the group devotes to sharing information about a task, the methods to be used, the interpersonal feelings that emerge, as well as the situations, targets, and plans. Figure 3-6 shows these six kinds of information in a matrix of nine combinations.* Examples of the kinds of statements that fall in each cell follow the figure.

FIGURE 3-6   Content of Subsystem Communication

Dimensions of problem analysis

		Situation	Target	Proposal
	Task	1	2	3
Level of analysis	Methods	4	5	6
	Interpersonal	7	8	9

*We are grateful to Fred Fosmire of the Psychology Department at the University of Oregon for describing this figure to us.

Cell 1:   There are more children in class A than in class B.

Mary doesn't like large classes.

Cell 2:   We ought to interest more children in taking class B.

Mary should have a smaller class at least one period a day.

Cell 3:   We can get more students to elect class B by adding two field trips.

Mary can have the first chance to encourage her students to transfer into that class.

Cell 4:   Our meetings always last too long.

The principal has insufficient time to observe in classrooms.

Cell 5:   We should come to meetings prepared to discuss agenda items.

The principal should spend more time in classrooms before evaluating teachers.

Cell 6:   We will start our meetings a half-hour later to give people time for preparation.

Teachers will rotate playground duty so that the principal is freed for observations.

Cell 7:   I'm pleased that everyone participated at this meeting.

Only half of us feel influential regarding decisions about X.

Cell 8:   We should always make sure that everyone who has something to say gets to speak.

We should reconsider who is to be involved in decision making about X in the future.

Cell 9:   The convener of the meeting will periodically ask if all who wish to speak have had a chance.

We'll give two days' notice before making another X decision so that interested persons can be contacted.

The ultimate payoffs for groups result from high-quality work in Cell 3, although high-quality task proposals do not come out of thin air; groups must share information in all cells on a fairly regular basis.

The amount of energy that a subsystem expends on each topic of communication is governed in part by communication norms. In some groups, for example, no one expects anyone to exchange information about the interpersonal feelings that emerge from their working together. Other groups might exhibit a norm supporting regular interpersonal-process debriefings. Norms also specify rewards for openness, communicating during emotion, and eliciting statements of personal resources. Subsystem norms specifying what people should or should not talk about greatly influence the degree to which interpersonal communication skill will be displayed.

It should be noted, however, that information is always distorted to some degree as it passes from one person to others. When most group members distort a message in the same way, as when a majority of group members believes an untrue thing to be true, a condition of pluralistic ignorance is said to exist. In many groups, for example, a majority of people say, "I'll tell almost everyone in the group when I'm feeling impatient, but very few will tell me when they're feeling impatient," notwithstanding that many of these people are mutually ignorant of what others say they will do. Especially where it misconstrues the expectations or intentions of others in the group, pluralistic ignorance tends to be self-maintaining, because when enough people believe an untrue thing to be true, everyone is discouraged from putting the matter to a test.

The OD consultant could collect interview or questionnaire data that illustrate this phenomenon. By feeding these data back to the group and encouraging discussion of obvious discrepancies, the consultant can help the client group to improve the accuracy of information at its disposal. To facilitate clearer communication, the consultant can also teach groups to use the following procedures or activities during their regular meetings.

1. *The Right to Listen.* Typically, meetings are run so that members have their say without much regard to whether they are understood by others. A procedure that can help to ameliorate this situation is to require a member before speaking to paraphrase its terms so that everyone is clear about the issues being considered. The convener can assume the duty of ensuring each participant both the right to be heard and the right to listen or to paraphrase.

2. *Time Tokens.* To assure that members initiate no more than their share of comments, poker chips can be equally divided among group members with the stipulation that one chip be tossed into the "pot" when a member begins to speak. In addition to sensitizing the group to frequency of participation, this procedure often leads members to make long speeches, so that the group also becomes aware of the negative effects of a series of prolonged monologues.

3. *High Talker Tap-out.* In this procedure, a group monitor notifies another member that he has exceeded a given time limit of speech, either by tapping him on the shoulder to signal that he is requested to stop talking or by giving him a card on which an explanation has previously been typed. At the monitor's signal, the person notified drops out of the discussion by moving back a few feet. When only two persons are left and have had their chance to contribute, the entire group discusses feelings and responses to the process. Such an activity often makes it easier to confront established patterns of discussion and decision making, offering an opportunity to discuss reasons for infrequent participation and perhaps to increase the number of persons involved in decision making.

4. *Thumbs Up.* It is often difficult for groups to carry on meaningful discussion and to monitor their group functioning at the same time. If group members have trouble recognizing when they are ready to make a decision, for example, members may give a thumbs-up signal when they are ready to state their opin-

ions and test whether others agree with them. If a group decides to monitor the use of a newly acquired communication skill, each member would display thumbs up when another member uses a skill effectively and thumbs down when an unhelpful comment is expressed. The use of this procedure can create stress, particularly when a unanimous thumbs-down signal is presented, but some of this stress can be productively harnessed if the group periodically discusses the procedure and its implications.

5. *Taking a Survey.* In a survey, one member of the group asks for the opinions of all others on a specific issue ("I'd like to know what everyone thinks of this proposal right now"); then some other member paraphrases the request until all members understand what they are being asked. All members in turn state their positions on the topic in two or three sentences. A member may express uncertainty, confusion, a desire to hear more, or admit that he has nothing to say. Each person must say something, however, and as soon as everyone has stated a position, someone summarizes the group's position, as: "Only two people seem to have reservations about the proposal," or "Only the third, fourth, and ninth ideas seem to have captured our interest." Group members should not confuse a survey with a vote, although a survey may be used in this way. Sometimes a survey is used to test the water instead of as a way of ascertaining commitment. In any case, the person requesting the survey should make clear what it is intended to accomplish.

Generally, a survey should be taken at the time it is requested, superseding any other activity. If group members using this procedure for the first time find it too cumbersome or mechanical, they might take a minute to plan their response before the survey starts, or flash thumbs up if they think a survey is a good idea at that time and thumbs down if they would prefer to wait. This procedure, like all others, should periodically be talked about by group members.

6. *Sitting in a Circle.* Because arranging group seating in a circle soon becomes automatic behavior for the consultant, group members sometimes forget the importance of this procedure and begin to place barriers, such as tables, between themselves. Close circular seating has two advantages: nonverbal behaviors are more easily sent and received when each person has an unobstructed view of everyone else, and equal participation is encouraged when there is no podium or head of the table to suggest that any particular member should assume leadership. When it is desirable to record information on a chalkboard or on newsprint, the circle can be opened into a horseshoe arrangement so that all may have an unobstructed view of the recorder.

7. *Fishbowls.* In larger groups too much air time may be used if everyone speaks on an issue. In this case the consultant may institute a procedure by which those in an inner circle talk while those in a concentric outer circle listen. Those on the out-

side may still contribute if there is an empty chair in the inner circle to which they can move when they have something to say or if those in the inner circle occasionally turn around to confer with or receive coaching from them.

8. *Video Taping or Audio Recording.* Video-taped and (less dramatic) audio-recorded segments of a meeting can provide excellent feedback and stimulate a group to review its own functioning. But both techniques require a skilled technician who can judge what to record and can quickly find important bits of interaction to play back. To replay a two-hour meeting is usually time-consuming and frustrating, while delaying the feedback until someone can edit the tapes may destroy part of the drama. Relying on transcription of tapes as the sole record of a meeting can cause frustrating delays when important decisions are being made. Nonetheless, well-made tapes are extremely useful for teaching group members to observe communication and other group processes.

ORGANIZATION-WIDE COMMUNICATION

Communication in the organization as a whole can best be observed by attending to the regularized procedures through which it occurs. The OD consultant looks at regular and legitimate channels of communication among subsystems, the regularity with which information from the organization's environment is discussed, the time that elapses between problem identification and responsive action, the regularity with which extra resources in one task group are used by another, and the like.

By formal channels of communication we mean interactions that are sanctioned by the organization and that carry information about organizationally relevant issues; announcements in bulletins or over the intercom, faculty or departmental meetings, and teacher-parent conferences are examples. Informal channels—such as coffee-break conversations among teachers, parking-lot debriefings of faculty meetings, or notes from teachers to parents—are neither required by the organization nor do they necessarily carry information that is relevant to the organization. Because problems arise when important information does not move through formal channels or when these are overloaded with irrelevancies, the OD consultant should help the organization to examine the relationships between its formal and informal channels. If certain information must be shared regularly, perhaps a new formal channel should be developed that is based on already existing informal channels.

Likert (1961) has distinguished a form of organizing that he terms *link-pin structure.* A link-pin function is performed by a person or subgroup that participates in two or more separate communication networks, carrying information across groups that would normally not otherwise communicate. To be sure, it is not unusual for a principal to attend teachers' meetings or student council sessions to report administrative-team decisions; but it is unique for a teacher or student to sit with an administrative team or for a group of people (instead of an individual) from one level to engage in face-to-face communication with a group from another level. The consultant should be alert to the possibility of building unique link-pin structures to promote an accurate flow of information within a school organization.

As chapter 12 will explain, a district cadre of part-time organizational specialists is an important link-pin structure because its members work in and among different subsystems, thereby gaining access to much important information. Further, representatives of cadre intervention teams serve as link-pins to the cadre coordinator through a steering committee. Finally, another report of our work (see Schmuck et al. 1975) has shown how OD consultation can create team-leader roles and how team leaders may serve as link-pins in multiunit elementary schools.

Katz and Kahn (1966) advise OD consultants to attend to the needs of the system before advocating changes in communication patterns. That is, however laudable increased information flow may be, it is more helpful to identify specific organizational problems first and only then to introduce changes aimed at helping the organization solve these problems. An organized system implies a restricted number of channels that can be used to perform a specific function, so that to move from a disorganized to an organized state may require new norms supporting the use of only certain channels while omitting others or reserving them for organizationally irrelevant purposes.

The larger the organization, the more important it is to provide clarity about channels that carry task-related information. In a group of six persons, for example, each must communicate with five others, so that there are only 15 channels to contend with altogether; an organization of sixty persons, by contrast, contains 1,770 possible channels. Unless people in larger organizations know clearly to whom they should go for what kinds of information, the results are likely to include overloaded channels, pluralistic ignorance, and insufficient information to do the job.

While we advocate clear definitions of, and limits to, channels used for formal organizational purposes, we also value freedom to use any channel for informal purposes. In our view, organizational life is better when hierarchical lines and differentiated subsystems do not prevent people from reaching out to one another for support, strokes, or good times. Although teachers may have to go to administrators for information about budget procedures, for example, they should not be prohibited by constraints either of time or of architecture from interacting with one another.

GATHERING DATA ABOUT COMMUNICATION

The following questionnaires and observation forms should be used by consultants for diagnosing problems of communication and as a guide when designing interventions, and by participants for gathering data from their own groups. In some cases, observations can be presented to the group immediately after they have been collected, or a questionnaire may be administered and scored during a single meeting. In other cases, the consultant or participants can summarize lengthy questionnaires or the data from several observation periods and present the summary to the group later. Guidelines for feeding data back to the group are detailed in chapter 10.

Knowledge and Use of Communication Skills

The questionnaire below was developed by Crosby and Wallen to assess a participant's recognition of communication skills.* Members of the group may wish to compare their answers and discuss their differences.

Concepts about Communication
Communication is much more than words. It includes tone of voice, facial expressions, posture, gestures, and eye contact or lack of it. But words are also important. If they match the tone of voice, etc., one's communication message is clear and congruent. This test is about communication by words. Please do not infer tone, etc., but rather focus on the words.

Section I: Description of the speaker's feelings. Before each sentence which represents a description of feelings below put an X. (Make no mark otherwise.)

1. _____ What a lovely day!
2. _____ I'm bored and confused!
3. _____ Cut it out!
4. _____ I feel like I'm on a pedestal.
5. _____ Why can't you ever be anyplace on time?
6. _____ You're a very interesting conversationalist.
7. _____ You shouldn't have bought me such an expensive gift.
8. _____ I feel that he didn't care if he hurt my feelings.
9. _____ Go jump in the lake!
10. _____ I feel this is an easy text.

Section II: Behavior description. Put an X before each sentence which represents a description of behavior.

11. _____ Joe interrupted Harry.
12. _____ Harry was sincere.
13. _____ Harry misinterpreted Joe.
14. _____ Joe was discouraged.

---

*Robert Crosby and John Wallen developed this questionnaire while they were consulting together. Crosby now has a private practice in Spokane, Washington; Wallen has retired.

15. _____ Harry's voice got louder when he said, "Cut it out, Joe."
16. _____ Joe was trying to make Harry mad.
17. _____ Harry talked more than Joe did.
18. _____ Joe was dismayed by Harry's statements.
19. _____ Joe said nothing when Harry said, "Cut it out."
20. _____ Harry knew that Joe was feeling discouraged.

Section III: Perception check of speaker's perception of another's feeling. Put an X before each sentence representing a perception check.

21. _____ Are you angry with me?
22. _____ I can tell that you're embarrassed.
23. _____ Why are you mad at me?
24. _____ Did my statement cause you to feel put down?
25. _____ What Jim said obviously upset you.
26. _____ You seem unhappy.
27. _____ Your feelings get hurt pretty easily, don't they?
28. _____ Oh, heck, are your feelings hurt again?
29. _____ What is it about Bill that makes you resent him so much?
30. _____ You're not getting mad again, are you?

Section IV: Personalness in which the speaker reveals something about his private life versus openness in which the speaker shares his reaction to the other person. Put an X before each sentence expressing openness.

31. _____ I've enjoyed our time together tonight.
32. _____ I'm annoyed at your making fun of me.
33. _____ I've never been able to cope with authority figures.
34. _____ I'm seeing a counselor regularly.
35. _____ Sometimes I feel so discouraged and frightened that I'm afraid I'll commit suicide.
36. _____ I envy you.
37. _____ I'm beginning to tune out because you are telling me so much detail.
38. _____ I'm afraid people would disapprove of me if they knew my background.
39. _____ I'm very fond of you.
40. _____ I felt hurt and disappointed when you said you didn't want to hear about my difficult childhood.

Cognitive awareness is insufficient in itself to ensure the use of communication skills. The observation form below can be used to provide information regarding the use of these skills by specific individuals and to obtain frequency counts for the use of each type of skill per unit of time. The latter measure can be used to compare use of the various skills by two different groups or by the same group on two separate occasions.

Instances of Use of Communication Skills

Identification of group: _____

Time at start of tally: _____ Time at end: _____

Tally each instance of initiation of each skill by each person.

Names or symbols of participants	Para- phrase	Behavior description	Description of feeling	Perception check	Give feedback	Ask for survey
_____	_____	_____	_____	_____	_____	_____
_____	_____	_____	_____	_____	_____	_____
_____	_____	_____	_____	_____	_____	_____
_____	_____	_____	_____	_____	_____	_____
_____	_____	_____	_____	_____	_____	_____

Actual and Perceived Participation

Participation in a group discussion may vary over the course of time because of differences in task involvement, in feelings about the group, or in such factors as fatigue or preoccupation with matters outside the life of the group. The consultant must sample participation several times during a meeting, and perhaps at several different meetings, before arriving at an adequate measure of actual and typical participation. The first form below can be used to sample actual participation in a task-centered group. The consultant may also wish to have group members provide subjective estimates of member participation by means of the second form below, even though the objective and subjective measures will often be highly correlated. In any case, the subjective data may be compared with an observer's more objective tallies, or it may be fed back to group members as a stimulus for group self-analysis. The estimates should represent participation during a specific time period, usually the time just prior to making the ratings.

Members' Participation: Observer's Form

(1) Take three ten-minute samples at early, middle, and late stages of each meeting observed. (2) Tally at ten-second intervals to indicate who is talking at that instant. (3) Write the times that observation begins and ends in the spaces provided.

Sample Observation Form

Observer: _____

Date: _____
Page no.: _____
Time begun: _____
Time ended: _____

Persons in group   Tallies of participation
(Name or code number)

Members' Participation: Estimate by Group Members

Each member should be given enough copies of the rating form to rate everyone in the group. After the ratings are completed, all members are given all the estimates of their participation so that they can study and total their individual ratings.

Sample Rating Form

Name of member being rated: _____ .
Please rate other members in the group on the following scales. Circle the appropriate number from 0 (low) to 6 (high).

1. How much did he or she participate?

0	1	2	3	4	5	6

None   A great deal

2. How well did he or she listen to other members?

0	1	2	3	4	5	6

Little or none   Very well

Norms about Communicating

If they are to perform effectively, all group members must know what behaviors other members expect. This section offers three questionnaires that can be used to identify norms about communication in the group and to determine the amount of agreement that exists about a specific norm.

Do's and Don'ts*

In any school district (or school or group), there are informal "do's and don'ts." They are rarely written down anywhere, but they serve as a kind of code, making it clear what people in the system should and should not do if they are to be accepted by others.

Below, there is a list of specific things that a person—an administrator, a teacher, a staff member—might do or say. We would like you to estimate what most people in your system would feel about each item. That is, we want you to tell us whether the predominant feeling of most of the people is that one should or should not do or say the thing in question. You can indicate your answer by placing a check mark in the appropriate column—should or should not—beside each item.

---

*From Matthew B. Miles, Center for Policy Research, Inc., New York, New York.

	Should	*Should not*
1. Ask others who seem upset to express their feelings directly.	———	———
2. Tell colleagues what you really think of their work.	———	———
3. Look for ulterior motives in other people's behavior.	———	———
4. Always ask "Why?" when you don't know.	———	———
5. Avoid disagreement and conflict whenever possible.	———	———
6. Question well-established ways of doing things.	———	———
7. Disagree with your superior if you happen to know more about the issue than he does.	———	———
8. Withhold personal feelings and stick to the logical merits of the case in any discussion.	———	———
9. Push for new ideas, even if they are vague or unusual.	———	———
10. Ask others to tell you what they really think of your work.	———	———
11. Keep your real thoughts and reactions to yourself, by and large.	———	———
12. Trust others not to take advantage of you.	———	———
13. Be skeptical about things.	———	———
14. Point out other people's mistakes, to improve working effectiveness.	———	———
15. Try out new ways of doing things, even if it is uncertain how they will work out.	———	———

The next questionnaire is excellent for checking the pervasiveness of pluralistic ignorance in a group because each person not only reports for himself but makes estimates of how others will respond as well. The content of the expectations can be changed to fit the situation. If, for example, teachers were asked how many parents they would be willing to work with and how many parents would like to work with them, parents in turn would be asked how many teachers they wanted to work with and how many teachers wanted to work with them.

112

Team Expectation Survey*

Estimate

1. Suppose someone in your group does not
   understand something you have just said.
   About how many will tell you about it
   when they do not understand something
   you said?   _____

2. About how many do you think will tell
   you when they like something you have
   done or said?   _____

3. About how many do you think will tell
   you when they disagree with something
   you said?   _____

4. About how many do you think will tell
   you when they feel impatient or irritated
   with something you said or did?   _____

5. About how many do you think will tell
   you when they feel hurt by something
   you said or did?   _____

6. Suppose someone says something you do
   not understand. About how many of the
   others will you tell when you do not
   understand something he has said?   _____

7. About how many of the others will you
   tell when you like something he has done
   or said?   _____

8. About how many of the others will you
   tell when you disagree with something
   he has said?   _____

9. About how many of the others will you
   tell when you feel impatient or irritated
   with something he said or did?   _____

10. About how many of the others will you
    tell when you feel hurt by something
    he said or did?   _____

11. Suppose someone has said something
    you do not understand. About how many
    of the others do you think are interested
    in knowing it when you do not under-
    stand something he has said?   _____

12. About how many are interested in know-
    ing it when you like something he has
    said or done?   _____

13. About how many are interested in knowing it
    when you disagree with something he said?   _____

*Taken from X-3 Questionnaire, Project 3002, Center for the Advanced study of Educational Administration (1970) and based on a form developed by Wallen (1966).

14. About how many are interested in knowing when you feel impatient or irritated with something he said or did? _____

15. About how many are interested in knowing when you feel hurt by something he said or did? _____

16. Suppose someone does not understand something you have just said. From how many are you interested in knowing when he does not understand something you said? _____

17. From how many are you interested in knowing when he likes something you said or did? _____

18. From how many are you interested in knowing when he disagrees with something you said or did? _____

19. From how many are you interested in knowing when he feels impatient or irritated with something you said or did? _____

20. From how many are you interested in knowing when he feels hurt by something you said or did? _____

In the third questionnaire below, questions 1 and 2 ask the respondent to predict the actions of others; questions 3 and 4 ask the respondent to predict his own response. The consultant may wish to write additional questions so that respondents provide both types of prediction for a single situation. The two predictions can then be compared to see how much the individual agrees with what he perceives to be a group norm and how much pluralistic ignorance exists in the group.

Communication in Problem Situations*

1. Suppose Teacher X feels hurt and put down by something another teacher has said to him. In teacher X's place, would most of the teachers you know in your school be likely to . . .

   1a. . . . tell the other teacher that they felt hurt and put down?
   ( ) Yes, I think most would.
   ( ) Maybe about half would.
   ( ) No, most would not.
   ( ) I don't know.

---

*Taken from X-3 Questionnaire, Project 3002, Center for the Advanced Study of Educational Administration (1970) and based on items originally prepared by John Wallen, Ray Jongeward, and Michael Giametteo for the Northwest Regional Educational Laboratory, Portland, Oregon.

1b. ... tell their friends that the other teacher is hard to get along with?
( ) Yes, I think most would.
( ) Maybe about half would.
( ) No, most would not.
( ) I don't know.

2. Suppose Teacher X strongly disagrees with something B says at a staff meeting. In Teacher X's place, would most of the teachers you know in your school ...

2a. ... seek out B to discuss the disagreement?
( ) Yes, I think most would do this.
( ) Maybe about half would do this.
( ) No, most would not.
( ) I don't know.

2b. ... keep it to themselves and say nothing about it?
( ) Yes, I think most would do this.
( ) Maybe about half would do this.
( ) No, most would not.
( ) I don't know.

3. Suppose you are in a committee meeting with Teacher X. The other members begin to describe their personal feelings about what goes on in the school, but Teacher X quickly suggests that the committee get back to the topic and keep the discussion objective and impersonal. How would you feel toward X?
( ) I would approve strongly.
( ) I would approve mildly or some.
( ) I wouldn't care one way or the other.
( ) I would disapprove mildly or some.
( ) I would disapprove strongly.

4. Suppose you are in a committee meeting with Teacher X. The other members begin to describe their personal feelings about what goes on in the school. Teacher X listens to them and tells them his own feelings. How would you feel toward X?
( ) I would approve strongly.
( ) I would approve mildly or some.
( ) I wouldn't care one way or the other.
( ) I would disapprove mildly or some.
( ) I would disapprove strongly.

Communication Networks

Questions like those following can be used to determine the number, size, and complexity of communication networks within an organization.* The second question provides data that can be used to see

*Questions are from a questionnaire of Project 3001, Center for the Advanced Study of Educational Administration (1968) (now CEPM).

A. Perhaps there are some people in your organization with whom you talk rather frequently about matters important to you. Please think of people with whom you talk seriously about things important to you, inside or outside formal meetings, once a week or more on the average. Write their names below. (If there are fewer than six people, write down only as many as there are; if none, write "none." If there are more than six, list just the six with whom you feel your conversations are the most satisfying.)

1. _____   4. _____
2. _____   5. _____
3. _____   6. _____

B. Now look back at question A. Each name is numbered. Listed below are all the pairs that can be made among six numbers. Perhaps you know whether some of the six people talk to each other about matters important to them. Please look at each pair of numbers below, look back to see what names they represent, and circle the pair of numbers if you have good reason to believe that the two people talk to each other once a week or more about matters important to them.

```
1-2
1-3    2-3
1-4    2-4    3-4
1-5    2-5    3-5    4-5
1-6    2-6    3-6    4-6    5-6
```

Feedback in the School

The following questions provide information about the availability of feedback.* Question B is less direct than question A, but if many teachers indicate that they do not know whether others agree with them on important issues, the consultant can be relatively certain that the level of interpersonal feedback is low.

A. Do you get any information from other professionals that helps you to tell whether you are doing an effective job of teaching?
(   ) No, none.
(   ) Yes, about once or twice a year.
(   ) Yes, about once a month, maybe.
(   ) Yes, about once a week.
(   ) Yes, more than once a week.

---

*Questions are from X-1 Questionnaire, Project 3002, Center for the Advanced Study of Educational Administration (1970).

B. Would you say there is some particular aspect of the school's functioning where new ideas are especially needed?
(   ) No, things are working about as well as they can.
(   ) No, no particular aspect more than another. We just need things polished up a bit all over.
(   ) Yes. If yes, please describe a feature of the school's functioning that needs attention:

1. _____
   _____

C. If you wrote in an answer above, how many people would you say agree with you.
(   ) Many.
(   ) Some.
(   ) Only one or two.
(   ) None.
(   ) I don't know.

Communicative Roles

Bales (1950) divided communicative activities in work-oriented groups into two general categories. The task-centered category includes acts that promote getting a job done; the social-emotional category includes acts that lower tension and increase group cohesiveness. In the following observation forms for task-centered and interpersonal processes, an observer may tally all group interactions during a specified time period or may focus on each of the members successively.

Categories for Task-centered Process

Tallies

I. Helps group collect data related to task
  A. Contributes data
    Defines terms, gives facts
    States objectives, goals
    Gives opinions, generalizations
  B. Asks questions, asks for survey
  C. Suggests actions, alternatives
II. Helps group use data
  D. Organizes data, combines, compares, points out relations in data
  E. Summaries: identifies points of agreement and disagreement
III. Tests for consensus
  F. Checks to see if group agrees

Categories for Interpersonal Process

I. Acts to increase shared understanding
   A. Paraphrases
   B. Impression check
   C. Helps others paraphrase or make perception checks
II. Acts to provide data about interpersonal process
   D. Describes interpersonal behavior
   E. Reports own feelings directly
      1. Positive feelings
      2. Negative feelings
   F. Helps others to describe interpersonal behavior or to report their own feelings directly

An observer may sometimes wish to code unproductive communication processes as well. The following list, while not exhaustive, includes some of the unproductive processes commonly seen in groups.

- Recognition seeking, claiming expertise because of longevity, etc.
- Self-confessing, apologizing repeatedly
- Pleading a self-interest that is irrelevant to the task
- Side talking
- Seeking help, asking for special favors

Another useful observation and feedback tool can be created from the matrix of figure 3-6. Observers can tally the incidence of communication about the situation dimension of the convening tasks, target statements about methods, proposals for improving interpersonal relations, and so on. They can also record the kinds of contributions made by each group member to give feedback on the roles that are or are not being filled in the group.

The role-perception questionnaire below, which can be completed by group members near the end of a work session, provides subjective data to complement the data collected by an outside observer.

Directions: For each of the ratings below, imagine that the value of the contributions from all members equals 100 percent. Then, beside each member's name, show what percentage of the total effort you would attribute to that person. You may give any member a score from 0 to 100 on each question. Remember that the scores for all members must add up to 100. Be sure to list your own name and to score yourself.

Question A: Show how much each member has contributed to making this a smoothly working, friendly, comfortable group by such acts as encouraging others to participate, showing interest in the feelings of others, helping to resolve tensions and misunderstandings, providing support when members were feeling uneasy or upset, and, in general, showing concern for how well the members of this group got along together.

	Members	*Score*
1.	_____	( )
2.	_____	( )
3.	_____	( )
4.	_____	( )
5.	_____	( )
6.	_____	( )

Total must equal 100

Question B: Show how much each member contributed to the group's achievement by such acts as providing good ideas, suggestions, and information, by keeping the group on the ball, by summarizing what had been accomplished and what still needed to be done, and, in general, by showing concern for productivity or getting a lot of work done.

	Members	*Score*
1.	_____	( )
2.	_____	( )
3.	_____	( )
4.	_____	( )
5.	_____	( )
6.	_____	( )

Total must equal 100

Again, the questions can be changed to reflect the observation scheme being used, as, for example:

A. Show how much each member contributed to clarifying the *situation* in which the group found itself by such acts as describing the purpose of the meeting, reporting an observation of how the meeting was going, or describing his or her own feelings toward another at the time.

B. Show how much each member contributed to making the *methods* used in this meeting effective by such acts as describing methods that were being used, suggesting better methods, or proposing that the group take a survey or meet in buzz groups.

EXERCISES AND DESIGNS FOR INTERVENTIONS

Basic Communication Skills

In practicing the following exercises the consultant should not only encourage correct use of the skills but should help group members learn ways of correcting one another. It is useful if participants identify their attempts to use the skills by stating, for example, "I'd like to paraphrase what I heard you say," and so on. Of course, all the exercises and designs presented to the end of this chapter will reinforce points discussed earlier, just as exercises and designs presented elsewhere in this book should highlight or otherwise encourage discussion of communication.

Paraphrasing. For the purpose of paraphrasing, members group into circles of no more than eight persons. The consultant or someone in the group suggests a topic that is relevant and important to the group, such as "what is the most important problem facing our team?" One member answers the question briefly; the next person in the circle accurately paraphrases this before giving his own answer, and so on around the circle. This exercise is also effective in two-person units, especially if the two join still another pair and each speaks from an understanding of his partner's answer.

A variation on this exercise can be particularly useful with a new group or with groups that have new members. Here, each person writes five to ten answers to the question "who am I?" on either a five-by-eight-inch card that is pinned to the person's chest or on a piece of newsprint that is taped to the wall. All members mill around for a few minutes silently reading one another's answers. Then, in partners or triads, individuals paraphrase items from the other persons' lists, perhaps limiting themselves to items that are most like or unlike items on their own list.

Impression Checking. Two exercises are useful for practicing impression checking. In the first, the consultant might ask group members to take turns conveying their feelings to others by means of gestures, expressions, and nonsense language and then ask others to check to make sure that they read the emotion correctly. In the second, called the "alter ego" procedure, half the group sit in a circle while the other half take their places behind specific members of the circle. While those in the center discuss some topic that has been agreed upon, those in the outer ring whisper their impressions to their partners ("Are you upset because you can't get a word in edgewise?" or "Am I correct in inferring that you're slumping because you're uninterested?"). Partners in the inner circle respond only by nodding their heads yes or no to these questions.

Describing Behavior. The nonverbal exercises in this book can provide data for practicing this interpersonal communication skill. After a five-member group completes the Five-Square puzzle, for example, members might begin their debriefing process by describing orally a

120

behavior that was conspicuous to them. If group members appear to be withholding significant oral reactions from one another, the consultant might ask each person to write a behavior description instead. The consultant then collects these statements and reads them aloud anonymously.*

Describing One's Own Feelings.   Many of the nonverbal exercises in this book arouse strong feelings that can later be expressed by means of an oral debriefing, a technique that works especially well when group members describe the nonverbal behavior that triggered their feelings. Written self-tests can also help clients in this skill. In the following example, group members individually mark a *D* by sentences that describe feelings and an *N* by sentences that convey but do not describe a feeling. When all participants have marked item 1, they share their responses in trios, then check against explanations of what is correct. The explanations appear in mixed order so that the eye is not drawn to the list of answers. After everyone in the trio understands the explanation, the trio marks item 2, and so on. This self-test takes about forty-five minutes to complete.†

Self-Test
1. (   ) a. Shut up! Not another word out of you!
   (   ) b. I'm really annoyed by what you just said.
2. (   ) a. Can't you see I'm busy? Get out!
   (   ) b. I'm beginning to resent your constant interruptions.
   (   ) c. You have no consideration for anybody else's feelings. You're completely selfish.
3. (   ) a. I feel discouraged because of some things that happened today.
   (   ) b. This has been an upsetting day.
4. (   ) a. You're a wonderful person.
   (   ) b. I really like you.
5. (   ) a. I feel comfortable and free to be myself when I'm around you.
   (   ) b. We all feel you're a wonderful person.
   (   ) c. Everybody likes you.
6. (   ) a. If things don't improve around here, I'll look for a new job.
   (   ) b. Did you ever hear of such a lousy outfit as this is?
   (   ) c. I'm afraid to admit that I need help with my work.
7. (   ) a. This is a very poor exercise.
   (   ) b. I feel this is a very poor exercise.

*To our knowledge, this procedure was first described in print by Pfeiffer and Jones (1970).
†Reprinted from Jung et al. (1972) by permission of the Northwest Regional Educational Laboratory.

(   ) c. I'm confused, frustrated, and annoyed by this exercise.

8. (   ) a. I feel inadequate when teaching that particular subject.

   (   ) b. I am inadequate in teaching that particular subject.

9. (   ) a. I am a failure; I'll never amount to anything.

   (   ) b. That teacher is awful. He didn't teach me anything.

   (   ) c. I'm depressed and discouraged because I did so poorly on that test.

10. (   ) a. I feel lonely and isolated in my group.

   (   ) b. For all the attention anybody pays to me I might as well not be in my group.

   (   ) c. I feel that nobody in my group cares whether I am there or not.

Answers and Explanations

Item 1:   *Expression a . . . N.* Commands such as these convey strong emotion without describing what kinds of feeling evoked the commands.

    Expression b . . . D. The speaker conveys his feeling by describing himself as annoyed. Thus, the statement not only expresses feeling; it also names the feeling.

Item 7:   *Expression a . . . N.* This statement expresses a negative value judgment. It conveys some kind of negative feelings without describing them.

    Expression b . . . N. Although the speaker begins by saying, "I feel . . .," he does not then tell what he is feeling. Instead he passes a negative value judgment on the exercise. Note that merely tacking the words "I feel" onto the front of a sentence does not turn it into a description of feeling. People often say "I feel" when they mean "I think" or "I believe." For example, "I feel the Red Sox will win" or "I feel it will rain tomorrow."

    Expression c . . . D. The speaker specifies that he feels confused, frustrated, and annoyed. He describes his feelings but does not evaluate the exercise itself.

    Although we can disagree with value judgments expressed by another person, we should not deny that he feels whatever he feels. If Joe says the exercise is poor and Jill says it is good, an argument may ensue about which it "really" is. However, if Joe says he was frustrated by the exercise and Jill says she was pleased and stimulated by it, no argument should follow. Each person's reaction is what it is. Of course, discussion about what causes each to feel as he does may provide important information about each person and about the exercise itself.

Many persons who say they are unaware of what they feel habitually express value judgments about others without recognizing that they are thereby expressing positive or negative feelings.

Item 10: *Expression a . . . D.* This statement conveys feelings by describing the speaker as feeling lonely and isolated.

Expression b . . . N. This statement conveys negative feelings without telling whether the speaker feels angry, lonely, disappointed, hurt, or any other specific way.

Expression c . . . N. Because it begins with "I feel," this kind of expression is often thought to describe the speaker's feelings. Notice, however, that the last part of the sentence really tells what the speaker assumes the others in the group feel about him and now what the speaker feels.

Expression *c* and *a* relate to each other as follows: "Because I believe or assume that nobody in my group cares whether I am there or not, I feel lonely and isolated."

Item 4: *Expression a . . . N.* This sentence states a value judgment. It conveys positive feelings toward the other without describing what they are. Does the speaker like the other, respect him, enjoy him, love him, or what? The expression does not tell us.

Expression b . . . D. The speaker conveys positive feelings by describing it as liking for the other.

Item 2: *Expression a . . . N.* Strong feeling is conveyed by the question and accompanying command, "Get out!," but the feeling itself is not described.

Expression b . . . D. The speaker's feeling is described as resentment.

Expression c . . . N. The speaker makes charges and accusations about the other. The accusations certainly convey strong negative feelings. However, because the feelings are not identified we do not know whether the accusations stem from anger, disappointment, or hurt feelings.

Item 6: *Expression a . . . N.* This statement conveys negative feelings about the organization without specifying them. It alludes to the condition of things in this organization but does not clarify the speaker's inner state.

Expression b . . . N. This is a rhetorical question that expresses a negative value judgment about the organization. It certainly conveys some kind of negative feeling but does not describe what it is.

Expression c . . . D. This is a clear description of how the speaker feels in relation to his job. He feels afraid.

Expressions *a* and *b* are attacks or criticisms of the organization that could result from the kind of fear described in *c*. Notice expressions that convey anger turn out to result from fear. Many expressions of anger result from fear, hurt feelings, disappointments, or loneliness, but because the speaker's basic feelings are not described the other person does not understand them.

Item 9: *Expression a . . . N.* This is another example of the subtle distinction introduced in item 8. The speaker is conveying strong negative feelings about himself ("I am a failure"). The statement does not describe his feelings, however.

Expression b . . . N. Instead of taking it out on himself, the speaker blames the teacher. His value judgment conveys negative feelings, but it does not describe what the speaker feels.

Expression c . . . D. This conveys feelings by describing the speaker's emotional state as depressed and discouraged.

Expressions *a* and *c* illustrate the important difference between labeling oneself and describing one's feelings. Feelings can and do change. To say that I am now depressed and discouraged does not imply that I will or must always feel the same. However, if I label myself as a failure, if I truly think of myself as a failure, I increase the probability that I will act like a failure.

One girl stated this important insight for herself this way, "I always thought I was a shy person. Now I have discovered that I am not shy although at times I *feel* shy." No longer did she keep herself from trying new things she wanted to by reminding herself that she was too shy.

Item 5: *Expression a . . . D.* This is a clear and specific description of how the speaker feels when around the other.

Expression b . . . N. Although this conveys positive feelings toward the other, it does not say that the speaker feels this way. To be a description of feeling, the statement should use "I," "me," "my," or "mine"

to make clear the feelings are in the speaker. Secondly, "you're a wonderful person" is a value judgment which does not specify what feeling is behind it
(see item 4a).

Expression c . . . N. The statement is not about the
speaker and his feelings but refers to everybody. It is
true that a feeling is named in the statement but the
speaker does not make clear the feeling is in him. A
description of feeling must contain "I," "me," "my,"
or "mine."

Note how much more personal and warm you
feel when another says to you that *he* likes you
rather than *everybody* likes you. Do you find it
more difficult to tell another "I like you" or
"everybody likes you"?

Item 8: *Expression a . . . D.* This conveys feeling by describing the feeling as one of inadequacy.

Expression b . . . N. Careful! This sounds much the
same as *a.* However, it really says the person *is*
inadequate. The person labels himself as inadequate.
True, he conveys negative feelings about himself,
but he does not describe them.

This subtle difference was introduced because
many people confuse *feeling* inadequate with *being*
inadequate. A person may feel inadequate when
teaching a certain subject and yet do an excellent
job of it. Likewise, a person may feel adequate and
competent in a subject and perform poorly. One
sign of emotional maturity may be when a person
functions adequately while feeling inadequate.

Item 3: *Expression a . . . D.* This describes the speaker as
feeling discouraged.

Expression b . . . N. Conveys negative feelings without describing what they are. The statement appears
to be about the kind of day it was when, in fact, it
is an expression of the way the speaker is feeling. We
cannot tell from this expression whether the speaker
is feeling depressed, annoyed, lonely, humiliated,
or rejected.

Giving and Receiving Feedback. This section offers three exercises
that enable people to practice giving and receiving feedback. In the
first exercise, group members form trios in which one member is
assigned to give feedback, the second to receive feedback, and the
third to observe the first two. The person giving feedback describes
two helpful and two unhelpful behaviors on the part of the receiver;
the receiver paraphrases, and the observer sees to it that the two continue to use communication skills correctly.

Another exercise demonstrates the importance of giving and receiving feedback by showing that close-mouthed behavior is more often interpreted as disapproving than as approving.* Participants select partners and decide which of them will be A and which will be B. The consultant tells A privately: "Your partner was supposed to contact you for lunch yesterday but failed to do so, and you are disappointed. On a scale of feeling ranging from 1 (extremely distant) to 9 (extremely close), portray a feeling of 3 in the one-minute conversation that you'll be having soon." To B the consultant says privately: "In the one-minute conversation that you'll soon be having with your partner, whom you like, respect, and value, pretend that you think it would be nice to share a ride to an evening meeting. You think the probability that your partner likes you is about 8."

The partners then come together to talk for one minute about whatever they choose. At the end of that time the consultant tells all Bs to assign their partners a number from 1 to 9 based on the scale of feeling from extremely distant to extremely close. Before it is divulged that all the A partners had been asked to portray a 3, all the B estimates are recorded on newsprint. Almost invariably, the average B estimate will be less than 2. The consultant can then initiate a discussion of why this is so, pointing out that silence or lack of candor about feelings can strain trust in even a one-minute interaction.

Friendly Helping, a third exercise that enables people to practice giving and receiving feedback,† is usually done in teams of four to six people (larger groups allow more practice but take more time). Each person fills in a chart like the one below by writing the initials of every other member of the group in or on the triangle, clearly indicating by the placement of the initials the writer's impression of either the typical, most impressive, or most distressing behavior of the others.

The Friendly Helping Handout

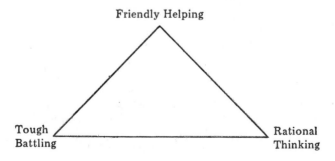

Friendly Helping

Tough
Battling

Rational
Thinking

---

*We are grateful to Fred Fosmire of the Psychology Department at the University of Oregon for this exercise.

†This exercise is adapted from one by Hale and Spanjer (1970).

Friendly Helping:	Expressing concern for the feelings of others; sharing personal feelings of anxiety, joy, sorrow; paying compliments; sympathizing, listening carefully
Tough Battling:	Sharing personal feelings of humor, anger, frustration; diving into problems; being action oriented rather than all talk; confronting whatever needs to be dealt with
Rational Thinking:	Expressing concern about identifying all parts of a problem; taking a logical figure-it-out approach; talking to reach understandings; interpreting

Group members take turns giving and receiving feedback in either of two ways: (1) all members tell where they placed person A, where they placed B, and so on, or (2) each person takes a turn to tell how he or she viewed all others. The consultant encourages givers of feedback to describe behavior and feelings and encourages receivers of feedback to paraphrase and check impressions. Although this exercise can promote typecasting or "labeling" behavior, this can usually be minimized if the equal importance of all three behaviors in groups is stressed and if group members are encouraged to replace such statements as "you're a battler" with "I see you serving the battling function in our group."

Unilateral and Transactional Communication

This section describes two exercises in unilateral and transactional communication. The first exercise (adapted from Bass 1966) is designed to provide a group with a springboard for discussions of communication in the school within a brief period of time. In this procedure, one member is designated as the coordinator; another is asked to be the sender; the remaining members are receivers. The coordinator signals when to begin, keeps track of how much time is spent during each phase of the activity, and observes the nonverbal reactions of the receivers.

To commence the activity, the coordinator gives the sender two patterns of rectangles, being careful not to show them to the receivers. The first pattern is presented to the receivers as a unilateral communication during which they must remain silent and refrain from asking questions as they draw the pattern as accurately as possible. The second is given through transactional communication during which the receivers are encouraged to break in at any time, to raise questions, and to interact verbally with the sender.

Handout for Unilateral and Transactional Exercise

Phase I: Unilateral Communication
Directions for sender:
1. Be sure that none of the receivers sees the overall design below.
2. Sit with your back to the receivers.

3. When you are ready to start, describe the diagram below so that the receivers can duplicate it on their own papers.
4. None of the receivers may communicate with you in any way at any time.
5. When you are through, take several minutes to record below your degree of satisfaction with the activity just completed.
6. Hand this sheet to the coordinator.

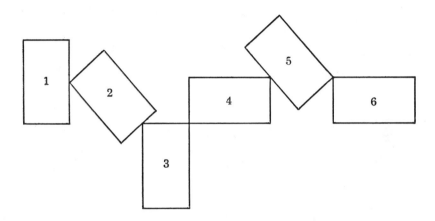

Satisfaction scale:

Very dissatisfied	Rather dissatisfied	Rather satisfied	Very satisfied	Don't know

What factors caused the reaction you circled above?

(end of sender's sheet)

Directions for receivers:

1. As receivers, sit with your backs to the sender.
2. Your task is to reproduce on this paper whatever the sender instructs you to.
3. Only the sender can talk. You may initiate no communications and make no audible signals of any type.
4. It is best to use only your own ideas about what the sender is saying. A neighbor's understanding of the task may be wrong.
5. When the sender has finished, answer the two items below and give paper to the coordinator.
   A. How many pieces of the diagram do you think you completed accurately?
   Circle the appropriate response: 1 2 3 4 5 6

B. If you felt any frustrations during the exercise, circle the number below that best describes your feelings:

1	2	3	4	5
Not at all frustrated	A little frustrated	Some real frustration	Very frustrated	Don't know

(end of receiver's sheet)

Directions for coordinator:

1. Prior to exercise:
   A. Check back-to-back seating so that receivers cannot see the sender's paper.
   B. You may answer questions before exercise begins.
   C. Encourage sender to begin when all are ready.
2. During exercise:
   A. Record starting time _____ ;
      completion time _____ ;
      elapsed time _____ .
   B. Record below apparent evidences (including nonverbal) of feelings such as satisfaction, frustration, interest level, high or low morale, etc., of:

Sender	Receiver

3. After exercise:
   A. Note elapsed time for exercise completion in 2A.
   B. Complete your own notes in 2B.
   C. Collect completed papers in your group.
   D. Record on the back of this sheet any on-the-job implications of exercise you have just observed.

Phase II: Transactional Communication

The handout for the *sender* differs from the one for unilateral communication only in two ways:

(1) Rule 4 now reads, "The receivers may interrupt your directions with questions or comments at any time."

(2) The diagram to be transmitted is this one:

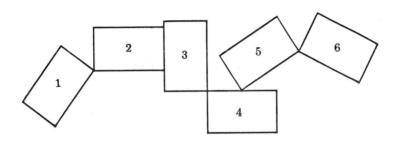

The handout for the *receiver* differs from the one for unilateral communication only in Rule 4 which now reads, "You may question the sender about instructions at any time and as often as you wish."

The handout for the *coordinator* is identical to the one for unilateral communication.

After the two episodes are completed, the coordinator assists the receivers in determining the number of correct placements in their drawings. A correct rectangle touches one or two other rectangles at the matching location on the sides of the other rectangles and should also be oriented vertically, horizontally, or diagonally as on the sender's page. One point is granted for each rectangle drawn correctly. Scores can range from 0 to 6 for each communication episode.

After the receivers score their own drawings, receivers and senders are asked to answer the following questions for discussion: With which communication were you most frustrated or tense? Which type would you prefer to use as a sender? Which type would you prefer to receive? (To each question, three alternative answers are possible: unilateral, transactional, or no difference.) The ensuing discussion can be guided by the coordinator, who may use the following questions as guides: When is unilateral communication efficient in our work, and how might we improve it? When is transactional communication necessary in our work, and what can we do to improve it? What are other implications of this activity for our work? What keeps us from using transactional communication more often in our work?

When using the exercise with multiple groups, each coordinator is asked to report the primary outcomes of his team to the entire staff so that all group members can discuss what they learned from the activity and recommendations can be made for continued work on improving communication clarity. Finally, before meeting with the total group, the consultant may meet with the coordinators during a scheduled break and prepare summary charts of the time required, accuracy, and attitudes associated with each communication mode in each of the groups. These summaries can be used to supplement individual reports by the coordinators during the meeting with the entire group.

The Blind Walk is another exercise that highlights the differences between unilateral and transactional communication. In this procedure, each member of the group is asked to pair with a person whom he does not know well or would like to know better. One member of the team is blindfolded, and the other silently guides him through, over, or around things. After several minutes the roles are reversed, but during this second phase talking is allowed. When the walk is completed, participants share their mutual reactions about the two ways of communicating and about their relationship. In a variation of this exercise, half the members of the entire group are blindfolded, and the sighted members choose a partner. Each leads one blindfolded member around without identifying himself, which seems to augment the impact of the nonverbal phase of the walk. Still another variation involves allowing no touching during the verbal phase, which makes clear verbal instructions imperative.

Interpersonal Styles

Several exercises are useful in helping group members explore the interpersonal orientations of themselves and of others with whom they work. In the exercise that follows,* group members complete sentence stems and various nonverbal activities to explore how much they want, as well as how they express, the three dimensions of interpersonal style—inclusion, control, and affection. Each of the three dimensions is explored in four steps.

To explore the dimension of inclusion, group members first complete the following sentence stems on paper.

- What I usually do when a new group begins . . . .
- I feel "in" with a group . . . .
- Being alone . . . .
- I invite others to do things with me . . . .

Second, they form trios or quartets to share their sentences. Third, all group members scatter about the room, avoiding eye contact, until the consultant tells them to find a partner nonverbally. Fourth, they discuss how active or passive they were in this activity and how it felt to seek and be sought.

To explore the dimension of control, group members first complete the following stems.

---

*The concepts in this exercise were drawn from Schutz (1966), the activities were first described to us by Fosmire of the Psychology Department at the University of Oregon.

- When I am with someone who has to have his or her way . . . .
- When another person leaves decisions to me and goes along with whatever I decide . . . .
- When a group expects me to take charge . . . .
- When another group member usually tries to take charge . . . .

Second, they report their responses in trios or quartets. Third, each person places his right hand on the left shoulder of a partner; when the consultant says "begin," partners nonverbally negotiate who will kneel in front of the other. Fourth, partners describe each other's behavior and state how each of them felt during the activity.

To explore the affective dimension, group members first complete these sentences.

- I feel closest to a person who . . . .
- I keep my distance from people who . . . .
- It's hard for me to express affection I feel when . . . .
- When others express affection for me . . . .

Second, the responses are reported in trios. Third, all group members form a large circle and at a signal from the consultant begin walking toward the center slowly or quickly, as they prefer, but all freezing in position when the first group member says "stop." The fourth step is to debrief the nonverbal activity with a partner by using interpersonal communication skills.

The total exercise can then be debriefed either with a partner or in small groups, with the focus on comparing experiences in the three dimensions. Questions such as the following may encourage this inquiry: Which of the three nonverbal activities was easiest for me? Which was the hardest? How was that like or unlike the way I usually feel? How did others behave in the three sets? How was that like or unlike what I usually observe?

The Five-Square Puzzle. The Five-Square puzzle exercise (adapted from Bavelas 1950) demonstrates cooperation in a group task characterized by nonverbal communication. It is administered to participants in groups of five. Observers are instructed to look for ways in which participants communicate nonverbally and for ways in which cooperation is helped or hindered.

Participants occupy five chairs around a table on which, before each person, there are some flat, mostly irregularly shaped pieces of plastic or cardboard. In an unordered pile before one person are three pieces marked A; before another are four pieces marked B; before another, two pieces marked C; before another, two marked D; and before the fifth person are four pieces marked E. The participants are told that there are exactly enough parts distributed among them to make five complete squares (see diagram below). The task is completed when a square has been composed in front of each member of the group.

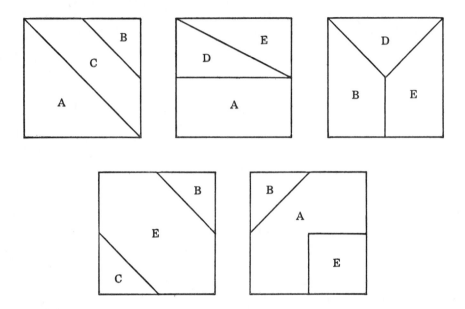

The procedural rules are as follows: (1) each member must construct one square at his own work place; (2) no member may talk,
signal, or gesture in any way that would provide guidance, direction,
or suggestions to any other member—for example, no member may
signal that he wants a piece from another member; (3) any member
may give any of his pieces to another member; (4) except for the one
piece that he is giving to another member, each member's pieces must
be in front of him at his work place. Only giving is allowed, no taking.

This exercise is frustrating for individuals who are accustomed
to managing others and also for people who are accustomed to guiding themselves by watching for signals of the expectations of others.
To the extent that the rules are observed (and it is very difficult for
most participants to apply this discipline to themselves), the exercise
focuses participants' attention on discovering ways in which they can
be helpful to one another. The most direct contribution that a member can make is to give an appropriate piece from his place to the
appropriate person, but he must allow the other person to find for
himself the way in which that piece fits with the others before him.

This exercise points up the great difficulty in allowing other
people to do things in their own way and the great extent to which
we rely on language to influence the behavior of others. At the same
time, it provides very useful information about how group members
act toward one another under the frustration the exercise produces.
When the performance is completed, the ensuing discussion should
focus on problems of coordinated effort and on the implications of
the exercise for relations among group members in their daily work.
To guide the discussion, the following questions might be asked:
What were some of your feelings during the exercise? Do you have

similar feelings when you are working in groups in the school district? Under what circumstances do these feelings arise? What implications does this exercise have for our work in the school?

Group Agreements. An exercise in making group agreements about communication not only encourages discussion about the behaviors that are expected from group members but also serves to introduce survey procedure. If it is feasible, members who will continue to work as a team should be grouped together for this exercise (adapted from one by Hale and Spanjer 1970). The exercise requires little preparation beyond providing each participant with a copy of the handout instructions shown below, although the consultant may wish to point out that the outlined agreements are only samples and not necessarily suggestions.

Handout for Group Agreements

Group functioning is improved when members have clear expectations of what kinds of behavior are expected of them as group members. Here are two examples of agreements that a group might accept.

1. *Directness:* If I am dissatisfied with the way the group is going, I will report my reactions directly to the group when it is in session. If, outside of a regular session, another member tells me of his dissatisfactions with the group, I will suggest that he bring the matter before the total group at a regular session.

2. *Sharing:* Any member may request a survey at any time. The requesting member states what he wants to know from the total group; another member paraphrases or otherwise clarifies the topic until all concerned are clear about what is being asked of them; then each person in turn states his current position on the topic in two or three sentences. A survey is not a vote that will bind the group or its members. A survey must be taken at the time that it is requested, suspending any other activity.

You should now discuss and decide whether you wish to conclude any group agreements and, if so, what they are to be.

Emotional Distance and Closeness. The purpose of this exercise is to heighten awareness of how degrees of distance and closeness in communication affect human relationships. The exercise is most effective if group members are skilled at describing their own feelings, objectively describing the behavior of others, and checking their own inferences about the feelings of others. Groups form two-person units to engage in a series of three-minute conversations on one of the following topics:

1. A topic that is of interest to only one of you and is unrelated to this day or event.

2. A topic that is of interest to both of you and is unrelated to this day or event.
3. A topic that is of interest to only one of you and is closely related to your life today or to this event.
4. A topic that is of interest to both of you and is closely related to your life today or to this event.
5. What is happening between the two of you right now— the way you are relating, your feelings, and your inferences about your partner's feelings. Emphasize your experience of this moment.

When the five conversations are completed, the debriefing may be guided by the following questions: How did your experiences change over the sequence of conversations? Did you find some conversations easier or more difficult than others? Why? What is happening between you right now? After the debriefing, the consultant may give a lecturette highlighting the dimensions of closeness and distance or distribute a handout similar to figure 3-3. The exercise can be concluded with a discussion in quartets of the ways in which emotionally distant and emotionally close communication affects the everyday lives and relationships of people, groups, and organizations. It should be emphasized that close communication does not require intimate friendship between persons and that emotionally close communication cannot be achieved immediately but is based on a step-by-step increase of mutual trust.

Improving Communication Skills

With the consultant's help, communication skills can be improved in both direct and indirect ways. As an example of the former, the following sequence of events emphasizing the use of these skills helps a group to identify issues and problems for additional work. The design takes about seven hours to complete and can be divided into morning and afternoon sessions.

The day begins with a general meeting introducing an overview of training goals and activities followed by an introduction to paraphrasing. The group is divided into small subgroups to discuss what should be changed to help their school operate more effectively. Following this discussion, members concentrate on paraphrasing and attempt to identify its difficulties and potentialities. After the unilateral and transactional communication exercise is introduced, participants discuss it within their subgroups, giving special attention to impression checking and describing one's own feelings. The total group is then reassembled, and the consultant reviews all the skills so far introduced before the group adjourns for lunch.

The afternoon session begins with an introduction to the Five-Square exercise, following which the group is again divided into small subgroups but of different participants. After completing the exercise, the subgroups discuss it using the skills of behavior description, impression checking, and describing one's own feelings. The total group reconvenes for an introduction to the group agreements exercise, and participants are reassigned to new subgroups. Emphasis is placed on using communication skills correctly during the task and during discussion as well. The small groups then report their various discussions to the total assembly.

The final activity of the day is introduced by a lecturette on the Johari Awareness Model, and the subgroups form helping trios to practice giving feedback on helpful and unhelpful behaviors. If time permits, group members may redistribute themselves into new helping trios and continue practicing. The consultant ends the meeting by reviewing the day's activities, distributing handouts on communication skills, and suggesting possible directions for future OD activities.

Occasionally a consultant will discover that processes other than those of communication are so impaired as to impede the school's functioning. In this case initial training efforts must be directed to these processes if the training is to benefit the organization. For the consultant who is designing a training sequence, however, this poses a problem because clear communication is essential to the success of other organizational training events. The solution to this dilemma is to plan the training activities in such a way that communication skills can be introduced even when the focus of the activities is elsewhere.

For example, the authors once worked with an elementary school in which conflict between parents and staff was so intense and goals so ambiguous that collaborative problem solving and decision making were impossible to initiate. To use the terms of Gibb (1961), the climate was defensive rather than supportive. Parents and staff were only interested in the amount and kind of communication skill training that would move them out of this situation rapidly. We decided to work separately with the two groups in a series of meetings distributed over two months.

At the first meeting individuals were asked to write behavior descriptions and statements of their own feelings about the situation in the school. Participants took turns sharing what they had written while others in their group practiced paraphrasing and impression checking. At other meetings we asked staff and parents separately to describe their behaviors and feelings when the school situation was as they wished it to be. Again they took turns sharing what they had written while everyone had a turn to practice paraphrasing and impression checking. At all these meetings we collected cards, eventually categorizing their content into seven major areas including the reporting system, building and grounds, extracurricular activities in the arts, and so on.

All staff and parents were given handouts describing interpersonal communication skills and a copy of an article by Gibb (1961) contrasting behaviors characteristic of defensive and supportive communication. According to Gibb, defensive climates are characterized by evaluation, control, strategy, neutrality, superiority, and certainty; supportive climates are characterized by description, problem orientation, spontaneity, empathy, equality, and provisionalism.

Both groups were encouraged to consider how their own behaviors contributed to defensive reactions by members of the other group.

After all participants had attended at least two meetings—in extra training events, the staff worked on organizational issues not directly related to relationships with parents—we brought the two groups together for a seven-hour meeting at which they performed the Imaging exercise described in chapter 5. This exercise required them to use the four communication skills to give and receive mutual feedback. The content of the feedback was then compared to the seven problem areas that we had identified to verify the problems that were most significant. Small problem-solving groups of parents and staff then met for several months to generate proposals which were finally reported back to the total group. Throughout these meetings we continually urged people to use the communication skills and taught them how to coach one another when they were improperly used.

Improved communication is a fundamental objective of consultation in organization development. Because a school's adaptability depends in part upon effective communication between persons, within subsystems, and in the organization at large, most OD efforts in schools begin with practice in new forms of interpersonal communication and proceed to the use of new communication skills, norms, and structures within the school's subsystems.

READINGS

What You Say Does Make a Difference

Jerry W. Valentine, Bradford L. Tate, Alan T. Seagren, and John A. Lammel

Administrators spend so much of their time communicating with teachers, students, and parents that the quality of their communication styles may be said greatly to affect their success. This article reports a study of communication styles and suggests those that are most effective in relation to specific aspects of the school environment.

From Jerry W. Valentine, Bradford L. Tate, Alan T. Seagren, and John A. Lammel. "What You Say Does Make a Difference." *NASSP Bulletin* 59, no. 395 (December 1975): 67-74.

The principal is clearly the one individual with the most influence on a school's "climate," "tone," or "environment." If a school's climate affects the quality of its educational program, the importance of analyzing the principal's behavior and its resultant effect is crucial.

Administrative Behavior Is Communicative Behavior

A major portion of an administrator's time is spent in communications, so in a broad sense administrative behavior is communicative behavior. Since the principal is a key link in the many communications systems making up the school environment, it is important that he understand the effect his behavior might have on others. Communication in general and, more specifically, "face-to-face" communication, has increased in recent years between the principal and the various population groups making up the school environment, particularly with the advent of widespread involvement in the decision-making process.

Most administrators realize that effective communications is a key to their success and that verbal behavior is the most significant form of communication. How then does the principal analyze and understand the influence his verbal behavior has on the organization? This article deals with that question and reflects the findings of a study of selected high school principals' verbal behavior with teachers, students and parents. The implications these findings and the processes used in the study have for practicing administrators are discussed.

The study of the verbal behavior between members of the school organization has long been of interest to educators. Although interest has been concentrated primarily on teacher-student verbal interaction in the classroom, the findings of Flanders and others have generated an interest in analyzing the verbal behavior of other members of the school organization. . . . Though only a limited number of administrative verbal behavior studies using prototypes of the Flanders' system have been concluded, these studies indicate that the Flanders' categories are applicable in analyzing administrative verbal interaction.

One instrument for analyzing administrative verbal behavior is the Administrative Verbal Interaction System (AVIS). The AVIS Instrument was developed at the University of Nebraska by a research team, under the direction of Alan T. Seagren. Originally designed to measure the verbal behavior of teachers and students in their leader-subordinate roles, this instrument was modified to measure administrators' interaction with others (students, teachers, parents, and other administrators).

A study of secondary high schools with student populations from 750 to 1,500 revealed that specific types of verbal behavior were related to specific aspects of the school environment. The areas of verbal interaction studies were principal/teacher, principal/student, and principal/parent interaction. School environments were measured by the Organizational Climate Index and the High School Characteristics Index and reflect the environment of the schools as perceived by teachers, students, and parents.

Principal-Teacher Verbal Interaction

The primary purpose of all public school principals should be to provide the best possible learning conditions for students under their supervision. Teachers are generally the primary means to achieve this end. The principal must therefore rely heavily on his influence with staff members in order to achieve the appropriate learning outcomes.

Principals who were more indirect in their verbal behaviors administered schools that were perceived by teachers as stressing practicality and friendliness. These principals used verbal behavior that increased the freedom of the teacher input by reducing restraints and encouraging participation.

The use of humor by the principal when interacting with his staff correlated to the amount of energy or effort displayed by the staff. In schools where the principal utilized more humor when interacting, there was a greater interest in achievement and a significant emphasis on hard work and a commitment to the goals of the school. There was also an emphasis on expressiveness of emotion or feelings and on reasoning and abstract thinking.

In schools where principals verbally stated their decisions to their staff, there was emphasis on recognition for accomplishments rather than feelings of inferiority or shyness.

One of the most significant verbal behaviors utilized by principals was statements of attitude or value. The more these behaviors were expressed by principals, the more the members of the organization became group-centered, desirous of public recognition for their accomplishments, and impetuous rather than reflective. . . .

One of the more obvious, direct administrative verbal behaviors was statements in which the principal gave directions to staff members. The more principals utilized this behavior following teacher talk, the more teachers perceived the organization as being constraining and restrictive with little opportunity for personal expression, less respect for the integrity of the person, and little personal autonomy. However, in the schools where more direction-giving was utilized, teachers expressed more respect for authority.

Principal-Student Verbal Interaction

In analyzing the interaction between principals and students, four groups of behaviors were found to be significant. These included the very indirect behaviors of accepting feelings and feedback; the cognitive domain, levels of content, analysis and value or opinion; the very direct behaviors of direction-giving and criticism; and self-initiated student questions followed by principal responses.

In schools were principals verbally expressed empathy or attempted to accept and understand what the student was saying, more evidence of assisting others and providing service in the organization was present.

Building on the ideas and statements of students and repeating or rephrasing student comments are the most common forms of feedback. In schools where these behaviors were more prevalent, more emphasis was placed on the physical well-being and safety of students with less emphasis on co-educational activities and relationships. In schools where feedback occurred following student answers to questions by the principal, there was more emphasis within the school upon practicality.

Behaviors related to questioning skills and the cognitive levels of content, analysis, and value or opinion were significant. In schools where there was more self-initiated student-talk at the content level, the students perceived the school as having few group-centered activities, little emphasis on achievement, hard work, and commitment to the goals of the school; and little organizational structure, procedural orderliness, and respect for authority.

A noticeable difference appeared between the environments of schools where more verbal behavior was at the content level and those schools having more analysis level behaviors. In the schools where there was more questioning, more answers, and more self-initiated student talk, there was an increased emphasis on change, flexibility, planning, and organization.

A difference was also present between the schools where more verbal behavior was at the value or opinion level as contrasted to the content level. The more principals expressed their own values and opinion, the more students perceived the school was assisting others and providing service.

The principal's verbal behaviors for the major areas of direction giving and criticism consist of statements of direction, emphasizing main points, statements of decision, and criticism or justification of one's authority. Typically, one would expect the relationship to be such that the more direction giving and criticism that are present, the more students would feel the school was oppressive and restrictive. However, in the schools where the principals made more use of direction giving, emphasizing main points, statements of decision, and criticism, the students perceived these schools as having an atmosphere where members of the organization assisted each other, provided useful services, and stressed group-centered social activities.

The fourth group of significant verbal behaviors was related to student-initiated talk, often in the form of questions, and principal-talk before and after questions. In the schools where students initiated more questions with principals, more change and flexibility were present. The more time principals spent in listening to questions and responding, the more the students perceived the schools as having a concern for the personal growth and development of individuals within the organization. As more students were given the opportunity to initiate questions following general information giving by the principal, less hostility and more effort and energy were present in the organization. The more students initiated all types of talk, the more the school was perceived as allowing the student self-expression and self-reliance.

Principal-Parent Verbal Interaction

As more and more emphasis is placed on the school's goals and objectives reflecting the community's attitudes, parent and other citizen involvement increases. This increase in involvement increases the need to work with parents, whether related to discipline, parent advisory groups, public relations, or simply discussing Johnny's school success or problems over coffee. The result is that the second-ary school principal must today, more than ever before, be able to communicate and relate to the lay population.

In studying the verbal behaviors utilized by administrators in talking with parents, several specific behaviors were significantly related to the parents' perceptions of the school climate. As was the case with Principal-Teacher and Principal-Student interaction, the cognitive levels of the discussion were important, i.e., content, analysis, decision making, and value or opinion statements. In schools where parents initiated more talk at the content level fol-lowing general information talk by the principal and questions by the principal, the parents perceived the schools as having little emphasis on group activities and on personal growth and develop-ment of individuals within the organization. Findings related to the analysis level can be contrasted to the content level: as parents initiated talk more at the analysis level following principal informa-tion giving, they perceived the schools as emphasizing reflection and contemplation.

The most apparent relationship between the verbal behaviors of the principals as they talked with parents and the parental percep-tion of the school was associated with the use of value or opinion statements. However, the relationship was the opposite of what one would generally expect. For example, in the schools where the principals expressed more value statements or opinions in talking with parents, the parents perceived the schools as lowest in concern for personal growth and development of individuals within the orga-nization. In the schools where parents initiated more value or opinion statements, there was less emphasis for hard work, per-severance, and a day-by-day commitment of the goals of the school. In the same schools, parents perceived the school image as being of a low profile nature.

In addition to the behaviors related to cognitive levels, three behaviors appeared important. In schools where parents were more willing to initiate talk following a question by the principal, rather than responding to the question directly, more emphasis on group-centered activities was present. In the schools where parents felt they needed to ask more questions of the principal, little respect for the integrity of persons and little personal autonomy was perceived. And, finally, in the schools where the parents spent more time responding to questions by the principal rather than initiating talk with the principal, the more the parents perceived the school as lacking in intellectual emphasis.

Summary of Verbal Interaction

This study of the verbal behavior of administrators revealed signifi-cant relationships between what the administrator said and the climate of the administrator's school. The perception of teachers, students, and parents alike correlated to the indirectness and directness of what the administrator said. Generally speaking, the more direct the principal, the more positive the attitudes of teachers, students, and parents.

Some specific behaviors were found to be more critical than others. The use of humor by the administrator and by those with whom he came in contact indicated a significantly relaxed, positive human-relations atmosphere. Another important behavior identified by the study was the expression of personal values or opinions by the administrator and those with whom he worked. Members of the group thus knew where they stood on issues—a factor adding to a positive working relationship. In a similar vein, the importance of the administrator's giving clear directions when appropriate appeared as another significant behavior.

The study also revealed that each administrator was consistently direct or indirect in the verbal behaviors that he utilized. This consistency was present in studying verbal interaction of different lengths, ranging from one minute to greater than five minutes. Consistency was also noted in analyzing the different types of situations in which the administrator was involved, i.e., administrators who were more directive in formal settings were generally more directive than indirective in informal spontaneous interaction. The administrators were also consistent in the directness and indirectness of their behavior as they discussed such varied topics as curriculum, policy, extracurricular activities, and discipline. For example, the administrator who was typically very directive in discussing the school curriculum was also very directive in the area of discipline. Consistency, whether through direct or indirect methods, was therefore one of the more revealing factors identified in this study of administrators.

Findings of the study further indicated that the influence of the verbal behavior of the principal was stronger with teachers than with students or parents. The number of interactions, the length of the interaction and the different content topics discussed supported the conclusion that the administrator more directly influences the teaching staff than he influences the student body or community. Logically, with the administrator-teacher influence being the strongest and because teachers have more direct contact with students and students have more contact with parents, the "domino effect " of the administrator's influence with the staff member is critical.

"What Does It Mean to Me?"

The obvious concluding question is, "What does this study actually mean to me, the practicing administrator?" The answer lies in two realms: (1) important specific behaviors of which the administrator should be aware, and (2) implication of the study beyond specific behaviors.

First of all, specific behaviors. The choice of what behaviors are most significant should be made by the individual administrator as he assesses the types of outcomes he desires. This study, not intended to be prescriptive, does not spell out a cookbook approach to administrator verbal behavior. However, it does provide the practicing administrator with useful data for assessing his *own* situation and deciding what behaviors are appropriate in his situation.

The significance of the study beyond the realm of specific behavior can be more important to the practicing administrator than the specific study data. This is emphasized because the study has shown the feasibility of effectively studying an administrator's verbal behavior in a methodology that is within the reach of any practicing administrator. An administrator can study his own personal behavior, make comparisons of his own behavior with other data, and then make more meaningful decisions about his own behavior's appropriateness.

This concept of self-assessment is certainly not new to administrators. Yet for too long we have self-assessed more through visceral feelings than hard data. Are not both types of assessment appropriate? In teacher evaluation, providing information about performance in the form of feedback is important if behavior is to be modified or changed. For the administrator, such feedback occurs through self-analysis or, as administration moves more toward the "team" concept, more help can come from a fellow administrator. Regardless of where feedback comes from, administrators need it. They can now more accurately identify the specific verbal behaviors utilized and then make their own judgments as to whether the behaviors were appropriate or inappropriate. As organizations grow and become more complex, it is the astute administrator who pauses long enough to question and study his own communicative ability in light of the outcomes he feels are desirable.

A Longer Look at Feedback

Larry Porter

In the following excerpt, Porter calls for improving the ways in which consultants and trainers teach clients to give and receive feedback. He urges us to risk reteaching when we believe it is needed, to emphasize receiving skills over sending skills, and to show empathy rather than impatience when delivering feedback that hurts.

Reproduced by special permission from *Social Change: Ideas and Applications.* "A Longer Look at Feedback," by Larry Porter, Volume 4, No. 3, NTL Institute, November, 1974.

Skill Building for Senders and Receivers

During the last few years of staffing a variety of workshops, I have observed considerable similarity in the way feedback issues are dealt with. It usually goes something like this: presentation of the Johari Window . . . ; brief lecture on "helpful feedback" . . . ; perhaps some assessment of written feedback examples to increase participants' grasp of concepts; use of this information in T-Group interactions. These activities almost always produce some payoff for individuals, at least with respect to conceptual gains and, in some instances, with respect to improved feedback skills.

Still, there doesn't seem to be much helpful feedback going on in the world. . . . I've been pondering why this is so and have concluded that perhaps we should continue doing what we've been doing, but pay greater attention to (1) continuing development of knowledge and skills related to feedback; (2) increased emphasis on receiver skills; and (3) acknowledgment of the fact that, despite skillful delivery, feedback can still hurt.

Continuing Development—Practice for the Real World

In my experience, most people are introduced to feedback skills and concepts at their first workshop. After that, participants see themselves as "experienced" and, therefore, in no need of further work on aspects already "covered"—a view first learned in traditional education, a process which chops content into pieces, to be learned the first time through or never. Moreover, many trainers . . . do not want to ask participants in their second or third lab experience to review or practice one of the building-block concepts. . . .

This assumption of expertise on the subject of feedback is produced by a collusion between "sophisticated" participants . . . and trainers, who function as though to do something twice is a capital offense against all experience-based learning theory. This, despite the fact that giving/receiving helpful feedback, which requires knowledge, skills, and behaviors that fly in the face of much of what we've learned as we've grown up, can be an enormously complex and threatening activity.

Perhaps one thing we need to do, then, is to assess thoughtfully the level of feedback skills existing in any group and, where they appear to need upgrading, to spend some time reviewing "what everybody already knows." For a profession which prides itself on innovation, this is risky behavior; but, then, we pride ourselves on risk-taking too, and in this instance I think the need is justification enough.

Receiver Skills—Modeling and Managing

Secondly, I think we need to modify the way in which we try to help people deal with the issue of feedback. Typically the emphasis has been on how to give helpful feedback. That seems a logical emphasis, but it may not be useful for many, particularly back home, away from "giving-helpful-feedback" norms. I now find myself making the fairly standard comments about "helpful" feedback, but focusing more on the implications for the receiver. The point I try to make is that giving feedback, however helpfully intended and skillfully delivered, may be risky or destructive in many situations; nevertheless, there are many situations in which knowledge about helpful feedback can be used to "manage" feedback received from others.

For example, I may not be able to tell my boss that I feel frustrated when he makes judgmental comments about me . . . because he'll think I'm weak . . . or that I'm retaliating against his comments. . . . What to do?

This is where "receiver skills" come in. Instead of giving my boss feedback, I try to exert some control over the feedback he gives me, using the same "helpful-feedback" concepts: "Could you give me an example or two of what I do that makes you uptight?" or "Next time you feel like that about me, I hope you'll let me know right away" or "Are there any other things I've been doing that make you see me that way? If so, maybe we need to talk about them."

This will almost certainly not deal with all the issues I have with my boss . . . , but it may help me deal with some of them. . . . Eventually, if this kind of modeling changes the way my boss gives me feedback, it may enable me to begin giving him feedback too.

The Recipient Has Rights

Taking on responsibility for "managing" both the style and the content of the feedback that comes to me is also likely to increase my control over what happens to me in this kind of interaction— I am much more apt to learn and grow in situations in which I feel I have some share of the control. I have often been surprised . . . at how "beholden" the recipient of feedback seems to be to the person(s) giving it, even when the feedback is delivered in nonhelpful ways. How rare to hear a "receiver" refuse to answer a leading question, indicate that it is useless because nothing can be done about it, or demand specific behavioral descriptions. In fact, how rare to hear the recipient demand anything! The trainer may point out what is going on and thereby get things back "on track," but this is more likely to focus on the sender's lack of feedback/delivery skills than on the receiver's lack of control over what is happening to him in the interchange.

Yes. Sometimes It Hurts!

Lastly, I think—by omission rather than intent—we minimize, overlook, or casually dismiss the pain connected with feedback. The unspoken point seems to be, "If you learn these 'rules' and practice them, you will be able to give negative feedback so effectively that it will help the recipient without hurting him."

The effect of this on participants as recipients of feedback is largely to confuse and sometimes to diminish them. "If the feedback is being given according to the 'rules,' and if it hurts me anyway— and wow! does it!—then there must be something wrong with me."

Poor fellow! He's getting negative feedback, which hurts; but he also has doubts about himself because it hurts! Two problems for the price of one, and all because it's so difficult to connect "helpful" with "hurtful," even though they sometimes do go together.

The effect of this on participants as givers of feedback is just as confusing: the feedback is given, the recipient behaves in ways which reveal his acceptance of it, but also transmit some pain, frustration, or even anger. . . . And then—one of the worst things that can happen at this point—the giver responds to the recipient's pain with impatience rather than with empathy. In addition, he may begin to see the concepts which he has just started to practice as phony or ineffective.

BIBLIOGRAPHY

Albertson, D. R., and Hannan, C. J., eds. 1972. *Twenty exercises for the classroom.* La Jolla, Calif.: University Associates.

These exercises were derived from human-relations training methodologies and are aimed at enhancing communication in learning groups. Activities include role playing, interracial role-reversal, estimating value judgments, and identifying leadership styles. The exercises can be used with a wide range of age groups and in a variety of school situations.

Havelock, R. G. 1969. *Planning for innovation through dissemination and utilization of knowledge.* Ann Arbor, Mich.: Center for Research on the Utilization of Scientific Knowledge, Institute for Social Research, University of Michigan.

By substituting the words *information* for *innovation* and *communication* for *dissemination*, the reader can learn about: (1) the advantages and disadvantages of unilateral directives and transactional communication within and among organizations, (2) the relationships between problem solving and communication, and (3) the place of change agents and consultants in improving communication.

Johnson, D. W. 1972. *Reaching out: interpersonal effectiveness and self-actualization.* Englewood Cliffs, N.J.: Prentice-Hall.

This useful, practical book provides concepts and skills related to communicating understanding, concern, support, and feelings. The contents include material on interpersonal skills, self-disclosure, trust, communication skills, listening and responding, confrontation, modeling, and interpersonal conflicts.

Jung, C.; Howard, R.; Emory, R. E.; and Pino, R. F. 1972. *Interpersonal communications.* Tuxedo, N.Y.: Xicom.

This is an instructional system that provides information and activities on such topics as face-to-face communication, communication style, and group and organizational factors that affect communication. Several of the exercises and guides can be used independently by organizational consultants.

Pfeiffer, J. W., and Jones, J. E., eds. 1973-75. *Handbook of structured experiences for human relations training.* Vols. 1-5. La Jolla, Calif.: University Associates.

These five volumes offer 122 structured experiences for learning how to improve human relations. Many of the experiences relate directly to communication, including listening and inferring, listening triads, leveling, nonverbal communication, status-interaction study, and role clarification. The activities can be reproduced, and the instructions and worksheets facilitate flexible use of the experiences. Since 1972, University Associates has also published an *Annual Handbook for Group Facilitators.* Most annuals have sections on structured experiences (exercises and simulations), instrumentation, lecturettes, theory and practice, and book reviews; some contain lists of persons and organizations.

Stanford, G., and Stanford, B. D. 1969. *Learning discussion skills through games.* New York: Citation Press.

In this practical guide for teachers, administrators, and consultants, the Stanfords give concrete suggestions for improving communication in the classroom and present solutions to some common interpersonal problems that arise in classrooms and the school.

Wyant, S. H. 1974. The effects of organization development training on communications in elementary schools. Ph.D. dissertation, University of Oregon.

Wyant's research shows that unless sufficient training is received, OD consultation can have deleterious effects on communication within a school faculty. The author recommends that schools undertaking OD training should ensure that more than twenty-five hours of training are obtained.

4

Establishing Goals

HAVING GOALS

Although most school participants are relatively unskilled at stating goals and reaching agreement about them with others, individuals, subsystems, and organizations are naturally goal oriented. They strive to move toward a condition that is perceived as more desirable than the present one, and in the gap between the here and there lies the motivation for change. Helping members of a school organization to establish clear goals, to note the differences between the current situation and the goals, and to commit themselves to reducing the discrepancy is a vital and difficult task for the OD consultant.

Statements of goals are, first, descriptions: they specify a distant state of affairs that is in some way different from the present condition. Second, the goal condition is seen as being better or more attractive to the group according to some set of shared values. Third, goal setting implies the presence of a standard of comparison for judging whether actions carry a group toward or away from the goal. Finally, stating a goal carries an implication of motivated commitment to bring the goal condition into existence. Thus in any consideration of goals, the consultant and group alike must be clear about the condition toward which the group is striving, why this condition is more desirable than the present one, how to judge whether the goal is being attained, and the degree to which group members are committed to attaining it.

Goals as Descriptions

Goal statements give form and shape to the end toward which a group is striving by describing the desired state specifically enough to indicate how the group will know when it gets there. Too often, however, goals are stated so ambiguously that it is difficult to determine whether they are in fact being achieved, and this imprecision creates several problems. While it is easy to agree on statements that either mean nothing or mean different things to different people, such pseudoagreements break down when people begin to act on their differing conceptions of what actually was agreed. Unclearly stated goals also make it difficult to describe the specific sequence of actions that will lead to the goal's attainment; time and energy are wasted on uncoordinated efforts and on maintaining the fiction that progress is actually taking place.

In contrast, clearly stated goals permit clear communication about the desired end, ways of deciding whether it is or is not being attained, and what must be done to attain it. A well-stated goal provides a standard against which the utility of actions can be judged and a value premise for decisions on whether to take this or another action. One of the hardest jobs for the OD consultant is to assist a group in stating goals that perform these functions effectively.

The consultant may find a group quibbling, for example, about whether to term a given state a goal, an objective, or an outcome. In this case it should be recognized that such terms are only matters of convention or of convenience; group members should quickly adopt a convention that clarifies matters for them and then move on. As long as the distinction between statements of smaller and larger scope is clear, the group need not be impeded by subtleties of terminology.

It is important to distinguish between means and ends, however—between goal states and alternative ways of achieving them—and the consultant must keep this distinction clear to the group at all times. Since there are usually several ways of meeting a goal, the group should seek alternative routes and not be stopped by an inability to agree on a particular means. It should also be recognized that in a group action of any duration and complexity there will be a progress of ends-means relationships in which one particular subgoal may be viewed as the means toward achieving a larger goal.

To the extent that subgoals are thus embedded within larger goals, it is also helpful to distinguish between terminal and instrumental goals. The former refers to that which the group is striving to achieve; the latter, to some of the activities undertaken to bring it about. Although one goal of an intervention may be to increase shared feelings among group members, for example, this is not an end in itself; it is instrumental to the larger goal of increasing the amount of valid information available to a group as it makes decisions and solves problems. Indeed, viewed in a broader perspective, even problem-solving effectiveness is not an end in itself but is instrumental to the larger goal of improving the quality of education that a school staff can provide. For the consultant and the group the key question here is whether accomplishing a certain goal constitutes an end in itself or whether it only marks progress toward a larger goal.

If organization members recognize that many instrumental subgoals are steppingstones toward terminal goals, they can avoid needless misunderstandings about the desired end condition. Thus in setting goals it is important to choose subgoals that are easily recognized when they are achieved and that can be achieved within a specified period of time. If a school faculty sets a goal that cannot be reached within three or four years, for example, faculty members who will have left the school by that time will be little motivated to help. We believe that, for a faculty, the longest period between subgoals should not exceed a school year.

Still another useful distinction may be made between operational and nonoperational goals. Operational goals are those exhibiting clear-cut, specifiable means-ends relationships and that guide action, provide a basis for decision making, and offer clear guidelines for problem solving. Nonoperational goals are the highly abstract, essentially meaningless goal statements that abound in organizational life and that cannot guide action because they are virtually empty of specific content. Groups often adopt nonoperational goals because they sound impressive to outsiders, project an appearance of competence, achievement, and group unity, provide a defense against conflict and criticism by obviating disagreement, and do not bind group members to any specific course of action. The OD consultant should discourage the proliferation of nonoperational goals and help a group develop the ability to set goals that clearly specify the terminal state desired, can be linked to actions that will bring about the goal, and have the definite commitment of group members.

Finally, discerning a goal that can genuinely be described as superordinate greatly facilitates moving a group toward clearer communication and more skillful problem solving. Superordinate goals are those that significantly satisfy the personal values of most members of an organization simultaneously. The goal of enabling children to learn certain basic skills, for example, can bring personal satisfaction to teachers and administrators alike, who, feeling competent in their own work and admired by their own publics, may band together to pursue this goal.

The goal of reorganizing a department, for another example, may enable some members to satisfy achievement needs in creating the new design, others to satisfy power needs by having influence over the redesign decisions, and still others to satisfy a need to work more closely with colleagues. The search for superordinate goals is especially important when individuals or subsystems are in competition or conflict. Finding a superordinate goal to which both can become committed allows them to direct their energies toward a terminal goal of mutual value that both can pursue without diminishing their individual values.

Goals as Values

Statements and discussions of organizational goals inevitably involve, and often engender conflict over, tenaciously held personal values, the more so in school organizations because education is itself an essentially moral enterprise. Most parents and teachers want schools to teach children what they regard as proper conduct and to inculcate in them the values most strongly held by their society. Problems arise, however, when people regard their personal values not as preferences but as inexorable facts inherent in the natural conduct of life, as they tend to do when they fear that their values are being in some way threatened or violated. At the same time, few individuals or groups consciously examine or articulate their values, with the result that discussions of goals often become confused and angry, bogged down for little apparent reason, with participants wrangling over seemingly innocuous points, unable to express their fears clearly.

During one of our projects, for example, the authors were asked to facilitate a meeting between some district officials, school board members, and teachers during a pother that followed cancelling the appearance of a radical left-wing speaker before a high school social studies class. The incident led to a year-long debate within the district concerning whether the purpose of education was to inculcate a given set of values or to expose students to a variety of values. During our intervention, however, the discussion centered on the outrage of one administrator who felt that the "permissive" course of action being considered by his colleagues not only profoundly violated his own religious and patriotic values, which he wished to see reflected in district policy, but also bound him as an administrator charged with carrying out policy to something that violated his own values. Further, because value differences within the group had not been articulated, he had mistakenly assumed that others felt as he did and had experienced a sense of betrayal on learning otherwise.

The OD consultant must recognize that goals arise from values, that values differ among people, and that the attractiveness of a goal to group members and the extent to which they will support it will depend upon the extent to which it accords with their own values. This is not to say that the organization is obligated to promote the personal values of all its members but only to suggest that it will find it impossible to achieve its goals if few members derive little personal satisfaction from the effort.

For this reason it is important for a consultant to assess accurately the degree to which organizational goals support or promote the personal values of organization members. The consultant should help a group to recognize its differing values and different ways of maintaining them, to make its conceptions of values public, to clarify how different values might be realized or violated by proposed course of action, and to steer a course that can promote different values in a common course of action. Establishing a plurality of goals is one way of assuring that personal values will be fulfilled. Ultimately, however, the consultant should strive to help the group accept and value its differences.

Goals as Motivators

Closing the gap between what is and what ought to be can be a highly motivating force because of the various kinds of benefits and satisfactions that it brings. Measuring oneself against a given standard of excellence may satisfy achievement needs. Associating and working with others in a common effort may satisfy affiliation needs. Gaining the approval of those whose admiration one values may satisfy power needs. Achieving a goal may mark progress toward a larger goal, release collective energies for attacking other problems, or enable a group to ease an uncomfortable situation. In addition, most organizations provide both tangible and intangible rewards for the achievement of goals.

For the OD consultant there are a number of implications in all this. First, goals that are stated clearly, specifically, and realistically have greater motivating power than those that are stated vaguely or appear extremely difficult to achieve. Further, clearly defined subgoals that mark progress toward a larger goal provide a sense of power and accomplishment when they are achieved and encourage continued striving toward the larger goal.

Second, since a variety of satisfactions may accompany achieving a common goal, the consultant should help group members articulate these satisfactions so that all members can understand one another's reasons for wanting to attain the goal. When agreement on goals does not come easily, the group can be encouraged to discuss what kinds of satisfactions are being sought and then find the kinds of goals that will provide these satisfactions.

Finally, although the tension aroused by stating the discrepancy between the present and desired condition produces motivation to reach the goal, in many cases relieving the tension becomes a goal in itself. A group may agree on a course of action for the sense of closure and achievement that it brings whether the action is wise and workable or not. The consultant must be aware of this possibility and assist the group in clarifying its reasons for coming to a premature agreement.

GOALS IN ORGANIZATIONS

Multiplicity of Goals

Although most school districts have a set of officially proclaimed goals and periodically attempt to establish formal system-wide goals, the goals that actually guide the actions of faculty members derive from far less systematic processes than these. The two major sources of most organizational goals are the external social environment and the organization's own subsystems. The short-term goals that usually command most attention and energy arise in response to a variety of social demands and pressures—in the case of school, from organized interest groups in the community, board members elected to promote particular points of view, agencies such as state legislatures and departments of education, federal programs that offer financial aid for the achievement of certain goals, and so on.

Functional differentiation causes organizational subsystems to pursue a variety of goals as well. Because they are organized to carry out different functions and are also responsive to different segments of the environment, subsystems often exhibit strongly held goals that not only differ from but may even conflict with official system-wide goals. Indeed, it is not uncommon for the goals of one subsystem to conflict with those of another with which it is interdependent. The goals of a district's business office, for example, might center on order, stability, and adherence to procedures, while those of an alternative school might center on continuing novelty, suspension of procedures in individual cases, and short-term responsiveness. To the extent that the two must interact, their differing goals provide a stage for intergroup conflict.

Because there is more cohesiveness within the subsystem and more pressure on individuals to commit themselves to subsystem goals, these provide a surer guide to understanding the actions of organization members than do the goals of the system as a whole. For the most part, however, it is rare to find all organization members pursuing a single organizational goal or even a small set of system goals. It is more common to find a good deal of diversity and conflict among the goals held by different parts and levels of an organization, and this is as true of school districts as elsewhere.

The OD consultant who finds that organization members deny or are unaware of this diversity and conflict should remember that when an organization does not have strong norms supporting creative conflict, the pretense of consensus serves a defensive function against the critical scrutiny of others. The consultant should also be aware that goals proclaimed are not necessarily goals pursued. Although official pronouncements seldom emphasize the disciplinary and custodial aspects of education, for example, observers of classroom and school behavior know that many teachers put far more effort into maintaining order and control than they put into pursuing the announced goals of education. When the discrepancy between official and actual goals grows too pronounced, almost everyone involved must waste energy maintaining the fiction that the official goals are intact. Staff members invent explanations of how their actions "really" carry out these goals, and the goals themselves must be reworded periodically to avoid obvious contradictions with actions.

It will also be found that some of the most powerful goals are not substantive goals but process goals—those related to the system itself—and the consultant should be alert to these if procedural ends are not to become more important than substantive ends. Process goals are concerned with: (1) security of the organization as a whole in relation to the social forces in its environment, (2) stability of lines of authority and communication, (3) stability of informal relations within the organization, (4) continuity of policy and sources of its determination, and (5) homogeneity with respect to the organization's meaning and role. In the eyes of organization members, especially administrators and supervisors who are trying to control the behavior of subordinates, these conditions are always imperfectly realized.

In diagnosing the ideal state toward which staff members are striving, the consultant can ask members directly about their goals, ask them what they think should *not* be permitted to happen, or ask them to list their goals and rank them in priority. Listing the amount of time spent on various activities each week usually reveals a sizable discrepancy between the goals people think they are pursuing and the amount of time actually devoted to other matters. Beyond this, however, the consultant must rely on observing and recording behaviors—another instance of the importance of collecting multiple indicators of the variable about which one wants information.

In view of the demands placed on school districts by a changing environment, it is not surprising that their goals are multiple or that for school participants the most salient goals tend to be those conceived in response to particular demands and pressures rather than those that are part of a long-range planning scheme. In addition, the consultant will often find a district or its subsystems simultaneously pursuing several goals that may be independent, complementary, or competitive. Generally, any given course of action will stay within the constraints imposed by the multiple goals; for example, a goal of lowering the student-teacher ratio cannot be pursued if fiscal resources are inadequate to this purpose. Thus the local school often steers a compromise course that approximates goal attainment while meeting the requirements and constraints imposed by other goals. Unless schools continually review their goals and seek ways of articulating them with those of the district, the result can be miscommunication, malcoordination, and a climate of confusion and distrust.

Levels of Goals

Although organizations and their subsystems are created to achieve certain ends, the consultant often finds their stated ends unclear to many members and ignored or even subverted by some of them. In such conditions members seldom experience the high satisfaction of achievement, subsystems function within the larger organization with no clear sense of purpose, and the organization limps along more or less ineffectively from day to day. Yet the organization can function more effectively if goals are harmonious at all three levels, and it is partly the consultant's responsibility to determine the nature of, and lurking conflict in, these goals.

Conflict arises in any organization when individual and subsystem goals seem to demand contrary directions of effort. A discussion of group goals is often the arena for a battle between individuals who, in fighting over proposed organizational goals, are at the same time fighting to fulfill their individual needs. The adaptive school must strike a balance between trying to satisfy member needs that might be fulfilled more efficiently outside the organization and trying to suppress the satisfaction of needs that might be harnessed to serve the organization's goals. How this balance can best be achieved depends on a number of factors, including the organization's goals, the assortment of needs typical of school personnel, the norms governing legitimate need-satisfactions within the district, the means of need-satisfaction outside the district, and the availability to the district of new personnel.

The consultant should ascertain how much agreement exists in the local school about one or more organizational goals. If sufficient agreement exists, work can proceed toward achieving these goals. If not, general agreement might be achieved in any of the following ways: participants can confer until an organizational goal is found that at least minimally satisfies each member's personal needs; dissatisfied participants can seek satisfaction outside the school for needs that are not met by organizational goals; or dissatisfied participants can leave the school altogether. In practice, all these methods are followed to some extent; but in schools, where most jobs require professional judgment and high involvement of self, the first and third methods are the more humane and efficient.

This is not to say that school people must be garrulous about all their goals and values, because it does not harm a school for an individual to conceal those that are unlikely to be satisfied within the organization. While it is wrong for individuals acting in their organizational roles to demand conformity to their own values from others or to demand satisfaction of their personal needs while pretending otherwise, it is nevertheless true that members who are frustrated in gratifying their needs may ignore or subvert the goals of the organization and pursue their own values and interests instead.

In a project conducted in a school district of Kent, Washington,* the authors trained a cadre of organizational specialists to function as part-time agents for OD, partly in the hope that they could thereby satisfy more needs than were satisfied by their ordinary jobs. Although several specialists found the work highly rewarding and sought to expand their opportunities for consulting within the district, a severe financial crisis in the district during the second year caused consulting opportunities to become very limited.

These conditions caused several of the specialists to turn elsewhere for need-satisfying activities. Some found consulting engagements in other districts; some pursued advanced degrees in related fields at nearby colleges; one expanded her organizational role with the teachers' bargaining agency. The point is that none of them sought to satisfy disappointed needs in other than professional settings, and cadre members sustained the cadre's existence as well as a good deal of its work for four more years—a total of six years in all.

---

*For details, see Schmuck and Runkel (1972); also Runkel, Wyant, and Bell (1975).

This example not only demonstrates the extent to which personal needs affect role performance in a school district but also shows that many personal needs are fully satisfiable only on the job. Dissatisfied needs give rise to new roles, and new roles offer opportunities for new satisfactions. In either direction, however, the time lag between identifying a need and finding a means of satisfying it can produce frustration, and the consultant is challenged to manage the change process in ways that will safeguard the satisfaction of personal needs during the period of transition and change.

To be sure, most staff members are always seeking fuller satisfactions, and no species of goal striving is going to be personally satisfying to everyone. That a certain amount of conflict will exist over goals and values is inevitable and obstructive insofar as it produces resistance to change. If conflicts are hidden, for example, norms must be established to keep them hidden, and such agreements not to communicate (as to refrain from assigning antagonists to the same committees) will inhibit attempts to work out new and better ways of functioning. The adaptive organization must continually ferret out goal conflicts, stimulate discussion of them, and do away with norms that have arisen to hide them. The consultant should help school people realize that by assisting one another in achieving consensual goals, those who find in them little of personal value can later elicit reciprocal support in pursuing goals that they do value personally.

Finally, certain kinds of goals that bear little relation to either the organization's needs or the demands of its environment may be the result of a history of poor choices and interactions that limit present action. Organizations that set and attain realistic goals generally establish for the next round equally realistic and attainable goals that are somewhat more challenging. In contrast, a history of failure in meeting goals leads to the setting of goals unrealistically low or high. The consultant should examine this history of high or low attainment and encourage the group to set challenging but realistic goals so that the OD experience progresses through a series of successes.

GOALS IN SCHOOLS

Ambiguity and Multiplicity of Goals

If the goals of education are to provide motivation and guidance to both the school and its environment, they must be described precisely enough with respect to their specific nature and duration for people to know whether they have been attained. Not only school members but members of the outside community, including parents, must be able to judge whether the attainment of these goals will serve their own personal or organizational goals as well.

It is helpful to coordination (as well as to productive conflict) between the two if the school states its goals in terms of the interaction between itself and its environment by noting some feature or process of the school, of the environment, and of the desired relationship between them. A secondary school, for example, might describe one of its goals as training students so as to supply a certain percentage of the community's need for carpenters each year, or as teaching social studies so that students can present outside the school evidence of change in their own behavior. Generally, however, public pronouncements of such goals are ambiguous and nonexplicit, while others, such as keeping children off the street for a certain amount of time each day, are not stated at all.

Some of the reasons for this ambiguity are not hard to find. First, there is little consensus about the nature of motivation and learning, and the changes in behavior and knowledge that schooling induces are not immediately apparent but occur over a long period of time. Second, it is more difficult to communicate about intangibles (such as decision making) than about tangibles (such as capturing a certain percentage of a sales market). Third, because society regards schools as essential, they are not faced with survival issues and therefore need not be as specific in their goal statements as other institutions. But there are other, less apparent reasons as well. Ambiguous goal statements are in part a defense against close inquiry or influence by outsiders, in part a defense against a sense of having failed to meet demands. The failure to set specific goals may also be the result of time pressures. The custodial function that requires a certificated person to be present with students, rigid time schedules (especially at the secondary level), and so on make it exceptionally difficult for educators to look beyond tomorrow's lesson plan. Finally, engaged as it is in shaping children and future society, education is inescapably a moral and political enterprise that raises emotions and values close to the surface; discussions of educational goals often take on a fuzzy if high-sounding moral tone to reduce value-violating possibilities.

Accepting ambiguous goals can only have deleterious consequences. While it is fairly easy to obtain a pseudoconsensus about abstract or fuzzy goals, when participants begin to act on their various perceptions and their actions diverge, conflicts will build, malcoordination will occur, and the agreement will fall apart. Again, when people feel dragooned into goal setting, they often produce statements that will satisfy whatever pressure is on the group, knowing that if the goal is vague enough, and since feedback about goal accomplishment is slow and unclear, it will be difficult to test their commitment or assess their performance. Accepting ambiguous goals also promotes ossification of procedures and a shift of attention to process goals, which are easier to recognize and discuss. Finally, without clear-cut goals, personal goals will play a large part in setting group goals and make unproductive conflict all the more likely.

Multiple environments that make varying demands on schools are the source of a rich variety of multiple goals; but unless the district and its relevant environments have strong norms for collaboration and can communicate clearly, too rich a variety can produce organizational paralysis. An organization that cannot set its own priorities cannot act.

Since schools are highly vulnerable to outside pressures, however, educators seldom have the opportunity of being proactive in setting district goals. Community group pressures, state-wide regulations, legislative mandates and rules often exercise greater direction over schools than do educators themselves. Further, an excess of external demands is usually reflected in differing and conflicting operational goals of subsystems. Finally, educators are themselves members of other formal and informal organizations and groupings whose differing values are often played out as conflict when educators consider a course of action.

In addition to being multiple in character, the environment also changes over the course of time, so that adaptive school organizations have often to recast goals stated only recently and to remake decisions repeatedly. The adaptable district should have a formal procedure for restating goals and committing its members and subsystems to new targets and actions.

Various reactions can occur when a school organization is frustrated in its efforts to achieve a goal.* First, the organization can intensify its efforts by devoting more time to the problem; but this is difficult in schools because the workday is tightly scheduled and extra time must be borrowed from other activities such as family life. Second, individuals can revise their perceptions of the problem to produce new paths to the goal. Third, the goal statement can itself be altered, either in its ultimate aim or in its more immediate instrumental means. Fourth, a variety of maladaptive reactions can occur. One is to exercise continuing compulsive effort to reach the goal in spite of evidence that it remains as remote as ever. Another is for individuals to redirect their energies toward satisfying personal needs by ignoring or subverting organizational goals and procedures.

People in schools entertain goals for others as well as for themselves, and it is only natural for them to hope that those for whom they care will pursue certain goals instead of others. Unfortunately, however, we too often convert these hopes into demands without consulting those whose behavior will be influenced, and much confusion, misunderstanding, resentment, and animosity can result.

Overcoming hidden agendas and backstage manipulation makes a great deal of work for the consultant. Early phases of OD work can profitably include discussions of what staff members hope from the behaviors of others and can clarify norms by ascertaining which hopes are being confirmed and which denied. Ascertaining the goals to which members of various parts of the school organization are willing to commit significant energies is another important step in clarifying communication, uncovering conflict, and preparing for

---

*The following list of possible reactions is adapted from one given for individuals by Krech, Crutchfield, and Ballachey (1962).

158

problem solving. Although none of these problems is insuperable, they cannot be ignored and they require an investment of time and energy fitted to the need.

The Self-renewing School

Although the specific goals and goal processes to which members of a school district commit themselves will vary from district to district and even from school to school, clear and shared conceptions of goals are vital. If OD consultants are to help local school members aid one another in reaching goals they value consensually, they must first discover the commonly valued goals that already exist and the processes that are followed at the interpersonal, subsystem, and organizational levels.

At the interpersonal level the essential process is that of converting frustrations into well-articulated problems that clearly identify the discrepancy between where participants are and where they want to be. For the self-renewing school, the essential condition is to provide opportunities for participants to articulate and examine personal goals and need-satisfactions related to the exercise of energetic activity, personal achievement, affiliation and enjoyment of the personal qualities of others, and of power and influence in managing the affairs of the school.

In a self-renewing school the following goal-related processes would be observed: (1) a continuing dialogue about individual needs, values, wants, and preferences and about ways in which these can either be legitimately realized within the organization or referred elsewhere; (2) skillful group interaction that draws out these articulations and attempts to integrate them with overall school and district goals; (3) the creation of formal and informal groupings to draw out goal articulations, match them with subsystem and organizational goals, and assess movement toward or away from these goals; and (4) time taken during discussions of present and proposed subsystem or organizational goals to ascertain their congruence with individual interests and values.

At the subsystem level the essential skill is that of attaining clarity and consensus about subsystem functions and goals, how these integrate the strivings of individuals, and how they are integrated with the goals of the larger organization. The primary concern at this level is an attempt to integrate individual, subsystem, and organizational goals. Stated goals are always regarded as hypotheses—reasoned guesses about desirable futures—that are subject to revision in the light of new information.

Thus in the self-renewing school one would see a periodic review and revision to keep working goals congruent with stated goals so that energy is not wasted papering over the discrepancy. Subsystem goals would be seen as neither immutable nor constricting but as empirical descriptions, however approximate or inaccurate, of the common directions of the group. Efforts would be made to clarify and state explicitly the objectives of the subsystem, to integrate these with individual goals, and to obtain commitment to the subsystem goals. There would be evidence that this and other subsystems create occasions for seeking and clarifying superordinate goals that define the contribution of each to the greater product, and, finally, there would be specific instances at which these kinds of actions occurred.

At the building-wide, institutionalized, organization level, the essential characteristic is goal focus. The ends toward which the staff as a whole is striving are clear, consensual, and appropriate both to environmental demands and to district resources. Goals are expressed in operational terms so that their attainment or nonattainment can be recognized. They are endorsed by most staff members, and there is agreement on them between the school and significant parts of its district and community. At this level, goals are regarded as temporary, recycleable, and contingent on environmental demand. The staff maintains strong norms legitimating a periodic requestioning of goals, and the pursuit of a goal is abandoned when it is widely affirmed that progress has been inadequate.

The self-renewing school therefore exhibits the following characteristics: widely circulated statements of the school's goals together with invitations to review them; widespread recognition of what constitutes acceptable and unacceptable progress; periodic formal gatherings of various parts and levels of the building staff to assess goals and progress; lively use of feedback channels; widespread involvement of affected members of the community in formal activities that help to articulate goals and assess progress toward them; the institution of problem-solving procedures when progress is found to be unsatisfactory; and the periodic institution of systematic efforts to monitor changes in the community and the demands that it makes.

At all levels, the goal statement must be clear enough for participants to know whether the goal is in fact being attained. There should be evidence of widespread commitment to goals, of attempts to integrate individual, subsystem, and organizational goals, and of strong norms legitimating the recycling of goals. One should expect in addition a balance of planning and action, with forethought to possible alternatives and consequences but not so much forethought as to leave no time for action.

It should be remembered that the ability to set clear, consensual goals at any level is inseparable from the effectiveness of other organizational processes—notably skill in communication, decision making, and problem solving, and the ability to elicit and consider the values of all organization members. In this respect, the ability to set and maintain effective goal processes is essentially a second-order capability in institutions. It should also be remembered that there are times when chaotic organizational action is better than orderly inaction, when planning overreaches predictable outcomes and some action, well-planned or not, must be taken. Action at least yields results and data to compare against desired states, while inaction often yields nothing more than a further proliferation of plans which may by now be out of touch with reality. In short, school people must know when to stop talking and start doing, even when they know that the proposed action falls far short of what is actually required.

CONSULTANT, CLIENT, AND PROJECT GOALS

All intervention strategies are based on an assumption that their probable outcomes will be desirable according to some set of values. For our part, we value finding work that satisfies human needs in productive collaboration with others and that in turn creates new and more adaptive human processes. Our subsidiary values include collaboration and cooperation instead of competition, tolerance for individual styles and differences, a sharing of power and influence, consensual group agreements, satisfaction of diverse motivational patterns in work, reflective examination of behavior, and organizational change through the involvement of all concerned. As OD consultants, our values and metagoals are closely associated with those of humanistic psychology and scientific inquiry. They have to do with expanded consciousness and choice, authenticity in interpersonal relationships, and the resolution of conflicts through democratic decision making and rational problem solving.

The consultant should be aware, however, that the values basic to our style of organization development are not necessarily the values most central to organizations themselves. Most OD consultants believe, for example, that with attention and training, individual satisfactions and organizational effectiveness can be optimized and that it is reasonable for people to expect the greatest possible rewards from their own work. Most school people, on the other hand, believe that satisficing—that is, making the best of a bad situation, perhaps by retreating into one's own tasks—is the best that can be hoped for. Satisficing at least assures stable if not very satisfying functional relationships, and consultants who suggest methods that offer greater rewards for greater risks will often encounter trepidation, if not outright reluctance, to engage in such methods.

Among client groups in schools the consultant is likely to encounter three convictions: that the most significant human relations are those dealing primarily with getting work done; that feelings matter less than thought in organizations; and that human relationships in organizations are most effectively influenced unilaterally, especially if they are supported by coercion or rewards from top management. In this regard, Miles (1965) has listed three norms that are uniquely influential in schools: (1) that teachers should be free from interference in their teaching; (2) that teachers should be treated as equals whether they are equals or not; and (3) that teachers should be friendly toward one another despite philosophical and pedagogical disagreements among them. It will readily be seen, however, that these norms often inhibit interpersonal feedback and assessment of a staff's strengths and weaknesses.

OD consultants should not impose their own goals on the client system and should recognize when they are subtly steering the group away from its main course. While they need not endorse client goals enthusiastically, they should gauge the possible range of outcomes of a consultation so that, if these outcomes are incompatible with their own values, they can decline to participate in the consultation. For their part, clients must feel that the consultant's goals are sufficiently compatible with their own to be able to commit enthusiastic energy to the project.

Intervention Goals

Organizational goals do not crystallize overnight but arise out of lengthy joint diagnoses by consultant and client, their discussions at the time of entry, and their mutual theories about organization and change. As the following example demonstrates, consensual group agreement, especially, takes time and must be informed, articulate, and internalized if it is to aid in accomplishing the complex technical work that schools perform.

In 1970 the Center for the Advanced Study of Educational Administration undertook a project to determine whether OD consultation would enable schools wishing to adopt a multiunit structure to convert to the new structure faster and better than schools that did not receive consultation. OD consultation was given to six elementary schools whose faculties, having discussed the desirability of the multiunit structure at length, decided to undertake the conversion. As consultants, we were committed to two goals—to making every effort to enable the schools to convert to the new structure but at the same time to enable each to reexamine its decision as factually and objectively as possible whenever it so desired.

For five or six months, with intermittent training in improving communication skills, faculty members were encouraged to express their hopes for the future, their currently unsatisfied needs, the actions they approved or disapproved in others, and other matters relevant to committing significant effort to common goals. At the end of this time, faculties of two of the schools agreed that they did not wish to adopt the multiunit structure after all. The OD work had changed their understanding of one another's personal and professional goals, had given them a more accurate view of what central office administrators meant by multiunit structure, and had given them a new conception of decision making in the context of this project. During the same period the other four schools reaffirmed their original decision and took first steps toward adopting the multiunit structure (for details, see Schmuck et al. 1975).

Argyris (1970) argues persuasively that change should not be the intervener's primary target. In his view, the consultant's task is to help the client generate valid information, make informed and responsible choices, and generate internal commitment to the choices. Change may be among the choices, but this is the client's, not the consultant's, choice. The consultant's job is to heighten the client's abilities for self-direction, recognizing that to take too strong a lead in promoting specific change may impair these abilities. The key is for consultant and client to collaborate in setting intervention goals during entry and also to consider specific ways in which progress can be measured or otherwise ascertained.

With the school district in Kent, Washington, for example, our macrointervention goals were:

1. To increase understanding of how participants in various parts of the district affect one another
2. To develop clear communication networks upward, downward, and laterally
3. To increase understanding of the various educational goals in different parts of the district
4. To develop new ways of solving problems through creative use of new roles in groups
5. To develop new ways of assessing progress toward educational goals
6. To involve more people at all levels in decision making
7. To develop new procedures for innovating practices both within and outside the school district

In an early intervention with an elementary school, the Kent cadre of organizational specialists pursued the following set of goals:

1. Having the total staff develop, understand, and agree to a philosophy of education that was compatible with individual goals for this school and that included consensual agreements about school policies on various matters
2. Developing clear communication networks, openness, and trust within and across teams
3. Facilitating constructive openness and helpfulness among staff members

OD Goals Compared with Those of Other Strategies

The consultant will often find that clients are engaged in, or at least aware of, three strategies—management by objectives, values clarification, and accountability—which strongly resemble OD in their attention to goals and values. Management by objectives, for example, has been described as "a process or system designed by management in which a superior and his subordinates sit down and jointly set a time frame and for which the subordinate is then held directly responsible" (Thomson, in Pfeiffer and Jones 1972). In this activity the superior describes to a subordinate organizational goals that have been handed down from a higher level, and the two jointly set the subgoals that will help to accomplish them. Management by objectives has the effect of forcing attention to results, inducing commitment to organizational objectives, and promoting thought about future organizational needs and how best to achieve them. The outcomes are usually stated in terms of greater control and coordination of effort and of greater commitment by subordinates to organizational objectives.

While it is true that subordinates must accept some goal direction if the organization is to carry out its goals effectively, management by objectives is too often just another way of increasing pressure on them to produce. Control from the top leaves subordinates little room in which to maneuver and virtually no occasion for articulating or exploring personal values that might be satisfied within the organization. With its single downward direction, it often prevents them from expressing ownership of their personal objectives or of experiencing the satisfaction that comes from sharing in the definition of the organization's larger goals.

Values clarification enables individuals to "discover through inductive group processes what their values are by structuring exercises that confront personal thinking" (Smith, in Pfeiffer and Jones 1973). Such efforts often include group-processes workshops and exercises and laboratory training in which consultants and values-clarification trainers draw on a common pool of structured experiences and procedures. This activity aims at providing a structure for individuals to use in shaping their thinking about personal values, goals, and priorities. Like sensitivity training, it focuses on personal growth and greater clarity about the bases of interactions with others. Smith suggests that values-clarification activities can be useful to an OD effort in negotiating the expectations that individuals have for themselves, their colleagues, and the organization, in setting goals and priorities that help an organization understand itself, in screening job applicants to determine whether their values are the same as the organization's values, and in team-building efforts.*

The current emphasis on accountability in schools is probably owing to the crisis in confidence that schools are now experiencing, as well as to the rapid escalation of educational costs. Accountability means essentially that schools should be answerable to their publics. State and local accountability programs often include PPBS, cost-benefit accounting, program and personnel evaluation, setting specific objectives at all levels, and including noneducators in goal setting. Schmuck and Miles (1971) suggest that an accountability-based OD program could collect data about student performance in schools and feed the data back to students, parents, and educators as a way of heightening interest, improving communication across roles, and redesigning the educational environment. In spite of the difficulties encountered by many accountability programs, including resistance from teachers who believe their job security to be threatened and a strong tendency to consider only easily measured results such as reading or mathematics competency scores, we believe that integrat-

---

*Two basic works on values clarification are Raths, Harmin, and Simon (1966), and Simon, Howe, and Kirschenbaum (1972).

ing some accountability techniques within the framework of an OD philosophy and strategy could be highly advantageous.

ASCERTAINING AND CLARIFYING GOALS

The theoretical distinction between ascertaining and clarifying goals and establishing goals is relatively arbitrary. The former suggests uncovering, clarifying, and making public goals that already exist; the latter, expressing a yearning for goals where none had existed previously. In practice, however, where there is no such neat distinction, the process is more like sharpening by means of public statements yearnings that were previously formless and then successively revising these statements at the same time that new directions and yearnings are being discovered and articulated.

For purposes of study, the procedures described in this section are generally directed at enabling the consultant to collect information about goals by means of some traditional and instrumental methods, while those in the succeeding section describe ways in which individuals, subsystems, and organizations can work together to create common directions. It should be noted that these procedures are only representative and that with a little practice consultants can devise others that work as well. Indeed, the consultant should modify any of the procedures given here or invent new ones that may be more appropriate for particular groups.

Instrumented Methods

Questionnaires. By ascertaining the goals held by all the members of an organization, questionnaires can provide information that may motivate individual members to reconsider their own goals. Merely answering a questionnaire can sometimes motivate respondents to reconsider their goals. For this reason it should not be assumed that the information gathered by questionnaire or interview one day will accurately reflect the respondent's views on another day.

Despite this and other disadvantages, questionnaires and interviews can provide a number of useful benefits. If they are systematic and thorough, they give each respondent an equal chance to be heard, at the same time that they avoid the biases that may surface in information that is volunteered or collected from arbitrarily chosen respondents. If the consultant's chief purpose is to survey the goals that group members are willing and able to express at a given moment, the use of questionnaires and interviews will maximize the chances of accuracy.

Questionnaires and interviews also permit quantitative comparisons that offer an objective measure of trends. The number of times that one person mentions or chooses an item from a list can be compared with the number of times others mention or choose it, and these individual or group responses can be compared with those of a later date. The item mentioned by one person is unaffected by hearing what others mention, and the quantitative measure cannot be charged off to distorted perceptions on the part of the data gatherer. If the counts from questionnaires corroborate other information, the consultant can be more confident of the accuracy of all the information. If they conflict with other information that is known to be incomplete, more information should be sought. As with all methods, it is best not to rely on a single source of information.

Some useful multiple-choice items are offered below, but the instructions for example 1 are not appropriate for all purposes. To determine which goals respondents feel to be worth their energy, the consultant should ask them to state exactly that. The instructions may be rewritten to obtain whatever kind of information is wanted.

Example 1*
Of the following items, which *three* do you consider most vital or important in your work as a teacher? (If you are not a teacher, please pick those you think would be most vital for you if you were teaching.) Write the number 1 beside the most important, the number 2 beside the second most important, and the number 3 beside the third most important. (If we have omitted an item you believe to be among the three most important, please describe it in the space provided at the end of the list.)

_____ Reduce the dropout rate.
_____ Improve the students' performance in basic skills.
_____ Develop an improved health education program, including sex education and programs dealing with tobacco, alcohol, and drugs.
_____ Introduce new programs for the culturally disadvantaged.
_____ Increase the percentage of college attendance by high school graduates.
_____ Improve the students' adherence to moral, ethical, or patriotic standards.
_____ Improve learning opportunities for gifted or talented students.
_____ Individualize instruction by introducing nongraded programs, flexible scheduling, or independent study.
_____ Change the emphasis from academic counseling to small-group guidance aimed at dealing with concerns of young people.
_____ Institute an in-service training program for teachers aimed at improving their performance in the classroom.
_____ Institute a training program in interpersonal relations and communication skills for all staff members.
_____ Develop a strong adult education program.
_____ Other:

*We are grateful to Max Abbott, Terry Eidell, and Roland Pellegrin of the early Program on Innovations at the Center for the Advanced Study of Educational Administration (now CEPM) for this item.

The second example offers another list of possible choices. The respondent and consultant may wish to regard these statements as terminal goals, or they may be treated as temporary expressions. A discussion of goals may be spurred by asking participants to respond to a list like this, telling them how many persons (anonymously) chose each item, and then inviting discussion. From the responses the consultant can determine not only which goals find favor with the respondents but also their degree of agreement about various goals. A tally of the number of responses to each item is an appropriate method of compiling results. In feeding back this information, the consultant may wish to rearrange the items from most to fewest tallies.

Example 2*
Write a Y (for yes) before those objectives you would be willing to try to achieve with others this year. Write an N (for no) before the objectives on which you do not want to spend any energy.

_____ Representing the school district's point of view to various community groups.

_____ Improving the measurable achievement of students.

_____ Dealing with medical or physical problems which might impair a child's ability to learn.

_____ Trying to identify those groups which speak for the community on different educational problems.

_____ Preventing classroom procedure from being disrupted.

_____ "Turning kids on" to learning.

_____ Dealing with absences of teachers and arranging for substitutes.

_____ Trying to determine the needs and demands of various groups in the community.

_____ Evaluating the effectiveness of new programs.

_____ Engaging representatives of the community in advising on school policy or plans.

_____ Helping a child better understand his mental and emotional self.

_____ Developing and submitting requests for funds to be used by the school system for new programs.

_____ Building support for school programs in the community and city.

_____ Working on problems which require new or different approaches.

_____ Identifying and dealing with psychological problems which might impair a pupil's ability to learn.

_____ Understanding and working with the needs and problems of student groups in the school.

_____ Experimenting with new materials and programs.

* Adapted from Derr (1971).

_____ Understanding and anticipating the implications of actions taken by groups or political organizations.

_____ Helping a child become aware of his future opportunities.

_____ Developing more relevant curriculum programs.

_____ Adapting materials and curriculum to students' needs.

_____ Taking into account the pupil's individual family situation and needs which affect his ability to learn.

_____ Working with outside organizations (e.g., universities) to develop new methods for teaching and learning.

_____ Considering the effects of a child's cultural, ethnic, or religious background on learning.

The third example attempts to ascertain whether respondents are satisfied with the school's functioning, with the goals toward which they think the school is moving, and where they want changes made. This questionnaire does not produce a direct statement of a goal but requires the consultant either to draw an inference from what was written or to proceed to more direct questions later. The advantage of this kind of item is that it calls for neither abstract thinking nor careful use of language by respondents, who can tell graphically just where they are hurting during their daily work.

Example 3
Would you say there is some particular aspect of the school's functioning where new ideas are especially needed?

(   ) No, things are working about as well as they can.

(   ) No, no particular aspect more than another. We just need things polished up a bit all over.

(   ) Yes. If yes, please describe briefly the features of the school's functioning that need attention:

1. _____

_____

_____

_____

2. _____

_____

_____

_____

The fourth example does not ascertain a particular goal but ascertains perceptions both of consensus and of the number of persons in contact with officially written goals. The answers to such an item could help the consultant devise more pointed questions for later use.

Example 4
Does this school have work goals with which almost everyone agrees?

Yes (   )   No (   )   I don't know (   )

If it does, are the goals written down anywhere?
Yes ( )   No ( )   I don't know ( )
If they are written down, do you have a copy?
Yes ( )   No ( )   I don't know ( )

An alternative way of generating a list of items to which respondents react is for the consultant to invite all faculty members to write one or more goals toward which they think the school should be striving. The statements in example 3 could serve as the basis for the list. The goals (with editorial revision to recast them in consistent form) then provide a list similar to those in examples 1 and 2.

Finally, the consultant can use the following items to check the frequency with which goals are discussed on formal and informal occasions in the school.

Example 5*
Please think about how often you discuss with other members of the staff what the school ought to be trying to accomplish with its students. How often do you yourself discuss goals of this sort in *formal* occasions (faculty meetings, committees, etc.)? Please make an X before the answer that comes closest to your case.
_____ Never
_____ Once or twice a year, maybe
_____ About once a month, maybe
_____ More than once a month but not once a week
_____ More than once a week
_____ I don't know.

How often do you yourself discuss goals of this sort in *informal* occasions (coffee room, corridors, while picking up mail, in the parking lot, etc.)? Please make an X before the answer that comes closest to your case.
_____ Never
_____ Once or twice a year, maybe
_____ About once a month, maybe
_____ More than once a month but not once a week
_____ More than once a week
_____ I don't know.

As already noted, the questionnaire has a number of disadvantages. Unless the devisor requires only X-marks in response to multiple-choice questions or only very brief written answers, the respondent's task becomes tiresome enough to be rejected. The disadvantage of asking for written answers, however brief, is that many respondents are unskilled at writing clear responses. At the same time, asking for X-choices confines the respondent to only those

---

*Again, we are grateful to Max Abbott, Terry Eidell, and Roland Pellegrin of the early Program on Innovations at the Center for the Advanced Study of Educational Administration (now CEPM) for this item.

answers that the questioner has framed in advance. If these are framed too simply or approached from the wrong angle, the respondent, instead of answering at length or to the point, may either select an answer that is the least bad of several bad choices or may skip the item altogether. Finally, because the questionnaire is probably the most widely used research instrument in schools, most school staffs feel surfeited with the instrument and may either reject it entirely or give flippant answers. The OD consultant must therefore convince clients that this is not just another instrument to be filled out and forgotten but that its results will be put to useful purpose that will genuinely affect their working lives.

Interviews. The interview, in contrast, allows the interviewer to rephrase questions in the interests of clarity and permits respondents in their own way to express views for which a questionnaire may provide no choice. The two-way communication that the interview affords not only enables the interviewer to ascertain the penetration of the question but also to seize upon and record fortuitous bits of information seldom elicited by questionnaires that may be useful in the course of further work with this particular organization. Below are examples of questions that OD consultants have asked about goals.

[To interviewer: Read words in parentheses only if necessary for clarity. Do not read words in brackets; they are instructions to you.]

1. What are the three most important things you do as a teacher? (The things that really count for something.)
   (a) _____
   (b) _____
   (c) _____
2. Do any of these enhance the (main) goals of the school? [Circle: yes, no.] [If yes,] which ones?
3. Do you feel the school is making progress toward its main goals? [yes, no] Can you elaborate on that? [Include sureness or confidence of answer if ascertainable.]
4. Are there any important things that you do in the classroom (things important to you) that you think wouldn't be thought as important by others? [yes, no] [If yes,] what things are those?
   _____
   _____
   _____
   _____
5. What are some things you'd like to see this school working toward that it isn't now?
   _____

[If names something:] What staff members do you think could help in accomplishing these things?

Interview questions such as these can and should be altered for close applicability to most school organizations. Other questions will emerge during entry processes, as a result of the consultant's own hunches about what is troubling the organization, or by asking a small group of teachers to suggest appropriate questions. In composing questionnaires or interview schedules, the two most important guides are to ask about only one simple thing at a time and to pretest the instrument for possible revision on a few nonparticipants before administering it to the participants themselves. For additional pointers on technical matters, see Kerlinger (1964, chap. 26), Phillips (1966, chap. 6), and Sjoberg and Nett (1968, chap. 8).

If interviews are to be conducted on objective matters or on topics that interviewees do not regard as threatening, organizational members themselves can conduct the interviews and obtain valid information. If delicate matters are involved or if the questions are likely to arouse high emotion, it is better to employ nonorganizational members with the understanding that they will turn over distributions of anonymous answers to the organization. In this case the information will usually be more dependable if the outside interviewers are people whom organization members know and trust. In school districts in which OD specialists and familiar outsiders are not available, it is prudent to employ new outsiders in several rounds of interviewing about nonthreatening matters before embarking on more emotional topics.

In general, the successful use of questionnaires and interviews rests on four conditions: (1) clarity between consultant and clients about who is to have access to the information and what use is to be made of it; (2) assurances that anonymity and confidentiality will be maintained; (3) allowance of sufficient lead time for compilation and analysis of results before they are put to use; and (4) clarity in the consultant's own mind about how intervention actions might be altered by the data findings. Consultants should ask themselves why they are asking certain questions, what they will do with the answers, and what decisions or intervention designs will be affected by the answers. If consultants only ask for information that might come in handy, they are asking respondents to pay in time and trouble for their own reluctance to take time and trouble.

Direct Observation. In instances when respondents seem too distrustful to give satisfactory answers to questionnaires or interviews, when school members are striving toward ambiguous goals, or when a school is so different from others that efficient instruments cannot be constructed until more is learned about the school, the consultant usually visits in order to watch and listen. An excessive amount of unguided watching and listening can be very wasteful, however. Observing can be most useful when it is guided by questions like those following.

For what activities do teachers spend the most time preparing? What kinds of topics are given the most time during meetings? What kind of aid from others do teachers accept with the most gratitude?

What presumed intentions on the part of others cause teachers to feel outrage or betrayal? Toward what ends to members encourage one another? The observer can watch for activities or episodes pointed up by such questions and, on encountering one, should note which goals seem at issue. This kind of observation is more reliable if several observers conduct observations at several places in the school at several times during the day and week, carefully compare their written notes, and obtain further information to resolve any contra- dictions.

Unobtrusive Measures.   The records that a school keeps for itself provide another tool for diagnosis. The consultant may wish to obtain a copy of the school's guiding philosophy or stated goals, a statement of goals by the school board, or a faculty-student hand- book that describes goals. Daily or weekly bulletins give a rough indication of what sorts of activities require attention and consume energy in the normal course of work. These official statements may enable the consultant to check for discrepancies between public announcements and actual strivings and may also provide the source of interview or questionnaire topics.

Multiple Methods.   While each of these four methods is useful in appropriate situations, all are better when used in combination. A single assessment of the goals of one group is inevitably unbalanced and incomplete for a number of reasons—because the goals of one group or school differ from those of another, because one method colors an assessment differently from another, and also because the history or circumstances of the assessments may differ.

For these reasons a single assessment should be accepted only tentatively. The roundness of the representation should be increased by balancing one method with another and by checking an assess- ment made on one kind of occasion with that made on another kind of occasion. Even when working with only one school, the consult- ant should assess the goals of another school to determine whether those of the client school are in harmony or in competition with its environment.

Uses of Information.   If diagnostic information about goals is to be purposive, the question of how to use it after it is obtained should be considered beforehand. First, information about goal processes can be used in designing the consultation. If the questions on goal processes reveal that the school does not spend enough time consid- ering goals, that norms do not promote the sharing of personal and organizational strivings, or that too little consensus on goals prevents primary decision makers from proceeding fruitfully, for example, exercises that generate consensus might usefully be included.

Second, the information can be used as a basis for data feed- back in a collaborative diagnostic intervention. In data feedback, the consultant compiles the information into a readily understandable form, such as a count of tallies or a presentation of simple graphs;

then, at a meeting with clients, the data are reported together with a lecturette on the variable in question that allows participants to interpret the data.*

Data will often show that an assumed consensus does not exist or that feelings held in private are actually shared by a wide variety of school participants. In this case an effective method for data feedback is to present the data in a general session, then to divide members into small groups to discuss the data's significance and to see which individual impressions are confirmed and which are not. This tactic, which highlights discrepancies between individual and subgroup impressions and helps to create an impetus for change by revealing the gap between the ideal and real situation, is especially useful when the consultant believes that pluralistic ignorance is preventing a staff from undertaking unified action.

Eliciting Goal Statements

The procedures that follow can be used to elicit statements of individual or organizational goals, although if members are to share their frustrations and yearnings openly, some prior work in communication norms and skills will generally be required. These methods convene the group so that members can share their perceptions with one another and with the OD consultant as well. Goal statements can be checked immediately to determine the amount of consensus on them, or they may be modified through dialogue.

Room Design.† In this procedure, participants are asked to close their eyes for three to five minutes of silence, to imagine in great detail a room or other physical space in which they would personally most like to learn, teach, or otherwise perform their work, and then to describe their visions to one another, answering the question of how this desired room would enable them to achieve what they are not achieving now. If this question does not elicit direct statements of goals, teachers will have no difficulty converting their answers into the desired form. The advantages of this procedure are that it gives participants another view of their goals by forcing them to use language other than abstract pedagoguese, provides views of further aspects of the goals, and yields paraphrases.

Projection into 1982. Another way to help individuals visualize their goals is to ask them a series of questions that lead them gradually toward clarification and specificity. The example below, which asks participants to project their goals five years from the year of the exercise, can be presented on paper for each participant to write his answers alone. To ascertain agreements and conflicts, individuals can be asked to read aloud to others those answers they care to reveal.

---

*For more detailed explanation and procedures, see McElvaney and Miles (1971, chap. 6), and chap. 10 of this book.

†We have adapted this procedure from Pfeiffer and Jones (1970, p. 98).

Again, for purposes of illustration, the example has here been written for teachers, but it can easily be rephrased for other positions in the school organization.

Projection into 1982*
Project yourself into the year 1982, and imagine that you are still working in this school district. If you had your fondest wish, what would your work here be like in 1982? We realize that we are asking no small feat of imagination, but please try to depict your vision of the future with as much specificity as possible in answering the following questions. In each case, tell how you would like it to be in 1982. You may or may not, as you prefer, temper your vision with what you think is realistically possible.

1. Now in 1982, my age is _____.
2. My position in the school district is _____
   _____
3. Some of the kinds of activities I engage in each day are
   _____
   _____
   _____
4. My responsibilities or functions are to _____
   _____
   _____

   Remember to be as specific and concrete as your imagination will permit.
5. What is it that you especially like about your work?
   _____
6. What results of your work make you especially proud?
   _____
   _____
   _____

Now look back at answers 1 through 6. Some of the things you are doing or results you are producing in 1982 are very different from those of five years earlier. Select the most important differences—not necessarily the biggest differences or those most difficult to achieve—but the differences you feel are the most valuable and satisfying.

7. What are the two or three things most worth accomplishing by 1982? _____
   _____
8. What are the chief sorts of satisfactions you feel from these accomplishments? _____
   _____
   _____

_____

*We have modified this procedure from one used by McBer and Associates.

Now leave 1982 and return to the present. Looking over your answers to the above questions, what do you seem to be saying about your goals for 1982 as a member of this school district? Please write two or three goals that you believe contain the more important elements of your answers above.

1. To _____ .
2. To _____
   _____
   _____ .
3. To _____
   _____
   _____ .

Delphi Method. Because many of the problems with which education deals are long-range, cross-disciplinary, largely without a theoretical basis, but urgent nonetheless, it is often difficult to select the best goal statements from a published text and too time-consuming to undertake a lengthy search for ways of ascertaining those most likely to be productive. The consultant who relies instead on the informed judgment of persons involved must select for his goal-stating group those who have a stake in the work for which goals are to be stated and who also bring a needed technical knowledge to the task (qualities often combined in one person).

In combining the judgments of various people to arrive at goals, face-to-face conferences and committee meetings offer certain disadvantages. The outcome is often a compromise reached under the influence of a heavily persuasive leader or a result of the bandwagon effect of majority opinion. The Delphi method is a way of replacing the committee with a sequence of individual interrogations interspersed with information feedback.

The Delphi technique requires individual participants to be segregated from one another, either in separate rooms or scattered over a large room, such as a cafeteria or gymnasium, beyond talking distance; the procedure can also be carried out by mail. In the first step, participants are asked to write the goals they believe to be most suitable for the school or group, or they may be given a previously prepared list of goals, such as that shown below, with instructions to mark individual preferences and write in any personally desired modifications.

- Encouraging creativity among students
- Maintaining an orderly and quiet classroom
- Enriching the course of study or curriculum of the classroom
- Giving individual attention to students
- Experimenting with new teaching techniques
- Diagnosing learning problems of students
- Coordinating classroom activities with other parts of the school program

- Ensuring that students learn basic skills
- Solving the personal problems of individual students
- Developing student ability in analytical reasoning and problem solving
- Developing the aesthetic potential of students
- Other—specify

In the second step, all the responses are collected and tabulated and a report is written, of which each participant is given a copy, telling which goals were chosen and how many participants either chose each goal or wrote very similar goals. Next, each participant is told to reconsider his previous answer for possible revision. New responses that deviate conspicuously from the goals recommended by the majority are noted and questioned for reasons, the reasons reported to the others along with the statements of goals and their frequencies. Asking people who deviate from the majority to give reasons causes those without strong convictions to move toward the median; those who feel they have good reason for deviant opinions are likely to maintain and defend them.

It should be noted that some goals can be expressed numerically. Some respondents, for example, might propose as a goal that the school should turn out a certain percentage of graduates each year who are capable of writing specified types of instructions for computers in the Fortran language with no more than one error among every 200 characters. Respondents might differ in the percentage of graduates they think ought to be able to do this, with the lowest recommendation at zero percent and the highest, let us say, at 50 percent. When goals differ numerically, as in this case, a certain percentage of respondents at the low and high ends may arbitrarily be regarded as "extreme" and be asked to state reasons for their positions. In cases where goals differ only qualitatively, a committee of nonparticipants may be asked to judge extremeness.

In either case, the consultant proceeds with two more rounds, repeating the previous round exactly and regarding the result of the fourth round as being as close to consensus as it is possible to get through purely rational processes. If the consensus is poor, participants may turn to face-to-face argument, divide into groups to pursue different goals, or propose another solution.

Tinkertoy. The Tinkertoy* procedure aims at eliciting group goals by nonverbal means and is most instructive if groups contain no fewer than three and no more than eight members each. Participants are divided into groups of fairly equal size, and each group is instructed to use Tinkertoys to produce a single symbolic representation of what it hopes the school will be like within a given period of time. When all groups have completed their constructions (allow thirty to

---

*Name copyrighted by The Toy Tinkers, division of A. G. Spalding & Brothers, Inc., 807 Greenwood Street, Evanston, Illinois 60204.

forty-five minutes for this activity), all participants gather round one of them. For five or ten minutes, those who did *not* build the model comment on the kind of school the symbolic structure suggests to them, while those who did build it reply and explain. The same procedure is repeated with all other constructions.

Since this procedure will not work well without a fair consensus on general goal areas within the groups building the structures, the consultant who has no previous information about the goals of individual respondents may wish first to survey the goals verbally. In addition to clarifying group goals, this method can also provide direct experience of how individuals participate in the work of the group. Participants can learn about their participative styles if time is allowed for debriefing the processes that occurred during the construction period; the consultant may also wish to assign someone in each group to act as an observer and make notes of pertinent acts and processes.

Individual Needs and Organizational Goals. This two-part procedure focuses on identifying individual needs and organizational goals and the extent to which they mesh. The first activity (for which approximately an hour should be allowed) is designed to make individuals aware of their personal work needs, the relationships among them, and the opportunities for meeting them.

In lists of brief phrases, individuals answer the question, What do individuals want from their work? (alternatively, What do you want from your work in this school district?). These items are compiled and posted on newsprint so that participants can copy the group list and rank-order each item as it applies to themselves in their jobs. Folding their papers so that they cannot see this ranking, they then rank-order each item in terms of the amount of opportunity their present work affords toward meeting these needs. Unfolding their papers, they compare the rankings to identify the greatest discrepancies.

The consultant may then wish to join individuals in pairs or small groups to determine commonalities among the lists. The resulting composite list, which can later serve as a basis for problem solving, should indicate the extent to which important personal needs are or are not satisfied in the organization. Finally, the consultant may deliver a lecturette on individual needs and their satisfactions as described in this and earlier chapters.

The purpose of the second activity is to identify organizational needs and goals to see how they compare or contrast with individual needs. First, lists of organizational needs are produced (typically including such items as conformity to rules and norms, commitment to organizational goals, maintaining stable authority relations, and so on). The compiled list is then posted next to the list of individual needs, and the consultant and group try to determine which items on the two lists are complementary or antithetical.

This procedure may have several outcomes: (1) it may highlight ways that were not previously apparent of satisfying individual needs within organizational goals; (2) it may suggest organizational goals that have no real commitment from individuals and that should therefore be revised or deleted; (3) it may uncover organizational goals that are imperative but not closely related to individual goals, in which case the result may be an agreement to share equitably the burden of working toward them; or (4) it may cause participants to find new superordinate goals that can enhance both individual and organizational striving.

ESTABLISHING GOALS

Conferences on Goals

The traditionally structured conference organized according to Robert's Rules of Order is probably the most common means by which people in school organizations establish and examine goals. Such a conference typically opens with the question, What are we trying to do here? but proceeds with little attention to methods of ascertaining understanding, priorities, assent, or commitment to goals. Members of school organizations who have voted in favor of a goal too often assume mistakenly that the vote will somehow cause dissenters to become committed to the goal preferred by the majority.

This type of conference can be profitable as part of a planned sequence of interactions, and, despite its weaknesses, the consultant should sometimes allow it to occur without interference. In particular, a meeting containing persons hostile to the consultant calls for prudent gentle movement. The consultant should pursue a traditional mode, suggesting no novel procedures for the discussion until the participants are prepared to believe that their dignity and welfare will be respected. In such a situation it is wise for the consultant to paraphrase (without naming), to describe behavior, and even to describe (in a soft voice) a few feelings of his own but not to ask for the feelings of others, suggest a systematic survey, or describe unusual methods for eliciting personal goals.

Beckhard (1969) has described a goal-confrontation activity that can be used both to discern relevant existing goals among individuals and subgroups and to obtain a final list of goals toward which both administrators and subordinates can take committed action. This design enables people who are not on the same hierarchical level to discuss their common interests. Increasing knowledge of goals, shared and deviant alike, increases realistic expectations about the behavior of others and allows problems to be more precisely delimitable. Beckhard describes this procedure as follows.

> Another form of organization goal-setting activity is what is called an "organization confrontation" meeting. This is usually a one-day activity which can be used to bring together a large segment of an organization in order to set priorities and action

targets. The activity is particularly appropriate in situations where an organization is in stress; where, for example, there is a new top management, where there has been a loss of a major customer, or where the organization is going into a new product or a new area of business. Organizationally, this meeting is most appropriate where the top group is relatively cohesive but there is a gap between the top and the rest of the organization.

The activity is designed to mobilize the whole organization in a very short period of time toward an action plan and priorities for change and improvement. It takes the following form.

Let us suppose that there are eighty people in the management from the general manager down through first-line supervision. This meeting includes all eighty members. The meeting itself takes between 4½ and 6 hours and could easily be divided into two time units—an afternoon and the following morning, or an evening and a morning. Let's assume we are using a night and a morning. The evening session has the following elements.

A general meeting includes a brief introduction by the general manager and possibly a statement by an outside resource if one is used. The statements define the purposes of the meeting, stress that this is an opportunity for everyone to influence the actions of the organization, and urge that people be open and say what they think. Assurances should be provided that no one will be punished for what they say and that anonymity will be preserved insofar as possible.

The group is divided into small groups of five or six people across organizational lines, so that no boss is in the same group with a subordinate or working colleague. The top-management group, excluding the general manager, meets as one group along with the heterogeneous subgroups.

The task of these groups is information collecting. The groups are assigned the following task: "Thinking of yourself as a person with needs and goals in this organization, and also thinking of the total organization, what are the behaviors, procedures, ways of work, attitudes, etc., that should be different so that life would be better around here?" Each group is asked to make a list of its items. They have about an hour for this task.

The total group then reassembles. The lists of the subgroups are placed on the board. From this total list, categories of problems are developed by the meeting leader. This marks the end of the evening meeting.

In the morning, another general session takes place. Each participant receives a copy of the information collected from the groups the night before, along with a cover page listing the category headings. The total group then participates in assigning category headings to each item on the list under the direction of the meeting leader and/or general manager.

The group then divides into functional groups under the leadership of those reporting to the general manager. For *example, everyone in the manufacturing area would meet together, chaired by the head of manufacturing; the same with finance, personnel, etc. These groups would have the following tasks:*

1. *Go through the entire list and select three or four items which most affect you or your group. Determine what action your group will take on those and the timetable for beginning work on the problems. Be prepared to report this out to the total group.*
2. *Go through the list again and select those items to which you think top management should be giving highest priority. (Criteria for inclusion on this list is that your group can't deal with it.)*
3. *Since this is a large meeting, and all of us are off the job, develop a tactical plan for communicating what happened at this meeting to those who are not here.*

The group reconvenes and each subunit reports out its list of three or four priority items and its plans for dealing with them. Then each group reports its suggestions for top management. A cumulative list of suggestions is developed. The top manager responds to this list, making some commitment on each item.

The top manager would then set a follow-up meeting for the near future, say, in five or six weeks; two hours should be allotted for such a meeting, in which the manager is committed to report progress on the items on his list and expects to receive reports of progress on other items from the various units.

The expectation of a follow-up meeting sustains "positive tension" in the system and keeps the whole organization focusing toward goals.

This model tends to produce rather dramatic organization results in a very short period of time (pp. 38–40).

Beckhard's goal-confrontation design can be used with overlapping groups: (1) when goals and decisions depend on lateral coordination, as is the case with most functions in a school organization; (2) when participants are sufficiently fluent in oral group discourse, as is the case with most certificated school personnel as well as with many noncertificated staff; and (3) when the task to be accomplished is complex, which is the case with most school tasks. Demanding, as it does, repeated discussions of complex tasks and subtle interdependencies, it might be more difficult to use with most custodial staffs, bus drivers, very young students, and so on.

Clear and Unclear Goals

Experiencing a simulation may be the best way of impressing on staff members the importance of clear goals. Later they can apply what they have learned from experiencing the exercise to actual goal setting within the school. The following exercise on goals has fifteen steps and takes about ninety minutes.

1. *Introduce the exercise.* Give a lecturette on the importance of group goals and an overview and outline of the sequence of events in the exercise.
2. *Conduct first activity.*
   a. *Form subgroups of six or seven.* Instruct the participants to get together with people with whom they are not well acquainted. Ask them to keep a balance between men and women in each group. Have them elect an observer in each subgroup. The observers should go to the corner of the room for instructions.
   b. *Instruct observers.* Have individual observation sheets prepared for each observer. Tell the observers your plan: you are going to give the groups two tasks with different goal statements. The first task will have an unclear goal; the second, a simple and clear goal.
3. *Observers return* to their groups.
4. *Brief total group as follows:* You have two jobs to do, both very brief. In both tasks you will discuss a problem. Your observer will not participate but will report to you at the end of the second task. Your first task will take about eight minutes. I'll give you a warning a minute or so before time to finish it. Your first topic is: "What are the most appropriate goals to govern the best development of group experiences in order to maximize social development in a democratic society?" It is unnecessary to appoint a leader.
5. *Groups carry out first task.* (Give warning at seven minutes —cut at eight.)
6. *Give groups second topic:* "In the next six minutes see how many names you can list of formally organized clubs or organizations that exist in a typical community." (Alternative topics: "List as many different functions as you can that take place in groups." "What can a leader do to make it easy for every member of the group to participate?")
7. *Groups carry out second task.* (Warn at five minutes— cut at six.)
8. *Ask observers* to give their reports on what happened during each task.
9. *Ask each group* to discuss the observer's observations. Instruct that the purpose is not to agree or disagree with the observer but to share perceptions among group members and help clarify what others in the group are reporting.
10. *Conduct second activity: a double-round Fishbowl.* Ask two groups of six or seven each to come together and form a cluster. Group A sits in the center; Group B sits outside Group A's circle of chairs, forming an outer circle.

11. *Brief all clusters as follows:*
    a. *Instruct Group A:* Your task is to produce a list of characteristics of good and bad goals. Ask one person to write them on newsprint. Use two columns.
    b. *Instruct Group B:* Your task is to listen to Group A, make notes, and be ready to add characteristics they have overlooked.
    c. *Group A works.* Group B listens and prepares to add to Group A's list.
    d. *Group B reports and critiques A's list.* Both groups select four or five good and bad characteristics they would give highest priority importance.
12. *Instruct Group B:* "This is your time to be in the center. Group A will observe your work. Your task is to list on newsprint as many *symptoms* as you can for each of the four or five bad and good characteristics your group chose."
    a. *Instruct Group A:* Your task is to listen carefully and think of any symptoms Group B is omitting.
    b. *Group B works.* Group A listens and makes notes.
    c. *Group B reports* and adds to Group A's list. Groups A and B as a cluster conduct a discussion of the work produced and prepare a brief statement explaining the nature of group goals according to the work produced by both groups. Each cluster elects a person to report.
13. *Reporters present brief statement.*
14. All newsprint from groups and clusters are posted on wall.
15. The consultant presents a summary using appropriate data produced by groups. Some ideas that groups are likely to come up with are as follows:
    a. Characteristics of good goals
       (1) Clear
       (2) Acceptable
       (3) Attainable
       (4) Amenable to modification or clarification
    b. Clear, acceptable, attainable goals cannot always be determined in advance. The first job of any group is to clarify and modify stated goals until they are clear and acceptable.
    c. Clear and acceptable goals make it easier for a member to diagnose needed roles and to accept responsibility for taking such roles. "We know what we are supposed to do."
    d. Possible symptoms of unclear or unacceptable goals
       (1) Tension
       (2) Excessive joking or horseplay
       (3) Voting or poll taking without discussion
       (4) Failure to support, use, or follow up contributed ideas
       (5) Lengthy discussion of unrelated topics

GOALS AND OTHER ORGANIZATIONAL PROCESSES

Goal Setting and Problem Solving

In the S-T-P method of problem solving, which is presented in detail in chapter 7, statements of problems, solutions, and goals are by nature inseparable, and the OD consultant should be alert to help a group explore their mutual implications. Goal statements in particular should meet two conditions: they should be general enough to state fully an end condition toward which activities will be directed, and they should be specific enough for group members to be able to agree on whether a target has been reached or not. During group S-T-P work, the consultant's actions should be directed toward ferreting out clear statements of goals as well as the implications of S and T statements by asking such questions as, (in the case of proposals) What do you accomplish by this action?, or (in the case of target statements) How would the situation appear if that problem were solved?

S-T-P problem-solving procedures are ways of increasing individual and group skills and of providing steps to facilitate the transformation of inchoate yearnings and frustrations into clear, consensual, specifiable goal statements. Their conscientious use should greatly increase the probability that consultants and clients will agree on goals that have the commitment of those who must transform them into actions and that present clear criteria against which to measure progress.

Inevitably, however—and especially when a group feels that it must either make progress or give up—the consultant will encounter a point at which the group is stuck, resistant to the "artificiality" of further exercises and procedures, and demanding to do something other than "play games." In this situation the consultant is likely to find the work stalled by underlying value and philosophical conflicts of which group members may be only partly aware, at the same time that they are unskilled at describing them and afraid of confronting them. This is a good point at which to determine whether group skills and processes are in sufficiently good shape to permit continued progress or whether they should be recycled before the group can proceed at its major task.

Although there is no magic wand or handy-dandy set of techniques for resolving this impasse, there are still a few steps that can be taken to resolve a value-conflict dilemma or to impose some form on chaos. One useful procedure described by Mager (1962) requires all the consultant's skill at clarifying communication and sharpening statements of frustration into clear statements of problems and skills. It also requires an ability to live with ambiguity for awhile and a good deal of patience as well.

In this procedure someone states a goal, no matter how fuzzily it may be worded, and this activity continues until the group finds a goal on which it can agree. Subgroups then list situations that would be indicators of goal accomplishment (the group can fantasize, refer to appropriate records and indicators, etc.); the lists are posted and duplications are eliminated. Next the group brainstorms specific performance criteria by which goal accomplishment could be measured, tests the original statements against these criteria, and rewords the statements as necessary until clarity and consensus are achieved. The point is that the consultant steers a movement away from the general and abstract toward the concrete and operational.

Group Processes in Establishing Goals

Other chapters discuss the advantages and disadvantages of drawing out ideas and actions from face-to-face groups. In this discussion of goal processes, however, it will suffice to emphasize three important points for the consultant: assess goals repeatedly, clarify conflicts, and obtain multiple expressions of goals.

As goals change for both the individual and the organization, the extent to which organizational arrangements satisfy personal needs and the extent to which environmental demands are met by the organization's goals will change as well. For members of school organizations, especially, it is important to check periodically on how well organizational goals encompass the personal needs of the staff and on the effects of the school's interaction with its community. Clarity and consistency of goals should be ascertained at least once a year. In cases of change from one form of organization to another, organizational goals should be surveyed at least twice a year and the findings fed back to the staff both orally and in writing.

When changing relevancies in the school's environment cause new goals to come into conflict with old—as, for example, the aspirations of administrators, teachers, students, and even cafeteria workers are currently being challenged by the ecological crisis, the resoluteness of militant minorities, the demands of humanistic youth, and other events in our changing society—the first necessity is to clarify the conflict. Is it more apparent than real? Is it unavoidable? Can consensus be reached without unanimity?

Certain conflicts, such as those involving goal commitments that are advantageous to the school but disadvantageous to some persons, cannot be resolved through organizational rearrangement, and these individuals must be asked to leave the organization. In schools, personnel must usually wait until the end of the year before departing their positions, which considerably delays the progress of organization development. It is nevertheless still highly desirable to get conflicts understood as soon as possible so that necessary steps can be taken either to reduce the conflict or, as the next chapter will suggest, to make constructive use of it.

Finally, because human longings are variegated, many-sided, often obscurely complicated, and always susceptible to change, it is very difficult for most people to make clear, tidy, succinctly formal statements of goals at any given moment. In one situation, only the most personally pressing aspect of a goal will be described; while, considered out of context, all aspects may appear to be so different from one another as to be virtually meaningless. In addition, we are not always clear or secure about our own desires. Describing a multifaceted goal in several ways may enable others in the group to discern which features are most desirable to the speaker; but for this reason alone the speaker may not wish to reveal personal goals too clearly. Personal knowledge of others yields a certain power over others, and assisting others in gaining this power involves taking the risk of being thwarted.

Individuals who can discern the rewarding relationship between goals that are extremely valuable to the organization and at the same time deeply satisfying to themselves may still resist committing themselves to these goals—because they may conflict with other personal goals that are valued even more highly, because the person doubts that others in the group value them equally and is unwilling to enter into contention with others in pursuing them, or perhaps because the individual believes rightly or wrongly that the organization lacks the resources to achieve the proposed goal.

For all these reasons the OD consultant should regard any brief, single expression of a goal as providing only tentative, incomplete, and dubious information, whether the individual has constructed the statement himself or has selected it as one alternative from a questionnaire. To increase the reliability of goal responses, consultants should question individuals about their goals repeatedly and sequentially. When dealing with a district, committee, school, or other groups, expressions of the organization's goals should be obtained from persons in various positions, and abundant opportunity should be allowed for paraphrase.

The principal message that OD consultants must convey to clients is that goals are rallying points and not fences. Strong norms supporting the recycling of goals at macro- and microlevels should be built into the design and operation of the school. Continuing discussion should metamorphose any and all goal statements. The crucial skill is that of conceiving the consummative state. At the end of a day a person should be able to say, "If goal X exists, I'll go home feeling that it has been a good day. What should happen to me on such a day is . . . ."

READINGS

Problems of Behavioral Objectives

Neil Postman and Charles Weingartner

Although goals and objectives should be stated as clearly and precisely as possible, there are nevertheless countless problems associated with the current emphasis on behavioral objectives and accountability. Postman and Weingartner illuminate some of these problems in the selection that follows.

One of the most significant consequences of the current demand for accountability in the schools has been the involvement of school people in a frantic effort to convert what used to be called "instructional goals" into what are now called "behavioral objectives." As the term suggests, behavioral objectives are an important part of the process of behavior modification which is in turn a new concept of teaching derived from behavioral psychology. In brief, the rationale for behavioral objectives goes something like this: School has a responsibility to the community to provide young people with certain skills, information and attitudes. The only way to tell if students are learning what the school is supposed to teach is by evaluating their behavior before and after the school has done its work. If those evaluations are to have any validity, they must be based on objective standards, so that everyone can agree on whether or not the students have in fact changed. The only way to have objective standards for measuring change is to spell out exactly what, after being taught, the student should be able to do that he couldn't do previously. This implies that what you want him to *do* has to be observable, and preferably measurable, as well. If, for example at the end of a year, 90 percent of the kids in a school can demonstrate 90 percent of the behaviors the school was supposed to teach, then the school is doing its job. If not—then someone's fouling up and ought to be replaced.

Sounds perfectly reasonable, doesn't it? And it might be too— if not for a couple of major problems. The first arises from the unhappy fact that the behaviors which are easiest to specify, observe, and measure (as well as modify) usually turn out to be trivial. A typical behavioral objective in "language arts," for example, might specify that "at the end of six weeks of institution, the student will be able to identify correctly, in a sample of ten sentences, fifteen words which function as nouns, ten which function as verbs," etc. A specific goal? Yes. Observable and measurable? Obviously. But is that really what we want kids to learn? And there's the trouble— the question that the movement to behavioral objectives does *not* address—namely, What's worth teaching? Inevitably, the behaviorally oriented curriculum is based, instead, on the answer to the question, What can we measure? And since the instruments available for measuring behavioral change are extremely limited, so are the behaviors such curricula set out to teach. So there's problem one. It could be solved, some say, by inventing more and better instruments for objective evaluation. Easily said. But the plain fact is that the most significant learnings cannot be translated into narrow behavioral objectives or measured on any standardized test. How would a school test, for example, whether its students are learning to rely on their own judgment, rather than on the pronouncements of authority? ("At the end of twelve weeks of instruction, 90 percent of the students refused to follow the school dress code 90 percent of the time"?) Or whether they are learning to be open-ended and tentative in their solutions to problems? Or whether they are enjoying the process of learning? The point is, of course, that where attitudes are concerned, change shows up in ways that are unique to each learner, and over times that range from a moment to a lifespan. Such change cannot be measured then, even in theory, by regularly scheduled standardized tests. And that's problem two.

There is, of course, much more to say about behavioral objectives—pro and con—than we can go into here. It is worth pointing out, though, that the danger in the current plunge toward behaviorism is *not* in the limitations of behavioral objectives, but in the schools' failure to recognize those limitations. In their efforts to be "scientific" about teaching, many school people are moving perilously close to the position that "If it can't be measured, there's nothing there." It would be difficult to imagine a view more *anti*-scientific, or more deadly to the learning experience, than that.

Issues about Objectives

Robert Stake

In this brief paper, Stake presents some important categories to keep in mind when setting goals and writing objectives.

Reproduced by permission from the author.

Ubiquity. All teaching has its purposes. Countless objectives are *simultaneously* pursued by every teacher. Some objectives are explicit; some are implicit. Objectives and purposes are also known as aims, goals, intents, and hopes. To understand the objectives people have, you also have to know something of their needs, their fears, their expectations, and their dreams.

Multiplicity/Diversity. People have more objectives than they can list. Different people have different objectives. Some people have objectives that are contrary to other people's objectives. Each person has objectives that compete with, and even contradict, some other of his own objectives. A list of objectives is an oversimplification of what the group wants and a misrepresentation of what any one individual wants. Nevertheless, it will sometimes be useful to have lists of objectives.

Behavioral Specificity. A stated objective always represents a *collection* of desired behaviors (or phenomena). The more specific the statement, then the smaller the collection, the less the misunderstanding about it, and the less useful it is to represent some of the complex purposes of education. The more general the statement, then the broader the collection of behaviors, the more the misunderstanding as to what is and what is not included but the more likely it can be used to represent some of the complex purposes of education.

There is no language that perfectly represents what a teacher aims to teach. It is helpful in some cases to state desired outcomes in terms of student behaviors—but not always. The people who hold the objectives should decide which language expresses their objectives best.

Responsibility. All teachers and all administrators are responsible for indicating the school's objectives just as they are responsible for arranging environments, providing stimulation, evoking student responses, and evaluating. But each teacher and administrator does not share equally in these responsibilities. To the extent that responsibilities are assigned, each teacher's assignment should capitalize on what he can do best. Few of us in the classroom are skilled in stating objectives. Those who are not should be invited—but not required—to develop the skill of stating objectives. A teacher's talents should be used to adapt teaching to the immediate circumstances, or to motivating students, or to appraising responses, or to whatever he is best at.

Obviously, stating objectives is not a prerequisite to effective teaching nor should it be considered a universal remedy for poor teaching. Sometimes—but not always—it will help matters to have a teacher state his objectives.

Priority. Different objectives will have different priorities. Priorities indicate how much effort (money, time, heart, etc.) should be allocated to each objective. Priority is based on need, resources available, and the probability that a given use of resources will alleviate a particular need. It makes little sense to be specific about objectives and vague about priorities.

Ephemerality. Objectives and priorities, for any person and any program, change with time. Statements of objectives, if to be used to mean something for an ongoing program, should be updated periodically.

Disclosure. Usually high-priority objectives should be apparent to both the teacher and the learner. Sometimes it will increase teaching-learning effectiveness to make the students more aware of objectives; sometimes it will not. It will not help to identify objectives which at the moment seem to the student irrelevant or contrary to his self-concept. The teacher should not deceive himself or his students by implying that he has indicated (or should or could) all the objectives involved in the learning. Of course, the teacher should candidly discuss the objectives with students who have a concern about them.

Evaluation Utility. Some knowledge of teacher objectives is necessary for a complete evaluation of a program. Specific statements may or may not help. The statement that evaluation cannot occur without specific statement of objectives is nonsense; evaluative judgment of merit and shortcoming does not require an awareness of objectives. Evaluation projects can be organized around learning activities, management decisions, or teaching problems just as well as around objectives. Objectives may be more usefully considered *after* studying program activities than before. The choice is made by deciding why the evaluation is being done and who it is being done for. It's a matter of judgment.

BIBLIOGRAPHY

Johnson, D. W., and Johnson, R. T. 1975. *Learning together and alone: cooperation, competition, and individualization*. Englewood Cliffs, N.J.: Prentice-Hall.

Goal structures call for different types of functional interdependence among coacting participants. The Johnsons thoroughly discuss three goal structures in relation to school behavior: (1) *cooperative goal structures*, in which participants perceive that they can reach their goal only if others with whom they are linked can reach their goal; (2) *competitive goal structures*, in which participants perceive that they can obtain their goal only if others fail to obtain theirs; and (3) *individualistic goal structures*, in which achievement of a goal by one party is unrelated to achievement of the goal by others.

March, J. G., and Simon, H. A. 1958. *Organizations*. New York: Wiley.

This book argues that subsystem goals are usually more powerful for individuals than are the goals of the overall organization and that they are tenacious and self-perpetuating even when they are unassociated or in conflict with overall organizational goals.

Miles, M. B. 1967. Some properties of schools as social systems. In *Change in school systems*, ed. G. Watson, pp. 1-29. La Jolla, Calif.: University Associates.

This article advances the view that educational goals are often affected by considerations having little to do with classroom teaching and learning. Three important influences are: (1) *moralism*—ideological statements often outnumber actual goal-directed efforts; (2) *value conflicts*—schools tend to lag behind community sentiments because of a conserving function and their vulnerability to local control; and (3) *financial emphasis*—in the absence of clear output criteria, heavy emphasis is placed on performing educational activities at the lowest cost.

Sarason, S. B. 1971. *The culture of the school and the problem of change*. Boston: Allyn & Bacon.

Sarason makes the point that educational innovations that are originally regarded as a means of achieving important terminal goals often become terminal goals in themselves, with the result that the means toward a goal may become a misleading criterion for assessing change. It is not necessarily true that schools are improving merely because they are innovating; indeed, curriculum reforms often do no more than substitute one set of books for another.

Silverman, D. 1970. *The theory of organizations: a sociological framework*. New York: Basic Books.

Unlike individuals, organizations are not easily characterized on the basis of their goals. In helping us to see organizations as goal-oriented systems, Silverman draws attention to the complexities of organizational life and suggests that collective goals are more related to the constraints that arise within an organizational structure than they are to the personal motivations of participants.

Weick, K. 1969. *The social psychology of organizing.* Reading, Mass.: Addison-Wesley.

Differing from many organizational theorists, Weick argues that most organizations behave in a stable, orderly fashion even in the absence of clear goals. In his view, goal agreement is not a necessary precondition for order and regularity. Because clusters of participants who behave in collective ways tend to define goals only after some task accomplishment has occurred, making sense of this accomplishment and ultimately rating it as important is how rational goal pursuit really takes place.

5

Working with Conflicts

Conflicts are ubiquitous within school organizations; they occur continually, arise for a variety of reasons, appear in a variety of forms, and affect the educational process both favorably and unfavorably. The presence of conflict is in itself neither good nor bad; it simply exists and should be expected. Both as clusters of people and as individuals, administrators, teachers, parents, and students not only react differently to conflict but react differently from conflict to conflict and from time to time, so that the most effective strategies for dealing with conflicts must also vary according to the conflict, the school, and the parties involved. That is, an appropriate conflict-management strategy will depend on the type of conflict, the intensity of the disagreement, the persons participating in the conflict, the seriousness of the issue for them, and the authority, resources, and knowledge they possess.

OD consultants must know how to seek out conflicts, how to conceptualize them and make them known, and how to help school participants generate creative solutions to them. The nature of the conflict-management strategy will depend in part on a careful analysis of the conflict itself and in part on the consultant's own skill in working with school people in conflict. This chapter is intended to serve as a guide for diagnosing and analyzing organizational conflicts in schools, for determining when it is appropriate for consultants to intervene, and for selecting designs and specific consultative techniques for managing school conflicts.

THEORY OF CONFLICT

One of the primary demands on any school organization is that its various parts should be linked together to achieve overall objectives. To accomplish common tasks and achieve multifaceted goals generally requires collaboration, and for most educational tasks the need for participant interdependence is great. Teachers in teams must work together; curriculum specialists at the district level must work with teachers; indeed, to facilitate a more open school, groups of teachers and administrators must work interdependently on committees and teaching teams that span grade levels.

Conflict is likely to arise when particular educational goals are perceived as being mutually exclusive (as when teachers believe that counseling is not benefiting students' cognitive learning); when activities undertaken to reach goals are regarded as interdependent (as when teachers and counselors alike believe that student self-concept is the key to cognitive learning); or when two or more parties draw upon the same limited resources to accomplish their goals (as when teachers and counselors compete for time with students).

More specifically, conflict occurs between persons when the goals of each are frustrated by the other, when each is competing for some reward at the other's expense, when they misunderstand or disagree with one another's expectations of conduct, or when they approach a problem from different points of view. Conflict occurs between working groups for many of the same reasons, and it occurs between organizations when they compete for scarce resources or when, as in the case of revolutionary movements, the legitimacy of an organization is challenged.

For the OD consultant, conflict should not denote individual distaste, disappointment, frustration, anger, or any of the common forms of miscommunication discussed in chapter 3. In these pages, conflict refers to a social condition in which two or more persons or groups cannot have the same thing at the same time. Further, OD consultants should regard school conflicts as natural unavoidable occurrences that cannot be expected to vanish of their own accord but that should be brought out into the open and managed by providing channels or occasions through which adversaries can introduce their conflicting claims, when these are relevant, into the business of the school.

If conflicts are legitimatized, compromises, trade-offs, and other negotiations can be conducted openly at problem-solving meetings; more realistic educational policies can be achieved, and conflict anxieties can be diminished as outcomes are more clearly foreseen. If they are not uncovered and managed, informal groups and underground networks which greatly distort the truth will arise to cope with them, often increasing destructive tension and personal hostility between conflicting parties. Thus in many schools teachers cluster together to criticize the work of counselors; counselors stay away from teachers, preferring to keep to their own offices and to enjoy informal breaks with one another; and only rarely do criticisms become public enough for problem solving to occur.

Before school conflict can be brought into the open for public discussion, some degree of interpersonal trust and constructive openness must exist. Most school participants, however, are unaccustomed to expressing open disagreement directly to those with whom they disagree. In many schools direct discussion of conflict is experienced as unpleasant and undesirable both by those involved in the conflict and by those only observing it, especially when it is difficult for staff members to differentiate between disagreeing with a colleague's opinion and "putting down" or rejecting that colleague. Indeed, in addition to personal predilections, the norms of many school organizations militate against the open expression of differences. The OD consultant should work toward making constructive openness and the open confrontation of differences new norms within the school. School participants will be more willing to discuss conflict openly when a consultant, whose own skill in dealing with conflicts can serve as an important model, is present to support and legitimatize the process.

To this end the consultant should first look for signs of hidden conflict among individuals and subgroups. In some cases, different parts of the school may be unaware that they are competing for scarce resources; in other cases, competitors may be aware of conflict but unwilling to communicate about it publicly or officially. Second, the consultant should ascertain tentatively to what extent the conflict may be obstructing educational goals, making procedures inefficient, and frustrating the personal needs of staff members, or, on the other hand, to what extent it satisfies the power and achievement needs of some members and demonstrates qualities of inventive resourcefulness in the school. Third, if the consultant decides that the macrodesign should include steps for bringing the conflict into the open, procedures precisely suited to the nature of the conflict, the school, and the school's participants should be devised to make it accessible to direct and constructive dealing.

Types and Sources of Conflict

In the S-T-P procedure for problem solving, the S (situation) refers to the essential features of a current condition; the T (target) to a desired condition toward which an individual or group is striving; and the P (proposals) to specific action-plans aimed at bringing about the desired condition. The S is commonly associated with facts, opinions, explanations, perceptions, and feelings; the T, with goals, aims, ends, values, purposes, and objectives; and the P, with plans, strategies, procedures, and implementation. This paradigm can be used to describe a three-part typology of conflict.

Factual conflict (type S) involves argument about the realities of a current situation—either debate over easily discoverable facts, such as the number of square feet in a classroom, or over facts more difficult to gather, such as the opinions of math and science teachers about current curricula. *Value conflict* (type T) encompasses argument over values, goals, or objectives ranging from highly specific phenomena, such as students' behavior or achievements, to more general events, such as debates between essentialist and progressive educational philosophies. *Strategy conflict* (type *P*) involves argument over the best way of moving from a present condition to a valued future condition with respect to either the major stages of a macrodesign or microaspects of a specific action-plan.

In the types of miscommumication described in chapter 3, true conflict, in the sense of differences of belief about facts, values, or strategies, does not really exist. Miscommunications—gaps between a message that is sent and the message that is received—frequently occur because the messages sent do not accurately reflect the sender's intentions or because individuals or groups are not arguing about similar *S*s, *T*s, or *P*s; thus the adversaries are misunderstanding each other rather than disagreeing.

The sources of school conflict, whether of fact, value, or strategy, can be categorized as: (1) differentiation of function among parts of the school, (2) power struggles between persons and subsystems, (3) role conflicts, (4) differences in interpersonal style among school participants, and (5) stress imposed on the school by external forces.

Differentiation of Function. Effective adaptation to the community requires school organizations to communicate with their environments through a number of specialized units, and this differentiation of function is often a major source of conflict. Members of different departments or subgroups who have access to different kinds of information from that of their counterparts in other departments are likely to take a different view of the facts of a situation and to entertain different strategies for accomplishing their primary tasks. When the same problem is tackled from widely diverging points of view, the presence of various cognitive, emotional, and attitudinal differences will produce interpersonal and intergroup conflict. All too often, however, conflicts arising from functional differentiation are misunderstood as arising from someone's personal incompetence. This is because school participants who interact every day are too close to their own organization to see the organizations of others clearly, and it is only natural for them to associate the source of the conflict with the person toward whom the frustration or irritation is directly felt.

An example of this type of misunderstanding once occurred in our work with a school staff. Over a period of months the staff had repeatedly complained that the counselor was doing such an inadequate job that they had begun to question his competence, although the principal and a school psychologist thought that he was doing a fine job and could not understand the staff's dissatisfaction with him. At a staff workshop designed by a couple of OD consultants, the issue was raised and dealt with as it had been many times before. Defensive, bewildered, and frustrated, the counselor knew that he worked hard but could somehow not get this across to the other staff members.

After listening to the discussion and asking several questions, it became apparent to the consultants that the problem had less to do with the counselor as a person than with the fact that his position and functions caused his primary energies to be directed toward community, parents, and other outside agencies. Because of the way their own tasks were organized, the teachers had had little contact with either the counselor himself or with those in the community with whom he worked and for this reason were largely unaware of the effects of his actions. The principal and psychologist, on the other hand, had considerable contact with the counselor and his work and were well aware of the effects of his actions. On the basis of this understanding the consultants were able to educate the staff about the effects of differentiation of function and clear the way for improved communication and understanding between the teachers and the counselor.

In their work on industrial organizations, Lawrence and Lorsch (1967) concluded that success in achieving both high differentiation and a high quality of collaboration is determined by the organization's processes for resolving conflict. When organizational mechanisms for resolving conflicts are ineffective, the conflicts caused by differentiation can be destructive. When conflict is openly confronted and resolved, both differentiation and collaboration are effectively promoted.

Power Struggles. A common cause of conflict in school faculties and districts, power struggles typically arise when some participants attempt to gain advantage over others. This can occur when adversaries compete for a commonly desired reward, such as a promotion or merit pay for good teaching; when self-interests conflict; when resources are scarce; and when opinions differ on the relative autonomy or interdependence of individuals or subgroups.

In one of our projects, for example, conflicting self-interests and a scarce resource brought about a power struggle over a scheduling problem in an elementary school. One team comprising teachers of the first and second grades, another comprising the third and fourth grades, and still another comprising the fifth and sixth grades all wanted a late-afternoon PE schedule. All had good reasons for this, but, as only one gymnasium was available for the afternoon periods, the conflicting self-interests involved developed into a full-scale power struggle.

Ideally, every teacher, administration, and group in a district should have all the resources needed for working effectively. Unfortunately, however, resources are usually scarce, and most school participants learn to fight for their share. In the case of this elementary school, the lower-grade units accused the upper-grade team of having dominated the afternoon schedule in the past, claimed that this domination had been typical of numerous other faculty interactions, and coalesced to demand a schedule change, in part because they wanted to exercise their right to a share of school-wide power. Feelings were heated, the upper-grade team resisted, and the ensuing conflict took six hours to resolve.

Power struggles also develop over conflicting views of the appropriate power relationships between members of a school organization —i.e., who should be accountable to whom, or who should tell whom what to do and when and how to do it. In another school in which we worked, for example, a conflict arose between the principal and the teaching staff over the institution of a new role of coordinator because the principal intended this role to include supervisory functions over the teachers, while the teachers thought that they had been teaching effectively without external supervision and believed that the principal was treating them unprofessionally.

Finally, power struggles may result from a desire to increase one's personal influence over educational goals (value conflict) or over the instructional program (strategy conflict). Some faculty members may wish to implant their personal influence on the school's philosophy and curriculum; others may wish to gain influence in order to be seen as more effective professionally or to spread their ideas to others. Whatever the particular social-psychological dynamics may be, such desires are typical in many schools.

Role Conflict.   Some social scientists argue that insofar as an organization is comprised of persons interacting in certain roles, much organizational behavior can be understood by understanding role relationships. Thus on joining a school faculty, new teachers usually attempt to learn what others expect of them by meeting with the principal, the team leader, other teachers in the same unit, district specialists, the counselor, the custodian, cooks, and students. These others constitute a *role set*, and the job-related behavior of new teachers will be strongly influenced by what these people expect them to be doing. It should be noted, however, that as some jobs allow more leeway than others for individual differences, neophytes have the power either to conform to these expectations, to resist them or to comply with them only partially.

Individuals may not conform to role-set expectations for a variety of reasons. First, they may receive from role senders conflicting or contradictory expectations about how they are to perform, so that following the principal's expectations, for example, might mean violating important norms of a teaching team. Persons within the role set might hold diverse expectations among which the individual will have to choose, as new teachers have sometimes to choose between the faculty's various goals and those they were themselves taught at school. These examples of *intrarole* conflict illustrate conflicting demands which an individual acting in a single role cannot satisfy simultaneously.

Second, *interrole* conflict—conflict between roles—sometimes prevents individuals from conforming to expectations. Because most persons perform multiple roles within a school organization, the individual will often have to choose among the known expectations of different role sets. For example, an individual may simultaneously be a teacher, the head of a curriculum committee, a member of a planning committee, a representative of the teachers' association, and the faculty member to whom most students express their dissatisfaction about how the school is run. If this individual is firm about leaving an important curriculum meeting as early as 4:30, members of the committee may express disapproval, while to stay past 4:30 without special arrangement for overtime pay might elicit disapproval or even disciplinary action by the teachers' association.

A third obstacle arises when the role expectations held by others conflict with an individual's own values, perception of the facts, or professional orientation, when they seem merely uninteresting, or when they accumulate to a greater amount of work than the individual alone can discharge. This condition can come about when recruiters overemphasize the favorable aspects of a job and underplay its unfavorable aspects, when recruits interpret the recruiters' messages to suit their own needs, or when there is a strategy on the part of new teachers to change the expectations of others by redefining the role once they are in the school.

During one of our projects a role conflict emerged when an elementary school staff sought to redefine the role of the school counselor. The three teaching teams in the school presented three different sets of targets and action proposals for the counseling role, none of which appealed to the counselor who maintained that the role, goals, and strategies she had adopted were based on her training as a counselor and offered a more responsible and useful version than those presented by the teaching teams. Hurt and angry, she finally mustered supporters to defend the ways in which she was currently carrying out her functions.

The problem in this case was threefold. First, the goals that the various subgroups held for counseling were themselves in conflict. Second, at the district level the counselor was considered to be performing well and meeting the expectations of that part of her role set. Third, the counselor disapproved of the action proposals made by the teaching teams, believing that her graduate training had prepared her well for what she was doing, that the values articulated by the teaching teams were unimportant, and that the suggested new roles would not be personally fulfilling to her.

Role conflict is a common cause of school-wide conflict, bringing together organizational, interpersonal, and personal factors as the individual and role set try to find expectations that will be acceptable to all. If the expectations of new teachers conflict with those of others in the school, their own expectations are likely to go unfulfilled. As time elapses, neophyte teachers will either conform to the expectations of members of their role set, change these expectations, or create a great deal of tension within themselves and the school as well. If the conflict remains strong, they will usually move to another kind of job within the field or leave the field altogether.

Differences in Interpersonal Style. All participants bring to a school a unique set of needs and experiences, styles of coping with stress, and a rhythm for getting things done. At times these interpersonal styles can work against one another, creating friction and conflict that may destroy productive collaboration. Several strategies can be effective in reducing or resolving these differences. As the following example demonstrates, encouraging open feedback between the parties involved may suffice to alter work patterns or interpersonal behavior for the better.

During consultation with the staff of a school in which we were working, it became evident that, with one exception, all the teachers had developed highly collaborative and flexible team-teaching relationships, while one teacher remained closed off from collaboration with the rest. Uncomfortably aware of the others' anger, he nevertheless did not know how to change the situation. An exercise encouraging open feedback revealed that this man habitually responded to serious matters with a joke. No one ever got a straight answer from him, and many had become so frustrated that they had stopped trying to communicate with him altogether. Bringing this feedback to light enabled him to begin to change his behavior and opened an opportunity for future exchanges of feedback between him and the rest of the staff.

Another common strategy is to arrange the duties of contending individuals in such a way that they need communicate but seldom and then only in very precise and objective terms. When it is feasible, this method often works well enough in the short run, although in the long run the reduction of communication may only increase hostility and cause it to spill over into communication with others. Still another strategy is to capitalize on the different styles in order to transform conflict into a variety pool from which to extract complementary and mutually supportive styles that will strengthen the capacity of the group as a whole.

External Stress.   What school district in America has not been in conflict with groups of citizens over new bond issues, controversial curricula, or issues of school control? Although some external stress may be induced intentionally, as when militant groups strive to produce revolutionary change in a school district, some stress inevitably accompanies social change, and the demands made by external forces and groups often create conflict for the school.

Disagreements will arise within the school district over the methods to be used in coping with external demands and assuaging external pressure groups, while diverse inputs from the community that lead to increased differentiation within the district will not only increase tension in the school but exacerbate conflicts already in existence. Whatever its source, external stress usually cannot be much reduced or effectively controlled by action within the school organization or by the efforts of a unit of the district, even by the department of public relations.

Organizing for Conflict Management

Some conflicts are natural and inevitable and may even provide a creative tension that has the effect of improving school performance;

others, although not helpful to the school, are not so destructive as to require the services of an OD consultant. Still others, however, can significantly weaken a school's instructional program and for that reason should receive a consultant's attention.

As they uncover conflicts between role takers or units in the school, consultants should answer two questions. First, are the conflicting parties required to work together to accomplish an important mission for the district? A teacher in a school with self-contained classrooms, for example, is not required to work much with other teachers on matters of instruction; similarly, the faculty of a school may have little to do with some of the personnel of the central office. Second, how interdependent are the parties who must work together? If a great deal of collaboration is required among them, the consultant should work toward making any conflicts accessible to problem-solving processes.

Whether conflicts should be uncovered at all depends upon the nature of the tension that is present. Some tensions enhance productivity, motivate change, and improve organizational functioning. If these tensions can be reduced through clear communication or effective problem solving, uncovering conflict is likely to have constructive consequences. On the other hand, where tensions can be reduced only over a long period of time, uncovering conflict may have debilitating or even destructive effects.

The likelihood of a destructive outcome is greater when participants exhibit low readiness for dealing with conflict. A low level of communication skill can cause the issues in conflict to become increasingly confused. A low level of skill in problem solving can leave people who feel inadequate in dealing with conflict even more distant and alienated than before the conflict was uncovered. A low level of mutual trust among participants can have similar consequences, especially if the consultant fails to realize that lack of trust and openness is not always the result of ignorance or lack of skill but is sometimes a realistic attitude on the part of individuals. In this case, a participant who was invited by the consultant to state the conflict orally might be punished in some way by the others for doing so, in which case the level of trust would decline even more, defensiveness would increase, and the consultant would be in a poor position to help resolve other conflicts.

Uncovering conflict, then, involves a certain risk for the consultant and school participants alike. The staff's attitudes toward conflict, the existing degree of openness and trust, the staff's skill in communication and problem solving and its experience with conflict in the past are all indicators of whether the risk is worth taking.

In addition to exhibiting staff readiness, schools and districts should themselves be structured to manage conflicts productively. Lawrence and Lorsch (1967) suggest that relatively simple organizations like elementary schools need only a well articulated, overlapping hierarchy for managing conflicts but that more complex organizations such as school districts should have special formal structures alongside the regular managerial hierarchy for this purpose.

In our view, two very productive structures for managing conflict are the multiunit structure for elementary schools and the cadre of OD specialists for school districts.

How the multiunit school is organized to manage conflict has been described in Schmuck et al. (1975). The key to this structure is that it offers a communicative link between each hierarchical level and each formal subsystem. Thus, for example, the leadership team includes the principal who connects with the school's central office, while team leaders connect the leadership team with teachers and students. Everyone in the school knows someone who can communicate directly with the leadership team, and this arrangement permits direct managerial contact with those who may be in conflict. To be most effective, multiunit structures must have administrators who are not only competent at conflict management but who communicate accurately about mundane matters by means of memos and bulletins to forestall or resolve minor day-to-day disagreements.

As chapter 12 will document, our research and development activities have shown that a cadre of OD specialists can make a major contribution toward managing district-wide conflict. OD specialists in the Kent, Washington, and Eugene, Oregon, school districts have helped to manage conflicts at building and district levels while working as permanent parts of their district structures.* The Louisville, Kentucky public schools and the York County schools in the suburbs of Toronto have both had OD departments that function in part to manage conflict.

Derr (1971) found that one big-city school district, which relied on a highly differentiated hierarchy for managing conflicts, had ineffective coordination between subsystems. Little direct contact occurred between administrators to deal with differences, and those in positions of authority were perceived by many personnel as incompetent to handle conflict. Clearly, such a district could benefit from an internal cadre of organizational specialists.

Effective school districts should have persons who are skilled at working with conflict and should provide for direct contact between these persons and the contending parties. They should have in addition a well-coordinated hierarchy, an effective formal procedure for settling small disputes, and should build appropriate conflict-management components—such as roles, teams, and departments, depending upon the degree of differentiation—into the fabric of the district.

GATHERING DATA ABOUT CONFLICT

Uncovering Conflicts. Collecting data through questionnaires, interviews, observations, or preferably some combination of all three and checking their validity by feeding them back to participants are

---

*See Arends and Phelps (1973) and Runkel, Wyant, and Bell (1975).

highly effective methods for uncovering organizational, group, and interpersonal conflicts in schools. While data should be collected in a formal systematic manner, it is not always important that they give a complete or balanced picture of the school; in some instances the only data necessary are those that allow the consultant to produce a picture of significant disagreements.

In giving data feedback the consultant should include interesting quotations from interviews together with tables of quantitative data derived from questionnaires, interviews, or observations. Participants will tell whether the data are correct and whether they agree with the weight the consultant is attaching to them. Data feedback may in itself engender meaningful conflicts that will help to move the consultation along, while the interaction that occurs within the representative group may mirror organizational conflicts that can be discussed at once. The following excerpt from Derr (1970) illustrates how one team of OD consultants used data feedback to uncover conflicts in a large urban school district.*

Following the organizational diagnosis, data feedback meetings were held with all department heads and other representatives (1) to confirm the . . . diagnosis and (2) try to obtain some group consensus about alternatives for improving the system. The use of the laboratory method or group dynamics enabled the MIT team to maximize participation and information exchange from those who attended the workshop. . . . The diagnosis was confirmed. In addition, it became obvious from observing the group that the sharing of information was a major issue (with whom and how much), that the norms of the system made it very difficult to disagree, that reverting to "professional standards" was a way to escape from and detour confrontive issues, and that official communication prior to the sessions themselves had been almost nonexistent, as some participants met others for the first time at the data feedback sessions.

Friday

We met briefly as a larger group of sixteen and four consultants (us). We divided into two small groups of eight plus two consultants and held meetings in two separate places. . . . One of the consultants led the discussion and fed back data while the other consultant processed the discussion. Four conclusions from the data were fed back and discussed:

1. *The departments are unsure about whether or not other departments both inside and outside of Special Services know what they do.*
2. *There appears to be too little vertical and horizontal communication. What interdepartmental communication there*

---

*This excerpt from C. Brooklyn Derr, 1970, Organizational development in one large urban school system, is reprinted from *Education and Urban Society* 2:403–19 by permission of Sage Publications.

is is done informally and in different degrees. Communication is more folkway (social) than formal.

3. *There appears to be a problem with trading information between departments. Some departments seem to hoard information and some, while willing to give it, have logistics problems.*

4. *The principal seems to have a key role in how Special Services programs really work in his building. His role is often confused, and sometimes he refuses to work with the SS people.*

The groups were asked to select three people whose purpose it was to summarize for the whole group what went on in each small group. This part of the design was to integrate smaller groups back into the larger group. The six representatives chosen from the two small groups, together with two consultants, took part in a fishbowl and talked about what had happened in the small groups. It was apparent that one group had refused to recognize that any of the problems really existed and the other group had seen the feedback data as being essentially correct. The central question arose: Why did our groups react so differently? One consultant then offered an analysis of the processes he saw going on in the working group of reporters and summarized. A decision was made by the whole group to hold a meeting on Monday.

Monday

The whole group began working in conjunction by having a consultant list on the board the "real" problems in Special Services as perceived by various group members volunteering their thoughts. These problems were followed by an open discussion of possible solutions. The consultants processed the meeting and helped bring out some of the basic differences between participants. The whole group then agreed on recommendations for a different form of organization for Special Services. They agreed that there should be more opportunities to relate as they had done during the workshop.

It was agreed that the consultants should draft a report which incorporated the thinking of the workshop participants and that this report would then be read and discussed by the participants at a future meeting.

Evaluating Collaborative Relationships. Conflicts can also be uncovered by asking school members to identify the quality of collaborative relationships among them. A questionnaire item (from Lawrence and Lorsch 1967) is cited below.

We would like to know about relationships that exist between various units in your organization.

Listed below are eight descriptive statements. Each of these might be thought of as describing the *general state of the relationship* between the various units. We would like you to select that statement which you feel is most descriptive of each of the relationships shown on the grid and to enter the corresponding number in the appropriate square.

We realize you may not be directly involved in all of the possible relationships about which you are being asked. However, you probably have impressions about those relationships. We are, therefore, asking that you complete all of the boxes in the grid—that is, put a number corresponding to a statement in each box. Relations between these two units are:

1. Sound—a fully sound relationship is achieved
2. Almost full relationship
3. Somewhat better than average relations
4. Average—sound enough to get by even though there are many problems of achieving joint effort
5. Somewhat of a breakdown in relations
6. Almost complete breakdown in relations
7. Couldn't be worse—bad relations—serious problems exist which are not being used
8. Relations are not required

3-4th grade team	1-2d grade team	Leadership team	Principal	
				5-6th grade team
				3-4th grade team
				1-2d grade team
				Leadership team

The same sort of grid might be compared in other ways. For example, the names of individuals might be used if one is concerned about interpersonal relationships within a unit with high interdependence, or the titles of groups both within and outside the school might be used to study possible conflicts between the school and the district office.

Ascertaining Interdependence. To determine the importance of conflicts to the school, information is needed on the degree to which conflicting parties must work together to accomplish educational tasks. (Even serious conflicts may not need attention if they arise between relatively autonomous parties.) The following questionnaire adapted from Lawrence and Lorsch (1967) gives examples of items that help to determine the amount of interdependence required by various units in an elementary school.

Questionnaire for Opinions about Others' Interdependence
We are interested in the degree of coordination which is required between the various units in your school.

1. Make an X by the statement that most nearly describes the extent to which the principal is able to carry out his or her job and make changes in it without having to bring others into the decision.

- The principal is able to choose his or her own job activities:
  - (   ) to an extreme extent
  - (   ) to a very great extent
  - (   ) to a considerable extent
  - (   ) to some extent
  - (   ) to a small extent
  - (   ) to a very little extent
  - (   ) not at all

- How about the first-grade team? They are able to choose their own job activities:
  - (   ) to an extreme extent
  - (   ) to a very great extent, etc.

- The second grade team? Its members are able to choose their own job activities:
  - (   ) to an extreme extent
  - (   ) to a very great extent, etc.

It is possible to continue with all the various grade levels until the same question has been asked of all of them. Afterwards the questioner might move to other major working groups:

- The leadership team (principal and team leaders):
  - (   ) to an extreme extent
  - (   ) to a very great extent, etc.

- The counselor:
  - (   ) to an extreme extent
  - (   ) to a very great extent, etc.

2. Make an X by the statement which most nearly describes the extent to which the principal is influenced by:

- The work of the first-grade team (or second or third, etc.):
  - (   ) to an extreme extent
  - (   ) to a very great extent, etc.

- The work of the leadership team:
  ( ) to an extreme extent
  ( ) to a very great extent, etc.
- The work of those in the central office:
  ( ) to an extreme extent
  ( ) to a very great extent, etc.
- Actions of community groups:
  ( ) to an extreme extent
  ( ) to a very great extent, etc.
- Actions of parents:
  ( ) to an extreme extent
  ( ) to a very great extent, etc.
- Actions of consultants and university persons:
  ( ) to an extreme extent
  ( ) to a very great extent, etc.
- Actions of professional associations and groups:
  ( ) to an extreme extent
  ( ) to a very great extent, etc.

The rest of the questionnaire will be abbreviated to present general ideas about the kinds of questions that are asked. It is possible in every case to ask a similar question for any particular group.

3. Make an X by the statement which most nearly describes the extent to which the various teams are influenced by:
- The work of other teams:
  ( ) to an extreme extent
  ( ) to a very great extent, etc.
- The work of the leadership team:
  ( ) to an extreme extent
  ( ) to a very great extent, etc.

4. Make an X by the statement which most nearly describes the extent to which the leadership team is influenced by:
- The work of the principal:
  ( ) to an extreme extent
  ( ) to a very great extent, etc.
- The work of those in the central office:
  ( ) to an extreme extent
  ( ) to a very great extent, etc.

An interview schedule also can be used to identify interdependencies as follows:

Interview about Own Interdependence with Others
[To interviewer: read words in parentheses only if necessary for clarity. Do not read words in brackets; they are instructions to you.]

1. To achieve the school's goals, is it necessary for you to work closely with others? [yes, no] [If yes,] which people? [Try to get names.]

   _____

2. Are there any important things that you do in the classroom (things important to you) that you think run counter to the school's goals? [yes, no] [If yes,] what things are those?

   _____

3. [If yes on item 2:] In achieving these personal interests in your classroom, is it necessary for you to work closely with any others? [yes, no] [If yes,] what people work closely with you?

   _____

4. Upon whom, inside or outside your school (not students), do you depend most to perform your job effectively?

   _____

5. [Taking each name separately:] Does [name] work closely with you? [Circle each name working closely.]

   _____

6. Now I want to ask you about the sorts of help you get from these people [taking each name separately:] What is the chief kind of help

   that _____ gives you?
   that _____ gives you?
   that _____ gives you?
   that _____ gives you?

Finally, the questionnaire below can be used to measure interdependence in the organization.

Questionnaire about Own Interdependence with Others
Please circle the response that best describes your job:
   5 = *very* characteristic of the job
   4 = *quite* characteristic of the job
   3 = *moderately* or *fairly* characteristic of the job
   2 = *not very* characteristic of the job
   1 = *not at all* characteristic of the job
   NA = does not apply or don't know

1. Other people have to come to
   me for decisions. 5 4 3 2 1 NA
2. On my job I meet pretty often
   with my boss. 5 4 3 2 1 NA

3. On my job I meet pretty often
with my subordinates.　　　　5　4　3　2　1　NA

4. On my job I am expected to
help other people.　　　　　5　4　3　2　1　NA

5. If I have to get help from someone, it's an indication I can't
do the work well.　　　　　5　4　3　2　1　NA

6. My job requires a good deal of
cooperation from others.　　5　4　3　2　1　NA

7. On my job I have to interact
with a lot of other people.　5　4　3　2　1　NA

8. My job depends on how well
others do their work.　　　5　4　3　2　1　NA

9. On this job (assignment) you
get to know other people
really well.　　　　　　　5　4　3　2　1　NA

10. I work amost exclusively with
other people.　　　　　　5　4　3　2　1　NA

11. I am frequently in contact with
other people.　　　　　　5　4　3　2　1　NA,

12. My ability to influence others
has to be used on this job.　5　4　3　2　1　NA

13. I spend most of my time
managing people.　　　　5　4　3　2　1　NA

Measuring Organizational Climate. In determining a school's readiness to deal with conflict it is important to know whether the organizational climate supports open confrontation of differences, receiving and giving feedback, and generally fosters an atmosphere of two-way interaction and discussion. Several questionnaires are useful for assessing these characteristics. One of these, entitled "Do's and Don'ts," was presented in chapter 3 and is described in greater detail in Fox et al. (1973). The following questionnaire also helps to ascertain informal norms or an organizational climate that can help or hinder staff members in uncovering and working with conflict.

Organizational Norms

1. Suppose Teacher X feels hurt and "put down" by something another teacher has said to him. In Teacher X's place, would most of the teachers you know in your school be likely to . . .
. . . tell the other teacher that they felt hurt and put down?

       (　) Yes, I think most would.
       (　) Maybe about half would.
       (　) No, most would *not.*
       (　) I don't know.

2. . . . tell their friends that the other teacher is hard to get along with?

      (   ) Yes, I think most would do this.
      (   ) Maybe about half would do this.
      (   ) No, most would *not.*
      (   ) I don't know.

3. Suppose Teacher X strongly disagrees with something B says at a staff meeting. In Teacher X's place, would most of the teachers you know in your school . . .
   . . . seek out B to discuss the disagreement?
      (   ) Yes, I think most would do this.
      (   ) Maybe about half would do this.
      (   ) No, most would *not.*
      (   ) I don't know.

4. . . . keep it to themselves and say nothing about it?
      (   ) Yes, I think most would do this.
      (   ) Maybe about half would do this.
      (   ) No, most would *not.*
      (   ) I don't know.

5. Suppose Teacher X were present when two others got into a hot argument about how the school is run. Suppose Teacher X tried to help each one understand the view of the other. How would you feel about the behavior of Teacher X?
      (   ) I would approve strongly.
      (   ) I would approve mildly or some.
      (   ) I wouldn't care one way or the other.
      (   ) I would disapprove mildly or some.
      (   ) I would disapprove strongly.

6. Suppose Teacher X were present when two others got into a hot argument about how the school is run. And suppose Teacher X tried to get them to quiet down and stop arguing. How would you feel about the behavior of Teacher X?
      (   ) I would approve strongly.
      (   ) I would approve mildly or some.
      (   ) I wouldn't care one way or the other.
      (   ) I would disapprove mildly or some.
      (   ) I would disapprove strongly.

7. Suppose you are in a committee meeting with Teacher X and the other members begin to describe their personal feelings about what goes on in the school. Teacher X quickly suggests that the committee get back to the topic and keep the discussion objective and impersonal. How would you feel toward Teacher X?
      (   ) I would approve strongly.
      (   ) I would approve mildly or some.
      (   ) I wouldn't care one way or the other.
      (   ) I would disapprove mildly or some.
      (   ) I would disapprove strongly.

8. Suppose you are in a committee meeting with Teacher X and the other members begin to describe their personal feelings about what goes on in the school. Teacher X listens to them

but does not describe his own feelings. How would you feel toward Teacher X?

(   ) I would approve strongly.
(   ) I would approve mildly or some.
(   ) I wouldn't care one way or the other.
(   ) I would disapprove mildly or some.
(   ) I would disapprove strongly.

Determining the Seriousness of Conflict. The consultant should attempt objectively to measure the seriousness of a dispute by asking participants, for example, to choose the position on the following scale that represents their perceptions of its seriousness:

1. Not at all serious
2. Not serious
3. Average
4. Serious
5. Very serious

A similar scale could be used to ascertain whether the conflict breeds creative or destructive tensions;

1. Makes me work much better
2. Offers encouraging competition
3. Doesn't affect me
4. Prevents me from being as effective as I could be
5. Is destroying our working relationships

Using an interview method, the consultant can gain a sense of the degree of conflict by asking participants to describe the worst thing that could happen if the conflict were worked on openly. Later, when resolution proposals are being presented, those opposed to particular proposals can be asked to describe their worst fantasies of what would happen if the proposals were undertaken.

Exercises on Conflict. The following four exercises are especially effective for uncovering conflicts, bringing them into the open, and working with them once they are public and shared.

The *Influence Line* is particularly useful when the consultant suspects that certain staff members are engaged in a power struggle. Participants are asked to line up according to their own perceptions of who is most influential (first) to who is least influential (last). How they line up and their behaviors and expressions while doing so constitute important information for the consultant; how they decide who should be placed where in the line offers data for later discussion. During the debriefing that follows the exercise, the data are presented and attempts are made to work through the conflicts that surface.

Hand Mirroring, described in chapter 8 in relation to its power motif, aims here at uncovering tensions that arise as a result of different leadership styles between partners. If, for example, one partner refuses to be led by the other, ask whether one is the other's boss or whether one feels that the other is a peer and not a figure of leadership authority. Whatever occurs during the exercise, the dyads should be asked to discuss whether they see any leadership struggles within their school. If feelings of trust and high involvement are present, they should be asked to talk about their own working relationship within the school.

The *Five-Square puzzle* described in chapter 3 can also be used to help a small, highly interdependent educational team talk about interpersonal conflict. During the debriefing, participants are asked to discuss whether there were any indications of conflict during the exercise and, whatever the answer, whether this was typical of how the group normally works. The participants are then pressed to give behavior and feeling descriptions in relation to interpersonal conflict within the team.

The *Planners and Operators exercise* described in chapter 8 can here be employed to uncover disagreements between superiors and subordinates in the school organization. Roles can be reversed—i.e., school superiors act as the operators for the exercise and subordinates act as the planners—to illustrate that such disputes are more often a result of conflicting roles and functions than of the personalities involved, or roles can be maintained to reveal how superiors actually deal with subordinates in the school. When this exercise is used to stimulate discussion of school-wide conflict, the consultant should take particular care during the debriefing period to see to it that observed conflicts are reported, that their relevance to the organizational life of school participants is clarified, and that the training includes further opportunities for dealing with the conflicts.

PROCEDURES FOR MANAGING CONFLICT

The procedures introduced in this section are designed to serve a variety of ends related to conflict management. These include uncovering conflicting expectations between individuals and their role sets, managing role conflicts, reducing individual conflicts and other disagreements, bringing subsystem differences into the open, testing the intensity of conflicts and obtaining a quick resolution of those that are easily resolvable, causing perceptions to be verbalized in order to dispel misperceptions and manage real differences, and suggesting structural changes for the effective management of school-wide conflicts.

Checking Expectations. This procedure is designed to reveal discrepancies between the expectations of individuals and their role set. Focal individuals are asked to write what they expect to be doing in their jobs in one year, five years, and ten years. Members of their role set are asked to write their expectations of what the focal persons should do to make the organization more effective. Consultants may then collate the data and feed them back to the participants to reveal any discrepancies between the two; or the parties can be grouped together to read their expectations aloud—the focal individuals first and the others second—and then react together to the discrepancies revealed. This procedure may also be used when two parties have differing expectations of the role of a third party.

Conflict Resolution Scale. This exercise helps to determine the seriousness of a disagreement and to resolve it quickly if it is not serious. Two parties who are in conflict over a specific issue are asked to rate the intensity of their sentiments on a scale from one to ten. If one party feels strongly and other does not—that is, if one marks a five on the scale and the other a nine—the conflict is resolved in favor of the stronger feeling. If both parties feel equally intense, they must debate the difference until they agree or at least reach a compromise. If both parties are very intense, the conflict between them may be serious and probably cannot be quickly resolved.

Imaging. Because it sets the stage for future problem-solving sessions and provides a good setting for the introduction of communication skills, Imaging can be the introductory activity in a sequence of training events. Depending upon the number of groups involved, Imaging typically requires a day and a half to two days. If more than two groups are involved it is best to work with them sequentially in pairs until all the combinations have had a chance to meet.

In introducing this procedure it should be emphasized that its purpose is to identify both the character of the relationship between the two groups and the problems that are contributing to their conflict. Participants are grouped into circles of six to eight persons with each group represented in each circle; the skills of paraphrasing and behavior description are introduced, and all participants practice them with the others in their circle.

The two groups are then given a two-part assignment. Each group is to meet separately to develop a descriptive image, both favorable and unfavorable, of itself and of the other group based on observed behaviors. These images are to be recorded on newsprint with two pages for each group—one page favorable, the other unfavorable—and the groups are to share these images when they reconvene. As participants develop the images, one or two consultants work with each group, encouraging it to focus on its relationship with the other group and to find behavioral examples that verify their images, reminding members that the newsprint sheets will be shown to the other group later.

When the images are completed, the two groups reconvene, post their sheets of newsprint, and share their images with the total group. Members of the group being described sit in a circle with members of the other group surrounding them. Someone in the outer group reads a behavior description, and a member of the inner group paraphrases. The members take turns, and when one group has finished, the groups exchange places and repeat the process. Vocal defensiveness is discouraged throughout this phase, and the groups are urged to paraphrase to be certain the images are clearly sent and received.

Next the two groups are again divided into several circles of six to eight people to review and practice the skills of checking one's perceptions of another's feelings and describing one's own feelings. The two groups are again asked to meet separately to accept the feedback they have been given and to recall examples of their behavior that support the favorable and unfavorable impressions of the other group.

When this task is completed, the groups reconvene to share behavioral evidence with the total group. Inner and outer circles are used as before, and participants are urged to use communication skills. The inner circle contains an empty chair for outer-circle participants who want more information from the inner circle. As their admission ticket, they must describe their perception of the present feeling of someone in the inner circle and ask for a check of this perception. Only after their perception has been verified or corrected may they ask their question or make a contribution.

After the evidence supporting the opposing group's impressions has been shared by each group, the two groups can work jointly with the consultants to identify the issues that require further examination, discussion, or resolution. This may be followed by a commitment to meet again to work on specific problem areas, or representatives may wish to consult with their constituents before making any agreements. Although it is unlikely that Imaging will bring about a complete resolution of existing differences, it does set the stage for future problem-solving sessions which, if they are carried out in good faith, can lead to increased trust and the development of a more collaborative relationship.

Confrontation Meeting.*   Primarily a goal-setting activity, the confrontation meeting offers three advantages for conflict management. First, the procedure works only when the system is experiencing stress because, as Beckhard (1969) suggests, "The energy present when the system is under stress is the energy needed to make the confrontation meeting work." Second, the procedure involves top management in a realistic way; any conflicts that arise can be examined within actual working relationships. Third, by bringing working groups together, the confrontation meeting increases the likelihood that any intergroup conflicts among them may be revealed.

Role Negotiation.   Assuming that most school participants prefer a fairly negotiated settlement to a state of unresolved conflict and that bargaining and negotiation are viable methods for helping adversaries change their behaviors, it is possible to help resolve role conflicts through role negotiation.

*See chap. 4 for a description of Beckhard's goal-confrontation procedure.

In this procedure, participants are asked to write three lists noting which actions the other person should increase in quantity and quality, which should be decreased in quantity, and which are helpful and should not be changed. Having collated these data, participants are allowed to question those who have sent messages but not to argue about the information received. "Communication is controlled in order to prevent escalation of actual or potential conflicts" (Harrison 1970). It is important at this stage to prevent the occurrence of any hostile, hurtful, or defensive emotional expressions.

When the messages are clearly understood, both sides choose issues to negotiate, each prepared to offer the other something of equal value in return for a desired behavior change. A list of negotiable issues can be compiled by asking each side to state its issue priorities, rank-ordering the items from most to least important (ordering the agenda is itself a negotiable issue); the items are then discussed in the order of preference. The negotiation takes the form of an exchange: If A does _____, B will do _____ in return. When all parties are satisfied that they will receive a reasonable return for what they are giving, the negotiation on one issue comes to an end, the agreement is recorded in writing, and another issue is negotiated.

Interpersonal Feedback. Interpersonal feedback is an important process for resolving conflicts that arise from differences in interpersonal style. Feedback refers to information that informs its recipient how close his behavior is to achieving its desired effect. Feedback must give information about progress toward a goal defined by the recipient, and it will not be effective unless the recipient specifically requests it. The following technique is designed to give recipients maximum control over the responsibility of requesting the feedback they are offered.

As the procedure begins, all participants list on newsprint which of their own personal behaviors they regard as strengths or weaknesses, or as helpful or unhelpful, in relation to their work situation. The lists are posted on the walls, and participants mill around reading them, adding additional helpful or unhelpful behaviors wherever appropriate. In this fashion all participants end with a list of their own helpful or unhelpful behaviors as others see them, and they then take time to read and think about this feedback.

Next the consultant explains that there are three options from which each individual may choose in deciding how best to make use of feedback. First, individuals may choose to consider their feedback personally to see whether any of the information will be useful to them for future behavioral change. (If everyone chooses this option, there will be no need to discuss others in the group context.) Second, an individual may request clarification from others if the feedback is unclear, insufficiently specific, or inadequately informative about others' perceptions. In the latter case, participants may ask which of their behaviors led to a given perception or may request a specific example of when a particular behavior occurred. In addition, a person may want opinions about feedback received from one or two others.

When participants choose to ask for clarification, it is their responsibility to initiate the request and to be clear about precisely what information they want from whom. A third option allows participants to contract for future feedback about a particular behavior if they believe they could benefit from knowing what was creating a particular perception of their behavior when that behavior was occurring. This is a useful technique for helping persons change behavior of which they are unaware and for clearing up interpersonal misunderstandings on the spot.

Throughout this process the consultant's role is to clarify and facilitate communication. When one person asks another for clarification, for example, the consultant may help the former to state the request clearly and ask the latter to paraphrase it. When the clarification is provided, the recipient might be asked to paraphrase it, to describe specific instances when such behavior occurred, or to check whether others agree that the behavior in question occurred in these instances.

Consultants should also be concerned with the group's emotional climate during this procedure. Realizing that people might be sensitive to feedback about unhelpful behaviors, they should intervene to ensure that it is given clearly, constructively, and attributes neither good nor bad intentions to the recipient. Consultants should be aware, too, of each person's level of receptivity to the feedback and should intervene to regulate the process if too much feedback is given at one time.

Third-party Consultants. To use third parties as consultants to individuals or groups in conflict, the district makes available to its members a list of organizational specialists who are qualified to play this role. When a conflict develops that they believe will be difficult to resolve, or when they deal with a conflict but are unable to resolve their differences, they can call on one of these specialists for help. The following excerpt from Walton (1969) tells how a third-party consultant helped some persons manage interpersonal conflict in an industrial organization. The example is easily related to school organizations.

> When Dave [the third party] did participate, he suggested that the interchange could be characterized as a negotiation, with Lloyd in effect saying, "Here are my needs or requests, which must be given due consideration if my staff is going to continue to contribute to [the organization]." Dave sharpened the three issues which Lloyd had put on the agenda, first citing Lloyd's view and then describing what he heard as Bill's answer. . . . After some further discussion of these points, they identified other areas of concern which were probably more basic to the conflict. . . .
>
> The outcome of the session was to schedule a meeting of both groups to review the work and to further explore how they could and should work together. . . . As the session con-

cluded, Bill expressed satisfaction with the meeting, indicating that he felt there was more understanding. Dave asked to meet with each person to discuss the meeting and to determine whether he would be of any further help. Both agreed that this was desirable.

The two [in conflict] had styles and skills that increased the likelihood of a successful confrontation. Although Lloyd often appeared dominating in interpersonal discussion, and although he sometimes resisted more personal interpretations of his own behavior, he had a directness and strength that was consistent with direct interpersonal confrontation. For Bill's part, his general skill at understanding the interpersonal process made him better able not only to hear Lloyd out, but also to challenge the latter's occasional domineering manner.

The third party performed a diagnostic function during and after the confrontation. He listened to each of the disputants discuss his views and feelings, and sharpened what he understood to be an issue, to which the participants responded in ways which tended to confirm or disprove that this was the underlying issue. An effort was made to state these issues in ways which made each person's position understandable, legitimate, and acceptable. One apparent effect of this understanding, legitimating, and sharpening of issues was to encourage Lloyd then to identify the more personal concerns he had about not being recognized as a competent person. . . .

The third party chose to play what he regarded as a minor role in regulating the process. Essentially, he let the parties run on their own. For example, he waited for Bill to deal first with the way Lloyd was dominating the discussion. Thus, he believed that the two parties had an opportunity to reveal or develop their own interaction equilibrium. Nevertheless, Lloyd attributed an active role to Dave. After reading this report he said:

"I believe the report understates Dave's effect as a third party and casts him more outside the process than I experienced him. Both his presence and his active, constructive participation influenced the process. For example, he turned me off once when I was getting long-winded, reminding me of the need to listen. When you hear something from a third party who doesn't have an investment in the issue at stake, you are more likely to respond to that advice, especially if it is given to you in a timely way on the spot. . . . In sum, for me, he was not only a catalytic agent, but also an ingredient in the situation" (pp. 22-24).

Structural Changes. An appropriate organizational structure is needed to resolve conflicts arising from differentiation. In particular, those in the upper echelons of the hierarchy should have direct contact with subordinates to work out their disagreements together. In highly differentiated organizations that require a complex articulated structure, cadres of OD specialists who are specially trained to manage conflicts and facilitate group processes may be important in achieving integration. Depending on how badly they are needed, some cadres will work full-time as members of a consultative department designated for this purpose; in other cases, cadre members may perform the function on a part-time or temporary basis as in our projects in Kent, Washington, and Eugene, Oregon.

We have also found that too much structural integration within a school can create tensions and conflicts, especially when the philosophies and instructional styles of faculty members are highly varied. In such schools, conflict may successfully be managed by allowing for planned pluralism or school structures in which there are several teams, houses within schools, even schools within schools. During the past decade we have observed a number of school plants that have within them several different structures for carrying out effective instructional programs. For schools that are seeking the qualities of self-renewal, deliberately decreasing interdependence and increasing differentiation is sometimes the best path to follow.

MICRODESIGNS FOR MANAGING CONFLICT

The purpose of this section is to suggest possible intervention strategies for resolving problems common to school organizations. When a conflict arises between two interdependent coworkers, determine whether the difference can be quickly resolved by using the communication skills described in chapter 3, since much of what appears to be interpersonal conflict can be due to miscommunication. If value or strategy differences are uncovered, test the intensity of the conflict by using a device like the Conflict Resolution Scale. If the conflict cannot be resolved by one person acceding to the stronger feelings of another, try methods of negotiation, bargaining, and compromise. A third-party consultant can be used to sharpen the conflicting issues and help the coworkers proceed through the role negotiation procedure. Finally, decreasing their interdependence should be formally agreed upon and tested for a defined period of time. The third-party consultant should later review how the relationship is going.

The Imaging procedure is most useful for uncovering and working with conflicts between interacting groups such as teaching teams or the district office and teachers' associations. In one very effective consultation we used this procedure to help bring parents and the educators at an elementary school into collaborative problem solving and decision making. Before a seven-hour meeting at which the parents and educators moved through most of the steps of the Imaging procedure, each group received training in communication skills. After this, each group offered its images of the helpful or unhelpful things that members of the other group were doing in relation to the school program.

At the meeting itself, six steps were followed: (1) verifying the images, (2) presenting the images, (3) identifying behaviors, (4) sharing the behaviors, (5) determining issues for problem solving, and (6) identifying the key problem for future work and forming problem-solving groups. In step 1, each group examined lists of cross-group images made out by the consultants and modified these images until they found their own list acceptable. In step 2, the two groups were brought together within a highly structured format to share their lists. In step 3, the two groups spent an hour separately describing examples of their own behaviors that might have contributed to the other group's image of them. In step 4, the two groups met to share the behaviors they had each listed during step 3. This stage completed a round of generating and validating factual data, and the participants were ready to move on to identifying targets.

In step 5, the consultant presented a tentative summary of the kinds of targets that parents and staff had been advocating. Then the participants divided into groups to list issues for problem solving, making use of the consultant's summary and their own ideas as well. Finally, in step 6, a list of seven major issues for collaborative problem solving was developed at a general meeting. For the next several months seven problem-solving groups composed of five to eight parents and one or two staff members met for five three-hour sessions each. Each group spent time carefully identifying its problem, considering the forces that prevented finding solutions, and locating resources that might be brought to bear. The problem-solving steps they followed are described in detail in chapter 7.

Although we have had little experience in managing conflicts with teachers' unions or rioting students, we believe that many of the procedures already described can be useful for dealing with such power struggles. We also think that a consultative design of multiple partisanship—in which the consulting staff divides according to its central involvements with particular clients—could be useful and should be researched. For other relevant suggestions, see McGrath's work (1970) on negotiations, and Chesler and Lohman (1971) on dealing with angry students.

READINGS

The Inevitability of Pain

Philip J. Runkel

In this article, Runkel argues that practitioners of organization development and practicing school people alike should forego the promise or hope that OD consultation will erase the personal pains ordinarily encountered in organizational life.

Reprinted from J. William Pfeiffer and John E. Jones (Eds.), *The 1974 Annual Handbook for Group Facilitators*. La Jolla, Calif.: University Associates, 1974. Used with permission.

Increasing the Profit of Pain

Despite the fact that we probably cannot reduce by much the total amount of pain with which we must cope, we can do a great deal to increase the profit we get from our pains. Much of our pain— certainly most of our psychological pain—is pain we give each other, and it is within our power to redistribute the occasions upon which pain arises. We can, through explicit agreement about responsibilities and the careful practice of new sorts of collaboration, share more equally the burden of pain. More than that, we can deliberatively and collaboratively choose the *purposes* for which we shall expose ourselves to pain, instead of finding ourselves ambushed by pain dumped on us by others; we can agree with our colleagues on what we hope to purchase with our pain.

To give a commonplace example, we can buy greater satisfaction in the work we do with our colleagues if we are willing to pay the cost in admitting to certain ineptitudes, learning some new role patterns, and persevering in the face of rebuffs. On the other hand, we can avoid risk, rebuff, and stumbling relearning if we are willing to pay the price in joyless work and in shrivelling withdrawal from our colleagues.

In short, we can often purchase longer-lasting satisfactions with shared pain than we can usually buy with hidden pain. Finally, once the necessity for honest pain is openly agreed upon, and once the risk is jointly undertaken with colleagues, we can learn that pain need not be seen as shameful and that it need not cripple action.

What OD can do is to move pain from one occasion to another and from one person to another. This is no small achievement. Our society is built to concentrate pain on certain segments of society and in certain behavior settings. Medical and psychological treatment is much more available to the rich than to the poor. The president's chair is more softly padded than the clerk's.

Necessity of Pain

Without saying very much about it, we all recognize the fact that the conduct of human business must cause pain among those who carry it on. In any large-scale engineering project such as erecting a building, a bridge, or a dam, it is taken for granted by the engineers that a certain number of people will be crippled and a certain number will die. When a large engineering project is completed without a death, engineers congratulate one another. When a stretch of highway is built, it is built with the firm knowledge of all concerned that some of the workmen will be hurt; beyond that, all know that the highway will soon be stained with the blood of some of its users.

People enter the profession of medicine with the sure knowledge that a certain number of them must catch the diseases of their patients. People enter business schools and go into high-pressure occupations under the known risk of psychosomatic ailments and various neuroses. Schools are built with the sure knowledge that those who "fail" in them will be psychologically damaged and marked for life.

Inappropriate Pain

We expect people to encounter pain and damage of certain sorts in certain places: miners in mines, executives in meetings, students in classrooms, spouses in families, motorists on the highways, and soldiers in war. But we do not expect that executives will suffer from cave-ins, spouses from failures on examinations, students from shrapnel wounds, or miners from psychosomatic ulcers; and when they do, we feel that something has gone awry. We are especially likely to be outraged, in brief, when a certain kind of pain occurs in an unaccustomed setting.

What OD Can Do

Organization development alters the settings in which pains appear and the persons upon whom they descend. Furthermore, OD raises questions about the propriety of the previously existing *distribution* of pain. Beyond that, it challenges the old ways of *coping* with pain.

When undertaking to change the distribution of pain and and the ways of coping with it, OD begins with what may be the hardest lesson of all; it begins by asking participants to expose their personal pains in the work group. This in itself, if only because it violates existing norms, is painful. Describing personal pains requires the participants to consider explicity both in words and actions what sort of pain is being paid for what sort of gain, and by whom. Significant OD cannot occur except through this step.

Another way to say all this is that OD does not and cannot merely "improve" organizations in the sense of making the wheels turn a little more quietly. It cannot leave organizations unchanged in their structure or norms and still make them "better."

Practitioners of OD are sometimes challenged (and properly) on the point of whether they are merely making life more comfortable for the bosses—merely giving management still more subtle ways to keep employees pacified. To the extent that practitioners go through superficial motions—such as arranging meetings where the employees are allowed to talk but where pains are not allowed to be shown—the charge is accurate.

Change—Cost and Reward

To the extent that members of the organization are enabled to uncover their reciprocal human resources, despite the risk of exposing the long resentment of an unproductive task or the grief of revealing a talent long wasted, the work will get done more surely. It will bring deeper satisfactions to workers—but only at a cost, if cost it is, of new relations and a new sharing of duties and powers between workers and bosses.

If the worker is to put "more of himself" into his work, he can do so only by finding satisfactions for more of his needs. This deeper transformation of the individual's relation to his work can occur only if it is supported by a corresponding transformation in the norms and processes of the organization.

This deeper transformation puts inevitable stresses on the old ways by which members of organizations have adapted themselves to organizational life. The change will inevitably be painful. And after the change, many people will find themselves facing new pains in new places.

Organization development, if effective, will not merely "improve" organizations—it will change them. It will produce new kinds of behavior settings, new kinds of norms, new potentialities, a new scope for achievement. The new way of life, the new collaboration, the new sharing of achievement and defeat, of joy and sorrow, will be exhilarating and fulfilling beyond what most people have known. But the new way will not be placid nor will it arrive comfortably; its price will be the acceptance of pain in unaccustomed places and the effort of learning to use pain in new ways.

Contrasting Views of Hostility in Groups
Cyril R. Mill

Social Change, the newsletter of the NTL Institute for Applied Behavioral Science, offers many useful ideas, strategies, and techniques for the OD consultant. Following are two complementary articles about group hostility that coach the consultant in very different ways. Mill's contribution should be read first.

Reproduced by special permission from *Social Change: Ideas and Applications.* "Working with Hostile Groups," by Cyril R. Mill, Volume 4, No. 1, NTL Institute, 1974, pp. 1-7.

Laboratory trainers and consultants are increasingly confronted by hostile groups. Every trainer encounters hostility from time to time, but he or she need not meet it unprepared. I raised this issue with several colleagues and we discussed various strategies for building a positive group climate. It is with the hope that our cumulative experiences will benefit others who face hostility and resistance that this paper is presented.

Sources of Hostility
The hostility referred to here may arise from many sources, chief of which is involuntary attendance at the training session. It is safe to

say that during the first decade or so of laboratory training nearly all participants came of their own free choice. This is still largely true of open laboratories offered to the public. The occasional presence of a participant who is sent by an employer, perhaps to get him "straightened out" or as a necessary step toward promotion, does not usually significantly affect the total climate of the laboratory. The hostility referred to in this paper is more pervasive. My concern is groups with so many hostile members that acceptance is a major initial issue for their trainers if any learning is to occur. Such a condition is more likely to be exhibited in a private training or organization development program done under contract for an organization. The trainees attend because others have decided that the training program would be a "good" thing. The trainees do not like it and have no reluctance in saying so.

Another source of hostility may be resentment amounting to a prejudice against experiential learning. Rightly or wrongly, "sensitivity training" has become a term of opprobrium. Many people are angrily opposed to exposing themselves to any sort of experiential learning, equating it with the horror stories which they may have heard or read about. If a trainer comes from an association connected with T-Group techniques or even if he is introduced as an "Applied Behavioral Science Consultant," he may meet considerable resistance, indicative of a conviction that nothing good will come of the effort.

Hostility may also occur when the laboratory method, and especially trainers who use such techniques, have been oversold. The wary but curious participants are sure that nothing can be that good. Nevertheless, they want to experience "real live trainers" (especially NTL trainers), just to say they have done so. But a self-fulfilling prophecy is imminent as they unwittingly subvert the procedures, cutting the trainers down to size and confirming their belief that laboratory training does not amount to much, after all.

There may be less complex reasons for negativism on the part of a group. Some organizations have so many workshops and conferences that the laboratory effort is seen as just one more in a series—and not much good has come from any of the others. The new techniques, quite different from traditional learning models, may be resented as an unwarranted violation of expectations. If the participants have planned to relax comfortably through this program, as they have during so many others, then the requirement of active participation in the learning process is received as an unwelcome intrusion.

Finally, in some instances the workshop is part of a major organizational change effort. As such, it can be expected to arouse many of the predictable resistances to change: people are unwilling to accept the need for changes that may disrupt their customary ways of behaving, thinking, and feeling.

Typical cases are described below.

1. A consultant to a large mental hospital was asked by a staff medical officer to attend a meeting of his "Community Committee," composed of 20 department heads. The medical officer had organized this com-

mittee to raise issues and provide feedback and recommendations to the chief officers of the hospital as a way of improving the living and working environment for patients and staff. Upon entering the room, the consultant noted that everyone was seated far apart, their chairs pushed back against the walls of the large room. While he was still mulling the thought, "beasts at bay," which the arrangement brought to mind, he was surprised to find that his host obviously expected him to take charge of the meeting. He quickly decided to rely upon a fundamental tenet of laboratory training: work on feelings before you work on task.

He asked the committee members to work in trios, just as they happened to be seated, and make a list of terms describing "How do you feel about being here?" After writing their reports on a blackboard and classifying them as positive or negative, not surprisingly, negative feelings were found to be dominant. Using the same trios, he asked, "How do you feel about my being here?" By this time the tasks and open request for feedback, unusual in this institution, had produced more positive reactions, such as "curious," "interested," and "welcome change." Finally, after a quick conference with the medical officer, he asked, "How do you feel about him [the medical officer]?"

Working in trios and surfacing feelings produced diagnostic data of such great importance that the group was launched into problem-solving the issues which emerged.

2. A two-day training session for new faculty members at a university was mistakenly billed as "Innovative Methods of Teaching in Higher Education." Sixty persons from the university were invited, but only about half that number came. During the initial socializing the trainers discovered high resentment of the whole affair. Faculty members felt that they had to give up a day of their weekend to attend a session whose title was seen as derogatory of their creative ability to produce their own solutions to instructional problems. They felt pressured to attend, however, because the program was said to be highly regarded by the university president and some of the deans. Many also expressed curiosity about experiential learning methods and trainers who use such techniques.

The trainers saw a parallel between this situation and that in many college classes where students attend under pressure of degree requirements, at scheduled times not of their own choosing, often subjected to content in which they have little initial interest. They decided to take time to build a contract with the participants, not only to clarify feelings and expectations but also as an example of an innovative (for this campus) classroom method.

Accordingly, small groups were asked to list their expectations of the staff, of the conference, and of themselves. The staff did the same. The sharing and negotiations that resulted as those lists were synthesized into a single document cleared the air and provided an open and relevant agenda for the remainder of the schedule. Negotiations became particularly tense over one staff expectation, which had been included in a spirit of verisimilitude to the classroom, i.e., "The participants must make a grade of C or better." It was deleted after the participants, who had received this with angry resentment, clearly showed that they knew now how students must feel about the games that are played around grades.

This technique of *formulating a contract* has been successfully used with many hostile groups. It goes much farther than the weak beginning so often used, "What do you want to learn?" and it models participative planning in a desirable manner.

Reducing Hostility

Many training events in the military, attended by both military and civilian personnel, present issues of both active and passive resistance which must be dealt with. A similar negative climate is often found in police training programs. The principles operating in these cases include a ready antagonism toward outsiders, especially of the middle-class, "egghead," professorial variety; and a belief in force, command, and authority as ways of getting things done. An extremely skillful approach is necessary to bring such groups to a point of readiness for a collaborative learning experience. Some of the methods that have been tried with varying degrees of success and that would have application elsewhere are dealt with in this section.

Begin immediately with an exciting, unusual, and perhaps competitive task such as the Tinker-Toy exercise or target game. The idea is to give the participants a quick exposure to the experiential model: action—process analysis—learning, and generalization. Further objections are then more likely to be based upon a mutually shared experience than on fantasy. To the extent that resistance to laboratory methods is based on a fear of the unknown, this technique provides a sample of such methods before resistance can be mobilized. Trust in the trainers is fostered, and subsequent directions from them are more readily accepted.

Open Staff Planning. The staff meets briefly in the center of the assembled body of participants, who hear the rationale for the initial activity, listen to a few assessments by staff of its view of the goals and design, and gather some data on how the staff uses theory to direct the flow of events. Sometimes an open chair invites participants to contribute their ideas. This method calls for a well-integrated, professionally secure staff.

Ask participants to write out their fears and hopes for the laboratory experience, discuss them in groups of four, and present a group report to all. This is followed by a form of contract building in which the staff reacts to these lists, indicating how it will take their fears into account in the design and how their hopes may be realistically achieved. Some people fear the T Group, for instance, in a laboratory where the staff has not even planned to use T Groups. Others may hope for unrealistic personal or psychic change.

Prepared Questions Directed at Staff. Some hostility may stem from unfamiliarity with the staff's background, its experience relative to that population and the focus of the training program, or even doubts about its competence. Trio groups can prepare questions they wish to ask of the staff (trios preserve some anonymity of the questioner); and the staff, seated as a panel in front of the group, may then respond to the questions or indicate that a question will not be answered.

This models a norm of openness and its limits for the laboratory. Depending on the type of program, the staff may choose not to answer questions about a few issues, such as salary or sexual behavior. Full, nondefensive answers, however, often build a bridge between staff and participants that becomes a basis for working together.

Flexibility in the technostructural features of the laboratory may prove to be advantageous for climate setting. One military group, for instance, moved from a grim barracks to a motel poolside. The focus, which was self-awareness in a traditional basic human relations format, was changed to ventilation of feelings about the Vietnam War from which the participants had all just returned. These changes transformed a potentially arid training event (it was poorly timed and erroneously directed, given the needs of the trainees) into an intensely moving and useful experience.

Cancellation of Training. Training programs once begun are so rarely cancelled that no such incident has come to my attention, but it need not be ruled out should all else fail. A confrontation between staff and trainees may be arranged to consider this possibility. In one instance this was done because the participants refused to apply themselves seriously to the program. Their norm for conferences was one of play (golf, fishing, bridge), with only nominal attendance at meetings. After one day of conflict and frustration, since the trainers felt obligated to try to meet the serious goals of this failing organization, an emergency session was called in which the participants were bluntly faced with their organizational shortcomings and presented with the alternative of working on them or cancelling the conference. The trainers were seen as serious and concerned. They immediately presented the conferees with a force-field analysis of the organization as they saw it, and that tool was picked up by the members for continuing application to individual problems during the remainder of the conference. The sessions ended on a note of confidence and enthusiasm.

The Trainer's Part

An optimum climate for learning was described long ago* and it is still presented to participants in many basic laboratories: (a) a willingness to experiment and withhold judgment; (b) an ability to take risks and to disclose one's behavior, attitudes, and opinions to others. Less frequently recognized is the need for trainers to contribute more than their design and training skills: they must actively take steps for climate-setting, especially when it is initially resistant and hostile. A "contract" between participants and trainers may need to be openly arrived at. An assessment of relevancy may require a change in focus to meet the needs of the trainees. Trainers may find it desirable to open their planning procedures and share some of their

---

*Mill, C. K., & Porter, L. D. Reading Book for Laboratories in Human Relations Training. Rev. ed. Washington, D.C.; NTL Institute, 1972, p. 1.

leadership functions, thus modeling qualities which they value highly among themselves.

The greatest danger lies in responding to hostility with hostility. Trainer hostility is less likely to be aroused if trainers perform a professional diagnosis of their groups' feelings and their sources. Diagnosis leads to problem-solving designs and avoids the development of manipulative and thus escalating strategies. Once feelings of negativism are allowed to surface, the energy which their tension created can be diverted into constructive channels for learning.

"Working with Hostile Groups": A Reexamination

James E. Crowfoot and Mark A. Chesler

Reproduced by special permission from *Social Change.* "Working with Hostile Groups: A Reexamination." Volume 5, No. 3, pp. 3-6. NTL Institute, 1975

A CLASSIC CASE OF "VICTIM BLAME"

. . . . In our view Mill's focus upon group hostility reflects a general concern for harmonious and well-controlled group processes rather than the specific ends of group learning or social change. His perceptions of the sources of group hostility to consultants and trainers are inadequate because they do not take into account the politics of the social unit involved and the politics of the training enterprise. What results is a classic case of "victim blame." Finally, Mill's suggestions for action represent an attempt to "cool out" the hostility, rather than meet and work with the underlying organizational and social change issues involved. In this article, we seek to reanalyze some of the explanations Mill offers, and to place them in an appropriate ideological and political context. Then we offer alternative suggestions for dealing with the same phenomena, actions we think are more in tune with concerns for fundamental social and organizational change.

Resistance Is Relative—from a Political Perspective

Mill's article is important because it represents a significant historical trend in the field of change-agentry. Well within the paradigms of analyzing resistance established by Watson (1966) and others, Mill essentially sees hostility as inappropriate or unfortunate—even basically irrational—in the well-ordered world of scientifically oriented planned social change (Bennis, Benne, & Chin, 1969).

In a recent article (1974), we located views such as Mill's within a professional-technical perspective on planned social change.* We

---

*Crowfoot and Chesler (1974) argue that the field of planned social change can be understood in terms of three distinct ideological perspectives: professional-technical, political, and counter cultural–redemptive. Each perspective has its own assumptions, value priorities, preferred strategies, clusters of practitioners, and explanations for resistance to change.

suggested that at the root of the value position of the professional-technical change agent lies a commitment to gradual change in the social order and a belief that progress always lies ahead, to be achieved through incremental and continuous adaptation. The recognition of partisanship and the legitimation of group goal conflicts is distasteful to practitioners and theorists of this persuasion. From this perspective, authorities are viewed as people of good will who for the most part seek the common good of all members of the systems for which they are responsible. Thus, resistance usually is seen as arising from inadequacy, fear, lack of information, or some other individual inability to adjust responsibly and rationally to the good and better future.

A political perspective on change, on the other hand, treats conflicts and resistance as natural and normal elements of the everyday contest of interests and values in a differentiated society. From this perspective authorities are recognized as protecting and advancing particular interests that are not necessarily synonymous with the interests of the different groups and parts of systems for which they are responsible. Resistance usually is seen as protection of one's interests in the face of reallocation of resources or encroachment on preferred values.

Mill fails to acknowledge the relativity of his analysis of resistance and the importance of perspectives different from his own. This is but one illustration of what has been the monolithic ideological character of publications such as *Social Change.* Our hope is that the "profession" of change-agentry can speak with more clarity and honesty about value differences and their important implications. As a step in this direction we propose to reexamine Mill's article in light of what other approaches—particularly the political perspective —have to say about the phenomena of group resistance and hostility.

Mill identifies the following sources of group hostility often directed at organizational trainers and consultants: (1) involuntary attendance at sessions wherein "others have decided that the training program would be a 'good' thing"; (2) prejudice against experiential learning per se; (3) the laboratory effort seen as just one more in a series of oversold events which have produced little in terms of significant change; and (4) the predictable resistance met whenever the training is part of a larger organizational change effort: people are unwilling to accept changes that may disrupt their customary ways of thinking, feeling, and behaving.

Involuntary Attendance versus Paternalistic Reassurance

Faced with the first source of hostility, the captive "subject," one might suggest "overcoming" it by mounting an offensive against the organizations or supervisors who so oppress their staff as to subject them to training without options. Certainly such action would be consistent with the rhetoric of free choice and democratic participation in training programs. But Mill neither elects nor mentions such an option; rather, he recommends a series of tactics for overcoming the hostility in the trainees. One tactic referred to is "contract building"—where participants share their fears and hopes with the trainers, who in turn, tell them how these will be taken care of. If this is really a "contract," it is clearly not a reciprocal one. Trainers don't share their fears and hopes; there is no bargaining or negotiating. Why not call this *paternalistic reassurance* or *professional supportiveness*, in which the authority conceals vulnerability while requesting clients to share or confess vulnerability and dependence, following which, the authority can respond, at his/her discretion, with reassurance.

Mill does discuss cancellation of training as a last resort, but he claims that he knows of no instance where training programs once begun have been cancelled. We cannot "buy" this "if all else fails" stance. Many problems of poor planning or manipulated recruitment call precisely for the termination of training on principle alone, perhaps after an initial session at which these problems and inadequacies are surfaced. The fact that the author knows of no such instances clearly tells us that in his view it is not in the consultants' interest to do this. If the training were cancelled, what would happen to the trainers' fees? Trainers and consultants in the service of organizational elites apparently feel they cannot afford to alienate these clients—nor to risk the loss of their own remuneration. This is collusion—whether the consultant realizes it or not.

Resentment, Prejudice versus Cooling-out and Diversionary Tactics

Mill's second source of hostility is "resentment amounting to a prejudice against experiential learning." We personally favor experiential learning: most of the time, although not all of the time, it has worked best for us. But it does not work well for everyone, for every cultural group, or for every situation. Sometimes, an experiential focus may emphasize individual subjective issues in ways that fail to clarify objective interests and "realpolitik." Such training can operate cooptively—and discouragingly—anchoring people further to status quo objective conditions while encouraging exciting subjective explorations. For Mill to label "resentment amounting to a prejudice" without including, even by implication, the possibility that different goals and different values about styles of learning also legitimately may be at stake, is almost to label *all* resistance irrational.

Client Expectations versus Trainer Control of Resources

The third source of resistance to specific training events is in part traceable to the tactics utilized by the broader social movement of human relations and OD training, which has sought to capture the market with extravagant claims. The consultant often feeds into these expectations by virtue of his/her own needs for recognition, acceptance, and employment. Mill's analysis is one-sided again, discussing only participant aberrance rather than trainer collusion as well. Frequently, professional trainers fail to identify and confront the inappropriateness of training due to their having been manipulated, their own carelessness, or their own pecuniary or status self-interests. After all, management's desires to "retrain" employees may suit their change objectives yet not advance those of their employees. Several exposures to these dominant biases in OD programs should generate in participants (employees especially) the feeling that nothing new is happening: basic power arrangements are not being altered, goals of top-level authorities are still being pursued, and so on.

Mill's diagnoses and suggestions for "overcoming" hostility and resistance are rife with the maintenance of trainer and professional authority and control. We review this later, but its presence is enough to convince the sensitive participant that the training workshop or OD program subtly represents the same power dynamics of the large organization—but in this case, the special power of the helping professions.

Pluralism, Competing Values versus Delegitimation

Any organizational change effort should be expected to meet resistance—resistance in the form of other persons or organizational units who hold values and interests that differ from those favored by groups (usually managing elites) who call in trainers and consultants. But rather than seeing such resistance as symptomatic of natural conflict within a pluralistic system, Mill seems to view the hostility engendered by it as stemming from an unwillingness or inability to accept the need for change. Maybe from the client's status and viewpoint, there is no need for change.

Trainers and consultants in the pay of organizational elites often come to adopt their employers' views as the only legitimate ones. Of course this is even more likely when the trainers and consultants themselves are white, male, and of the same status, background, and value orientations as are the governing elites. The net result is that differences are seen as illegitimate, as resistance to the legitimate and rational goals for change stressed by managers and consultants.

We believe that social change is always a political process. It involves the alteration of organizational norms, styles, policies, structures, and resource distributions; it also involves the pursuit of cherished values or interests. In the pursuit of one's own priorities and the influence or alteration of others', various technologies and tools are used. When some of the tools of change (money, status and power of "professional" change agents, scientific information or knowledge) are captured by one competing party, they become weapons in that party's defense and advancement of its own interests. (One example of this is when professionals create articles, training designs, analyses of hostility, and myths about conflict that delegitimize resistance to managerial and consultant goals.)

Of course the profession of change-agentry has its own politics and power issues. The commitment to maintain professional control is clear in Mill's recommendations of ways trainers may overcome hostility. For instance, he recommends a quick exposure to exciting, unusual, and perhaps competitive tasks to dispel participants' fantasies about what will occur. He does not say that such techniques can divert attention from basic conflicts in the trainer-trainee relationship. Another technique he recommends is open staff planning (in reality a canned substitute of actual staff planning), but even there he warns that this is a technique only for a "well-integrated, professionally secure staff." What happens if the staff is not well integrated? One assumes that in Mill's view, differences among themselves and uncertainties should not be shared with participants. Why not? Or at least why not be open that the reason they should not be shared is fear of surfacing staff conflict and thus making the staff more vulnerable in the staff-participant contest?

Tokens and Euphemisms: No Power Parity

As a contingent strategy to be used only if the trainers' initial effort at establishing a positive climate is unsuccessful, "a contract openly arrived at" is suggested by Mill. He describes it equivocally: "Trainers *may find it desirable* to open the planning procedures and *share some of the leadership* function . . . " with participants. One wonders why this would not be desirable *all* of the time; why share only some of the leadership functions? And why should not trainees decide that? The entire line of argument here poses alternative strategies for maintaining trainer control with token target participation in "leadership." A "positive climate" here means one in which *learners will comply* with professional direction, and thus becomes a euphemism for trainer control.

In the vast majority of instances, trainers do have control over whether or not the training event goes on, what will be covered, and how. The kind of control the participants have is to be absent from sessions, late to sessions, present in sessions but not participating, present in sessions and participating in obstructive ways, and so on. That is, the only forms of power and control participants in general have available to them may center on the options of resisting or being "hostile." To set participant hostility within the paradigm of power and control over the workshop or change design requires consultants to see themselves as responsible parties in a power relationship, not as bystanders watching the irrational hostility of participants. Mill's suggestions maintain the power differential between consultants and trainees in the workshop: he elects corrective action at the level of communication and interpersonal relations rather than power parity between trainers and participants or renovation of program goals and structures.

Another technique Mill recommends is prepared questions directed at the staff. A staff panel "may then respond to the questions or indicate that a question will not be answered. . . . Depending on the type of program, the staff may choose not to answer the questions about a few issues, such as salary and sexual behavior."

Why shouldn't *all* questions be answered? After all, the salary of trainers is important data in disclosing who they are, what their priorities are, to whom they are accountable. Likewise, in a situation where participants anticipate vulnerability, risk-taking, experimentation—what the laboratory method calls for—staff members' sexual preferences and outlooks (like their race, age, and class) may be exceedingly important information in determining the reality of potential trust relations and the probability of one's being taken advantage of.

Democratizing the Professions

Mill's recommendations emphasize trainers' needs for techniques for overcoming resistance instead of exploring new structures, roles, decision-making processes, and distributions of power in a training situation. Further, the underlying theme in these recommendations is that trainers establish and preserve control through distraction, pretended openness, increased interpersonal communication, i.e., a united trainer front.

Change traditions other than the professional-technical now seek to democratize the professions and to create situations where clients/targets control their consultants rather than the reverse. Mill's gentle and decent recontrolling efforts would be inappropriate in such a scenario, wherein change agents are expected to provide partisan advice, support, and expertise to clients who control them and determine how to use them. In target groups committed to social-justice objectives, Mill's suggestions perpetuate concealment of the real effects of racial, class, and sexual power—impotence of the oppressed and rage at continual oppression by the elite. For such groups, and perhaps for us all, getting in touch with that rage is an essential element of our personal liberation and a key source of energy for social change.

Hostility as a Source of Energy and Growth

Apart from the seriousness of Mill's failure to understand and articulate his own political bias, and perhaps even to propose alternative perspectives, he demonstrates a limited understanding of the role played by hostility and negative feelings in individual and system change. While Mill judges that hostility should be eliminated from the change situation, we feel that *hostility can be a major source of energy and personal growth* (Fanon, 1963; Laing, 1967). Such hostility can indicate investment in a situation, and when legitimated can be manifest in engagement and encounter. With this expressed energy is the potential for discovery of related feelings, revised perceptions, altered behaviors, and deepened passion and commitment to cherished values. Hostility—latent or actualized—in intergroup conflicts can be a vehicle for achieving new systemic boundaries, revision of goals, and clarified, renewed, or terminated group and individual commitment.

Deutsch (1969, p. 35), certainly no advocate of escalated personal or social conflict, indicates: "Harnessed rage or outrage can
be a powerful energizer for determined action, and if this action is
directed toward building one's own power rather than destroying the
other's power, the outrage may have a socially useful, constructive
outcome." And he notes that both rage and fear "are rooted in a
sense of helplessness and powerlessness." Constructive responses to
them will require renovation of existing personal and social power
arrangements—in the society, in small-group role relations, and in
organizational training programs.

REFERENCES

Bennis, W., Benne, K., & Chin, R. *The planning of change.* New York: Holt,
    Rinehart & Winston, 1969.

Crowfoot, J., & Chesler, M. Contemporary perspectives on planned social
    change: A comparison. *Journal of Applied Behavioral Science,* 1974,
    10, 278–303.

Deutsch, M. Conflicts: Productive and destructive. *Journal of Social Issues,*
    1969, 25 (1), 7–41.

Fanon, F. *The wretched of the earth.* New York: Grove Press, 1963.

Laing, R. D. *The politics of experience.* New York: Ballantine Book, 1967.

Mill, C. R. Working with hostile groups. *Social Change,* 1974, 4 (1), 1–4.

Watson, G. Resistance to change. In G. Watson (Ed.), *Concepts for social
    change.* Washington, D.C.: National Training Laboratories. National
    Education Association, 1967. Pp. 10–25.

BIBLIOGRAPHY

Blake, R. R.; Mouton, J. S.; and Sloma, R. L. 1972. The union-
    management intergroup laboratory: strategy for resolving inter-
    group conflict. In *The social technology of organization devel-
    opment,* ed. W. W. Burke and H. A. Hornstein, pp. 101–26. La
    Jolla, Calif.: University Associates.

This article describes a consultative design for confronting the
    intense intergroup antagonism between management and a
    union and for moving the relationship toward effective problem
    solving. The groups are led through a series of systematic steps
    to examine their relationship in depth. Initial confrontations
    lead to joint problem solving, which leads to new, shared inter-
    group agreements.

Derr, C. B. 1972. Conflict resolution in organizations: views from
    the field of educational administration. *Public Administration
    Review* 32: 495–501.

Outlining methods that an administrator may use to develop a
    strategy for conflict resolution, this article identifies the most
    common kinds of organizational conflicts, underscores the
    importance of differentiating between conflicts (e.g., between
    those that foster creative tension and those that are potentially

destructive to the organization), and presents a model for determining the degree to which conflicts are important and should be resolved.

Fromkin, H. L., and Sherwood, J. J., eds. 1976. *Intergroup and minority relations: an experiential handbook.* La Jolla, Calif.: University Associates.

This practical handbook reports procedures for helping members of different groups expand perspectives of themselves and of members of other groups. Activities on clarifying values, intergroup awareness, intergroup communication, and intergroup problem solving are included together with instruments, photographs, and other resource materials.

Kahn, R. L., and French, J. R. P. 1970. Status and conflict: two themes in the study of stress. In *Social and psychological factors in stress,* ed. J. E. McGrath, pp. 238-63. New York: Holt, Rinehart & Winston.

Endemic to organizational life, role conflict can be especially acute in schools. This article specifies three types of role conflict—intrasender, intersender, and interrole conflict—and discusses the kinds of organizational dynamics that evoke such conflicts as well as the psychological conflicts that result.

Lohman, J., and Wilson, G. 1977. *Social conflict and negotiative problem solving.* Portland, Ore.: Northwest Regional Educational Laboratory.

This is an instructional system designed to help teachers, administrators, and others increase their capability of recognizing and handling conflict arising from value differences and self-interest. A structured, experience-based design, parts of which could be fit into tailored designs, it covers such topics as social conflict, power, assertiveness, self-interest, and negotiative problem-solving skills.

Schmidt, W. H., and Tannenbaum, R. 1972. Management of differences. In *The social technology of organization development,* ed. W. W. Burke and H. A. Hornstein, pp. 127-40. La Jolla, Calif.: University Associates.

This article offers suggestions to managers on how to handle disagreements and conflicts, presents ideas about diagnosing differences, designing a strategy, and working out the differences through problem solving, and ends with advice on maintaining managerial objectivity.

Walton, R. E. 1969. *Interpersonal peacemaking; confrontations and third-party consultation.* Reading, Mass.: Addison-Wesley.

This book covers designs, techniques, and evaluation procedures of use to third-party consultants in managing conflicts. In suggesting ways to help conflicting parties learn to handle future conflicts on their own, it can be an invaluable resource to organizational specialists in school districts.

6

Improving Meetings

While all channels of communication in a school can be useful, meetings are singularly important in providing a setting in which school members can communicate and coordinate information about problems and decisions and at the same time satisfy emotional needs for activity, achievement, affiliation, and power. Meetings provide an opportunity for participation not found in memos, newsletters, loudspeaker announcements, and the like. They enable an immediate check of reactions to what another person has just said and to one's own immediate utterances as well. If managed effectively, meetings can be the principal channel for bringing staff members into collaboration to reach common understandings and for that reason can be highly productive and satisfying events in the life of the organization.

Yet most school staffs and subgroups use meetings infrequently and ineffectively, often inhibiting clear communication and wide participation. Indeed, since many educators regard meetings as a dull waste of time or as a burden to be endured while more interesting work awaits elsewhere, it is not surprising that mismanaged meetings can arouse distaste and even hatred. Holding meetings merely because they are scheduled, clinging strictly to Robert's Rules of Order, not dealing with feelings, not allowing members to help plan the meeting or compile the agenda, not keeping a record of things done, attempting to cover too many items on an agenda, allowing a few members to do all the talking, allowing only those with high status to conduct the meetings, neglecting to carry the group's decisions into action—all are traps that prevent meetings from reaching their potential.

OD .consultants, who conduct most of their training in meetings and who will also be called on in the course of the school year to give help and consultation at ordinary school meetings, should not only be aware of the feelings that staff members have about meetings but should attempt to make their training sessions models of effective meetings. This chapter introduces methods that consultants can use to help school people organize meetings for the most effective mobilization of human resources.

PURPOSES OF MEETINGS

Most educators recognize the potential benefits of forming committees, departments, and teams for organizing curricula and developing policy. They see, too, that present trends in school organization, such as team teaching and differentiated staffing, will bring about more problem solving and decision making by groups. Although individuals can usually reach more efficient decisions on issues that are relatively simple in structure, have objective and easily separable elements, and require a strict sequence of acts that can readily be performed by one person, on more complex issues groups have some advantages over individuals working alone.

Where issues with many alternative subtasks are involved, where elements are not easily conceptualized, where one person cannot perform a subtask without relating to others, and particularly where efficiency depends on the continued coordination and interaction of a number of persons, a group decision will almost always be superior to one produced by even the most capable individual. Groups can usually produce more ideas, stimulate more creative thought among members, pool ideas to develop more realistic forecasts of the consequences of decisions, and generally produce bolder plans than can individuals working alone. Perhaps most important, group members can commit themselves to action in one another's presence.

In a school organization that requires intelligent coordination among staff, one-way communication is not enough; the percentage of people responding constructively to messages must be high. It is important for an organization member to know how many people "bought" a message, who these people are, and why they found the message to be either inspiring or distasteful. Beyond getting a message accepted, it is often important for many people to know firsthand that the transmission occurred and that others know it occurred. The face-to-face meeting is the only setting in which all these functions can occur quickly.

Perhaps the greatest value of meetings is that they draw out and coordinate staff resources for a systematic exchange of creative ideas. They can also be useful for planning action that will require the consistent coordinated effort of several staff members. Even the simplest matters, such as using audio-visual equipment or art supplies, are often difficult for staff members to coordinate and could be facilitated by staff discussions. If the transmission of simple information at meetings wastes valuable time, another mode of communication, such as a clearly written memorandum, would be more appropriate, require less time, and be available for later reference. Chapters 7 and 8 provide further discussion of the assets and debits of participative involvement in problem solving and decision making.

Finally, meetings provide one of the few means by which people in schools can come together to satisfy emotional needs. Observers such as Jackson (1968) and Lortie (1975) have noted the social isolation, the vagueness of outcomes, and the relatively low degree of power associated with teaching and working in schools. The traditional self-contained classroom requires teachers to work apart from other adults most of the time. Vague but demanding educational goals are often set by the larger society of which the school is a part but on which teachers have little influence. Joining with other adults in meetings to solve mutual problems and share common frustrations can greatly improve the chance that school members can take initiative, feel successful, experience affiliation with others, and feel that they are exercising some influence over their own and shared fates.

Because meetings are confined in time, space, and membership, they bring many group processes that are elusive in the larger organization into full view for the consultant to observe. Thinking of meetings as microcosms of the organization will enable the consultant to anticipate many of the norms manifested outside meetings. Moreover, in initial contacts with clients, consultants should make observations at regularly scheduled meetings at which real work is taking place. It is better to see clients in action than to hear them talk about how they work together, and meetings are among the most easily observable group actions in schools.

By observing interpersonal interaction at meetings, consultants can discern roles and norms that reflect the organization's goals, approved procedures, and affective climate. The kinds of communication encouraged at meetings, for example, can reveal the expectations and skills that members use to coordinate their efforts. The amount of time devoted to goal setting can indicate the importance that members attach to this in relation to other activities. Shared assumptions about the functions of conflict can be noted in the ways in which opposing views are uncovered and handled. To understand how staff members have organized to accomplish their tasks, comparisons of problem-solving and decision-making activities can be made at staff meetings, smaller group meetings, and informal sessions. Finally, consultants can watch the degree to which participants comment on how they conduct their meetings and how they assess changes in their group processes.

Meetings that are handled ineffectively often have unfortunate repercussions elsewhere in the school. Principals who receive a policy decision at a district meeting without a clarifying discussion may misinterpret the policy and transmit wrong directions to teachers.

When educational goals are seldom discussed at building meetings, teachers may find themselves working at cross-purposes. When small conflicts over disciplining students are not discussed at staff meetings, they may grow into hostilities. When problem solving and decision making during meetings are confined to only a few staff members, nonparticipants are likely to experience frustration and tune out; those who stay out of the discussion may be unwilling or unable to carry out the action steps that others have developed. Finally, if staff members fail to discuss changes that are occurring in the community and student body, their instructional programs will lose effectiveness.

EFFECTIVE MEETINGS

Effectiveness at meetings is not common, especially when issues are not easily resolvable. But ineffectiveness should not be punished when it occurs. Instead, consultants should go beyond helping groups to develop effective meetings and on occasion help them to lower their expectations so that mutual recrimination does not consume an inordinate amount of time.

Four Features

Effective meetings include at least four features: task and maintenance functions, group orientation and self-orientation, leadership roles, and follow-through. To have effective meetings, groups must learn to fulfill task functions, which carry forward the meeting's work requirements, and maintenance functions, which help group members develop satisfying interpersonal relationships. Task functions include initiating ideas on work procedures, seeking information or opinions from others, giving information or opinions, and summarizing what has occurred in the meeting. Maintenance functions include ensuring that others have a chance to speak, ensuring that listeners have a chance to check on what they have heard, reconciling disagreements, sensing group mood, and being warm and responsive toward others.

Meetings are most effective when some members attend to how well the group is accomplishing each part of its work and others stop working on their tasks periodically to discuss the group's process. Symptoms of difficulty include excessive nitpicking, repetition of obvious points, ignoring suggestions for improvement, private conversations in pairs or subgroups, domination of discussion by two or three people, polarization of members, general inability to paraphrase another's point of view, attack against ideas before they are completely expressed, and apathetic participation. When such symptoms occur, the group should set aside the original task and place emerging maintenance issues on the agenda. It must also learn to deal effectively with its processes and to shift easily back to its main work. Most if not all staff members should be capable of performing both task and maintenance functions.

A second feature of effective meetings that consultants can observe is the degree to which members engage in self-oriented rather than group-oriented behavior. Unproductive behaviors such as fighting, withdrawing, blocking, avoiding, depending on the formal leader, expressing indifference, sandbagging, and keeping agendas hidden are directed toward individual needs rather than toward the task at hand. Schein (1969) theorizes that self-oriented behavior occurs when groups fail to recognize or to deal with any of four underlying emotional issues of members: identity, control, needs and goals, and acceptance of intimacy; it also probably reflects low trust in the group.

Self-oriented behavior may be a problem when it delays accomplishment of the main task and leaves members dissatisfied; but groups often allow individuals to take the time of everyone else for individual purposes. If this can be done aboveboard, the group should not avoid it and an individual should not be afraid to ask. Everyone should be clear that it is happening and be willing to delay the original group task so that a discussion of the individual's concern, like attention to group process, will pay off later.

A third way to look for effectiveness in meetings is to observe how leadership is supplied within a single meeting or over a series of meetings and how group members share the leadership. We define leadership as any behavior that helps the group carry forward its work or satisfy members' needs in constructive ways. Leadership is needed for: (1) planning and preparing for the meeting, (2) setting goals by building an agenda, (3) coordinating task business, (4) keeping records of what happens, (5) helping attend to group and interpersonal processes, (6) evaluating how well activities have met goals, as well as how satisfying and helpful interpersonal processes have been, and (7) planning ways of following through on plans.

In our view, these functions should be shared by all members of a group at the same time that individual members are assigned primary responsibility to see that certain special roles are performed effectively. These special roles—meeting organizer, convener, recorder, process observer, and follow-up monitor—will be described later in this chapter.

Follow-through, the fourth readily observable feature of meetings, occurs after the meeting. If requests pour into the secretary's or principal's office for information about items discussed at the meeting, the meeting was probably ineffective in relaying that information. If staff members grumble in the faculty room about a decision made at a meeting, they probably did not feel free to contribute their own views. Tasks that are implemented with commitment and dispatch, however, give evidence of adequate preparation at the meeting.

Consultant Roles and Functions

Two factors make it possible for meeting skills to be worked with successfully at a very early phase of an OD effort. First, although most school staffs cannot easily call off work, even for brief periods, to practice new group and organizational processes, consultants can often gain admission to regularly scheduled meetings to help with the ongoing work of the school. Second, any initial successes achieved at moving group members from chaotic to productive meetings can increase their trust in the consultant's competence and encourage them to work toward resolving the larger issues confronting their organization. The following section briefly discusses four methods the consultant can use to improve meetings: modeling an effective group member, providing information about effective meetings, providing training, and providing consultation and feedback.

By attending the meetings of a school staff or other group within the client system, consultants to some extent become temporary members of these meetings and, as such, may act as models of effective group members. If members seldom clarify one another's statements, for example, consultants may repeatedly clarify what others are saying. If agendas are loosely described and consultants are themselves on the agenda, they may insist that the purpose of their agenda topic be clarified and that definite time requirements be imposed for them. If a group leaves decisions dangling with no clear indication of who is to be responsible for follow-up actions, consultants can ask leading questions that focus on this lack of specification.

For purposes of modeling, consultants can sometimes assume important leadership roles as well. As convener, the consultant can demonstrate assertive behavior, help the group warm up, organize its agenda, and encourage wide participation; in other roles, consultants can exhibit careful recording of events or observations of group processes. Unless considerable trust exists between members and the consultant, however, this type of modeling should be avoided. The role of consultants is not to furnish leadership functions for the group but rather to help the group establish effective meetings by passing on their own skills to group members.

If group members already perceive the nature of their problems, consultants can often help by providing information about the characteristics and procedures of effective meetings, especially the guides for conveners, recorders, and process consultants described later in this chapter. After giving this information, they can lead discussions about the advantages and disadvantages of the recommended procedures or techniques and then coach members as they conduct their meetings in new ways. In this way, too, consultants can help a group find resources that none of its members individually can provide by assisting in a search beyond the group for other people and materials.

When group members are unhappy with their meetings and have committed themselves to improving them, the consultant is in a good position to offer training in alternative modes and roles. Training events can be set up at which members practice the exercises and procedures connected with various leadership roles and functions described in this chapter.

238

Finally, group members are often unaware of how they are influenced by group norms and processes. Members of a faculty, for example, may know that their meetings are going poorly but may not understand why. Some members may be upset because the group cannot work effectively on its agenda in a brief period of time; others may criticize meetings because they are all work and no fun. In such instances, process consultants can collect and feed back data about meeting processes so that members can perceive, understand, and act in ways that will improve their meetings. Detailed guides for process observation and feedback are given in chapter 10.

GATHERING DATA ABOUT MEETINGS

This section presents several questionnaires, interviews, and observation schedules that we have found useful for gathering data about meetings in schools. We have tried to state the context in which each instrument works best and the settings in which many have been used successfully. Many of the instruments can be adapted to meet special situations. Items from the Group Expectation Survey, for example, might become part of an interview schedule or suggest behaviors that the consultant can observe and report in a process feedback session.

Instruments for Diagnosing Problems

Meetings Questionnaire. We have used the Meetings Questionnaire, developed by Matthew Miles for the Cooperative Project on Educational Development, in numerous settings to diagnose the quality of the client's meetings. In the normal procedure, each member of a group that meets regularly responds to the thirty-seven items on the questionnaire. The consultant can then tabulate and display these data on newsprint to present means and frequency distributions for each item. Members can be encouraged to diagnose their own meetings by discussing items on which high agreement exists or items with mixed responses. In the questionnaire below, the introductory paragraph can be modified to suit the type of meeting to be described.

Questionnaire on Meetings
Schools hold a lot of meetings, and much depends on their quality. Please think specifically of the meetings you have in your school.

How often are these   Length of
meetings usually held? _____.   typical meeting _____.

Now, please consider what usually or typically happens in these meetings. Some possible happenings in meetings are listed below. Before each item below, please write one of the following numerals to indicate how usual or typical it is in your group.

5 This is very typical of the meetings; it happens repeatedly.

4 This is fairly typical of the meeting; it happens often.

3 This is more typical than not; it happens sometimes.

2 This is more untypical than typical, though it happens now and then.

1 This is untypical; it rarely happens.

0 This is not typical at all; it never happens.

1. _____ When problems come up in the meeting, they are thoroughly explored until everyone under-stands what the problem is.

2. _____ The first solution proposed is often accepted by the group.

3. _____ People come to the meeting not knowing what is to be presented or discussed.

4. _____ People ask why the problem exists and what the causes are.

5. _____ There are many problems which people are con-cerned about which never get on the agenda.

6. _____ There is a tendency to propose answers without really having thought the problem and its causes through carefully.

7. _____ The group discusses the pros and cons of several different alternate solutions to a problem.

8. _____ People bring up extraneous or irrelevant matters.

9. _____ The average person in the meeting feels that his ideas have gotten into the discussion.

10. _____ Someone summarizes progress from time to time.

11. _____ Decisions are often left vague—as to what they are and who will carry them out.

12. _____ Either before the meeting or at its beginning, any group member can easily get items onto the agenda.

13. _____ People are afraid to be openly critical or make good objections.

14. _____ The group discusses and evaluates how decisions from previous meetings worked out.

15. _____ People do not take the time to really study or define the problem they are working on.

16. _____ The same few people seem to do most of the talking during the meeting.

17. _____ People hesitate to give their true feelings about problems which are discussed.

18. _____ When a decision is made, it is clear who should carry it out and when.

19. _____ There is a good deal of jumping from topic to topic—it's often unclear where the group is on the agenda.

20. ____ From time to time in the meeting, people openly discuss the feelings and working relationships in the group.
21. ____ The same problems seem to keep coming up over and over again from meeting to meeting.
22. ____ People don't seem to care about the meeting or want to get involved in it.
23. ____ When the group is thinking about a problem, at least two or three different solutions are suggested.
24. ____ When there is disagreement, it tends to be smoothed over or avoided.
25. ____ Some very creative solutions come out of this group.
26. ____ Many people remain silent.
27. ____ When conflicts over decisions come up, the group does not avoid them but really stays with the conflict and works it through.
28. ____ The results of the group's work are not worth the time it takes.
29. ____ People give their real feelings about what is happening during the meeting itself.
30. ____ People feel very committed to carry out the solutions arrived at by the group.
31. ____ When the group is supposedly working on a problem, it is really working on some other "under the table" problem.
32. ____ People feel antagonistic or negative during the meeting.
33. ____ There is no follow-up on how decisions reached at earlier meetings worked out in practice.
34. ____ Solutions and decisions are in accord with the chairman's or leader's point of view but not necessarily with that of the members.
35. ____ There are splits or deadlocks between factions or subgroups.
36. ____ The discussion goes on and on without any decision being reached.
37. ____ People feel satisfied or positive during the meeting.

Group Expectation Survey. The Group Expectation Survey* enables group members to discover what kinds of information they want from others in the group and what kinds of information they are willing to give to others. Fosmire and Keutzer (1968) discuss protocols collected from a wide range of groups showing: (1) that group members usually say they are receptive to interpersonal feed-

---

*Developed by John Wallen and adapted from Hale and Spanjer (1972).

back but perceive others as unwilling to give it, and (2) that group members usually say they would report their feelings candidly but ·doubt that others would do so. Fosmire, Keutzer, and Diller (1971) explain that the survey is useful not only for measuring and reporting data for discussion but for showing group members that attempts at openness might be safer than they had formerly believed. We have used this survey with a variety of school staffs and subgroups that meet regularly. When each member has completed the questionnaire, we compute the mean scores for each item and feed the results back to the group for analysis and discussion. Figure 6-1 illustrates how the data might be displayed for feedback.

Group Expectation Survey
Directions: Before each of the items below, put a number from the rating scale that best expresses your opinion.

Rating Scale
    5 = all members of this group
    4 = all members except one or two
    3 = a slight majority of the members of this group
    2 = slightly less than half the members of this group
    1 = one or two members of this group
    0 = none of this group

How many members of this group do you expect will candidly report the following information during future group sessions?

_____ 1. When he does not understand something you said?
_____ 2. When he likes something you said or did?
_____ 3. When he disagrees with something you said?
_____ 4. When he thinks you have changed the subject or become irrelevant?
_____ 5. When he feels impatient or irritated with something you said or did?
_____ 6. When he feels hurt—rejected, embarrassed, or put down—by something you said or did?

To how many members will *you* candidly report the following information in future group sessions?

_____ 7. When you do not understand something he said?
_____ 8. When you like something he said or did?
_____ 9. When you disagree with something he said?
_____ 10. When you think he has changed the subject or become irrelevant?
_____ 11. When you feel impatient or irritated with something he said or did?
_____ 12. When you feel hurt—rejected, embarrassed, or put down—by something he said or did?

In your opinion, how many in this group are interested in knowing . . .

_____ 13 When you do not understand something he said?
_____ 14 When you like something he said or did?

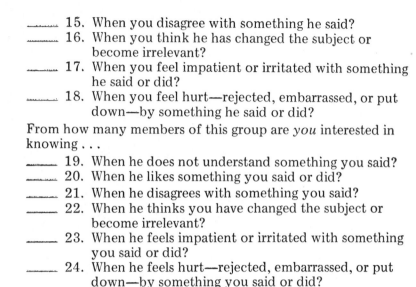

15. When you disagree with something he said?
16. When you think he has changed the subject or become irrelevant?
17. When you feel impatient or irritated with something he said or did?
18. When you feel hurt—rejected, embarrassed, or put down—by something he said or did?

From how many members of this group are *you* interested in knowing . . .

19. When he does not understand something you said?
20. When he likes something you said or did?
21. When he disagrees with something you said?
22. When he thinks you have changed the subject or become irrelevant?
23. When he feels impatient or irritated with something you said or did?
24. When he feels hurt—rejected, embarrassed, or put down—by something you said or did?

FIGURE 6-1 Displaying Results of the Group Expectation Survey

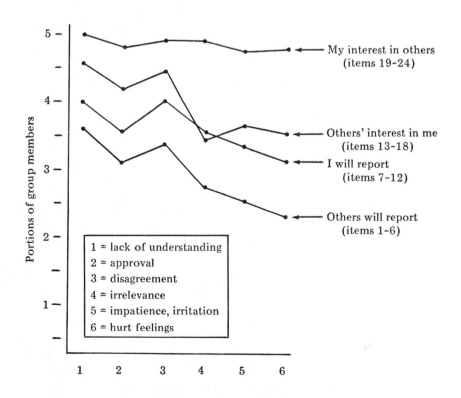

Instruments for Process Observation and Consultation

The instruments in this section consist mainly of observation schedules that the consultant can use to facilitate process consultation during meetings. With these instruments an observer can record both descriptive and quantitative data during a meeting, and these can later be fed back to group members for their own analysis and discussion.

Observing Participation. Effective groups make use of their members' resources during meetings. All members participate although in different and complementary ways. By means of the observation schedule illustrated in figure 6-2, the consultant can record the frequency with which individuals speak to other individuals, to the total group, or not at all.

FIGURE 6-2   Observer's Frequency Chart: Patterns of Communication

Record at the bottom of the chart the time interval during which the observations are made. Label the circles with the names of group members. The first time a person speaks to another person, draw an arrow from the speaker to the receiver of the message. The first time a person speaks to the total group, draw the arrow to the center of the cluster of circles. Additional messages from the speaker to that individual or to the total group may be indicated with tally marks on the arrow. An X can be placed in a person's circle if he or she interrupts another to speak. A $\sqrt{}$ can be put in the circle to indicate that the person's remark encouraged another to participate.

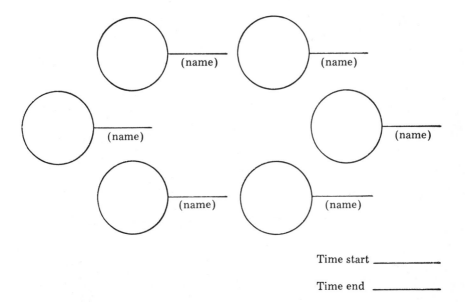

Time start _____

Time end _____

SOURCE: Adapted from Johnson and Johnson (1975, p. 119).

FIGURE 6-3 Leadership Functions in Meetings

While observing each group, make a tally mark every time you hear or see behavior (verbal or nonverbal) that approximates in your estimation the following categories:

Categories	Member					
	S	W	E	R	J	O
1. Setting goals		3				
2. Proposing problems	8	2		20	3	12
3. Asking for information	3	8				2
4. Giving information		2	1	2		2
5. Proposing solutions	4			2		2
6. Asking clarification	2	1				
7. Giving clarification	3	1		15	3	6
8. Testing for consensus		1				
9. Supporting				1		
10. Asking about group progress			1			
11. Summarizing		1		2		
12. Evaluating	5	1		20	2	9

Observing Leadership Functions. The following observation schedule can be used to observe particular leadership functions in groups. In this instance, the observer makes a tally every time a member performs a leadership function in the specified categories listed in the schedule. At the end of the meeting, tallies can be counted and fed back to members as illustrated in figure 6-3.

Interaction Process Analysis. Another way of observing and analyzing leadership functions in meetings is to collect information on the task and socioemotional behavior of group members. Bales (1950) developed an instrument with categories similar to the task-maintenance functions described earlier in this chapter. His categories were:

FIGURE 6-4   Cumulative Interaction Form

Date _____ Group _____

Time: _____ to _____   Observer _____

	Behavior	Members										Totals
Positive Emotions {	Shows solidarity											
	Shows tension release											
	Agrees											
Task {	Gives suggestions											
	Gives opinions											
	Gives orientation											
	Asks for orientation											
	Asks for opinions											
	Asks for suggestions											
Negative Emotions {	Disagrees											
	Shows tension											
	Shows antagonism											
	Totals											

SOURCE: Johnson and Johnson (1975, p. 51).

Social-Emotional Area: Positive
1. Shows solidarity, raises others' status, gives help, rewards.
2. Shows tension release, jokes, laughs, shows satisfaction.
3. Agrees, shows passive acceptance, understands, confers, complies.

Task Area: Neutral
4. Gives suggestions, direction, implying autonomy for others.

5. Gives opinions, evaluation, analysis, expresses feeling, wishes.
6. Gives orientation, information, repeats, clarifies, confirms.
7. Asks for orientation, information, repetition, confirmation.
8. Asks for opinions, evaluation, analysis, expressions of feeling.
9. Asks for suggestions, direction, possible ways of action.

Social-Emotional Area: Negative

10. Disagrees, shows passive rejection, formality, withholds help.
11. Shows tension, asks for help, withdraws, leaves the field.
12. Shows antagonism, deflates others' status, defends or asserts self.

The consultant can collect information on these categories using the observation schedule in figure 6-4. The data can be reported to group members, who can discuss the task and socioemotional activities they usually perform or identify those they would like to practice to gain greater proficiency.

Instruments for Evaluating Meeting Effectiveness

The following questionnaires measure participants' reactions to meetings. The first three were developed to help a group analyze a single meeting; the fourth has been used to measure perceptions and expectations about a series of meetings.

Example 1. Several consultants have used this questionnaire for survey feedback to school groups. We learned of it from Rosalie Howard, a consultant with Smith, Murray, and Howard, Inc., of Eugene, Oregon.

Directions: Mark an X before each item in the box that best shows your reaction to this meeting.

Agreement		Disagreement		
Strong	Mild	Mild	Strong	
( ) YES!	( ) yes	( ) no	( ) NO!	1. The results of this meeting were worth the time.
( ) YES!	( ) yes	( ) no	( ) NO!	2. I was given adequate opportunity to state my beliefs about subjects discussed by the group.
( ) YES!	( ) yes	( ) no	( ) NO!	3. Our meeting was efficient.

Agreement		Disagreement		
Strong	Mild	Mild	Strong	
( ) YES!	( ) yes	( ) no	( ) NO!	4. I am satisfied with the attention and consideration that others gave to my ideas and opinions.
( ) YES!	( ) yes	( ) no	( ) NO!	5. We wasted too much time in this meeting.
( ) YES!	( ) yes	( ) no	( ) NO!	6. The group effectively used my knowledge of the subjects discussed.
( ) YES!	( ) yes	( ) no	( ) NO!	7. The most important topics were never discussed.
( ) YES!	( ) yes	( ) no	( ) NO!	8. I had adequate opportunity to influence our conclusions and decisions.

Example 2. The following items were developed by Runkel in 1966 to measure responses of educators at a problem-solving meeting:

1. Do you feel that anything of value happened during this meeting?
   ( ) Yes, quite a lot.
   ( ) Yes, something.
   ( ) Not much.
   ( ) Nothing.

2. If you found something of value in this meeting, does any particular happening or idea stand out in your mind?
   ( ) Nothing of value happened.
   ( ) It was a valuable meeting, but no particular thing stands out.
   ( ) Yes, something does stand out for me, namely:

   _____

3. If you found something in this meeting to be of *no* value, was there a particular happening or idea that stands out in your mind as being valueless?
   ( ) Most everything was of some value.
   ( ) Some parts of the meeting had no value, but no particular thing stands out.
   ( ) Yes, something stands out for me as having no value, namely:

   _____

4. Was there any feature about the way this group operated that you thought particularly effective?

    (   ) No.   (   ) Yes, namely:

_____

_____

5. Was there any feature about the way this group operated that you thought particularly *ineffective*?

    (   ) No.   (   ) Yes, namely:

_____

_____

Example 3. This form is based on an instrument developed by Schein (1969).

Answer the items according to *your own opinions* about the meeting. There are no right answers. Circle the number on the scale that corresponds to your opinion.

1. Goals of the meeting

    Poor   1   2   3   4   5   Good

    (conflicting; unclear; diverse, unacceptable)   (clear; shared by all, endorsed with enthusiasm)

2. Participation in the meeting

    Poor   1   2   3   4   5   Good

    (few dominate; some passive; some not listened to; several talk at once or interrupt)   (all get in; all are really listened to; open and lively discussion)

3. Leadership of the meeting

    Poor   1   2   3   4   5   Good

    (group needs for leadership not met; group depends too much on one or a few persons; no direction or no leadership)   (a sense of direction; leaders allowed to emerge as needs for leadership arise; everyone feels free to volunteer to lead)

4. Decisions made during the meeting

    Poor   1   2   3   4   5   Good

    (no decisions were made; decisions were made to which I feel uncommitted; bad decisions were made)   (good decisions were made; everyone felt a part of the decision-making process; people feel committed to the decision)

5. Your feelings during the meeting

    Poor   1   2   3   4   5   Good

    (I was unable to express my feelings; my feelings were ignored; my feelings were criticized)   (I freely expressed my feelings; I felt understood; I felt support from the participants)

6. Organization of the meeting
   Poor___1_____2_____3_____4_____5___ Good

   | (it was chaotic; it was too tightly controlled; very poorly done; I felt manipulated) | (it was very well organized; it was flexible enough so we were able to influence it; all went smoothly) |

7. Relationship among meeting participants
   Poor___1_____2_____3_____4_____5___ Good

   | (my relationship with them is the same as before; I feel antagonistic toward many of them; I don't trust them; there is little potential for a future relationship) | (our relationship is much improved; I trust them more than I did prior to the session; I feel I got to know and understand many of them better; there is good potential for the future) |

8. Attitude about the meeting
   Poor___1_____2_____3_____4_____5___ Good

   | (boring; it was a waste of time; I don't like the way it was presented, disliked it) | (interesting; was helpful, liked it) |

9. Content of the meeting
   Poor___1_____2_____3_____4_____5___ Good

   | (uninstructional; did not learn much; not informative; too much process; not enough content) | (learned a lot; was informative; I'll be able to use the content; content appropriate to our needs) |

10. Productivity of the meeting
    Poor___1_____2_____3_____4_____5___ Good

    | (didn't accomplish much; no useful ideas emerged; it got us nowhere) | (got a lot done; very fruitful; something will come of this session) |

Example 4. The following survey can be given to group members to assist them in analyzing individual members' contributions to group effectiveness. The information is sensitive for groups with low degrees of trust, so the consultant should take care in deciding when to use it and in designing procedures for feeding back the information.

Role-Perception Survey
"Guess Who"

Who, in your judgment, contributes most to the group's effectiveness by

. . . acts of encouragement, warmth, friendly interest, and support? _____ (name)

. . . producing ideas, information, and suggestions?

_____ (name)

. . . helping us stay on the track, summarizing, checking to make sure we understand each other? _____ (name)

EXERCISES AND PROCEDURES FOR IMPROVING MEETINGS

This section offers exercises and procedures that consultants can use either in formal training sessions or during regular meetings. Although some might prefer another scheme, we have categorized these exercises and activities according to their effectiveness in helping group members: (1) warm up for meetings, (2) plan, conduct, and evaluate meetings, (3) analyze leadership and group behavior, (4) broaden participation, (5) stimulate creativity, and (6) deal with hidden agendas and game playing. Consultants will want to adapt them to their own particular applications, although each has been successfully tried as described here.

Helping Members Warm Up

Fatigue, illness, or other preoccupations may prevent participants from becoming involved in the tasks at hand. Procedures that help them to become attentive to the here and now will increase the efficiency of meetings. To this end, we have found the five warm-up activities that follow to be effective.

Naming. This activity enables strangers to learn the names of others in the group at the same time that their own names are being learned. One person states his or her own name; the next person to the left or right repeats this name and adds his own; the next person repeats the first two names and adds his own, and so on until all names are given. Because connecting names and faces (or whatever other aspect of appearance is mnemonic) requires alertness, it has the effect of focusing eyes on people instead of on note paper or out the window.

Hearing Goals. This activity, which is also designed to focus attention on persons and their directions of thought, can be used superficially or to greater point according to the mood of the moment. Each person addresses a particular other person, expressing some goal he would like to see the group achieve during the session, whether the goal is an agenda item or not. It might be a desire to finish a given plan, to discuss "why I only get paired with Joe and Clarence on field trips," or to be given a feeling that some conclusion is reached at the end of the session. In any case, the answering person must say something in response that is more than a mere acknowledgment of the first person's utterance.

Milling. In this procedure, each person walks about the room looking at other members without speaking to them. After a few minutes, participants are asked to choose someone they would like to know better and to talk with this person. After another few minutes the milling begins again and someone else is chosen with whom to repeat the activity.

Billy Goat.   This activity is helpful for loosening people up in preparation for some creative task. The group stands in a close circle; the consultant steps into the center of the circle and explains: "When I point to someone and say 'billy goat,' that person must place her hand beneath her chin to resemble a goat's beard and bleat *baa*. The persons to her immediate left and right must at the same time form a goat's horns by each holding an index finger to the head. The last person of the three to do this must then step to the center of the circle and choose the next billy goat." After a few rounds the facilitator may introduce variations such as Elephant (middle person makes a trunk by holding two fists to his nose while neighbors form floppy ears) or Kangaroo (middle person makes a pouch by cupping hands while neighbors hop up and down). There are endless variations, and the group should be encouraged to create a few.

Walk across the Circle.   In this exercise, eight to twelve persons are seated in a circle and, at a signal from the consultant, all walk across the circle and sit in the chair of the persons opposite them. But only one step may be taken at the first signal, only one step at the second signal, and so on. After each single step, participants must hold their positions until the next step is called. As soon as everyone has taken one step, call the next step promptly although not while someone is still finding his balance. Keep calling until the last person has reached a chair and sat down. You may join the exercise yourself while calling the steps. After the first step, participants will get in one another's way and will have to choose whether to circumnavigate or to plow through the scrimmage. Those who prefer bodily contact will get it; those who do not will easily avoid it. This exercise requires only an average feeling of friendliness and good will among group members. During the debriefing, some of the participants will quickly offer descriptions of behavior and feelings.

Helping Members Plan, Conduct, and Evaluate Meetings

The leadership functions needed for effective meetings and several leadership roles that should be assigned to individual members in rotation have already been noted in this chapter. Here we discuss how consultants can help members plan, conduct, and evaluate their meetings and how they can strengthen the ways in which leadership functions are managed and leadership roles are assumed.

Planning and Preparing.   Before a meeting is called, attention should be given to clarifying goals, to issues of appropriate membership, and to matters of time scheduling and physical facilities. If the purpose of a meeting is clear to everyone involved, appropriate members can prepare relevant contributions toward accomplishing that purpose. If goals are unstated or unclear, some persons whose presence is necessary may not be invited; some will discover that their presence is unnecessary; others may feel little desire to attend the meeting at all; while many who attend will present concerns irrelevant to the major purpose.

Goals must also be kept in mind as a decision is made about how to schedule time. A group that wants to generate fresh ideas for teaching should probably not plan to meet at 3:00 P.M. after a hard day's work. Attention should be given to time allotments as well. Too often groups spend hours discussing a five-minute report only to find themselves forced to make a major decision in a few minutes. Finally, most meetings for problem solving and decision making require physical arrangements that encourage participation. Chairs should be placed in circles or around tables so that face-to-face communication can occur, and materials such as newsprint and felt pens should be available for illustrating and recording members' contributions.

As simple as these items appear, in many schools they are ignored by those responsible for meetings. Consultants can help to improve meetings by going over the planning prerequisites and also by encouraging an individual member, not necessarily the formal leader, to assume responsibility. The three planning sheets displayed in figures 6-5, 6-6, and 6-7 were developed by Schindler-Rainman, Lippitt, and Cole (1975, pp. 23-25) and can be used by meeting organizers to increase the effectiveness of their efforts.

Organizing an Agenda.   Most meetings involve several topics or activities that will vary in their respective time requirements. Some items will be presented for information only; others will require longer discussion and planning for action. Efficiency can be greatly improved if a group spends a brief time at the beginning of the meeting to set priorities, designate time allotments, and decide what kind of action each item requires. Unfortunately, many people are inexperienced at running meetings in a disciplined way. Those accustomed only to the free-for-all style will need repeated explanations of the disciplined step-by-step method and will learn faster if others in the group help to model and explain this style.

The following procedure allows everyone to contribute to building an effective agenda. (1) Ask group members to name the items they want to deal with at this meeting. (2) When you are reasonably sure that all members understand each item, order the items according to their similarities and place them in homogeneous clusters. (3) Select the order by asking group members for their priorities, trying at the same time to establish rough time estimates to be spent on each agenda item. Some of this can be accomplished before the meeting begins by posting an agenda sheet in a central location and encouraging group members to write on it items for the next meeting's agenda. In this way participants can not only contribute their own items for the group's consideration but can also think about

FIGURE 6-5   Diagnostic Planning for Designing Participatory Meetings

Thinking about the participants or members (e.g., how many, subgroups and individual differences, needs, readinesses, interests, expectations)	Some desirable outcomes of the meeting (e.g., skills, information, values, concepts, actions, plans, recommendations, decisions)	Ideas for activities, experiences, resources, to facilitate the outcomes (e.g., exercises, projects, resources, facilities, work groups)
*Star most important characteristics and differences among participants to keep in mind in designing	*Star highest priority outcomes	*Star what seem to be most appropriate, effective, feasible ingredients of design

Summary statement of desired outcomes:

FIGURE 6-6   The Meeting Design

Time estimate	Activities, methods, groupings	Who responsible	Arrangements of space, equipment, materials

1. Premeeting and start-up of the meeting

2. Flow of session after start-up activities

(continue on additional sheet as needed)

FIGURE 6-7   Commitments, Follow-ups, Supports

1. *Plans for ending the meeting* (e.g., closing activities, evaluation, reports of back-home plans, deadline commitments, etc.)

2. *Follow-up* Who? Will do what? When? Where?
   (e.g., often a directory of names, addresses, telephone numbers of participants is very important at this point and getting any follow-up dates recorded in everyone's calendar)

3. *Clean-up and other immediate commitments*
   (e.g., what has to be returned, thank-you calls made, bills paid, etc.)

---

other people's items so that they can offer more informed questions and decisions.

The best strategy we have found for helping groups improve their ability to organize an agenda is to assign the responsibility for this function to the convener, gain the group's agreement to use the procedure described above, and then coach the convener over several meetings. Consultants may recommend that the convener use the meeting format exhibited in figure 6-8 or some modification of it.

Convening. Using a chairman or convener to lead discussion and rotating this role throughout the membership are common procedures for providing some of the leadership functions previously discussed. Conveners have the legitimate authority to conduct the meeting. They should facilitate discussion by gatekeeping, asking brief questions, and summarizing concisely. They should move groups efficiently through their tasks, steering discussions of group processes

FIGURE 6-8   Sample Agenda Format

Agenda item	Order	Time	Person	Required action
United Fund	4	5	Sue	information only
Hall passes	2	10	Lee	discuss, appoint study committee
Selection committee for new vice principal	1	15	Lynn	advise principal on membership criteria
New science textbook	3	35	Task force	consensual decision
Debriefing	5	10	All	discuss

when that appears helpful, bringing hangers-back into the discussion, though remaining conscious of the necessity of moving the group along. They should see to it that recording minutes, writing on the chalkboard, and assigning tasks to individuals and subgroups are being done. Although they should be forceful and definite, not hesitant and apologetic, conveners should be aware that their role is to facilitate, not to dominate, and they should avoid arguing down others or writing on the board only that which meets their approval.

The convener's primary duty is to remind the group of its pact to discuss certain items during the meeting and to stop at a stated time (although this pact can be altered by common consent). If the group is taking too much time on one item, the convener should call this to attention, asking something like, "Do you wish to subtract time from other items, cancel one or more items, extend the meeting, or what?" Conveners should not choose or even suggest a solution but should demand procedural decisions from the group. When the group is not capable of making such decisions, it is useful to discover this fact.

Over a series of meetings each group member can practice guiding the group. This procedure is most helpful if group members give the convener feedback after the meeting about how well this individual has met their needs. We have found the following guide for the convener to be very easy for those with a fair amount of previous experience at conducting deliberative meetings. Conveners should think about all these tasks but should not try to use them all if the meeting is brief or attended by very few.

Guide for the Convener
Before the meeting:
- Review the agenda.
- Make sure a recorder is assigned to document proceedings at the meeting.

During the meeting:
- Get it started promptly.
- Lead the group to establish priorities among items on the agenda and to specify the time to be spent on each item.
- Keep the group at the task (i.e., monitor discussion and inform group when it strays from the agenda item at hand).
- Keep the group to its time commitments for each agenda item.
- Be attuned to feelings of confusion and try to clarify them.
- At the end of each agenda item:
  - Check to be sure that everyone who wanted to has had a chance to contribute to the discussion.
  - Check whether anyone is not clear about where the matter now stands.
  - Summarize or ask someone else to summarize. Be sure that the recorder has recorded the summary.
- Take process checks whenever they seem appropriate (if a process observer is present, employ that person's services):
  - Regarding satisfaction of group members with their participation.
  - Regarding decision making being done.
- Conduct or ask someone else to conduct a debriefing session during the last ten minutes of the meeting.

Recording Activities and Decisions. Activities initiated at a meeting are seldom completed at the same meeting because most such issues require some sort of procedure for storage and retrieval of information at a future time. Since groups cannot rely on individual memories, recording and distributing minutes are crucial for continuity. Effective groups assign recording tasks to one individual but rotate the role throughout the membership just as the convener role is rotated. The following guide is appropriate for most school meetings but can be adapted for brief informal meetings attended by few people.

Guide for the Recorder
Before the meeting:
- Review the agenda and record of previous meetings for unfinished agenda items.
- Gather materials necessary to record what happens at the meeting (e.g., pencil and paper, large newsprint and felt pens, and perhaps a video or audio recorder).

During the meeting:
- Describe the setting for the meeting (places, dates, time and list the participants.

- Copy down the agenda in the order finally agreed upon.
- During each agenda item, record the major views expressed and points of information shared.
- At the end of each agenda item, record short summary including decisions made, understandings achieved, or action to be taken.

After the meeting:

- Collect any newsprint used by group members during the meeting (e.g., for brainstorming ideas) and prepare to attach a typed copy to the record.
- Meet with the convener to check the clarity and complete-ness of the record.
- Have the records typed, duplicated, and transmitted to group members.
- Make sure a debriefing item gets on the agenda.

Facilitating Process. Meetings can be more effective if a group ap-points one of its own members to be a process observer with func-tions that complement those of the convener and if its consultants have been successful in transferring to group members the skill and responsibility for observing and analyzing their own process. The consultant can coach the process observer over several meetings by using the guide below and by helping this person become proficient in using the instruments for process observation and feedback de-scribed earlier in this chapter. Groups new to process observation and discussion might take a look at how they are doing every twenty to thirty minutes, with the observer leading a brief discussion at each process break about how satisfying and productive the meeting has been so far. The following guide suggests important tasks for the process observer, who should not attempt to squeeze them all in at once but should choose among them, taking the size and type of meeting into account.

Guide for the Process Observer

Before the Meeting:

- Collect and practice using appropriate observation sched-ules for gathering data on meetings.
- Ask the group what kind of information it would like you to look for and when you might make a process check or report back observations.

During the meeting:

- Attend to the process rather than to task functions of the group.
- Record your observations and impressions about why the meeting is going as it is. Watch for communication pat-terns, breadth of participation, atmosphere of the group, apparent satisfaction of group members, decisions being made.

- Organize your observations so that they can be shared with the group. Coding similar observations may help to make sense out of a clutter of notes.
- Report your observations to the group when appropriate, and make sure you describe observed behaviors to support your interpretations of what was happening in the group.
- If the group gets bogged down at any point, ask members to stop and discuss what is preventing them from accomplishing their purposes.

At the close of the meeting:

- Conduct a debriefing session during the last few minutes of the meeting, asking members to consider the following:
  - Did we accomplish our goals for this meeting?
  - Did we use our resources effectively?
  - Did we avoid pitfalls such as wasting time?
- Ask members for feedback about how well you served as their process observer.

Group Agreements. Rewards and punishments arise when groups have definite but inexplicit norms about behavior. If people believe that they will suffer rejection or punishment by failing to conform to these norms, it will be difficult for them to practice new behavior or to take creative risks unless doing so is explicitly encouraged. Hence norms controlling collaboration, use of power, and especially openness about feelings should be made explicit if they are to exercise a salubrious influence on meeting effectiveness. If, for example, group members deal with feelings of boredom or frustration when they arise, the conditions that produce these feelings can be changed to create a better climate for accomplishing the tasks at hand. The following procedures are helpful for clarifying norms.

1. *Forming group agreements.* Each member states a norm or custom that he would like others to practice. The group discusses each proposal until consensus is reached on several of them. Because it is important to describe the behavioral content of a proposed norm, the consultant may wish to provide samples like the two that follow.
   (a) For directness, I will report dissatisfactions with the way the group is going during the meeting. I will not discuss these dissatisfactions with nonmembers. If outside a regular session another member tells me of his dissatisfaction with the group, I will suggest bringing the matter before the total group at the next meeting.
   (b) Any member may ask for a survey at any time. The member will state what he wants to know from the total group, and someone else will paraphrase the request. Each person will state a position in two or three sentences. A survey is not a vote and will not bind us. A survey must be taken when it is requested and will suspend any other activity.

Establishing group agreements is the way new norms are made. Members discuss the explicit ways in which they have been rewarding and punishing one another for certain behavior in the past. They say that they want to give up some of the behavior that was maintained in that way, that they want certain other behaviors to be rewarded, and that they will join in new common patterns of encouraging and discouraging one another's behavior. It's as simple and as difficult as that.

2. *Continuing group agreements.* Periodically a group should review its agreements and discuss whether they are being kept. Agreements should not be regarded as sacrosanct. An effective group will change its agreements often and will plan actions to build commitments for new agreements. Above all, the group should be clear and explicit about what kinds of behaviors are expected.

3. *Listing inhibited and induced behaviors.* Each group member answers the following questions in writing:

   (a) What have I wanted to do in this group but have not done because it seemed inappropriate?

   (b) What have I done in this group that I didn't want to do but to which I couldn't say no?

   After sharing these answers aloud, the group looks for common patterns that suggest norms. The members then make consensual agreements about which existing norms are dysfunctional and which new norms would be better. In the final step, members plan for instituting the new agreements by stating steps and dates for actions that will reflect them.

Evaluating Group Effectiveness. Few people publicly evaluate the meetings they attend, and seldom is all available information used to ascertain how well the group is doing or where improvements could be made. Most meetings would be improved if they were interrupted periodically to give participants, observers, or buzz groups an opportunity to discuss where the group is, where it should be going, and how it can get there. Evaluation procedures described elsewhere in this book can be used at several points during a meeting to help a group find ways of reaching its objectives. Here we wish only to encourage group members to discuss evaluative information.

Analyzing Leadership

Effective meetings occur when group members assume and share leadership functions necessary for carrying forward the work and interpersonal processes of the group. Consultants can help them understand their own leadership and group behavior by asking them to complete either or both of the following questionnaires* and by

---

*From Johnson and Johnson (1975, pp. 18-20 and 245-46).

leading a discussion of similarities and differences among the responsibilities of individuals. The group may list behaviors that are seldom in evidence, and individuals may set personal goals to try performing one or more of the behaviors in the group.

Checking My Group Behavior.   This questionnaire asks group members a series of questions about their behavior in the group. The consultant encourages them to be as honest as they can and tells them that there are no right or wrong answers.

1. I offer facts, give my opinions and ideas, provide suggestions and relevant information to help the group discussion.
   Never   1 : 2 : 3 : 4 : 5 : 6 : 7   Always
2. I express my willingness to cooperate with other group members and my expectations that they will also be cooperative.
   Never   1 : 2 : 3 : 4 : 5 : 6 : 7   Always
3. I am open and candid in my dealings with the entire group.
   Never   1 : 2 : 3 : 4 : 5 : 6 : 7   Always
4. I give support to group members who are on the spot and struggling to express themselves intellectually or emotionally.
   Never   1 : 2 : 3 : 4 : 5 : 6 : 7   Always
5. I keep my thoughts, ideas, feelings, and reactions to myself during group discussions.
   Never   1 : 2 : 3 : 4 : 5 : 6 : 7   Always
6. I evaluate the contributions of other group members in terms of whether their contributions are useful to me and whether they are right or wrong.
   Never   1 : 2 : 3 : 4 : 5 : 6 : 7   Always
7. I take risks in expressing new ideas and current feelings during a group discussion.
   Never   1 : 2 : 3 : 4 : 5 : 6 : 7   Always
8. I communicate to other group members that I am aware of, and appreciate, their abilities, talents, capabilities, skills, and resources.
   Never   1 : 2 : 3 : 4 : 5 : 6 : 7   Always
9. I offer help and assistance to anyone in the group in order to bring up the performance of everyone.
   Never   1 : 2 : 3 : 4 : 5 : 6 : 7   Always
10. I accept and support the openness of other group members, supporting them for taking risks and encouraging individuality in group members.
    Never   1 : 2 : 3 : 4 : 5 : 6 : 7   Always
11. I share any materials, books, sources of information, or other resources I have with the other group members in

order to promote the success of all members and the group as a whole.

Never   1 : 2 : 3 : 4 : 5 : 6 : 7   Always

12. I often paraphrase or summarize what other members have said before I respond or comment.

Never   1 : 2 : 3 : 4 : 5 : 6 : 7   Always

13. I level with other group members.

Never   1 : 2 : 3 : 4 : 5 : 6 : 7   Always

14. I warmly encourage all members to participate, giving them recognition of the contributions, demonstrating acceptance and openness to their ideas, and generally being friendly and responsive to them.

Never   1 : 2 : 3 : 4 : 5 : 6 : 7   Always

Broadening Participation

Most meetings could be more effective if all group members were encouraged to participate actively. Accurate communication demands active listening, and effective decision making requires at least minimal participation by those who will carry out decisions. Members should not have to guess what others think of their ideas; if they are to improve the way they participate in the group, they must know the effects of their remarks on others. The following procedures are useful for broadening participation.

The Chance to Listen. By time-honored democratic tradition, the right to speak is everyone's basic right at a meeting. But parliamentary rules and procedures do not ensure our right to understand what has just been said. To ask a question for clarification, you are first required to "get the floor," and getting the floor is hedged about with numerous rules, restrictions, protocols, customs, and protections. By the time you have fought through the channels to be allowed to ask your question, you have had a ten-minute debate with the meeting's chairman or parliamentarian, three other speakers who were awaiting their turn at the floor have made long speeches, and the earlier speaker of whom you wished to ask your question has gone out to lunch.

One way to alter this situation is to insist during crucial periods that before someone speaks, he or she must paraphrase the person who just finished speaking. Before a proposal is decided upon, several people should paraphrase so that everyone is clear about what is being decided. The chance to listen means that you are allowed at any moment to interrupt a speaker for clarification. This only works, however, when the group as a whole genuinely values mutual understanding.

High-Talker Tap-out. It is not uncommon to find during small-group discussions that only a small percentage of the group is involved in a large percentage of the interaction. The High-Talker Tap-out deals with this problem by making the balance of participation more even. Appoint someone to monitor the group to see whether any participant is dominating the interaction. If one or two are, the monitor gives them notes asking them to refrain from further content comments, although comments on group process may be permitted.

Time Tokens. The Time Token is another device for dealing with people who contribute too little or too much. Distribute tokens to participants, each token to be redeemed for a specific amount of discussion time—say fifteen seconds each. When a participant uses up his tokens, he may say nothing more unless other members are willing to give him some of their tokens. This less obtrusive procedure has certain advantages over the tap-out. It allows an exceptional contributor to overcontribute with the consent of the other group members; it makes each member's degree of participation obvious and salient; it urges participants to make their contributions more concise; participants monitor their own talking and need not wonder what the silence of certain other members means.

Beach Ball. Still another procedure for dealing with those who contribute too little or too much is the Beach Ball. Only the person holding the ball is permitted to speak. Others who wish to contribute must nonverbally attract the attention of the person with the ball and induce the speaker to toss it to them. Instead of a beach ball, a wad of newspaper or other harmless object can be used.

Fishbowl. A procedure that employs some of the advantages of the small-group discussion within the setting of a larger meeting is the Fishbowl. In this procedure, a small group forms a circle within a larger group and discusses whatever is on the agenda as the other participants observe. To allow wider participation, empty chairs can be provided in the central group so that any observing members can join the discussion, with the understanding that this will only be temporary. The onlookers are themselves arranged in a circle so that everyone can see and hear the inner group clearly and also get quickly to a visitor's chair.

This procedure is useful when those in the encircling group can see an obvious reason why those in the interior circle were selected— if, for example, they are a regularized group within the organization, if they are temporary or regular representatives of segments of the onlookers, or the like. If members of the inner group have no obvious special differences from the rest, assigning them special seating will usually seem unjustifiable.

Buzz Groups. Buzz groups are effective in diffusing participation in a large group, especially when important decisions must be made and some members hesitate to express opposing views before the entire assembly. Suppose, for example, a faculty is at the point of setting priorities among several goals. Some teachers have stated their preferences but most have remained silent. The chairman may interrupt the meeting temporarily while groups of four to seven persons form to discuss the issue briefly to discover whose opinions are opposed and whether they are ready to reach agreement. When feelings are difficult to bring out, have reporters from each buzz group summarize the ideas and feelings of their groups without indicating which persons expressed them. Such summaries also make it difficult for any one group of members to dominate the flow of interaction.

Encouraging Participation Exercise. The following eight-step exercise* shows the importance of maintenance functions in a decision-making group, emphasizes the necessity of involving all members in group decision making, and gives practice in observing leadership behavior in a group. It concentrates on encouraging group members to become involved in group activities.

I. Introduce the exercise by reviewing the task and maintenance functions in a group and by telling participants that the exercise focuses on leadership behavior in a decision-making group. Inform them that there is a "best" solution to the problem, based on research, which they will learn after they have completed the first six steps.

II. Form groups of ten to fourteen members—large groups are essential in this exercise—with two additional observers for each group. Distribute copies of the following case study.

Overcoming Resistance to Change
In American industry, competition makes change necessary— like changing products and the way in which jobs are done. One of the most serious production problems at the Sleep-Eze pajama factory has been that production workers have resisted necessary changes. The upshot has been grievances about the piece rates that went with the new methods, high job turnover, low efficiency, restriction of output, and marked aggression against management. Despite these undesirable effects, methods and jobs must continue to change at the Sleep-Eze company if it is to remain a competititor in its field.

The main plant of the Sleep-Eze Manufacturing Corporation is in a small town in a southern state. The plant produces pajamas and, like most sewing plants, hires mostly women; there are about 500 women and 100 men employees. The workers are recruited from the rural areas around the town, and they usually have no industrial experience. Their average age is twenty-three, and their average education is ten years of formal schooling. Company policies in regard to labor relations are liberal and

---

* Originally created by Hall (1969), here adapted from Johnson and Johnson (1975, pp. 39–40 and 351–54).

progressive. A high value has been placed on fair and open dealing with the employees, and they are encouraged to take up any problems or grievances with the management at any time. Sleep-Eze has invested both time and money in employee services, such as industrial music, health services, lunchroom facilities, and recreation programs.

The employees of Sleep-Eze work on an individual-incentive system. Piece rates are set by time study and are expressed in terms of units. One unit is equal to one minute of standard work: 60 units per hour equal the standard efficiency rating. The amount of pay received is directly proportional to the weekly average efficiency rating achieved. Thus, an operator with an average efficiency rating of 75 units an hour (25 percent more than standard) would receive 25 percent more than the base pay. The rating of every piece worker is computed every day, and the results are published in a daily record of production that is shown to every operator.

The average relearning time for workers who are transferred to a new job is eight weeks. The relearning period for experienced operators is longer than the learning for a new operator.

The company now recognizes that the time has come to make changes again. Although they are to be minor ones, changes heretofore have been met with extreme resistance by the employees involved. Such an expression as "when you make your units [standard production], they change your job" is heard all too frequently. As in the past, many operators will refuse to change, preferring to quit.

Some examples of the changes to be made are:

1. Eighteen hand pressers have formerly stacked their work in half-dozen lots on a flat piece of cardboard the size of the finished product. The new job calls for them to stack their work in half-dozen lots in a box the size of the finished product. An additional two minutes per dozen will be allowed (by the time study) for this new part of the job.

2. Thirteen pajama folders have heretofore folded coats with prefolded pants. The change calls for the pants to be folded too. An additional two minutes per dozen will be allowed.

3. Fifteen pajama examiners have been clipping threads and examining every seam. The new job calls for pulling only certain threads off and examining every seam. An average of 1.2 minutes per dozen will be subtracted from the total time.

What is the best procedure for management to take to make sure the least amount of resistance results from these needed changes? Listed below are several different ways of handling this problem. Rank these alternatives in terms of their effectiveness for bringing about the least resistance to change. Place a 1 by the most effective alternative, 2 by the second most effective, and so on through 5, the least effective. Remember that after the exercise you will be told what researchers have found to be the "best" ranking.

_____ By written memo, explain the need for a change to the employees involved, and allow extra pay for transfers to make up for the usual drop in piece rate after a change.

_____ Before any changes are made, hold meetings with large groups of the employees involved, and give a lecture explaining that the change is necessary because of competitive conditions. Have the time-study man thoroughly explain the basis of the new piece rate. Then put in the change as planned.

_____ Before any changes take place, hold meetings with large groups of the employees involved. Using demonstrations, dramatically show the need for change. Present a tentative plan for setting the new job and piece rates, and have the groups elect representatives to work with management in making the plan final.

_____ By written memo, explain the need for the change, put the change into operation, and make layoffs as necessary on the basis of efficiency.

_____ Before any changes occur, hold meetings with small groups of the employees involved. Employing demonstrations, dramatically present a tentative plan for setting the new job and piece rates, and ask everybody present to help in designing the new jobs.

III. Meet with the observers and give them copies of task and maintenance functions observation sheets. Explain that their role is to give their attention to the leadership and decision-making behavior of the group.

IV. Give the groups thirty minutes to arrive at a decision on the case study, indicating that their decision should be based upon accurate information and facts.

V. At the end of the thirty minutes, have every group member fill out the form below:

1. How much did you participate in making the decisions reached by your group? I participated:
   7 = Completely or thoroughly.
   6 = A lot more than others.
   5 = More than others.
   4 = About as much as most others.
   3 = Less than others.
   2 = A lot less than others.
   1 = Not at all.

2. How satisfied did you feel with the amount and quality of your participation in reaching a joint decision? I felt:
   7 = Completely satisfied.
   6 = Generally or mostly satisfied.
   5 = A little more satisfied than dissatisfied.

4 = Neutral, as satisfied as dissatisfied.
3 = A little more dissatisfied than satisfied.
2 = Generally or mostly dissatisfied.
1 = Completely dissatisfied.

3. How much responsibility would you feel for making the decision work? I would feel:
   7 = Completely responsible.
   6 = Generally or mostly responsible.
   5 = A little more responsible than irresponsible.
   4 = Neutral, as responsible as irresponsible.
   3 = A little more irresponsible than responsible.
   2 = Generally or mostly irresponsible.
   1 = Completely irresponsible.

4. How committed do you feel to the decision your group made? I feel:
   7 = Completely committed.
   6 = Generally or mostly committed.
   5 = A little more committed than uncommitted.
   4 = Neutral, as committed as uncommitted.
   3 = A little more uncommitted than committed.
   2 = Generally or mostly uncommitted.
   1 = Completely uncommitted.

5. How much frustration or fulfillment did you feel during the work on the decision? I felt:
   7 = Completely frustrated.
   6 = Generally or mostly frustrated.
   5 = A little more frustrated than fulfilled.
   4 = Neutral, as frustrated as fulfilled.
   3 = A little more fulfilled than frustrated.
   2 = Generally or mostly fulfilled.
   1 = Completely fulfilled.

6. How good was the decision your group made? It was:
   7 = Completely accurate.
   6 = Generally or mostly accurate.
   5 = A little more accurate than inaccurate.
   4 = Neutral, as accurate as inaccurate.
   3 = A little more inaccurate than accurate.
   2 = Generally or mostly inaccurate.
   1 = Completely inaccurate.

7. How much influence did you have on the group's decision? I influenced:
   7 = Completely or thoroughly.
   6 = A lot more than others.
   5 = More than others.
   4 = About as much as most others.
   3 = Less than others.
   2 = A lot less than others.
   1 = Not at all.

8. When members had differences of opinion, to what extent were all sides carefully listened to and the conflict directly faced and resolved?

7 = Completely listened to.
6 = Generally or mostly listened to.
5 = A little more listened to than not listened to.
4 = Neutral, as listened to as not listened to.
3 = A little more not listened to than listened to.
2 = Generally not listened to.
1 = Completely not listened to.

9. To what extent are you willing to work effectively with this group in the future?

7 = Completely willing.
6 = Generally or mostly willing.
5 = A little more willing than unwilling.
4 = Neutral, as willing as unwilling.
3 = A little more unwilling than willing.
2 = Generally or mostly unwilling.
1 = Completely unwilling.

VI. On the basis of the response to question number one, divide the reaction forms from all groups into two categories as follows: Place in the high-participator category any person who responded 5 or higher on the first question and in the low-participator category anyone who responded 4 or below. For each category, determine the mean response to the rest of the questions by totaling the responses for each question and dividing by the number of persons in the category. Enter the mean response in the table below.

	High participators	Low participators
Amount of satisfaction obtained from participation	_____	_____
Feelings of responsibility for making the decision work	_____	_____
Feelings of commitment to the group's decision	_____	_____
Amount of frustration felt during group meeting	_____	_____
Appraisal of decision quality	_____	_____
Influence felt on the group's decision	_____	_____
Direct dealing with conflict	_____	_____
Willingness to work with the group in the future	_____	_____

Present the results to the participants, ask each group to discuss them, and propose a theory concerning both the effects of participation in group decision making on the implementation of a decision and the effects of maintenance functions (especially encouraging participation) on group decision making. Give each group up to thirty minutes to formulate its theory.

VII. Have groups share their theories and encourage a general discussion about the importance of maintenance functions in groups. Only after this discussion, present participants with the correct ranking of alternatives presented in the case study as below:

> *This case study was an actual situation studied by Coch and French in the late 1940s. From the results of their study, they considered the correct ranking to be 4, 3, 2, 5, 1. The two principles involved are: (1) group discussion is more effective than lectures and memos in influencing change, and (2) belief that one is participating in making the decision leads to commitment to putting the decision into practice.*

VIII. Have each group analyze the leadership behavior in its group using the information gathered by the observers. Review the leadership behavior of group members in terms of the theories just formulated in step VI. Of special interest should be information on who encouraged the participation of other members.

Brainstorming. Members of groups have a wealth of ideas about most problems, but their ideas too often remain untapped. The purpose of this technique is to get as many ideas as quickly as possible and to elicit ideas that would remain hidden in free-for-all criticism. The consultant can help group members identify the problem to be brainstormed and then discuss the following principles with them. (1) Groups will be more productive if they refrain from evaluating ideas at the time they are proposed; critical judgment should be suspended until all ideas are out. (2) Group production of ideas can be more creative than separate individual production of ideas. Wild ideas should be expected, and people should build on one another's contributions. (3) The more ideas the better. Quantity is more important than quality during brainstorming.

Self-inquiry Method. Schindler-Rainman, Lippitt, and Cole (1975) have used the self-inquiry method to help members think through those problems that might inhibit open communication and inquiry during meetings. The steps include explaining the purpose of the activity, having members spend a few minutes alone answering the questions:

- What are some of the factors in this meeting that will inhibit free and open exchange?

- What might a member like yourself propose to reduce the barriers to openness and creativity?

and, finally, having members share the results of their self-inquiry with others at the meeting. If certain factors are repeatedly identified or if group members want to find ways of carrying out their individual proposals, group problem solving might follow.

Dealing with Hidden Agendas

Consultants will sometimes observe behavior that has nothing to do with the immediate goals of the group or with the agenda posted before the meeting. Perhaps two teachers have had a running feud for years and delight in putting each other down at every opportunity. The principal may have information that members need but is withholding it, afraid of some or other consequence. Two members may be carrying on a flirtation with each other. When these relationships are played out in meetings, we say that people are dealing with *hidden agendas*, and the energy that goes into these agendas saps energy from the public agenda of the group.

The following exercise is designed to create an awareness of hidden agendas and how they affect the accomplishment of group goals.* The exercise requires a minimum of five role players and two observers and can be done within an hour.

1. Introduce the exercise as a way to think about differences between individual and group goals. Select five role players and two observers (or multiple sets of seven with large groups).
2. Present the following instructions to all role players: Read your instructions alone, and do not reveal them to other role players. When thinking about how you will play your role, think of ways to emphasize the role while remaining natural and not overacting. You are all playing actors at a meeting of a special fact-finding committee of the Community Action Program (CAP) Governing Board in Middleburg. Your committee was established to study the suggestion that CAP revise its procedures for electing board members. At present, representatives are elected for three-year terms and must run in a general-area election. Your committee is to consider two questions: (1) What would be the best electoral basis? the general-area election? smaller district elections? even smaller neighborhood elections? (2) How long should representatives serve? The chairwoman of your committee is LaVerne Turner who will make your recommendations to the city council.
3. Present the following instructions to individual role players:
   (a) Instructions for Carol Stone: You are a social worker with the Middleburg Department of Welfare and would

---

*Adapted from Johnson and Johnson (1975, pp. 91–92 and 365).

like some of your welfare clients to become active in CAP. You want some of your clients elected to the CAP governing board so that your department head will be impressed with your efforts and you will have more power in CAP. Because your assignment and those of other social workers are determined by districts, you want board members to represent districts and the terms of board representatives to remain at three years.

(b) Instructions for LaVerne Turner: You own and operate a store and are an ambitious community leader. You think poor people are lazy and want their representatives on the CAP governing board to be divided about goals so that business and professional members can run things their own way. You support city-wide elections for board members so there will be more representatives without support from small-interests' groups and one-year terms to minimize continuity among members from poverty areas.

(c) Instructions for Roberta Stevens: You are a mother of five on [a federal benefit called Aid to Dependent Children] and want a greater role for poverty representatives on the CAP governing board. You support the concept of neighborhood elections and one-year terms for board members so that more people from poverty areas get a chance to serve. You want more poverty representatives on the board to minimize the influence of business and professional members.

(d) Instructions for Lou Haber: You are a dentist who is also on the city council. You feel that government officials and professional people know what they are doing and should have a greater voice on the CAP governing board. Your objective is a weaker group of poverty representatives on the board; so you would support general-area elections and one-year tenure for board members.

(e) Instructions for Ed Simon: You are vice president of the chamber of commerce and are not really interested in this committee. You joined only to meet Carol Stone so that you can ask her for a date. During the meeting you plan to agree with and support every point she makes. Your behavior is guided by your desire to impress her.

4. While individual role players are studying their individual instructions, tell the observers that they are to answer the following questions:

- What is the basic goal of the group? How did each member contribute to or hinder goal accomplishment?
- Toward what goals were the individual members working?
- What task and maintenance behaviors were present and absent?

- What was the group atmosphere like? Did it change from time to time?
- Was participation and influence distributed throughout the group? If not, who dominated?
- How far did the group get in attaining its goal?

5. Set the stage for role players by reviewing the situation and setting up the space for the meeting of the fact-finding committee. Instruct them to begin.
6. End the role playing after fifteen minutes whether the group has come to a decision about what to recommend to the city council or not. Ask observers to report, and encourage role players to join in a discussion of the observers' questions.
7. Have role players read their individual instructions with Ed reading his last. Then ask role players and observers to discuss answers to these questions:
   - How do hidden agendas affect the group; how do they affect each group member?
   - What are some of the indications that hidden agendas are operating?
   - Is the recognition of hidden agendas necessary to understand what is going on in the group?
   - How can hidden agendas be productively handled to help in accomplishing the group's goals?

READINGS

Factors Affecting Change-agent Projects
Paul Berman and Edward W. Pauly

In volume II of *Federal Programs Supporting Educational Change*, Berman and Pauly report seven major factors affecting four types of implementation outcomes at the classroom level in 293 change-agent projects funded by the federal government. The four types of outcomes were: "the perceived success of the project (percentage of goals achieved), the fidelity of implementation (the extent to which the project was implemented as laid out), the extent of teacher change, and the difficulty of implementation" (pp. v-vi). The following reading presents two excerpts from this volume. The first describes the seven major findings; the second elaborates on the fifth finding, which related staff meetings and staff training as factors affecting implementation outcomes. We include these excerpts because they confirm our conviction that meetings are important and profitable arenas for school change.

From P. Berman and E. Pauly. *Federal Programs Supporting Educational Change, Vol. II: Factors Affecting Change-agent Projects.* Santa Monica, Ca.: Rand, 1975, pp. viii-ix and 60-63.

The following results were obtained from a multiple regression analysis of the factors affecting project implementation outcomes at the classroom level:

1. The effective implementation of innovative projects depended primarily on a supportive institutional setting and on an implementation strategy that fostered the mutual adaptation of the staff to the project's demands and of the project's design to the reality of its setting.

2. Projects funded by the same federal program showed considerable variation in their implementation strategies and institutional settings. These within-program variations affected project implementation more significantly than did the differences between federal programs.

3. Projects using similar educational methods of technologies varied considerably in their implementation strategies and institutional settings. These variations affected project implementation more significantly than did the differences between the educational methods or technologies themselves.

4. Superintendents, who tend to be organizationally remote, provided a generalized support that may have made schools receptive to innovations. such receptivity may be essential to Title III projects. Elementary school principals appear to have been "gatekeepers" of change, either facilitating or inhibiting implementation.

5. The following elements of implementation strategies promoted teacher change:
    a. Staff training.
    b. Frequent and regular meetings.
    c. Staff meetings held in conjunction with staff training.
    d. The quality and amount of change required by the project.
    The following elements of implementation strategies inhibited perceived success or teacher change:
    a. The lack of the above elements.
    b. Teachers not participating in day-to-day implementation decisions.
    c. For Title III projects, the lack of local material development.
    The following elements of implementation strategies were not significantly related to implementation outcomes:
    a. The *quantity* of planning.
    b. Participants' freedom to alter the basic project design on difficult projects.
    c. Part or full pay for training.

6. Elementary school projects were more effectively implemented than junior or senior high school projects and were more likely to produce teacher change.

7. Within the range of variation of differential funding considered here, a project's funding level did not have significant effects on teacher change or perceived success. Projects that serve most of, or the entire, student body of elementary schools were

unlikely to produce teacher change. The more concentrated were the resources of Title III projects, the more likely was teacher change to occur. . . .

Implementation Strategies. Almost independently of the educational technology or method involved, implementers of innovations have considerable freedom in putting their projects into practice. Each implemented project develops its own strategic mixture. Thus, to investigate an individual project, it is appropriate to observe its characteristic implementation strategy or syndrome. However, for statistical purposes, we need to analyze the strategic elements separately. The following material discusses the effects on implementation outcomes of each strategic choice in turn but defers synthesizing the results until the conclusion.

Planning. Beginning with the first listed element of implementation strategies, the percentage of the project's budget spent in planning and project design was not significantly related to implementation outcomes. Projects varied considerably in the amount of planning they did, and it would appear that the extremes of virtually no planning and of almost all planning in the first year or two were not characteristic of effectively implemented projects. . . . Unless the implicit planning model is congruent with the realities of project implementation, we hypothesize that teacher change and other goals will not be advanced.

Staff Training. The more staff training (i.e., the time project teachers spent in training), the more likely was teacher change, particularly in Title III projects. But the amount of staff training by itself did not significantly increase perceived success and tended toward decreasing success in elementary school innovations.

Our fieldwork experience suggests an explanation for this discrepancy between change and perceived success. Many projects, including staff development projects funded by Title III, do not seem to have linked training in new methods to application in the classroom. For example, pullout or pre-service training may not have been able to anticipate day-to-day activities during implementation. More important, staff training that is not integrated with other strategic components that reinforce the teacher's attempts to implement a newly learned approach may have little lasting effect. We will return to this hypothesis when we consider the interactive effect of training along with staff meetings.

Meetings. The positive significance of staff *meetings* for all the implementation outcomes, for all levels of schools, and for projects on all federal programs is clearly shown. This finding is particularly important in light of the strong dependence of implementation on organizational climate. Regular and frequent meetings can facilitate communications and coordination and also enhance morale and the teachers' commitment to the projects, when teachers believe that the meetings contribute to the essential activities of the project.

Meetings-Training Interaction. The value of meetings operating in conjunction with other elements of implementation strategy can be examined statistically by analyzing "interactions." In particular, preliminary analysis shows that although the amount of staff training time by itself is not significant for perceived success or fidelity of implementation, its interaction with meetings increases both perceived success and fidelity, as well as marginally enhancing teacher change. This result reinforces the hypothesis suggested earlier: Pre-service training, including technical assistance by consultants and outsiders, may be less effective than in-service and ongoing training linked to regular and frequent meetings of the project staff.

Participation. Considering the emphasis we have placed on involvement and participation, the next finding is to be expected: If teachers felt they did not participate in day-to-day decisions as the project was implemented, implementation was more difficult, and the chances of success, of fidelity to the project design, and of teacher change were reduced. This result was particularly strong for Title III projects, perhaps because of their local initiation.

Flexibility. Project design flexibility would seem a priori to be a desirable trait. We operationalized this flexibility (in gross terms) by measuring the freedom of project directors, principals, and teachers to alter the project design. None of the measures produced significant and stable results, although teacher flexibility had somewhat stronger effects than the others and is therefore shown in the tables. This statistical result may be due to measurement error; or it may be that flexibility did not affect implementation outcomes; or it may be that flexibility should not be considered by itself (i.e., there is a specification error) but rather must be treated as part of complex leadership relationship characteristics in the first year of the study. Project leadership and flexibility remain areas in which additional research is needed.

Local Material Development. The development of materials locally by project participants is shown by the case studies to have a considerable effect on implementation. Unfortunately, our measurement of this variable is simply whether a project did or did not develop its own materials (as reported by the project director). This measurement is contaminated by the tendency of projects to "reinvent the wheel"; that is, most projects tend to adapt even prepackaged material to their own setting. Consequently, our operational measure is probably more accurate for projects that accepted prepackaging in toto and, in this sense, did not develop their own materials. Given these definitions, not developing local materials (i.e., using prepackaged materials without adaptation) was not significantly related to implementation outcomes, except for Title III projects where it decreased perceived success.

Projects Located in Special Units. Projects that were primarily located in special units outside of classrooms tended to be "pullout" projects in which either selected students or a whole class spent one class period, once a week, in the project's laboratory or resource center. Although the statistical data are not significant, the effects of the pullout projects seem to depend on whether they were intended for remedial purposes (e.g., in reading or math in elementary schools) or for enrichment (e.g., career education often in junior or senior high schools). The enrichment units tended to be implemented as laid out and positively affected the percentage of goals achieved; the remedial laboratory was often difficult to implement. In either case, projects not located in the classroom usually did not engage the teacher in the project and were thus less likely to result in changes in teachers' behavior.

Project Coverage. Of the 104 projects in the Rand sample that served high schools, 65 also served elementary schools. These broad subjects included some Title III, Right-To-Read, and Vocational Education projects. Such broad project coverage had a strong negative effect on the effective implementation of projects, particularly those funded by Title III.

These projects seemed to have had severe management and administrative problems resulting from the attempt to integrate similar goals and treatments across different types of schools. For example, some reading projects spanning school levels promoted complex and ambitious plans for diagnostic and prescriptive methods. Although some of these projects did produce significant change in teacher behavior at the elementary level, where teachers view reading as one of their central teaching tasks, they may not have gained the necessary commitment of high school teachers. The net result was the apparent failure of the project to realize its high expectations.

Change or Effort Required of Teachers. In addition to staff training and meetings, the implementation strategies most likely to increase teacher change involved those requiring change. This important finding held whether the required change involved a specific teaching technique or an overall change in teaching style. Projects requiring teacher change and extra effort were difficult to implement and generally did not adhere to the initial project design. Perhaps because of their ambitious nature, they tended—although the estimates are not significant—to have a negative effect on the achievement of project goals.

Mutual Adaptation Strategy. Thus far we have discussed the findings for the effects of implementation strategies item by item. However, each project employed its own combination of strategic choices that defined its particular implementation strategy. Although we cannot statistically analyze individual combinations, the data do suggest characteristics of an implementation strategy that might be more likely to result in high levels of teacher change and achievement of project goals. In particular, frequent and regular staff meetings, staff training held in conjunction with meetings, and project requirements placed on teachers to alter their behavior appear to be elements that worked together so that project participants could adapt to the project and vice versa. This combination seemed to comprise key components of an implementation strategy that might be called a *mutual adaptation* strategy.

Leadership Principles for Problem-solving Conferences

Norman R. F. Maier

Having skillful discussion leaders or meeting conveners is very important if groups are to become effective both at conducting meetings and at solving their problems at meetings. Norman R. F. Maier here describes nine principles useful to leaders or conveners who want to increase the problem-solving abilities of their groups.

Reprinted by permission from the May, 1962 issue of the *Michigan Business Review*, published by the Graduate School of Business Administration, The University of Michigan.

It is possible for a discussion leader to increase the ability of a group of people to solve problems by means of the application of certain principles. No claim is made that the nine principles described below constitute a complete list, and it is also possible that the number eventually may be reduced to fewer and more fundamental principles. The reader may find that some of the principles overlap in certain respects. Nevertheless, the principles stated below are adequate in their present form to serve as a guide to the discussion leader.

Principle 1. <u>Success in problem solving requires that effort be directed toward overcoming surmountable obstacles.</u> If we think of a problem situation as one in which obstacles block us from reaching a goal, it follows that some of these obstacles will be more readily overcome than others. As a matter of fact, a problem will be insoluble if attempts are made to reach a goal over an insurmountable obstacle. This means that persistent attempts to overcome some obstacles might be doomed to failure. Success in problem solving, therefore, depends on locating obstacles that can more readily be overcome.

It is the common tendency to persist in following an initial approach to a problem. In other words, a particular obstacle is selected and pursued despite the fact that it cannot be overcome. Usually this obstacle is the most obvious or is one that previous experience has suggested. For example, medical research reveals that the inoculation of a serum to create immunity has been a successful approach for dealing with some diseases, so it tends to be followed for others. In business it is not uncommon to approach new problems with approaches previously found successful. Yet difficult problems require new and unusual approaches; if they did not, they would not be difficult problems. . . .

Principle 2. <u>Available facts should be used even when they are inadequate.</u> A solution that was effective in one situation becomes favored and is used in new situations even when the similarity between the old and the new situation is superficial. The assumption that the situations are the same tends to detract from a careful examination of the facts that are available.

When a good deal of information is available, problem solvers are more prone to work with the evidence. There is then enough information given to permit them to reject some solutions. However, in the absence of adequate information, it becomes more difficult to be selective and as a consequence imagination and biases dominate the problem solving.

Principle 3. The starting point of a problem is richest in solution possibilities. The solution of a problem may be envisaged as a route from the starting point to the goal. The process of thinking about a solution is like proceeding along a particular route. Once one starts in a particular direction, one moves away from certain alternatives and thus reduces the number of possible alternative directions that may be pursued.

Each route may confront one with obstacles. As discussion of a problem proceeds, successive obstacles present themselves. A group may have successfully by-passed two obstacles along the way and then find difficulty with others that face them at their advanced stage of progress. Because of this partial success in moving forward, it is difficult for them to revert and start all over again, yet a new start is the only way to increase the variety of solution possibilities. For example, a great deal of progress was made with propeller-driven planes; however, they had limitations. They were not able to fly above a certain height because of the lack of atmosphere. Increasing their power and design could raise the flying ceiling somewhat; nevertheless, the need for atmosphere limited the ceiling for propeller-driven craft. A plane with an entirely different power plant—the jet engine—represented a fresh start in aviation. . . .

In order to get a better appreciation of the starting point of a problem, a discussion leader should ask himself why he wishes or favors a certain solution. What purpose does my solution serve? Such a question may suggest the nature of the starting point of the problem. Spending time with the group to explain the prime objective, therefore, represents a procedure for finding the starting point.

All solutions represent methods for reaching a goal, but frequently sight is lost of the starting point. Rather the goal becomes an ideal toward which to strive. Practical consideration, however, requires that we reach a goal from the point at which we find ourselves. It may be unrealistic to get to an ideal goal from certain points. If one could start over again, more problems could be solved, or more ideal goals could be reached, but this is not realistic problem solving. A solution always is a path *from* the starting point *to* a goal, and sight of this starting point should not be lost.

Principle 4. Problem-mindedness should be increased while solution-mindedness is delayed. By nature, people progress too rapidly toward a solution. This is what is meant by solution-mindedness. This tendency is similar to the phenomenon known as the Zeigarnik effect. Once a task is begun, psychological forces are set up to push the task to completion. The reader will understand how he himself resists being interrupted while engaged in a task and how he worries over unfinished activities. It is only natural, therefore, that since the goal of a problem is to find a solution, energy and activity toward accomplishing this end is set in motion.

This means that in almost any discussion the responses of various persons tend to interrupt the thinking process of one another, and this is often disturbing. It is only natural for a dominant person to push through his ideas, and when he happens to be the leader, the value of group participation is lost. . . .

It is apparent that a discussion leader can cause a group to be more problem-minded. Usually he is a strong force in encouraging solution-mindedness. He must not only inhibit this tendency, but encourage problem-mindedness in his group in the process of improving his discussion leadership.

Principal 5. Disagreement can lead either to hard feelings or to innovation, depending on the discussion leadership. Two strong forces make for conformity: fear of the leader's unfavorable judgment and fear of unfavorable responses from the group to which one belongs. These factors unfortunately operate only too frequently in group discussion, so that the leader must be prepared to deal with both of them. Experimental evidence in support of this conclusion is to be found in several of our recent studies.

Almost everyone has learned that he can get into more trouble by disagreeing with his boss than by agreeing with him. This is the kind of learning that develops "yes-men." In most organizations, conferees need a great deal of encouragement to feel free to disagree with the boss. This does not mean that disagreeing is a virtue. Rather the subordinate must feel free to disagree if he is to contribute the best of his thinking. The leader takes the first steps in reducing conformity by withholding judgment, entertaining criticism, and trying to understand strange ideas.

The dangers of disagreeing with the majority members of one's own group or with society in general is less readily learned. The dissenter and the innovator sometimes find themselves popular and sometimes unpopular. For this reason, any hard feelings created by disagreement are not too apparent. However, an additional factor also operates. This is the security gained in "going along with the crowd." When people are unsure of themselves, they are particularly prone to follow group opinion rather than risk a deviant opinion. Conformity to group standards becomes unfortunate when it inhibits free expression or when the group rejects the person who innovates without examining or understanding his contributions. A majority does not have to prove or justify itself because it does not have to change minds, but a minority can be laughed down and hence is denied the opportunity to prove itself. Original ideas are new, so the original person frequently finds himself in the minority. This means that he may not only be a lonely person, but will have to justify many of his views.

When one person disagrees with another, the latter is inclined to feel that he has been attacked. As a consequence he feels hurt, defends himself, or becomes angry and counterattacks. Such emotional reactions lead to interpersonal conflict, and this type of interaction tends to worsen. As a result, some people avoid hurting others. Good group members, therefore, tend to be sensitive to group opinion, and to become careful is to avoid disagreeing. People who get along with other participants by conforming may be good group members, but they also become poor problem solvers. Members cannot learn from one another by agreeing. They can avoid generating hard feelings but eventually they may become bored. Satisfaction in group problem solving should come from task accomplishment, otherwise the group activity is primarily social.

We therefore are confronted with the fact that because disagreeing with others frequently leads to injured pride and interpersonal conflict, it is considered to be poor manners. In attempts to avoid trouble, people learn to refrain from disagreeing and hence move toward conformity. However, this alternative also is undesirable. The resolution of this dilemma is not only to prevent the suppression of disagreement but to encourage a respect for disagreement and thereby turn it into a stimulant for new ideas. How is this to be done?

First of all, each individual can learn to be less defensive himself, even if he cannot expect this tolerance from others. This is not much of a gain but it can be a personal one. A group leader, however, can accomplish a good deal in this respect. The leader of a group discussion can create a climate where disagreement is encouraged, he can use his position in the group to protect minority individuals, and he can turn disagreements among group members into situational problems. This is a second of the important skill areas for reducing the undesirable aspects of conformity, and in addition this skill in group leadership makes for innovation by using disagreement constructively.

Group thinking has a potential advantage over individual thinking in that the resources making for disagreement are greater in a group. Group thinking also has a potential disadvantage in that the dominant thinking may be that of the majority. The leader's responsibility is to capitalize on the advantages and avoid the disadvantages of group processes. . . .

Principle 6. The "idea-getting" process should be separated from the "idea-evaluation" process because the latter inhibits the former. "Idea-evaluation" involves the testing and the comparison of solutions in the light of what is known, their probability for succeeding, and other practical considerations. It is the practical side of problem solving and is the phase of problem solving when judgment is passed on solutions. "Idea-getting" requires a willingness to break away from past experience. It is this process that requires an escape from the bonds of learning and demands that we search for unusual approaches and entertain new and untried ideas. . . .

Creativity requires the ability to fragment past experience to permit the formation of new spontaneous combinations. In contrast, learning requires the ability to combine or connect elements that have been contiguous to each other in our experience. Since these two abilities are basically different, they do not necessarily go together. One person may possess an unusual learning ability and be uncreative; another may be unusually creative but not be outstanding in learning ability. Both the abilities to learn and to fragment experience are necessary for good problem-solving. However, the second of these has been largely overlooked because of our emphasis on the study of learning. . . .

The acquisition of knowledge, such as college training, actually may give an individual a mental set that reduces his creativity in certain respects, even though such knowledge is valuable in other ways. This is because the educated person may attempt to solve a problem by applying what he knows, and although this would be a successful approach on some occasions, it would not be a creative solution. This set prevents him from making up unique solutions and thereby developing a combination of parts that cannot be found in his past. Thus a potentially creative person . . . might be dimmed . . . by a knowledge of standard or known approaches to a problem.

Past learning, practical considerations, and evaluation all tend to depress flights of imagination—the forward leap that is based on a hunch (insufficient evidence). Creative thinking is a radical rather than a conservative look at a problem situation and requires encouragement if it is to be nurtured. To demand proof of new ideas at the time of their inception is to discourage the creative process.

However, creative ideas and insane ideas sometimes are difficult to distinguish. Both represent a departure from the common and traditional ways of thinking; both are new and unique to the person. But there is also a difference. The creative idea has a basis in objective reality, even though the evidence to convince others is inadequate; in contrast, the product of the insane mind is made up of elements derived largely from internal stimulation, such as hallucinations and imagined events.

The discussion leader can delay a group's criticism of an idea by asking for alternative contributions, and he can encourage variety in thinking by encouraging the search for something different—something new. Turning ideas upside down, backwards, trying out different combinations of old ideas all represent ways to encourage the expression and generation of new ideas.

Principle 7. <u>Choice-situations should be turned into problem-situations.</u> The characteristic of a choice-situation is one of being confronted with two or more alternatives. As a consequence, behavior is blocked until one of the alternatives is selected. The characteristic of a problem-situation, on the other hand, is one of being confronted with an obstacle that prevents the reaching of a goal. Behavior is blocked until the obstacle can be removed or surmounted. Creative alternatives tend to be overlooked in choice-situations because a choice is made between the obvious alternatives. The fact that such alternatives exist directs the energy toward making a choice and thus detracts from the search for additional alternatives.

Creative or unusual alternatives, not being among the obvious ones, are unlikely to characterize behavior in choice-situations

because activity is directed toward a choice between existing alternatives. Something must be done to delay this choice until the possibility of additional alternatives is explored. This is something the
discussion leader can do. Since the unusual alternatives are not
readily apparent, it is necessary to encourage considerable searching.

The discovery or creation of solutions is inherent in the nature
of problem-solving. This means that the discussion leader should
approach each choice-situation as one in which the possibility of
additional alternatives exists. When he encourages this searching
behavior in group discussion, he is turning a choice-situation into
a problem-situation. Only after other alternatives are found or
invented should the process of making a choice be undertaken.

Principle 8. Problem-situations should be turned into choice-
situations. Because problem-situations block behavior, the natural
reaction for people is to act on the first solution that is obtained.
The objective in problem-situations is to remove or get around an
obstacle. As a consequence, the discovery of the first successful
possibility tends to terminate the search. The fact that one solution
is found does not preclude the possibility that there may be others,
yet people frequently behave as though this were the case.

If the leader accepts the first solution as a possibility, he may
then ask the group to see if they can find another solution. If a
second and even more solutions are obtained, the problem-situation
will have been turned into a choice-situation. The opportunity to
make a choice must necessarily improve the final decision because
a choice between alternatives is permitted and the better one
can win. . . .

Principle 9. Solutions suggested by the leader are improperly
evaluated and tend either to be accepted or rejected. When the discussion leader conducts a discussion with his subordinates, he is in a
position of power so that his ideas receive a different reception than
those coming from participants. This point is basic to the group
decision process. In this connection, an experiment by Solem nicely
illustrates the principle. He found that discussion leaders acting as
superiors had more successful conferences when they did not have a
chance to study a problem beforehand. When they studied a problem
and reached a decision before the discussion, they tended to express
their ideas. As a result, the discussion was diverted into a reaction to
their ideas so that alternatives were not generated. The tendency of
members was either to show acceptance or rejection reactions to the
leader's ideas. Thus the leader's previous study of a problem caused
the group to reach less acceptable and poorer decisions.

Even when the discussion leader has no formal authority over
the group, his position is seen as one of power. Actually such a
leader exerts considerable power by merely approving or disapproving of ideas that are expressed. Thus a leader's suggestions are either
blindly followed or resented rather than weighed.

The best way to avoid these two undesirable reactions is for
the leader to refrain from introducing his views or passing judgment
on the ideas expressed by participants. His job is to conduct the

discussion and show his proficiency in this regard. In applying these principles his position becomes analogous to that of a symphony orchestra conductor. He plays no instrument but makes use of the instruments of the participants. Similarly, the discussion leader uses the minds of conferees and is interested in the best end results. At this point the analogy breaks down because the orchestra conductor has a particular outcome in mind, while the discussion leader strives for acceptable and high-quality solutions, not his particular one.

Conclusion

Quality and *acceptance* are essential dimensions in decision making. The quality dimension refers to the objective features of a decision— in other words, how does it square with the objective facts? The acceptance dimension refers to the degree to which the group that must execute the decision accepts it—in other words, how does the group feel about the decision? High quality and high acceptance are both needed for effective decisions. This means that group discussion must effectively deal with both facts and feelings.

A major problem is raised because the methods for dealing with facts are quite different from those for dealing with feelings. The skilled conference leader must recognize when he is dealing with facts and ideas and when he is confronted with feelings and biases. The difference is not always too apparent because feelings are often couched behind made-up reasons or rationalizations. Diagnostic skill therefore is one of his leadership requirements.

Once he is able to make diagnostic judgments, his next step is to deal effectively with each. The skills for removing conference obstacles in the form of feelings and in the form of ideas are quite different, and each set of skills has its place.

The problem-solving principles discussed in this paper are primarily relevant to handling the intellectual aspects of discussion. In dealing with emotional aspects the leader performs a more permissive function and serves more in the role of a group counselor.

The skill requirements in conference leadership are not difficult to learn. The problem lies more with the interference caused by old habits. Once one can break away from these and get a fresh start, the battle is half won. The first step is to recognize the existence of qualitative distinctions. No one skill is best for all purposes. If the basic distinctions are made, progress in each area becomes relatively easy.

BIBLIOGRAPHY

Burke, W. W., and Beckhard, R., eds. 1970. *Conference planning.* 2d ed. Washington, D.C.: NTL Institute for Applied Behavioral Science.

This collection of papers offers a variety of concepts and techniques for improving meetings, placing special emphasis on planning and conducting large conferences and meetings. Section 4, on "Training Group Discussion Leaders," is especially valuable when read alongside our ideas about convening. In general, this book provides ways of enhancing active participation at task-oriented meetings.

Fordyce, J. K., and Weil, R. 1971. *Managing with people: a manager's handbook of organization development.* Reading, Mass.: Addison-Wesley.

This handbook offers practical concepts and specific techniques on how industrial managers can promote a higher quality of life in their organizations. An entire section is devoted to the techniques of running different types of meetings and conferences and how these can serve as arenas for planned change.

Parnes, S. P. 1967. *Creative behavior guidebook.* New York: Scribner's.

The creator of the procedure of "brainstorming" includes here a potpourri of techniques and designs for stimulating creativity and divergent thinking in individuals and groups. The book also has an excellent bibliography. (A companion volume is cited in our bibliography for chapter 7.)

Pino, R. F., and Emory, R. E. 1976. *Group process skills.* Portland, Ore.: Commercial Educational Distributing Services.

This collection of group skills and structured exercises aims at improving group processes in task-focused groups and organizations. For the organizational consultant there are many helpful tips and techniques, and several of the exercises can easily be adapted to help intact groups improve their meetings.

Schindler-Rainman, E.; Lippitt, R.; and Cole, J. 1975. *Taking your meetings out of the doldrums.* Columbus, Ohio: Association of Professional Directors.

A self-help manual for those who take responsibility for conducting meetings, this book includes many useful suggestions, techniques, and job aids for small-group meetings, conferences, programs, classes, workshops, seminars, and conventions and can be used by organizational consultants and participants alike.

Schwartz, M.; Steefel, N.; and Schmuck, R. A. 1976. *The development of educational teams.* Eugene, Ore.: Center for Educational Policy & Management.

Although team meetings are but one aspect of the broader issue of team building, many concepts and techniques in this booklet focus on indicators of meeting effectiveness and on procedures for conducting successful meetings. Because all the examples and practical suggestions relate directly to educational teams, this document is especially useful to educators and consultants who work in public schools.

7

Solving Problems

Although every chapter in this book should provide some help in identifying and solving organizational problems in schools, this chapter offers specific designs and techniques for organizing groups of people to analyze school problems and to build collaborative action plans for solving them. It describes useful ways of conceptualizing problems, some origins of organizational problems in schools, ways in which educators typically handle organizational problems, and some social-psychological forces that constrain or facilitate effective group problem solving. Finally, the chapter presents a sequence of effective problem-solving activities and points out flexible ways to use either the whole or selected parts of the sequence.

THEORY OF PROBLEM SOLVING

Because every successful OD effort improves the problem-solving abilities of the school as a whole and of its important subsystems as well, it is very important for the OD consultant to apprehend problems clearly and be able clearly to communicate problem-solving concepts to participants. We view as a problem any discrepancy between an actual state of affairs (situation) and some ideal state to be achieved (target). Since both situation (S) and target (T) are in flux, problem solving must be a continuing process. Organizations and their subgroups should be detecting and working on problems continually, not just during times of crisis, failure, extreme tension, or pain, and should be aware that their understanding of situation and target will change as they work toward solutions. As group members reach new clarity about the problem that brought them together, they will become aware of problems they had not apprehended earlier. This process, however natural in human awareness and thinking, has stages, and it is a responsibility of the OD consultant to provide a systematic method that will enable a group to agree on its present stage and to move in a coordinated manner from stage to stage.

Working toward a target not only tests how well a plan has been conceived but also how well the original situation has been understood. New information that is brought to light while carrying out a plan for change may call for a change of plan, a modification of target, or bring about revised ideas about the desirability of the target as first conceived. As people approach their target and form a clearer picture of what living in the ideal state might actually be like, they may not find it as desirable as they had originally thought, or perhaps reaching it will have come to seem too costly. This does not necessarily mean that they planned poorly or chose the wrong target; it means that no plan or target stays good for very long and that if the group's vision does not change, circumstances will.

For this reason, participants should tackle concrete problems first, pick targets of moderate scope, and avoid the trap of overplanning. The danger of large-scale planning is that after devoting an immense amount of effort to it, people feel reluctant either to "waste" any of it or to put still more effort into reconceiving the goal or changing the plan. If they succumb to the temptation to carry out the plan to the last detail even though the facts show that things are going badly, they face the worse danger of losing the norms and skills of openness. Thus, instead of planning on the grand scale, we advocate incremental planning that is informed by regular feedback and replanning. School participants should build their new world in moderate steps, repeatedly resurveying both the wider horizon and the immediate path.

School problems can be classified in several ways. First, they can be classified by whether they chiefly concern: (1) relationships within a school plant (lack of sufficient role clarity, for example, or unclear lines of authority); (2) relations within the district (inadequate understanding of how to use staff specialists or poor communication between elementary and secondary levels); or (3) relations between the school or district and subsystems in the community (poor articulation of educational goals with parents, lack of sufficient student involvement in building innovative curricula, or inability to make effective use of community resources for learning).

A second scheme of classification specifies the magnitude of a problem according to how many people should be involved in the various stages of dealing with it. That is, most problems can be categorized according to whether they reside predominantly within one person (intrapersonal), among very few people (interpersonal) within a group, between two or more groups, throughout a larger subsystem, or among several subsystems. In fact, however, most organizational problems in schools exist at several of these levels at once. When a faculty is concerned about a discrepancy between its current and an ideal set of disciplinary procedures, for instance, there is a discrepancy not only at the level of the entire school but also among various grade levels, among several sets of individuals, and within many individuals. In addition, this problem can involve district policy and discrepant expectations among parents, students, and staff.

A third way is to classify problems according to organizational processes as this book has been organized. Although a problem can be categorized chiefly within a particular issue such as goal setting or conflict management, each content area is interrelated with all others, as, for example, goal setting overlaps with issues of communication, conflict management, running meetings, and making decisions. Since schools are multifaceted and their organizational problems are multidetermined, solutions will necessarily be multiple as well.

A fourth way of classifying school problems is to identify them according to how school participants perceive discrepancies between the present situation and an ideal state. In a recent study of organizational problems in urban schools, for example, we found staff members talking about the gap between the current level of student achievement in the school and a target for performance based on national norms; the gap between the current amount of parent involvement in the school and a target of high parent participation in the educational process; and the gap between the low use of outside resources at present and a target of enlisting much more help and support from key actors in the school's environment.

Whatever the classification, people usually become aware of the symptoms of a problem—incidents or conditions that evoke dissatisfaction, frustration, tension, or other unpleasant experiences—and respond to the symptoms before they have a clear understanding of the discrepancy between the S and T. People who encounter frustration commonly leap to two conclusions—that something must be going wrong somewhere, which is not always true, or that the source of their troubles is to be found in people who are above or below them in the organizational hierarchy, which is not necessarily true either.

Organizational life inevitably brings people into conflict over matters of time, space, materials, money, and other resources precisely because organizational life and its problems are highly interactive. When organizational stress arises, people should ask themselves whether the normal functioning of the organization will eventually remove what may be only a temporary source of frustration or whether unusual steps may be necessary to resolve the disquiet.

At present, attempts at solving organizational problems in schools typically begin when an administrator discovers that "something is wrong." Perhaps she receives phone calls or letters complaining about some policy, or perhaps a budget election fails several times in succession. In such cases, the person in authority, usually after consulting a colleague or the next person in authority, issues a directive or policy statement in an effort to remove the difficulty. It is *not* typical for the directive to include definitions of the *S* and the *T*.

Consultants can sometimes help just by reminding people to ask these questions. When people do not themselves have enough information to answer them, consultants can sometimes build faster working channels for information flow. That participants will sometimes blame their own discomfort on others in the hierarchy is perhaps inevitable, but helping people become aware of their own part in producing, perpetuating, and solving problems is itself a good part of the consultant's job. If, however, anxiety remains high, important motives for achievement, affiliation, and power remain unsatisfied and the equilibrating processes of the organization promise to be too slow, special measures should be introduced.

Problem solving in schools, then, is typically begun too late (when the discrepancy between *S* and *T* has reached the crisis stage) or too soon (before an adequate conceptualization has been made of the *T* and before valid information has been gathered on the *S*). In either case, few of the potential resources available for effective problem solving are mobilized within the organization, and members of such schools seem unable to make productive use of outside resources to this end. Finally, problem solving may also be hampered because schools face certain constraints imposed by time, social-psychological factors of groups, organizational factors, and a changing environment.

Time presents a major obstacle to participants and clients alike. Some school problems reach a crisis level before they are even recognized as problems; others remain unsolved because members lack the time to work on them. For their part, consultants must work around the client group's regular schedule. Even then, school people usually feel pressed to get their problems solved quickly and become impatient when asked to learn a new procedure at the expense of losing time that they believe could be better spent taking actual steps to solve the problem.

Another set of constraints arises from certain difficulties of collaborative problem solving in face-to-face groups. As suggested in chapter 6, although the advantages of group problem solving are considerable, several social-psychological blocks arise when people work in the presence of others. Some staff members may keep their ideas and feelings private for fear of ridicule or punishment from members of higher status.* Groups may do a poor job of forecasting consequences because of fear of criticism, and individual members may fail to ask for needed data because they are afraid to appear ignorant. A frequent impediment to group action is the difficulty of getting warmed up so that members can stay in tune with one another dur-

---

*See Bridges, Doyle, and Hahan (1970) for a study of the effects of the presence of principals on teachers' work groups.

ing each phase of a problem-solving sequence. In many groups, for example, it is common to find that some members have not yet brought their attention to the task, while others are struggling to define and understand the problem, while still others are eagerly proposing solutions.

Perhaps the most significant difficulty that affects group problem solving in schools is the failure of participants to distinguish between the process of problem solving and the act of making a decision. We apply the term *problem solving* to the kind of exploration and sorting that is facilitated by the *S*, *T*, and *P* concepts; we use the term *decision making* to denote choosing a particular plan of action, the persons who will carry it out, and the schedule for doing so. Because planning and action go better when groups can agree explicitly on which of the two phases they are pursuing, we have found it effective to teach these two phases to participants under different labels.

Organizational factors—such as lack of internal resources, lack of access to external resources, and lack of skill in using channels to either type of resource—can also constitute restraints on effective problem solving. Often, important information is either not available from organizational members or is available but is not tapped. Even when there is time to ascertain who has important information, group members frequently do not think of eliciting it. In addition, school faculties often suffer from an absence of synchronization between members with resources and their colleagues with particular needs. If a science teacher has ordered some technical equipment that could be useful in many other areas of curriculum, for example, and if this teacher is the only person who knows how to use the equipment, it is difficult to decide whether the science teacher should use available time to teach others how to use it, to help others develop ways to apply it to their own needs, or to search for scientific specialists in the district who could help others use it.

Perhaps the most formidable constraint on effective problem solving in schools is imposed by the changing external environment. No sooner have science teachers and their colleagues worked out high-quality solutions to mutual problems than technological change makes their new equipment obsolete. No sooner does a principal prepare a policy to please complainants in the community than some other community group raises different complaints. Not only are organizational environments of all types becoming increasingly turbulent,* but schools in particular are becoming increasingly interdependent with their external environments. Confronted with severe environmental complexity, the efforts of any problem-solving group within a school will often appear feeble. Indeed, some organizational theorists conclude that, in view of the power of the external environment, internal planning and organizing for problem solving are useless. On the contrary, however, we believe that since both the

---

*For evidence, see Emery and Trist (1965), and Terreberry (1968).

external and internal environments of schools are in continual flux, organizational problem solving must become a way of life if the school is to be self-renewing.

GATHERING DATA ABOUT PROBLEM SOLVING

Assessment of problem-solving activities receives attention elsewhere in this book. Chapter 4 includes guidelines for constructing questionnaires, interviews, and observation categories and provides examples of items to measure goals or target states. The sections on instruments in chapters 3, 5, and 8 provide forms for collecting information about particular types of problems. Chapter 2 gives information on assessing changes in organizational problem-solving competencies. Finally, chapter 6 gives information on gathering data about group effectiveness in problem-solving meetings. This section presents some additional interview questions and another form for helping problem-solving groups discuss their effectiveness.

Interview Questions for Identifying Problems

1. What are some things you would like to see this school working toward that it isn't doing now?
2. [If named something:] Which staff members do you think could help accomplish these things?

_____   _____

_____   _____

3. Have you received any information recently about your work or about the school that you found surprising? [Yes, no] [If yes:] Please describe one or two such kinds of information:

_____

_____

4. To make things operate more effectively, which people do you think ought to work together more closely? [Write names. Show each cluster of names respondent says should work more closely by encircling that cluster.]

_____

_____

5. What are some aspects of the current situation in the school that need changing?

_____

_____

6. What are some target conditions that you would like to see your staff attempt to achieve?

_____

_____

_____

7. Do you have any proposals for action in mind right now for moving toward these targets?

_____

_____

_____

Questions to Check on Group Effectiveness.   The following questions are used between stages of the S-T-P problem-solving sequence to encourage process discussion.

You have been working on a task. Like an automobile, a group needs maintenance. While working on a task, a group needs to stop occasionally to be explicit about its *interpersonal processes.* Please fill out the three scales below by circling one number in each.

What I say is prized and valued here.	6	5	4	3	2	1	What I say is being ignored here.
Our group is falling into traps.	6	5	4	3	2	1	Our group is avoiding traps.
I have participated often.	6	5	4	3	2	1	I have participated very little.

Discuss your answers on the three scales with the group. Try to be helpful. You will tend to be *helpful* when you are specific (e.g., "I felt valued by you, John, because you often asked me to say more when I spoke," or "An example of when I thought we fell into a trap was . . . ," or "I felt put down when you . . . "). You will tend to be *unhelpful* if you are general and evaluative (e.g., "You're the kind of person who puts people down," or "This group isn't working well," or "This group is the greatest I've ever been in").

PROMOTING EFFECTIVE PROBLEM SOLVING

Although the constraints on organizational problem solving in schools are many and strong, educators can do a better job by regarding problem solving and decision making as parts of a single cycle and by giving attention to both the quality of the action-plan and the degree of commitment of those who will carry out the actions. This section discusses concepts and ways of promoting high-quality work on organizational problems in schools; subsequent sections provide tools that consultants can use to facilitate improved problem solving. Concepts and techniques of effective decision making are described in chapter 8.

The following guidelines, adapted from Maier (1962), under-score particular functions for the conveners of problem-solving groups.

1. Because problem-solving groups typically progress toward solutions too rapidly, encourage problem-mindedness by checking that everyone understands the problem. The convener should encourage the group to achieve clarity about S and T before attempting to generate Ps. If most of the participants are ready to brainstorm Ps, however, let them do so for a while, but bring them back to considering Ts before evaluating Ps.

2. Because disagreement can be a valuable tool for creative problem solving, encourage respect for its use as a stimulant for new ideas. The convener should help group members distinguish among disagreements over beliefs about facts (S), disagreements that involve different value positions (T), and disagreements concerning different proposals for action (P).

3. Because evaluation and criticism inhibit the generation of ideas, delay criticism by seeking alternative contributions. The convener should help group members distinguish between critical appraisal and brainstorming, in which all ideas are acceptable—indeed, wide-ranging and creative ideas are encouraged. The convener should understand and be able to use stimulating discussion techniques that encourage creative thinking in the group.

4. Because conveners have great power even when they lack formal authority, be aware of your domination as a convener and try to limit it.

5. Because leadership is a set of functions, the convener should encourage the group to share responsibility for these functions.

Effective problem solving demands attention to three questions —Where are we now (S)? Where do we want to be (T)? How can we get there (P)?—but since school problems are multifaceted, the answers to these questions cannot be simple. Consultants can cope with this complexity by means of three stratagems. First, a group should analyze a problem in both its cognitive and affective aspects. Second, it should take into account the several social-psychological levels at which the problem exists. Third, it should recognize that a multidetermined problem requires multiple solutions.

In other words, the consultant should help the group look for information at the intrapersonal, interpersonal, group, and organizational levels, help the group locate and quickly integrate informed outsiders, and help the group attack the problem on several of its existing levels. If, for example, a staff must respond to complaints from students and parents, ask that students and parents be invited to collaborate in the problem-solving process. Better yet, form temporary problem-solving teams as the need arises, and include enough heterogeneity of membership on each team to handle the complexities of the problem.

In addition to dealing with a particular problem at hand, problem solving usually has the beneficial side effect of clarifying the differentiated and integrated functions that people perform in school organizations. How tasks should be divided while at the same time maintaining needed coordination among them will vary according to the problem, but differentiation and integration must both be included in the design. Differentiation can generate long-run variety for adapting to future problems, and integration can provide the joint commitment appropriate to the interdependencies in most problems.

Finally, effective problem-solving groups will usually reach a tentative working agreement about what constitutes the present situation and ideal target before considering alternative plans for reaching the target, and these initial working agreements should be checked and revised frequently. Most of the facets of any problem are in flux: the angry parents may change their minds tomorrow, the science teacher may take a new job, or the bond issue may not pass. The group must recognize that problems are seldom solved permanently and that every solution should be viewed as tentative—as an appropriate set of efforts given the constraints of time and available information and of environmental pressures or change. Group members should therefore be ready to assess changes and to revise plans for action, keeping in mind that problem solving is a way of life for the self-renewing individual, group, organization, and community.

THE S-T-P SEQUENCE FOR PROBLEM SOLVING

The Sequence

The following procedure for helping a team of educators solve organizational problems in schools consists of seven stages: (1) identifying the problem, (2) analyzing the problem, (3) generating multiple solutions, (4) designing plans for action, (5) forecasting consequences of intended actions, (6) taking action, and (7) evaluating the actions. These stages parallel the nine generic skills of organizational adaptability described in chapter 1.

Participants should have the definitions of their S, T, and P clearly in mind before setting to work on Stage 1. To underscore these definitions, it is useful to post them on newsprint and to review them before commencing the problem solving; in addition, group members should be encouraged to suggest illustrations of the three definitions. It is essential to use communication skills effectively throughout all stages and to be explicit about interpersonal processes while the group is performing its task. It is usually helpful as well to intersperse special occasions for discussing the group's effectiveness and its interpersonal processes—for example, to check how the interpersonal processes are going after each of the problem-solving stages. At least, however, interpersonal processes should be discussed after Stage 3 and Stage 5. Briefly, the seven stages include the following activities.

Stage 1. Post two sheets of newsprint in front of the group, writing *Situation* on one sheet and *Target* on the other. (A third sheet headed *Proposals* might be added if this will relieve participants from feeling penned in by an overrestrictive procedure. Usually, however, it is best for proposals to be held in abeyance until all group members are clear about the S and T.) As group members attempt to state aspects of the S and T precisely and specifically, record their contributions on the appropriate sheets while encouraging other group members to make still more contributions. Thoroughly check understandings, perceptions, agreements, disagreements, and personal goals.

Stage 2. Hang a large sheet of paper with the situation indicated in the middle and the target on the far right-hand side (see figure 7-1). At the top left, write *Facilitating Forces*; at the top right, write *Restraining Forces.* (1) Think of all the restraining forces that are keeping the group from moving closer to its target. (2) Think of all the facilitating forces that are helping the group to move toward its target. Ask all group members to think about helps and hindrances. (3) Number the forces in order of their power to help or hinder. (4) Mark the forces that are unalterable.

Stage 3. Select one or more restraining forces that you believe can be weakened by appropriate action and that, when weakened, will permit you to make significant progress toward your goal. Although an adequate list of restraining forces will be of more help to generating proposals than to working with facilitating forces, try, too, to think of actions that will help the more powerful facilitating forces work for you when restraining forces have been reduced. Use brainstorming to generate proposals, and record all ideas on newsprint. During brainstorming, group members should not render evaluative judgments about the proposals for action that are offered.

Stage 4. Make a specific plan of action listing all the most practical and feasible proposals that were generated during Stage 3. Specify who will do what, when, and in what sequence. Be sure to gain the help of those who will implement the plan. Encourage the group to schedule the first step the day after Stage 5 or as soon as possible.

Stage 5. Try to imagine and anticipate the many obstacles that might impede successful implementation of the plan. Simulate parts of the plan, get feedback from others, and revise the plan if necessary.

Stage 6. Put the plan into action. Take the first step, and alter the plan according to how well it works.

Stage 7. Evaluate the effects of the group's work together in terms of both problem-solving effort and interpersonal processes. Determine what has been most successful about the group's processes and what should be done differently when the group works the next time. Assess the changes that have occurred in the problem. If necessary, return to Stage 1, begin again, and persevere. Remember that one of the most important functions of an OD consultant is to lend energy and support to the group in its continuing efforts to improve its problem-solving ability.

Two Examples

We here give examples of how groups in two schools have used the problem-solving sequence. These are reproductions of actual work by teachers who had received five days of training, mainly in communication skills, group and intergroup exercises, and the problem-solving procedure. Each group spent approximately one-half the total training time on problem solving.

To Clarify Roles.   The following example is taken from the problem-solving activities of a team of teachers and principal in an elementary school. Although the statements below do not include everything the groups wrote on newsprint, they do include those that enabled the groups to move from stage to stage.

Stage 1. Identifying the problem.
Where we are: Lack of clarity in the role of the principal.
Where we want to be: We (the staff) know where the principal stands, and he knows where we stand.
Our task: To clarify the role of the principal.

Stage 2. Analyzing the problem.
Forces that are helping us get toward our target:
1. Many of the staff are open and want to know about the principal's philosophy.
2. The staff's willingness to be open is enhanced by our new communication skills.
3. The principal is willing to clarify his philosophy and his role.

Forces that are blocking our movement toward where we want to be:
1. Lack of time.
2. Some staff members' willingness to be the principal's "mouthpiece" and the feeling that he does nothing to discourage this.
3. Lack of complete openness of the staff, including the principal.
4. Confusion about our own roles.

Stage 3. Generating multiple solutions.
The most important ideas that we brainstormed were as follows:
1. We need more time for process and problem-solving meetings.
2. We need to practice openness.
3. We should let the principal know if we like something he is doing.
4. We should let the principal know if we do not like what he is doing.
5. We want the principal to give us feedback.
6. We need to clarify roles and expectations of each other and with the kids.

Stage 4. Planning for action.

Our intended actions, developed from elaborations on our brainstormed ideas, are as follows:

1. The principal will make a statement to the staff about his educational philosophy and role expectations, and the staff will have a chance to interact with him. Observers [names specified] will record the interaction and check on the communication processes between the principal and staff. All will evaluate the process and progress at the meeting. These actions will occur during our forthcoming workshop.

2. During the last week of summer vacation, we will go to Mabel's place on the Klakitaw River for a debriefing and planning session after the leaders' workshop. The whole staff is invited.

3. A school handbook will be written with everyone participating. It will contain:
   a. Role descriptions.
   b. A statement of how we hope to operate (openness).
   c. The principal's philosophy and expectations.
   d. Each group's summary of what it did and felt during this workshop.
   e. Operational procedures.
   It should be flexible and changeable and written in behavioral terms.

4. A teacher's workday in the fall (statewide In-service Day) will be used to do follow-up consultation with the whole staff in communication with the help of a few outside consultants—preferably in some location away from the school.

5. During the first week of school we will conduct a day of orientation for children and:
   a. Take students on a tour of the total building (nothing, including faculty areas, will be out of bounds).
   b. Introduce all the staff to students.
   c. Provide some heterogeneous group activity (mixed-grade groups) for students.

6. On the first day of school, the students, interested parents, and staff will report to the gym for an hour of welcome.

7. Following all staff meetings, communication and procedural matters will be checked by:
   a. Having a couple of people observe the meeting and report back on how we did.
   b. Including total staff in staff meetings.
   c. Training students to answer the phone and to greet visitors.

8. All students will be sent home at lunchtime on the last Friday of each month. Staff will bring sack lunches, eat together, and practice sharing communication skills and ideas. On those days all students will leave school at the same time.

9. One meeting a month will be set aside for sharing ideas, innovations, and failures. Seating will be arranged to prevent staff teams from isolating themselves.

Stage 5. Forecasting consequences of intended actions.

[The group presented the information reproduced above to the rest of the staff and asked for reactions and criticisms.]

Stage 6. Taking action.

[The staff implemented Action-Plan 7 (evaluating staff meetings) immediately. They also formed several ad hoc groups to develop the other plans and to try them out.]

Stage 7. Evaluating the actions.

[Most of the ideas for action had built-in evaluation plans. The staff was careful to allow time for evaluation as each sequence of actions unfolded during the school year.]

To Share Strengths and Encourage Variety. The second example is taken from the problem-solving activities of a group of teachers who were attempting to move from teaching in self-contained classrooms to teaching in teams. The experience of this group illustrates our admonition not to give up when things seem not to be going according to plan. For a time, the group seemed to have stalled after Stage 5, but the returning consultants gave enough help for the group to be able to proceed to action and evaluation.

Stage 1. Identifying the problem.

Situation: Lack of established procedures for sharing innovative ideas and supporting one another in experimentation. Target: We shall have adequate procedures for developing, sharing, supporting, and protecting innovations.

Stage 2. Analyzing the problem.

Facilitating forces: (1) physical plant conducive to sharing within units; (2) staff is willing to try new things; (3) principal encourages innovation; (4) new staff is willing and enthusiastic; (5) young staff has good ideas; (6) interns and others have experiences that will bring in outside ideas; (7) experienced staff is supporting changes and participating in them; (8) there is ready access to equipment that can be used for innovations; (9) there is willingness to know and communicate because of our new staffing arrangements (esprit de corps); (10) shared experiences brought us together during planning weeks; (11) kids serve as communication channels for ideas; (12) kids are very open to new experiences and sharing them; (13) some parents are very supportive; and (14) consultants work directly with students.

Restraining forces: (1) noise carries; (2) units are physically cut off from one another; (3) three of four units (or unit rooms) are separated; (4) some kids resist sharing; (5) facilities are overcrowded; (6) procedures for flexible use of space have not been worked out; (7) there is limited access to consultants for planning and execution; (8) failure to pass budget threatens many contracts (e.g., consultants and interns); (9) funds are lacking for supplies and field trips; and (10) the fear of a lack of supplies sometimes leads to hoarding. [In addition to the above, the group listed the most important restraining forces in this order:]

1. Lack of procedures for sharing knowledge between and within units about what each teacher has done, can do, and wants to do regarding innovations.
2. Competition and a lack of procedures for seeking support result in feelings of inadequacy, mistrust, and failure among staff members.
3. Teachers feel inadequate to innovate and are forced to fall back on traditional methods when confronted with large groups of students.
4. Some parents lack a view of the total picture at the school, and they feel apart from what we are doing; consequently, teachers fear parental nonacceptance.

Stage 3. Generating multiple solutions.

[The group brainstormed ideas for overcoming each of the most important restraining forces.]

Stage 4. Planning for action.

[The group reviewed its list of solutions, discarding many ideas and categorizing the rest as follows:]

1. Procedures for sharing knowledge:
   a. Ideas for immediate action: (1) take a survey at a staff meeting of each person's desires and strengths, (2) set up a card file of past and future ideas for innovations, and (3) set up tours. Ensure that staff members get to walk through the building to all rooms regularly.
   b. Ideas for future committee action: (1) make a list of strengths and have staff members put a check by the ones they feel they possess; (2) release each teacher once each week to go around and visit other classes (i.e., observe and interact); (3) have everyone tack a big sheet of newsprint up with his own strengths and hopes; (4) allow each person to add to other lists by writing perceptions of others' strengths; (5) put the lists into a file of "resources" in our building; (6) share lists stating "what I feel like doing today"; (7) keep a record of what is being done (include critiques); (8) update the outside resource file; and (9) use outside resource people more often.
   c. Ideas for future individual or team action: (1) inform your team leader about what you have done, can do, want to do; (2) establish time at each team meeting for sharing such information; (3) set up memory refreshers throughout the year; (4) send your students to find out

what is going on elsewhere in building; (5) use intercom to invite others to visit your lesson; (6) create central displays about what is going on in your team; (7) tape-record events and let others listen; (8) make posters advertising all events; (9) encourage classes to visit other classrooms; and (10) set up and exchange student programs within and between teams.

2. Procedures for seeking support, decreasing competition, and reducing feelings of inadequacy, mistrust, or failure:

   a. Ideas for immediate action: (1) use direct expression of feelings; (2) acknowledge own or others' feelings; (3) hold brainstorming sessions on these problems; (4) wear signs saying how you are feeling; (5) keep signs saying "I need support," and wear them when you do; (6) wear button with smile on one side and frown on the other; and (7) help staff to share crazy ideas.

   b. Ideas for future committee action: (1) arrange staff parties, (2) arrange demonstrations by faculty (e.g., of lessons), (3) plan a trust-building day, and (4) use student questionnaire on feelings and evaluation.

   c. Ideas for future individual or team action: (1) establish positive reinforcement outside building; (2) eat right, get sleep; (3) survey periodically for feelings; (4) know own strengths and limitations; (5) give positive reinforcement to your colleagues; (6) accept others' limitations; (7) work together in unit groups; (8) let others accept you—be open-minded; (9) openly express feelings; (10) try to get success from apparent failure; (11) talk about your failures and weaknesses; (12) avoid secrecy; (13) share feelings with your team leader; (14) paraphrase, describe behavior, and check perceptions; (15) share long-range plans across units; (16) establish as a goal the expression of a certain number of statements about your feelings; and (17) share your feelings with principal and auxiliary staff.

3. Ways to facilitate innovations with large groups and overcome teachers' feelings of inadequacy:

   a. Ideas for future committee action: (1) set up a committee to implement the use of student helpers; (2) set up procedures for using parent volunteer groups, and pass them around the building for additional information; (3) talk to people at other schools doing similar things; (4) enlist help of student teachers, university students, and high school students for large meetings; and (5) observe other large groups.

   b. Ideas for future individual or team action: (1) use the skills of a partner; (2) plan with auxiliary staff to cooperate during large meetings; (3) use rooms as research centers; (4) strive to use new materials; (5) forget that you are a teacher; (6) use district coordinators; (7) try one new method each week; (8) visit the Curriculum Materials Center more often; (9) look for successes, point them out to your colleagues, and praise one another; (10) appreciate individual differences among teachers (e.g., let some work with large groups and some with small); (11) value student concerns and student feedback; (12) use large groups to free staff; (13) remove or re-arrange furniture; (14) have principal help teachers; (15) use machines; (16) read; (17) lengthen school day; (18) innovate in area where you are comfortable; (19) teach outdoors; and (20) have a problem-sharing session each week.

4. Ways to increase the support of parents:
   a. Ideas for immediate action: (1) evidence a lack of phoni-ness, (2) complete parent questionnaires, and (3) con-sider that parent knows something about his child.
   b. Ideas for future committee action: (1) set up newsletters; (2) set up conferences (have parents come to school for feedback about students); (3) use room helpers; (4) hold an open house; (5) establish a teacher-parent social time (parents bring nonparents); (6) present precise informa-tion about student progress to parents; (7) hold parent workshops; (8) work cooperatively with Education Center in framing news items for the press; (9) plan care-fully for meeting with parents (e.g., work in role-playing situations with others and critique, meet with public during staff meeting, and establish sessions in which teachers role-play parents and parents role-play teachers); (10) keep school facilities open for community use during nonschool hours; (11) do not combine too many activi-ties in one parent-teacher meeting; (12) plan for greater informality at PTA meetings; and (13) plan Dad's Night and Mom's Night.
   c. Ideas for future individual or team action: (1) invite parents to observe special projects; (2) encourage school visits any time and at special times; (3) make phone calls to children's homes when all is going well; (4) ask parents for suggestions and use them; (5) plan teacher-parent–team potlucks; (6) send room newsletters home; (7) send notices about new team planning; (8) be open with children; (9) have kids write letters to parents; (10) establish school newspaper; (11) take an interest in parents' interests; (12) have a parent "share day"; (13) learn to live with parental nonacceptance; and (14) encourage team mothers to meet.

Stage 5. Forecasting consequences of intended actions.
[Unfortunately, members of this group neglected to anticipate the barriers to carrying out their plans. Excited and committed to following up their ideas, they did not recognize the many

constraints that would hold them back when school began, with the result that most of the ideas they developed were either lost or placed in suspended animation. As it happened, they had written their ideas in a form they could retain, so that later in the school year they were able to recapture many of these plans and use them effectively.]

Stage 6. Taking action.

[The group wrote out its plans on ditto masters, assembled booklets for each staff member, and described its work to the rest of the staff at a special meeting.]

Stage 7. Evaluating the actions.

[This stage received scant attention. During the follow-up OD consultation in the fall, the group reconvened to assess the current state of its problems. Several members were too busy to attend; the remaining members attempted to act on some of the simpler plans, but they, too, soon abandoned the task. Seven months later, however, the school staff was ready to recoup many of the resources they had discovered during the summer. Staff members spent a good part of one Saturday in April reaffirming the goals they felt to be most urgent and finding others with whom to collaborate in planning for action. For a description of the microdesign used on that Saturday, see chapter 8.]

The Sequence in Detail

This section reviews each stage of the problem-solving sequence in detail and recommends specific actions for carrying out each stage effectively.

Identifying the Problem.   Defining a workable problem is the most difficult stage of the problem-solving sequence. Indeed, we have devoted all of chapter 4 to techniques for setting goals ("targets" in terms of the S-T-P) and much of the rest of the book to discussing ways of thinking about current situations. Summarized here are some procedural suggestions for identifying a problem in a small work group.

1. Generate multiple problem statements in terms of Ss and Ts. Describe a number of problems (discrepancies between S and T) as concretely as possible, mentioning actual people, places, and resources. Elicit as many statements of problems as people are willing to give. Write the statements where everyone can see them—for example, on a chalkboard or sheet of newsprint. Avoid arguing about whether a problem is perfectly stated or about how to solve it.

2. Refine the problem statements, restating each so that it describes the situation as it is now and the ideal target that is not being reached. Reduce the number of statements to the fewest possible, setting aside those with unrealistic objectives. Select one problem that has top priority for the group, and work until the group has agreed that the problem is important, urgent, and solvable. If group

members want to work on more than one problem, take them through each one separately.

Analyzing the Problem. Of the numerous forces at work during problem solving, some will encourage and others will impede reaching solutions for change. Using figure 7-1 to complete a Force-Field Analysis is the central task of Stage 2. Following are guides for this task.

Figure 7-1   Force-Field Analysis

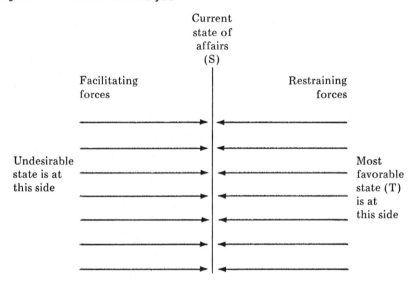

1. Thinking of the present state of affairs as being held stationary by two sets of opposing forces, try to list all the facilitating forces, including psychological, interpersonal, institutional, and even societal factors; then list all the restraining forces including both psychological and group factors. Place special emphasis on uncovering all restraining forces. If a restraining force seems to be a complex of multiple separate obstacles, list each element separately. Check whether group members believe they have a complete list of forces. At this stage, avoid argument and suspend critical judgment; let your mind expand by understanding the views of others. Create in your group an accepting, inventive mood rather than a fighting, competitive mood.

2. Rank the restraining forces, agreeing on those (perhaps three to six) that you think are most important. Rate these for their solvability, and circle the important ones. Avoid arguing about unsolvable items or about opinions before you have sufficient data. If you have doubts, collect data from colleagues outside the group or from other persons who have pertinent information. A group that attempts to

solve a problem without vital information is asking for failure; so take whatever time is necessary to get it.

Generating Multiple Solutions.   This stage offers a time for creativity and fun. Adopt a psychological set for brainstorming, and withhold critical judgment and evaluation; rather, try to encourage others to be creative, playful, even wild. Consider each restraining force in turn, and think of ways to reduce its strength. Act on the following suggestions to increase your own creativity.

1. *Get ready.* Loosen up. Stretch your body, and reach for the ceiling. Try some warm-up activity, such as Billy Goat described in chapter 6.
2. *Get set.* Have lots of newsprint tacked to the wall. Appoint a recorder who can hear well and write rapidly. When you are ready, appoint two recorders.
3. *Go.* Brainstorm ideas for eliminating the first restraint. Be silly and wild, and pool your wildness. Don't say no to any idea or even take time to express approval beyond exclamations like "Hurray!" "Hear! Hear!" "Wow!" or "Go! Go!" Proceed to the next force in the same way.

Planning for Action.   When all possible solutions have been generated, the group should use critical judgment in building concrete plans for action. The following points are helpful.

1. Choose the brainstormed ideas that seem best.
2. Decide which groups or persons should expedite them.
3. List the materials and other resources needed.
4. Place the ideas and necessary actions into a time sequence.
5. Plan to begin the sequence as soon as possible.
6. Estimate specific dates for the actions to occur.
7. Make plans for commencing the action sequence. Who will do what?
8. Make plans for periodically evaluating the effectiveness of actions as they are implemented.
9. Be prepared to revise the plans as the action sequence unfolds; specify dates for review.

Forecasting Consequences of Intended Actions.   Many fine ideas arising from problem-solving sessions vanish, never to reappear. Use the following suggestions to anticipate barriers to carrying out action plans.

1. Weigh the probabilities for success against the labor required for implementation.
2. Try to imagine all possible things that might go wrong. Simulate the actions by asking friends to role-play persons who will be affected by the planned action, and ask them to give you feedback about their reactions.

3. Go directly to the people who will be affected, and involve them in criticizing the plans.
4. Remember to anticipate barriers from environmental sources.

This work is arduous, and we are all tempted to forego the checks; but you will save yourself later frustration if you carry them out at the right time.

Taking Action. Do not delay taking the first action step. Since most of the forces affecting the problem are themselves in a state of change, the analysis and plans for solutions may not remain appropriate for long. Remember that problem solving is tentative and continual, and have the courage to be imperfect.

Evaluating the Actions. Premature evaluation can inhibit effective planning, but failure to evaluate the effects of actions once begun can be disastrous. Planners should establish criteria for evaluating the effectiveness of their actions and review their progress as each action step occurs. Procedures for evaluation are discussed at length in other chapters, notably chapters 2 and 11. Criteria may include costs, time, undesirable side effects, valuable by-products, risks, support, and acceptability. In addition, look for changes in conceptions of the focal problem.

Some General Guides. In summary, the following suggestions may facilitate group performance on problem solving.

1. Help the group achieve valid information, free choice, and commitment to their choices.
2. For larger problems, organize the task before the group begins by helping members plan how they want to work together and how much time they can afford for various subtasks.
3. Attend to the feelings of the members as they engage in the task.
4. Encourage serious consideration of the problem, and delay deciding on solutions until the problem is thoroughly diagnosed.
5. Help direct efforts toward overcoming surmountable barriers.
6. Post ideas on newsprint as they are generated.
7. Treat disagreements as variety-generating and not as trouble.
8. Do not allow critical judgment to inhibit the generation of ideas.

The Sequence in a Brief Session

Improving problem-solving technique is a basic part of any effort at OD consultation. The sequence we have described can be modified for use by an individual, group, or larger subsystem; it can be used effectively in part or in total; and it can run from two hours for short-range concerns to a year or more for major organizational issues. Here we present a microdesign developed as a brief introduction to the process of solving educational problems that are of concern to the whole group and that can be decided in about two hours. This is not an adequate substitute for the more complete process but may be used for demonstration purposes or when a group has already had sufficient training to solve problems quickly.

Stage 1. Either someone *states* the problem and the group agrees by survey that it is a problem—teach the survey technique at this point if the group has not been previously introduced to it—or the group *stages* a problem and confirms by survey that it is a problem.

Stage 2. Ask the group to think of as many alternatives as it can for resolving the problem, and have someone record the ideas on newsprint. Brainstorming is a time for suspending critical judgment. Let the ideas flow freely; any idea is a good one at this stage.

Stage 3. By voting, determine the priority of each of the items listed, raising your hand only if you think the item is an important workable solution to the problem. Do not vote for more than seven or eight alternatives. Then, by discussion and consensus, choose from among the ten most preferred alternatives the five that the group feels are the most important and workable. In arriving at a consensual group decision: (1) everyone should feel free to state his reasons for including one or more items among the five, (2) the communication skills learned earlier should be used, (3) a survey should be taken when the choices are actually made, and (4) every member of the group should own or be willing to support the five alternatives finally chosen.

Stage 4. For a suitable questionnaire on checking the group's effectiveness, see the questions on group effectiveness presented earlier in this chapter.

Stage 5. Using critical judgment, the group should now be able to design concrete action plans for the five solutions chosen earlier.

1. Examine the alternative solutions one at a time and decide by consensus which should be implemented first, which second, and so on. If you wish to divide up the work at this stage, small groups can each work on one or more solutions. In this case it will be necessary to reserve time for later reporting back to the whole group.
2. Estimate specific dates for the actions to occur.
3. Decide which groups or persons should be responsible for expediting each alternative.
4. Make plans for beginning the action. How will it happen?
5. By brainstorming, try to imagine all the things that could go wrong.
6. Reexamine the action plans for possible revision as a result of step 5.

Stage 6. By now the group will have been working together on problems for two hours or so, and members will have observed some behavior by others that helped the group work better together. At this stage:

1. Put as many sheets of newsprint on the wall as there are persons in the group, with the name of each person at the top of each sheet.
2. Each person should write on someone else's sheet a helpful behavior that that person has exhibited during the work and sign his name or initials beside the comment. Although it is best if the helpful behavior occurred during the problem-solving session, a helpful behavior shown elsewhere is also acceptable.
3. Finally, everyone present at the workshop reads everyone else's sheet. Anyone adds to any sheet as he wishes.

READINGS

The Principal as Convener of Organizational Problem Solving

Richard Schmuck and Jack Nelson

Self-renewal within a school building can be greatly facilitated if the principal learns and uses skills of convening problem-solving groups. Schmuck and Nelson describe this new role and suggest ways to implement it.

Richard Schmuck and Jack Nelson. The principal as convener of organizational problem solving. Research Reports in Educational Administration, 1970, 2(2), pp. 5-12, 18-19. Center for Field Services and Training, School of Education, University of Colorado, Boulder.

. . . Performing effectively as the convener of problem-solving places new demands on the principal. Benevolence and warm paternalism are no longer virtues. Rather, empathic understanding is required along with willingness to enter into uncomfortable confrontations. The communication skills of paraphrasing, describing behavior, describing own feelings, perception checking, summarizing, and gatekeeping are important behaviors to establish constructive openness during problem-solving. Unilateral decision-making is not usually appropriate, but openness about one's own feelings engendered by the role of principal is needed to strengthen trust with the staff.

When teachers are confronted with behaviors of a principal that are at variance with what they have come to expect, it is quite understandable that they should be distrustful. Much of their experience has taught them that authority figures not only do not behave democratically and trustfully, but that in many instances they should not do so. Our interpretation of teachers' behavior is that they initially react to an innovative principal as a phoney or as "playing a game" to protect themselves from the risks implicit in potential engagement on more democratic terms. It is important for the principal taking the new role to persist in it over a long period of time to gain the confidence of his staff.

Perhaps the most important behavior necessary to carry out the new role effectively has to do with guiding group problem-solving. It seems fair to assume that most principals and teachers have been trained to take positions of high control and to direct single-handedly the activities of the staff or of a group of students. But they have not been trained to work collaboratively with adult professionals. . . .

Support for the New Role

Research in social psychology lends support to the role of the principal as a convener of problem-solving. Findings reveal that it is possible to create relationships among individuals comprising a face-to-face group so that the group exhibits properties different from those properties observed in typical committees, staff groups, or task forces in everyday organizational life. The more effective groups have leaders who allow for greater participation, wider initial divergence of expressed judgments, and greater acceptance of diverse decisions. Moreover, effective leaders have been shown to encourage minority opinions and conflict to a greater extent than less effective leaders. Also, it has been shown that group participants with little influence over a decision not only fail to contribute their resources to the decision but usually are less likely to carry out the decision when action is required.

Evidence comes directly from research on schools also. Gross and Herriott examined the consequences of the professional leadership exhibited by elementary school principals on the operation of their schools. To measure the effects of the leadership behavior of principals on their staffs the researchers examined the relationship between the principal's scores on a measure of Executive Professional Leadership (EPL) and three characteristics of schools that are widely accepted as meaningful criteria of effectiveness: staff morale, the professional performance of teachers, and the students' learning. Gross and Herriott found positive and significant relationships between EPL and each of these three variables. EPL was defined as the efforts of a principal of a school to conform to a definition of his role that stresses his obligation to improve the quality of the performance of his staff. This role has many similarities to the role of the convener for problem-solving. . . .

Examples of New Role

Although the role of principal as convener of organizational problem-solving is just beginning to take shape as a viable role, a few examples of this role in action have been documented.

(1) In a junior high school, we helped form the Principal's
Advisory Committee into more of a problem-solving group. The
principal served as the group facilitator. The group met bimonthly
for one hour before classes began. At the committee's request an
additional 6:30 A.M. breakfast meeting lasting two and a half hours
was scheduled the last Friday of each month. Members very rarely
missed these meetings. When an area chairman could not attend, he
asked a member of his subject area to take his place. On several
occasions, general faculty members were invited to attend these
meetings; typically two or three would appear and participate. This
Advisory Committee facilitated organizational problem-solving in
the school in several ways. The principal acted to help decisions,
to keep communication flowing, and to help less active teachers to
participate. . . .

(2) In an elementary school [in a southern suburb of Seattle
in 1968–69], we helped the staff form into a multi-unit structure.
The principal formed a leadership team with five unit leaders (master
teachers), a curriculum resource librarian, and a counselor. Each unit
leader formed a team with three or four other teachers and several
aides (either student teachers from a nearby university or volunteer
adults from the community). No self-contained classrooms existed
in the building. The principal served as a convener for the leadership
group, which, in turn, integrated the instructional efforts of the
various units. Key decisions for new instructional strategies were
made by the units, and innovations in overall curriculum and organizational policies were decided upon by the leadership group. Power,
in general, was placed more in the hands of teams of teachers. The
principal kept the whole communication process active and clear.

(3) In an experimental high school in Portland, Oregon, the
principal became concerned that low achieving students, primarily
a group of culturally disadvantaged black students, were not advancing very well in the basic skills (especially reading and writing). He
decided to hold a meeting with a group of black students to discuss
how they saw the school. Most of these students reported that they
liked the freedom in the school, but they also wanted to learn to
read and write so that jobs would be easier to get. Unfortunately, the
teachers in this experimental school wanted to teach problem-solving
and systematic inquiry, mostly in lieu of teaching remedial reading.
The principal was able to work as a convener of problem-solving by
arranging for the black students to give their feedback directly to
the relevant teachers. He set up a meeting and used several techniques described elsewhere.

(4) In another high school in Eugene, Oregon, the principal has
decided to take a leave of absence for one year to go to graduate
school at the University of Oregon to learn skills of consulting. With
the permission of his staff, he will serve as an organizational consultant to his own school during that year. He hopes to help the staff to
organize itself for organizational decision-making so that the teachers
and specialists will become involved in more and more decisions in

small teams. He wants to construct the role of the principal as convener of organizational problem-solving.

Implementing the New Role

The introduction of a more democratic, team-oriented, teacher decision-making structure calls for very direct and decisive action on the part of the principal. He must be ready to initiate the sort of organizational process he believes will yield the most productive results; the ultimate responsibility for decisions in buildings lies with him. The special effect of the new role we have been discussing, however, results from the principal's facilitation of problem-solving by others and from his restraint from doing jobs that might be done by others closer to the point of application.

Our assessment of the existing role indicates that there are many opportunities for the principal to be a convener. He can organize a formal decision-making body that best fits his style. It may be charged with topics ranging from spending discretionary funds to the best use of rooms. Through such a group, a large faculty can be represented effectively, and knowledge of a problem can be widely shared well in advance of the time action is to be accomplished. In this setting, the principal does not need to be the "boss," but can assume the role of facilitator. A regularly scheduled bimonthly meeting has proved to be effective.

Another opportunity for the principal as convener can almost always be found among the chief administrative jobs of the school. In a weekly meeting, information concerning the general management of the school can be shared, such as information from the central office, desires from the faculty, and information from informal channels. By determining the best solutions, many problems involving poor communications among the staff can be avoided. A second regular half-hour meeting can be used for rapid collection of up-to-the-minute news for the bulletin. Pertinent information about the next week's events can get to the total staff before their departure for the weekend.

Another opportunity occurs early in the fall. At that time, in regularly scheduled meetings, the principal and first-year teachers can explore their unique concerns and problems. The principal can use this opportunity for open discussion of school policy, generation of mutual respect and trust, and a sensing of potential difficulties.

The principal can employ volunteer interest groups within the faculty to do a great deal of pre-planning for curricular innovation. He should not overlook ad hoc groups to work on special problems such as orientation of new students, problems unique to scheduling parental visits, and public relations with the community. He can contribute his expertise to these groups, as well as that of district consultants, curriculum specialists, and other resources available. Problems relating to budget, personnel, and space can be discussed before concrete proposals are formulated. These groups should be convened in the early spring or fall to meet budget deadlines for the following year. . . .

Possible Consequences of the New Role

Once the principal uses the problem-solving process and once a new decision-making pattern has been established, a number of consequences can be predicted that are not necessarily related to the new role itself. For example, after the principal has shared power with others on some important matters, he cannot easily retrieve it by fiat. Thus, while he makes the decision initially to share his power, it is typically risky for him to reverse his stance; the probable result is organizational stress and a lowered trust from teachers.

Another consequence of the new role is an increase in the amount of time that will be consumed in solving problems and making decisions. Problems that the principal may have decided on his own in a short time may take hours of the group's deliberation. This can be frustrating and the principal must be able to deal with his own frustration and that of his teachers. The willingness of the principal to tolerate this increase in time may even sometimes seem to the teachers to corroborate their fear that he is "playing a game" and is only waiting for them to fail. The principal must be able to suffer through these periods.

Changing the formal structure also has consequences for the informal structure. For example, a danger is that decision-making teams working with the principal can become "inner circles." The members have easier access to power than the rest of the faculty. This suggests that unless this development is foreseen and plans made to deal with it, a large group of staff members may drift toward the periphery. The main issues of importance seem to be (1) to ensure a free flow of data about suspicious and negative feelings, (2) to diagnose the nature of the problems that appear, and (3) to initiate appropriate actions to resolve problem situations.

The difficulties listed above are ever present, but they can be met with determination and skill on the part of the principal and his advisors. It is our belief, backed by the studies and experiences already cited, that greater use of the human resources throughout the school and a greater commitment by the staff to the school's goals will emerge when the principal acts regularly to convene problem-solving activities and makes use of objective problem-solving procedures.

Solving Organizational Problems from the Outside

Shirley Terreberry

Terreberry proposes a systems approach, urging interveners to locate problems and solutions in the environment.

Shirley Terreberry. Overview on organizational intervention. University of Oregon, 1970 (mimeo).

From a systems point of view, organizational change means change in the kind or quantity of the organization's output (i.e., its products or services to the environment).

That sounds too simple, and yet it's true for all living systems. For example, we note that an individual has changed only by observing change in his behavior (his output). We can tell that a small group has changed only by observing change in its task performance (its output).

In other words, system change is best observed from *outside* the system.

When we are *inside* a small group we are aware of the behavior of other *individuals* in the group. We may even change the behavior of some individuals. But this will not often change the task performance (output) of the group as a whole. This is because the group's output is mainly a function of input to it from the environment, and feedback from the environment.

Similarly, when we are inside an organization we are aware of the behavior of other individuals and other groups. We may even change the behavior of some individuals or groups. But this will probably not change the product or service (the output) of the organization as a whole. Again, this is because an organization's output is mainly a function of input to it from the environment, and feedback from the environment.

In other words, there is a difference between problems *in* organizations, on the one hand, and organizational problems on the other. But let's start with problems *in* organizations, since these are so common.

Many problems *in* organizations are problems of individuals. This usually means that the individual's behavior (output) differs from the output that is defined as desirable. For example, suppose you are a welfare worker and you discover that one of your co-workers frequently makes mistakes in figuring welfare grants. Which definition of the problem do you prefer:

1. He's stupid, or
2. He makes mistakes in figuring budgets.

Let's analyze this example.

Input origins. There are three categories of explanation for any system's problem. One is *input*. Suppose you find out that your co-worker's mistakes stem from failing to include a laundry allowance when appropriate. Which explanation do you prefer:

1. He's hostile toward clients, or
2. The page on laundry allowances is missing from his manual.

Feedback origins. The second category of explanation, of any system's problem, is *feedback* concerning *output*. Suppose your analysis shows that your co-worker is making a lot of mistakes in adding. Which explanation do you prefer:

1. He's sloppy in his work, or
2. He doesn't realize he's making mistakes.

Throughput origins. The third explanation is *throughput*. We can diagnose a problem as throughput *only* when we have exhausted all possibilities of explaining it in terms of input or feedback re output. But it may be that the guy simply doesn't know *how* to add. His prior training (input and feedback) simply haven't equipped him to do this kind of throughput. *Now* what? Well, if you see problems simply as problems of individuals then you may not recognize that you have bumped into an *organizational* problem: how come the organization *inputs* an individual who can't *throughput* the work? We'll come back to this kind of problem later.

Many problems *in* organizations are problems of *groups*, which are subsystems of the organization. This usually means that the group's task performance (its output) differs from the output that is defined as desirable. For example, suppose that you are an assistant city manager and you discover that the city planning department is spending all of its time on long-range land-use plans, although the City Council's priority is low-income housing, and the City Manager has asked the planning department to recommend sites for low-income housing. Which definition of the problem do you prefer:

1. The planning department is uncooperative, or
2. The planning department is working on the wrong task.

Input origins. Again, as in the case of individuals, there are three categories of explanation of any system's problem. The first is *input.* Suppose you study the problem and you find out that the planners didn't realize that the city's present priority is low-income housing. Which analysis do you prefer:

1. The planners are resistant to change, or
2. The city's message wasn't "loud and clear."

Feedback origins. The second possible explanation is lack of *feedback* [concerning] *output.* You talk to the planners and discover that they assume the others can *infer* the best location for low-income housing on the basis of their land-use plans. Which explanation would you prefer:

1. The planners are conceited bastards, or
2. They don't understand that others don't understand *them.*

Throughput origins. Again, this third category of explanation cannot be determined until we are certain that the planners received the necessary inputs and feedback. But it could be that the planners don't understand problems of low-income housing.

Now it's time to pause. In all of the examples above, the *first* alternative is what we commonly choose: that the person or group is stupid, hostile, sloppy, uncooperative, resistant to change, or conceited. Do these sound familiar? We make these kinds of "diagnoses" all the time. They're easy. And they are cop-outs. Note that all of these "explanations" have two things in common: (1) they are emotional and evaluative, and (2) they locate the problem *inside* the person or group, rather than in the environment which provides input and feedback.

The second alternative, in all the examples above, is quite different: (1) it is descriptive and analytic (rather than emotional and evaluative), and (2) it requires collecting *additional information* rather than making a snap judgment. This is what distinguishes the professional, in my opinion. Notice that all of the second alternatives above have another useful feature: *each implies the appropriate intervention!!*

For example, suppose your analysis of the welfare worker's problem is that he doesn't realize he's making mistakes, so he needs feedback on his output. Of course it takes some skill to give *good* feedback. Which of these do you prefer:

1. "Alex, you're careless in your arithmetic," or
2. "Alex, these budgets aren't coming out right."

The first implies that there's something wrong *inside* of Alex (carelessness). The second focuses attention on the output ("these budgets"). What might you say next to Alex:

1. "You ought to be more careful," or
2. "I had the same trouble until I started adding every budget twice."

Consider the second example, about the city planning department. Suppose your analysis shows that the department is working on the wrong task because the City Council's priority wasn't made clear. What intervention do *you* propose?

Now we will shift from problems *in* organizations to genuine organizational problems. As with individuals and groups, an organizational problem usually means that the organization's products or services (outputs) differ from the output that is defined as desirable.

The most common problem of organizations is often stated as "not enough money." But this is a premature diagnosis, rather than a problem definition. The real problem is that the organization is not producing the kind or quantity of output that is defined as desirable. If we short-circuit the process of defining a problem by leaping to a conclusion, we automatically overlook alternative explanations and interventions.

For example, some years ago all the family counseling agencies in the country were waving lengthy waiting lists at Community Chests and demanding more money (more input). Then two researchers did a cost analysis of a family agency and found that *one-third* of the total budget went for case recording: i.e., paying caseworkers to dictate lengthy case records, and paying typists to type them, and paying supervisors to read them. Similar studies were conducted in other agencies with the same results. So agencies began to curtail their case recordings, and waiting lists soon disappeared. (Was this a problem of organizational input, throughput, or feedback re output?)

Here's another example. For several decades, federal and state legislatures rather glibly cut welfare allocations when funds became scarce. Welfare commissions and employees often complained bitterly about "not enough money," to no avail. But this is changing. Mechanisms for *feedback re output* are beginning to develop, and to be effective. Can you think of one example?

The purpose of these two illustrations is to emphasize the importance of defining organizational problems in terms of kind or quantity of *output,* as we did in the case of persons and groups. This helps prevent us from leaping to premature conclusions, overlooking alternative analyses and interventions.

Let's select an organizational problem and see if we can apply the same three categories of explanation (input, feedback, through-put) as we did for the welfare worker's behavior and the planning department's performance. The organization is a mental health clinic, and the problem which you have defined is: service (output) is given mainly to middle- and upper-class clients, to the neglect of the working class and poor people.

Input origins. Suppose you find out that the agency's Board is comprised only of middle- and upper-class people. Which analysis do you prefer:

1. Board members are biased, or
2. The Board is not representative of the community.

Or perhaps you discover that the Board *is* broadly representa-tive, but the agency's personnel are all from middle- and upper-class backgrounds. Which analysis do you prefer:

1. Our staff is prejudiced against the lower class, or
2. Our staff lacks familiarity with lower class people.

Feedback origins. Suppose you find that the Community Chest and the agency Board and staff all agree that service should be dis-tributed equitably to all segments of the community. In talking with these people, however, you find out that they believe service *is* equitably distributed. Which conclusion do you prefer:

1. They don't want to deal with reality, or
2. They don't realize what is happening.

Throughput origins. If you have thoroughly analyzed the prob-lem, and there is no way of explaining it in terms of input or feed-back, then it may be a *throughput* problem. Perhaps the kind of problems which plague poor people simply don't lend themselves to techniques of mental health treatment. Or perhaps there are only two staff members who *are* effective with lower-class clients, and the problem can be solved by having these two people specialize in lower-class clients, rather than having clients randomly assigned to *any* staff member.

In the examples above, the first alternative is the one we too commonly choose: that the organization is biased or prejudiced or unrealistic. As in the case of persons or groups, we make these kinds of "diagnoses" all the time. This kind of "analysis" tends (1) to be emotional and evaluative, (2) to locate the blame *inside* the organiza-tion rather than in the environment which provides input and feed-back, and (3) to be a cop-out, because it excuses us from doing anything about it.

The second alternative, in the examples above, is (1) descriptive and analytic, (2) requires collecting additional information, and (3) implies a strategy of intervention.

For example, suppose your analysis of the mental health clinic's problem is input: i.e., the clinic is not hiring staff who have skills in working with lower-class clients. Let's suppose that the clinic director is the one who makes personnel decisions, and he shares your concern about the clinic's failure to serve poor people. (If he *doesn't*, then you've made an error in your analysis of the problem.) So you prepare a report, probably in writing, in which you describe and analyze the problem, and you suggest a change in hiring policy. If your analysis is correct, and your proposal is feasible, then change is probable.

BUT!! Here's the common rub. The director says: "You're right. I agree. But none of the applicants *have* skills in working with these people." Maybe he's wrong and you can find out and correct his information. But maybe he's right. So you've taken the problem all the way to the organizational boundary, where input decisions are made, and you've discovered that the solution lies *outside,* rather than inside, the organization. (In my opinion, this is the case with most organizational problems.)

Do you quit now? Or do you keep going? If you were a "bureaucrat" you wouldn't have gotten even *this* far. So let's continue.

You ask the clinic director: "Where do our job applicants come from?" and he says: "From the U of O Counseling Department and the P.S.U. School of Social Work." So now you have to analyze *these* organizations, since they produce the outputs which your clinic inputs. Maybe you discover that they *do* produce some of the kinds of graduates that your agency needs. So you and the director arrange for them to start referring these kinds of graduates to your agency. Or you help create a field placement in your clinic for students who want to do mental health work with poor people.

On the other hand, you may discover that these schools are *not* producing the kind of persons you're seeking. You can search the environment to see if there are other schools that *do.* Perhaps there are. Or maybe you'll find that this kind of output isn't being created *any*where. You can quit there, or you can tackle this *new* problem. Why don't schools output the kind of input you are seeking? Is it *their* inputs (admissions policies)? Is it their throughputs (dropouts, or that schools turn all inputs into middle-class outputs)? Or is it feedback concerning output (schools don't know what agencies need)?

Intervention with organizational problems is considerably more complex than intervention with individuals and small groups. It is more difficult but also more important, in my opinion, because organizations are—increasingly—the "social actors" that make the social system what it is.

Each of us has a choice: we can damn "the system" or we can develop strategies of intervention (skills in defining, analyzing, and intervening) to *change* the parts of the system that we *can* change.

Are you a "bureaucrat" or a "professional"?

BIBLIOGRAPHY

Gordon, W. 1961. *Synectics.* New York: Collier.

This classic explains how analogy, metaphor, and simile can be used to find better ways of solving problems. Specific techniques are offered for defining problems, for dealing with them systematically, and for behaving differently as a consequence. Synectics assumes that subjective response is more important to creativity than is objective, a priori knowledge.

Kaufman, R. 1976. *Identifying and solving problems: a system approach.* La Jolla, Calif.: University Associates.

This book deals with identifying and solving problems using the techniques of system analysis. It offers easy-to-use tools for analyzing the gap between current and desired goals, offers a variety of techniques for selecting and testing alternative means of reaching goals, and includes selected instruments for assessing to what degree a goal has been reached.

Koberg, D., and Bagnall, J. 1972. *The universal traveler: a soft-systems guide to creativity, problem solving, and the process of reaching goals.* Los Altos, Calif.: Kaufmann.

This book, which offers an array of concepts, techniques, and insights for creative problem solving, is stimulating, practical, and fun to read. Topics include blocks to creativity, problem-solving steps, measuring outcomes, creativity games, self-hypnotism, and painless criticism.

Lighthall, F. F. 1973. Multiple realities and organizational nonsolutions: an essay on anatomy of educational innovation. *School Review* 81: 255-93.

Because effective organizational problem solving requires staff members to share an understanding of the complexities of their school's problems, innovation is likely to fail when administrators offer solutions without leading staff members to see the problems. In this review of a failure in educational innovation, Lighthall illuminates a mismatch between the narrow reality of a particular innovation and the manifestly multiple reality of a complex staff.

Nagle, J. M., and Balderson, J. H. 1974. *Group problem solving: the D-A-P approach.* Eugene, Ore.: Center for Educational Policy & Management.

This booklet offers a systematic procedure for group problem solving, including phases for generating designative information (D), appraisive information (A), and prescriptive information (P). These phases are the same as problem identification, plan development in terms of goal setting, and plan development in terms of implementation. The booklet presents succinctly detailed substeps within each of the major phases.

Parnes, S. P. 1967. *Creative behavior workbook.* New York: Scribner's.

Together with its companion volume—the *Guidebook* described in the bibliography for chapter 6—this practical book is written for those who wish to help others become creative in problem solving. Designed for use during a creative behavior workshop, it provides the reader with opportunities to review and practice the principles and procedures of creative problem solving.

Schmuck, R. A.; Chesler, M.; and Lippitt, R. 1966. *Problem solving to improve classroom learning.* Chicago: Science Research Associates.

Describing how a problem-solving sequence can be applied in the classroom, this book contains sections on diagnosing problems and on taking action, showing how the dynamics of learning groups can be altered constructively.

Decision Making

The previous chapter described problem solving as a process of identifying situational and target information and of generating proposals that will move school participants from their present state of affairs to an ideal state of affairs. Problem solvers become decision makers when they determine which situational information is valid, select their preferred targets, or choose among alternative plans of action. In other words, decision making follows problem solving whenever a choice arises. Problem solving involves gathering, filtering, and processing information; decision making involves assigning priorities and acting on them.

Although problem solving and decision making are often viewed as a single process, we have chosen to distinguish the latter for four reasons. First, we believe that increased awareness of decision-making processes can alleviate the tensions and frustrations that arise when these processes are imperfectly understood, when decisions are made by default, or when decisions are made but not implemented. Second, we believe that people who are aware of how decisions are made can participate more effectively in making those that require their aid and that such decisions are the more likely to be carried out. Third, we think that a school group that has been trained to employ multiple decision-making modes effectively can better select the mode most appropriate to the kind of decision to be made. Fourth, we believe that school resources will not be adequately shared unless school participants in all important roles can at least sometimes take part in collaborative decision making.

Although a school's ability to maintain access to resources, to act responsively, and to assess its movement toward goals is critically linked to the clarity and explicitness of its decision-making process, few schools regularly examine their norms, structures, o· procedures for exerting influence or making decisions. This chapter describes concepts and skills that can clarify these processes for the purpose of achieving shared influence and collaborative decision making in schools.

INFLUENCE AND DECISION MAKING

Traditional theories of organization located the major sources of power at the top of the organizational hierarchy and consequently limited the power and influence of those at lower levels. This is because early organizational and management theorists believed that workers were motivated primarily by economic incentives and job security, that efficient organizations developed rational rules and procedures to keep subordinates under control and protect the organization from human caprice, and that participation in decision making and shared influence were incompatible with organizational effectiveness.

For many existing organizations, however, these traditional views are mistaken. In particular, there are school districts in which power is not located exclusively at the top but is shared with principals, teachers, students, and even parents, and there are schools with very active neighborhood boards which include educators and parents in equal numbers. Indeed, there is a good deal of evidence that a wider distribution of influence yields measurable benefits. In addition, problem solving and decision making are not always sequential, deliberate, orderly, rational processes carried out by people tightly connected with one another. We support the view of Weick (1976), who describes schools as loosely coupled systems rather than "coupled through dense, tight linkages." Using Weick's imagery, consider the implications of this view.

> Imagine that you're either the referee, coach, player, or spectator at an unconventional soccer match: the field for the game is round; there are several goals scattered haphazardly around the circular field; people can enter and leave the game whenever they want to; they can throw balls in whenever they want; they can say "that's my goal" whenever they want to, as many times as they want to, and for as many goals as they want to; the entire game takes place on a sloped field; and the game is played as if it makes sense. . . .
>
> If you now substitute in that example principals for referees, teachers for coaches, students for players, parents for spectators, and schooling for soccer, you have an equally uncon-

ventional depiction of school organizations. The beauty of this depiction is that it captures a different set of realities within educational organizations than are caught when these same organizations are viewed through the tenets of bureaucratic theory.

Consider the contrast in images. For some time people who manage organizations and people who study this managing have asked, "How does an organization go about doing what it does and with what consequences for its people, processes, products, and persistence?" And for some time they've heard the same answers. In paraphrase, the answers say essentially that an organization does what it does because of plans, intentional selection of means that get the organization to agree upon goals, and all of this is accomplished by such rationalized procedures as cost-benefit analyses, division of labor, specified areas of discretion, authority invested in the office, job descriptions, and a consistent evaluation and reward system. The only problem with that portrait is that it is rare in nature. People in organizations, including educational organizations, find themselves hard-pressed either to find actual instances of those rational practices or to find rationalized practices whose outcomes have been as beneficent as predicted, or to feel that those rational occasions explain much of what goes on within the organization. Parts of some organizations are heavily rationalized, but many parts also prove intractable to analysis through rational assumptions (p. 1).

If entire states, districts, or even large schools are unlikely to be moving in the same direction at the same time, it is important for groups solving problems and making decisions to be substantially independent of other subsystems while they marshal their commitment and take first steps. It is also unrealistic to believe that people in loosely coupled systems are able to commit themselves to one another over long periods of time. For this reason, problem solving and decision making must occur in brief cycles in which people take small first steps, assess progress, and only then move to further action.

Making decisions means using power to influence selection among choices. We think that power can be attributed to individuals and groups at any organizational level; indeed, we choose to develop multiple power sources in organizations. French and Raven (1959), from whom we have borrowed some of our ideas about power sources, postulate five potential sources of power that people can use to influence others in social settings:

1. *Reward Power:* the control and distribution of rewards valued by others.
2. *Coercive Power:* the control and withholding of rewards valued by others.
3. *Legitimate Power:* authority legally vested in or assigned to a position.

4. *Expert Power:* the expertise of special knowledge, skill, or experience.
5. *Referent Power:* personal attractiveness or membership in someone's primary reference group.

In general, the more of these sources the more powerful they will be, although expert and referent power tend to be especially important. Bachman, Smith, and Slesinger (1966) have shown, for example, that the satisfaction and performance of subordinates improve as organizational leaders rely increasingly on expert and referent power bases. According to Hornstein and his colleagues (1968), teachers find more satisfaction working under principals who employ expert or referent power than under those who impose legitimate or coercive power. These findings support Weick's position that reward, coercion, and legitimacy are only loosely coupled to action.

The OD consultant can help clients to identify the sources of power at their disposal, to develop sources they do not have, and to rely more often on those that have strong intended effects and few undesirable side effects. For example, the consultant can help a parent group gain legitimacy by getting them school-board approval to make input to the school. For another example, staff members can describe one another's resources and rewarding behaviors in order to become aware of these sources of influence. The consultant can also help those in positions of legitimate power—principals, for example—to begin distributing part of their power to others. Forming new organizational structures such as special decision-making bodies or ad hoc steering committees can encourage teachers and others to assume leadership and responsibility for what goes on in the school. Particular problems in moving toward more shared influence are discussed later in this chapter.

Again, it is not necessarily true that if some people become more influential, others must become less so. Powerful people who subscribe to this view often fear organizational development as a threat to their power. In the effectively functioning organization, however, members of all hierarchical levels can gain in power and influence as the power and influence of their subordinates increase. In other words, influence is reciprocal in effective organizations.

March and Simon (1958) theorize that expanding the influence of lower echelons not only increases the power of these members but also allows management to participate more fully. According to Likert (1961, 1967), who describes much the same phenomenon in terms of his link-pin model for organizations, more influence is given to subordinates by communicatively linking all organizational levels. Researching the relationship between organizational power and effectiveness, Tannenbaum (1968) found it feasible for more influence to be exercised at every hierarchical level in what he called *polyarchic organizations* and has shown that when more people exert influence, the extent to which they are influenced by others increases as well.

The creation of management or leadership teams and multiunit structures are attempts by people in schools to organize themselves according to these principles. The multiunit school developed by the Wisconsin Research and Development Center for Cognitive Learning provides procedures for teachers to work in teams rather than in isolation and creates the position of team or unit leader. Regular meetings between the principal and unit leaders provide a forum for broader involvement in decision making and a communicative link between unit teachers and the principal. The total organization becomes more integrated as information goes directly from its source to where it is needed, and all levels gain more actual operating power from the increased interaction.

Of course this increased influence should not be relentlessly exercised every minute of every day. It is better, for example, to place a leadership team between the teachers and the principal than to have the total body of teachers making demands on the principal every week. In the latter case, the principal, learning too much about every week's details, would be tempted to get into the teachers' roles, which would destroy necessary differentiation. For the same reason, it is better for principals to meet the superintendent with serious demands every month or two instead of every week. The OD consultant can help clients explore how influence is distributed in their organization and compare this to their images of ideal distributions. By helping them learn to exert and receive influence, give and receive feedback, and recognize the existence of interdependencies, the consultant can help clients create more effective and satisfying decision-making structures.

Finally, several organizational theorists have challenged the traditionalist notion that participation deters rather than enhances organizational effectiveness. Lewin (1951) and Coch and French (1948) indicate how participation satisfies social needs; Maslow (1954), Schein (1965), and McGregor (1967) suggest that participation satisfies growth needs as well. Research carried out in industry, voluntary organizations, and schools alike has demonstrated that the satisfaction of organization members increases when they can influence decision making.*

We believe that people in schools not only want but need to offer critical input and participate in decision making. Like members of other organizations, teachers who have access to powerful people in the district feel better about their jobs and the schools in which they work and are more willing to display their capabilities to others. Teachers report greatest satisfaction with principals when they perceive some degree of mutual influence. There is even a positive correlation between student satisfaction with school and their perceptions of mutual influence with teachers.

But organizational effectiveness means more than satisfied people; it means improvement in the quality of decisions and increased likelihood of implementation as well. Maier (1970) provides some of the best evidence that shared decision making produces

---

*See Bachman, Smith, and Slesinger (1966); Hornstein et al. (1968); and Argyris (1970).

higher quality, more acceptable decisions than those made by individuals alone. Participative decision making enhances organizational effectiveness because people who feel the support of a group are more willing to take risks in pursuit of creative solutions and also because the possibility of finding the best solution is greater in a group than with an individual. In short, decision-making procedures that allow more people to risk sharing their good ideas can yield decisions that are worth implementing. To this end, OD consultants can help clients explore the kinds of decisions that are made in school, pinpointing those that must be of high quality and that require high acceptance for implementation, and calling attention to situations in which participative decision making is especially important.

GROUP DECISION MAKING

Three Modes

How influence is distributed in an organization depends upon how decisions are made in face-to-face groups. Although groups vary considerably in their composition and procedures, three decision-making modes occur most often: (1) decisions made by a single person or by a minority, (2) decisions based on the ability of a majority to overrule a minority, and (3) decisions based on acquiescence and support of the total group after discussion and debate (here called the consensual process). Although it is difficult to obtain these patterns in their purest forms even under controlled laboratory conditions, behavioral studies indicate that each affects a group's performance differently.

Although many kinds of school decisions are best made by one person or by a small committee, these are either about matters that do not require committed action by all or most of the members of the school, are not so complex as to require subtle coordination and understanding among those implementing the decisions, or are those whose outcome is a matter of indifference to most people. Examples include the form on which to report absences, the date on which a particular school assembly will be held, the time to call a committee meeting, or the advice to give architects of the new home economics wing. The efficiency of such decisions is widely understood and does not require discussion here.

Relegating discussions to a minority subgroup is the method most frequently practiced in everyday school life, however, and these decisions are the least effective in using members' resources, obtaining their commitment, or in achieving high quality. Decisions made by one or a minority of persons may be welcome when contestants find strife so unpleasant that merely resolving the matter is more attractive than the quality of the solution. It is nevertheless true, however, that when only a few members contribute to making a decision, the final decision will depend upon the limited resources of only these few.

When problems are too complex to be solved by simple sequential decisions, a minority does poorer than the total group, partly because it lacks the total group's resourcefulness and partly because the mutual probing and stimulation of the total group are missing. The inferiority of minority decision making is especially evident in complex organizations like schools whose central organizational tasks cannot be carried out in small face-to-face groups involving most of the members.

Because it allows more resources to be introduced into discussion, decision by majority vote is superior to minority decision making in producing decisions that require wide commitment for implementation. Where commitment by everyone is not required, a majority vote can also serve very well. If, for example, a school faculty decides to hold a picnic on a certain day with the understanding that not everyone will attend and that there will be no penalty for nonattendance, a majority vote will enable the picnic to be held with no damage to the undertaking by those in the minority.

It should be remembered, however, that a majority vote ascertains only those alternatives that people find more or less preferable; unless there is extended discussion, it does not uncover the alternatives that certain people find insupportable. To the extent that the outvoted or uninvolved minority is unable to use its resources to influence the decision, some resources are still not being brought to bear on the decision. Indeed, when nonsupport or sabotage by one or more members could seriously damage an undertaking that requires total group support, a decision by majority vote could be dangerous.

Group consensus is, for us, a process in which: (1) all members can paraphrase the issue under consideration to show that they understand it, (2) all members have a chance to voice their opinions on the issue, and (3) those who continue to doubt or disagree with the decision are nevertheless willing to give it a try for a prescribed period of time without sabotaging it. Consensus is therefore different from a unanimous vote. It does not mean that everyone agrees or even that the decision represents everyone's first choice; it means that enough people are in favor of it for it to be carried out and that those who remain doubtful nonetheless understand it and will not obstruct its implementation.

Because consensus requires fairly advanced skill in two-way communication, in coping with conflict, and in the use of paraphrasing and surveying, it is more difficult to achieve than majority vote, although its emotional benefits in many ways outweigh the cost. Majority vote hides pain. A member who may be hurting silently votes one way or another without having to reveal his dismay, with the result that the group is unaware of his pain and is surprised by subsequent foot-dragging and sabotage. But pain is far more likely to find expression and to be dealt with during the consensual process. Thus majority rule sacrifices pain to efficiency, while consensus takes pain into account but at the expense of considerable time and discomfort.

Where there are pronounced status differences among staff members, a minority decision is often employed in the hope of short-circuiting conflict and saving time. For avoiding conflicts that arise from differences of opinion, the majority vote holds great attraction for many. Consensus, however, is designed neither to avoid conflict nor to overcome group resistance in the short run and is perhaps for that reason often discounted as impractical or unfeasible. Although consensus usually results in more resourceful decisions for complex tasks, it is a form of decision making seldom attempted in schools.

For our part, we are convinced that decisions about instructional matters, for example, can be made more effectively when staff members are able to stimulate and encourage use of one another's resources during decision making. To this end, a number of procedures described in this book are extremely useful for uncovering minority views that might otherwise not surface easily. Surveying, for example, can be carried out by tactfully inviting silent members to express their views. Paraphrasing, summarizing, and checking the feelings of others can also be used to elicit responses. Those who hold the majority position can assume the role of the minority and express this view to the rest of the group, asking minority members to say whether the expression of the role player was accurate. Other techniques for stimulating minority participation include Time Tokens and HIgh Talker Tap-out, both described in earlier chapters.

Alternative Structures

Members of teaching teams and small faculties whose members hold similar value orientations can readily learn to use the consensual mode of decision making. But techniques and procedures that facilitate consensus in small groups are difficult to apply successfully when value orientations are pluralistic or when the group is too large for easy interaction in face-to-face discussion. In such organizations, the OD consultant and organization members may wish to create alternative structures that allow for different modes of decision making. Three alternative arrangements that have been used in large organizations include the management team, the decision-making body, and ad hoc groups.

We know of a senior high staff of seventy teachers, for example, that was involved for several years in an OD effort. The administrative team composed of the principal and three vice principals found that some staff did not wish to be involved in shared decision making, viewing the process as too complicated, time-consuming, and frustrating. After considerable experimentation, the administrative team agreed to continue providing overall leadership to the staff.

Each member of the team now holds certain fixed responsibilities related to student services, physical plant, curriculum, and so on, but avoids making unilateral decisions about matters that have ramifications for someone else's responsibility. For example, the vice principal in charge of student services does not decide that students can hold an assembly in the gym without first conferring with the vice principal in charge of physical plant to see that the gym is available. The group still meets regularly, any member can suggest items for the agenda, and all decisions are made by consensus.

In this same school most decisions are made by a group called the DMB (decision-making body). Composed of all department chairpersons, head teachers, the principal, and the three assistant principals, this body meets regularly to make school-wide policy, curriculum decisions that affect more than one department, and to allocate the total budget of the school. Any staff member or student may initiate agenda items and speak on any issue during open meetings. The positions of convener and recorder are rotated every nine weeks so that everyone shares in leadership roles. The principal's voice counts only as a member of the group unless he clearly states in advance that he will take responsibility for making a unilateral decision; otherwise decisions are made by consensus.

In the same senior high, staff or students who think that the administrative team and DMB are inadequate forums for a particular issue have the right to form ad hoc groups whose proposals are placed before the total staff for a majority vote. This arrangement, while seldom used, is nevertheless always present as a backup when consensus for decision making appears to be too costly to someone involved. We also know of a large research and development organization that used an ad hoc group when it was faced with a major policy decision about its mission and organizational staffing pattern. The creation and use of this group involved a four-stage activity spread over two days.

First, the program's director described the issues and problems facing the organization. All professional staff, assisted by two OD consultants, discussed this presentation and the extent to which any means of resolving the issues would affect organization members until they were able to report clear understanding. In a method approximating consensus, they used a survey to agree that no solution would be acceptable until everyone in the group could vote 3 or 2 on a scale in which 3 meant wholehearted support, 2 meant support with some reservations, 1 meant too many reservations to implement the solution, and 0 meant no support for any part of the solution.

Second, an ad hoc group was formed of individuals who stated either that they had special resources or expertise to contribute to decision making or that they cared greatly about the decision's ultimate outcome; a survey identified these persons among the total group. Third, the ad hoc group met in a Fishbowl until its members agreed consensually to recommend a single proposal to the total group. An open chair in the Fishbowl allowed persons in the outside circle to make process observations or comments about the proposal being developed. The consultants monitored reactions of other group members, occasionally providing feedback to members of the ad hoc group.

Fourth, the ad hoc group presented its proposal to the total group. When a survey of the total group indicated that several people were still reluctant to support the proposal, the ad hoc group reconvened to refine it and to plan a way of taking the reservations into account. Again, all other group members could occupy the empty chair in the Fishbowl or otherwise observe the meeting. A second presentation was followed by a survey indicating that the proposal now had sufficient support to become the basis of a new policy statement.

Changing Modes and Structures

Changing the norms and procedures associated with decision making is easy for neither consultants nor clients. Discussions of how influence is exercised and received are often the most prolonged, painful, and conflict-producing parts of an intervention; indeed, as influence becomes more dispersed through collaborative decision making, more rather than less conflict can occur. This does not mean that consultants should avoid dealing with the decision-making process but only that they should be aware of several potential difficulties.

First, the amount of participation in joint decision making by people in schools is determined in part by the leadership style of the formal leader—e.g., the principal, team leader, or department chairperson. Schmidt and Tannenbaum (1958) identify six leadership styles:

Telling: The leader makes the decision autonomously, announcing only its substance.

Selling: The leader makes the decision autonomously but provides rationale to encourage others to go along with it.

Testing: The leader makes a tentative decision and elicits reactions before deciding finally and autonomously.

Consulting: The leader elicits input before making the decision and explains how input was used or why it was ignored.

Joining: The leader asks others to take an equal part in decision making and agrees to go along with what the group decides.

Abdicating: The leader lets others make the decisions either by delegating the responsibility or by default.

Evidence from several of our projects indicates that unless the formal leader is willing and able to join with others, efforts toward joint decision making are likely to fail. In one school that was moving toward a multiunit organizational structure, for example, decision-making authority was to rest within grade-level teaching teams that were to be coordinated by a special leadership team composed of the principal and three team leaders. But satisfaction with the principal and the school declined over the course of the OD project, primarily because of the principal's unwillingness to allow others to exert influence on decisions affecting the school.* In another school pursuing the same goal, the principal valued joint decision making. Initially lacking the skills to join effectively with others, he went through a period of indecision that led to staff frustration and dissatisfaction, although in the second year he gained enough skill and confidence for himself and the staff to work out a way in which decisions could be made to their mutual satisfaction.

OD consultants should carefully assess the readiness and capability of formal leaders to join others in decision making and may arrange a variety of special experiences to help them become more comfortable and skillful in doing so. These experiences might include special skill-practice sessions, opportunities to discuss leadership behaviors, or coaching. The consultant can also serve as a counselor merely by being supportive or by actually helping a leader link with other leaders in a peer-support system.

In one project in which parents were forcing a principal to share influence, we helped him not only to plan meetings and develop interpersonal communication skills but also arranged for him to talk with the principal of a neighboring school about the problems of sharing influence and of joining with others in decision making. In another project we brought principals from several elementary schools together on a monthly basis to share their concerns and to role-play difficult situations that they were facing. To some of these principals we gave special coaching, sitting with them as they convened decision-making meetings, sharing our observations of the group's dynamics, and making suggestions about what they might do to improve participation and performance.

Second, because few teachers are trained to make decisions outside their classrooms, it is not surprising that many members of a school staff or team may themselves lack the motivation or competence needed to make shared decision making work. Some teachers may lack commitment to school goals, be uninterested in or untouched by certain decision issues, distrust the formal leader's motives, or otherwise have little investment in finding solutions or taking action.† Since the spread of mutual influence is likely to increase conflict, some group members may be unwilling to pay the cost of involvement in time and energy. Finally, some teachers simply prefer being at home with their families to participating in long decision-making meetings.

Many of the instruments presented in the next section of this chapter can be used to assess the readiness of group members to participate in joint decision making, while several of the exercises presented in the final section can be used to build this readiness when it is low. Group members can see the advantages of using the consensual process by participating in exercises like Lost on the Moon and can specify the areas of decision making that are most im-

---

*See Schmuck et al. (1975, chaps. 4, 6, and 13).

†See Flynn (1971); Wood (1973); Alutto and Belasco (1972); and Belasco and Alutto (1972).

portant to them by helping to develop a decision-making matrix; procedures such as surveying can alleviate many of their fears about inability to handle conflict.

Third, several factors within the larger organization or larger environment may impede movement toward joint decision making. Members of school districts or communities that exhibit highly diverse goals, unsupportive polarized subgroups, and a history of continued conflict or management by crisis may hesitate to change their decision-making norms and structures. In such cases, the consultant might provide evidence that groups in the environment are not invariably obstructive or might collect data from these groups to help in designing a new decision-making structure. The Imaging exercise described in the preceding chapter can help to clarify real environmental constraints and identify those that are only imagined.

Finally, if they are to recommend or select appropriate decision-making modes and procedures, consultants and clients alike must be aware of the kinds of decisions that are made in schools and the kinds of problems that may result from decisions so that they can plan in advance how further problem solving is to be done. Although consensus is preferable when quality and wide acceptability of decisions are important, even those that do not require everyone's effort for implementation may profit from the added attention that consensual decision making provides. That is, decision makers often need help with formative and summative evaluations of their decisions— the more so when decisions are risky either because the means of implementation are unclear or because the consequences of the decision will be difficult to assess.

For example, those who are deciding whether to change from a closed campus (students admitted from 8:00 A.M. to 3:00 P.M.) to an open campus (students free to come and go as they wish) must also consider ways of assessing the reactions of students, parents, staff, other schools, community businesses, the police department, and others to the consequences of their choice. Whose opinion should be sought? When? How? For another example, deciding whether to add community-based work-experience courses to the curriculum is not a self-contained decision but part of a larger decision that includes the question of how this might be done. Even if additional staff can be provided so that other programs are only minimally disrupted, consensual decision making that includes those who are only indirectly involved may still be necessary. Although there are model programs that might be copied, it is likely that the school will have to adapt one to suit its own needs or create an entirely new kind of program. In any case, the greater the pool of resources that can be brought to bear on solving the problems that arise from efforts to implement a decision, the better.

GATHERING DATA ABOUT DECISION MAKING

Several questionnaires and observation schedules can help in assessing an organization's ability to make group decisions. Using the instruments included here, the consultant can design intervention strategies or gather information to feed back to clients.

Actual and Preferred Decision Making

The following questionnaire reveals how respondents think decision making *is* handled and how they think it *should* be handled at three levels of the organization—the team or department level, the school level, and the overall district level. Discrepancies between what is and what ought to be provide a focus for group problem solving around decision-making processes and procedures.*

> Instructions: Check one space in each column to the right of each statement.

	The way things are			The way things should be		
	Always	Sometimes	Never	Always	Sometimes	Never
1. Decisions are made through teamwork.						
2. Facts from those who know are used to make decisions.						
3. You take a part in making decisions that affect you.						
4. You or your peers help make decisions.						
5. When decisions are made, they are based on information that you think is right and fair.						
6. Decisions are made by those who know most about the problem.						
7. The people who make decisions that affect you are aware of the things you face.						

*These questions were adapted from Mullen and Goolsby (1974).

| | The way things are | | | The way things should be | | |
	Always	Sometimes	Never	Always	Sometimes	Never
8. Decisions are made in such a way that you do not mind carrying them out.	___	___	___	___	___	___
9. Leaders work with their peers and people below them to make the decisions.	___	___	___	___	___	___
10. Things are organized so that you or your peers can help make decisions.	___	___	___	___	___	___

Actual and Preferred Influence

In the first example below,* the first question measures the amount of influence a staff member believes occupants of different positions in the school district now exert. The second question measures how much influence the respondent thinks each occupant ought to have. Results from the two parts can be compared and used for feedback to members of the school organization. Discrepancies between the two parts can stimulate discussion and problem solving to reduce the differences. Other phrases may be substituted for "in determining what innovations get attempted in your school." For example, the consultant might ask about influence in determining curriculum policy, influence in determining codes of conduct, or influence in determining what books, supplies, and equipment will be purchased.

1. In general, how much actual influence do you think each of the following groups or persons has now in determining what innovations get attempted in your school? Please indicate how much influence each person or group has by circling the appropriate number.

	None	A little	Some	Con-sider-able	A great deal
Local school board	1	2	3	4	5
The superintendent	1	2	3	4	5
Principal of your school	1	2	3	4	5

*These questions are adapted from a questionnaire by Max Abbott, Terry Eidell, and Roland Pellegrin of the Center for Educational Policy and Management, University of Oregon, Eugene, Oregon (undated mimeo).

	None	A little	Some	Consider able	A great deal
You yourself	1	2	3	4	5
A small group of teachers	1	2	3	4	5
Teachers in general	1	2	3	4	5
Curriculum personnel (supervisor, director, or coordinator)	1	2	3	4	5
Students	1	2	3	4	5
Parents	1	2	3	4	5
Teacher unions	1	2	3	4	5
PTA	1	2	3	4	5
Other (specify)	1	2	3	4	5

2. How much influence do you think these groups or persons *ought to have* in determining innovations attempted in your school?

	None	A little	Some	Con- sider- able	A great deal
Local school board	1	2	3	4	5
Your superintendent	1	2	3	4	5
Principal of your school	1	2	3	4	5
You yourself	1	2	3	4	5
A small group of teachers	1	2	3	4	5
Teachers in general	1	2	3	4	5
Curriculum personnel (supervisor, director, or coordinator)	1	2	3	4	5
Students	1	2	3	4	5
Parents	1	2	3	4	5
Teacher unions	1	2	3	4	5
PTA	1	2	3	4	5
Other (specify)	1	2	3	4	5

In the next example, the first question asks the respondent about stated policy, the second about what actually happens, and the third about how the respondent would prefer things to be done. Similar items could be written to obtain these three types of information concerning policies on many different matters.

1. Is there an official policy about who should plan and develop the school curriculum?

   No (   )

   Yes (   )   If you answer yes, please indicate below who the policy says should do this by marking X before one or more of the persons or groups named.

   _____ Citizens' or parents' committee
   _____ Board of Education
   _____ Superintendent
   _____ Principal
   _____ Department head or grade chairperson
   _____ A group of teachers
   _____ The individual teacher
   _____ Counselor(s) or guidance director
   _____ A student committee
   _____ Other (specify) _____

2. Regardless of the official policy, who *actually* plans and develops the school curriculum? Please mark one or more choices below regardless of whether your choices are the same as the previous question or different.

   _____ I don't know who actually does this
   _____ Citizens' or parents' committee
   _____ Board of Education
   _____ Superintendent
   _____ Principal
   _____ Department head or grade chairperson
   _____ A group of teachers in an instructional unit
   _____ The individual teacher
   _____ Counselor(s) or guidance director
   _____ A student committee
   _____ Other (specify) _____

3. Regardless of policy or who now does it, whom would you *prefer* to plan and develop the school curriculum? Please mark one or more choices below.

   _____ I don't care much who does it
   _____ Citizens' or parents' committee
   _____ Board of Education
   _____ Superintendent
   _____ Principal
   _____ Department head or grade chairperson
   _____ A group of teachers in an instructional unit
   _____ The individual teacher
   _____ Counselor(s) or guidance director
   _____ A student committee
   _____ Other (specify) _____

Group Effectiveness and Decision Making

The following items measure respondents' reactions to decision-making procedures typical of their meetings.*

Name of the group you are considering _____ .
How often does it usually meet? _____ .
Length of typical meeting _____ .

Now please consider what usually or typically happens in a meeting. To each of the items below, assign one of the following numbers.

5   This is *very* typical of a meeting; it happens repeatedly.
4   This is fairly typical of a meeting; it happens *quite often.*
3   This is more typical than not, but it *doesn't happen a lot.*
2   This is more untypical than typical, though it *does happen some.*
1   This is quite untypical; it *rarely* happens.
0   This is *not* typical at all; it *never* happens.

1. _____ Decisions are often left vague—as to what they are and who will carry them out.
2. _____ The group discusses and evaluates how decisions from previous meetings worked out.
3. _____ When a decision is made, it is clear who should carry it out and when.
4. _____ When conflicts over decisions come up, the group does not avoid them but really stays with the conflict and works it through.
5. _____ There is no follow-up on how decisions reached at earlier meetings worked out in practice.
6. _____ Solutions and decisions are in accord with the chairperson's or leader's point of view but not necessarily with that of the members.
7. _____ There are splits or deadlocks between factions or subgroups.
8. _____ The discussion goes on and on without any decisions being reached.

Participation in Decisions

Answers to the first three items below help to draw a picture of influence structures and networks of interdependence. Item 4 elicits perceptions of the power of various people in the school and helps assess

---

*These items are taken from a questionnaire first formulated as part of the Cooperative Project on Educational Development; other items from this questionnaire are included in chapter 6.

how autocratic, democratic, or polyarchic the influence structure is perceived to be by the staff. Item 5 elicits the staff's perceptions of the principal's sources of power. Is the principal influential because of his expertise, his attractiveness, or what?*

1. Please mark an X before the *one* statement below that best describes *your* part in deciding upon the teaching methods you use.

    _____ I choose my own teaching methods without assistance or direction.

    _____ The final choice of teaching methods is left to me, but there are others whose job includes making recommendations or suggestions.

    _____ Within certain limits I can choose my own teaching methods.

    _____ As a member of a group or committee, I share with others the job of deciding the teaching methods to be used.

    _____ I do not choose my own teaching methods. They are laid down for me by others.

2. If you choose answer 2, 3, 4, or 5 in the question just above, you were indicating that some other person or persons were somehow involved in deciding upon the teaching methods to be used in your classroom. If you chose answer 2, 3, 4, or 5, please write below the names and positions of the other persons involved.

    Name   Position

    _____   _____

    _____   _____

    _____   _____

3. When you want to receive approval in your school for an idea you are proposing, it is sometimes helpful to enlist the support of certain individuals in your school. Please list below, by name and position, the individuals whose support would help most in obtaining approval for your ideas.

    Name   Position

    _____   _____

    _____   _____

    _____   _____

---

*These questions were developed at the Center for Educational Policy and Management by Max Abbott, Terry Eidell, and Roland Pellegrin, University of Oregon, Eugene, Oregon (undated mimeo).

4. Please check the column that indicates your best estimate of the influence of teachers and principals on the areas of school life listed at the left.

In general, how much influence . . .

	None	A little	Some	Considerable	A great deal
. . . does the principal have on how the school is run?	____	____	____	____	____
. . . do teachers as a group have on how the school is run?	____	____	____	____	____
. . . does the principal have with teachers when it comes to activities and decisions that affect the performance of their classroom duties?	____	____	____	____	____
. . . do teachers have on the principal's activities and decisions?	____	____	____	____	____

5. Listed below are five reasons commonly given when people are asked why they do what their superiors suggest or want them to do. Read all five, then number them according to their importance to you as reasons for doing what your principal suggests or wants you to do. Write 1 by the most important factor, 2 by the next, etc., using each of the numerals 1 through 5 only once.

I do what the principal suggests or wants me to do because:

_____ I admire the principal's personal qualities and want to merit his or her respect and admiration.

_____ I admire the principal's competence, good judgment, and experience.

_____ The principal can give special help and benefits to those who cooperate.

_____ The principal can apply pressure or penalize those who do not cooperate.

_____ The principal has a legitimate right, considering his or her position, to expect that suggestions will be carried out.

Observing Decision Making

Groups make decisions all the time—some of them with conscious attention to the processes being used, some of them without awareness. It is important to assess both the appropriateness of the method to the decision being made and the consciousness with which the method is chosen. The following observation schedules can help the consultant observe meetings and not how decisions are made. Observations can be summarized and fed back to the group to start a discussion of decision-making procedures (see chap. 10 for advice about carrying out a data feedback session).

Decision-making Procedures

Tally the frequency with which the following procedures are used or note names and example-statements that indicate when these procedures are used in the meeting.

Plopping. A person's proposal goes unnoticed by others, as when Joe says, "I think we should introduce ourselves" and no one does.

Self-authorizing. A person's proposal is implemented only by that person, as when Lee says, "I think we should introduce ourselves. My name is Lee House."

Handclasping. A person's proposal is immediately implemented by one other person, as when Joe says, "I think we should introduce ourselves," and Lynn responds, "My name is Lynn Hale."

Vetoing. One person explicitly denies a proposal made by another, as when Pete says "I don't agree" after John proposes that people ought to introduce themselves, and no one else sides with the proposal.

Majority-Minority Voting. The decision is made when a specified percentage of persons indicate support or rejection of the proposal.

Surveying. Everyone is polled to determine where they stand on a proposal; may be done as a straw ballot or for a vote.

Consensus Testing. Similar to surveying but with genuine exploration to test for opposition to determine whether those opposed will go along or feel the need to sabotage the decision.

Decision-making Interactions

This observation schedule works best with relatively small groups. Listen for proposals to use or not to use, to do or not to do, and check or code one column in the row beside the proposer's name.

	No One	Individuals	Total Group
Responders → Proposers ↓	P = Plop S = Self- authorized	H = Handclasp V = Veto	S = Survey V = Vote C = Consensus

EXERCISES AND PROCEDURES IN DECISION MAKING

The exercises presented here can be used to highlight influence patterns, decision-making procedures, the behavior of decision makers, or some combination of these. Ideas for sequencing or combining these exercises with those in other chapters appear in the final section of this chapter.

Nonverbal Procedures and Exercises

The following four procedures and exercises work only with pairs of persons. Repeating them with a sequence of partners can generate data for considering how individual influence in decision making varies in different situations.

Hand Mirroring.   Spread out so that their outstretched arms do not collide, participants face their partners and present their hands palms out and fingers up about two inches from the other's hands. When they have agreed who will lead the first round, the leader moves his or her hands and arms while the partner follows as in a mirror image. After three minutes the partners reverse roles. For the final round, roles are left unspecified, and partners agree nonverbally on who will lead and who will follow. At the end of each round, partners describe their feelings and check their impressions of the other's thoughts and feelings. At the end of the exercise, all describe thoughts and feelings.

Thumb Wrestling. As in Hand Mirroring, partners face each other and clasp right hands leaving their thumbs free. Each attempts to pin the other's thumb with his own thumb. After several pins, participants discuss their thoughts and feelings about winning and losing, defeating and being defeated.

Shoulder Press. Partners face each other, each placing the right hand on the other's left shoulder. At a signal they nonverbally negotiate which will kneel before the other. When one has knelt, they might repeat the sequence or debrief by considering differences in their respective intentions and actions. The one who has the most influence is not always the one who remains standing. Participants might then discuss the advantages and disadvantages of such influence styles as holding firm, acquiescing, or appearing to acquiesce. Practice of communication skills such as behavior description and impression checking is important for good debriefing.

Influence Line. Participants nonverbally arrange themselves in rank-order according to the amount of influence that each one has. The rank-order can be recorded on newsprint before the group debriefs its experience. Questions to guide the debriefing might include: In what ways does the rank-order surprise or not surprise anyone? What are the consequences of this particular influence structure on the way the group makes decisions? How did it feel to be where you were in the line?

Resource-sharing Exercises

The two exercises that follow emphasize the need for coordination and information sharing by all group members.* Unless everyone participates in making the decision, they will almost inevitably be in error.

Card Discovery Problem. The consultant prepares a deck of thirty cards for each group of six participants. Each card has printed upon it a 12 X 12 matrix of points, and each point is designated either X or O. If each of the 144 points is randomly assigned either an X or O, the problem is very difficult and time-consuming. The problem is simplified by assigning the same symbol to all the points in some small area. For example, the 12 X 12 matrix can be divided into 36 smaller 2 X 2 squares with all 4 points in a given square containing the same symbol; the 12 X 12 display can also be divided into 3 X 3, 4 X 4, and 6 X 6 squares. The examples in figure 8-1 show that the complexity of the display diminishes as the size of the squares increases. The difficulty of the problem is further reduced by labeling one edge of the card as its top. Finally, to facilitate quick verification that the group has solved the problem correctly, a number

---

*These exercises have been described in Fosmire (1970).

identifying the pattern is printed on the back of each card, with identical cards receiving the same identification number.

The deck contains varying numbers of duplicate cards representing the several levels of complexity. Figure 8-1 lists the types of patterns making up the deck. Note that the deck contains more than

FIGURE 8-1   Several Levels of Display Complexity

Two cards of a 6 x 6 pattern
Two of another 6 x 6 pattern
Two of a 4 x 4 pattern
Three of another 4 x 4 pattern
Two of a 3 x 3 pattern
Two of another 3 x 3 pattern
Four of still another 3 x 3 pattern
Two of a 2 x 2 pattern
Two of another 2 x 2 pattern
Three of still another 2 x 2 pattern
One card of yet another 2 x 2 pattern
Two of a random pattern
Three of another random pattern

```
O O O O O O X X X X X X        O O O O O O O O O O O O
O O O O O O X X X X X X        O O O O O O O O O O O O
O O O O O O X X X X X X        O O O O O O O O O O O O
O O O O O O X X X X X X        X X X X X X X X X X X X
O O O O O O X X X X X X        X X X X X X X X X X X X
O O O O O O X X X X X X        X X X X X X X X X X X X
O O O O O O O O O O O O        O O O O O O X X X X X X
O O O O O O O O O O O O        O O O O O O X X X X X X
O O O O O O O O O O O O        O O O O O O X X X X X X
O O O O O O O O O O O O        X X X X X X O O O O O O
O O O O O O O O O O O O        X X X X X X O O O O O O
O O O O O O O O O O O O        X X X X X X O O O O O O
```

| 6 x 6 | 3 x 3 |

```
X X X X X X O O O O O O        X O X O O X X X X X O
X X X X X X O O O O O O        O X X O O X O O O X X X
O O O O O O X X O O X X        X X O O O O O X O O O X
O O O O O O X X O O X X        X O X X X X O O O X O
X X X X X X X X X X X X        X O X X X X O O O X O
X X X X X X X X X X X X        X O X O O X X O O O X X
O O X X O O O O X X X X        O O O O O O O X X X O
O O X X O O O O X X X X        X X X O X O O X O X O O
O O X X O O X X X X O O        X X O X X X X O X O O O
O O X X O O X X X X O O        O X O X O O O X X O X X
O O X X X X O O O O X X        X X X X O O O X X O X O
O O X X X X O O O O X X        O O X O X X O O O O X X
```

| 2 x 2 | random |

one card of every pattern except one; one card is unique. The consultant introduces the exercise by reviewing the instructions below with the group. He then mixes the deck of cards and distributes five to each participant. Forty minutes is an average time for solving the problem.

Card Discovery Problem

Instructions: A set of cards will be distributed among you. One card in the set is a singleton; it is unique. In other words, each card in the entire set has one or more duplicates except the singleton card. Your task as a group is to discover the singleton card in the entire set. When your group indicates that the unique card has been identified, the task is ended whether or not you are correct; so be sure that everyone is confident of your choice before you declare.

You may organize yourselves any way you wish to complete this task, with only the following restrictions:

1. You cannot show your cards to another member.
2. You may not pass cards to another member.
3. You must not look at another member's cards.
4. You cannot draw pictures or diagrams of the designs.
5. Do not refer to the numbers on the back of the cards.
6. Do not pool your discards (i.e., keep your own discards in your own separate pile).

While it is very important that you do not make an error in selecting the unique card, you will be scored also for the amount of time it takes you to complete the task.

After a decision is reached, participants should discuss the influence and decision making that occurred during the exercise, compare their way of working on this problem with the way they usually work as a group, and attempt to identify the barriers that reduced effective use of group resources. Fosmire (1970) has noted four common errors among groups that try to solve this problem: (1) failure to agree on a common language for describing the displays, (2) attempting to work in pairs or trios instead of remaining in a single group, (3) passive listening, and (4) silent acceptance of nonunderstanding. The two latter he describes as follows:

If one member describes a card and another replies, "I've got one; let's throw it out!" the group may be making two mistakes. First, the member may not be hearing the description correctly, but he does not paraphrase, so no one catches the error. Second, there may be a third card in the set. If a more passive member has the third card, he may fail to speak up to double-check his suspicion that he holds the card, silently accepting his nonunderstanding, only to run the risk of erroneously identifying that card as the singleton later in the task (pp. 21-22).

The consultant should watch for these errors, although not prevent them from happening, and should present his observations to the group for discussion during the debriefing phase of the exercise.

Mine Field.   This exercise also requires special equipment and can be scored for both accuracy and speed. It differs from the preceding exercise in offering 144 possible decisions so that the influence of individuals can change over time and be examined.

The game board is a 12 X 12 matrix made so that individual cells can be uncovered in sequence to reveal either a "safe" or a "mined" step.* Permanent markings on a smooth board can be covered with gummed stickers, or two colors or beans can be covered with small inverted paper cups. A more elaborate board requires drilling 144 ½"-diameter holes in ¼" plywood, and 144 identically placed wells in ½" plywood. Put colored markers in the wells in the thicker board, and cover it with a sheet of paper. Place the thinner board on top so that you have a sandwich with the paper between the boards. Participants use the blunt ends of pencils to poke through the holes and paper to reveal differently colored markers in the wells. The board can be used again and again merely by changing the paper, and the pattern can be changed by reassorting the markers. The only caution is to use colors that are bright and varied enough to be seen through the punched paper.

The pattern of safe and mined steps on the game board is unimportant, but there should be only one safe path on which to proceed from the left side of the board to the right. In the following diagram, for example, shaded spaces indicate safe steps, and unshaded spaces indicate the location of mines.

The game is played best by a team of four to six players. In addition to the game board, participants receive an individual sheet of instructions, each of which reveals a *different* 6 X 6-cell portion of the board. Instruction sheets list the following rules.

1. You may not show this sheet to any other member of your group.
2. You must memorize the pattern on this sheet in two minutes, surrendering it to an observer after that time.
3. You cannot draw or copy the pattern on your sheet.
4. As a group, you will decide which of the twelve steps on the left edge of the board to take first. When you have made a decision, one person will remove the sticker (or lift the cup or punch the hole).
5. If the space underneath appears shaded, you will have taken a safe step in the mine field. If the space underneath is unshaded, the person who has revealed it will be considered "dead" and can no longer participate.

---

*Boards for this game are commercially available from Professor Fred R. Fosmire, Department of Psychology, University of Oregon, Eugene, Oregon 97403.

6. The group will then make a second decision about where to step, then a third, then a fourth, and so on. Each step must be next to the one before, either to the right or the left, above or below, or on one of the four diagonals. No jumping over steps will be allowed. As before, the person revealing a mine will become "dead."

7. You will continue taking steps across the board until the path beginning on the left edge ends up on the right edge.

8. Each person in the group is currently reading this same set of directions. However, each person has a different diagram to memorize. Each diagram shows only a portion of the board, but each diagram correctly depicts that portion. It will be necessary for group members to pool their knowledge so as to complete a group walk across this mine field in the shortest possible time. As a group you have all the information you need; your individual maps, if fitted together, would show the whole path.

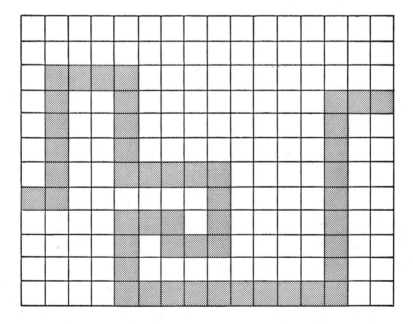

In addition to recording the amount of time needed to complete the task, the consultant and other observers can record the following information for each step taken by the group: Who first proposed this step? Who explicitly agreed that this step should be taken? How was that decided? It is also possible to describe the behavior of participants, perhaps concentrating on one person per step. While any or all of these observations can be reported to the group at the end of the exercise to encourage debriefing, it is best to let the participants begin the debriefing by discussing questions like the following: How did the group make decisions in this exercise? How did people feel as they worked on their tasks? What prevented the group from crossing the field faster or with fewer errors? In what ways was the decision making in this exercise like or unlike the way the group usually works?

Consensus Exercises

The five exercises in this section allow participants to practice and consider the process of consensual decision making. The first exercise is described in complete detail, but others have been condensed by eliminating some information about procedures. Using the first exercise as a pattern, the consultant can create handouts and scoring sheets for the others.

Lost on the Moon. Imagining themselves to be members of a space crew who have crash-landed on the moon some 200 miles from where the mother ship waits, participants are given sheets of paper listing fifteen critical items left intact after the landing and are asked to rank-order them according to their importance in helping the crew reach the rendezvous point. As the exercise begins, each participant is given a copy of the sheet headed "Lost on the Moon." Further instructions are included in the exercise description.*

Lost on the Moon
Instructions: You are a member of a space crew originally scheduled to rendezvous with a mother ship on the lighted surface of the moon. Because of mechanical difficulties, however, your ship has been forced to land at a spot some 200 miles from the rendezvous point. During the rough landing much of the equipment aboard was damaged, and, since survival depends on reaching the mother ship, only the most critical items aboard must be chosen for the 200-mile trip. Below are listed the fifteen items left intact and undamaged after landing. Your task is to rank-order them in terms of their importance in enabling your crew to reach the rendezvous point. Place the number 1 by the most important item, the number 2 by the second most important, and so on through number 15, the least important.

_____ Box of matches
_____ Food concentrate
_____ Fifty feet of nylon rope
_____ Parachute silk
_____ Solar-powered portable heating unit
_____ Two .45 calibre pistols
_____ One case dehydrated milk
_____ Two 100-pound tanks of oxygen
_____ Stellar map (of the moon's constellation)

---

*This exercise is adapted from Hall (1971).

_____ Self-inflating life raft
_____ Magnetic compass
_____ Five gallons of water
_____ Signal flares
_____ First-aid kit containing injection needles
_____ Solar-powered FM receiver-transmitter

Next each participant is given a sheet of "Instructions for Consensus." After reading this, participants are instructed to reach a consensual decision of the best rank-order of the fifteen items.

Instructions for Consensus
Consensus is a decision process for making full use of resources and for resolving conflicts creatively. Consensus is difficult to reach, so not every ranking will meet with everyone's complete approval. Complete unanimity is not the goal—it is rarely achieved. But each individual should be able to accept the group rankings on the basis of logic and feasibility. When all group members feel this way, you have reached consensus as defined here, and the judgment may be entered as a group decision. This means, in effect, that a person can block the group if he thinks it necessary; at the same time, he should use this option in the best sense of reciprocity. Here are some guidelines to use in achieving consensus:

1. Avoid arguing for your own rankings. Present your position as lucidly and logically as possible, but listen to the other members' reactions and consider them carefully before you press your point.
2. Do not assume that someone must win and someone must lose when discussion reaches a stalemate. Instead, look for the next most acceptable alternative for all parties.
3. Do not change your mind simply to avoid conflict and to reach agreement and harmony. When agreement seems to come too quickly and easily, be suspicious. Explore the reasons, and be sure everyone accepts the solution for basically similar or complementary reasons. Yield only to positions that have objective and logical foundations.
4. Avoid conflict-reducing techniques such as majority vote, averages, coin flips, and bargaining. When a dissenting member finally agrees, don't feel that this person must be rewarded by having his or her own way on some later point.
5. Differences of opinion are natural and expected. Seek them out and try to involve everyone in the decision process. Disagreements can help the group's decision because, with a wide range of information and opinions, there is a greater chance that the group will find a better solution.

Allow groups approximately forty-five minutes to reach consensus about their rank-orderings, and then ask them to tabulate the

346

results. In each group let one person act as secretary. As each member of the group calls out his private rank-orderings of the fifteen items, the secretary records these on the scoring sheet shown in figure 8-2. When each person's rank-ordering has been recorded, the

FIGURE 8-2   Scoring Sheet for Lost on the Moon

	Individual rankings										Sums of indv. rankings	Ranking of sums	Consensual ranking	NASA's ranking
	1	2	3	4	5	6	7	8	9	10				
Box of matches														15
Food concentrate														4
50 feet of nylon rope														6
Parachute silk														8
Solar-powered portable heating unit														13
Two .45 calibre pistols														11
One case dehydrated Pet Milk														12
Two 100 lb. tanks of oxygen														1
Stellar map (of the moon's constellation)														3
Self-inflating life raft														9
Magnetic compass														14
Five gallons of water														2
Signal flares														10
First-aid kit containing injection needles														7
Solar-powered radio FM receiver-transmitter														5

secretary sums the ranking for each of the items and rank-orders the sums, thus arriving at an average rank-order for the group. (This could represent the rank-order that might have been obtained had the group merely voted and not held a discussion.) The secretary also records the rank-order that the group has reached by consensus.

It is best if all groups work in one large room in circles that are separate to minimize mutual distraction. When the secretaries in each group have completed their work, the correct answer to this exercise according to NASA is announced. The secretaries also record this rank-ordering on their sheets. Each group then computes three scores by summing the arithmetic discrepancies between the correct rank-order and the rank-order obtained through consensus, the average rank-order of the group before discussion, and the individual rank-order that came closest to the NASA rank-order. Each group then sees whether its "best" individual, its average produced before discussion, or its consensual product is superior.

After the participants have inspected and informally discussed the charts for a few minutes, each group should discuss three questions. The highlights of these discussions should be made known to the total assembly of participants.

1. What were my reactions to the exercise? How did I feel? What was I thinking?
2. How similar were our behaviors here to our usual behaviors in school? How different? What are the implications of this exercise for our staff?
3. How well did we use our group resources? What prevented us from using them better? How could the obstacles to better use of resources have been avoided?

Twelve Angry Men. This exercise in group decision making, based on a motion picture released in April 1957 by United Artists Corporation, requires participants to predict the order in which the jurors in *Twelve Angry Men* will change their votes from a guilty to a not-guilty verdict. The movie is shown for about thirty-eight minutes, until just before the second vote of the jurors is taken. While viewing the first part of the film, participants fill out the rank-ordering form below; after this is completed, the group is asked to produce a new rank-order consensually. The correct rank-ordering is discovered by viewing the remainder of the film, and scoring and debriefing are carried out as in the previous exercise.

Twelve Angry Men
Instructions: You have just seen the first part of the movie *Twelve Angry Men* and have begun to develop some feelings, attitudes, and hunches about each of the jurors. Throughout the rest of the movie the jurors change their votes from guilty to not guilty, one at a time, until the total jury votes not guilty at the end. You do not know what facts will be produced or what discussion will take up, but you do have sufficient information at this point to make a good guess as to the sequence with which jury members will change their vote. Who will be first? Who will be last? Place a 1 after architect (Henry Fonda) since we know that he is the first to vote not guilty. Now place a 2 after the juror you think will change next, a 3 for the third person to change, and so on to 12. Be sure your own name and group are at the top of the paper.

Foreman (Assistant Coach)	——	Baseball Fan	——
Advertising Man (Glasses)	——	Painter	——
Watchmaker (Mustache)	——	Slum Kid	——
Bigot (Ed Begley)	——	Broker (E. G. Marshall)	——
Elderly Man	——	Bully (Lee J. Cobb)	——
Architect (Henry Fonda)	——	Timid Man	——

Grievances of Black Citizens. In the long form of this exercise, participants predict the order in which a large group of mostly black citizens identified the most significant grievances of American blacks. Distribute to participants the instruction sheet headed "Grievances of Black Citizens." As in the earlier exercises, participants first rank-order the items individually and then discuss them to achieve a consensual order. Use instructions for consensus and guided debriefing as before. The ordering of the grievances given by the National Advisory Commission on Civil Disorders (1968), from most to least grievous, is as follows.

1. (D) Discriminatory police practices
2. (H) Unemployment and underemployment
3. (E) Inadequate housing
4. (A) Inadequate education
5. (G) Poor recreational facilities
6. (L) Unresponsive political structure
7. (B) Disrespectful white attitudes
8. (I) Administration of justice
9. (J) Inadequate federal programs
10. (C) Inadequate municipal services
11. (K) Discriminatory consumer and credit practices
12. (F) Inadequate welfare programs.

Grievances of Black Citizens
During the fall of 1967 the research staff of the National Advisory Commission on Civil Disorders (the Kerner Commission) studied conditions in twenty cities that had experienced riots during 1967. The group of twenty cities consisted of nine cities that had experienced major destruction, six New Jersey cities surrounding Newark, and five cities that had experienced lesser degrees of violence.

In each city the black residents living in or near the disorder areas were the greater portion of those interviewed. Also interviewed were persons from the official sector (mayors, city officials, policemen and police officials, judges, and others)

and the private sector (businessmen, labor leaders, and community leaders). Altogether, more than 1,200 persons were
interviewed, but the large majority were black citizens living
in or near the riot-torn areas.

Using the answers to the interviews, the investigators
identified and assigned weights to the four types of grievances
that appeared to have the greatest significance to the black
community in each city. For each city they made judgments
about the severity of particular grievances and assigned ranks
to the four most serious. Their judgments were based on the
frequency with which a particular grievance was mentioned, the
relative intensity with which it was discussed, references to
incidents exemplifying the grievance, and estimates of severity
obtained from those interviewed.

Four points were assigned to the most serious type of
grievance in each city, three points to the second most serious,
and so on. When the point values were added for all cities, a
list of twelve grievance types emerged, rank-ordered. The type
of grievance considered the most serious in the most cities was
number 1. The one that seemed generally least serious was
number 12. Following are the twelve grievance types reported
by the Kerner Commission. Your task is to guess how they
were ordered by the commission staff.

Put a 1 beside the type of grievance you believe the staff
judged that black citizens felt to be the most serious to them
across all twenty cities. Put a 2 beside the second most serious
and pervasive, and so on down to a 12 beside the least widespread and least serious.

_____ A. Inadequate education: de facto segregation, poor
quality of instruction and facilities, inadequate
curriculum, etc.
_____ B. Disrespectful white attitudes: racism and lack of
respect for dignity of blacks.
_____ C. Inadequate municipal services: inadequate sanitation
and garbage removal, inadequate health care facilities, etc.
_____ D. Discriminatory police practices: physical or verbal
abuse, no grievance channels, discrimination in
hiring and promoting blacks, etc.
_____ E. Inadequate housing: poor housing code enforcement,
discrimination in sales and rentals, overcrowding.
_____ F. Inadequate welfare programs: unfair qualification
regulations, attitude of welfare workers toward
recipients.
_____ G. Poor recreational facilities: inadequate parks and
playgrounds, lack of organized programs, etc.
_____ H. Unemployment and underemployment: discrimination in hiring and placement by organizations or by
unions, general lack of full-time jobs, etc.

_____ I. Administration of justice: discriminatory treatment in the courts, presumption of guilt, etc.

_____ J. Inadequate federal programs: insufficient participation by the poor, lack of continuity, inadequate funding.

_____ K. Discriminatory consumer and credit practices: blacks sold inferior-quality goods at higher prices, excessive interest rates, fraudulent commercial practices.

_____ L. Unresponsive political structure: inadequate representation of blacks, lack of response to complaints, obscurity of official grievance channels.

The short form of this exercise can be carried out more rapidly by offering participants only eight grievances to rank instead of twelve. The same instructions can be used, but all designations of twelve should be changed to eight. The eight items we have used and their correct ranking are as follows:

1. (C) Discriminatory police practices
2. (F) Unemployment and underemployment
3. (D) Inadequate housing
4. (A) Inadequate education
5. (H) Unresponsive political structure
6. (B) Disrespectful white attitudes
7. (G) Inadequate federal programs
8. (E) Inadequate welfare programs

Occupational Prestige in the United States. The following sheet of instructions can be used in the same way as the foregoing exercises as an exercise in consensus. The numbers in parentheses are the correct rankings and should not appear on the sheet given to the participants at the outset.

Occupational Prestige in the United States
Instructions: In 1963 the National Opinion Research Center at the University of Chicago conducted a study of the prestige according to ninety occupations. A national sample of the American adult population was interviewed, and each person interviewed was asked for his personal opinion of the general standing of each job. Below is a list of fifteen occupations included in this study. Your task is to rank these in the same order of prestige as did the sample of the American public. Place the number 1 by the occupation that you think was ranked as most prestigious by the national sample; place the number 2 by the second most prestigious occupation, and so on through the number 15, which is your estimate of the least prestigious of the fifteen occupations.

_____ Priest (8)
_____ Nuclear physicist (2)
_____ Author of novels (11)
_____ Banker (9)
_____ Member of the board of directors of a
large corporation (7)
_____ Carpenter (15)
_____ Owner of a factory that employs about 100 people (10)
_____ Physician (1)
_____ Electrician (13)
_____ Lawyer (5)
_____ Architect (6)
_____ College professor (4)
_____ Official of an international labor union (12)
_____ State governor (3)
_____ Undertaker (14)

Below is an alternate list of occupations taken from the same source as the one above.

_____ Banker (6)
_____ U.S. representative in Congress (2)
_____ Public school teacher (8)
_____ Railroad engineer (11)
_____ Sociologist (7)
_____ Musician in a symphony orchestra (10)
_____ Dentist (3)
_____ Radio announcer (14)
_____ Insurance agent (15)
_____ Minister (4)
_____ U.S. Supreme Court justice (1)
_____ Farm owner and operator (12)
_____ Policeman (13)
_____ Airline pilot (5)
_____ Building contractor (9)

Characteristics of a Successful Teacher. The following sheet of instructions can also be used as an exercise in consensus. Although there are no correct rankings, the topic is of real relevance to people in schools, and reaching consensus on the most important characteristic of a successful teacher often brings out major value differences that can be used as foci for discussion.

Characteristics of a Successful Teacher
Following is a list of eleven characteristics of a successful teacher plus one space for adding any characteristic you think has been overlooked. Rank-order the characteristics according to your opinion of their importance in contributing to successful teaching.

Your rank-order		Group rank-order
_____	Encouraging creativity among students.	_____
_____	Maintaining an orderly and quiet classroom.	_____
_____	Enriching the course of study or curriculum of the classroom.	_____
_____	Giving individual attention to students.	_____
_____	Experimenting with new teaching techniques.	_____
_____	Diagnosing learning problems of students.	_____
_____	Coordinating classroom activities with other parts of the school program.	_____
_____	Ensuring that students learn basic skills.	_____
_____	Solving personal problems of individual students.	_____
_____	Developing student ability in analytical reasoning and problem solving.	_____
_____	Developing the aesthetic potential of students.	_____
_____	Other (specify): _____	_____

Exercises to Explore and Clarify Values

Decision making of any kind, but particularly decision making by consensus, is difficult when those involved hold different values about the purposes of education and the ways of schooling. It is all the more difficult when organization members are unaware of these differences and their influence on the way in which collaborative work is carried out. The consultant can help school people clarify their values and explore important value differences by means of the two exercises that follow.

Personal Coat of Arms. In this procedure,* the consultant draws on newsprint the following facsimile of a coat of arms.

Participants are then asked to answer six questions by drawing a picture, design, or symbol in the appropriate area of their own coat of arms.

1. What do you regard as your greatest personal achievement to date?
2. What do you regard as your family's greatest achievement?
3. What is the one thing that other people can do to make you happy?

---

*This exercise is adapted from Simon, Howe, and Kirschenbaum (1972, pp. 278-80).

4. What do you regard as your own greatest personal failure to date?
5. What would you do if you had one year to live and were guaranteed success in whatever you attempted?
6. What three things would you most like to be said of you if you died today?

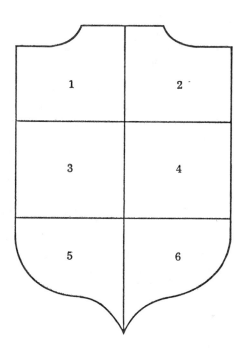

Participants can then discuss their drawings in small groups, explaining the significance of the symbols and how these express their values. The consultant can further focus the discussion by asking participants to note similarities and differences in one another's coat of arms.

Fall-out Shelter. Simon, Howe, and Kirschenbaum (1972, pp. 281–86), from whose work this exercise is adapted, report that Fall-out Shelter "is often a very dramatic example of how our values differ: how hard it is to objectively determine the best values; and how we often have trouble listening to people whose beliefs are different from our own" (p. 281). If there are many participants, divide them into groups of five to ten each before describing the following situation.

Your group members are of a department in Washington, D.C., that is in charge of experimental stations in a far outpost of civilization. Suddenly World War III breaks out and bombs

begin dropping. Places all across the globe are being destroyed.
People are heading for whatever fall-out shelters are available.
You receive a desperate call from one of your experimental
stations asking for help.

It seems there are ten people, but there is only enough
space, air, food, and water in their fall-out shelter for six people
for a period of three months, which is how long they estimate
they can safely stay down there. They realize that if they have
to decide among themselves which six should go into the shelter,
they are likely to become irrational and begin fighting. So they
have decided to call your department, their superiors, and leave
the decision to you. They will abide by your decision. But you
have only a half-hour before you must get to your own fall-out
shelter; so you have time to get only superficial descriptions of
the ten people before you will have to go to your own shelter.

As a group, you must decide which four of the ten will
have to be eliminated from the shelter. Before you begin, I want
to impress upon you two important considerations. It is entirely
possible that the six people you choose to stay in the shelter
might be the only six people left to start the human race again.
This choice is therefore very important. Do not allow yourself
to be swayed by pressure from the others in your group. Try to
make the best choices possible. On the other hand, if you do
not make a choice in the time allowed, then you are in fact
choosing to let the ten people fight it out among themselves
with the possibility that more than four might perish. You have
exactly one half-hour. Here is all you know about the ten people.

1. A sixteen-year-old girl of questionable IQ, a high school
   drop-out, pregnant.
2. A policeman with gun, thrown off the force for police
   brutality.
3. A clergyman seventy-five years old.
4. A thirty-six-year-old female physician unable to bear
   children.
5. A forty-six-year-old male violinist, narcotics user.
6. A twenty-year-old male black militant with no special skills.
7. A thirty-nine-year-old former prostitute, retired for
   four years.
8. An architect, homosexual.
9. A twenty-six-year-old male law student.
10. The law student's twenty-five-year-old wife, spent the
    last nine months in a mental hospital, still heavily sedated;
    they refuse to be separated.

After the groups have made their choices, post the lists for all
groups to observe so that each group can discuss its choices with the
others. The consultant can then ask participants to disregard the
content of the activity but to examine its process and value implications on the basis of several leading questions. How well did

people listen to one another? Did people allow themselves to be pressured into changing their minds? What do the final choices say about similarities or difference of values in this group?

Intergroup Exercises

The two exercises that follow require more than one group. Suggestions for forming the groups are included in each description.

Planners and Operators. By simulating problems that arise when one team makes decisions about another team's work, this exercise demonstrates the difficulties of using a formal hierarchy in group problem solving.* Participants learn about the processes of team planning, about communication problems between a planning and an implementing group, and about the problems an implementing group confronts when carrying out a plan that is not its own.

The exercise is performed by clusters of nine to twelve persons divided into three subgroups of four planners, four operators, and one to four observers. The planners decide how they will instruct the operators to perform the task; the operators carry the task through as best they can; the observers watch the process, making notes of efficiencies and difficulties. The task consists of joining sixteen puzzle pieces designed to form a 12" square, leaving an empty 1" X 1" square in the center. The diagonal lines on the diagram are thicker than the others to hint to the planners how they might organize their instructions for the operators.

FIGURE 8-3　Planners and Operators Puzzle

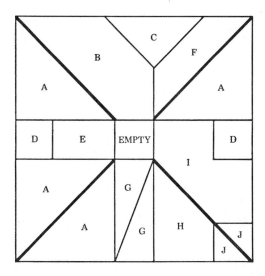

---

*We are indebted to Warren Schmidt of UCLA for the general design of this exercise (also called the Hollow Square) and for some of the information about the activity that typically follows it. The exercise can be purchased by writing to Dr. Richard A. Schmuck, Center for Educational Policy and Management, University of Oregon, Eugene, Oregon 97401.

Each member of the planning team has four pieces of the puzzle; the planning team has the diagram shown in figure 8-3. In placing the pieces in four piles, the exact distribution is not of great importance; the following combinations are possible—(1) A, B, I, G; (2) A, C, D, H; (3) A, D, F, J; (4) A, E, J, G—although the actual pieces should not be labeled. The key restriction on the planning group is that its members may not move the pieces, put the puzzle together, or give a drawing of the design to the operating team; they may only plan how the pieces can be arranged to form the design in the least amount of time. A detailed description of the exercise follows.

- Explaining that this is a simulation in which planners instruct operators to carry out a task, the consultant divides the group into four-person planning teams, four-person operating teams, and observers. Observers leave the room to be briefed by a consultant later. Operators go to another room. Planners gather around their tables to get acquainted.

- Out of hearing of both the planning and operating teams, the consultant briefs observers on what to look for in the planning, communicating, and implementing stages of the exercises, giving each a copy of the "Briefing Sheet for Observing Team."

- The consultant hands out briefing sheets and puzzle materials to planning teams, reads the briefing sheets aloud, and emphasizes that the planning must end in forty minutes. The planning now gets under way.

- The consultant then goes to the operating teams to distribute briefing sheets that explain their task during the waiting period. Essentially this task is to discuss how they feel while waiting to be instructed and how they can prepare themselves for an unknown task. They are told that their planning team may summon them at any time but that if they are not called by five minutes before the task is to begin, they are to report for work anyway. If participants ask about visiting the other group or passing notes, some consultants will carry notes between groups and allow planners to visit operators (but not vice versa).

- When the planning is completed, whether in forty minutes or sooner, the planning team calls in the operating team and gives instructions.

Briefing Sheet for Observing Team
You will observe a planning team deciding how to solve a problem and giving instructions to an operating team that will carry out the solution; you will also observe the operating team. The problem consists of assembling sixteen flat pieces into a square containing an empty square at its center. The planning team has a diagram of the assembled pieces. This team may not assemble the pieces itself but must instruct the operating team on how to do so in a minimum time. You will observe silently throughout the process.

Suggestions:

1. During the planning period, watch for the following behavior:
   a. Is there balanced participation among team members?
   b. What kinds of behavior facilitate or impede the process?
   c. How does the planning team divide its time between planning and instructing? (How early does it summon the operating team?)
   d. Does the team decide that certain members should do one thing and other members do other things during the instructing? If so, how is this decided?
2. During the instructing period, watch for the following behavior:
   a. At the beginning of the instruction, how do the planners orient the operators to their task?
   b. What assumptions made by the planning team are not communicated to the operating team?
   c. How effective are the instructions?
   d. Does the operating team question the planners?
3. During the assembly period, watch for the following behavior:
   a. What evidence do operating team members exhibit that instructions were clearly understood or misunderstood?
   b. What nonverbal reactions do planning team members exhibit as they watch their plans being implemented or distorted?

Briefing Sheet for Planning Team

Each team member sits by a packet containing some puzzle pieces. When all the pieces from all four packets are properly assembled, they will form a large square containing a small empty square at its center. A sheet displaying a diagram of the completed puzzle is provided. Your task is to do the following.

1. Plan how the sixteen pieces distributed among you can be be assembled to form the square.
2. Plan how to instruct your operating team to carry out your plan for assembling the square.
3. You may call the operating team and begin instruction any time during the next forty minutes. Hide the diagram before calling in the operators.
4. The operating team must begin assembling the square forty-five minutes from now, and you are required to give them at least five minutes of instruction.

Before you begin, read these rules.

During planning:

1 Keep your pieces before you at all times.
2. Do not touch the pieces or trade with other persons now or during the instruction phase.

3. Do not assemble the square; that is the operators' job.
4. Do not mark any pieces.

During instruction:

1. Give all instructions in words, either aloud or in writing. Hide the diagram from the operators; do not draw any diagrams yourselves, either on paper or by gestures.
2. The operating team must not move the pieces until a signal is given to start.
3. After the signal is given, you may not give further instructions but should stand back and observe.

Briefing Sheet for Operating Team
1. Your team of four people will be responsible for carrying out a task according to instructions given by your planning team.
2. Your task will begin in forty-five minutes.
3. Your planning team may call you in for instruction at any time during the next forty minutes.
4. If you are not summoned in forty minutes, you must report to the planning team at your own initiative at the end of forty minutes.
5. Once you have begun the task, the planning team is not allowed to give you further instructions.
6. Finish the task as rapidly as possible.
7. You may send notes to the planners, and they may send notes in reply.
8. While you await a call from the planning team, do the following:
   a. Individually, write the concerns that you feel while awaiting instructions.
   b. As a group, think of anything that might help or hinder you in following instructions.
   c. Write the things that are working for you on one sheet of paper and the things that are working against you on another.
   d. Keep these sheets handy because you may find them useful during the discussion that follows completion of the task.

- The consultant now calls time to begin, instructing planners to step back from the table and to remain silent as the operating team begins its work.
- Operators complete the task according to their instructions, taking as much time as necessary.
- Discussion includes reports from the observers, planners, and operators and observations of similarities between the exercise and other organizational and group experiences.

Planners and operators both experience several kinds of learning in the course of this exercise. Planners learn that it is frustrating to plan a task that someone else has to carry out and which they are themselves prohibited from performing. They frequently spend so much time planning the activity that they do not allow enough time to communicate their plans adequately to the operators, with the result that a good deal of the planning effort is wasted. In addition, planners often place limitations on themselves that are not in their instructions and fail to use all the resources at their disposal. Indeed, their very preoccupation with giving information under pressure often reduces the efficacy of the communication. They sometimes use geometric or other terms that the operators do not understand, and they frequently give cumbersome instructions in writing instead of taking the time to give them aloud. At the same time, planning is a very seductive task which so absorbs the interest and attention of planners that they often forget what the operators are experiencing, fail to take into account their anxieties, their need to feel physically comfortable in the environment, and so forth.

For their part, operators often feel anxiety about performing an unknown task and usually develop some antagonistic feelings toward the planning team. This is particularly true when several groups are engaging in the exercise in one large room and one operating team is called by its planners after seeing other teams called in earlier. Sometimes an operating team sets up its own organizational structure, selecting a leader to receive their instructions and give them guidance; but this structure is typically ignored by the planners, who usually never suspect that such an organization exists.

When the exercise is completed, the ensuing discussion may be guided by questions such as the following: Did you feel that your behavior during this task was typical, or were you surprised by some of your behaviors or feelings? Which actions of the planners and operators surprised you? What was most frustrating about the task, and what do you think is the key to its successful completion? What could planners or operators have done to improve their own or the other group's performance? What occurred during the exercise that was like or unlike what occurs at our school? Did any ideas arise that might be used to improve our school's organizational functioning? If no one else does, the consultant may summarize the important points raised during the discussion.

Prisoner's Dilemma. This exercise simulates a risk-taking situation like that experienced by two guilty prisoners being questioned separately by the police. Each is told what the other has confessed and that a similar confession will get them both off easier. The prisoner's dilemma is whether to confess. The exercise allows groups to explore win-lose zero-sum influence situations and dramatizes the merits of collaboration and competition in intergroup relations.*

---

*This exercise is adapted from Pfeiffer and Jones (1974, pp. 52-56).

Two teams of three to eight persons are seated far enough apart so that they cannot overhear or communicate with each other unless told to do so. One team is designated Red and the other Blue. The exercise consists of ten rounds, in each of which the Reds vote either an A or B and the Blues vote either an X or Y. Teams have three minutes to make the decision for each round before reporting their choice and discovering their score.

Points are awarded for each round as follows: (1) if Reds choose A and Blues choose X, both teams win 3 points; (2) if Reds choose A and Blues choose Y, Reds lose 6 points and Blues win 6; (3) if Reds choose B and Blues choose X, Reds win 6 and Blues lose 6; (4) if Reds choose B and Blues choose Y, both teams lose 3 points.

Points won or lost are doubled in the fourth round and quadrupled in the ninth and tenth rounds. Points for each round and a running total for each team are recorded on newsprint. If desired, each team may appoint a representative to "negotiate" before the fourth and eighth rounds. Negotiators meet for one minute where they cannot be overheard by either team. Other than imposing a time limit and designating the meeting place, the consultant does not limit what happens in these sessions.

Final debriefing can begin with questions like: How were decisions made in our team? Who was most influential in our team? What were the advantages and disadvantages of collaborating with, competing with, being suspicious of, trusting, defeating, or losing to the other team? How was the way we worked in this exercise like or unlike everyday life in this organization?

Examining Influence and Participation

The next three procedures can be used in sequence to examine influence and group participation patterns. Like High Talker Tap-out, Beach Ball, and instruments such as Communication Roles (see chap. 3), these procedures provide good transitions from communication skill to decision-making process.

Influence Group. Participants form three groups of equal size composed respectively and exclusively of high influencers, moderate influencers, and low influencers, the members deciding among themselves by consensus who should be in which group. Consensus on the final grouping is very important and ends the active part of the procedure. Debriefing can begin in a Fishbowl arrangement with each group taking a turn in the center to discuss how it feels to be in this group and how its members feel toward the other two groups. The total group then explores the likely effects of the grouping on the functioning of the subgroups and total group.

Self-assessment of Participation. Group members form three groups of equal size composed of high talkers, moderate talkers, and low talkers, each group to discuss a regular item on the agenda in the presence of the two other groups. The Fishbowl arrangement allows all members to see how persons of high, middle, and low talkativeness deal with issues and also to see what the problems of communication are in these three groups.

Knutson (1960) has demonstrated that highly loquacious persons get the greatest attention from others, including their own kind; that worthwhile contributions from low talkers are often inhibited or buried by the garrulousness of high talkers; and that high and low talkers alike come to believe that low talkers have little to offer. Asking high talkers to be quiet while low talkers speak can expand possibilities for both listening and interaction.

After every subgroup has had its turn in the center, the entire group discusses what has happened (Knutson's points will usually emerge in the discussion). Finally, the entire staff proceeds with the rest of the agenda. At the end of the meeting, members are asked whether the exercise had any effect on the later portion of the meeting.

Influence Roles. Two kinds of influence or group functions must be present for meetings to be effective: task functions, which answer the work requirements of the meeting, and maintenance functions, which help the group with its interpersonal feelings and internal cohesion. Ideally, all staff members should be capable of performing both of these functions. Usually, however, only a few perform task functions and even fewer perform maintenance functions. In this exercise, group members individually nominate one person as the one who most often performs one or the other function in their group. Twelve names are written down, one for each influence role below, and all nominations are listed on newsprint.

Influencing Task
1. Initiating: proposing tasks or goals; defining a group problem; suggesting a procedure for solving a problem; suggesting other ideas for consideration.
2. Information or opinion seeking: requesting facts on the problem; seeking relevant information; asking for suggestions and ideas.

3. Information or opinion giving: offering facts, providing relevant information; stating a belief, giving suggestions or ideas.
4. Clarifying or elaborating: interpreting or reflecting ideas or suggestions; clearing up confusion; indicating alternatives and issues before the group; giving examples.
5. Summarizing: pulling related ideas together; restating suggestions after the group has discussed them.
6. Consensus testing: sending up trial balloons to see whether the group is nearing a conclusion or whether agreement has been reached.

Influencing Maintenance
1. Encouraging: being friendly, warm, and responsive to others; accepting others and their contributions; listening; showing regard for others by giving them opportunity or recognition.
2. Expressing group feelings: sensing feeling, mood, relationships within the group; sharing one's own feelings with other members.
3. Harmonizing: attempting to reconcile disagreements; reducing tension by oiling troubled waters; getting people to explore their differences.
4. Compromising: offering to compromise one's own position, ideas, or status; admitting error; disciplining oneself to help maintain the group.
5. Gatekeeping: seeing that others have a chance to speak; maintaining group discussion rather than one- , two- , or three-way conversations.
6. Setting standards: expressing standards that will help the group to achieve; applying standards in evaluating group functioning and production.

Debriefing can focus on individual feelings and behavior either causing or resulting from the nominations, or on consequences for the group of the centralized or dispersed structure described by the nomination pattern.

This exercise can also be combined with Self-assessment for Participation as follows. After the group has divided into equal subgroups of high, moderate, and low talkers, there will be twice as many observers as participants in the Fishbowl. Each inside participant can have one outside colleague watching for task functions and another outside colleague watching for maintenance functions, each to give him feedback on which functions he did or did not carry out in the group.

If this procedure is repeated several times, the person being observed can tell the observers about several functions that he would like to try, and they can give feedback in subsequent observations or meetings on whether they have seen him attempting to perform these functions. One of the most significant concepts to be learned from such an activity is that many contributions are influential and helpful to the group even when they are not focused directly on the task. In addition, the dispersion of influence is likely to increase as more members learn how to keep the discussion circulating widely through the group.

Decision-making Roles. This exercise provides a vehicle for achieving group agreements about the roles each member should assume in decision making.* In the matrix that follows, the columns represent different jobs or status levels within the organization; the rows represent functions about which decision making occurs. Participants choose their own jobs and functions.

	Principal	Assistant principal	Counselors	Teachers	Service personnel	Students
Determining goals	_____	_____	_____	_____	_____	_____
Ordering materials	_____	_____	_____	_____	_____	_____
Sequencing procedures	_____	_____	_____	_____	_____	_____

Next, the consultant describes six kinds of influence that persons can have on a decision and tells the group to complete the matrix by discussing the kind of influence appropriately exerted on each function by each position. The kinds of influence are as follows.

Kinds of Influence

Label

Blank   May recommend or suggest. Because it is understood in a healthy organization that any person in any position may make recommendations to the person who can authorize action, we enter no special symbol for recommending and suggesting.

I   Must be informed. *I* means that the position holder must know the results of a decision in order to take appropriate coordinating action. *I* usually shows that a position will be affected by a decision or that the position holder will have to implement the decision.

C   Must be consulted. The position must be given an opportunity to influence the process of decision making by presenting information, demonstration, or proof. Those with *C* power should be consulted early enough so that their information can make a genuine difference in the final decision.

---

*This procedure has been adapted from Wallen (1970).

P   Must participate. *P* means that position holders must take part in making the decision and that at least a majority vote of all those with a *P* is necessary before the decision can be final.

V   Veto power. *V* means that position holders have veto power over the function and that their agreement must be obtained before the decision can be made.

A   Authority to make decision. *A* represents the greatest power of all. Those with *A* power can make the decision, and others must go along with it.

Macrosequences for Decision Making

In designing macrosequences from the exercises in this chapter, four guidelines will be helpful: (1) begin with feedback, (2) sequence according to the social-psychological level of emphasis, (3) move from exercises to closer approximations of the group's real world, and (4) repeat or provide similar experiences to assess progress.

To help a school group move toward discussion of decision-making processes, first collect systematic data on meetings using the meetings questionnaire or observation categories presented earlier in this chapter. Next, report a summary of the data to the staff. Finally, the staff might do the Self-assessment of Participation exercise to highlight their own contributions or lack of contributions to decision making at meetings.

Two sequences are useful for acquainting trainees firsthand with how the dilemmas of power and decision making look at the interpersonal, group, and organizational levels. One starts with an interpersonal exercise such as Hand Mirroring, moves on to a consensus exercise such as Lost on the Moon, and ends with the Planners and Operators exercise at the intergroup or organizational level. Another sequence moves in the opposite direction, beginning with the organizational emphasis, proceeding to the face-to-face group, and ending at the interpersonal level.

Which sequence should be chosen depends upon the level of interaction that participants are most eager to explore at the beginning of a training event and upon the goal toward which the consultant wishes to lead them. Generally, we believe that moving from the interpersonal to the organizational level is the more effective procedure. Participants can easily think about interpersonal influence at the beginning of training and, by proceeding from small group to organization, can be encouraged to analyze the issues of power and decision making in their organization more carefully.

Moving from exercises to procedures helps a group make use of the lessons learned from the exercises. After a consensus exercise such as Lost on the Moon, for example, the consultant can give the group a comparable period of time in which to reach consensus on some actual group issue that requires clarification and decision. In the course of the real decision making, the consultant can ask them to take a Self-assessment of Participation. After the group has had ample time to reach a decision, participants can discuss how well they used members' resources, diffused participation, and made decisions. Occasional interruptions by the consultant to offer comments about processes help participants to become more aware of their actual methods of making decisions.

Presenting two or more of the five exercises on consensual decision making one after the other can be particularly useful when trainees can meet for only two or three hours at a time and the times are spread over several months or more. Lost on the Moon, Twelve Angry Men, and Characteristics of a Successful Teacher, for example, can be presented sequentially, each followed by a discussion of how well the group used its resources in making the decisions. The repetitive pattern encourages group members to remind one another of the new norms about discussion and decision making that these exercises expose. In addition, a series of exercises makes improvement visible. By seeing how well they perform in subsequent exercises, group members are less likely to deceive themselves about the difficulty of making effective decisions consensually.

READINGS

Social Psychology of Organization
Daniel Katz and Robert Kahn

In the concluding chapter of *Social Psychology of Organization*, Katz and Kahn point out the difficulty of involving people in decision making in our present large-scale organizational structures. We agree that such structures are blocking involvement at a time when our expectations for involvement are increasing. The nine solutions suggested by Katz and Kahn deserve closer attention.

Perhaps the greatest organizational dilemma of our type of bureaucratic structure is the conflict between the democratic expectations of people and their actual share in decision-making. Though the great majority of decisions have to be made by leaders, their followers can participate in the process psychologically if they can share in the information about decision-making. By being informed, individuals, moreover, can mobilize public opinion to affect the decision process, and even if given groups are unsuccessful in achieving all they want, they may experience satisfaction in having meaningfully participated. The need for such involvement has been stimulated by democratic teaching in the home and the school and reinforced by the values of the culture. Increasingly, the level of expectation has been raised so that people in all organizations from the local recreation club to the nation state want to feel some relationship to the policy formulation which affects their lives.

As organizations grow in size and complexity, however, the decision centers become more removed from the people, and the information needed to make decisions becomes more the exclusive property of the leaders. There is the further difficulty . . . of individuals at the top of the hierarchy talking mostly with a small group at their own level and reinforcing each other in their views. Often these people are under constraints of time in informing their followers and bringing them along to view things from the leadership point of view. But there are other constraints as well. Officials often believe that to share information would tie their hands in that the public or specific interested groups would press for certain alternatives. Such public dissemination of information might also give competing outside structures too much knowledge of an organization's plans. Finally, even where there is the desire to communicate fully to followers, the means of reaching people effectively are not always available. Not only are appropriate mechanisms for sharing information often weak but the audience, remote from the specifics of the problem, may lack the cognitive basis for receiving the message and often the motivation to listen.

The effects of the conflict between rising expectations of involvement and the difficulties of communication and participation in a complicated structure of decision-making can have three maladaptive effects: (1) It can produce apathy or alienation among certain elements, who see themselves hopelessly outside the system. (2) It can produce blind conformity among those who accept the system and its normative requirements as demands external to themselves and for which they have no responsibility. (3) It can result in ferment without form, rebels without a cause, demonstrations with no appropriate target. Students, for example, can riot in aimless fashion because they feel frustrated by the system but do not know what is wrong or what the possible remedies are.

Adaptive solutions to this conflict . . . include some of the following changes: (1) Most organizations can profitably move toward some decentralization of decision-making in substructures. (2) Democratic forms can be introduced not so much through consultation of leaders with followers as through a shift in the source of authority from the officials to the members. (3) Distinctions between classes of citizenship can be broken down. (4) The Likert principle of overlapping organizational families can improve communication. (5) Feedback from organizational functioning can include systematic communication from organizational members. (6) Closed circuits of information which make captive their own initiators can be opened up through operational research. (7) Role enlargement is often possible within existing structures and, with automation, may be a significant trend of the future. Such enlargement increases the sense of participation of members. (8) Group responsibility for a set of tasks can ensure greater psychological involvement of individuals in organizations. (9) More explicit recognition is needed of the nature of bureaucratic systems. They are by nature open systems, and the tendency to act as if they were closed, rigid structures makes people their servants rather than their masters. We have not as yet fully exploited the true character of the bureaucracy—namely its openness as a social form.

The Japanese Touch
Newsweek, 8 July 1974

This *Newsweek* article reports that Japanese managers encourage a more participative style of management than do their American counterparts and are willing to take the time to arrive at consensual decisions. It is interesting to note that the Japanese language equates the word *decision* with the action stage of problem-solving as we have tried to do in this chapter.

An American semiconductor firm owns a plant in Dallas and one in Japan. Both are virtually identical—using the same technology, the same manufacturing procedures and the same number of workers. There is one obvious difference: the plant in Japan outproduces the one in Dallas by 15 per cent.

The conventional explanation for the difference is that Japanese workers are simply more industrious than Americans. But if that is true, how is it that 200 American employees now working at the television-assembly plant Sony has built in San Diego manage to produce just as many color sets as their Japanese counterparts at an identical Sony operation in Tokyo?

Outclassed: The difference between the American workers in San Diego and in the Dallas semiconductor plant is that the Sony employees work under Japanese managers—and that, says a recent study by two Stanford Business School professors, makes all the difference in the world. "The Japanese simply outmanage us when it comes to people," declares management specialist Richard T. Johnson, who wrote the study along with organizational theorist William G. Ouchi. "We've done very well coping with the inanimate elements of management. But a shocking number of American managers are really inept in dealing with people."

What the Japanese have that Americans by and large don't is a finely cultivated sense of the importance of looking at the corporation as a social organization, not simply as a profit-oriented enterprise. This perspective has led to a system of management techniques that Westerners may find strange but one that has made Japanese productivity the envy of the world. And Japanese firms have been able to transplant this key cultural outlook by filling top managerial positions of their U.S. subsidiaries with Japanese nationals.

While Japanese management techniques foster high productivity, they can also make life difficult for American-born managers who must contend with what seems a topsy-turvy world. For one thing, the Japanese conceive of management as a process in which the most important information flows from the bottom up, rather than from the top down. Japanese managers expect change and initiative to come from those closest to the problem, from salespeople and assembly-line workers rather than from top executives.

More baffling to Westerners is the Japanese style of decision making. It involves a lengthy process of achieving consensus, and it often takes days or weeks to arrive at a decision that an American manager might make by himself in minutes. But in the process, practically everyone who will be affected by the decision is consulted. Thus, notes trade official Masahiro Soejima, "when Japanese businessmen finally do reach a decision, they are ready to act with great speed." No time need be wasted trying to convince colleagues that the decision is correct, since they helped make it. In fact, Soejima points out, "the word 'decision' doesn't have the same meaning in Japanese. We call 'decision' the 'action stage'."

Beer: But the most telling aspect of Japanese management is its concern for workers as individuals. "Our philosophy is that you must care about the individual," says chairman Yu Mizuki of NTN Bearing Corp. of America, a suburban Chicago subsidiary of a Japanese manufacturing concern. "Human relations are just as important to us as production." Often after a period of successful operations at NTN, work is halted early so that everyone—including top management—can gather in the warehouse to celebrate with beer and sandwiches. Some Japanese-run firms hold monthly birthday parties for employees at which the chairman personally presents gifts. And almost all Japanese managers make a practice of knowing the names of as many subordinates as possible.

Predictably, workers thrive under such treatment. Says the Stanford study: "American workers employed by Japanese companies report that they like the feeling of having many ties rather than just a work contract with their employer. The notion that the company is interested in their over-all affairs and even in the well-being of their family is flattering and comforting." Indeed, it works so well that several American corporations have already adopted similar managerial styles—among them Eastman Kodak, IBM and NCR.

All this seems to indicate that America's traditional antagonism between management and labor may well be anachronistic, Stanford's Johnson told *Newsweek*'s Gerald C. Lubenow. And if American workers would indeed welcome a closer, more encompassing relationship with their employers, the implications for American business—and society—could be profound.

BIBLIOGRAPHY

Emory, R. E., and Pino, R. F. 1975. *Interpersonal influence.* Tuxedo, N.Y.: Xicom.

Designed with educators in mind, this instructional system aims to help teachers and administrators explore the nature of interpersonal influence in schools. Exercises focus on various styles of influencing others and on effective ways of accepting the influence of others. School consultants can easily adapt several of the exercises for use within tailored designs.

Florida Department of Education. 1973. *Shared decision making.* Tallahassee, Florida.

This training manual grew out of the press for collaboration that is experienced in schools moving toward differentiated staffing and team teaching. It aims to help educators understand shared decision making and to assist them in establishing effective group decision making within the school. The manual includes both conceptual papers and concrete practical techniques as well as a lengthy bibliography.

Hall, J., and Williams, M. S. 1970. Group dynamics training and improved decision making. *Journal of Applied Behavioral Science* 6: 39–67.

Research on the effects of various kinds of experiential training on decision making in face-to-face groups revealed that groups trained in communication skills, consensus procedures, and the like consistently performed better than untrained groups on measures of decision-making quality. Consultants can incorporate some of the insights and procedures of this report into their designs.

McGregor, D. 1960. *The human side of enterprise.* New York: McGraw-Hill.

A classic on the management of human resources, this book places great emphasis on decision making within organizations. In addition to introducing McGregor's thinking about "Theory X" and "Theory Y" as important philosophies of leadership, it advances his views on how to enhance collaboration and move toward more consensual decision making in tough situations.

Vroom, V. H., and Yetton, P. W. 1973. *Leadership and decision making.* Pittsburgh: University of Pittsburgh Press.

Different organizational tasks call for different leadership styles and decision-making procedures. Effective leadership is flexible, and effective decision-making procedures are appropriate to the problems being confronted. Vroom and Yetton offer a contingency theory of leadership and decision making and suggest ways of helping leaders learn how to match their influence attempts and decision procedures to the organizational tasks at hand.

9

Macrodesigning

The overall sequence of a comprehensive OD intervention includes stages of entering, contract building, macrodesigning, implementing and monitoring microdesigns, evaluating outcomes, and institutionalizing the client's capability to continue changing as needed. Of all these interdependent stages, the two designing stages determine the greatest part of the success or failure of most interventions.

A *macrodesign* comprises the overall structure and outline, sequence of parts, and general forms through which activities flow. An example would include improving organizational skills, changing norms through problem solving, and changing the organization's structure; another example can be found in the basic steps of the Imaging procedure described in chapter 5. This chapter tells the consultant how to build comprehensive macrodesigns. *Microaspects* refer to the specific activities played out during any limited period of consultation. Some microdesigns for training in skills, exercises, and procedures are offered in chapters 3 through 8; chapter 10 will give the consultant some guidelines for microdesigning.

In addition to requiring clear understanding of objectives, accurate diagnostic data, and foreknowledge of the probable effects of various intervention techniques, design building requires a delicate balance of insight into one's own motives on the one hand and empathy for clients on the other. Although fitting macroaspects and microaspects to specific objectives and clients in effective combinations is an important skill of the OD consultant, a rarer skill is the ability to monitor one's own proclivities. Recognizing one's own defenses, for example, and being able to use this recognition as information about the conduct of the consultation will greatly enhance a consultant's effectiveness.

INTERNAL FEATURES

OD consultations consist of a series of organized social events carried out by school people who have continuing, committed interrelationships with one another. Consultants, too, look forward to continuing interaction with their clients and with one another during most of a macrodesign. If the consultation is of sufficient length and scope, all participants become in effect a temporary society which not only serves as a vehicle for the OD work but can itself exemplify many of the interpersonal procedures and structural forms that consultants want to teach.

When designing an OD intervention, consultants should see to it that this temporary society maintains in good condition the four organizational features that must be taken into account to enhance interpersonal and subsystem effectiveness: (1) differentiation and integration, (2) norms, (3) role relationships, and (4) satisfaction of motives within the organization. They should also see to it that the macrodesign presents clients with conceptual lessons that can be used to support organized action.

Differentiation and Integration

People in schools perform a variety of differentiated functions, from receiving and transmitting information about the working of the school district to shaping students and materials, and the consultative event can raise both differentiation and integration to the level of conscious awareness in a number of ways. First, selecting for participation people from a variety of jobs and then communicating across this variety invariably reveals to clients the profit to be found in integrating diverse functions. Indeed, that people from heterogeneous but interdependent positions are even included in the same intervention events helps to make the concept of integration salient.

Second, rotating combinations of people through the various subgroups that form during a consultation so that everyone will eventually have interacted at least once with everyone else can have an important multiple effect. In the course of an intervention, people from every level of the school or district will reveal both competence and incompetence in performing OD tasks, in perceiving organizational functioning, and in perceiving how OD tasks relate to everyday life in the organization. By interacting with many people with whom they have either never before communicated or have communicated only superficially, clients learn that differentiation of role and function is primarily an organizational reality and not necessarily a matter of personal endowment, that effective interpersonal and group performance is not necessarily more difficult in some positions than in others, and that other people are as worried about their interdependence with them as they are worried about their interdependence with others.

Depending upon the complexity of the macrodesign, rotation can often be achieved by instructing clients to form themselves into groups in which there is at least one person with whom the individual has not interacted before. When the sequence of consultative events is complicated and the consultant wants the clusterings to satisfy goals other than mere spread of interaction, it may be prudent to lay out beforehand a complete schedule with names and groupings minutely specified.

Finally, consultants may design exercises and other activities so that both division of labor (differentiation) and active collaboration among different roles (integration) can occur. For example, the Fishbowl technique can be used to bring together multiple link-pins from different teams, or each subgroup can appoint its own convener, recorder, and process observer before a meeting and give these people time to debrief how they worked together and with others in their subgroup. In a very large event requiring four or five or more consultants, the use of the consultants themselves can be designed to exhibit differentiation and integration.

Norms

A school organization becomes able to change its routines by learning how to replace old norms with new. Conceptually, this is done by reaching agreement in the relevant groups on what the new norm should be, simulating the new action patterns a few times, and then trying out the new actions a few times on the job. When clients feel rewarded by the new pattern, the new norm has become a reality. In practice, however, establishing new norms causes stress, not only because it means discussing matters that are seldom publicly discussed, but also because older norms may not support the changes that are being attempted. Clients are less likely to withdraw from an OD design either physically or psychologically if the consultant guides them through a series of steps each of which arouses less anxiety than those preceding. Specifically, a design can move staff members to new norms if it begins with structured, gamelike interpersonal exercises, proceeds to group simulations, and then moves to real procedures.

At the beginning of one senior high school project, for example, staff members told us through interviews that their school had no problems and ran like clockwork. At a series of discussions with all department heads, however, after it was agreed that further discussions could be profitable, members began to discuss the organization for which the consultant worked and their school as a whole. At a later meeting they mentioned problems that they had had in the past and problems that they regarded as other people's, in the course of time moving closer to people who were present, and from problems present somewhere in the school to their own present problems. Over the series of meetings the time perspective moved gradually from the past and a vague future someday to the present and to specified future dates ("Ted and I will see the principal on Friday to tell him what we want to do about this").

As simple as it is in both concept and action, the latter statement could not have occurred at the first meeting because the group's norms did not support it at that time. Uncertain of the extent to which their frustrations were shared or of the degree to which others were willing to invest energy in change, having as yet no reason to trust the consultant, the group had regarded committed action involving themselves and the principal as inappropriate and too risky at the outset. For these reasons, early discussions had been conceptually vague and general and interpersonally distant, concerned with other people and other times. For the same reasons, early steps in a design encouraging clients to try new norms must allow them, at least initially, to practice at some distance from their ordinary daily involvements.

Working with functioning units or subsystems, in which group norms tend to be very powerful, we do not typically place two different faculties into close interaction with each other, or members of two separate central office departments into the same training group. Instead we bring together interdependent persons who either have the same supervisors or are bound to one another by some shared function such as supervising the playground or selecting new staff members. In this way clients are already much closer in their interdependence or common fate than are strangers from different subsystems.

Specifically because they are closer, however, it is important that they be given some protective distance from one another—a distance that allows them to protect their views of themselves, that requires no commitments affecting other parts of their lives, that does not require them to take a stand on matters of school policy or to make specific commitments about what they will do on the job. One way of placing protective distance between school members is to begin a consultation during the summer hiatus when the routines and commitments of the new school year are not yet fully established. Another way is to remove clients from the building or rooms in which they usually work, away from telephones or other continual interruptions (although we have found little to be gained by moving them out of town or to a nonschool ambiance). Probably the best technique is to be found in the highly structured game such as those described as exercises in chapters 3 through 8, which, in relation to their daily work on the job, can be seen as "then and there" rather than as "here and now." If exercises are to be effective in changing norms, however, they must be introduced as an early OD activity.

For example, exercises offered early with an OD design can facilitate establishing a norm that supports *debriefing*—i.e., examining the effectiveness of interactive processes in a group soon after every meeting. Even when done during make-believe activities, debriefing encourages adaptability because it makes explicit the norm that procedures are alterable. That is, if a survey during debriefing shows agreement that a certain procedure is impeding progress toward a goal, the question of whether to change the procedure arises, which opens the door to productive self-renewal. Thus exercises that facilitate debriefing, if conducted after every meaningful unit during the first few hours of consultation, can cause debriefing to become an accepted norm among the clients. Further, the consultant should provide time for debriefing on all written agendas and encourage its use by listing a number of leading questions for group discussion.

The consultant can also confront norms among clients by modeling behavior that is contrary to their norms—for example, by exhibiting openness, directness, and authenticity about the organization's dynamics to clients who are unwilling to do so themselves. To this end the macrodesign of data feedback is a useful strategy. The consultant interviews organization members individually about the variables discussed in chapters 3 through 8 and subsequently feeds group data back to all members of the school using a style that is direct and open, using living examples, and asking for clients' reactions. Clients are often sufficiently relieved that someone is finally telling them the truth about the school to begin concerted problem solving on the newly revealed problems.

Roles

Because role taking always occurs in interactions with other role takers, an OD macrodesign should address itself not only to relationships among organization members but also to the relationship between the consultant and clients (many of whom may expect an "expert" to behave in a more authoritarian manner). At an early stage of execution of the macrodesign, consultants should therefore distinguish between their own goals and those of the clients in order to distinguish between their respective roles as well.

The role of clients is to state the problems and goals of their school or district, to assign priorities, schedules, and deadlines, and to choose whom they will work with and trust. The consultant's primary goal is to maximize the clients' ability to deal consciously and purposefully with their own organizational processes. On the question of appropriate group processes, clients will usually defer to consultants; but on matters of substance, deference will be given to the clients themselves. In addition to drawing attention to role structure during consultation, arriving at this understanding will exemplify the introduction of new group-process activities, such as debriefing, that will later prove useful to clients.

Clients can gain wider practice in putting new roles into effect if consultants treat them equally, without regard to previous deference patterns in the school or district. This is not to say that they should ignore the jobs that people hold or the realities to which they will return but only that they can give practice in flexible role taking if they give special privileges to no one. They should not ask administrators, for example, to act as leaders more often than others or excuse their absences more readily. Treating everyone alike demonstrates that a role relationship established for one purpose in one subgroup of the organization need not apply for other tasks or in other parts of the organization.

Motives

Although individuals differ in the extent to which they attempt to satisfy activity, achievement, power, and affiliation needs in their jobs, clients and consultants alike bring their own motives with them to a consultation, and consultants should not allow their own needs to bias them against the needs of others. Indeed, consultants who work with, not against, the needs of all parties will maximize their influence on a consultation. Let those who crave activity become involved in the implementation of new programs; let those with strong achievement motives be initiators and planners; let those who enjoy power be coordinators and conveners; let those enjoy the warmth of affiliative satisfactions who wish to do so.

One way in which the activity motive can be expressed is through the exercise of charismatic leadership, a quality that is more cultural than psychological in its dynamics and that can characterize a group as well as an individual leader. In our view,* the attraction of the charismatic leader (or group) rests on three principles, all related to the activity motive. (1) The charismatic leader expresses for other people their own mute longings in a way that makes these longings clear to them. (2) The charismatic leader shows people that the object of their longing is not only attainable but within their own power to attain. (3) The charismatic leader inspires people with the conviction that significant action can be taken now, today, not next year or in heaven.

Insofar as the achiever seeks to reach a goal or outcome, and the achievement of specifiable outcomes is a school's raison d'etre, the achievement motive, especially, can energize the planning of innovative programs. Achievement motives are active when problems are real and important, so that requiring clients to choose realistically attainable goals provides the best possible field of action for people with high achievement needs. Indeed, the high achievement motivation of many educators, parents, and students is one of the forces acting in the consultant's favor. When asked to state their goals, most people can reply with some specificity. When they are asked to do so, many groups of teachers can seek consensus on some near subgoal. When asked to construct plans for reaching a goal, most groups of teachers will put in extra hours in the eager hope of reaching a subgoal.

---

* Adapted from David Berlew, 1971: personal communication.

376

At the same time, however, program planning and problem solving may not satisfy people whose primary motivations are power or affiliation. These motives are somewhat more difficult to use because many educated Americans believe that it is somehow shameful to exhibit them in public, although inhibiting norms can be considerably weakened by the use of appropriate warm-up activities such as those described in chapters 3, 5, 6, and 8.

Even action- or achievement-motivated people may not enjoy large-scale problem solving if their motives have been repeatedly frustrated and their patience for finding gratifying outcomes has grown short. Such people are less likely to seek a problem-solving approach to real problems than to indulge any of several common attitudes: the scapegoat attitude (blame or punish someone for the problem, and the problem will go away); the savior attitude ("Don't worry, our leader will take care of us"); the prayer-wheel attitude ("If we continue doing what we've always done when threatened, after a while the problem won't look as bad"); or the rabbit attitude (freeze, and maybe the problem will go away without noticing you).

Bridging the gap between consultation and independent action is the most far-reaching way of making use of clients' motives. That is, never design a consultation so that clients go away feeling satisfied and fulfilled because this leaves them no reason to undertake further action. Design each event so that they have committed themselves to action, have formed a clear plan of action and a clear picture of the nature of the action, have expressed mutual expectations, and have perhaps made a first step in the action phase, but have neither completed nor approached completion of the action; this leaves them with the motivation to act even in the consultant's absence.

Learning Themes

When designing a macrosequence, consultants should consider the abstract significance of even the most mundane events in the interests of leaving clients with one or more conceptual lessons that support organized action. While the exercises described in chapters 3 through 8 teach small lessons, it is in the larger lessons taught by the OD event as a whole that consultants demonstrate their ability at macrodesigning.

The Planners and Operators exercise, for example, teaches among other things that, no matter how carefully people may organize their lectures, one-way instructions are less effective than most people believe them to be. The larger session that includes this exercise, however, may carry the additional lesson that principals either do or do not care about the effect of unilateral communication on their relations with teachers and that they are or are not willing to take action on the matter. This further lesson is likely to be clear and strong if the exercise is conducted with principals and their actual teachers, if it is preceded by a few activities centered on communicative efficacy, and if it is followed by activities and exercises that cause clients to probe their present relationships so that participating principals are given an opportunity to demonstrate their own perceptions and hopes.

Again, a consultative session that aims at moving into action innovative ideas that require the collaboration of teachers and administrators might convey the following related lessons. First, while the ordinary routines of the school do not facilitate conferring, gathering information from those with veto power, arranging logistics, or planning committed action to begin on a certain date, it is nevertheless possible to design a setting that does facilitate these steps. Second, the behavior of staff members toward one another is almost always more a function of organizational structures and the given situation than it is of individual interests and personality styles.

A macrodesign that presents clients with cognitive messages that they can carry into the school can leave them feeling that their potentialities are different or that their relationships with others are new. By this we mean specifically that new actions are now possible and that some old actions are now less probable. We mean, for example, that during the next few days the principal and a committee will invent and try out some new modes of bilateral communication, systematically assessing the results of their efforts; that within a few days clusters of teachers will begin doing new things on a collaborative basis; and that the principal or superintendent will collaborate in supporting these new ventures. In short, the lesson we seek always to impart is that new and more worthwhile interdependent actions are not only conceivable and feasible but are imminent.

By participating in one particular aspect of a group's plan of actions, consultants can also help clients move behaviorally toward their goals. If, for example, teachers in a group set a goal of learning how to construct meeting designs which they can themselves carry out with students, a particular part of their macrodesign might consist of a planning session in which outside consultants sit in as facilitators, intervening only when asked or when the meeting process appears unproductive. Participating teachers should leave this kind of OD activity feeling closer to their goal than before and more competent to make progress toward it in the future.

The problem-solving sequence described in chapter 7 (stylized earlier in this chapter as the movement from skill practice to exercise to application) provides a useful learning theme which we used in 1970 during the first week of a design to launch the conversion of several schools from traditional individuated structures to multiunit team-teaching structures. Essentially, the design comprised four stages.

(1) During the first five days, skill practice, exercises, and focused training aimed at helping the faculty articulate its present and ideal conditions, reach group agreement both for subgroups and for the school as a whole, and to be clearer with one another about their yearnings and frustrations. (2) The staffs were asked next to state formally some problems that were within their power to solve. (3) While working on actual school problems, they were taught tne problem-solving sequence. By the time their plans had been detailed

and first steps taken in accordance with the plans, the week had ended. (4) During the final day, staff members told one another about the faculty strengths that they believed would help move the school toward its new goals. By adding personal abilities to the list of helping forces, this activity also made some of the variety pool more accessible.

SUCCESSFUL MACRODESIGNS

This section describes eight techniques that can be built into macro-designs to enhance clients' skills in communication and problem solving, in openness, responsiveness, and accessibility of the variety pool. Included are seven steps for building a macrodesign, a discussion of the composition and process of the design team, and ten questions that should be asked before using a design.

Eight Techniques

1. *Include key members.* Especially with small subsystems such as teams, departments, committees, cabinets, and building staffs, designs for OD consultation work best when all group members begin and participate in all phases together; even a few days' difference can raise barriers between those who participate and those who come late. When all members experience the intervention goals, skills, and activities simultaneously, they are better able to remind one another of what happened at the workshops and better able to transfer what was learned to the school situation.

When the organization is large, it is not feasible to include all members in one event. It is difficult, for example, to induce all members of a large secondary school to attend an individual OD event, and it is logistically impossible for all members of a school district to attend all training events. The nonparticipant will understand that a great number of people cannot be accommodated at one meeting and will not feel threatened when an OD event is held with one fraction of the district before others.

Thus when beginning an OD project with a large organization, invite key members—those who are regularly interdependent and who hold formal positions of power in the district—and select them in ways that will be viewed as legitimate and appropriate. If you ask teachers or students to attend a district OD event with the superintendent's cabinet, for example, either invite those holding formal positions of leadership, or invite a random group, or choose the participants by some other method that will cause them to be viewed as legitimate representatives and not as chosen by some faction. If people do attend an OD event as representatives of a larger body, see to it that they regularly report the content of the consultation to their constituents.

2. *Clarify OD goals, theory, and technology.* The ultimate aim of OD is to develop in the school a self-renewing culture in which

discrepancies between actual and ideal conditions are viewed as problems for work and in which creative practices are sought both inside and outside the organization as problems arise. To this end the macrodesign should include both explicit descriptions (cognitive) and lively experiences (affective) that bring these goals to life. Clients should see that clarifying communication and developing new group norms for working together more effectively are prerequisite to carrying out innovative educational programs, and they should come to view defining and solving problems as a regular repetitive cycle in the school. An assortment of handouts can be employed to introduce and clarify these concepts (an example of such a handout is to be found later in this chapter).

3. *Move from structured activities to application.* Skill exercises effectively demonstrate organizational issues of role relationships, group norms, and human motivation in microcosm. They allow staff members to become actively involved with little personal risk and anxiety, at the same time that they can be real enough to lead to discussions of how any given experience was either similar to or different from what really happens in the school. Indeed, structured exercises enable organization members who attend a training event out of duty rather than by choice to find new interpersonal modes more easily than do freer experiences that demand more personal commitment and initiative. Exercise results often stimulate thought about familiar problems and thus encourage problem solving about real issues as a next step. By means of skillful debriefing, the consultant can bring participants to the realization that more work is needed to improve oral and written communication, to overcome difficulties in listening, and to gain skill in working together in groups.

4. *Move from shared information to action planning.* Reporting systematically collected information back to appropriate organizational units as a basis for diagnosis, problem solving, and planning is one of the most important intervention modes for OD projects in schools. In both data feedback and confrontation designs, start by sharing important information within and among appropriate subsystems and role takers. Then help group members practice communication skills to assure a flow of clear information across subsystems and persons. Move next to problem solving, and lead clients toward making specific action plans. Continually point out this macrosequence, which can be labeled *action research*, in the hope that clients will adopt it as a regular organizational process.

5. *Rotate subgroup memberships.* When small subsystems such as a building staff or smaller groups are involved in OD consultation, successful macrodesigns rotate participating members through different groups, especially during the opening days of the intervention, for several reasons. Rotation increases the potential networks of workable relationships on the staff, diminishes the possibility that groups in relative isolation from one another will come to perceive an in-group and out-group (which can occur with surprising speed), and helps to increase members' identification with the whole staff.

The latter is necessary to sustain motivation through the project's follow-up phases and to increase group cohesiveness so that members pull together and share resources during problem solving.

When consulting with large groups, such as the staff of a very large building or a complex district made up of people with a number of jobs, rotating subgroup memberships is impractical. In this case it is best to begin with homogeneous job groups, introducing occasions for them to communicate about their performances during the exercises and skill activities. Next arrange a period when they can discuss district organizational problems similar to those in the exercises, allowing each group to list its own problems and to tell the others about them. Next arrange problem-solving activities within heterogeneous job groups. Finally, schedule planning of the application of OD techniques to school situations for homogeneous groups in which new skills, norms, and actions can be practiced. Later consultation should bring heterogeneous groups together again to assess how well the problem solving has been going.

6. *Treat all ranks equally.* People in educational institutions are generally attributed higher or lower status on the basis of impressions of how much or how well they contribute to valued group goals. Some status differences are both relevant and useful, as when parents are accorded high status for knowing their way around the community or when principals are accorded high status for knowing their way around complicated budget procedures. Other status differences are meaningless, however—as when it is believed that only an administrator can convene a meeting or that only the school secretary can take minutes—and an effective macrodesign reduces such unnecessary differences in the context of the OD events. That is, the consultant responds to organization members in terms of their performance in intervention activities and not in terms of their job titles.

Consultants should explain that every participant is potentially important in carrying out a task and that stereotypes based on job titles can impede effective group functioning. Rotating participants through groups can bring teachers, administrators, and nonprofessional personnel into closer communication with one another and thus reduce the distance between them. Equal treatment during an OD event will bring them closer psychologically, a prime prerequisite to achieving openness and improved communication for performing the tasks of the school.

To be sure, consultants sometimes offer special coaching or training to people in certain positions. For example, a principal might welcome recommendations for building bilateral communication into a personal supervisory role. For other examples, we have trained a parent group to give feedback in ways that aroused less defensiveness among teachers and have also helped students to practice effective meeting procedures before joining teachers and parents on a school's advisory body. Consultants should not encourage clients to ignore status or other differences that enrich a school's variety pool or resources. Instead, they should together create norms that support retention of differences that are relevant and useful for accomplishing the school's work.

7. *Exemplify new organizational forms.* A successful macro-design deliberately includes activities that, in their own structure and process, exemplify organizational forms potentially useful to clients. Practice in summarizing, group exercises in decision making, procedures such as the Fishbowl or problem solving—all should be living representations of techniques that can be used in the everyday life of the school. In other words, the consultant should plan activities that give clients new and improved organizational structures that they can bring to their regular work.

8. *Set out continuing work for the future.* The effective macro-design should culminate with work specifications that clients will be facing as they leave the OD event. That is, consultants should design in such a way that school people feel some sense of closure about matters learned and interim tasks completed but so that they also feel some unresolved tension concerning important tasks still incomplete. A shared feeling of incompletion, the conviction that continued problem solving will be useful, and a sense of urgency to get on with it are all powerful motivations for self-renewal.

The Design Team

Intervention teams are typically composed of one consultant to ten or fifteen clients. When the target group offers special challenges or when less-experienced consultants are included in the consulting team, working in pairs can increase the ratio to one consultant to six or seven clients, lend emotional support and additional skill to the consultants, and leave each client-unit less susceptible to errors.

Especially during brainstorming, the design team will gain in total strength if it is composed heterogeneously with regard to information, skills, interests, and personal styles. Because such diversity can also create difficulties in building openness and interdependence, the team should spend time developing itself as an effectively functioning adaptive group, and the consultant should strive to create the kind of team culture that is expected of the target group. Both of these goals require frank discussion of process as the team fashions the OD design.

No matter how large the team becomes, it is important that consultants who will implement the design should participate in some of the planning, although it is unnecessary and often inefficient for all team members to be involved in all phases of planning. When the design team exceeds four members, a division of labor is required. Subteams of two, for instance, can work on diagnosing the target group, defining OD goals, and developing alternative sequences.

Before the rest of the macrodesigning takes place, the whole team should react to the diagnosis and goal setting and should brainstorm microdesigns for increasing facilitating forces and reducing restraining forces. Finally, the whole group should react to the proposed sequences, select one, and enlist members for refining and implementing each microaspect of the design. After this is done, individual members or two-person subgroups may finalize the specific steps of each small part of the total design.

Seven Building Steps

The seven steps for building an effective macrodesign are not unlike the steps employed in problem solving (see chap. 7).

1. The design team starts by discussing its general view of organizational self-renewal, using as guides the concepts introduced in chapter 1 of this book. Talk about conceptions of adaptability in relation to how the target group will look at the end of the OD consultation. Important aspects of this discussion will already have occurred during the entry-and-start phase when the contract with the target group was being built.
2. Using the instruments and data-collecting procedures described in chapters 3 through 8, collect data on selected organizational attributes of the target group, and seek information about the clarity of communication and educational goals (chap. 3), hidden intergroup and interrole conflicts (chap. 5), and meeting effectiveness (chap. 6). Although these data can be collected by means of questionnaires, interviews and observations are generally more useful for consultants, allowing them to gather sufficient additional data on the spot to commence characterizing the target group during the interviewing or observing process.
3. List for the particular event that is being designed consultative goals that are more specific than those discussed during entry. Ideally, observable behavioral evidences for the goals are specified in advance (see chaps. 3 through 8).
4. List forces present in the target group that will facilitate or restrain the achievement of OD goals. These forces can be categorized as group, interpersonal, or intrapersonal (see chap. 7 for a discussion of Force-Field Analysis).
5. Use brainstorming to generate microdesigns that might increase facilitating forces or reduce restraining forces (see chap. 10 for details about microdesigning).
6. Prepare alternative sequences for the microdesigns.
7. Finally, accept one sequence and assign implementation duties for each microaspect to a specific member of the consulting staff. Let the consultant responsible for each microaspect refine the design of his or her part.

Ten Questions

Designing an OD event requires creativity, knowledge, and flexibility; it is in many ways the most challenging and exciting part of the intervention process. Although the history of designing OD events is brief and its empirical basis is limited, there are nevertheless ten questions that should be answered affirmatively before any design is put into action.

1. Will the design allow clients to feel rewarded, challenged, up-lifted, and inspired?
2. Does it clearly connect training and consultation to the actual work of the target group
3. Will it increase communicative clarity, a sense of pulling to-gether, and energy for continuing collaborative work?
4. Does it aid in clarifying problems involving unclear roles, norms, and decision-making procedures?
5. Does it offer activities through which achievement, activity, affiliation, and power motives can be satisfied?
6. Does it offer a description of some goals of the total organiza-tion so that members can recognize and identify with super-ordinate goals?
7. Does it feature a learning theme to leave clients with one or more conceptual lessons?
8. Does it include procedures for monitoring consultative events as they are occurring?
9. Does it build structures and schedules that will continue after consultation?
10. Does it offer a sense of closure while leaving some tension re-lated to work still to be accomplished?

EXAMPLES OF MACRODESIGNS

Although the number of possible macrodesigns is virtually infinite, we have here chosen to present those that have shown promise in our own work. Some of these (organizational training for a school faculty, consultation for launching multiunit elementary schools) have been evaluated carefully; others (demonstration to define OD at entry, consultation for bringing parents and students into school manage-ment) are presented because they include components and design principles that we have previously found effective.

Portraying OD during Entry

Some organization members think of OD as involving highly emo-tional sensitivity training; others think of lectures and discussion on administrative science and group dynamics; still others think of relaxed fun and games having little relevance to the real life of the school. Most clients probably hold no very clear idea about OD, and these unclear expectations often plague the entry, start-up, and contract-building phases of an intervention. By helping a target group to understand OD theory and to experience OD technology, the following design for a demonstration workshop should increase the reliability of the decision whether to continue into consultation in earnest.

FIGURE 9-1   Handout for Entry Demonstration

Organization development (OD) can be defined as a planned and sustained effort to apply behavioral science for system improvement using reflexive, self-analytic methods. OD involves system members themselves in the active assessment, diagnosis, and transformation of their own organization. The following matrix shows some of the training activities that take place during OD interventions.

—Organization development enables the school to become more receptive and responsive to its community—by

—Improving its capabilities to modify its own
  (1) Differentiation and integration
  (2) Norms
  (3) Roles
  (4) Motivational patterns
        —through

—Building more effective
  (1) Communication patterns
  (2) Goal clarity
  (3) Ways of working with conflicts
  (4) Meetings
  (5) Problem-solving procedures
  (6) Joint decision making
        —by experiencing

—The consultative strategies of
  (1) Training in skills, exercises, and procedures
  (2) Data feedback and action planning
  (3) Confrontation and problem solving
  (4) Process observation and feedback

The demonstration requires two days, and clients—either the entire body of a small system or those members of a large system who possess formal authority—are told that it is being presented to help them determine whether they would like to become involved in an OD project at all. They are asked to suspend judgment until the two days are over because the demonstration events must move along a bit before a clear picture of OD will emerge. Demonstration goals include: (1) developing clients' enthusiasm for the possible benefits of OD to their organization; (2) presenting a picture of what a self-renewing organization is like; (3) helping members of the client group see how they can confront current problems through OD methods; (4) helping them understand the unique functions of OD in contrast to those of management consultation or sensitivity training; (5) presenting them with a picture of skills that can be gained through OD training; and (6) establishing the beginning of a collaborative relationship between clients and consultants, communicating that the former are expected not only to influence the project but eventually to own and run it themselves.

GURE 9-2   Handout for Entry Demonstration

ι intervention for organization development (OD) is a planned and sustained effort to
ply behavioral science for system improvement using reflexive, self-analytic methods.
ι organization consultant involves system members themselves in the active assessment,
ιgnosis, and transformation of their own organization. The following chart shows some
the activities that can occur during an OD intervention.

	Consultative strategies				
	Group exercises	Skill training	Data feedback	Intergroup exercises	Procedures
Decision making	Black grievances	Survey for consensus	Delphi	Planners-Operators	Consensus; ensuring listening
Communi-cation	One-way–two-way	Practicing communica-tion skills	Socio-metric survey	Imaging as game	Buzz groups; ensuring listening; Fishbowl
Norms	Group agreements	Preparing training	Group expecta-tion survey	Role negotia-tion	Problem-solving sequence
Group effective-ness	Five-square puzzle	Practicing leadership functions	Staff meeting question-naires	Planners-Operators	Problem-solving sequence
Uncover-ing con-flicts	Helpful and unhelpful acts	Behavior description	Actual and preferred procedures	Planners-Operators	Imaging for real

Early in the event, following some warm-up and getting-acquaint-
ed activities, group members are given the handout shown in figure
9-1 or the alternative in figure 9-2. A consultant guides them through
the material, telling them that some of the activities, theory, and
technology of OD will come alive for them during the next day and a
half and calling attention to supplemental reading materials available
on a display table.

After introducing the handout, the demonstration proceeds to
episodes that involve more active client participation. Every remaining microaspect should begin with experiential activity and be followed by debriefing with the help of client or consultant observers,
the debriefing to focus on both the here-and-now aspects and interpersonal dynamics of the experience. Clients are then asked to comment on the similarities and differences between the OD activity and
their actual school experience. Finally, the consultant points out
relevancies to the real organization, presents some research concepts
and results related to the activity so that group members can apply
these to their organization, and hands out (or otherwise makes avail-

able) more detailed readings on relevant theory and research. This sequence from experience to comparison to theory may be used profitably with every episode or microaspect of the demonstration.

Many alternative macrosequences can be effective as well, including the following: (1) practice in communication skills; (2) feedback on the results of a survey of norms, using, for example, the Group Expectations Survey; (3) exercise on group decision making using the Lost on the Moon exercise; (4) exercise on effectiveness between groups using the Planners and Operators exercise; and (5) practice in uncovering conflicts using the Imaging procedure. If Imaging is used toward the end of the two days, time must be allowed to commence collaborative problem solving so that conflicts do not remain virulent at the end of the demonstration. Problem-solving sequences can usefully be introduced as the last object for group study.

As a final event, a twenty-minute audio-tape slide show on OD in schools (Arends et al. 1973) can be presented for purposes of summary and of providing a springboard for group questions and discussion. In addition, an Arends, Phelps, and Schmuck (1973) booklet on OD in schools can be handed out at the end of the demonstration in preparation for a discussion of whether the staff should enter a full-fledged OD project.

OD Training for a School Faculty

The following design, carried out in a junior high school, is fully reported in Schmuck and Runkel (1970); its purposes were to stimulate improved group problem solving among faculty members and generally to help the school, as a human organization, to become more responsive to students and parents. The training began with a six-day laboratory in late August 1967 with almost the entire building staff present. The fifty-four trainees included all the administrators, all but two of the faculty, plus the head secretary, the head cook, and the head custodian.

The first two days were devoted to group and intergroup exercises and communication skills—e.g., Lost on the Moon, the Five-Square puzzle, and the Planners and Operators exercise, along with paraphrasing and other communication skills described in chapter 3—all of which aimed at increasing awareness of interpersonal and organizational processes and at demonstrating the importance of effective communication in accomplishing tasks collaboratively. After each exercise, small groups discussed how the experiences were like or unlike their normal relations in school. All staff members then pooled their experiences and analyzed their relationships as a faculty. Each small group chose its own way of reporting what it had experienced, and the consultants supported openness in giving and receiving feedback about perceptions of real organizational processes in the school.

During the next four days the faculty pursued a problem-solving sequence, working on real issues that were thwarting the school's organizational functioning. After a morning of discussion and decision (which also served as practice in decision-making skills), three significant problems emerged on the third day and three groups formed, each to work through a problem-solving sequence directed toward one of the problems.

Working substantially on its own, each group followed a five-step procedure: (1) identifying the problem through behavioral description, (2) further defining the problem by diagnostic Force-Field Analysis, (3) brainstorming to find actions likely to reduce restraining forces, (4) designing a concrete plan of action, and (5) trying out the plan behaviorally by means of a simulation activity involving the entire staff. The consultants served as facilitators, seldom made substantive suggestions, and never pressed for results. The first six days of training culminated with a discussion in which members described their own strengths and those of their colleagues and reflected on what their school could be like if all faculty resources were used.

Early in the fall, during the active school year, the consultants interviewed all faculty members and also observed several committees and subject-area groups to determine what uses were being made of the earlier six-day training. Data gathered at this point indicated that problems still unresolved were closely related to communicative misunderstanding, an overload of duties in some jobs, and a limited capability for group problem solving.

At the next follow-up consultation with the entire staff, held for one-and-a-half days in December 1967, the consultants sought to increase the effectiveness of area coordinators as communication links between teachers and administrators, to increase problem-solving skills of the area groups and the principal's advisory committee, to help the faculty explore ways of reducing its duty overload, and to increase effective communication between service personnel and the rest of the staff. OD activities included communication exercises, problem-solving techniques, decision-making procedures, and development of skill in observing and giving feedback to work groups.

On the first day, departmental groups applied problem-solving techniques to their own communication difficulties and received feedback from other observing groups. The problems raised were brought the next day to a meeting of the principal's advisory committee held before the staff. The staff observed the committee in a Fishbowl arrangement, participated with its members in specially designed ways, and later reflected on how effectively the committee had worked and how accurately its members had reflected them.

The main objectives of the third follow-up event in February 1968, which also lasted one-and-a-half days, were to evaluate staff progress in solving the problems of resource utilization, role clarity, and staff participation and to reanimate any lagging skills. A group discussion was held for each problem, and all teachers were invited to work in the group considering the problem that interested them most. Each group discussed the favorable and unfavorable outcomes associated with its problem and wrote examples of improvement, instances of no change, and cases of regression. The groups tried to devise ways to halt backsliding by modifying the school's organizational procedures. Faculty members continued with this activity in small groups during the spring without help from the consultants.

The Charismatic Day

The personal qualities of a charismatic leader, who excites the imaginations of others, encourages them to share in feelings of relevance and power, and imparts a sense of urgency to them, can also become part of the culture of a group. The Charismatic Day, a one-day macrodesign built on this concept, can be carried out with a school faculty (or groups of parents or students) late in a year-long OD effort, following a series of training and consultative events such as those described in this chapter.* The intent of the design is to excite the hopes and imaginations of staff members, to help them feel powerful and confident, and to instill in them a pervasive sense of urgency. It encourages organization members to put new ways of working together into immediate action and is also useful in stimulating a staff to upgrade classroom group processes in new ways.

First, the outside consultants, with the help of insiders who have participated in planning the event, quickly list in the form of goals some changes currently under serious consideration in the school, each of which must have the vocal support of at least one small group. Staff members are asked to express their understandings and feelings about these goals in buzz groups and soon afterward to report the discussions to the total staff.

Again in a small group, each person is asked to tell others specifically and realistically what he personally wants to do to achieve these broader goals. Then each individual prepares a list headed "what I can contribute toward achieving my preferred action plan"; the lists are posted, and staff members try to find others with whom they can profitably work to achieve their personal plans. Clusters of four staff members are encouraged but not required, and time should be allowed for the clusters to form.

To induce a sense of urgency, each cluster is asked to produce a plan of action that can be initiated next week. After an hour or two of planning, participants are asked to talk about the new things they believe they can do with others in school as a result of this procedure. If nothing they have done in planning has been important or if they feel discouraged about their action plans, they are asked to talk about their disappointments. The design can end here, or, if group members seem ready, ten to fifteen minutes can be spent at some trust-building procedure.

Establishing OD Specialists in a School District

As part of a two-year intervention from 1968 to 1970 (described in detail in chap. 12), consultants from the Center for Educational

---

*For our use of this macrodesign, see Schmuck et al. (1975).

Policy and Management (CEPM)—then known as the Center for the Advanced Study of Educational Administration (CASEA)—attempted to establish an internal cadre of organizational specialists within a target district. Before this was begun, however, organizational training events for several key parts of the district were carried out by CEPM consultants for one year. (Although most district personnel were aware of the project, about 30 percent were never directly involved owing to the consultants' limited time and resources.) The goal of the OD events was to increase the communication and problem-solving skills of teams of personnel in a variety of influential positions, with the early auxiliary goal of articulating the complex relationships between line and staff personnel. The results of this district-wide effort are described by Runkel, Wyant, and Bell (1975).

Training Personnel with Line Functions. In April 1968 the CEPM consultants invited all the key personnel performing line functions in the district to the first training event. These included the superintendent and his cabinet, the elementary and secondary school principals, and selected teachers who were leaders within the local education association. At least one teacher from every building attended the meeting along with the higher officers in the association. The event lasted four days, but only the superintendent's cabinet was present all the time.

On the first day, before others had arrived, the superintendent and his cabinet discussed ways in which their communication was breaking down, the lack of clarity in their role definitions, ambiguous norms within the cabinet, and also their strengths as a group.

On the second day, the principals joined the cabinet in a specially designed imaging procedure that brought into the open the organizational problems that each group felt involved the other (see chapter 5 for details). The issues uncovered were earmarked for future problem-solving. Now the cabinet and principals divided into three units: cabinet, elementary principals, and secondary principals. Each group met separately to consider helpful and unhelpful work-related behaviors of the other two groups toward their own group. At the end of two hours, all agreed-upon behaviors of the other groups were written in large letters on sheets of newsprint. This session ended with a brief period of training to sharpen the communication skills of paraphrasing and behavior description.

Next, one of the three groups sat in a circle surrounded by members of the other two groups. Those in the outer ring read aloud the descriptions they had written of the inner group. A member of the inner circle then paraphrased the descriptions to make sure they were understood by all his or her colleagues. After all items describing the inner group were read, each of the remaining two groups took its turn in the inner circle. Throughout this procedure, inner-circle members were *not* allowed to defend their group against the allegations made by the others.

Next, the three groups met separately to find evidence supporting the descriptions—i.e., to recall examples of their behavior that could have given the other group its impressions. Returning to the Fishbowl arrangement, each inner group reported evidence it had recalled to verify the others' perceptions. Again, inner-group members were asked simply to describe the evidence without attempting to defend themselves.

On the evening of the second day, teachers joined the principals and cabinet so that for four hours all the line personnel in the district with formal authority were together. A modified Imaging procedure was carried out, culminating in a meeting at which the three groups specified the organizational problems that they believed existed in the district. Discussion was lively, penetrating, and constructive; most had never so openly confronted persons in other positions with their perceptions of district problems. The principals returned to their buildings the next day leaving time for teachers and cabinet to interact. On the fourth day the cabinet met alone to schedule dates for problem solving.

Training Personnel with Staff Functions. Personnel in staff roles in the divisions of Student Personnel Services and Curriculum Development attended a three-day conference in September 1968 during which they were joined for a half-day by the principals. This event began with the staff of Student Personnel and Curriculum meeting separately to discuss the helps and hindrances occurring within each of their groups, with special attention to interpersonal helps and hindrances easier to see. Afterward, the two groups, with the principals as a third group, participated in a period of confrontation. As in April, the confrontation unearthed a number of problems for work. Finally, each group undertook a systematic process of problem solving, planning to continue these efforts back home.

Demonstrating OD Consultation to Selected School Staffs. From September 1968 to April 1969 CEPM consultants worked with five different school staffs in the district. Especially as compared with the trainings with line and staff personnel, these brief OD events demonstrated to many of the teachers the benefits of consultation in reaching district subsystems. Although as demonstrations they were probably not as successful as the demonstration portraying OD during entry, they had the effect of increasing awareness of the meaning and procedures of organization development. Perhaps the most significant result of these events was that many of the volunteers to be trained as future specialists came from the buildings in which consultation took place.

Preparing the Specialists. In the spring of 1969 district personnel were informed that a workshop would be held in June 1969 for those who wished to become OD specialists. A mimeographed circular stated that the trainees would become skilled and knowledgeable in group processes, would serve on committees to give feedback, or would serve as trainers for special groups within the district. The CEPM consultants solicited applications from all hierarchical levels of the district, and the twenty-three persons selected represented a wide cross-section of the district, including teachers, counselors, elementary and secondary principals, specialists in curriculum and student personnel, and assistant superintendents who were members of the superintendent's cabinet.

The first (and major) training event was a two-week workshop in June 1969. The goals of the first half of this workshop were to introduce the trainees to many of the skills, exercises, and procedures to be found in the first edition of this book, to provide them an opportunity to explore the effect of their behavior on a group, to establish the cadre as a cohesive, supportive unit, and to give them practice in leading training activities.

Trainees spent the first three days experiencing many exercises in small groups, rotating the role of cotrainer for training experience. Each exercise focused on a certain type of group process, such as interpersonal control, sharing of resources, or coordinating efforts to make certain "lessons" easy to comprehend. During the last two days of this week, group members designed exercises that would help strengthen their group as the cadre of specialists. They carried out the exercises with their peers, engaged in critical discussion afterward, and reviewed and practiced the skills of paraphrasing, behavior description, describing one's own feelings, and checking one's impressions of the feelings of others.

For the second week, they divided into six subgroups, each convened by a CEPM consultant. The entire group determined potential target groups within the district, and each subgroup chose one for its work. Among the targeted groups were several schools that were changing their programs in the coming academic year, the principal and department heads at a senior high school, the principals and counselors serving elementary youngsters, and a community advisory group made up of parents. The remainder of this week was spent establishing goals for the training to be conducted with the target groups, gathering diagnostic data about them, analyzing the data to determine the forces operating within the target groups, and designing training events. The CEPM consultants worked closely with these subgroups, anticipating the follow-up they would give during the academic year.

During the first two-thirds of the 1969/70 academic year the CEPM consultants continued to work with the new specialists, withdrawing in March 1970. Thus many training events engineered by the specialists were observed and criticized by the outside consultants to support the development of training skills within the cadre. Approximately ten different training events occurred with their assistance, most of them successful in raising district interest in improving communication, group processes, and organizational problem solving.

Launching Multiunit Elementary Schools

Future elementary schools are likely to be increasingly characterized by a multiunit structure in which teams of teachers work in flexible ways with large collections of students. Ideally, this format will make fuller use of individualized instruction, differentiated staffing, and group decision making; but the transition from the self-contained to the multiunit style will not be easy, nor will the abilities and customs developed in the traditional school be sufficient in themselves to make the new organization work. Relying on differentiated staffing and dispersed decision making will require well-understood roles and norms, as well as greater attention to coordination among teachers; this in turn will require higher skills in communication and group problem solving on the part of all staff members.

The following design aims at helping a largely self-contained school move effectively toward the multiunit structure. The intervention calls for a series of consultative events over about nine months. The first, week-long event of approximately forty hours occurs in August and is followed by several events during the academic year aggregating another forty hours.

The first five days in August commence with group exercises, such as Grievances of Black Citizens (chap. 8), and a diagnosis of the school's organizational structure through the use of Tinkertoys in groups, at the same time that consultants teach clients communication skills to use during debriefing. To generate organizational concerns, consultants attempt to make group agreements in teaching teams by means of intergroup exercises. On the third day, problems are identified and problem solving occurs in heterogeneous groups. Finally, staff strengths are identified and shared. Staff members discuss their group agreements within teams and continue problem solving in the heterogeneous groups after they return to school. Consultation during the school year should emphasize four major themes in this sequence, with approximately ten hours of process facilitation devoted to each theme.

1. *Supporting successful performance of the heterogeneous problem-solving groups.* As a skill, problem solving will not be successful unless it leads to reduced frustrations and new satisfactions among the staff. The plans made during the last few days of the first week of consultation should now be reexamined to meet the schedules of the school day. In general, plans should either be carried through, modified as necessary, or dropped by explicit agreement.

2. *Helping the teaching teams work effectively.* Continued organizational problem solving depends upon norms of interpersonal openness and helpfulness in the teaching teams. During this phase the teams should be strengthened by continued consulting and coaching in communication skills, group agreements, meeting skills, and decision making.

3. *Building the leadership team.* The aim of any OD consultation should be to build new functions, roles, procedures, or policies so that the new structures become part of the basic fabric of the school. Because the principal, team leaders, counselor, and resource teacher constitute "carry-roles" crucial to success or failure in the new organization, special process consulting should be extended to

them in such functions as the role of the effective group convener, the role of process analysis during a work session, and differences between being the leader and merely performing leadership functions.

4. *Involving the leadership team in designing an OD learning experience for the rest of the staff.* Consultants should attempt to establish expectations and skills within the two staffs that support continued consultative efforts initiated and carried out by fellow staff members. During this phase the outside consultants might coplan and coconsult with the leadership team to help the staff solve problems, to help the staff improve group processes in its subgroups (e.g., teaching teams), and to help the entire staff improve organizational processes across subgroups.

Improving Classroom Group Process

Although little has so far been written on the matter in this book, successful OD consultation for a school can have favorable effects directly in the classroom (for evidence, see Schmuck 1971 and Bigelow 1971). As Schmuck and Schmuck (1974) point out, macrodesigns that deliberately plan for the transfer of OD training and that also include consultation on classroom group processes will have greater impact. This section offers two illustrative designs of different durations.

The first design, which lasts eighteen months, commences with an OD event in late August, just before the beginning of the school year. The design for this laboratory could resemble that described in "OD Training for a School Faculty." Teachers are then asked to volunteer for a program of consultation and training in classroom group processes, and a consultant skilled in interpersonal relations theory and classroom processes works with them two hours each week throughout the academic year. During the following summer a teacher development laboratory is held which might include communication skills, group techniques, problem solving, and role playing as applied directly to the classroom. Follow-up discussions could occur during the fall semester to help the teachers try out new procedures and to reinforce any insights or new skills developed during the previous year.

The second design, which lasts about six months, is launched with a one-week OD laboratory two weeks before school begins and is followed by a week of consultation in classroom group processes. Since many districts now grant some days before the opening of schools for in-service training, it may be possible to use these as part of the second week, which is devoted to facilitating the translation of group processes found useful during the OD phase into classroom innovation. During the fall semester, supportive discussions can be led by consultants who emphasize the problem-solving process and encourage teachers to implement their plans in the classroom.*

---

*For action plans for the classroom, see Schmuck and Schmuck (1975).

Bringing Parents and Students into School Management

The gap between the sporadic, generally ineffective ways in which parents and students currently participate in educational decisions and the well-organized procedures available to this end constitutes a major problem in contemporary public schooling. As the following sketchy macrodesign indicates, however, the methods of OD consultation can be adapted to narrow this gap. First, train each separate body—educators, parents, and students—in communication skills, establishing objectives, uncovering and working on conflicts, conducting meetings, solving problems in groups, and collecting data. Second, bring all three together to explore goals, uncover differences, and agree on problems that impede joint decision making and other uses of human resources. Third, allow small heterogeneous problem-solving groups (with students, parents, and educators all represented as members) to work collaboratively on problems previously identified. Fourth, build new structural arrangements out of the multiple realities shared during the second and third stages and as part of the solutions to problems worked out during the third stage.

READINGS

The Client as Theorist

Lee Bolman

Kurt Lewin's dictum that there is nothing as practical as a good theory applies to the consultant and the client alike. The macro-designs of OD consultants should emanate from a theory and should in turn help the clients to become better theorists.

Reproduced by special permission from Lee Bolman, "The Client as Theorist: An Approach to Individual and Organization Development," in John Adams (Ed.), *Theory and Method in Organization Development: An Evolutionary Process.* Arlington, Virginia: NTL Institute, 1974.

If our own theories as applied behavioral scientists are rudimentary, our clients' theories are more rudimentary still, and we have provided them little help to develop better theories. Partly, this stems from the fact that many OD professionals do not have an explicit and consistent theory of their own. The lack of such a theory increases the likelihood that their behavior will depart from their espoused values and makes it very difficult for them to help clients develop cognitive clarity.

Such cognitive clarity—in both consultants and their clients— is critical because of the important functions which an effective theory of action can serve, functions which are not likely to be carried out effectively in the absence of such a theory.

First, the real world is impossibly complex, and cannot be negotiated without the use of concepts and theories. Man has no

choice but to theorize—it is simply a question whether the concepts he uses, and the assumptions he makes, provide an optimal map
of the world he needs to negotiate.

Second, a reasonably consistent and integrated theory provides
guidance to an individual when he encounters significant choice-
points. Such guidance makes it much more likely that his choices
will form a coherent pattern which is validly linked to the individual's basic goals.

Third, an effective theory builds in tests of its own validity by
being explicit about the predictions it makes at significant choice-
points, and about the assumptions which underlay those predictions.
When experience proves inconsistent with prediction, the individual
is clearly alerted to a problem either in the theory or in the consistency between theory and behavior. When a person is not explicit
about his predictions at significant choice-points, then his theory is
empty in the sense that it cannot be invalidated and he cannot learn.

Fourth, an effective theory is communicable to others. Com-
municability opens the theory to the possibility of dialogue, and
increases the probability that the theorist can learn from others. For
consultants, it is particularly important that their theory be communicable in a form that clients can understand since this is critical
to the client's ability to make intelligent choices among consultants.

If we grant the importance of helping clients to develop better
personal theories of action, several questions emerge: (1) What is a
theory of action? (2) What differentiates effective and ineffective
theories of action? (3) What methods can be used to help people
become better theorists? The remainder of this paper is addressed
to those questions.

Theories of Action

Any behavior can be viewed as implying a theory of action, which
includes at least the following elements:

1. *Goals.* A goal is simply an event or state of affairs which is preferred
   by the actor to other events or outcomes.
2. *Assumptions.* An assumption is a belief or hypothesis about the
   world—it may be a belief about oneself, about people, about situational contingencies, etc.
3. *Strategies.* A strategy is here defined as a recurrent pattern of behavior, as something which the actor does repeatedly or consistently.
4. *Outcomes.* Outcomes are simply consequences of an interaction.

A simple model of the relationship between goals, assumptions,
strategies and outcomes is the following:

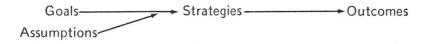

In other words, an actor begins with a set of goals he hopes to achieve, and a set of beliefs which he holds. These goals and beliefs jointly determine the strategies he uses, and the strategies produce outcomes (which may or may not be congruent with the original goals). . . .

Effective and Ineffective Theories of Interaction

The Peter Principle (Peter and Hull, 1969) is only one of a number of plausible but misleading hypotheses which have been offered to explain "why things always go wrong." Actually, things do not always go wrong, but they go wrong often enough in most organizations. A fundamental reason for this is a widely-shared, pervasive theory of effective human interaction which is, unfortunately, an ineffective theory.

This theory of effective interaction has emerged as the predominant theory-in-use for every population with which I have worked in the past year—including graduate students (in education and business), helping professionals (psychiatrists, psychologists, social workers), clergymen and company presidents. There are, of course, substantial individual differences in interaction style, yet there seems to be little variation around certain basic assumptions.

This pervasive theory, as I have inferred it from more than 100 "personal case papers" (which I will describe in detail in the next section of the paper) has the following elements:

A. *Goals for interaction*
In most interactions, each actor has some substantive goal that he can specify to a reasonable degree. In addition, most actors seem to pursue the following interactional goals:

1. Unilateral influence and/or unilateral management of the interaction;
2. Achievement of own goal as initially defined, without testing that goal against new information or against the goals of others;
3. Protection of self;
4. Winning, or avoidance of losing;
5. Suppression of emotion.

B. *Assumptions*
The following are the most common assumptions, in approximate order of frequency:

1. "I am right, the other person is wrong";
2. It is too risky or harmful to be open about one's own feelings;
3. People are most effectively influenced through persuasion and logical argument;
4. Other people's emotions are most effectively influenced through logical, rational appeals;
5. When people resist influence, it helps to intensify the persuasion and logical argument;
6. Others can easily use and respond positively to advice.

C. *Strategies*

Given the goals and assumptions outlined above, it is not surprising to find that the following are the most common strategies:

1. Present logical arguments, try to persuade and "sell";
2. Punish others, tell them they are wrong, threaten them;
3. Withhold one's own eelings, remain calm and rational;
4. Ask for additional substantive information (but not for feedback);
5. Meet resistance with additional persuasion, increased pressure;
6. Avoid the exploration of other people's feelings and perceptions (particularly when they disagree);
7. Give advice;
8. Defend self against criticism;
9. Compliment others, start with the "bright side";
10. Lean on authority, give orders, make demands.

D. *Outcomes*

The following are the most common outcomes from the cases I have worked with:

1. Case-writer accomplishes own initial goal (occurs in about 50% of cases);
2. Relationship deteriorates or stays poor;
3. No learning or minimal learning (case-writer's assumptions are not tested, no feedback about his behavior);
4. Other's commitment to outcome is external (because case-writer managed process, influenced unilaterally);
5. Reinforcement of norms for non-openness, manipulation, mistrust;
6. Self-esteem of participants to interaction declines.

For simplicity, I shall refer to the above cluster of goals, assumptions and strategies as the "competition theory" of human interaction. It is based on the assumption that interpersonal relations are inherently competitive, and tends to guarantee that they will be. Kelley and Stahelski (1970) have shown that competitive theories of interaction tend to drive out cooperative ones, even in settings where, objectively, a cooperative relationship would produce more optimal outcomes for all parties concerned. That is one reason that the competition theory persists, despite the fact that it rests on a number of shaky assumptions and is a recipe for human ineffectiveness.

There are other reasons that it persists: (1) it is an effective theory in many routine interactions; (2) in more complex situations the theory is partially reinforcing, since people accomplish their initial goals about half the time; (3) the theory creates self-fulfilling prophesies, and minimizes the likelihood of having to learn an alternative theory. . . .

Methods for Training the Client as Theorist

Everyone has theories about all sorts of things, but few people view themselves as theorists. For this reason, most people cannot respond directly to a question of the form, "What is your theory of X?" (where X might be "organization development," "management," "watching television," or whatever). It does not help that the concept of theory is popularly associated with such adjectives as "abstract," "impractical," "intellectual" and "hard to understand."

Two influential theoretical approaches in social psychology converge to suggest a route. Self-perception theory (Bem, 1967) suggests that persons determine their beliefs and attitudes at least in part by making inferences from their own behavior ("I must enjoy television because I watch it a lot"), while attribution theory suggests that each of us makes inferences about the beliefs and attitudes of others by watching their behavior. This suggests the possibility that an individual can be helped to explicate his own theories-in-use through a dialogue between himself and others, which centers on trying to make inferences from his behavior.

To provide a starting point for such a dialogue, it is helpful to ask the client to write a paper which can be called a "micro-theory paper" or an "intervention case paper." The client is asked to write this paper under a set of instructions like the following.

1. Select a situation in which you attempt to influence, educate or change another person or persons. The situation should be one which you see as genuinely challenging for you and of significant relevance for your professional functioning. It might be one that you have already experienced, are currently facing or that you anticipate facing in the future.

2. Present a brief description of the case situation (in a few paragraphs sufficient to allow someone unfamiliar with the situation to understand its basic elements).

3. Indicate your goals or objectives in the situation. In other words, indicate what you consider to be a successful outcome.

4. In the following format, present one or two pages of dialogue between you and the other person(s) in the situation.

Dialogue	Underlying thoughts, feelings
Me:	
Other:	
Me:	
Other:	

The left side of the page should contain an actual script for a conversation between you and the other person(s) in the situation. The right side should indicate the underlying thoughts, feelings, inferences, and so on, that you would be having during the course of the dialogue. Please try to write a dialogue which is representative of the important issues you see yourself facing in the situation. As an alternative to the written dialogue, you may also submit a tape recording, transcript, or video tape of an actual conversation.

5. Review the dialogue, and try to specify what you think were your basic strategies for achieving your objectives.
6. What assumptions underlay your strategies?
7. Finally, how would you evaluate your intervention? Where did you succeed and why? Where were you unable to achieve your goals and why?

Over the years, behavioral scientists have had discouraging experiences with the validity of self-report measures, and that raises questions about the usefulness of such a case paper. Does it really reflect anything significant and valid about the individual? Conclusive evidence on this question is difficult to obtain, but experience so far suggests that the answer is very definitely yes. Rosenbaum (1972) compared group predictions based on individual case papers with the individual's behavior in discussions of that paper. He concluded that the case paper frequently represented an accurate preview of the individual's interpersonal style. In my own experience, the following cases are illustrative.

Case A: "A" wrote a paper centering around the difficulties he had with a co-worker, which he tended to blame on the hostile and rigid attitudes of that co-worker. A's description of his own behavior clearly suggested that he dealt with conflict primarily by avoiding it. Two weeks later, a situation involving serious conflict between A and another individual arose. A reacted by physically withdrawing from the program for several days.

Case B: "B" wrote a case paper depicting a situation in which he tried to persuade an organizational superior to save a project from extinction. B's behavior, as he described it, consisted of a sales pitch about the merits of the project, which he intensified in response to any signs of resistance from the superior. In a residential program, he consistently received feedback from others indicating that they saw him as manipulative and resistant to input from others.

Such cases rest on "clinical judgment," and do not constitute conclusive evidence of the validity of the approach. But experience with such papers so far suggests two things: (1) it is relatively easy for individuals to "misrepresent" (often unintentionally) what they do when they describe it in relatively global and inferential terms; (2) it is much less likely that the person can actually write a script with himself in it which is equally misleading. For example, a person may write that: "My basic strategy is to communicate to the other person that I want to hear his views and give him a chance to have a say in the decision," yet write a script in which his behavior is unilateral and non-listening. Experience with such papers suggests that the reader is well-advised to suspect the rhetoric and trust the script.

A Case Example

A university-based consulting team was working with a small school system. One member of that team wrote an intervention case paper describing the team's approach, and, in lieu of the written dialogue, submitted a tape recording of a meeting between the consulting team and the Superintendent of Schools. The paper indicated three major objectives for the consulting project: (1) helping the staff direct its energies and commitment to system-wide problems more effectively and systematically; (2) develop new problem-solving structures in the system and help them work cooperatively on manageable objectives; (3) assist the system to use existing resources more effectively and to seek needed additional resources from outside.

The team's espoused strategy included the following elements· (1) increase the effectiveness of the superintendent in his role; (2) involve teachers in the renewal of the system; (3) help the system make linkages to other institutions which could provide needed resources. The team diagnosed the system as suffering from serious conflicts which were rarely discussed openly. The superintendent was felt to encourage the non-openness by continually asking for "dialogue" and "sharing of opinions" but behaving in ways that did not encourage such openness.

The writer of the paper submitted a tape recording of a meeting between the consulting team and the superintendent. He indicated that the team was not satisfied with its handling of several parts of the meeting, although they did not have a clear sense of what had gone wrong.

At the beginning of the meeting, the superintendent discussed visits he had made earlier in the day to two of the schools. He indicated that he was upset by some of the things he had seen happening (for example, teachers who sat in their lounge after the bell had rung). He received the following reply from a consultant:

> Consultant A: Certainly one of the keys now will be the method and the technique of your intervention. At one extreme you might intervene in such a way that there will be less communication, less structure for action, and therefore a situation which will be a greater problem. What we really want to see—and when I say we I mean all of us because there's no doubt that what you want, and what we want, and what all educators should want, is precisely the same, and this is an immediate remedy for problems that can't be immediately remedied. So it we can discuss this a little bit—the possibilities of intervention in the schools, emphasizing a positive entry, and perhaps the specific techniques so that there can be a very profitable use of the next few minutes.

If the superintendent were to learn from the consultant's behavior, he would presumably conclude that a "positive entry" consists of lecturing to others, and telling other people what their goals are. Perhaps the superintendent was confused by the apparent inconsistency between the substance and the process of the consultant's intervention. At any rate, the intervention was followed by a half-minute of silence, which was broken by a second member of the team, who turned to the superintendent and asked him if he wished to say more about the schools he had visited. The first consultant cut this off by saying, "Well, I don't know if we should be moving to specific schools. If we're talking about the specific problems of schools, these are things that should be brought out already." This consultant went on to provide additional human relations advice to the superintendent, of which the following is an example:

> Consultant A: I wonder if it might be more profitable if we discussed a structure beginning on Monday for attempting specifically to attack the problems so that by Tuesday someone is acting. Such as you meeting with the principals, again in a positive context, without just inviting them in and saying, "Your school is in miserable shape and these are the problems." That alienates these men and puts them in a bad light with the others. If somehow this can be put in the context of the strength that exists and the desire of the chief executive to do all in his power to help.

The consultant implies that the superintendent has minimal interpersonal skill and sensitivity (why else would the superintendent need such simplistic advice?), but does not say so directly, and provides no evidence to support such a contention. Without testing the superintendent's reactions to this message, the consulting team then decided that the superintendent would be helped by role-playing a situation in which he was interviewing an underqualified job applicant. The superintendent indicated that he would be open in expressing his feelings that the applicant was underqualified. One consultant apparently felt this was a breach of good human relations principles and punished the superintendent for behaving in this way. Another consultant then asked the superintendent if he felt helped by the experience, and he indicated that he felt it had been useful.

During the meeting, a considerable part of the consultants' behavior was controlling, advice-giving and occasionally punitive, even though the substance of their statements continually urged cooperative and open communications between the superintendent and his subordinates. Some members of the consulting team felt uncomfortable with this consultant dominance, but none of them said anything in the meeting about their discomfort. The consulting team thereby provided an unintended model of the system's problems (non-openness in dealing with conflict), and managed to extract from the superintendent a statement that he felt helped by such consultation.

In preparing to work with the case-writer around the theory underlying the intervention, I prepared a "reconstructed" theory (see figure 9-3). I included in the model the goals, assumptions and strategies which the consultants stated for themselves, and these appear in the top half of each of the three boxes labeled "goals," "assumptions," and "strategies." Then, when I felt that the consultants' behavior implied assumptions or goals which were not explicitly stated, I made inferences as to what these might be.

402

FIGURE 9-3   Reconstructed Theory: Case Example

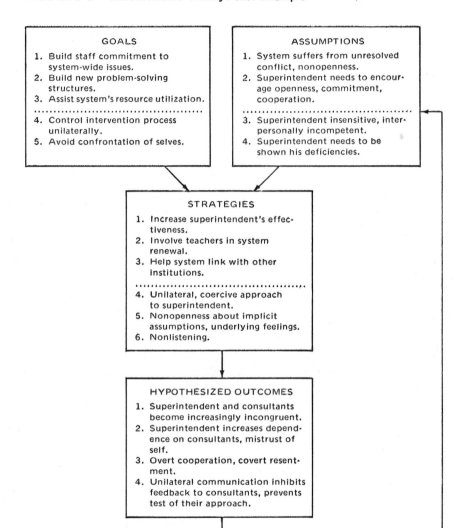

GOALS
1. Build staff commitment to system-wide issues.
2. Build new problem-solving structures.
3. Assist system's resource utilization.
....
4. Control intervention process unilaterally.
5. Avoid confrontation of selves.

ASSUMPTIONS
1. System suffers from unresolved conflict, nonopenness.
2. Superintendent needs to encourage openness, commitment, cooperation.
....
3. Superintendent insensitive, interpersonally incompetent.
4. Superintendent needs to be shown his deficiencies.

STRATEGIES
1. Increase superintendent's effectiveness.
2. Involve teachers in system renewal.
3. Help system link with other institutions.
....
4. Unilateral, coercive approach to superintendent.
5. Nonopenness about implicit assumptions, underlying feelings.
6. Nonlistening.

HYPOTHESIZED OUTCOMES
1. Superintendent and consultants become increasingly incongruent.
2. Superintendent increases dependence on consultants, mistrust of self.
3. Overt cooperation, covert resentment.
4. Unilateral communication inhibits feedback to consultants, prevents test of their approach.

As one example, the consulting team's rhetoric emphasized staff commitment, involvement and cooperative problem-solving. This implies a consulting process with the same qualities; yet the tape recording showed a process which was dominated by the consultants, in which there was little communication and feedback to the consultants and in which the consultants were willing to confront the superintendent but not one another. From this behavior, I inferred latent goals of controlling the intervention process and avoiding confrontation of self. Similarly, the consultants did not explicitly state that they viewed the superintendent as interpersonally naive, but they treated him as if they were making such an assumption, and I added this to the list of consultant assumptions.

In subsequent discussions with the case-writer, I presented my version of the reconstructed theory underlying the intervention. As I presented it, I emphasized two things: (1) I did not assume that my reconstruction was necessarily valid, since there were numerous ways in which I might have misunderstood or distorted what was happening; (2) I believed that the best way to test differences in our inferences was to refer directly to the original data—the case paper, and the behavior in the meeting. The ensuing dialogue was characterized by a high degree of openness and mutuality from which both I and the case-writer derived considerable learning. He indicated, for example, that the consulting group had been concerned for some time about undue dependence in the client-consultant relationship, and were aware that the superintendent tended, at least overtly, to buy "whole hog" whatever the consultants presented. The consultants had never confronted this issue because they were unsure how to do it without making both themselves and the superintendent defensive. At the case-writer's request, time was spent role-playing alternative ways to try to confront this issue with the superintendent.

The strongest evidence for the case-writer's learning from this process was a subsequent case paper he wrote, in which he was able to present his theory much more explicitly, and to behave more consistently with it. Equally important, he showed considerable insight into gaps between his espoused theory and his behavior, and was able to discuss the latent goals and assumptions which caused him to depart from his desired behavior.

In this situation, I chose to work with the case-writer client by presenting a reconstructed theory that I had developed independently. This has the advantage of providing a coherent and specific model to which the client can react, and also helps the client to get a sense of what is meant by a "theory of action." On the other hand, some clients are overawed or unduly threatened by such a presentation and are likely to become too dependent or too rejecting in responding to the model. An alternative is to work jointly with the client in using the case to develop a model from scratch. This is often a difficult and frustrating process in its initial stages, but is likely to help the client develop a clearer sense of how to get from behavior to the underlying theory, thereby making him less dependent on someone else to do this task for him.

In either case, I try to work with the client until we can arrive at a model which he and others can agree is a reasonable approximation of the theory underlying his behavior in the case. Where agreement cannot be reached, I try to make certain that each of us clearly understands the nature of the disagreement, and the position of the other. Because the case is brief and written, problems of perceptual distortion or faulty memory are considerably less troublesome than in discussions of here-and-now behavior, and this makes it considerably easier to reach agreement.

Once agreement is reached, two things are usually apparent: (1) the reconstructed theory differs markedly from the client's espoused theories, usually in ways which the client finds distressing; (2) the disparity between the two theories frequently results from self-defensive strategies and from deficiencies in the interpersonal skills of the client. At this point, the client can begin work on the twin objectives of developing a theory which is more consonant with his personal values and goals, and developing the behavioral skills which will enable him to implement the improved theory.

The objective of increasing the behavioral capabilities of the client can be attacked through a number of available techniques in individual and organizational development. The objective of helping the client develop a more adequate theory is one about which relatively little is known. We have used three primary methods: (1) presenting the client with an example of an "ideal" theory of action (developed by the consultant), in order to provide at least one model of what a better theory might look like; (2) presenting a conceptual framework to help the client understand some of the properties of a good theory and criteria for evaluating a theory; (3) asking the client to write a second case paper in which he tries to incorporate learnings from discussion of the previous case. However, when deficiencies in the original theory stem from defense reactions or lack of skill in the client, the client needs to learn to deal with these before he is able to write a better theory. For example, if a client's only known way to influence others is through covert manipulation, he will be unable to write a consistent non-manipulative theory, much as he might like to develop one.

Individual or Organization Development?

The methods discussed in the previous section were developed originally within the context of professional education, with a focus on the individual professional and his own theories for intervention. In this form, it is particularly relevant in the education of organization development consultants, managers, and laboratory educators.

I am convinced the goal of working around theories for action is equally relevant as a technique for organization development. Just as the patterns in an individual's behavior imply a theory-in-use, the regularities in behavior in any social unit imply a theory-in-use for that unit. Experience in working with organizational units is still in a very early stage, and the methods which are appropriate to individual development may not be equally effective with organizational units.

For example, the "intervention case paper" has been found extremely helpful as a starting point for inferring an individual's theory-in-use, but this method is much less applicable to larger social systems. In working with a larger system, it is possible to develop the espoused theory from written materials and from interviews with key decision-makers. The theory-in-use can be determined by looking at the structure and behavioral norms of the organization: its control systems, its interpersonal norms and its personnel policies.

In working with a hospital-based drug treatment unit, I have developed an espoused theory from their verbal descriptions of their approach and from the one written statement which they have produced. I have also reconstructed a theory from the staff's interactions with one another, and this theory departs in several respects from the espoused theory. As one example, the espoused theory emphasizes open expression of feelings by both patients and staff, but the staff often has difficulty being open with one another. In working with the staff I have asked them to become more explicit about their espoused theory, and to explore gaps between what they espouse and what they do. I am using progress on these tasks as an index of the success of the consultation: we will terminate when the staff feels satisfied with its theory and with its ability to implement it, or when the consultation is no longer providing significant help on the task.

Conclusion

I have argued that human relations and organization development professionals can become substantially more effective by developing better personal theories of action for themselves, and by helping themselves to develop such theories. Currently, most clients adhere to a "competition theory of interaction" which emphasizes unilateral influence and self-protection. The prevalence of this theory is an important cause of the organizational ills which created the need for organization development. My experience suggests that consultation and educational process which do not focus explicitly on those theories usually have little effect on them, and, therefore, on the ways that people behave.

The effectiveness of action cannot be separated from the effectiveness of the theories underlying that action. We can and will develop better theories, and we can certainly help our clients to become better theorists. In this paper, I have outlined some approaches to the problem of more effective theory and action. The approaches are admittedly formative and rudimentary. But I hope that the paper is sufficiently clear that its shortcomings can be seen by readers, who can then begin the process of dialogue through which the theory underlying this paper can develop.

REFERENCES

Bem, Daryl J. "Self-perception: an alternative interpretation of cognitive dissonance phenomena." *Psychological review,* 1967, 74, 183-200.

Blake, Robert R., Mouton, Jane S., Barnes, Louis B., and Greiner, Larry E. "Breakthrough in organization development." *Harvard Business Review,* 1964, 42, No. 6, 37-59.

Kelley, Harold H. and Stahelski, Anthony J. "Social interaction base of co-operators' and competitors' beliefs about others." *Journal of personality and social psychology,* 1970, 16, pp. 66-91.

Peter, Laurance J. and Hull, Raymond. *The Peter Principle.* New York: Bantam, 1969.

Rosenbaum, J. "Report of results of 'evaluation of intervention' questionnaire." Unpublished manuscript, Harvard University, 1972.

Schon, Donald A. Seminar discussion, Summer clinical program in educational administration, Center for Educational Leadership, 1972.

Vail, Peter B. "Practice theories in organization development." Paper presented at NTL Conference on New Technology in Organization Development, Washington, D.C., December, 1972.

Camping on Seesaws: Prescriptions for a Self-designing Organization

Bo L. T. Hedberg, Paul C. Nystrom, and William H. Starbuck

Organizational consultants are not only called upon to design effective action sequences for training and consultation but also to design innovative structures and procedures to fit the goals, technology, and people of the client organization. The current plethora of alternative schools attests to the popularity of creative organizational designing in education. The following article is intended to stimulate the OD consultant's imagination about alternatives for designing self-renewing school organizations.

B. L. T. Hedberg, Paul C. Nystrom, and William H. Starbuck: "Camping on Seesaws: Prescriptions for a Self-designing Organization," *Administrative Science Quarterly,* V. 21, No. 1, March 1976, pp. 41-65.

An organization's history can be broken down in segments of all kinds. One can focus upon single members' activities in their jobs, or upon the activities involving single functional or geographic units. . . . One can discuss social and intellectual domains. . . . One can attend to contiguous events, such as what happened during January 1962. . . .

An alternative method for analyzing dynamics is to concentrate on the generators of behavior—processes. Processes are the media by which an organization creates future acts out of its past experiences. . . .

WHY DESIGNERS SHOULD HELP OTHER PEOPLE ERECT AN ORGANIZATIONAL TENT

Designing is widely thought to belong outside the stream of routine activities. Designers are technical specialists who value their non-involvement. They enter a situation, inventory the problems and capabilities, go off and explore alternative solutions in the abstract, return with an optimal solution, and finally implement their solution. Since implementation requires changes, effective designers initiate and control changes. If the organization adopts these changes, the designers are judged successful. . . .

Designers can be even more successful if they will discard this generally accepted concept of their role. One reason is that changes start complex causal chains that are hard to predict. . . . Predicting an organization's future well enough to control it reliably requires greater analytic capability than designers, or any other people, possess.

Another reason designers can benefit from a new role is that their direct influence over organizational participants' behaviors is weak. Although it is possible to influence activities, . . . activities are ultimately controlled by those who perform them, and participants often begin repealing designers' manipulations as soon as the designers withdraw.

Designing Process Hierarchies

Rather than seeking to shift how an organization behaves, designers can concentrate on altering the processes that accomplish changes. . . . Indeed, truly effective modifications of processes would improve an organization's propensities to learn, to correct flaws in its design, and to experiment with alternative structures and strategies.

Designs can themselves be conceived as processes—as generators of dynamic sequences of solutions, in which attempted solutions induce new solutions and attempted designs trigger new designs.

Process designs will both enhance an organization's flexibility and responsiveness and enhance the aesthetics of design activities. The perception of design as a problem-solution-implementation sequence misrepresents how solutions evolve; and the notion that designs require implementation leads designers astray. Transplanted designs arouse rejection mechanisms that thwart implementations. Moreover, while nonparticipant designers are off inventing solutions, the problems may change or even disappear. . . .

Designers can at best catalyze an organization's self-designing: not only would the organization's members define problems for themselves and generate their own solutions, the members would also evaluate and revise their solution-generating processes. . . .

Erecting Tents or Palaces?

. . . Designers . . . have long promoted skill specialization, integration, clear objectives, and unambiguous authority structures. These widely accepted values assert that an organization should be internally differentiated and yet harmonious, should use explicit communication channels and explicit decision criteria, and should act decisively and consistently. . . . In constant surroundings, one could confidently assemble an intricate, rigid structure combining elegant and refined components—an organizational palace.

Yet change is one of the world's dominant properties. . . . An organization's environment does change. Evolving cause-effect relations render today's methods obsolete, and what has been learned has to be replaced. . . . Designers who erect an organizational palace had better anticipate problems caused by shifting subsoils. . . .

One approach to eliminating mismatches between a rigid structure and a changing environment is systematic remodeling. . . . However, systematic procedures offer weak protection against unpredictability, just as increased rigidity does not effectively prepare a building for earthquakes. Some flaws of systematic procedures are inherent in the concept of strategic planning: drafting plans, dismantling an old structure, and erecting a new structure take so long that designers need to forecast how the environment will shift. Since forecasts are only conjectures derived from past experiences, greater reliance on forecasts induces greater design errors. . . . Systematic procedures also sap an organization's flexibility by strengthening its rationality. Interdependence originates when harmony is imposed on contradictory subgoals and disordered activities, and a change in part of an interdependent structure requires changes throughout. The result is an organization that embodies more forecasts and that responds more sluggishly when its forecasts manifest their errors.

Camping in a Tent

Residents of changing environments need a tent. An organizational tent places greater emphasis on flexibility, creativity, immediacy, and initiative than on authority, clarity, decisiveness, or responsiveness; and an organizational tent neither asks for harmony between the activities of different organizational components, nor asks that today's behavior resemble yesterday's or tomorrow's. Why behave more consistently than one's world does?

An organizational tent actually exploits benefits hidden within properties that designers have generally regarded as liabilities. Ambiguous authority structures, unclear objectives, and contradictory assignments of responsibility can legitimate controversies and challenge traditions. . . . Incoherence and indecision can foster exploration, self-evaluation, and learning. Redundant task allocations can provide experimental replications, and partial incongruities can diversify portfolios of activities. . . .

Those who live in an organizational tent can use good alarm clocks, wash-and-wear clothes, and the ability to plan itineraries quickly. They invent sensors for alerting themselves to significant events, and ceaselessly question their present assumptions and habits. . . . They remain ready to replace old methods, and they discard even adequate old methods in order to try new ones, looking upon each development as an experiment that suggests new experiments. They hear descriptions of what exists as statements about the past, and fantasies about what might happen as opportunities to create reality. . . .

HOW PROGRAMS TETHER AN ORGANIZATION TO ITS ENVIRONMENT

When environmental activities seemingly threaten, an organization can adjust its behaviors to accommodate the environment. Processes by which an organization maps its environment into itself can be labelled adaptive. The adaptive processes include selecting environments, monitoring and predicting environmental changes, consulting outsiders, learning, and buffering fluctuations in the flows of resources across organizational boundaries. . . . Alternatively, when an organization sees opportunities arising or believes its environment is pliable, it can undertake to remodel environmental elements. Processes by which an organization impresses itself into its environment can be called manipulative. The manipulative processes include constructing desirable niches and negotiating domains, forming coalitions, educating clients and employees, advertising to potential clients and customers, and resolving conflicts. . . .

Tethering with Programmed Chains

Real processes are never purely adaptive or purely manipulative, of course, and since an organization always misunderstands itself and its environment to some degree, processes inevitably spawn unanticipated effects. An intended manipulation is only the first link in a vaguely forecasted chain of adaptations and manipulations. . . .

Programmed behaviors loosen the tethers between an organization and its environment. Activity programs supply little self-doubt and few occasions for reconsidering conventional reactions. . . . When the situation differs radically from any encountered before, trying out old programs delays attempts to generate entirely new modes of behavior. In essence, an organization has to unlearn its previous activity programs by exhausting the processes that keep behaviors static, before it starts analyzing an unfamiliar situation and devising appropriate new activity programs. . . .

An organization can choose how it uses programs as tethers between itself and its environment. An unusually dynamic organization shifts products, clients, technologies, or territories because it sees its environment as benevolent. It perceives and investigates abundant opportunities: it develops new products, services, clients, and suppliers; it creates new subunits and realigns old ones; it continuously changes methods, technologies, and task assignments. . . .

Another sort of organization—the usual one—makes changes, but makes as few as possible, and does so only to satisfy environmental pressures. The organization sees its environment as rather static and minimally benevolent, offering few opportunities, but erecting many constraints, and emitting just enough threats to disrupt complacency. . . . Because the organization responds lethargically and with the least innovative responses feasible, its environment must threaten and constrain to elicit action; and because the organization does not exploit opportunities, opportunities are offered to it fleetingly and diffidently, if at all. To the organization, proposals for changes are criticisms of how things are, its environment appears to change little, and programmed behaviors appear fully adequate to cope with the changes that occur. The organization can elaborate its program repertoire into a palatial hierarchy. But the palace is built on a bit of flotsam in a sea of social and technological changes, and the flotsam is constantly being eroded by impinging events.

Drifting into a Decaying Backwater

Every so often, a bit of flotsam gets washed away, out of the mainstream. An organization drifts along in an environment which it believes is placid and somewhat more than minimally benevolent—until one day it bewilderedly realizes its environment has evolved into a stagnating backwater. Unperceived changes have carried the organization into niches that are decaying and becoming infertile. Even though the niches are not yet totally stagnant, the organization's continued survival suddenly depends on making drastic changes. Processes tethering the organization to the stagnating environment have become dangerous and must be dismantled. New processes are needed, first for creating or discovering a vital environment, then for mating together organization and environment, and later for reestablishing a dependable, nutrient equilibrium. Although this new equilibrium, if achieved, may not bring forth such extremely self-confident insensitivity as characterized the former equilibrium, the organization will have metamorphosed out of a nonreflective state in which manipulative processes were comparatively dormant and adaptive processes automatic, will have generated pervasive efforts to manipulate and to adapt, and finally will have extinguished the most extreme and disruptive processes. . . .

HOW TO CONVERT A CRISIS INTO A LETHAL TRAGEDY AND OCCASIONALLY SURVIVE

. . . Success, or the appearance of it, breeds somnolence. . . . The organization gradually slides so far out of touch with what is happening, both within itself and in its environment, that a potentially fatal disaster develops unseen. Then when reality begins to intrude, the organization misapprehends its difficulties and responds in ways that amplify the crisis. Of course, a stagnating environment is a diagnosis by an organization which is nearly blind: the critical defects do not lie in the environment at all, and environmental deterioration is only ordinary technological and social evolution which the organization meets ineptly. Studies of organizations in stagnating environments . . . suggest that an organization's reactions divide into three heuristic phases.

Weathering the Storm

At the outset, an organization does not entertain the notion that its environment has irreversibly changed. The environment is only temporarily deviating from its usual, benevolent state. . . . This deviation presents something of a challenge: everyone must pull together, work as a team, and tolerate temporary constraints. However, the trouble originates outside the organization, and a return to normal is imminent. Since the organization itself remains strong, the challenge can be overcome through intensified efforts—do as before, but more. . . .

As time passes, the spirit of jauntily facing a challenge together fades. Shortages of liquid funds force more stringent economies, and actions are taken to improve the accounting statements. Excised are superfluous goals, such as intercollegiate athletics, job tenure, egalitarian decision making, high wages, organizational image, high admission standards, pollution control, full product lines, or equal employment opportunities. Short-run improvements are sought at the expense of long-run progress. . . .

Moreover, if an organization succeeds in eliminating the signs of distress from its formal reports, it brakes its efforts to reform, and discounts the need for fundamental strategic changes over the long run. Things are improving. Not only have the temporary obstacles been overcome, but the primary means to success have been centralized control and adherence to those activity programs that have traditionally formed the strategic core. The effectiveness of activity programs and the wisdom of top management have been demonstrated once again. The organization's structure has been pared of unproductive and burdensome fat—redundant machines and buildings, nontraditional products and services, excessively skilled personnel, the football team, advertising and research specialists, preventive medicine and diagnostic clinics, and informal communication channels.

Unlearning Yesterday

Perhaps the funds shortages, negative profits, and falling revenues never cease, or perhaps they disappear and then reappear in an organization that no longer has the resources to buy delay. In either case, the permanence of change manifests itself, and the organization's members must decide what permanent actions to take.

The first step toward new behaviors is unlearning old behaviors. The effectiveness of existing activity programs and traditional strategies is disconfirmed, and the processes binding the organization to today's behavioral patterns are disengaged.

Unlearning actually began, but was not recognized as such, while measures were being taken for weathering the storm. . . . When members discover that their organizations may not survive, unlearning mounts: doubts multiply concerning the organization's appropriate domain, and followers abandon their leaders, especially the leaders associated with past programs and strategies. . . .

It is nearly impossible for an organization to survive through this nadir. Changes in structure, strategy, personnel, and ideology must now be revolutionary; marginal, gradual modifications that fit into historical trends will no longer suffice. Reality has to be discovered. A new environment must be found, and the organization must restyle itself to match this environment. . . . Yet the organization was riddled with defects before the recent threats demonstrated themselves, and since then, the organization has not only been centralized and further routinized, but stripped of its creativity, heterogeneity, and mutual trust. Almost no human or financial resources can now be marshalled for information gathering or experimenting.

Inventing Tomorrow

Nonetheless, a rare organization does make it. To do so, it must act swiftly and decisively. It realistically assesses today's desperate plight, yet simultaneously arouses the courage to seek out tomorrow's opportunities. . . . It emphasizes contests to wrest more resources from external sources instead of intraorganizational contests over the limited resources already at hand. It shoots out sensors for perceiving potential new niches, and strives boldly to manipulate its environment. It finds entrepreneurial personnel, gives them discretion, and avoids punishing them for taking risks. Disregarding precedents, it takes on a fluid and ambiguous structure in which there is much communication and minimal consensus. It sets priorities and makes wise choices about the projects that should come first. It counteracts dissension and inefficiency with participation, coordination, and trust. . . .

Both adaptive and manipulative strategies are fundamentally inadequate. An organization in a stagnating environment dare not adapt to its present niches, for that would reinforce its burdens. . . .

Methods for reducing uncertainty become increasingly plausible as an organization achieves mastery within its new environmental niches. Surveillance of the environment can be routinized. Thought can be given to frequently arising situations, and activity programs developed for dealing with them, thus ensuring that the heterogeneity of solutions matches the heterogeneity of problems. Activity programs that arise spontaneously can be made compatible with one another. Subunits can be set up to encompass crucial contingencies in the flow of activities and to manage the boundaries between organization and environments. Subunits' capabilities can be tailored to the tasks they regularly perform, and plans, programs, and inventories can replace informal communications as the primary means of coordination. Consensus can be fostered among members as to what goals the organization will pursue and how it will develop over the long run. . . .

Of course, someone who stayed with an organization while it drifted into a stagnating environment and then had to fight its way out, might wonder, "Are we going to go through it all again?"

HOW AN ORGANIZATION CAN FLY
WITHOUT FLYING APART

The reactions of an organization in a stagnating environment suggest several inferences about the ways processes interact with one another, about the guidelines these interactions follow, and about the rules for effectively managing processes.

Different processes hold different potentials for change. Change is often accelerated by such processes as enlisting new members, appointing new leaders, acquiring subsidiary organizations, buying complete packages of methods, or consulting outside experts. These accelerators either increase the speed of change in present directions or divert change into new directions; they enable an organization to absorb new experiences and concepts rapidly, they reinforce or inhibit forces acting on an organization's environment, and they stimulate new visions and experiments. Active processes, such as evaluating the past performances of people or subunits, retiring, firing, or retraining members, competing with other organizations, or consulting outside experts, often decelerate by reducing the speed of change in present directions. These active decelerators erase memories of past events and weaken organizational traditions; they sever links between an organization and its environment; they confront fantasy with reality and raise doubts about the usefulness of today's practices. Many other decelerator processes act passively, in that they tie an organization to its past states but do not aggressively oppose the accelerating forces. Some processes that can passively decelerate are indoctrinating new members, accounting, investing pride in the skills used to perform current tasks, and myth making. Finally, some processes stabilize speeds and directions of change and weave strands of consistency through behaviors at different times. These stabilizer processes characteristically include reinforcing the use of activities that seem to succeed, standardizing procedures, training, switching around among activity programs, limiting people and subunits to specialized activities, and ignoring small variations in perceived events.

Interactions between accelerator, decelerator, and stabilizer processes generate contests in which coherence struggles against fragmentation. An organization does not automatically travel along as one compact cluster of activities; it tends to separate into fragments flying at different speeds in divergent directions. Continued viability requires that an organization remain coherent without becoming rigid, and requires that an organization's speeds and directions of change approximate those of its environment. Outlying fragments have to be restrained, diverted, stimulated, or chopped off, and dynamic balances must be struck among the diverse forces.

However, an organization has much discretion among ways to achieve viability. It can strive to adapt promptly to the motions of its present niches, or it can set out to construct, through manipulative acts, a sequence of environments that will nurture its evolution along a planned flight path. Neither of these extreme strategies is likely to succeed, because adaptive and manipulative acts complement one another. Somewhere between the extremes is a balanced organization that regards its environment as partly an unknown to be discovered, partly a set of constraints to be satisfied, partly an alternative to be selected, and partly a setting to be resculptured. . . .

An organization finds itself in a stagnating environment because it failed to stay balanced on fulcra. . . . Survival becomes possible only if the organization finally discovers fulcra and dynamically balances its processes.

HOW TO RECOGNIZE FLYABLE SEESAWS

Processes should balance on six fulcra—more or less. All six fulcra are so closely related that adjacent ones could be merged; and each of the six could be partitioned into two or more components. . . .

To emphasize the difficulties of staying balanced, the fulcra are stated as if an organization ought to seek minimal amounts of desirable characteristics. Although it would be equally correct to say an organization should seek minimal amounts of the opposite characteristics, this latter approach might be misinterpreted as only reaffirming the values that an organizational palace is intended to maximize.

Minimal Consensus

An organization can extract advantages from both consensus and dissension simultaneously. Balance implies that consensus does not become regimentation and dissension does not become warfare.

Since the usual organization seeks more consensus than is useful, since it often settles for superficial symbols that subordinates are properly submissive, and since it suppresses conflicts that could be genuinely resolved, additional dissension would confer benefits. . . .

Dissension stimulates reconsideration of implicit or conventional assumptions, encourages strategic diversification, and deters maladaptive stresses from aggregating into crises. . . . However, excessive dissension debilitates. . . .

Minimal Contentment

The usual organization seeks happy, contented members. At least, this is the policy enunciated for public consumption. An organization strives to satisfy its members, and its failures to make everyone completely contented result from unavoidable competitions among claimants, from inexorable constraints imposed by the environment, or from the unrealistic demands of some members. Observers voice doubts about this overt policy after noting that people who allocate resources often behave selfishly: unions bargain for higher wages than labor's productivity deserves, managers pay themselves excessive salaries and sit smugly in plush offices, and faculties assign themselves light teaching loads. But these doubts concern the ways satisfactions are distributed; though the doubters suggest some members ought to receive smaller or larger pieces of the satisfaction pie, they do not challenge the desirability of an organization satisfying its members.

It is vital that people be at least minimally contented with their personal rewards, with their current activities, and with the organization's long-run goals and prospects. An organization loses essential heterogeneity if members grow so discontented that they refuse to participate. . . . In effect, minimal contentment can buffer against the short-run reductions in satisfactions and expectations that changes involve. On the other hand, excessive contentment incubates crises. Low levels of contentment sharpen an organization's perceptions. . . .

Minimal Affluence

Discontent generally decreases as an organization gains affluence. . . . Everyone can receive a little more, mutual self-satisfaction grows, and self-confident complacency sets in. Insensitivity toward environmental and organizational happenings accumulates and spreads. Since the usual organization is seeking as much affluence as possible, it can be charged with striving to maximize its unawareness of reality.

Affluence does offer advantages. It affords a margin which absorbs consequences of failure and which loosens the tethers between organization and environment. Opportunities can be given to display initiative and to experiment. Long-run goals can be pursued and strategies analyzed, and decisions need not be made immediately, without reflection. Members can be retrained and their knowledge updated. Alternative structures can be tried within the organization.

So a small buffer of flexible resources is an asset. However, excessive affluence can be as serious a liability as is poverty. An organization requires reminding that its environment is partly unknown, evolves, and sometimes turns hostile. . . .

The case studies of organizations in stagnating environments suggest that insufficient affluence is the most frightening signal emitted by error-monitoring processes, and that insufficient cash rouses special excitement. This doubtless indicates that an organization in a stagnating environment has such rudimentary monitoring processes that it does not realize something is awry until it has run out of cash. . . .

Minimal Faith

An organization should plan its future but not rely on its plans. Plans and long-run goals allow an organization to anticipate what will be required tomorrow, and the more realistic the organization's problem-solving processes, the more tomorrows it can accurately anticipate. . . . Plans also serve as the key premises for appraising potential environments, for constructing performance measures that take account of future costs and benefits, for deciding which short-run demands actually warrant attention, for reacting to immediate problems in ways that do not destroy desired opportunities, and for reassuring members that changes will turn out well.

However, an organization needs balanced criteria for developing plans and goals. Because every organization fails to predict some events, extremely detailed plans or plans extending far into the future waste problem-solving capacities and also discourage responsiveness. . . . Moreover, plans and goals are frequently too systematic and rational; useful goals are somewhat unclear, and useful plans are somewhat disorganized, erratic, and uncertain. . . .

A realistic organization keeps itself ready to replace plans and goals in order to match and to exploit environmental unpredictability. . . . Events that disprove invalid hypotheses or suggest useful conjectures might emerge at any time, alertness snares knowledge and flexibility captures opportunities. Experiments can breed opportunities and expose nascent challenges; they help an organization alternate between practical assessments of what it is and ideas about what it can become. . . .

Minimal Consistency

The usual organization behaves as if it prefers revolution to evolution.

Some changes can be postponed but not escaped; other changes are desirable. If an organization avoids changes, its effectiveness degrades, its capacity to accept changes weakens, and needs for change build up. By the time changes can no longer be held off, needs may have accumulated to revolutionary proportions, and the organization may have lost most of its ability to take changes in stride. Yet the usual organization systematically avoids changes through inflexible policies, strict conformity to standard procedures, indoctrination programs for new personnel, clear and rationalized goals, reward structures that discourage risk taking, sharply delineated responsibilities, blocked communication channels, punishment of dissent, insistence upon overt consensus, and centralized control. Activities and strategies are reinforced, rewarded, inhibited, or eliminated because of consequences they seemingly have already produced, or because of their consistency or inconsistency with precedents. Monitoring processes are carefully tuned to the signals from current and former environments, and internal communications are channeled for efficiently executing former and current tasks. . . .

What an organization should be avoiding is drastic revolutions. Since sudden changes do not allow enough time for each subunit to adjust to the recent behavioral changes of other subunits, coordination efforts may founder. . . .

The primary requirements for evolutionary change are ideological, conceptual, and procedural. An organization can never be satisfied to continue behaving as it has, for perfection itself justifies dissatisfaction. Even in the face of apparent optimality, incremental experiments are needed to sharpen perceptions, to test assumptions, and to keep learning processes vital. . . .

At the same time, an organization can generally avoid abrupt leaps to radically different procedures. . . . Improving procedures as quickly as possible ultimately produces less benefit than does breaking down major improvements into small increments spread out over time. When each increment is small enough to leave intact most of the activities and perceptions of most people, and small enough to uncover only partial conflicts of interest and only marginal contradictions among goals and responsibilities, an organization avoids the mammoth losses that revolutions impose. Incremental changes also limit the trust placed in current knowledge, leave time for analyzing the results of experiments, and preserve latitude for taking advantage of new discoveries. Balanced and continuous innovation aims at rates of acceleration and deceleration that interpolate between what the organization has been assimilating and what it expects. An organization needs either awareness of its unique past or, better, a stable concept of its destiny, because these help it attain identity as a distinct subculture and focus members' loyalties toward this subculture. . . .

Minimal Rationality

The organization has traditionally been viewed as a vehicle for rationality, and bureaucracy has been characterized as the most rational of social systems. The self-designing organization advocated here is anything but bureaucratic, however. In a self-designing organization, objectivity should be fostered, responsibilities delegated, and conflicts resolved impersonally on substantive critera; but also, expertise should be diluted, authority ambiguous, statuses inconstant, responsibilities overlapping, activities mutually competitive, rules volatile, decision criteria varying, communication networks amorphous, behavior patterns unstable, analytic methods unsophisticated, subunits conflicting, and efficiency a subordinate goal.

Indeed, rationality itself warrants cautious pursuit. One danger lies in oversimplifying models. . . . A related danger is emphasizing means to the exclusion of ends. When solutions are generated and evaluated, criteria of excellence often have more to do with how analyses are conducted than with what results the analyses produce. . . . Still another related danger is developing rational answers to the wrong questions. Questions may be asked solely because ways appear for answering them . . . ; then the people who invent answers shackle themselves to their answers. . . .

The general point is that rationality is not easily identified. The usual organization pursues a superficial image of rationality which understates the value of imperfection. Not only can every organization expect imperfection, a self-designing organization should seek it. . . . A self-designing organization can attain dynamic balances through overlapping, unplanned, and nonrational proliferations of its processes; and these proliferating processes collide, contest, and interact with one another to generate wisdom.

BIBLIOGRAPHY

Arends, J. H. 1975. Problem solving for staff, parents, and students of an urban junior high school: a case study in organization development. Ph.D. dissertation, University of Oregon.

This study describes in detail the macrodesign of an abortive effort to establish improved relationships among staff, parents, and students; the design included establishing a cadre of OD specialists within the school. A number of recommendations about intervening are offered to organizational consultants and educators.

Doll, R. C.; Love, B. J.; and Levine, D. U. 1973. Systems renewal in a big-city school district: the lessons of Louisville. *Phi Delta Kappan* 54: 524–34.

Describing a macrodesign for system renewal in Louisville along with a history of the change efforts and suggestions for other school districts, the authors conclude that: (1) the macrodesign must be closely interwoven with the regular academic schedule, (2) change plans falter when insufficient resources are provided, and (3) accountability techniques are useful only in calling attention to problems, not in helping to solve them.

Lake, D. G., and Callahan, D. M. 1971. Entering and intervening in schools. In *Organization development in schools*, ed. R. A. Schmuck and M. B. Miles, pp. 139–53. La Jolla, Calif.: University Associates.

Poorly conceived and executed beginning stages constitute a major pitfall in designing. This article draws attention to the first things that occur when a school staff and OD consultant meet and begin work together. It describes a consultative failure caused by inadequate start-up and suggests how consultants can improve their entry work.

Schmuck, R. A. 1974. Bringing parents and students into school management: a new program of research and development on organization development. *Education and Urban Society* 6: 205–21.

This essay proposes a macrodesign for establishing problem-solving and decision-making interfaces among parents, students, and educators and delineates the steps by which OD consultation could be used to bring about such structural changes.

Schmuck, R. A.; Arends, J. H.; and Arends, R. I. 1974. *Tailoring OD interventions for schools.* Eugene, Ore.: Center for Educational Policy & Management.

The sixteen guidelines for macrodesigning offered in this study take into account the special attributes of schools, the sequential and cyclic nature of OD, the dynamics of entry, diagnosis, and microdesigning. Many of the guidelines are embedded in the present chapter.

Schmuck, R. A.; Murray, D. G.; Smith, M. A.; Schwartz, M.; and Runkel, M. 1975. *Consultation for innovative schools: OD for multiunit structures.* Eugene, Ore.: Center for Educational Policy & Management.

This monograph, which offers many recommendations for consultants, describes the results of applying two contrasting macrodesigns for helping elementary schools adopt team teaching and the multiunit structure.

10

Microdesigning

While macrodesigning is concerned with the overall structure, sequence of parts, and large events of OD consultation, microdesigning refers to particular elements within the structure, specific events in the sequence, and the minute-to-minute steps and activities within any event. Although these are interrelated activities, the OD consultant is more concerned in microdesigning with the *logistical, substantive,* and *methodological* details of the consultation.

By logistical details, we mean the organization of materials and physical facilities before a consultative event begins. For some events this may involve only providing enough newsprint, masking tape, and felt pens; for others it may require preparing materials for an exercise or simulation, writing and practicing lecturettes, arranging tables and chairs, assigning participants to groups, providing a timepiece, bringing refreshments for activity breaks, or preparing to take messages so that participants will not be interrupted in their work. A location, too, should be carefully chosen in advance. If it is furnished with tables and adult-sized chairs, a classroom or the school library is suitable. For very large groups, a school's cafeteria or gymnasium may be used if its acoustics permit both small group and individual work.

The substantive details of a microdesign include the particular content of a training event, the interview data to be collected for data feedback, the context of an intergroup confrontation, and certain special variables to which the consultant pays attention during process observation and feedback. The nature of these details will depend upon what the consultation aims to accomplish and what will be required to produce significant and lasting change. As consultants turn from macro- to microdesigning, attention to the intervention's ultimate goals and a perspective on what is needed to achieve them are the only matters that should not be allowed to become "micro."

This chapter focuses on methodological details and guidelines for microdesigning in relation to the four types of OD consultation—training, data feedback, confrontation, and process observation and feedback—that should bring about collaborative problem solving and a willingness to try out new actions. The descriptions that follow are intended to highlight their distinguishing features, some important considerations for microdesigning, guidelines for carrying out OD consultation,* and examples of effective microdesigns of each type. The chapter ends with a discussion of the importance of involving clients in microdesigning.

TRAINING DESIGNS

Chapter 1 introduced the view that improved interpersonal skill, subsystem effectiveness, and organizational functioning must be present before an organization can become genuinely self-renewing. As one possible macrosequence to this end, chapter 9 suggested improving interpersonal communication skills, changing group norms through problem solving, and changing organizational structure to support these new skills and norms. Training designs consist of step-by-step plans to produce cognitive, behavioral, and normative change. They are used primarily when the consultant aims to refurbish interpersonal, group, or organizational functioning in one or more ways, and they assume that individuals and groups alike can learn to use new behaviors, norms, and structures.

They assume that long-lasting individual change can occur when a person internalizes new concepts and is encouraged to behave in new ways and that the organization likewise changes when its norms and social structures are altered correspondingly. Cognitive and normative change can be stimulated by means of information presented in the form of lecturettes or written handouts. Behavioral and structural change arises from experiential learning..

The high-profile consultant, presenting information and experiences based on what ought to be occurring in an effective group, should maintain a directive stance so that group members can infer discrepancies between the ideal way of working together and their present way of working together. Similarly, the consultant should structure temporary training events in such a way that the organi-

---

*Guidelines for designing are also discussed in Schmuck, Arends, and Arends (1974).

zation as a whole can try out new norms and practice new ways of functioning successfully in real organizational life.

Experiential Learning

Since Kurt Lewin's research during the 1930s and early 1940s showed the importance of active group participation in helping people to learn new skills and attitudes, much social-psychological research has strongly supported behavioral tryouts or experiential learning, which is basic to OD training. Experiential learning places the responsibility for learning directly on the client. Only by actually trying out new role behaviors and by reflecting on the generalizations and conclusions that they produce can individuals make cognitive or behavioral changes in their interpersonal competencies. Only by means of active practice and conscientious self-reflection or debriefing do groups develop norms in support of surveying or of creating the roles of convener and recorder. Likewise, new organizational structures, such as steering committees, link-pin arrangements for communicating information, or the regular use of buzz groups and Fishbowls in goal-setting conferences, do not happen unless the organization can experience their utility.

The consultant's job is to structure the training situation so that learners can experiment with their behavior, trying out new skills and ideas, to make their own generalizations. By providing appropriate input, the consultant helps clients summarize and build frameworks that organize what they have learned. In other words, learning occurs as a result of both the experiences themselves and conceptualization of the meaning of the experiences. But OD consultation assumes further that cognitive and behavioral change on the part of individuals is insufficient without normative and structural system change as well. That is, subsystem and organizational change will not occur unless experiential learning opportunities teach new procedures, give practice in operating with new norms and roles, and allow reflection on organizational structures.

Experiential learning involves above all a deep commitment to client self-determination. Because democratic values and procedures pervade the experiential learning strategy, consultants must clearly communicate their own intentions so that clients are forewarned about the direction of the consultation; this can be done by means of the demonstration techniques described in chapter 9. Because the commitment to client self-determination further requires the consultant to respect the client's choice of whether to become involved at all, we also encourage clarity and specificity during the contract-building process and a survey of all participants to determine whether enough of them will go along with a consultation.

In addition, consultants should not label the client's interpretation of what has been learned as either inaccurate or wrong. Clients who perform an exercise for one purpose but who offer debriefing comments on other matters, for example, should be shown how these apparently disparate matters in fact relate. Denying clients' interpretations not only violates the consultant's commitment to client self-determination but also makes it unlikely that important or lasting learning experiences will result.

Finally, it takes more than just skill to facilitate experiential learning successfully. Knowing how to give directions for an activity or exercise, knowing how to ask questions that stimulate thorough debriefing, knowing how to structure a session so that participants gain practice in new organizational forms—all these are important, but other qualities and conditions are required as well.

1. Trainers should have internalized a repertoire of conceptual maps and theory, an understanding of research, and so forth. Understandings of how organizations work that provide a context for consultation, sophistication about the methods and substance of consultative inputs, and an understanding of the processes and probable outcomes of various kinds of interventions all provide cognitive support to the skillful trainer.

2. Of the several kinds of support that trainers need, one is client readiness to benefit from the training. For clients to take responsibility for their own learning, they must want to do so, know how, and understand why, at least to some degree. Saturen's findings (see Runkel, Wyant, and Bell 1975) indicate that the ready client organization exhibits norms in support of collaboration and the expression of variety and individual differences. If it does not exhibit these norms of readiness, pre-readiness events may be vital for even the most brilliant and skillful trainer to have the environmental support necessary to pursue an effective consultation.

3. Membership in a consultative team can bring forth a third quality that trainers need, and this may be called will, courage, guts, chutzpah, self-initiating action, or "hanging in." Unfortunately, trainer burnout occurs all too often in OD work. Without clearly differentiated and integrated roles, without norms in support of lending a hand and giving feedback, consultants will find it impossible to accomplish their tasks or to maintain themselves as a cohesive team.

Guidelines for Training

Chapters 3 through 8 offer numerous exercises or games that can be part of a microdesign for OD training. Each exercise is in some way different from the others. For example, the Friendly Helping exercise in chapter 3 allows practice in giving and receiving feedback, while Lost on the Moon in chapter 8 provides an opportunity to gain group skill in consensual decision making. For another example, the exercise in chapter 6 for increasing participation is intended for use in groups, while Imaging, described in chapter 5, is used when two or more groups are brought together. At the same time, however, all exercises have basic similarities. All provide some lesson to be learned by practicing with an artificial or trainer-determined content, and all require particular behaviors on the part of the trainer. Some concepts that trainers should keep in mind and some behaviors that they should exhibit are suggested below.

Beginning the Activity. Carefully introducing an exercise or activity helps clients to know what is expected of them as well as how they might interpret the experience. Imaging, for example, might be introduced by explaining that its purpose is to identify the character of relationships between two groups and the problems that are contributing to conflict. Because paraphrasing and behavior description are important in this exercise, consultants might review them briefly or encourage a ten-minute practice session in each group. Next the consultants might present a brief overview of all phases of the exercise, giving greatest attention to the first phase and explaining that detailed instructions for each subsequent phase will be given as these begin. Approximate times for beginning each phase might be posted in some visible place, such as on newsprint or on a blackboard.

If the exercise requires participants to assume different roles, the behaviors expected of each role player and the differences between them should be clarified at the outset. When performing the one-way-two-way communication exercise described in chapter 3, for instance, it is important to clarify what senders and receivers can expect of each other as well as what both can expect of observers. It is often helpful to encourage group members to paraphrase instructions. All questions about the consultant's expectations should be answered, but those whose answers would reveal the solution to the simulated problem or puzzle should be fielded with the explanation that the purpose of the activity is for clients to discover that for themselves. Inaccurate paraphrasing or repeated questioning need not be annoying if the trainer regards this as evidence that the directions were ambiguous in the first place for those who need most to understand them.

Modeling the expected product of the exercise often helps participants understand what they are supposed to do. In explaining Hand Mirroring, for example, we have sometimes selected partners from among participants to demonstrate what we mean. To introduce the Blind Walk, we have used pairs of consultants to demonstrate their individual styles for the purpose of stressing that many variations are possible in this exercise. If we expect participants to make lists on newsprint during the activity, we might exhibit a possible format or a sample created by another group in a previous workshop.

During the Activity. Many relatively uncomplicated exercises allow participants to complete their work without interruption. For more complicated exercises such as Imaging or the Planners and Operators exercise, consultants may have to remind clients of the rules or explain next steps throughout the event. In such cases you should do only what you said you would do at the beginning, as interruptions to give an overlooked instruction or unsolicited comment can be annoying and disrupting to the participants' experience. This is not to say that attention to every detail before and during an exercise will prevent a flop but only to reiterate that careful planning is very important. At the same time, however, overplanned designs which leave no wiggle room for surprises, freak accidents, or unanticipated side trips can produce a highly "tasky" atmosphere that leaves no room for ownership of learning, inventiveness, or "soul."

On one occasion, for example, we planned for the staff of an elementary school a half-day of training in giving and receiving interpersonal feedback, beginning during the first half of the morning with the Friendly Helping exercise and planning after a break to ask participants to brainstorm the organizational forces that prevented them from doing this on their own. Watching the exercise unfold, however, it became clear to us that many people resisted either hearing themselves described or telling others that they were regarded as tough battlers and, in addition, that many people seemed to want much greater influence than they currently had over decisions about staffing and assigning students to classes. During the break, several participants told us that there was a "vague something" about our design that did not quite meet their needs. After a brief huddle, we initiated the second half of the event by occupying the center of a Fishbowl and replanning the design. We ended by proposing, with the clients' agreement, that the discussion change to the issue of interpersonal influence in the group.

The rest of the half-day included an activity in which staff members rank-ordered themselves (i.e., lined up) according to the amount of influence they believed they had, following which the total group discussed where it believed various individuals should have placed themselves. As in the earlier exercise, we again encouraged giving and receiving feedback. It developed that our willingness to redesign the second exercise on the basis of data collected informally during the first part of the morning spared us the necessity of conducting a training event from which group members would have learned little of importance to them.

Following the Activity.   At the end of an activity in experiential learning, consultants should provide concepts that enable clients to connect their generalizations and conclusions with OD theory, and this phase begins with debriefing, in which participants share their observations, state their interpretations, or raise issues that the experience brought forth. The consultant may sit in on debriefing merely to observe or to paraphrase what is being said or, more important, to provide reluctant or unskilled debriefers with leading questions, behavior descriptions, or impression checks that will help them to get started. Debriefing should not, of course, focus on descriptions of feelings or behaviors indefinitely. Questions like, What patterns did you notice . . . .? or What generalizations can be drawn . . . .? raise the discussion to a higher level of analysis. Final debriefing questions can encourage a group to focus on how its performance in, or satisfaction with, the exercise is like or unlike what typically occurs at group meetings.

Once participants have discussed their experiences, trainers may wish to call attention once again to the main purposes of the exercise, relating these to organizational theory. A lecturette to this end may require no more than restating or summarizing what has already been said during debriefing, or this phase may take the form of a prepared presentation with only occasional reference to participants' comments. Examples of lecturettes that we have used include the Johari Awareness Model from chapter 3, task and maintenance leadership functions from chapter 6, and types of decision making (minority rule, voting, consensus, etc.) from chapter 8.

The nature of the consultant's comments during the wrap-up will naturally depend upon the group's success in performing the exercise or activity. To a group that completed the Five-Square puzzle rapidly, and in which members greatly appreciated one another's helpfulness, the trainer may wish to note only helpful behaviors. Providing a wrap-up for a less effective group may require very different tactics, however.

For example, we once asked an elementary school staff to divide into small groups for the purpose of building Tinkertoy models of "who talks to whom on this staff." Only one of three groups was able to build such a model; another group's model collapsed as members attempted to describe what it meant to them; after five minutes the third group abandoned the effort altogether and returned their Tinkertoys to the container. The debriefing of the total staff revealed great discouragement and frustration with a task which they had thought would be fun. Blaming one another was commonplace during the debriefing.

The lecturette that we delivered after these events highlighted the need for sufficient, adequate channels of communication and reassured participants that many groups had far too few such linkages. We asked them to discuss who talked to whom in the school and who ought to be talking more. The thrust of the lecturette and the shift away from the frustrating Tinkertoy experience freed staff members to discuss issues that were especially relevant to their group.

Designing for Transfer of Learning.   Because training aims to equip persons and groups with skills that will enable them to function successfully in real-life situations, it is important to design microevents that include simulations or games for transfer of learning. Too often this is complicated by the "cultural island" approach to training events; that is, groups are typically distanced from their workaday worlds to help "unfreeze" daily sets, patterns, and expectations in order for them to take a fresh look at themselves in their home settings. Events that require a teaching group to make decisions about surviving on the moon, for example, or that require an administrative team to assemble the Five-Square puzzle provide this kind of distance.

When designing for transfer of learning, several guidelines are helpful. First, do not assume that transfer is automatic, but plan for it and discuss it with participants. Second, immediately after the debriefing of an exercise, allow participants plenty of time to consider its implications for their home setting. Third, include several of what classical learning theorists call "identical elements." For example, a large staff at a retreat might be grouped into its natural teams for an exercise.

For another example, teaching some faculty members to design questionnaires for assessing the organizational climate in their school, we divided the group into two teams, each of which was to play both "consultant" and "client" to the other. Each team was given diagnostic information about the "client" team, including a description of the group's own history and problems. By designing questionnaires about and for themselves, the participants learned how to select and combine items to assess dimensions of climate. After trying out their first efforts and getting feedback from their "clients," the total group worked together to design an instrument for others in the school.

Fourth, make sure the participants can learn the cognitive, affective, and motoric aspects of what they are expected to transfer. Helping members of a student council to become better representatives of their homeroom constituencies, for example, we attended to the cognitive aspects of representation by giving a lecturette on what a good representative would and would not do. We encouraged thought about the affective aspects of being a representative in small-group discussions of hopes, fears, and concerns. Motoric aspects were taken into account as each member made to the rest of the group a practice presentation about the meeting that had just occurred; other council members were told to simulate a homeroom environment with one student portraying the teacher.

Fifth, after the behavioral tryout, provide opportunities for debriefing in the real situation. The next meeting of the group could begin with a discussion of "how we have worked as a group since our last meeting" and could go on to establish a next set of learning goals.

Themes and Designs for Training

If it is to succeed in teaching something of importance without eliciting cries of "input overload," a training intervention, regardless of its length, should be organized around some major theme. In the interests of clarification, we have often found it helpful during training events to post an agenda listing times, the name of the exercise, and the kinds of concepts the exercise is intended to teach. Note that we do not tell clients *what* they will learn (e.g., "You will learn that transactional communication is superior to one-way communication"); instead, we reveal the topic and purpose of the exercise (e.g., "To explore the relative advantages of one-way and transactional communication and to relate the exercises to communication in the school").

The number of possible themes is virtually limitless. Some themes organize content according to consultation objectives, as many of the microaspects of the Charismatic Day in chapter 9, for example, sought to help participants understand the concept of charisma in order to behave toward one another in more charismatic ways. Other themes take into account the activity, achievement, affiliation, and power motives of group members as described in chapter 1.

Role-playing certain behaviors before they are to be tried in the real setting is one way of taking activity motives into account. A staff that is talking about someday holding parent conferences, for example, may be helped to take initiative in doing so by pairing up and demonstrating such a conference to other pairs. Another design might call for enthusiastically praising the first group member who volunteers to try out the role of convener or those who take initiative in giving feedback to the consultant on how the training session is going.

Achievement themes might include an activity like "strength bombardment," in which each person describes the special strengths that he perceives in every other person. Praising or otherwise acknowledging individual achievements that do not directly concern group work—for example, praising faculty members who complete home improvement projects or who stay on their diets—can satisfy achievement motives by establishing the expectation that work well done will be rewarded. We have also encouraged groups to display activity charts on which to check off each task as it is completed, or to take time during the training event to proliferate visible products, such as newsprint lists, to demonstrate to even the most product-oriented people that something is in fact being accomplished.

The best way of satisfying the achievement motive, of course, is to help group members find real solutions to real problems. In one of our projects, for example (see Schmuck et al. 1975), first and second grade teachers in a multiunit school had agreed to find a way for each teacher to teach reading to only half a class at a time while the other students engaged in interesting activities as part of a large group. But a lack of space and of additional personnel to run the large groups impeded achieving this goal; in addition, schedules would have to be changed for the music teacher's visits to first and second graders and for use of the gym by third and fourth graders.

By brainstorming all possible space arrangements and by choosing those requiring the fewest people to move each day (an important criterion for the group), one problem was solved. By soliciting parent-volunteers, sufficient personnel were found. Finally, other staff members were contacted so that the necessary schedule rearrangements and trade-offs could be negotiated. As a result of finding these solutions, the teachers in the first and second grade unit were very proud, not only of their new reading program but of their success in overcoming real problems that had stood in their way.

Opportunities to laugh together while working collaboratively on low-risk tasks can help groups build cohesion that satisfies members' needs for experiencing friendship. Affiliation themes are particularly important in brand-new groups or at the start of temporary systems such as workshops; thus we often include warm-up activities that encourage people to become better acquainted or to get ready for trying out new behaviors.

The Who Am I? exercise described in chapter 3 is especially useful at the beginning of the school year when people have been separated for some time or when a group has new members. The Billy Goat exercise described in chapter 6 allows people to try out unusual or unreal role behaviors before the serious work begins of experimenting with real day-to-day role behaviors. We have divided faculties into temporary teams to plan games that all could play together. One team devised a relay for building the tallest sandpile on a nearby beach in four minutes; another made materials so that everyone could play a popular TV game show; still another wanted each group to write a song parody about group life. We have also asked groups to make chalk murals on large sheets of butcher paper and have suggested physical exercises like jumping jack or leapfrog to others. In short, affiliation themes can and should be fun to design and carry out.

Power motives can sometimes be satisfied by pointing out a group's range of goals and encouraging members to think about how influential they are or wish to be either within or beyond this range. On one occasion, for example, we worked with a parent-staff problem-solving group that was distressed about the unattractiveness of their school building and grounds. Complaining specifically about the drabness of the walls and the blacktop on the playground, their first ideas included placing flowers on the secretary's desk and posting colorful exhibits in the display case.

When the consultants pointed out that they were not talking about painting walls or tearing up blacktop to plant a few trees, group members replied with *yeahbuts:* "*Yeahbut* the district has a policy about who should do the painting," or "*Yeahbut* the steering committee coffers are too empty to pay for landscaping labor or materials." By continually prodding the group to check whether their suggestions matched their complaints, the consultants encouraged the members to get district policy changed so that they could do the painting if they used regulation-quality paint, to sponsor a workday on which parents and teachers were invited to bring tools and seedlings for playground refurbishment, and in general to expand their area of influence.

Many of the goal-setting activities described in chapter 4 can help groups think about the areas of their environments that they wish to influence. Hand Mirroring and the Influence Line exercises described in chapter 8 can be used when issues of interpersonal influence are salient. Imaging (chap. 5) and the Planners and Operators exercise (chap. 8) are particularly useful in uncovering issues related to intergroup influence.

DATA FEEDBACK DESIGNS

Designs for data feedback assume that collaborative functioning can be enhanced if organization members share a common understanding of what is happening in a group, what they think ought to be happening, and which proposals will move the group from where it is to where it wants to be. Using the S-T-P problem-solving procedure, consultants elicit and structure information from individual group members, emphasizing discrepancies between what is actually occurring in the group, what group members think is occurring, and what they would like to see occurring. For consultants, this involves: (1) collecting the data, (2) organizing the data for feedback, (3) creating the behavioral setting in which feedback will occur, (4) presenting the feedback and helping members identify discrepancies around which problem solving will subsequently occur, and (5) facilitating the actual problem-solving effort.

Just as experiential learning is important in the work of the trainer, inquiry learning is crucial for the consultant using data feedback. Inquiry learning seems complicated because it aims to help learners understand a particular concept and at the same time to develop their skills for inquiring into other, discrepant data. Basically, however, data feedback strategies are based on a simple principle—don't tell or interpret for clients what you can get clients to tell or interpret for themselves. Questions that ask, Why?, What theories do you have to explain this?, or What evidence can you present to support that generalization? encourage clients to examine and interpret data.

Guidelines for Data Feedback

Although there can be no question about the importance of collecting and feeding back data to client organizations, it is not surprising that using these methods presents a major challenge to most OD consultants because of the extraordinary skills required.* First, they must be clever enough to collect relevant, valid data and be able to put this information into a form that is at once understandable, engaging, stimulating, and tension producing. Second, they must raise these mundane facts to a level of quintessential significance so that participants regard them as worthy of notice. Third, and perhaps most important, they must introduce the data into the ongoing ebb and flow of organizational life at opportune times. The more naturally and spontaneously they can do this, the more helpful they will be.

Collecting Data. Scientifically trained consultants may well envy the skill with which the world's great novelists make perceptive observations about human behavior, transform them into word pictures of brilliant clarity and detail, and at the same time create a sense of universality that is larger than the lives of their characters. Amassing relevant data and overcoming the scientific myopia for distant, abstract, and general phenomena constitute major challenges for OD consultants, who, like anthropologists, must perceive the relationships

---

*For this section, we are indebted almost entirely to Schmuck (1973).

between highly particularized organizational events and infer from them larger principles about organizations in general.

To assist clients in solving their unique problems while helping them recognize that they are in many ways like all organization-kind, the consultant continually collects data, by both formal and informal means, that will yield insights into the operation of the organization. Self-report questionnaires, interview schedules, and observational categories constitute the primary formal methods for survey feedback. At the same time, however, organizational letters and memos, informal conversations with organization members, and observations made during even the most casual visits offer important information as well. Ideally, consultants allow their first impressions, however they are obtained, to guide their selection of formal questionnaires, interviews, and observations, the results of which will be embellished by insights gained from data collected more informally.

The following principles offer helpful guidelines for formal data collection and feedback.

1. Interviewing clients before collecting data via questionnaires helps to establish rapport and trust between clients and consultant, which in turn supports more authentic responses by clients on self-report questionnaires.
2. When using an interview or questionnaire, ask general questions before specific ones. Pointing first to specific issues often gives clients new ideas about how to answer general questions so that valid answers are not given.
3. Modeling the communication skills of paraphrasing, describing behaviors objectively, checking impressions of the client's feelings, and describing your own feelings when appropriate during the interview will facilitate the introduction of these skills later.
4. When using questionnaires, collect some data that can easily be quantified and other data that render quotable phrases. For as many clients who prefer numbers, an equal number are captivated by the catchy phrases of their colleagues. Ideally, numbers and phrases will support similar themes.
5. Employ the same open-ended questionnaire item several times throughout a sustained consultation in order to engage participants in discussions about how things are changing within the organization. Force-field analyses of the same phenomena, for example, might be drawn several months in succession.
6. Use only a few categories for feedback. Ten are plenty, but it is better to use even fewer and to keep the tallying process simple. Clients' arguments over an ambiguous instrument typically siphon off energy and motivation better used for self-analysis.
7. After formally observing a meeting, interviewing a few of the participants about which events were usual or unusual will give you a more balanced understanding of typical interaction in the group's meetings.
8. Carefully sift data before presenting them, give only small

amounts at a time, and try to elicit discussion about their meaning for the organization.

9. Finally, observe the client group as it discusses meanings of the data, voice your observations to encourage the group to discuss its interactions during the data feedback, and ask how typical these interactions are.

Making Feedback Significant. In addition to these principles for increasing the validity and usefulness of data feedback, there are several ways of giving concrete items in the feedback more significance for participants.

First, the feedback activity should be guided by a simple theory that applies to other social settings as well. "Gunny sacking," for example, is likely to apply wherever two or more persons become reasonably intimate, in the home as well as on the job. The term refers to an accumulation of pent-up and hidden frustrations, irritations, and resentments which participants rehearse to themselves, afraid that their exposure would be emotionally overwhelming. Built-up interpersonal tensions lead to ineffective collaboration, but they can be reduced by talking openly and directly about them, especially if the consultant points out that interpersonal irritations are inevitable and characteristic of all organizations, including the family. Such a clear, reasonable, simple theory can be used during data feedback to emphasize the importance of exposing even the most trivial on-the-job frustrations and irritations.

Second, the significance of variables being measured can sometimes be increased by clustering them under a label that is interesting to the clients—for example, "Five Features of Organizational Health" or "Three Facets of Organizational Climate." The organization's productivity, its morale, and its use of human resources are other useful summary designations.

Third, particular data sometimes take on higher significance if they are compared with data from similar organizations. Pressures for understanding and action seem to be strongest when members of the client organization view themselves as lying somewhere between the worst and best of the comparison organizations.

Incorporating Feedback into Macrodesigns. To incorporate data feedback into the natural flow of a consultation, consultants should have two basic capabilities. First, they should have (both in mind and in their files) a large and diverse collection of formal questionnaires, interview items, and observation categories. The instruments presented in chapters 3 through 8 are an excellent basic set; also very useful are instruments contained in Fox et al. (1973), several volumes of training aids (including data-gathering techniques) by Pfeiffer and Jones (1969-74), and the *Annual Handbooks for Group Facilitators* (1972-76). As the following five examples will show, the second capability consists of remembering that methods and instruments for formal data collection and feedback can and should be woven into each of the primary stages of a macrodesign.

1. *During entry, when data can be used to develop understanding and agreement about the intervention's objectives.* Consulting with the staff and a large parent group in an elementary school,* we first attended a meeting with a representative group composed of the principal, a few staff members, and representatives of the parent group. Before agreeing that we would help, we met separately with the total staff and total parent group to learn what they hoped to gain by working together and by having us work with them. At a second set of separate meetings we reported a summary of the data collected during the first meetings, and each group discussed differences in how they perceived the purposes of the consultation. We then met again with the small group of representatives and proposed what the consultation could accomplish in light of these differences. The small group concurred with our proposal and agreed to serve as a steering committee to make decisions about the direction of the macrodesign over the next several months.

2. *During the first major consultative event, when data previously collected might be fed back as part of the planned design, or might be collected on the spot and fed back immediately.* In an intervention with a junior high school faculty, we were invited to conduct a two-day event on the topics of improving meetings and clarifying decision making. Before the event, we interviewed all staff members to find out how they defined meeting and decision-making problems. At the beginning of the event, we fed back a summary of these data and asked the staff to decide which specific problems were most important to deal with now. At the end of their meeting, when they had selected four problems for work, we gave them feedback about how the meeting had gone and how they had decided which problems to attack first. This on-the-spot feedback confirmed their view that the major problems with their meetings and decision making included infrequent use of listening skills, lack of group agreements about roles in meetings, sloppy procedures for meetings, and lack of understanding about who was to decide what.

3. *After the first consultative event but before the initial follow-up event.* With another junior high school faculty we pursued a two-day consultative event in August, with small-group interviews in September.† The interview questions were intended to identify faculty subsystems with the highest degree of mutual interdependence. Determining from these data that the pupil personnel subsystem (comprised of counselors and the school psychologist) and the administrative subsystem (comprised of the principal, vice principal, and two grade-level coordinators) were more recognizable than various departmental teams and more in need of coordinating their efforts than either was of coordinating its efforts with any other group, we proposed to continue consultation on their interaction and to abandon immediate efforts to consult with the total faculty. To enable

---

* For details, see Phelps and Arends (1973).

† For details, see Arends (1975).

other interested individuals to continue working with us, we proposed establishing a new subsystem that would be trained to serve as process consultants to any other faculty group requesting help. These proposals were accepted at a brief meeting of the total faculty in October.

4. *In doing process coaching with an organizational subsystem during one of its regular work sessions.* This is by far the most common setting in which we have used data feedback designs—so common, in fact, that we have provided many examples of such designs later in this chapter. At this point suffice it to say that we have frequently distributed abbreviated questionnaires during meetings, quickly tabulated the results, and reported the findings to the total group as a means of focusing debriefing. Our questions have included: To what degree have members' ideas been listened to at this meeting? How satisfied are you with your participation so far? Describe one thing that someone has done during the meeting that has been helpful to you. On a scale of one to ten, ranging from very unproductive to very productive, how much do you think the group has accomplished during this meeting?

5. *After the consultant has completed work with the organization.* Most of our longer macrodesigns have concluded with a report that typically recounts the major events of the macrodesign, summarizes major findings from data collection during and after the consultation, and makes recommendations either to the clients or to other consultants who would undertake similar work. When this is prepared for an audience other than the client group, we not only shield the identity of the individual participants but sometimes prepare two versions of the report—one for the client group and another for outsiders. Returning to the school to answer questions about either or both versions, we have often had to explain how data are displayed and the meaning of any research or statistical jargon used.

CONFRONTATION DESIGNS

Confrontation designs are based on the assumption that effective team functioning cannot occur in the absence of information about how a focal individual or group client is perceived by others. Because they are most often used in cases of difference or conflict, this information usually includes a description of the conflict's dimensions, an analysis of the source of the differences, and a consideration of the consequences of the conflict for both parties. Confrontation designs enable consultants to help either or both parties express their perceptions of the other's actions, focus on their differences, and engage in problem solving to resolve their differences. The elements of such designs usually include creating a setting for confrontation, uncovering and clarifying differences, and encouraging problem solving that leads to agreements for managing conflict.*

---

*Confrontation designs are explained in great detail by Walton (1969).

Structuring the Setting. The elements of a confrontation design that can be influenced by consultants include the place in which the confrontation occurs, the amount of time allotted, and the amount of privacy provided. The place, for example, can be selected to give an advantage to one or to neither party. Neither party would feel more comfortable if Imaging were performed by elementary and secondary school principals in the district's central office. On the other hand, staging an Imaging exercise in the school cafeteria might make outnumbered teachers more receptive to a large and angry parent group, and a teacher-principal confrontation might be appropriately set in the teacher's classroom to offset the principal's power advantage.

A highly formal setting is particularly useful when two large groups are brought together in a confrontation. On one occasion we arranged two sets of chairs facing each other—one set in two rows of six chairs each, the other in six rows of six chairs each. By requiring persons in each front row to move to the back and all others to move forward a row every ten minutes, we equalized participation within each group and minimized the effects of differences in total group size. Participants in the smaller group said that it was less threatening to be "six against six than twelve against sixty."

The amount of time allotted for a confrontation should be sufficient, specified in advance, and as free of interruption as possible, especially if the consultant is to help the parties understand their differences, consider how much can realistically be accomplished in the time available, or how much time they wish to set aside to accomplish their goals. In other words, it is possible to begin with a clear time limit or a clear goal, but one or the other should be known in advance.

The consultant should consider in advance whether adding extra people will help or hinder a confrontation and should have an alternative plan if the initial one is not effective. Although extra persons can add relevant insights and be viewed as a source of support for either or both of the confronting parties, a private event avoids the risk that a fourth person or third major group may inhibit the confrontation or complicate the process with other needs and goals.

Three-way confrontations effect a compromise between maintaining privacy and including others. To this end, we once divided the eighty participants in a district demonstration event into three groups—central office personnel, building administrators, and teachers—to do an abbreviated Imaging exercise in which each described its images of the other groups and examined their images of it in return. We then asked each to identify problems between the other two, finally combining the three lists to find common problems. In addition to accomplishing the purposes of Imaging, this strategy gave a considerable number of people some initial experience in acting as third-party consultants to groups in conflict.

Functions of the Third Party. As third parties to a confrontation, consultants can perform a number of vital functions. First, they can equalize the energy that the parties bring to the confrontation by, for example, giving the more impatient party something constructive to do while working with the more passive or frightened party. In one case we planned a practice session in paraphrasing for the group with the clear agenda while helping the less prepared group make up its list of demands.

Second, consultants can equalize the situational power of the two parties. If one party is more verbal than the other, they can suggest a nonverbal activity or require both parties to put their ideas on paper first. Many of the suggestions for structuring the setting are intended to equalize situational power. Conducting a role-clarification and negotiation session between the counselors and administrators of a secondary school, for example, and aware that the administrators wrote annual performance reviews for the counselors, we held the session in a room in which counselors sometimes worked with students and at a time immediately after school when the administrators, but not the counselors, were still on duty.

As it turned out, however, this attempt to make the counselors feel more secure about confronting the administrative team had the effect of shifting the power advantage too much the other way. Although the familiar setting gave the counselors confidence, repeated interruptions by teachers and students looking for an administrator caused the meeting to adjourn after two hours with very little accomplished. An evening meeting, or even a daytime meeting during which students and teachers were otherwise occupied, might have enabled both groups to focus more intently on their work.

Third, the consultant as third party can help participants achieve similar definitions of issues before suggestions are made for resolving the conflict. The S-T-P procedure is useful in this regard; posting three sheets of newsprint labeled "Situation," "Targets," and "Proposals" and asking each group to complete the first two before working on the third can frequently prevent premature decisions being made about solutions. By encouraging paraphrasing and impression checking, the consultant can also reduce possible misunderstandings between parties, so that the expression of an unpleasant feeling by one party can be correctly interpreted either as an attempt to perpetuate the conflict or as a gesture of trust.

Fourth, the consultant can maintain an optimal level of tension so that a sense of urgency produces an exchange without the occurrence of either rigidity or distortion. Encouraging the parties to persevere while the information is fresh or suggesting a break may both be appropriate in the same consultative event. During a two-day event in which three groups used the Imaging exercise to uncover and find solutions to common organizational problems, we ended the first day by brainstorming a list of specific problems. Leaving the newsprint on the wall overnight, we encouraged participants to think about major categories that would guide the brainstorming of cross-role groups as they created proposals and action-plans to recommend to the larger group.

Fifth, the third party can employ procedures and language that ensure clear communication. Use of the interpersonal communication skills described in chapter 3 is essential. The third party may have to be particularly active with paraphrasing and impression checking for clients to use these skills; it may also be necessary to ask questions that require each party to describe feelings or to describe the other's behavior.

The sixth function of the third party is often performed inexplicitly. Simply by being present during the course of a confrontation, the OD consultant can provide emotional support. This way of saying that it is all right to express disagreements and very productive to try to do something about them can be extremely important in organizations whose norms do not support these behaviors.

Encouraging Follow-through. One way of stimulating follow-through on agreements or further dialogue after the initial confrontation meeting is to make explicit the techniques and principles that are being used as the meeting proceeds. By attempting to teach the means of effective confrontation, the consultant should increase the clients' ability to continue or to repeat the confrontation on their own. But this must be well planned and carried out because it cannot be assumed that parties to a conflict will themselves normally think about how to avoid future unproductive interchanges.

Another way is to attempt to change the larger organizational context in which the parties to the conflict must survive. In order for them to continue their dialogue or carry out their conciliatory plans, it may be necessary to plan ways of informing others in the organization about the outcomes of the dialogue or to confront others about their lack of support. If participants have strong feelings about keeping their confrontation confidential, their wishes should be respected. In any case, the follow-up behaviors of consultant and clients alike should be clear before a confrontation meeting is regarded as complete.

A third means of ensuring continuation of the dialogue or implementation of action-plans is simply to "stick around." Just being available may give the parties confidence or remind them of agreements they have made. If the consultant cannot be present continually, it may be wise to build another third party into the process at the beginning. If participants and the extra third party are willing, all may attend the initial encounter to become more familiar with the procedures of third-party consultation. Of course, the most obvious way of facilitating follow-through is to ensure that the parties make an appointment to get together again, making clear both the time and the purpose of the future meeting.

PROCESS OBSERVATION AND FEEDBACK DESIGNS

Much has been written about process observation and feedback (or more simply, process consultation) because many consultants believe that they constitute the heart of any macrodesign.* Designs for

---

*Some ideas in this section are treated in greater detail by Schein and Bennis (1965), and Schein (1969).

process consultation focus strongly on the immediate functioning of the group and reflect the view that effective functioning is inseparable from the group's ability to see its problems while actually working on them. Otherwise uninvolved in the group's task, OD consultants monitor group processes and individual behaviors and present the data so collected in the form of behavior descriptions, questions, hypotheses, or speculations about why the group works as it does. Consultants encourage participants to report their own observations and attempt at the same time to shift attention from a consideration of tasks to a consideration of processes.

In contrast to training designs, process observation and feedback designs emphasize the inductive approach to learning. By reflecting on many behaviors in one meeting or on many phenomena over several meetings, group members increasingly understand how to improve their methods of working together. In contrast to the trainer, the process observer maintains a low profile, is generally nondirective, reacts to what is happening rather than to what should be happening, and intervenes to help solve a particular process problem rather than to help beef up group functioning in general.

Foci. The titles of chapters 3 through 8 suggest one basic set of foci for process observation and feedback. As the theme of a particular event, the consultant may choose the group's interpersonal relationships. Calling a group's attention to its cliques and coalitions, for example, leads to a different kind of discussion than do comments about dispersion of influence, struggle between group goals and individual satisfactions, clarity of communication, or phases of problem solving. Interpersonal or group process may also be enriched by focusing on the structure of the organization, including its integration and differentiation of roles, allocation and limitations of material resources, time-task relationships, intergroup linkages, and the like.

Opportunities. The strategy of process observation and feedback involves making the group aware of its own dynamics, usually by getting a discussion of process on its agenda. During the initial consultative events it may be suggested that fifteen minutes be allocated for a process debriefing at the end of a meeting; during the later stages, consultants can offer their own comments when any group member makes an observation about group processes. It may take repeated efforts before a group will agree to an agenda item for discussing how they worked together on other agenda items, but getting them to do so is the process observer's basic function and responsibility.

Because of the immediacy of observational feedback, the process observer seldom has the luxury of building a design with as much care as the trainer, of analyzing data with as much leisure as the feeder back of data, or of structuring a meeting to the extent that a third-party consultant must. At the same time, however, any occurrence in a group provides the process observer an opportunity for feedback, and this quality of "winging it" often gives process consultation an advantage in flexibility. By this means clients come to

use their own learnings, to invent creative solutions to their problems, and to find the zeal and confidence to continue. In addition,
process consultation can easily include time for clients to analyze
and criticize both the behaviors of the consultants and the overall
nature of the consultation itself.

Timing.   Knowing when to comment on a group event and when to
let it pass is a crucial skill for a process observer, and its effective
exercise depends upon several factors. Consider, for example, the
observer who, having the group's permission to interrupt whenever
something "significant" occurs, notices that one member has interrupted another member for the third time in a half-hour.

First, the observer must judge how ready the group is to consider its interpersonal processes at this point. If a slow meeting has
only just begun to accelerate, the time may be wrong for process
examination; if the interrupted member has complained about interruptions in the past, however, the time may be right. In any event,
a group will ignore a consultant's comments until its members are
ready for them, and nothing is gained by premature feedback that is
ignored or resisted. If the observed event is genuinely significant, it
is likely to recur repeatedly.

Second, observers must take their own feelings into account,
recognizing that body language may reveal these feelings to clients
and therefore make them the property of the group. Whether to be
transparent or opaque about such feelings is a matter of personal
preference. Some observers prefer to initiate a process discussion by
saying, "I feel uncomfortable because Joe has interrupted Maria
three times so far"; others will prefer to ask Maria how she feels
about being interrupted or may ask the total group to discuss who
has spoken, who has been interrupted, and who has remained quiet.
Although the choice between relative opacity or transparency is
largely one of style, consultants should be aware that the choice is
theirs and should pay attention to the consequences for the group of
speaking out or remaining silent about their own internal state.

Third, process observers may decide either to offer or to withhold feedback in the interests of dependency reduction. The ultimate
aim of OD consultants is to work themselves out of a job by building
into the organization a capability for monitoring its own processes
and eliciting its own feedback. Thus, on one occasion, observers may
withhold feedback to allow a group member with skill and understanding to do so instead; on other occasions they may encourage a
group to examine a particular phenomenon in order to sensitize
members to that kind of issue, to reinforce something previously
taught, or to model appropriate ways of giving feedback. In both
cases the rationale centers ultimately on dependency reduction.

In addition to group readiness, the consultant's preference for
personal transparency or opacity, and the need to reduce client
dependency, a fourth factor depends upon the culture of the group.
Groups that regard the singling out of individuals as taboo, for
example, are not likely to appreciate attempts at behavior descrip-

tion or impression checking. Some groups are more apt to discuss their processes when regularly interrupted to do so, while others seem to profit more from widely spaced interventions. Faculty groups that maintain a slow steady pace and whose norms militate against contributions that lack citations of literary, historical, sociological, or biological data will prefer feedback that is rich in abstract concepts and observable behaviors, while a quickly paced group may profit more from feedback given in small bits.

Although we have spoken throughout this chapter as if OD consultants alone make decisions about microdesigning, we recognize that they value taking a collaborative stance with clients in the real world. For that reason, this chapter concludes with a brief section on ways of working with clients as an intervention is designed, implemented, and evaluated.

INVOLVING CLIENTS IN MICRODESIGNING

To the extent that diagnostic data are collected and used, clients can be said to influence the designing process before a consultative event actually begins. But there are several more direct ways in which the consultant can allow clients to influence the event in its early stages. Prior interviews that assess the group's organizational, group-process, and interpersonal problems can also provide information about what the consultant should or should not do during the consultation. During interviews, for example, we have asked clients whether they prefer to work all together or in small groups most of the time. In questionnaires we have asked for advice about when and where workshops and retreats should be held. We have also begun a few training sessions by proposing several different designs and asking clients which would best suit their needs.

Clients can also greatly influence microdesigning in the course of a consultative event. For example, they might refuse to record all their ideas on newsprint but choose instead to record only each person's best idea. They may choose to interrupt the consultant during a feedback presentation instead of waiting until the end; or, as in one of our more devastating experiences, they may reject the consultants' proposals in favor of using the time in their own way. Consultants who pay attention to the clients' behaviors during a consultative event can collect a great deal of diagnostic data for later use; indeed, all the factors related to the timing of process observation and feedback have application in this regard.

The importance of involving clients in the designing process in the interests of increasing a staff's capacity for self-renewal has been abundantly demonstrated by our own experience* and by much research as well. In a study supported by the Rand Corporation, Berman and McLaughlin (1975) coined the phrase *mutual adaptation*

---

*For example, review the collaboratively built follow-up design for our project with multi-unit schools described in chapter 9.

to describe a condition in which a project is modified to fit a local school situation at the same time that the local school is changing in the direction of project goals. They found, in addition, that this condition is associated with a number of other conditions.

First, projects which clients view from the beginning as responsive to their needs and as a means of solving their problems have much more staying power than those that begin merely because money or other resources are available. Second, it is important that the project be supported from the beginning by group members whom others regard as having a thorough knowledge of particular local conditions; in other words, most clients believe that the suitability of a project depends primarily upon local conditions. Third, and most important for this consideration of client involvement in designing, mutual adaptation is accompanied by a planning process that establishes channels of communication between project staff and clients, sets forth initial goals and objectives with the assistance of representatives of the client group, and is maintained continually throughout the project.

Fourth, it is important that practical, how-to-do-it, here-and-now topics have precedence over theoretical or inspirational content during the course of the project. Both design and consultant are likely to be judged unfavorably if they do not meet the clients' immediate needs. Fifth, projects are most often successful when they include what Berman and McLaughlin call "local development of materials." That is, the quality of the finished product, whether it is to be an understanding of what is going on in the organization or a document outlining group agreements, is much less important than is the chance to participate in developing the product. Sixth, mutually adaptive planning and mutually adaptive interventions are likely to occur only when a critical mass of individual staff members is involved.

Finally, we believe that by asking clients to collaborate in the designing process and to criticize the design before it is executed, while it is in progress, and after it is completed, consultants can gain important information that will enable them to do a better job next time. We believe that clients will take the risks involved in criticizing and evaluating if time is allowed for this purpose and if consultants are receptive to their feedback. Collaborative planning can begin by asking clients what they think can be done to meet a list of intervention goals and by referring back to these goals during postintervention debriefing, asking to what degree each has, in fact, been met. Another method of ensuring that clients give feedback to the consultants is for clients to help design a postmeeting reaction questionnaire before the event begins and to use this questionnaire when the session is ended.

Collaboration is not over five minutes after the last microintervention is ended. Chapter 11 explains how it continues as summative evaluations are completed. Chapter 12 describes how clients and consultants make joint decisions concerning how to institutionalize the OD capacity in the client group before the consultants have exited.

READINGS

Rules of Thumb for Change Agents

Herbert A. Shepard

In the following reading, Herbert A. Shepard tells neophytes and old pros alike what to keep in mind as they attempt to bring about change. Shepard, whose account is informed by his many experiences as a consultant, writes with both specificity and humor. Following his advice can save many consultants from disaster.

Herbert A. Shepard, "Rules of Thumb for Change Agents," *OD Practitioner* 7 (3), November 1975.

The following aphorisms are not so much bits of advice (although they are stated that way) as things to think about when you are being a change agent, a consultant, an organization or community development practitioner—or when you are just being yourself trying to bring about something that involves other people.

RULE I: STAY ALIVE

This rule counsels against self-sacrifice on behalf of a cause that you do not wish to be your last.

Two exceptionally talented doctoral students came to the conclusion that the routines they had to go through to get their degrees were absurd, and decided they would be untrue to themselves to conform to an absurd system. That sort of reasoning is almost always self-destructive. Besides, their noble gesture in quitting would be unlikely to have any impact whatever on the system they were taking a stand against.

This is not to say that one should never take a stand or a survival risk. But such risks should be taken as part of a purposeful strategy of change, and appropriately timed and targeted. When they are taken under such circumstances, one is very much alive.

But Rule I is much more than a survival rule. The rule means that you should let your whole being be involved in the undertaking. Since most of us have never been in touch with our whole beings, it means a lot of putting together of parts that have been divided, of using internal communications channels that have been closed or were never opened.

Staying alive means loving yourself. Self-disparagement leads to the suppression of potentials, to a win-lose formulation of the world, and to wasting life in defensive maneuvering.

Staying alive means staying in touch with your purpose. It means using your skills, your emotions, your labels and positions, rather than being used by them. It means not being trapped in other people's games. It means turning yourself on and off, rather than being dependent on the situation. It means choosing with a view to the consequences as well as the impulse. It means going with the flow even while swimming against it. It means living in several worlds without being swallowed up in any. It means seeing dilemmas as opportunities for creativity. It means greeting absurdity with laughter while trying to unscramble it. It means capturing the moment in the light of the future. It means seeing the environment through the eyes of your purpose.

RULE II: START WHERE THE SYSTEM IS

This is such ancient wisdom that one might expect its meaning had been fully explored and apprehended. Yet in practice the rule—and the system—are often violated.

The rule implies that one should begin by diagnosing the system. But systems do not necessarily *like* being diagnosed. Even the *term* "diagnosis" may be offensive. And the system may be even less ready for someone who calls himself or herself a "change agent." It is easy for the practitioner to forget that the use of jargon which prevents laymen from understanding the professional mysteries is a hostile act.

Starting where the system is can be called the Empathy Rule. To communicate effectively, to obtain a basis for building sound strategy, the change agent needs to understand how the client sees himself and his situation, and needs to understand the culture of the system. Establishing the required rapport does not mean that the change agent who wants to work in a traditional industrial setting should refrain from growing a beard. It does mean that, if he has a beard, the beard is likely to determine where the client is when they first meet, and the client's curiosity needs to be dealt with. Similarly, the rule does not mean that a female change agent in a male organization should try to act like one of the boys, or that a young change agent should try to act like a senior executive. One thing it does mean is that sometimes where the client is, is wondering where the change agent is.

Rarely is the client in any one place at any one time. That is, s/he may be ready to pursue any of several paths. The task is to walk together on the most promising path.

Even unwitting or accidental violations of the empathy rule can destroy the situation. I lost a client through two violations in one morning. The client group spent a consulting day at my home. They arrived early in the morning, before I had my empathy on. The senior member, seeing a picture of my son in the living-room, said, "What do you do with boys with long hair?" I replied thoughtlessly, "I think he's handsome that way." The small chasm thus created between my client and me was widened and deepened later that morning when one of the family tortoises walked through the butter dish.

Sometimes starting where the client is, which sounds both ethically and technically virtuous, can lead to some ethically puzzling situations. Robert Frost* described a situation in which a consultant was so empathic with a king who was unfit to rule that the king discovered his own unfitness and had himself shot, whereupon the consultant became king.

Empathy permits the development of a mutual attachment between client and consultant. The resulting relationship may be one in which their creativities are joined, a mutual growth relationship. But it can also become one in which the client becomes dependent and is manipulated by the consultant. The ethical issues are not associated with starting where the system is, but with how one moves with it.

RULE III: NEVER WORK UPHILL

This is a comprehensive rule, and a number of other rules are corollaries or examples of it. It is an appeal for an organic rather than a mechanistic approach to change, for building strength and building on strength. It has a number of implications that bear on the choices the change agent makes about how to use him/herself, and it says something about life.

Corollary 1: Don't Build Hills as You Go

This corollary cautions against working in a way that builds resistance to movement in the direction you have chosen as desirable. For example, a program which has a favorable effect on one portion of a population may have the opposite effect on other portions of the population. Perhaps the commonest error of this kind has been in the employment of T-group training in organizations: turning on the participants and turning off the people who didn't attend, in one easy lesson.

Corollary 2: Work in the Most Promising Arena

The physician-patient relationship is often regarded as analogous to the consultant-client relationship. The results for system change of this analogy can be unfortunate. For example, the organization development consultant is likely to be greeted with delight by executives who see in his specialty the solution to a hopeless situation in an outlying plant. Some organization development consultants have disappeared for years because of the irresistability of such challenges. Others have whiled away their time trying to counteract the Peter Principle by shoring up incompetent managers.

---

* Robert Frost, "How Hard It Is To Keep From Being Kind When It's in You and in the Situation." In The Clearing, pp. 74-84. New York: Holt, Rinehart and Winston (1962).

Corollary 3: Build Resources

Don't do anything alone that could be accomplished more easily or more certainly by a team. Don Quixote is not the only change agent whose effectiveness was handicapped by ignoring this rule. The change agent's task is an heroic one, but the need to be a hero does not facilitate team building. As a result, many change agents lose effectiveness by becoming spread too thin. Effectiveness can be enhanced by investing in the development of partners.

Corollary 4: Don't Overorganize

The democratic ideology and theories of participative management that many change agents possess can sometimes interfere with common sense. A year or two ago I offered a course, to be taught by graduate students. The course was oversubscribed. It seemed that a data-based process for deciding whom to admit would be desirable, and that participation of the graduate students in the decision would also be desirable. So I sought data from the candidates about themselves, and Xeroxed their responses for the graduate students. Then the graduate students and I held a series of meetings. Then the candidates were informed of the decision. In this way we wasted a great deal of time and everyone felt a little worse than if we had used an arbitrary decision rule.

Corollary 5: Don't Argue if You Can't Win

Win-lose strategies are to be avoided because they deepen conflict instead of resolving it. But the change agent should build her/his support constituency as large and deep and strong as possible so that s/he can continue to risk.

Corollary 6: Play God a Little

If the change agent doesn't make the critical value decisions, someone else will be happy to do so. Will a given situation contribute to your fulfillment? Are you creating a better world for yourself and others, or are you keeping a system in operation that should be allowed to die? For example, the public education system is a mess. Does that mean that the change agent is morally obligated to try to improve it, destroy it, or develop a substitute for it? No, not even if he or she knows how. But the change agent does need a value perspective for making choices like that.

RULE IV: INNOVATION REQUIRES A GOOD IDEA, INITIATIVE, AND A FEW FRIENDS

Little can be accomplished alone, and the effects of social and cultural forces on individual perception are so distorting that the change agent needs a partner, if only to maintain perspective and purpose.

The quality of the partner is as important as the quality of the idea. Like the change agent, partners must be relatively autonomous people. Persons who are authority-oriented—who need to rebel or need to submit—are not reliable partners: the rebels take the wrong risks and the good soldiers don't take any. And rarely do they command the respect and trust from others that is needed if an innovation is to be supported.

The partners need not be numerous. For example, the engineering staff of a chemical company designed a new process plant using edge-of-the-art technology. The design departed radically from the experience of top management, and they were about to reject it. The engineering chief suggested that the design be reviewed by a distinguished engineering professor. The principal designers were in fact former students of the professor. For this reason he accepted the assignment, charged the company a large fee for reviewing the design (which he did not trouble to examine), and told the management that it was brilliantly conceived and executed. By this means the engineers not only implemented their innovations, but also grew in the esteem of their management.

A change agent experienced in the Washington environment reports that he knows of only one case of successful interdepartmental collaboration in mutually designing, funding and managing a joint project. It was accomplished through the collaboration of himself and three similarly-minded young men, one from each of four agencies. They were friends, and met weekly for lunch. They conceived the project, and planned strategies for implementing it. Each person undertook to interest and influence the relevant key people in his own agency. The four served one another as consultants and helpers in influencing opinion and bringing the decision-makers together.

An alternative statement of Rule IV is as follows: Find the people who are ready and able to work, introduce them to one another, and work with them. Perhaps because many change agents have been trained in the helping professions, perhaps because we have all been trained to think bureaucratically, concepts like organization position, representativeness or need are likely to guide the change agent's selection of those he or she works with.

A more powerful beginning can sometimes be made by finding those persons in the system whose values are congruent with those of the change agent, who possess vitality and imagination, who are willing to work overtime, and who are eager to learn. Such people are usually glad to have someone like the change agent join in getting something important accomplished, and a careful search is likely to turn up quite a few. In fact, there may be enough of them to accomplish general system change, if they can team up in appropriate ways.

In building such teamwork the change agent's abilities will be fully challenged as he joins them in establishing conditions for trust and creativity; dealing with their anxieties about being seen as subversive, enhancing their leadership, consulting, problem-solving, diagnosing and innovating skills; and developing appropriate group norms and policies.

RULE V: LOAD EXPERIMENTS FOR SUCCESS

This sounds like counsel to avoid risk taking. But the decision to experiment always entails risk. After that decision has been made, take all precautions.

The rule also sounds scientifically immoral. But whether an experiment produces the expected results depends upon the experimenter's depth of insight into the conditions and processes involved. Of course, what is experimental is what is new to the system; it may or may not be new to the change agent.

Build an umbrella over the experiment. A chemical process plant which was to be shut down because of the inefficiency of its operations undertook a union-management cooperation project to improve efficiency, which involved a modified form of profit-sharing. Such plans were contrary to company policy, but the regional vice president was interested in the experiment, and successfully concealed it from his associates. The experiment was successful; the plant became profitable. But in this case, the umbrella turned out not to be big enough. The plant was shut down anyway.

Use the Hawthorne effect. Even poorly conceived experiments are often made to succeed when the participants feel ownership. And conversely, one of the obstacles to the spread of useful innovations is that the groups to which they are offered do not feel ownership of them.

For example, if the change agent hopes to use experience-based learning as part of his/her strategy, the first persons to be invited should be those who consistently turn all their experiences into constructive learning. Similarly, in introducing team development processes into a system, begin with the best functioning team.

Maintain voluntarism. This is not easy to do in systems where invitations are understood to be commands, but nothing vital can be built on such motives as duty, obedience, security-seeking or responsiveness to social pressure.

RULE VI: LIGHT MANY FIRES

Not only does a large, monolithic development or change program have high visibility and other qualities of a good target, it also tends to prevent subsystems from feeling ownership of, and consequent commitment to, the program.

The meaning of this rule is more orderly than the random prescription—light many fires—suggests. Any part of a system is the way it is partly because of the way the rest of the system is. To work toward change in one subsystem is to become one more determinant of its performance. Not only is the change agent working uphill, but as soon as he turns his back, other forces in the system will press the subsystem back toward its previous performance mode.

If many interdependent subsystems are catalyzed, and the change agent brings them together to facilitate one another's efforts, the entire system can begin to move.

Understanding patterns of interdependency among subsystems can lead to a strategy of fire-setting. For example, in public school systems it requires collaboration among politicians, administrators, teachers, parents and students to bring about significant innovation, and active opposition on the part of only one of these groups to prevent it. In parochial school systems, on the other hand, collaboration between the administration and the church can provide a powerful impetus for change in the other groups.

RULE VII: KEEP AN OPTIMISTIC BIAS

Our society grinds along with much polarization and cruelty, and even the helping professions compose their world of grim problems to be "worked through." The change agent is usually flooded with the destructive aspects of the situations he enters. People in most systems are impressed by one another's weaknesses, and stereotype each other with such incompetencies as they can discover.

This rule does not advise ignoring destructive forces. But its positive prescription is that the change agent be especially alert to the constructive forces which are often masked and suppressed in a problem-oriented, envious culture.

People have as great an innate capacity for joy as for resentment, but resentment causes them to overlook opportunities for joy. In a workshop for married couples, a husband and wife were discussing their sexual problem and how hard they were working to solve it. They were not making much progress, since they didn't realize that sex is not a problem, but an opportunity.

Individuals and groups locked in destructive kinds of conflict focus on their differences. The change agent's job is to help them discover and build on their commonalities, so that they will have a foundation of respect and trust which will permit them to use their differences as a source of creativity. The unhappy partners focus on past hurts, and continue to destroy the present and future with them. The change agent's job is to help them change the present so that they will have a new past on which to create a better future.

RULE VIII: CAPTURE THE MOMENT

A good sense of relevance and timing is often treated as though it were a "gift" or "intuition" rather than something that can be learned, something spontaneous rather than something planned. The opposite is nearer the truth. One is more likely to "capture the moment" when everything one has learned is readily available.

Some years ago my wife and I were having a very destructive fight. Our nine-year-old daughter decided to intervene. She put her arms around her mother and asked: "What does Daddy do that bugs you?" She was an attentive audience for the next few minutes while my wife told her, ending in tears. She then put her arms around me:

"What does Mommy do that bugs you?" and listened attentively to my response, which also ended in tears. She then went to the record player and put on a favorite love song ("If Ever I Should Leave You"), and left us alone to make up.

The elements of my daughter's intervention had all been learned. They were available to her, and she combined them in a way that could make the moment better.

Perhaps it's our training in linear cause-and-effect thinking and the neglect of our capacities for imagery that makes us so often unable to see the multiple potential of the moment. Entering the situation "blank" is not the answer. One needs to have as many frameworks for seeing and strategies for acting available as possible. But it's not enough to involve only one's head in the situation; one's heart has to get involved too. Cornelia Otis Skinner once said that the first law of the stage is to love your audience. You can love your audience only if you love yourself. If you have relatively full access to your organized experience, to yourself and to the situation, you will capture the moment more often.

Bringing a School Staff and Parents into Effective Interaction

Jane H. Arends and Richard I. Arends

This reading summarizes a much longer paper describing the process and outcomes of an intervention that we helped carry out during the 1971/72 school year. The consultant team included members of the Program on Strategies of Organizational Change and representatives of a school-district cadre of OD specialists like the one described in detail in chapter 12. The reading is included at this point to illustrate some of the detailed planning that is required for microdesigns of OD interventions.

Prepared especially for this volume.

THE CONTEXT OF THE MICRODESIGN

Thomas Elementary School, one of 32 elementary and twelve secondary schools in the district, had a student population of 250 that was drawn from a middle and upper-middle-class neighborhood. Students had traditionally scored well above national norms for achievement and both the parents and staff had expressed pleasure with the school's academic rigor for a number of years.

In the early seventies, some parents began to echo the concerns of popular educational critics who argued for parent involvement and humanized education. About 90 of these parents at Thomas School attended informal neighborhood meetings in the fall of 1971 to discuss concerns they had with the school. The outgrowth of these meetings was the formation of a group that called itself the Parents' Advisory Committee.

The Committee sent a letter to the school's principal in November that described "wide-spread concerns with school-to-parent communication, curriculum—especially in the arts—and the quality of the staff and its training." The principal passed on the letter to the twelve teachers in the school who greeted it with disbelief, resentment, and disappointment. The principal then called upon the coordinator of the district's cadre, asking for "assistance in dealing with the parents' complaints."

The coordinator of the cadre called together a team of consultants from inside and outside the district to outline a macrodesign that would guide the intervention. The team came up with a design that had as its overall theme a confrontation between parents and teachers. Within the basic theme were elements of training, data feedback, and process observation and feedback. The macrodesign included the following six stages:

Stage 1: Form and meet with a Steering Committee comprised of some teachers and a few parents to explain the macrodesign and get approval to proceed.

Stage 2: Provide demonstrations of OD to the staff and to all interested parents so they understand the goals and procedures of the intervention.

Stage 3: Train parents and staff separately in the skills of interpersonal communication and group problem solving and help each group identify top-priority concerns. Collect data on impressions of intergroup climate and influence.

Stage 4: Bring the two groups together and feed back data on climate, concerns, and influence. Help the groups clarify intergroup communication and agree upon top-priority mutual concerns.

Stage 5: Form problem-solving groups of parents and teachers to design proposals to solve important mutual problems. Serve as process consultants to these groups.

Stage 6: Bring all problem-solving groups together to share their proposals and to make decisions and plans for implementation.

According to the macrodesign, Stage 1 was to begin in November and Stage 6 was to be completed by June of the same school year.

FEATURES OF THE MICRODESIGN

The six stages of the macrodesign did get carried out as scheduled. The following sections describe the microdesign elements that made that possible. This article concludes with a description of the intervention's outcomes and some ideas of things to consider when tailoring the design for other situations.

Meeting with the Steering Committee

On December 14, the consultants met with the newly-formed Steering Committee, a group comprised of three teachers, the principal and seven parents. The principal had identified these people as representative of the school and community and as both influential and energetic in their respective groups. Giving special attention to the parents' impressions of the needs of the school and the consultants' definition of their role, the two-hour meeting began with a presentation and discussion of the macrodesign. Steering Committee members were surveyed and agreed that the consultants should proceed with the demonstration events. Parents on the committee agreed to extend invitations to other parents and the principal agreed to have the consultants attend the next faculty meeting. All Steering Committee members agreed to meet about once a month throughout the school year to discuss progress with the intervention and to give feedback to the consultants.

Demonstration Events for the Staff and Interested Parents

Two members of the consultant team met with the total staff the following week. After informing the staff of decisions made by the Steering Committee, the principal introduced the consultants. The demonstration meeting had two main purposes: to explain OD and the consultants' roles and to elicit the staff's commitment to proceed. A slide-tape presentation on OD, a lecturette on consultants as multi-partisan helping agents,* and a question-and-answer session served the first purpose. A total group discussion that concluded with a survey of individuals served the second.

The survey revealed that staff members were generally hesitant and unwilling to become involved because they were concerned about the time it would take for training, whether the parents already involved were "truly representative of all parents," and whether they "as professionals" should listen and respond to parents. In addition, the consultants became aware of the fact that teachers did not trust each other to take a united stand should parents' demands be difficult to implement. The consultants paraphrased these concerns, but did not attempt to influence the staff, but the principal did *not* take the same stance; he pressed the staff to approve of the project, saying, "We really have no other choice." A second survey showed that all teachers were willing to proceed but were skeptical about possible outcomes.

The first demonstration event for parents occurred at an evening meeting attended by 51 parents. The PTA president and the principal opened the meeting with a short business session and introduced the

---

* Multi-partisan helping agents was a term coined by the consultants for this intervention to emphasize that (a) they would not side with parents to attack the staff any more than they would side with the staff to ignore parents' demands, and (b) they were group process and organizational consultants who would not tell teachers how they ought to teach or parents what to do in the school.

consultants. After the consultants gave a brief history of the intervention to date, described the interests and roles of the consultants, presented a slide-tape show explaining OD, and outlined the macrodesign, parents formed small groups with members of the consultant team for question-and-answer sessions. A summary of each group's discussion was reported to the total group after about half an hour.

The summaries revealed skepticism on the parents as to the staff's commitment and ways to involve other parents. Recognizing a need to keep other parents informed and at the same time to avoid spending a lot of time continually bringing newcomers on board, the parents agreed that all parents should be informed of a second demonstration and that attendance at this or the next meeting be considered a prerequisite for being on the mailing list for future involvement. Parents on the Steering Committee ended the meeting by agreeing to send out invitations to all parents for the next meeting.

The second demonstration for about 50 parents began with a review of what had happened at the first meeting to bring the 15 newcomers up to date. A lecturette on S-T-P problem solving was followed by work in pairs to describe frustrating situations and valued targets. After 20 minutes with two different partners, parents formed eight groups to list common situations and targets on newsprint. The consultants urged paraphrasing and describing situations and targets in behavioral terms. The evening concluded as some parents volunteered to host training seminars for parents in their homes and all were given a questionnaire intended to elicit their impressions of who had influence in the school as well as handouts on S-T-P problem solving, communication skills, and an article on defensive communication (Gibb 1961).

Training for Staff and Parents

Training for the staff occurred at a two-day workshop in January when teachers had released time to prepare semester reports. The session began as communication skills were introduced through an exercise which required three groups of teachers to build Tinkertoy models depicting how staff members typically communicated with each other. After the models were assembled non-verbally, the staff used communication skills to describe what they represented. During the second half of the first day, staff members completed the Group Expectations Survey and were interviewed individually by the consultants. The second day began with feedback of data collected and a lecturette on S-T-P problem solving. The staff formed small groups to more precisely define problems related to staff and parent relationships. The consultants urged the staff to postpone brainstorming solutions until the gap between situation and targets was clear. The day concluded with practice in small-group problem solving using the Five-Square puzzle exercise and as staff members listed their individual resources on large sheets of newsprint.

In early February, eleven seminars for groups of four to six parents each were hosted in the homes of volunteer parents. Warm-up exercises and introductions were followed by reviews of communication skills. Parents then described experiences they had had at the school so all could practice the skills. After the S-T-P problem-solving model was reviewed, parents summarized their experiences as a definition of the situation and listed their individual goals. By paraphrasing and surveying, the interest which others had in their individual goals was ascertained.

There was more training for staff members as they met later in the month for two hours after school in three small groups. These meetings included time for additional practice in communication skills and S-T-P problem solving as well as time to administer the questionnaire on impressions of influence that had been given to parents.

Identifying Mutual Problems

In March a seven-hour meeting was held at the school in the afternoon and evening for parents and the staff.* The session began with feedback of data collected through the questionnaire on influence. The consultants emphasized that both groups saw the other as more influential than either saw itself and explained that this protocol is usually indicative of a history of poor communication. One trainer was assigned to meet latecomers at the door to catch them up; approximately 45 parents and thirteen staff members were present when the session began and only five or six parents came late.

The Imaging exercise proceeded through the following six steps:

Step 1: Parents and staff went to separate rooms to verify lists of helpful and unhelpful behaviors they thought the other group exhibited. These lists had been prepared in advance by the consultants as their summaries of the comments which had been repeatedly voiced by parents and teachers in earlier sessions. Each group modified its list until they found it acceptable.

Step 2: The two groups came back to the large multipurpose room and sat in chairs that had been arranged so five parents in the front of the parent group would face five staff members in front of their group. The groups took turns presenting items from their lists and a member of the receiving group was asked to paraphrase as each item was read. The consultants did not allow debate, explanation or justification of any item. Twice during the session, participants played "musical chairs" so new people got the front-row seats where they were allowed to talk. This structure was designed to equalize participation between two groups that were very unequal in size.

Step 3: The two groups again went to separate rooms for an hour to discuss examples of their own behaviors that might have contributed

---

*Students were sent home at noon so teachers and parents could be ready at 3:00. Parents had arranged for their own babysitters at home and the Steering Committee had called everyone to bring something for a potluck supper.

to the other group's image of them. The consultants urged them to avoid defensiveness and to concentrate on why they had been viewed as unhelpful rather than to insist that they hadn't wanted to be.

Step 4: The parent group and the staff each picked six people to represent them in reporting the discussions that had occurred in step 3. The twelve representatives sat in a Fishbowl for this discussion. Parents and staff members took turns reporting items from their lists and a paraphrase was allowed and encouraged after each item.

Step 5: The consultants reported five target areas they had summarized from all earlier staff and parent comments. Participants then divided into four groups in the four corners of the room: parents and teachers of first and second graders, parents and teachers of third and fourth graders, parents and teachers of fifth and six graders, and the principal and auxiliary staff with the parents from the Steering Committee. Each group listed five to ten major issues they wished to see become topics for collaborative problem solving. Each problem was stated in the form, "There is a lack of" and was written on newsprint.

Step 6: Members of the consultant team, in a Fishbowl, summarized the issues raised in the four groups. One consultant acted as convener until the 40 specific problem statements were combined into a list of seven. The seven were listed on separate sheets of newsprint and parents and staff members signed up to work on the one that interested them most. The Steering Committee members spread themselves among the seven groups and agreed to serve as linkers across the groups over the next two months.

Joint Problem-solving Groups

During March and April, the seven problem-solving groups comprised of five to eight parents and one or two staff members met five times in homes of parents. Each group chose its own convener and recorder and had the same consultant each time. During the course of the two months, each group made and worked with its own procedural agreements, carefully defined its problem, considered facilitating and restraining forces operating on the problem and its ability to find solutions, and located resources that might be brought to bear to solve the problem. One group prepared a questionnaire which its members administered to other parents and students while other groups contacted people in other schools and the district's central office whom they had identified as appropriate technical consultants. Each group brainstormed possible solutions to its problem and planned what would be required in terms of financial, physical and human resources if its proposal gained acceptance from others.

Total Community Sharing

At the last regularly-scheduled PTA meeting of the year—in May —each group presented its proposal. The meeting was planned and convened by members of the Steering Committee so that proposals could be considered in some logical sequence. The proposal to restructure the PTA and to write a new constitution was quickly adopted and followed by election of PTA officers. Proposals to establish a parent volunteer program, make improvements to the building and grounds, and to start an after-school program for students, an artist-in-residence program, a handbook for students and parents, a regular newsletter, and a party for welcoming new and foreign families were then presented and adopted. Parents and staff members then signed up for committees that would oversee implementation of the proposals. The evening ended as the new PTA president convened a Fishbowl meeting of PTA officers to review summer activities.

OUTCOMES OF THE INTERVENTION

Three kinds of outcomes of the intervention were documented by the consultant team with methods that included follow-up interviews with 40 participants in March of 1973. The first set of outcomes had to do with implementation of proposals designed by the parent-staff problem-solving groups. Within a year, there were: (1) a new parent organization that included parents in the process of making decisions about curriculum and staffing, (2) new forms of written communication from school to home, (3) improvements to the building and grounds, (4) parties for welcoming new and foreign families to the community and school, (5) many parent volunteers in classrooms and the library, and (6) an artist-in-residence program. Parents and teachers favorably evaluated these innovations.

A second set of outcomes had to do with improvements in the climate of interaction between staff and parents and in the climate of interactions among staff members. After the intervention, parents reported that they had better impressions of the school, could now get the information they wanted, and that they thought their input was welcomed by the staff. When asked about changes that they saw in the school, more than two-thirds of the parents singled out the atmosphere as being very different.

Staff members reported being much more comfortable about having parents in the school, inquiring about the school's activities, and being effective in the PTA. Teachers did not totally endorse parental participation in other than subordinate roles as volunteer aides, but they did appreciate the efforts of some parents to make the library a more accessible place for students. In addition, over two-thirds of the staff reported a year later that working conditions and relationships within the school had improved. They were proud of their first steps at team planning and thought that their individual resources were being put to better use since they had started communicating openly with each other.

The third set of ourcomes concerned changes in perceived and attributed influence. Parents perceived an increase in their own influence after the intervention and did so without attributing less influence to the staff. Staff members, by contrast, didn't think they had gained or lost influence but attributed more influence to parents. To both parents and the staff, the PTA in its new structure was the vehicle through which the total amount of influence available to be shared had been increased.

CONSIDERATIONS FOR TAILORING

What happened at Thomas School cannot be expected to occur without alteration in other settings. In this case, the involved parents were motivated and competent to confront and collaborate with the staff even though they had been frustrated in their prior efforts to do so. In addition, the staff came to realize—quite early in the intervention—that confrontation and collaboration were inevitable and not as painful as they had expected them to be. Important questions remain, however.

(1) What happens with a staff that has even stronger norms in support of autonomy, lower competence in interpersonal and problem-solving skills, a greater inability to recognize the implications of their posture, and more unwillingness to regard the parents' efforts as legitimate than the staff at Thomas School?

(2) What happens when parents are not motivated or competent to make their wishes known, to suggest proposals to remedy important problems, or to pitch in and help implement new programs?

(3) What happens when it is impossible to form a consultant team of district personnel who have credibility and legitimacy with the staff and outsiders who have credibility and legitimacy with parents?

(4) What happens with logistics when a higher percentage of parents are employed in nine-to-five jobs, are spread over a much larger community than was the case at Thomas, don't have phones, or don't volunteer their homes as meeting places?

(5) What happens if the school, instead of being one of the "best" in the district, is known to be one of the "worst," so that parents and staff members feel discouraged at the outset and have to deal with basic needs before being creative about new, add-on programs?

(6) What happens where there is more diversity within the community so that finding a representative group of parents is a chore rather than a fairly easy task?

Some of the consultants who carried out this intervention began almost immediately to seek answers to these questions. And some of the answers were forthcoming after an intervention conducted by some of the members of the team during the 1973/74 school year.* In this second intervention—another pilot effort in the sense that it

---

* For details of the process and outcomes of this second intervention, see Arends (1975).

was the team's first in an inner-city school serving seventh and eighth grade students—the outcomes sought were not achieved. Efforts to establish a Steering Committee to oversee the project were abandoned midway through the year and efforts to train a group of teachers as group facilitators were to no avail in the sense that the group disbanded as soon as the consultant team left. Nonetheless, several lessons were learned in this project that answered questions left over from the Thomas School intervention. These lessons were derived both from inferences grounded in the comments of participants and by comparing the project to the "ideal" described in theory and research on OD in schools. Seven major lessons were:

1. Involve the total staff in decisions to conduct a demonstration event about the OD process. Don't take the word of a few—even if they are administrators—to decide that the staff is ready to be helped.

2. Retain initiative for contacting parents until the staff or other parents volunteer to take over this function. Don't leave notification of parents about meetings to chance.

3. Provide training to volunteer subsystems or to ad hoc groups of individual volunteers. You need not wait until the whole staff is ready to be helpful to some people about some things.

4. Establish new subsystems only when a "critical mass" of the staff agrees and funding to continue training is assured. Don't start to build a new group until others are ready to adjust to its presence and you are ready to stick around and help it become a more permanent structure.

5. Be extremely clear about project goals by portraying the ideally functioning school in a variety of ways. Find out which portrayal best matches the priorities and sequences of priorities that staff members have in mind.

6. Include a variety of people on the intervention team, e.g., local people as well as outsiders, curriculum consultants as well as process consultants. Keep the differentiation among roles clear and present enough variety so differentiation is visible to clients.

7. Provide training that allows staff members to "distance" themselves from traumas of the on-the-job world before encouraging application of learnings. Teachers, in particular, invest so much energy in "keeping school" that they find it hard to think of change when they are in the midst of things as they seemingly always have been.

To be sure, not all of the questions left over after the Thomas School intervention were answered by this second intervention. The consultant team from Thomas School still looks forward to the day when they and other OD consultants will have a swifter and surer technology to bring about parent involvement in schools. In the meantime, they keep the questions in mind, keep reading new research, and are careful never to assume that what worked at Thomas School or any place else will work in the same way or with the same outcomes in yet another school.

BIBLIOGRAPHY

Chesler, M., and Flanders, M. 1967. Resistance to research and re-search utilization: the death and life of a feedback attempt. *Journal of Applied Behavioral Science* 3: 469-87.

This article describes the interpersonal events of a successful and an unsuccessful feedback session with educators. The importance of trust and clarity of purpose are emphasized, and suggestions are made concerning how the consultant can prepare educators to receive feedback so that the information is put to constructive use.

Cohen, A. M., and Smith, R. D. 1976a. *The critical incident in growth groups: theory and technique.* La Jolla, Calif.: University Associates.

This text offers concepts and techniques for sharpening a consultant's intervention strategies and skills and provides a system for clarifying consultative interventions according to level, type, and intensity. Although the system is simple, it can be powerful and easily tailored to the particular needs of school consultants.

_____. 1976b. *The critical incident in growth groups: a manual for group leaders.* La Jolla, Calif.: University Associates.

This companion volume presents sixty-one typical incidents in groups. As the manual allows trainees to select their intervention styles and to compare their selections with those of the authors, it can be especially useful for purposes of self-study and reflection.

Eiben, R., and Milliren, A., eds. 1976. *Educational change: a humanistic approach.* La Jolla, Calif.: University Associates.

Dozens of brief articles are here classified under group techniques, psychodrama and role playing, change strategies, open classroom and other structural interventions, and in-service programs. All articles contain down-to-earth guides for action; many contain simulations or games.

Friedlander, F. 1968. A comparative study of consulting processes and group development. *Journal of Applied Behavioral Science* 4: 377-99.

Friedlander presents data indicating that, in the long view, pre-work and postwork processes surrounding a workshop are more potent than the content of the workshop itself. The article stimulates consideration of the importance of integrating macro- and microdesigns.

Golembiewski, R. T., and Blumberg, A. 1967. Confrontation as a training design in complex organizations: attitudinal changes in a diversified population of managers. *Journal of Applied Behavioral Science* 3: 525-47.

This article reports on several applications of the Imaging procedure described in chapter 5 of this book. The authors offer a range of variations on implementing the procedure and present evaluative data from organization members who have enacted the procedure.

Johnson, D. W., and Johnson, F. P. 1975. *Joining together: group theory and group skills.* Englewood Cliffs, N.J.: Prentice-Hall.

This compendium of group theory and group exercises for skill development offers many activities that OD consultants can integrate into their repertoires. The principal topics of interest to OD are decision making, group goals, communication within groups, controversy and conflict, cohesion and norms, problem solving, and team building.

Pino, R. F.; Emory, R. E.; and Jung, C. 1976a. *Preparing educational training consultants I: skills training.* Portland, Ore.: Commercial Educational Distributing Services.

This instructional system includes materials, designs, and procedures for eighty-eight hours of instruction. During the first forty-four hours, the basic concepts are learned; during the second forty-four hours a workshop is conducted for others in group process skills. Many elements of this system can be incorporated into tailored designs.

_____. 1976b. *Preparing educational training consultants II: consulting.* Portland, Ore.: Commercial Educational Distributing Services.

This system increases trainees' skills in diagnostic and intervention strategies that help an organization or other group to add or strengthen a function needed for goal attainment. It also helps participants to assess their own competencies and to derive an explicit rationale for the consultant role. The total instructional time is eighty-four hours.

11

Evaluating Outcomes

When clients ask, "Has something happened here that was worth our money and effort?" the kind of information being sought is called summative, and that is the topic of this chapter. The pages that follow will describe several kinds of outcomes of interest to consultants, funders, taxpayers, teachers, parents, and other audiences. They will suggest ways of assessing satisfactions, organizational adaptability, and other possible results of organization development and will describe a number of difficulties and enigmas encountered by those who evaluate outcomes.

It should be remembered, however, that any piece of information can be part of diagnosing context for one person or group, of monitoring progress for another, and of evaluating outcomes for another. Clients subject themselves to the rigors of organization development with different goals in mind, so that an activity or ability that is an interim step toward a goal for one may be the goal itself for another. Some clients may be content to stop where they are; certain funders may have got what they want by now; certain groups of parents may judge that their point is proven. The difference between interim and total achievement lies less in the objective nature of the activity or ability than in the client's viewpoint and needs. Although we usually think of outcome evaluation as following larger units of work and monitoring progress as following smaller units, in distinguishing progress from outcomes the audience for the data is more relevant than the magnitude of the work.

KINDS OF OUTCOMES

First, an outcome can be small in scope and near in time, or it can be vast and realizable only in a distant future, or it can be something between. Examples: Did the consultation at a series of eight faculty meetings succeed in making the last one more productive than the first? Did a two-year project to establish team teaching at a school succeed in bringing about the interactive pattern set forth as a criterion of success at the beginning of the project? At the end of a seven-year project, did a school district find itself solving problems by preventively anticipating them at the hierarchical levels where they would cause the most pain, using resources outside the usual channels, and maintaining alertness for problems that might recur or change into new ones?

Second, when recording outcomes, consultants and clients should be alert to unanticipated effects, whether they are immediately pleasing or not. In one of our projects, for example, six elementary schools received OD consultation to help them realize their intention of converting from the traditional self-contained classroom structure to a multiunit structure with differentiated staffing.* After four months, two of the schools withdrew from the project, the principal of one of them reaching his decision after a day-long conference with a dozen other elementary school principals on the topic of their relationships with one another, especially as these were affected by the project. His culminating statement was to the following effect: "I realize that I've never been entirely clear about why I got into this project. Now I know that this is not what I really want to do. The project does not fit with the way I have to operate. I want out."

The other principal felt much the same way. At both schools, too, many teachers felt that the project was interfering with special thrusts of work which they were already pursuing. Did the project fail in these two schools? Did the schools extricate themselves from an environmental pressure to get involved in something that was not right for them? Did the consultants help them to extricate themselves sooner than they would otherwise have done? Who succeeded or failed at what? Who won or lost?

Third, that multiple goals produce mixed benefits is axiomatic. Because participants bring different goals and values to an OD project, an event that is a heady success for one may be viewed as a humiliating frustration by another. Any OD project will engender different opinions and satisfactions among its participants, and consultants must be alert for those who are not sharing in the benefits felt by the majority. Consultants (or specially hired evaluators) will perform a great service by designing their evaluation of outcomes not only to determine how close they came to meeting their clients' and their own chief goals but to ascertain any desirable or undesirable outcome whatsoever. It is important to learn what gains and losses

---

*Reported by Schmuck, Murray, Smith, Schwartz, and M. Runkel (1975).

are perceived, regardless of whether they were included among the original goals.

Finally, an expensive and time-consuming organizational change should, within reasonable limits, produce an outcome durable enough to resist decay or hostile onslaught. Many consultants will feel a project to have been a failure if the procedures, norms, and esprit de corps that they so carefully built and nurtured over several years vanish shortly after the arrival of an unsympathetic new principal or superintendent. We feel that if we had imbued the school with enough strength and unity, it would have stood up to the new administrator and not have capitulated so soon. Runkel, Wyant, and Bell (1975) have written with pride, for example, about the Kent cadre of organizational specialists, which continued to do its work for five years after administrative support was removed.

But look at the durability of a new organizational form from the viewpoint of the new principal or superintendent. Would you want to become principal of a school in which you had almost no chance of influencing the staff? The very concept of a school that makes itself unresponsive to influence, even from its own principal, contradicts the concept of organizational adaptability. Such a school is like the Sorcerer's Apprentice who conjured up a water-carrying device so effective that it later resisted his every effort to stop it from carrying water. For consultants, then, the question arises: How strong do we want our magic to be?

Limited Outcomes

Throughout this book, organizational adaptability has been identified as the ultimate goal of OD, at least in the long view of the theorist; in addition, chapters 9 and 10 indicated how every step of training and consultation can more firmly lay the basis for the eventual realization of this goal. At the same time, however, organizational development could not occur unless its methods brought certain satisfactions to clients long before they approached that distant goal. Limited outcomes are often vitally important to members of a school or district and can have great value for clients in money, time, productivity, or satisfaction. Excerpts from two articles by Duffin, Falusi, and Lawrence (1972), who at that time comprised the Organizational Unit of the York County Board of Education in Ontario, Canada, will illustrate.

> The York County Board ... had all the classic behavior and attitudes of any large-scale merger: mutual suspicion, cries for autonomy, generalized hostility to the head office, competition for resources, and a collection of principals who were clustered in groups that were somewhat isolated from each other and from the total system. ... All of the outcomes described are one which have not only persisted for two years or more, but ones which have grown and developed during this time. ... In general, there have been four major results:

(1) the development of a York County identity;
(2) the development of a relatively distortion-free vertical chan-
     nel of communication for planning and decision making;
(3) more effective planning, problem solving, and conflict
     resolution;
(4) job enrichment (pp. 34–35).

Although these are not the characteristics of organizational
adaptability that we described in chapter 1, they are characteristics
that are likely to be found in a school organization of high adaptability. As the following additional excerpts illustrate, the point is
that these outcomes were highly valued by Duffin, Falusi, and
Lawrence.

> There is more resolution of conflict now by members who share
> the conflict rather than kicking the problem upstairs. For exam-
> ple, two neighboring high school principals met recently and
> resolved their conflicts over budget resources. The meeting was
> initiated by them, the conflicts were resolved by them, it was
> done quickly and amicably, and it saved the area a substantial
> amount of money. . . .
> The Administrative Committee . . . have cut the number of
> items on their weekly agenda from well over thirty to no more
> than five. They have reduced the length of their meetings with-
> out increasing their frequency, the climate of the meetings is
> now much more relaxed, and much more gets done. . . .
> At the area level, before teachers were allotted to individ-
> ual schools, . . . the principals were able to divide the available
> number of teachers in the way that made the most sense to the
> whole area. They also perceived that it made good sense to
> leave a reserve to be used at the discretion of the superintend-
> ents so that unforeseen circumstances could be dealt with other
> than by crying for additional resources from the Board or by
> upsetting the planned structure in other schools. . . (p. 36).
> The discovery that certain textbook titles were being
> reordered in one school while another school was taking the
> book out of service or had a surplus for some other reason led
> to the question of . . . the possible saving inherent in rebind-
> ing . . . and in the consolidating of extra copies. . . . Before
> September 1971, approximately 46,000 books that were
> usable, or usable if rebound, were picked up and delivered. . . .
> This is the sort of development where one might well expect a
> falling-off. On the contrary, . . . in 1972, we have [53,369]
> usable books to be distributed and . . . to be rebound. . . . Here
> we have a clear example of what can happen when people col-
> laborate in terms of needs and resources in an atmosphere of
> trust (pp. 62–63).

Other limited outcomes that school people have found valuable
include reducing the boredom of meetings, finding previously
unknown capabilities among colleagues, clarifying central-office roles

enough to reduce administrators' fears of broaching topics with the wrong people, increasing two-way communication between teachers and students, making student council meetings more productive, enabling parents to find roles in the school that bring them satisfactions, enabling teachers to find roles vis-a-vis parents that bring satisfactions to both, helping a principal to become aware of personal acts that forfeit the confidence of staff members, reducing vandalism, reducing hazing among high school students, and building solidarity in teaching teams. Many other such limited benefits have resulted, at least in part, from the use of OD methods, and local people are understandably happy when these benefits occur, notwithstanding that no single problem solved can give assurance that the school is sufficiently lively and resilient to cope well with the next problem that comes along.

Three Levels of Outcomes

Because OD projects usually seek to improve skills at interpersonal, subsystem, and organizational levels, these three levels can also be used to classify outcomes. Here we use them to relate this chapter to others in this book.

Figure 11-1 shows diagramatically by what means first-level skills can be altered. Concepts about old and new skills, the trainees' present skills, exercises that help to unlearn old skills and to learn

FIGURE 11-1   Altering Interpersonal Skills

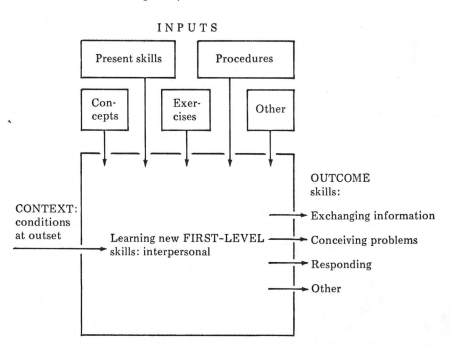

FIGURE 11-2   Altering Subsystem Skills

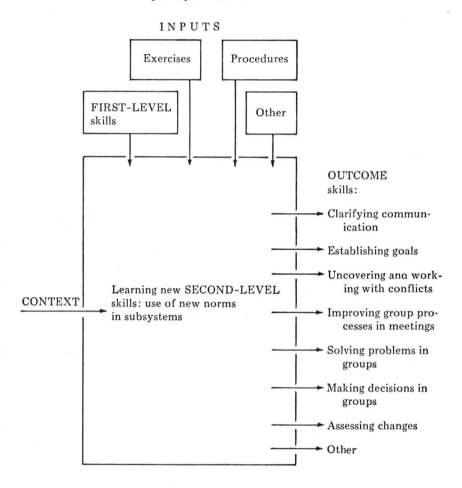

new ones, and procedures that enable new skills to be fitted into daily work—all are brought to the training or consultation situation as inputs, sometimes through formal university courses, sometimes in do-it-yourself packages, more often in the hands of a trainer or consultant. "Other" is included among the inputs and outcomes to remind us that there are always influences on learning other than those to which we give immediate attention. We introduced the concepts of old and new interpersonal skills, exercises and procedures in chapter 1, described some practical procedures and exercises in chapter 3, and discussed assessing input and design in chapter 2.

That learning always takes place in a preexisting context is indicated at the left of figure 11-1; for a discussion of diagnosing context, see chapter 2. Consultants diagnose context so that they can design training that works with, not against, the context. When diagnosis is valid and the training properly designed, context and training

FIGURE 11-3   Altering Organizational Skills

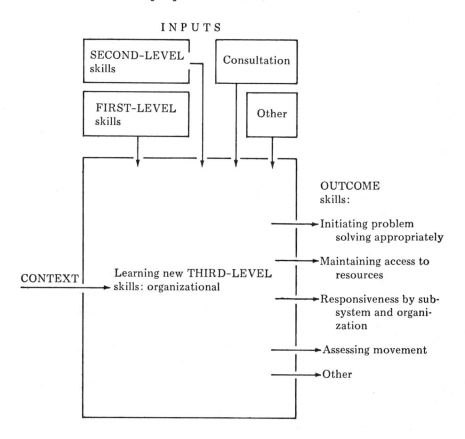

carry learning in the same direction. Chapter 2 also mentioned monitoring progress; particular methods for doing so were given in chapters 3 through 8. The outcome skills named at the right of the figure were described in chapter 1. Methods for assessing the three interpersonal skills were offered in chapters 2 and 3.

Figure 11-2 shows how second-level skills can be altered. Here the inputs are the first-level skills together with exercises that teach trainees how to build second-level skills on the basis of those of the first level, and procedures that enable them to be carried into daily work.

The context at this level may differ from that at the lower level. If a school staff has undertaken OD training and has elevated its first-level skills, these skills are now part of the input. But the fact that all the staff went through recent training in first-level skills together is now a part of the context that was not there previously. A school staff in that context would require a different design for later consultation than one in which members had received training in first-level skills at different times or not recently. The second-level skills named at the right of figure 11-2 are the topics of chapters 3 through 8, which also have sections on assessing them.

In figure 11-3, the inputs at the third level are the first- and second-level skills, along with consultation to help organization members and subsystems find or build new patterns of differentiation and integration among subsystems, organization, and environments. The skills named at the right are those described in chapter 1. Methods of assessing them are suggested in this chapter together with some comments on the difficulties of choosing and assessing ultimate outcomes.

Each of the three figures shows outcome skills that can be taken as summative evaluation (i.e., as outcomes to be valued in themselves); that can be used to solve "content" problems such as conflicts over budget, expensive duplications of textbooks, enabling parents to become influential members of the school community, and so on; or that can cumulate to produce a versatile and lively organizational adaptability.

Academic Achievement

Despite some evidence that organizational adaptability has effects related to academic performance by students, the link between the two is complex and tenuous, and the lag between them is long. In our opinion, an OD project lasting from one to three years and restricted to staff members should not be expected to have quick or significant effects on students' academic performance, and consultants should not lead educators to hope otherwise. This section will review some of the effects of OD on students and give reasons why we believe long-term projects of large scope are required to effect significant change in academic performance.

Effects on Students. Comparing communication between students and teachers in the classrooms of two junior high schools, Bigelow (1971) found: (1) that communication initiated by students rose in the classrooms of teachers who had received OD training but did not rise in those of untrained teachers, and (2) that feelings of mutual attraction rose among students in the classrooms of trained teachers and declined in those of untrained teachers. These results indicated that trained teachers were able to transfer OD techniques to affect communication in their classrooms. Bigelow cited other studies showing that in classrooms having climates like those of the trained teachers, students recalled more academic material, did more homework, showed higher achievement in cognitive, affective, and behavioral domains, and liked their classroom life more.

Schmuck and Runkel (1970, pp. 85-87) found that some junior high school teachers who had received OD training made numerous applications of the training to the conduct of their classes. Teachers reported such applications as "using nonverbal exercises to depict feelings about the subject matter being studied," "using a paraphrase exercise to point out how poor classroom communications are," "using the problem-solving sequence in social studies classes to learn more about social problems," and "using small groups for giving and receiving feedback about how the class is going."

Saturen (1972) found that teachers in OD-trained elementary schools used a student committee to develop regulations for student conduct much more often than did teachers in untrained schools. Nelson (1971) taught some elementary school teachers to observe one another's teaching, record objective data, and report the data to the teacher observed. While this had the effect among teachers of improving openness, clarity of decision making, and satisfaction with working conditions, students expressed *lowered* attraction toward the school and academic subjects during the same period. We suspect that the latter was only a temporary condition, although the duration of the study was too brief to provide an answer.

The League of Cooperating Schools* in the Los Angeles area has long used theory and methods similar in important respects to those of most organization development projects. Reporting data from the League's experience, Seeman and Seeman (1976) conceived teachers' participation in the organizational life of the school in terms of dialogue, decision making, and action taking.

> *The instrument was based on the view that schools would be able to respond most effectively to their changing needs and environment—whatever the specific nature of the change involved—if they had a well developed and more or less institutionalized process favorable to ongoing and renewable change. We conceived of that process, which every school has in more or less degree, as a three-step complex composed of dialogue, decision making, and action taking (DDA). The basic idea was that the character of the communication, the quality of the decision making, and the ability to move into an action phase (the outcome of this process being continually evaluated and repeated as necessary) were essential ingredients in the school's receptivity to, and capability for, effective change (p. 28).*
>
> *Perhaps the defining feature in this conception of DDA is that it is a process through which the teachers exercise some degree of control over the direction and assessment of change in their schools. When the dialogue-decision-action process works properly, the teachers are participating in the power structure of the school—a fact which should have considerable consequence, if the recent literature is any guide. It should, for example, have some repercussions on the teachers' general sense of control over their own destiny; and recent evidence suggests that the sense of control (the feeling of helplessness or mastery in the community or in organizations) is a critical factor in performance (p. 29).*

---

*Supported by the Charles F. Kettering Foundation through its affiliate, the Institute for the Development of Educational Activities.

Seeman and Seeman reported statistically significant correlations between teachers' participation in DDA and favorable attitudes toward learning, school, and self on the part of their students. They showed evidence that students' attitudes were not correlated significantly with several characteristics of teachers' background (age, level of education, years of experience) or personality (dogmatism, powerlessness, morale). Finally, they cited several studies showing correlations between the kinds of student attitudes they assessed and academic achievement.

Although the Seeman and Seeman study was not based on interventions by OD consultants, we cite it here because of the similarity of its theory to that in this book, because studies of the effects of OD projects on students are few, and because studies of the effects of the organization on the academic achievement of students are likewise few and inconclusive. The effects reported in the studies mentioned above were not strong; all the studies were short-term, and we do not know whether the effects were sustained in later years.

Because our topic is the organization of the school, we cite no pedagogical studies here; but they are no source of pride either. Although some techniques have shown great promise, follow-up investigations have, to our knowledge, seldom revealed a significant continuing elevation of academic performance. Most pedagogical improvements fade out after two or three years, and all are gone after a decade—a notable instance is to be found in the investigation of the new math by Sarason (1971) and Sarason and Sarason (1969). We believe that the most effective pedagogical improvements are too well adapted to existing classrooms, so that their effectiveness declines as student populations and social problems change. What we need are not temporary "improvements" but schools that are self-renewing.

Competition and Cooperation. Bowles and Gintis (1976), among others, believe that academic performance in not wholly—perhaps not even largely—determined by pedagogy and that school organization, having strong effects on many other aspects of school life, may have strong effects on academic achievement as well. When OD training succeeds in replacing competitive with collaborative ways of getting staff work done, work gets done more quickly and competently and the school becomes a more attractive place for those who work in it. Oddly enough, however, teachers can thoroughly learn and carry out more cooperative ways of working together while students continue to sweat in a jungle of competition.

Competition has been a central feature of school life for centuries as teachers, administrators, and parents have rewarded, helped, and encouraged students who get higher grades and have failed to help or have otherwise discouraged those who lag behind. But only one or a few can win in a competition, and the longer students go to school, the more they separate into skillful haves and unskillful have-nots by a pattern of reinforcement. It is not true that all students begin each new day with an equal chance of getting A-grades.

When this pattern is repeated day after day and year after year, the more hopeless it becomes for those who fall below the average level of skill in the school ever to overtake the others. The reason they do not learn to read, write, or figure very well is not in most cases a lack of intelligence on their part or ineptitude on the part of their teachers. The far more common, pervasive, unremitting reason is that the organization, in its functioning, has been telling them that they are in effect second-class citizens in schools and are not really wanted.

After reviewing decades of literature on cooperation, competition, and individualistic relationships among schoolchildren, Johnson and Johnson (1974) write:

> A large number of educators, psychologists, and popular writers have challenged the notion that it must be an inevitable part of American education that a large proportion of students experience failure. . . . Holt . . . states that, for the student, the most interesting thing in the classroom is the other students. However, in a competitive goal structure, the student must ignore the others, and act as if these other students . . . are really not there. . . . In many schools he can't talk to other students in the halls between classes [or] during lunch. Holt states that this is splendid training for a world in which, when you are not studying the other person to figure out how to do him in, you pay no attention to him (pp. 224–25).
>
> For the teacher who is truly interested in intellectual functioning, one of the saddest probable consequences of the continual use of competitive goal structures is that the intrinsic motivation for learning and thinking will become subverted. A highly competitive person does not learn for intrinsic reasons; learning is a means to an end, the end being "winning." Intellectual pursuit for itself becomes unheard of because having knowledge that does not help one "win" becomes a waste of time (p. 226).

Necessary Alterations. Recent years have brought a great deal of investigation of working conditions in industry. One of the most thorough reviews of this literature was made by Argyris (1973), who gave special attention to the effects of strong control by those in authority, of splitting up and routinizing work, and of fostering competitiveness—features that strongly correspond to the position of students in schools.

> The impact of these factors can be summarized as decreasing the individual's experience of control over his immediate work area, decreasing his use of the number of abilities, and increasing his dependence and submissiveness. To the extent that individuals seek to use their more central abilities and to be autonomous, they may adapt by reactions ranging from absenteeism to withdrawal and noninvolvement, aggression, and increased emphasis on instrumental rewards, and a decreasing

emphasis on intrinsic rewards. These conditions tend to increase in frequency and scope as one goes down the hierarchy. The lower-level worker is in a psychologically deprived condition. . . . Organizations are unintentionally designed to discourage the versatile and involved worker (p. 150).

In our language, the impact of the noncooperative structure of tasks, formalization of rules, strong specialization of tasks, and authoritarian style of management was to reduce opportunities for achievement, power over one's own fate, and feelings of companionship among those at the bottom of the hierarchy. As these conditions are not uncommon in schools, it should not be surprising when students react as employees do, with absenteeism, noninvolvement or aggression, and a diminished interest in the joy of learning.

From the organizational point of view, academic have-nots will be able to summon renewed energy and hope only when their depressed place in the school organization is changed. It will not do merely to urge them to study harder and climb over the haves, because students as a body would remain where they are now, with only different names in the featured roles. We need schools that do not have to rank-order students, to reward those at the top and punish those at the bottom. But to bring such schools into being requires radical and formidable reorganization. First, the school would have to enable all students to find rewards at school, which means that grading systems would have to be rethought, classroom procedures radically altered, and new domains of trust built. Second, principals, counselors, central office personnel, and parents would have to alter their priorities and practices to suit; both time and social support, and probably training as well, would be necessary to help them change their present beliefs to beliefs justifying the new structures. Finally, time would have to be allowed for academically unskilled students to react to their new world and begin to increase their skills.

Even if these arguments are only half correct, we urge consultants not to make optimistic promises about the effects of an OD project on indicators of academic achievement, such as scores on standardized tests. Only a long-term project that gradually shifts the norms of students, parents, and school people from competitive to cooperative, at the same time giving students more control over their working (learning) lives, could have a chance of bringing all students into an attractive school culture in which academic learning would be regarded as rewarding by all students.

This is not to say that such a long-term project is a hopeless dream. We have cited several studies showing that, even within the present competitive structure, changes of organizational norms among staff can have beneficial effects on students' attitudes toward the school and on their interaction with one another. Increasing students' attraction to the school is a good place to start. If more students want to be in the school physically and psychologically, that alone could encourage teachers and administrators to attempt further revisions of the organization. Gradual changes of this sort, with students and staff making mutual adaptations and checking progress as they go, could lead step by step to classroom practices more encouraging to all students and thereby to higher achievement by students.

ASSESSING OUTCOMES AMONG STUDENTS

How students view their school and their place in it, the attraction they feel toward it, and the potential benefits they see in being there are crucial to the kind and amount of learning they can acquire. In a school with strong organizational adaptability, students and staff will know with reasonable accuracy what is pleasing or plaguing to each other. But it is not always easy to elicit information from students, especially from those who believe that the staff cares little about them and is likely to misuse any information about them that they acquire. For this reason, maintaining anonymity in the data and a reputation for integrity in handling data are vital.

If students are being included in an OD project, progress can be monitored by using the suggestions for data gathering given in chapters 3 through 8, altered to suit the student's age and language comprehension. In pluralistic countries like the United States, the language of students contains many more dialects than the language of teachers. Thus, an interview written for tenth-graders will not work well with third-graders; an interview for inner-city black high school students will work less effectively for suburban white high school students; an interview written for students in Plaquemines Parish, Louisiana, will not work as well for those in Westchester County, New York. Consultants who use the questions in this section, even though they are presented in the form of questionnaires, should convert them to interview schedules, guides to direct observation, topics to guide a search among documents, or to whatever form is best suited to their purpose and clientele.

If summative evaluation is needed concerning the relations between students and the rest of the school, consultants will want to ascertain communicative relations between students' subsystems and staff's subsystems. They will want to know about the mutual responsiveness of students and staff and about how each makes use of the other's resources. They will want to know how students, staff, and parents join in mutual problem solving and assess progress toward their goals and how they decide when to do so.

Fox, Luszki, and Schmuck (1966) and Schmuck and Schmuck (1975) have described several straightforward ways of obtaining information about students as well as from students in classrooms; in addition, Simon and Boyer (1967) have produced fifteen volumes describing systematic methods for observing students in classrooms. Consultants can use techniques and instruments directly from these books and others or borrow ideas from them for constructing their own methods. We offer two lists of questions below in the same spirit.

Organizational Functioning

In 1976 Warren Bell and Ann Burr developed a questionnaire to ascertain the functioning of the school organization from the point of view of students, taking ideas for many of their questions from Fox and others but rewriting them in simpler language. The Bell and Burr questionnaire did not include the subheadings used below; they are included here for the convenience of consultants who may not wish to use the entire questionnaire.

Questionnaire for Students
on Organizational Functioning
This is not a test. We want to find out about how it feels to be in your school. If the words seem to be true about your school, circle "Yes"; if they don't, circle "No." If you don't know what the sentence is about, circle "I DK" (I don't know).

Circle your answer

People notice when something goes wrong; they try to make it right.	YES	NO	I DK
There is no one here who will help me when I have a problem.	YES	NO	I DK
Teachers plan a lot together when a change needs to be made.	YES	NO	I DK
People here are interested in ideas from everyone.	YES	NO	I DK
Teachers don't solve problems; they just talk about them.	YES	NO	I DK

Goals

People talk about the way they want the school to be.	YES	NO	I DK
I have certain things I want to do in school this year and I have told someone else about them.	YES	NO	I DK
Parents were not asked to help set school goals.	YES	NO	I DK
What we do here is because of "goals."	YES	NO	I DK
This school does not try to get better.	YES	NO	I DK

Conflict and Variety

People listen to each other even if they are not friends.	YES	NO	I DK
No one else will help me if a teacher is unfair to me.	YES	NO	I DK

Most people here believe there is more than one way to take care of problems.	YES	NO	I DK
The principal will not listen to our "side" of an argument.	YES	NO	I DK
When we disagree here, we learn from each other.	YES	NO	I DK

Open Communication Up and Down

Teachers find it easy to talk to the principal.	YES	NO	I DK
I do not find it easy to talk to the teachers.	YES	NO	I DK
The principal talks with us frankly and openly.	YES	NO	I DK
I can easily get help from teachers if I want it.	YES	NO	I DK
People do not talk to each other here if they are from different parts of the school.	YES	NO	I DK
Teachers say mean things about each other.	YES	NO	I DK

Decision Making

Teachers help decide which adults will work at this school.	YES	NO	I DK
Parents do not help decide about new school programs.	YES	NO	I DK
People from this school give advice to the superintendent and his staff before things are decided about the school.	YES	NO	I DK
I do not get to help decide what to do here in school.	YES	NO	I DK
None of the students gets to help decide what to do.	YES	NO	I DK

Responsiveness

In this school, it is OK to have a problem.	YES	NO	I DK
Teachers don't try "new" things here.	YES	NO	I DK
Students with special problems get help.	YES	NO	I DK
Students with new ideas are ignored.	YES	NO	I DK
The new things we do at this school are just what we need.	YES	NO	I DK

Attractiveness of the School   Circle your answer

I would rather go to school here than
in most other schools in this city.   YES   NO   I DK

Students here have a good feeling
about each other.   YES   NO   I DK

New students and new teachers are
ignored or "put down."   YES   NO   I DK

Teachers and students feel good about
each other.   YES   NO   I DK

People here do not care about one
another.   YES   NO   I DK

Learning Environments

Anderson (1973) has made available for students a list of 105 questions in booklet form. In this booklet the student marks one of four answers: strongly disagree, disagree, agree, or strongly agree. Since at this writing the booklets are easily available from Anderson at small cost, we reproduce only a few examples here.

Questionnaire for Students
about the Learning Environment
The class has students with many different interests.
Certain students work only with their close friends.
The students enjoy their classwork.
There is constant bickering among class members.
The better students' questions are more sympathetically
    answered than those of the average students.
Every member of the class has the same privileges.
Most students want their work to be better than their friends'
    work.
The work of the class is frequently interrupted when some
    students have nothing to do.
Students cooperate equally with all class members.
The better students are granted special privileges.
Only the good students are given special projects.
Class decisions tend to be made by all the students.
The students would be proud to show the classroom to a
    visitor.
Some groups of students work together regardless of what the
    rest of the class is doing.
A few of the class members always try to do better than the
    others.
There are tensions among certain groups of students that tend
    to interfere with class activities.
Students are asked to follow strict rules.
The class is controlled by the actions of a few members who
    are favored.

ASSESSING SATISFACTION

Most of us believe that a strong, resilient organization that meets internal and external challenges with competence and vigor will be composed of people who come to work in the morning feeling confident and eager, who go home feeling good about their day, and who are in general well satisfied with their lives as part of the organization. Indeed, because work preoccupies so much of our lives, many people believe that being happy on the job is a worthwhile end in itself. For these reasons, many social scientists and industrial psychologists regard the satisfaction of organization members as a touchstone for organizational health and adaptability. For their part, OD consultants design interventions for change projects to include activities that bring immediate satisfactions so that participants will be encouraged to continue working toward a more satisfying organization.

Job Satisfaction

Two questions should be asked when assessing the job satisfaction of individuals separately or of a department or school as a whole: (1) Do they like things as they are now, or do they wish things were different? (2) If they wish things were different, in which direction do they wish to move? Let us examine some ways of assessing job satisfaction and see how they answer these two questions. Both in everyday conversation and in scientific studies, a common way of assessing satisfaction is by asking a direct question, such as:

- How satisfied would you say you are with your present job?
  _____ Very satisfied
  _____ Somewhat satisfied
  _____ Neither satisfied nor dissatisfied
  _____ Somewhat dissatisfied
  _____ Very dissatisfied

The answer will usually give you a fairly good impression of how each individual feels about the overall satisfaction the job brings compared to what the individual imagines the job _could_ bring. While useful surveys have been conducted using this kind of item, it works best when all or most of the dissatisfied respondents are dissatisfied for the same reasons and when all or most have roughly the same picture of the greatest degree of satisfaction that a job could bring, for it is in exactly these two ways that the item may yield misleading information.

The "how satisfied" question cannot tell you what to offer to make the dissatisfied respondent more satisfied—a shorter workday, for example, or four ten-hour days a week? Does the respondent want more or less responsibility? and so on. The "how satisfied" question also cannot tell you what the respondent's aspirations are. If I find my job boring but think that it could never be otherwise, if I think that any job I might get would be equally boring, and if I am resigned to holding this kind of job for the rest of my life, then "very satisfied" might mean "about all I can expect." If, in contrast, my job is boring but I am taking a correspondence course with the hope of making it big in radio, I am going to answer something less favorable than "very satisfied."

Not surprisingly, people who express more satisfaction with routine jobs in answering this question tend to stay in these jobs longer. As Argyris (1973) writes: " . . . The greatest dissatisfaction on a routine job occurs during the first years. After three to five years, the individual becomes adapted and satisfied. . . " (p. 162). This matches the fact that the greatest number of people who leave the teaching profession do so after their first year or two of experience.

Interpreting expressed dissatisfaction as a gap between the respondent's present condition and the condition in which she would like to be does reveal the direction in which she wants to move but does not yield information of the "how satisfied" type. Consider the following paired questions, for example.

- How much opportunity to use your own judgment would your ideal job offer?
  _____ A great deal of opportunity
  _____ Some opportunity
  _____ A little opportunity
  _____ No opportunity

- How much opportunity to use your own judgment does your present job offer?
  _____ A great deal of opportunity
  _____ Some opportunity
  _____ A little opportunity
  _____ No opportunity

If the respondent says that her ideal job would offer "some opportunity" to exercise personal judgment and that her present job affords "no opportunity," we know what kind of job would attract her, but we do not know whether she regards the gap between some and no opportunity as trifling or terrible. Paired questions bracketing a gap give us little confidence in concluding that one person's gap is worse than another's.

Although the direct question method need not specify a particular dimension of satisfaction (such as "opportunity to use your own judgment"), the discrepancy method must, if it is to make sense. If, using the discrepancy method, you attempt to ask about the ideal without specifying some dimension, the question will be silly—e.g., How satisfactory would your ideal job be? ———Very satisfactory? In sum, the direct question tells us how the respondent feels but not what to do about it. The discrepancy method tells us where to move but not how strongly the respondent feels about moving there.

Consultants can use either of these methods, despite their faults, if they have reason to believe that the conditions that evoke the faults exist to an insignificant degree in their current project. If they have respondents with exceptional patience, they can use both methods. To approach precision, evaluators usually want to ask about several dimensions of satisfaction; but by the time respondents have answered three or more questions along each dimension, they begin to grow confused by the complexity of the procedure, resentful of the number of questions, or both. As the questions in the following section will demonstrate, however, there is a way of combining the two methods to advantage. These illustrations of each of the four dimensions of need are not presented as the "best" forms but should be altered in content and phrasing to suit local need.

Satisfaction of Needs

In general, *power* means having control over one's important choices and reasonable control over one's own fate. On the job, it means being able to do the things one cares about without having to ask permission or having a judgment contradicted or overturned by someone else. In particular, it means having reasonable control over one's own actions within the agreed limits of the job. The following examples of how to query people about this kind of power should be rephrased or otherwise redirected to suit your own circumstances.

- How much independence (control) do you have in the way you go about your teaching?
  _____ I have about the amount that I prefer.
  _____ I'd like more independence.
  _____ I'd rather have less independence.
- How do you feel about who makes the decisions about what you should do?
  _____ I like the degree to which I myself make decisions about my work.
  _____ Other people make too many decisions for me; I'd like to be making more.
  _____ I am expected to make too many decisions; I'd like to leave more of them to others.

Once again, a questionnaire is not always the best way of obtaining information; we set out examples in this form only because it is convenient. Consultants should use their own ingenuity in converting these items to other methods of data collection.

The next two examples are useful in assessing satisfaction of the need for *achievement*.

- How much of your own ability, skill, or creativity can you put to use in your teaching (job)?
  _____ I can put my abilities, skill, and creativity to use to about the degree that I want.

_____ I wish I could put more of my abilities to use than my
job now allows.

_____ I wish my job did not demand as much of my abilities
as it does.

- How much opportunity do you have in your work to feel proud
of what you have done?

  _____ I get ample opportunity to feel proud of things I do.

  _____ I wish I had more occasion to do things of which I could
  feel personally proud.

  _____ I wish there were fewer occasions when people expect
  me to take pride in what I do.

By _activity_, we mean the need to initiate, explore, and pursue
goals with vigor. Initiation, exploration, and vigorous pursuit can be
intellectual as well as physical, as the following questions illustrate.

- How do you feel about the amount of variety and new experience that you get in your work?

  _____ I get the amount of variety and new experience that
  I like.

  _____ I wish that my job had more variety and new experience
  in it.

  _____ I wish that my job had less variety and new experience
  in it.

- How do you feel about the energy, vigor, or go-get-it that your
job calls for?

  _____ I like the amount of energy or go-get-it that my job
  calls for.

  _____ There isn't enough opportunity in my job to expend
  energy or to have a go-get-it feeling.

  _____ My job calls for too much energy; I'd like to take it
  a little easier.

The need for _affiliation_ is the most difficult to assess. Although
we know that cooperative effort in achieving a shared goal typically
evokes strong feelings of mutual trust and affection, there seems to
be a norm in this country supporting the view that doing good work
on the job is irrelevant to feeling warm and friendly toward coworkers. To assess the need for affiliation, consultants might begin with a
few warm-up questions.

- Some people feel that they work with a really great bunch of
people; others don't feel that way at all. How do you feel
your bunch might compare with those in other schools?

- When something really good happens at work, people sometimes give one another a big hug. Has that happened where
you work?

- Sometimes people feel that they have to work past or around
other people or look out for them because they might do some-

thing that could hurt one, or something like that. On the other hand, people sometimes feel that where they work is sort of one for all and all for one. How is it where you work?

After a few such warm-up questions, you might proceed to the following.

- How do you feel about the friendliness of the people with whom you work?

  _____ I like the amount of friendliness we have at work; it's not too much and not too little.

  _____ I wish we had more of a feeling of friendliness and togetherness at work.

  _____ There is too much buddy-buddy straining to be friendly where I work.

- Do you feel relaxed and warm with your colleagues at work?

  _____ The bunch at work is a nice, comfortable group of people about whom I feel very good.

  _____ The bunch at work are not very comfortable to be with. I wish they could relax more, be less businesslike sometimes and more human-to-human.

  _____ The bunch at work is more chummy than I like. I sometimes wish they'd accept the school as a place where people work and let it go at that. We don't all have to be pals.

Insofar as satisfaction means satisfaction of needs, using power, achievement, activity, and affiliation needs as criteria seems to us the most direct way of assessing on-the-job satisfaction. The answers to these questions enable us to determine whether the respondent finds acceptable the degree of satisfaction of each need, whether corrective action is necessary, and, if so, which direction corrective action should take. They do not enable us to say that one respondent is more dissatisfied than another, however. If the consultant should want that information, the following kind of question usually makes respondents' answers roughly comparable.

- How much independence do you have concerning the way you go about your teaching?

  _____ I have about the amount that I prefer.

  _____ I'd like a little more independence:

    _____ only a little more

    _____ some more

    _____ a lot more

  _____ I'd rather have less independence:

    _____ only a little less

    _____ some less

    _____ a lot less

ASSESSING ORGANIZATIONAL ADAPTABILITY

To assess the outcomes of an OD project and the satisfaction it produces for you or another audience, you must: (1) specify the desired outcomes, (2) get information about the actual outcomes, (3) determine how much the actual outcomes differ from those desired, and (4) decide how much deviation between them is acceptable to you or to others. While it is not necessary to follow this particular order, we urge you, in the interests of intelligent designing, to specify as precisely as possible the outcomes you are seeking before an intervention begins. We do not recommend deciding on outcomes, however, before you reach the entry stage of mutual agreement on outcomes with alients or before you have collected data that will help you decide which outcomes are feasible and worth pursuing. Finally, you need not hold rigidly to outcomes set at the beginning. Feel free to give up hope for an outcome that ceases to look feasible; feel free to add or substitute another partway through the project if it comes to seem more feasible or desirable.

Determining how much an actual outcome differs from one hoped for and knowing beforehand how much deviation from a goal will be acceptable are not easy, and the assessment methods available to OD consultants are neither precise nor totally reliable. As we describe various methods of assessment, we shall not give dogmatic criteria for determining success or failure. Although some indicators can yield numerical scores, a score that is acceptable to one audience will often be unacceptable to another. We can only hope, as consultants amass and write out more of their experiences with outcomes and indicators, that future consultants will be able to evaluate outcomes more easily than we do today.

Collecting Data on Outcomes

The forty-one questions below, which include indicators of problem solving, access to resources, responsiveness, and assessing movement, can serve as a check list. For convenience, we have written them in interview form. Feel free, however, to add other questions more suitable to your project and locality and to get the information by interview, from existing documents, overheard conversations, simulations during training, direct observation, or any other suitable source. Questions 1-7 deal with targets in problem solving; questions 8-15 deal with the situation as problem solving begins; questions 16-18 deal with the planning aspect of problem solving.

Problem Solving. 1. Does this school have goals for its work with which almost everyone agrees?
2. Are the goals written down?
3. Do you have a copy?
4. Have you received any particular information during the past few months that has helped you think about the school moving toward its goals? From whom did you get the information?

5. Please think about how often you discuss with other members of the _____ what the school ought to be trying to accomplish with its students. How often do you discuss goals of this sort with others on occasions such as _____?
6. What are some things you'd like to see this school working toward that it isn't working toward now; What other persons do you think could help to accomplish these things?
7. Have you heard about the _____ project? Can you tell me its purpose—what it is trying to bring about? Do you think the project will help the school move toward its goals?

Questions 1, 2, and 3 are intended to indicate whether people in the school give goals enough attention for them to be in writing and whether people are sufficiently aware of the written form to know whether they have a copy. These three items revealed important differences in a project that we conducted to help elementary schools move from self-contained classrooms to multiunit structure (see Schmuck, Murray, Smith, Schwartz, and M. Runkel 1975, pp. 163-66 and 305-307). Questionnaire items similar to question 5 have yielded information about uses of communication in schools (see Runkel, Wyant, and Bell 1975, chap. 8, items 48 and 89). The other questions have served to gather information informally during interventions. Further information about targets might be obtained by inquiring in the directions indicated by questions 8, 9, 10, 12, and 13.

8. As things are now, what do you think this school fails to do for children that it ought to do?
9. As things are now, what do you think makes life difficult for teachers in this school?
10. As things are now, what do you think worries parents who send their children to this school?
11. As things are now, is there anything you think causes strain between this school and the central administration?
12. What strengths does this school have—what does it have going for it—that could help it do better things for students in the future?
13. What strengths does this school have that could make life better for its teachers in the future?
14. What strengths does this school (community, organization, group) have that could make parents feel better about the school in the future?
15. How many others would you say agree with you about _____? How do you (could you) find out the extent to which others agree with you on _____?
16. Would you say that there is some particular aspect of the school's functioning in which new ideas are especially needed? How many others would you say agree with you about that?
17. Are there people on the staff (among students, parents, _____) who sometimes come up with really new and different ideas?
18. In this _____, do you think the right people get together to plan things?

Access to Resources. 19. What groups make decisions in your school?

20. Sometimes it is easier to get a job done if a well-coordinated group works on it instead of a single individual or a series of individuals. Some people are especially skillful at getting such a work group together and organized into an effective team. Are there some members of the staff (students, parents, _____) who clearly have this special coordinating ability?

21. Sometimes it is necessary for one person to tell another person something or to raise a question that is embarrassing or otherwise difficult. Some people seem better able than others to open this kind of conversation in a spirit of helpfulness. Are there some people on the staff (students, parents, _____) who clearly have this special ability?

22. Are there some people on the staff (students, parents, _____) who seem especially confrontive, personal in a challenging way, or especially willing to open topics that arouse anxiety?

23. When people get into strong conflict at a meeting, what do you think is the best thing to do about it?

24. If your group encounters difficulty in working together or in understanding one another, is there any person or group to whom they can turn for help?

25. When this project is over, will the school have any capabilities that it did not have before? What will they be?

(Other questions that might yield information about access to resources are: 4, 6, 7, 10, 12-14, 16-18, and 24-26.)

Responsiveness. 26. We were talking about [some activity or task in the school]. Are the right people usually involved in this activity?

27. Since the _____ project started, have any new jobs, positions, roles, or sets of duties come about? Which?

28. What do people give you approval or disapproval for that they didn't before the project began?

29. Have some people lost or gained power since the project began? Are any changes in power now under way or planned?

30. Suppose someone on the staff has an idea that he or she seriously thinks could help the school. What steps should this person take to make sure the idea gets a hearing where it counts?

31. Has any new structure, organization of the school, or new interconnection of jobs or roles come about since the project began? Are any now under way or being planned?

32. What will keep your new capabilities being used? What will prevent them from fading out?

33. Will there be some new structure to maintain the new capabilities—that is, new jobs or connections between jobs, new roles, new sets of duties, new committees, new kinds of liaison with groups or agencies outside the school, or the like?

34. How will the functions now performed by the OD consultants be performed after the project is over?

35. [For larger projects:] What is being done to prepare people for the end of the project?

(Other directions of inquiry that could yield information about responsiveness are represented by questions 6, 13, 19, and 20.)

Assessing Movement. 36. Are people doing what they said they would do?
37. Have things that were planned been carried into action? What things have actually happened that were planned to happen?
38. Are the things you are doing carrying you toward the goals that you set?
39. Do you think out new goals to be set now?
40. Who is keeping track of progress?
41. Do you get any information from other professionals that helps you to tell whether you are doing an effective job?

(The information yielded by questions 5, 9, 15, 27-29, and 31-32 might also help to assess movement.)

Directly Observable Evidence

Although conducting interviews and questionnaires at the end of a project will bring interesting information, the most direct route is to observe whether clients are actually doing what you hoped they would be doing: discussing problems in terms of situation, target, and plan; using the systematic problem-solving method in choosing and trying out solutions; probing resources and playfully exercising abilities that are not usually demanded by their jobs; trying out courses of action instead of explaining away problems defensively; regularly assessing the progress of their action plans and testing whether they are going where they wished to go; and periodically reassessing their goals.

In addition to observing whether these things are being done, consultants must judge whether they are being done more often, more judiciously, and more successfully than they were being done before or in greater degree than they are done by those who have not received consultation. You will want to judge, too, whether the changes or the differences from other schools were worth the cost of mounting the project. Although your judgment will sometimes differ from that of your clients or of other audiences, the necessity for judging cannot be removed.

Judging whether clients are better off than they were or better off than others who have not availed themselves of OD consultation should be guided whenever possible by comparing rates or frequency of certain actions at the end of a project with those exhibited at the beginning of the project. Such comparisons are seldom numerical and are often intuitive, based on what "everybody knows" to be the typical rate in most schools or districts. Although some evaluators belittle nontallyable evidence, it often gets more directly to the point than data extracted from questionnaires, is frequently more convincing to some audiences than more scientific data would be, and can be used to validate data that are countable. All the examples of directly observable evidence that follow make explicit or implicit comparisons with base rates.

Problem Solving. We can regard the problem-solving criterion of the adaptive organization as having been satisfied if we observe: (1) that systematic group problem solving is used frequently throughout the school organization, (2) that plans and commitments made in groups are not often remade by organization superiors, and (3) that plans and commitments made by individuals, whether superiors or subordinates, are not often remade by groups. Although a group may become so enamored of the problem-solving steps or so ritualistic about them that it uses the entire sequence for even routine matters which everyone would prefer to leave to some individual's judgment, such overuse declines as understanding grows regarding the advantages and disadvantages of the various ways of using individuals and groups in decision making.

Our first example of highly adaptive problem solving comes from the report on the Highland Park project by Schmuck and Runkel (1970).

> *An incident in the latter part of February, 1969, illustrated Highland Park's problem-solving abilities. The central office asked Highland Park if it could provide room for approximately 100 educators who would be participating in a conference sponsored by the Northwest Regional Educational Laboratory. Other schools in the district, citing insufficient space, turned down the central office.*
>
> *The principal called together the area chairman for physical education, the cafeteria manager, the assistant principal for curriculum, the vice principal, and the chief custodian. A solution was found within an hour. A class in physical education, usually taught separately for boys and girls, could be taught with both groups together in the gymnasium except for the lunch periods, when the gymnasium had to be used as a dining hall. During these periods, however, the band room was available. The cafeteria manager decided she could provide lunch for the visitors with the addition of one temporary person to her staff. The plan was described to the central office, who sent a representative to meet with the Highland Park group and work out a detailed schedule for the occasion.*
>
> *During the actual conduct of the visiting conference, the principal was out of town. The assistant principal for curriculum acted as host. Though there was some inconvenience to the music department, members of the conference expressed gratification with the hospitality they received. The central office sent the Highland Park staff a letter of appreciation, stating that it would not have been able to host the conference without the problem-solving ability of the Highland Park staff (pp. 373–74).*

This example shows how a natural occurrence can fit nicely into the logic of the base rate. Other schools with no less space per student than Highland Park had been asked to host the conference, and all had the same eager support from the central office, the same financial compensation (none), the same time of year, and so on. The other schools provided the base rate against which Highland Park stood out as unusual. Of course, one problem well solved does not bespeak organizational adaptability; but when a school solves several problems with unusual resourcefulness, one should take special notice. An example of unusual problem solving is here cited from Duffin, Falusi, and Lawrence (1972).

> . . . One area superintendent used his area supervising caretaker in the maintenance budget planning. The caretaker actually participated in the planning in his own area of accountability rather than submitting a report or a set of requisitions to his bosses. Consequently, a much better maintenance budget was produced in short order and there has been a saving of $2,600 in grass cutting alone. The superiors were amazed at the quality and quantity of data which the supervising caretaker had. This sort of task-relevant involvement of people has been repeated in other areas, in schools, and so on. Almost without exception, the results have been better in quality of decision and degree of commitment and execution (p. 64).

Access to Resources. The following two examples of a use of resources seldom found in most schools or districts are both from Schmuck and Runkel (1970).

> As the Principal's Advisory Committee became more of a problem-solving group, they felt that meetings should last long enough to permit in-depth examination of problems. They got this block of time by meeting at 6:30 A.M. once a month at a local restaurant. These meetings ran for two and one-half hours. This schedule continued throughout 1968–1969. Members very rarely missed these meetings; when an area chairman could not attend, he asked a member of his subject area to take his place and he paid for the breakfast of his substitute. On several occasions, general faculty members were invited to attend these meetings; typically, two or three would appear and participate (p. 373).

> The superintendent cancelled regular meetings with his "cabinet" and established a new sort of meeting in their stead. The new weekly meeting was attended not only by assistant superintendents, but by anyone in the district who wished to attend. A memorandum was sent out especially encouraging schools, departments, and any other sort of group to send representatives to the meetings. The purposes were to review the problems faced by the district and exchange information with the superintendent about the problems. The superintendent

486

does not act as chairman of the meeting. Two organizational specialists were present at each meeting to act as "process observers" and make interventions to help keep the meetings productive (p. 375).

Responsiveness. Schmuck, Murray, Smith, Schwartz, and M. Runkel (1975) tell how consultants spurred responsiveness in a school staff that had become mired in talk halfway through an OD project. The consultants designed a workshop that would help participants articulate goals in terms of the values they cherished as a group, help them communicate to one another a high sense of strength, competence, and influence over their environment, and impart a sense of urgency to them. The following is a brief description of the workshop.

8:00 A.M. Introduction: . . . The need to take actions soon— very soon—was stressed.

8:15 A.M. Each member of the leadership group described one or two of the intervention goals in two minutes.

8:30 A.M. Buzz Groups: The staff formed into buzz groups. Each group shared positive and negative feelings about the list of goals. [The consultants] and the leadership group left the room for a few minutes to facilitate openness. . . .

8:50 A.M. The . . . consultants and the [leadership group] returned to the room; reporters from each buzz group read aloud the group feelings about the goals.

9:00 A.M. Each group was told to make a list of things to do that could attain these goals. Keeping in mind what people liked and did not like about goals helped them to think of things to do with others. They were told to remember that this was not game playing. If they listed something someone else liked to do, others were told to call on that person to do it. Each group was to make a list on newsprint of whatever anyone named. After 20 minutes, they were told to stop. Then each person put his name at the top of his own newsprint and put down just those things he'd like to do.

9:30 A.M. Individual preferences were posted on the walls. Participants got coffee and milled around to find other persons who had similar preferences.

9:50 A.M. Each member of the staff was asked to make an individual list of "What I can contribute toward achieving my preferred action plan."

10:10 A.M. The lists of contributions were posted together with the lists of preferences. Each staff member moved around, trying to find others with whom he would like to work to achieve personal plans. The consultants encouraged clusters of at least four to form. The clusters were made up of people who wanted to work together immediately on action plans.

10:30 A.M. Clusters were formed and were told to produce a plan of action that could be initiated the next week.

10:45 A.M. Several isolates were worked with individually by a few . . . consultants.

12:15 A.M. . . . All Spartan [school] faculty members milled around the room, making statements about their plans for action.

This completed the formal part of the consultation. The teachers remained in the room for some time, talking about their new plans and commitments, and consultants took notes of what they overheard. Here is a selection from several dozen comments that were recorded.

- *We've been talking for months and I thought we never would do anything, but now we're really going to act.*
- *I am just astonished at how fast this faculty can move—and how fast I can move, too.*
- *We accomplished something; we have plans to do a thing I've been wanting to do. Of course, there are some things that are wrong that we haven't even touched on, too.*
- *I feel so much better! I never would have realized that other people were so ready to join together!*
- *We actually have times set next week when we're really going to start doing it!*
- *We cleared up so many things!*
- *I'm amazed at what we did in one hour. . . .*
- *I feel really good about what our group accomplished, but even better that I could have worked with any other group and done just as much.*
- *We can finally do what we've wanted to do all year.*
- *Each of us knows what we will do and what the others in our group will do.*
- *My ideas really got used—I've been afraid to mention them sometimes because I feared they would sound silly.*
- *We used one another's strengths—really listened well.*
- *Somebody reported feeling very good about being able to start something new in the middle of the year—not bound by fall-to-fall time perspective.*
- *Several people said that what they got out of the day was not anything new but the opportunity to do things that they had been wanting to do. . . .*
- *This has been one of the greatest times I've had since being at Spartan.*
- *I was amazed we could move so fast when we made up our minds to do it.*

Assessing Movement. In the summer of 1969, the Center for Educational Policy and Management established in the school district at Kent, Washington, a cadre of organizational specialists who became highly skillful at examining their goals, at assessing their position in relation to their goals, at planning, and at taking corrective action. Those skills became vital when the district suffered a severe financial setback the year after the cadre was formed. From the report by Runkel, Wyant, and Bell (1975), we briefly describe a few meetings from a longer series in which the cadre assessed its movement toward its goals. The point is not to show what assessments were made but to show the kinds of activities and setting through which the cadre undertook to make assessments.

> *12–13 December 1969. Meeting of cadre for renewing group solidarity and refurbishing coordination. The crisis in the district (they said) pervades our conference. Furthermore, physical distance makes it difficult for us to communicate rapidly. When composing subteams for interventions we must consider the personal acceptability of members. Will staff resent being asked to give extra time when their hours are already being overclaimed by budgetary stresses? Should we revise priorities?*
>
> *27 May 1971. Meeting of entire cadre "to discuss status of the group at this time and where it is going." Ideas for future activities were generated. Consensus seemed to be that "the group feels it has a tremendous service potential, but it needs a boost from funding support, etc." No facilitator from outside was employed.*
>
> *5 February 1972. Meeting of entire cadre for a self-renewal session to formulate goals, clarify expectations, choose maintenance tasks and projects, and plan budget. Maury Pettit of Central Washington State College was facilitator.*
>
> *8–9 September 1972. Meeting of entire cadre for a self-renewal session on interpersonal blocks and goals for the future. Runkel and Murray . . . were facilitators. They reported: "In our opinion, the workshop was exciting and stimulating. They were very receptive to giving one another feedback and ready to proceed with work toward new goals. They showed great maturity and adaptability as an organization."*
>
> *30 October 1972. Meeting of entire cadre to clarify the balance between goals and resources. Maury Pettit was facilitator.*
>
> *7–8 September 1973. Meeting of the entire cadre for "team building." Twenty cadre members attended. John Goff and Bob McGlone were facilitators. Included exercises, lecture, and planning.*

SOME DIFFICULTIES

Although initiating problem solving, maintaining access to resources, exhibiting responsiveness, and assessing movement toward goals all help to ascertain the degree to which a school has approached organizational adaptability, assessing an outcome as complex and distant as organizational adaptability presents special difficulties, some of which will be explored in this section. Some of these difficulties will directly concern the OD consultant, while others will not. Some of the ideas given here will best serve consultants by helping them talk with professional evaluators.

Time and Change

Assessing organizational adaptability does not necessarily require sophisticated techniques, but it often does require that one or several people linger long enough to count and chart typical rates of change. It takes considerable time to lift a school from its original level of capability to a level of high capability with regard to the four criteria of organizational adaptability, and a school district can make an excellent investment in its future by setting aside resources for counting instances that evidence continued gradual growth in these criteria. Unfortunately, however, someone must pay salaries, and it is difficult to persuade government agencies and the comptrollers, chairpersons, and boards of local school districts to provide money over a three- to ten-year period that would enable the effects of a training project to be charted in respect to the criteria for organizational adaptability.

In addition, schools show considerable variation in their year-to-year progress toward organizational adaptability. Studying the kinds of innovations reported by elementary school teachers in two school districts near Seattle over four years and four administrations of questionnaires, Runkel (in Runkel, Wyant, and Bell 1975, chap. 8) divided the innovations into five classes—structural, collaborative, curricular, cloistered, and none. Omitting answers of "none" and examining the class of innovation reported by the greatest percentage of teachers that gave data over at least two years in each of twenty-two elementary schools, Runkel found that six schools reported the same type of innovation over three consecutive years, five schools reported the same type of innovation over two consecutive years, and eleven schools changed every year. These statistics indicate that outcome evaluators should watch at least three elementary schools to find one sticking with one type of problem for as long as three years. Even then, we must recognize the fact that sticking with one type of problem does not necessarily mean solving it well and that solving problems is only one of the four criteria of organizational adaptability.

Murray (1973) has also presented data showing why we should not expect to make a reliable assessment of organizational change after only a year of effort.* Two elementary schools had made use of OD consultation to help them move from self-contained classroom structure to multiunit structure. Assessing several features of their

---

*Murray's results are abridged in chapter 6 of Schmuck, Murray, Smith, Schwartz, and M. Runkel (1975).

organizational functioning before the consultation began (spring of 1970), after a year of continuing consultation (1971), and after a second year of discontinued consultation (1972), Murray's data revealed different sequences of effects in the two schools. Discussing these results, Schmuck, Murray, Smith, Schwartz, and M. Runkel (1975) write:

> *Spartan and Palmer differed significantly in how the organiza-*
> *tional change processes proceeded over a two-year period. The*
> *Palmer staff members began quickly to implement team teach-*
> *ing and other sorts of collaborative educational arrangements*
> *during the first year of the project. Later they ran into diffi-*
> *culties in maintaining these change attempts, and the following*
> *year saw the innovation beginning to fade. In contrast, the*
> *Spartan staff members first spent effort in developing commun-*
> *ication skills, group norms, and problem-solving procedures,*
> *moving much more gradually than Palmer into the multiunit*
> *structure. After one year of consultation in OD, the Spartan*
> *staff was ready to benefit from technical consultation and*
> *multiunit structure. The Spartan staff then moved quickly in*
> *that direction and stayed there during the second year (p. 358).*

> *Successful establishment of a multiunit structure requires two*
> *school years. Consultation in organization development should*
> *be designed to last at least for the first year, with instructional*
> *innovations emphasized the second year. . . . Gradual, incre-*
> *mental changes within the school may support more sustainable*
> *changes in structure than rapid alterations in staff arrangements*
> *(p. 191).*

In brief, when assessing progress toward organizational adaptability, consultants or evaluators must always strive to ascertain a trend and refuse to be satisfied with an evaluation that takes data only once before an intervention and once afterward. Had Murray assessed the functioning of Spartan and Palmer schools only before and after, in 1970 and 1971, he would mistakenly have concluded that Spartan had improved slightly but that Palmer had leapt far ahead, whereas the 1972 assessment showed that Palmer had bitten off more than it could chew while Spartan had increased and made firm its gains. Ascertaining a trend requires at least three years and often more.

Finally, it is impossible when working with human affairs to predict confidently what will happen in a new situation before it arises. Professors of educational psychology who tell teachers-to-be that any particular action will evoke a particular reaction all or even most of the time are teaching falsely. Predictions are worth making because we can take them to the brink of our next interaction and use them to help us look for *likely* action. But we must at the same time be alert for on-the-spot information that will confirm or disconfirm our predictions, and we must search out additional information so that we can the more surely increase or decrease our confidence in our predictions.

Thus, even when using research studies and experience, we should never suppose that the next week or year or the next innovation will go like the last but should make careful diagnoses, select possible courses of action, specify some likely reactions, and then move into the week, year, or innovation alert for every corroboration or contradiction, prepared to abandon one prediction and to substitute another at a moment's notice. We should act only when our best guess about what will happen sufficiently exceeds our confidence in our next best guess.

Audiences and Confidentiality

In addition to OD consultants and the clients, an interested audience for evaluation reports can include students and parents, the staffs of other schools, other administrators and other districts, professors, social scientists, taxpayers' organizations, chambers of commerce, police and juvenile authorities, aldermen, legislators, and federal agencies. Consultants must be as responsive to their audiences as they are to their clients, keeping in mind that the kinds of data and analyses that will satisfy some will seem irrelevant to others. Using the term *responsive evaluation* to mean taking the viewpoints of audiences into account, Stake (1975) speaks to professional evaluators, although his remarks are useful to OD consultants as well.

I prefer to work with evaluation designs that perform a service. I expect the evaluation study to be useful to specific persons. An evaluation probably will not be useful if the evaluator does not know the interests and language of his audiences. During an evaluation study a substantial amount of time may be spent learning about the information needs of the persons for whom the evaluation is being done. The evaluator should have a good sense of whom he is working for and their concerns.

An educational evaluation is responsive evaluation (1) if it orients more directly to program activities than to program intents, (2) if it responds to audience requirements for information, and (3) if the different value perspectives of the people at hand are referred to in reporting the success and failure of the program. In these three separate ways an evaluation plan can be responsive.

To do a responsive evaluation, the evaluator of course does many things. He makes a plan of observations and negotiations. He arranges for various persons to observe the program. With their help he prepares brief narratives, portrayals, product displays, graphs, etc. He finds out what is of value to his audiences. He gathers expressions of worth from various individuals whose points of view differ. Of course, he checks the quality of his records. He gets authority figures to react to the importance of various findings. He gets audience members to react to the rele-

vance of his findings. He does much of this informally, iterating, and keeping a record of action and reaction. He chooses media accessible to his audiences to increase the likelihood and fidelity of communication. He might prepare a final written report; he might not—depending on what he and his clients have agreed on.

Many of my fellow evaluators are committed to the idea that good education results in measurable outcomes: student performance, mastery, ability, attitude. But I believe it is not always best to think of the instrumental *value of education as a basis for evaluating it. The "payoff" may be diffuse, long delayed; or it may be ever beyond the scrutiny of evaluators.*

Instead of objectives or hypotheses as "advanced organizers" for an evaluation study, I prefer issues. *I think the word* issues *better reflects a sense of complexity, immediacy, and valuing. After getting acquainted with a program, partly by talking with students, parents, taxpayers, program sponsors, and program staff, the evaluator acknowledges certain issues or problems or potential problems. These issues are a structure for continuing discussions with clients, staff, and audiences. These issues are a structure for the data gathering plan. The systematic observations to be made, the interviews and tests to be given, if any, should be those that contribute to understanding or resolving the issues identified.*

Consultants and evaluators too often find themselves preparing a report for the wrong audience. If they wish to capture the interest of more than one audience, they must collect data that each will find important and prepare the report in a style that will communicate with each. To this end it is usually helpful to have two or three members of the audience review the report before it is cast into final form.

Before they entrust you with information about themselves, however, your clients will want to know whether you can keep information confidential. To demonstrate that you can, protect your information in every conceivable way. Do not ask for respondents' names if you can avoid doing so. Keep questionnaires and notes about the school constantly in hand or in a briefcase within reach; never leave notes about clients in an unattended room or hallway, even if they are locked in a briefcase or box, because these can easily be carried off. Do not gossip with friends about juicy bits of data. Allow only those office personnel to see data who must see them to process them; any names should be converted to numbers as the first step in data processing, and so on. It is impossible to be overcareful in protecting clients from the exposure of information they expect to be kept confidential.

If any of your work has federal financial support, it is important to know that any agency of the Department of Health, Education, and Welfare requires you to submit a detailed plan showing how you intend to protect your clients from harm. This is a legal requirement that cannot be violated without penalty. As of February 1976, the chief federal documents governing the protection of human subjects are the following:

> DHEW Publication no. (NIH) 72-102, December 1971: The Institutional Guide to DHEW Policy on Protection of Human Subjects.
>
> DHEW Part 46. Protection of Human Subjects, Federal Register, vol. 39, no. 105, 30 May 1974.
>
> DHEW Part 46. Protection of Human Subjects, Technical Amendments, Federal Register, vol. 40, no. 50, 13 March 1975.

SOME TECHNICALITIES

This section explores several topics that in most textbooks come under the heading of "experimental design." Consultants will be able to make direct use of many of these ideas. Some that apply more to large-scale experiments, or to evaluations of a scope that few OD consultants have the budgets to mount, are included so that the consultants will be conversant with them on encountering other professionals—directors of research or evaluation in the school district, for example—who use them in their work.

Before and After

It is not enough for OD consultants to find after consultation and training that the client group is showing a certain desired pattern of behavior, because it is possible that they exhibited the same pattern of behavior before consultation or training. To determine whether this is so, the consultant takes an assessment both before and after the intervention. In the following notation borrowed from Campbell and Stanley (1963)—O_1 X O_2—the symbol O_1 represents a measurement made before the intervention, X stands for the intervention, and O_2 represents a measurement made after the intervention. The difference between O_1 and O_2 is an indication of the effect of X.

When the consultant is evaluating the effect of a small cycle, the O_1 observation may be very informal. During the early phases of training, for example, the consultant might suggest that a few members of the group state in their own words whatever consensus they believe has so far been achieved and might use their responses as rough indicators of their understanding of the concept of consensus and of paraphrasing skill. Again, having heard during entry frequent complaints about the lack of success of certain groups in making decisions for carrying out tasks, the consultant might compare this very rough indication of low productivity in group problem solving with three or four consecutive instances of successful task completion after training.

Some kinds of outcomes require greater precision in measurement than these. If there is hope of reducing the number of disciplinary cases in a school, for example, it is important that everyone agree on the marks by which a disciplinary case is to be recognized and also on the manner in which cases are to be observed and reported. If the report of a reduction in discipline cases is to be believed, the consultant must be able to demonstrate that a change in students' behavior is a more likely explanation for the change in the count than a change in the characteristics used by teachers to identify cases.

If differences between conditions at two or more different times are to be compared and assessed objectively, the measurements should be made by methods as alike as possible—that is, if a questionnaire item is used at O_1, the same item should be used at O_2. This is not to say that several different methods may not be used but rather that any method used at O_1 must be replicated at O_2 if a difference in measurement is to be attributed to the behavior of the people observed and not to the method of measurement. Typically, before-and-after information is collected by means of questionnaires, prestructured interviews, or direct observations; but whatever the method used, both the method and the decision about what kind of data to take must be planned long before the actual intervention begins.

A disadvantage of the $O_1 \ X \ O_2$ design is that effects other than those arising from X may have produced the difference between O_1 and O_2. For example, if a consultant gives training in face-to-face communication to a department in a high school at which many other innovative things are occurring at the same time, the eagerness to join others in exciting new activities may produce increased openness of communication even without the training.

Comparing the behavior of the trained group with the behavior of another group that did not undergo training, as:

$$\text{Group 1:} \quad X \ O_2$$
$$\text{Group 2:} \quad \ O_4$$

checks on this weakness. If both groups belong to the innovative school, and the group receiving training shows the greater openness of communication, it is reasonable to infer that the training caused it. Unlike the first design, however, which may check on level of skill at the outset, the second design does not show where the two groups started with respect to the behavior to be altered. If the first group ends by showing greater skill than the second, it may be because we happened to select two groups that began with different degrees of skills, so that in actuality the training has had no effect.

The strengths of these two designs for assessment can be combined using two groups, with measurements taken in both groups before and after the training, but with training given to only one group:

$$\text{Group 1 (experimental):} \quad O_1 \ X \ O_2$$
$$\text{Group 2 (control):} \quad \ O_3 \quad O_4$$

If you wish to be sure that the training is imparting listening skills, for example, you can obtain evidence of the training's effect by assessing group skill both before and after training—perhaps by posting an observer to tally instances of paraphrasing and other specific skills during preplanned ten-minute intervals—and complement this evidence by observing the use of listening skills in one or more groups that do not undergo training. These designs can be used equally well at any stage of the consultant's work, whenever there is time for advance planning.

Applying these designs for assessment to more distant goals requires only the appropriate measures and longer periods of time. In proposing a program of organization development, for example, you might argue that the training would make teachers more aware of the valuable knowledge and skills possessed by others and would give them practice in calling on these human resources in collaborative problem solving, especially during times of stress. After a period of operating with the new collaborative mode, members would form clear opinions about the actual availability of skilled aid from others and would perceive that others had clear opinions about it as well. As one way of assessing the availability of human resources, you might assign interviewers to ask the following questions before training, soon after training, a year afterward, and two years afterward.

When it becomes difficult to keep the school operating smoothly, what people can you count on to pitch in with some extra work?

1. _____ 4. _____
2. _____ 5. _____
3. _____ 6. _____

[If named any:] Now I want to ask something more about each of these people. Take [name no. 1]. How do you think *that person* would answer the question you just answered? (Whom would *that person* feel he or she could count on to pitch in with extra work?)

Whom would no. 2 name? _____
Whom would no. 3 name? _____
No. 4? _____
No. 5? _____
No. 6? _____

In schools operating under a strict hierarchy of authority, with only vertical channels of communication, most teachers are likely to answer the first part of the question with "I don't know" or "No one" or by naming only one person. We would expect little change in this pattern immediately after training except for the addition of the names of persons who attended training with the respondent. (If everyone in the school underwent training, there might be a widespread increase in the number of names mentioned at this point.) A year later, however, respondents should be giving more names in answer to the first part of the question and indicating more perceptions of congruent opinions on the part of other teachers in answer to the second part. If the new pattern of collaboration remains stable, we could expect a similar pattern of answers after the second year.

Certain further measurements, such as checking whether the training actually produced the immediate conditions expected, will bolster the consultant's case. Were teachers more aware of the knowledge and skills possessed by their colleagues than they were before training? Were they more realistic in their judgments of the advantages and risks of collaborative work? In both cases, a simple question asked before and after training could suffice. If these conditions were not produced, the claim that the training led to the later increase in use of human resources collapses.* A control group can be used to check whether some event other than the training may have brought about the expanded use of human resources. A school organization that is not being trained but that is subject to the same influences as the trained school organization could also be measured to produce the pretest–posttest–control-group design described earlier.

The purpose of using a control group is to provide a base rate against which to compare and measure the effects of an intervention. Often, however, a base rate is so well known that little is to be gained by measuring it again. For example, a consultant might use techniques of OD to enable teachers to engage in management by objectives (MBO). Although certain parts of the MBO procedure are being used in a number of schools in this country, the fact that few schools or districts use the entire MBO prescription is such common knowledge among educators that it is hardly worth the trouble to find a control group to demonstrate the absence of full-scale MBO in them.

On the other hand, while the infrequent use of communication skills such as paraphrasing would have been an example of a widely known base rate only a few years ago, many teachers have gained communication skills since then from one or another kind of laboratory training, including such packaged programs as that by NWREL-XICOM (1970). Thus, consultants can no longer assume that teachers whose schools have not undergone OD training will be unacquainted with contemporary concepts and techniques of face-to-face communication. Consultants should be wary, in any case, of resting on their own beliefs about what is or is not widely known. When comparing outcomes with a base rate that is believed to be common knowledge, it is prudent to check your assumptions about the base rate with several professionals, several nonprofessionals, and with the educational literature to be sure that they agree.

Trends, Series, and Sequences. The sequence of causation from the beginning to the end of an OD project of large scope, however, is too

---

*Charters and Jones (1973) have explained this point well.

complicated for simple before-and-after assessments. Consultants should be able to present data justifying their claim that a given outcome took shape through a series of planned and deliberate steps, each of which was instrumental in making more advanced steps possible. To this end they should assess the condition and functioning of the client subsystem after every important step, noting the dates on which important interventions occurred, the dates on which pre- and postintervention assessments were made, the designations of the subsystems from which data were taken, and the abilities, qualities, or conditions assessed.

Careful documentation will reveal the causal chain leading from one step to the next. If a documentation can show that the steps exhibited immediate results that approximated, at each step and more or less in order, the interim outcomes that were planned, it is much easier for the consultant to claim that the intervention or some part of it produced the final outcome, and that the outcome was not produced by some condition (such as the availability of extra money) that existed simultaneously with the intervention. It will usually not be easy to argue that the outcome of any one particular step produced the necessarily right conditions for the next step to have its effect in turn. But if the interim outcomes can be shown to move fairly steadily toward the eventual outcome, it would be excessive for anyone to claim that the whole catenation fell together by chance or was produced by some background factor. The inference from such a chain is always stronger than an inference from any one of its links.

Consider, for example, a hypothetical consultation designed around the Imaging procedure (chap. 5) to enable two opposing groups to agree on the mutual behaviors or subproblems that are obstructing the solutions of larger problems. Suppose that before the intervention, and especially before the Imaging, the consultation data showed for these groups very low or even zero rates for bringing out unpleasant facts, trying to understand each other's positions, asking each other's views on disagreements, or agreeing on common problems whose solutions would benefit both, and that after the Imaging they were better able to do these things. Suppose, too, that a skeptic remarks, "But after ten hours of talking and game playing together, maybe they were ready to make progress anyway, and the Imaging itself was irrelevant." Because there are always alternative hypotheses that might be true, the consultant might not be able to make an air-tight case for the Imaging alone.

Suppose, however, that the consultant had been tracking and documenting the consultation over the weeks and could point to the actual steps at which problems had been conceived in a new way, at which joint steps had been taken by groups that had never done so before, at which the two groups had joined in discussion and work that many had believed impossible at the start, at which they had appealed to information and skills presented during the consultation, and at which they had coordinated their actions by referring to their planning and comparing their actions with that planning. Because of the

498

concatenation of these events and the clients' use of the "products" of the events for coordinating later events, a reasonable critic would have to admit that the chain of events had had a strong causal effect on the outcome.

The "Good" School. On occasion, when a school succeeds in making a complex, difficult organizational change, an onlooker will say, "Sure, but that school was good when the project started; the change didn't have far to go," implying that insofar as the school was already "good," the observed change was a foregone conclusion and required little thought, effort, or help from a consultant.* Although some schools already moving toward a good or better condition are more ready than others to profit from OD consultation, this does not necessarily mean that they are already very close to a state of lively and constructive organizational adaptability. A school with high skill in organizational adaptability seems capable of meeting any problem with aplomb, vigor, and cheer and of making a success of almost everything it undertakes. But a "good" school is seldom good in all the ways necessary for strong skill in organizational adaptation, nor is a "good" school this year automatically likely to be equally good or better next year.

Every year, in any school district, it is inevitable to find one school that is superior in some single respect, as in standing out from the crowd in percentage of last year's graduates enrolled in the next higher level of education, for percentage of staff contributing to the Community Chest, for having a curricular innovation in operation for several consecutive years, and so on. Equally inevitable is the fact that in any year one school must stand out for having the lowest percentage of last year's students going on to more education, and so on.

In any cluster of schools, at any given time, some will be found far in one direction or another from the "average" at the center; at another time most of those that were at the periphery will be somewhere closer to the center, while those that were earlier at the center will now be out at the edge of things. The typical school oscillates between the edge and the center; the unusual school stays in the same place for long periods; but it is remarkably unusual for a school to stay at the top (or bottom) of some list year after year and still more remarkably unusual for it to stay at the top of more than one list. In sum, a school that looks good this year is not ordinarily to be expected to be good next year as well. It takes special ability or special help to remain "good."

The Routine Year. Because the aim of OD is to help people in organizations do things for themselves, consultants cannot claim that a project has reached a successful outcome while they are still offering

---

* This discussion is indebted to chapters 10 and 14 of Runkel, Wyant, and Bell (1975).

their help. The outcome must be evaluated after the clients are on their own and amid the same conditions under which they will be carrying out their work in the new way. At the subsystem and organizational levels, skills are exercised on a yearly cycle. If a school wishes to improve its problem-solving capacity as a total organization, for example, the new skill will be tested throughout the turning of the academic year; but its first single trial must be another year in duration, and its first adequate trial will come in the first "routine" year—usually at the end of the third year after the consultants' departure.

The first routine year occurs when a school can say, "This is how we customarily do things," meaning that the preceding year was just like the present one. The first year after the consultants' departure is not routine because, although the clients will now be doing the new thing on their own, the consultants had been present the previous year. The second year is not routine because the clients had spent the previous year testing whether they could get along without the consultants. The third year is the first possible routine year because it is the first in which the preceding year can be said to be just like the present one.

An assessment at the end of the third year gives an estimate of how well the new thing works under ordinary conditions, but it does not tell us whether skill with the new thing is increasing or diminishing. To ascertain that trend, the consultants should take further assessments at the end of the fourth year and—since two points are a poor basis for projecting a trend—at the end of the fifth year as well. The necessity for longer study arises especially in schools in which other active projects may significantly affect the conditions within which the first project must operate. In other words, some schools have no routine conditions into which a new way of doing things can settle. Under these circumstances, the outcomes of your project should be assessed for a much longer time to reduce the possibility that the stir aroused by some other project is giving your project a vital boost or holding it below its potential.

Few projects intended to produce organizational change in public schools are evaluated with such thoroughness; but when evaluations are made over a shorter time, consultants are only making guesses about the future. Whether a project is worth evaluating for five or more years depends on several factors, including: (1) whether the changes to be brought about do, in fact, rest on a yearly cycle; (2) whether the project shows auspicious signs of achieving success; (3) how long it will probably take for the project to achieve success; (4) what kind and degree of profit will result from a successful project; (5) what its cost will be; and (6) what the costs of evaluation will be. If a project has cost a great deal of money and is showing fair or better signs of success, if the potential profit is good and the costs of evaluation are moderate, continuing to evaluate is likely to give the most benefit for the least cost, while discontinuing evaluation would waste much of the original investment.

Validity, Generalization, and Sampling

The relationship between consultants and clients constitutes a difference between OD projects and many purely research or innovative projects. In many research projects, from pretests through posttests, the attitude of school people toward the data collector is one of distant acquaintanceship and irritable tolerance. In even a very brief OD project, however, the client-consultant relationship becomes increasingly intimate, trusting, and committed as time passes, especially when clients feel they are receiving a clear benefit. Consultants who are also the collectors of evaluative data will get different answers to the same questions at different times, not only because external factors may have changed in the interim but also because clients who have grown more trusting will confide at a later date what they had been unwilling to confide earlier. Indeed, clients will often transfer this growing intimacy and trust to professional evaluators who, unlike the consultants, have no other interaction with them.

When consultants first collect data on job satisfaction, for example, before they have carried out any consultation, respondents will season their answers with a large measure of protectiveness ("Sure, I like it here OK; I have no complaints"). Given multiple choices, they will usually check a favorable item, even if it is not the most favorable response offered. They do that because, at first acquaintance, school people do not know whether their answers will be passed on to their superiors; parents (especially those in poverty) do not know whether their answers will be passed on to school authorities, social service agencies, or the police; and students have no way of knowing whether their answers will be passed on to all the above. Clients tend initially to withhold information about unhappy feelings, but as trust grows they begin to open up about their unhappiness with their school, their jobs, their working conditions, and the people with whom they work. Therefore clients will frequently answer questions about satisfaction more unfavorably several months after consultation begins than they did before it began, even though they may be feeling more hopeful than they felt before.

Another feature of OD work may exacerbate this effect. When social science researchers ask their "subjects" for information, for example, they have usually been authorized to do so because their entry into the organization has been legitimized by someone of authority within the organization: "Dr. Scaramouche is here from the university to conduct a very important study, and we can be a key source of information. I want you to give him your full cooperation." No matter how gently researchers may talk, this mode of entry inevitably gives them a measure of power or authority over the subjects—a relationship almost impossible to avoid as long as the researcher makes unilateral decisions about what to investigate, who will be studied, what the instructions will be, what will be done with the data, and so on.

In contrast, the consultant-client relationship gradually comes to approximate a partnership.* At the beginning of an OD project, many if not most clients expect to be treated as they have been by researchers; at the end, they find themselves being treated as peers and allies, so that it is not surprising that their later answers to questioning should differ from their earlier ones. The point is that if, in striving for objectivity and uniformity in their relationships with subjects, researchers have reaped one kind of contamination of data, OD consultants reap another kind of data contamination as they grow into partnership with their clients. For researchers and consultants alike, the important thing is to be alert for the kind of distortion of data that can be expected.

We have been discussing several difficulties that consultants encounter in maximizing the validity of the information they need; but the core meaning of validity is different for consultants and researchers. Researchers distinguish between internal and external validity.† *Internal validity* denotes how confident we can be that our data have told us something about those from whom we have taken the data. How confident can we be that people in a certain group learned paraphrasing? that people in this school are ready to deal constructively with conflict? that the conversation at last week's meeting affected the course of the planning at this week's meeting? *External validity*—also called *generalizability*—denotes how confident we can be that our data have told us something about those from whom we collected *no* data. How confident are we that our method of teaching paraphrasing would work as well in another school or city? that the indicators of readiness which correctly predicted ability to deal constructively with conflict in this school will predict correctly in another school or another year?

School practitioners are greatly interested in the internal validity of their information but are seldom interested in generalization. The local superintendent on this side of the river, who comes to a conclusion about the best next step to take on the basis of data collected in this district, ordinarily has little curiosity about whether this would also be a good step to take in the district across the river. Researchers, on the other hand, are almost always interested in generalizability and are interested in internal validity only insofar as it bolsters generalizability. Ordinarily the researcher in the district on this side of the river is halfway across the river in spirit before the last questionnaire from this side has been filled out.

OD consultants must be as concerned as practitioners are with the internal validity of their evaluations and will often be concerned

---

* A good example of this is given in chapter 4 of Schmuck, Murray, Smith, Schwartz, and M. Runkel (1975). Argyris (1968) has poignantly described the parallels between being a subject in an experiment and being a worker in a job that is strongly "defined, controlled, evaluated, manipulated, and reported."

† For fuller discussion, see almost any book on experimental or research design in the social sciences—for example, Runkel and McGrath (1972, pp. 44-59 and 158-72).

to some degree with generalizability as well, although not in the same way as many researchers are. That is, they will seldom need to make a statement such as: "I am 98 percent confident that if I repeated in 100 schools the training I just conducted in 10 and that if the 100 were randomly selected from the same population of schools as these 10, the mean scores on the posttests in 98 of those schools would lie between 67 and 83."

The kind of statement the consultant makes is more like: "When I go into a school that differs from these 10 in respect to _____, _____, and _____, the variables to assess that would probably yield the most useful diagnostic information (after which I would take trial steps and then gather more diagnostic information) would be _____, _____, and _____." In other words, the consultant does not expect to draw the next school randomly from a population, does not wish to make a statement about what this school would be like or what might happen there before collecting diagnostic information about it, could not specify confidence in such a statement in any case, and is not interested in the number of schools out of 100 about which some preconceived statement might be correct.

Nevertheless, consultants, too, want to learn from experience how to go into the next school able to make diagnoses that are more valid, quicker, and less of a nuisance to school people than in the last school. It is therefore very important that they keep records of their experiences, periodically publish them in some formal or informal way, and urge other consultants to do likewise. In this way a body of lore can be assembled to help us all choose a likely set of hypotheses when we open conversations with the next client.* The records will be more useful, of course, if they are kept in the detail illustrated in this book. That is, consultants should record dates and places for all important events, methods of data collection used, rates of return of questionnaires (if used), numbers, percentages, and types of persons from whom data were collected, rationale for gathering answers into clusters or categories, descriptions of all important features of training sessions and other interventions, and so on.

For reasons of cost, researchers must often content themselves with observing or querying fewer people (or whatever unit they are studying) than they would prefer. When they take a sample from all the units that interest them, their concern with generalizable conclusions requires them to draw their samples in very special ways.† Interested in a different kind of generalization, OD consultants have little need to sample from very large or infinite populations, although a few facts may be useful to them concerning sampling from small and finite populations.

---

*This book is an example of one kind of repository of lore; another example is the *Annual Handbook for Group Facilitators* published by University Associates Publishers, 7596 Eads Avenue, La Jolla, Calif. 92037. Other examples include some of the journals cited throughout our references, addresses for which can be obtained from your library.

†Of the many tomes full of ingenious reasoning and mathematical formulas about sampling, see Kish (1965) for an example. For a brief introduction, see Runkel and McGrath (1972) or almost any book on research methods or experimental design.

Accustomed to reading surveys of public opinion in the public press, we have come to accept the fact that the balance of opinion among hundreds of millions of people can be estimated with fair accuracy from a sample of only 2,000 or even 1,500 people—less than .001 of 1 percent of the nation's population. The same percentage does not apply to small populations, however. You cannot accurately estimate among 100,000 people the proportion who would answer yes to some question by querying only one of them, although that would be the same percentage as 2,000 out of 200 million.

Table 11-1, which is provided for easy reference when you are sampling from a small population, answers a question of this type: From how many cases will I have to take data if I want to have no more than X-percent error either way in my estimate and if I want to be confident that my error would not exceed that in at least 95 out of 100 samples of the size that I would draw? That is, if you were going to query a certain number of people and were going to take that sample 100 times, drawing different people but the same number every time, you would get different proportions of people answering yes from sample to sample. Small errors (deviations from the proportion in the population) would be frequent, but large errors would be infrequent. The table is constructed to tell you the sizes of samples that would give you errors (above or below the population proportion) no greater than those shown at the tops of the columns in at least 95 percent of 100 samplings.

When they are feeding back data to clients about the clients' school or district or when they or their evaluator colleagues are evaluating outcomes, OD consultants often wish to make close estimates of opinion. When they want to be fairly accurate in their estimates, they should choose a small error and draw a strictly random sample. For other purposes, consultants can accept considerable latitude in their estimates. They may be thinking, for example: "If opinion X is held by only three or four people in this school, we won't have to make special allowance in the training plans but can explore the effects of their opinion with these few persons individually. But if the number of persons holding that opinion reaches 20 percent of the staff, we'd better take time out to explore personal needs." In

.TABLE 11-1   Sample Sizes Required to Estimate Specified
Errors in at least 95 of 100 Samples

Population	Error of 2.5 percent	Error of 7.5 percent	Error of 15 percent
1000	606	146	41
300	251	109	37
100	94	63	30
50	48	38	23
20	20	18	14

this case the consultants do not wish to get a close estimate of the percentage holding that opinion; they only want to know whether the percentage might reach 20 or anything beyond.

To work out this example, let us suppose that we are working with a school having 100 staff members. Looking at the table under 15 percent error, we find that we can get an estimate within 15 percentage points by querying 30 people. If we randomly select and interview these people and if only 2 of them answer yes, the estimate of the population proportion on the basis of our sample would be 2/30 = 7 percent. And we know that in 95 out of 100 samples of 30, the actual population proportion will be 15 percentage points larger or smaller than that estimate. Adding 7 to 15, we find that the population proportion could be as high as 22 percent in a few of those samples.

On the basis of this sampling, we can be fairly confident that the actual proportion among the 100 people is very little beyond 20 percent, if at all. Thus interviewing only 30 members of a faculty of 100 persons has saved us a great deal of work. On the other hand, if 6 of the 30 persons had answered yes, it might still be true that no more than 20 among the 100 would answer yes, but we can no longer be 95 percent confident of this. If we do not wish to risk an important decision about the design of the training on a low-confidence estimate, we must enlarge the sample, select more people randomly, and ask them the question.

In sum, if you want to be fairly accurate about the responses of 50 or fewer people, interview them all. If you want to be fairly accurate about more people than that and want to draw a sample instead of interviewing them all, remember that these calculations apply only to samples drawn with strict randomness—by drawing names from a hat or using a table of random numbers. It takes trouble, of course, to list all the people in your population, to draw a random sample, and then to buttonhole exactly these people. In borderline cases, sampling can be more trouble than it is worth. With a population of 120 or 130, for example, it might be less work to interview everyone than to draw a sample of 111 or 119.

READINGS

Justice in Evaluation

Ernest R. House*

In this paper, House deals with some of the most stressful self-questionings that evaluators of outcomes encounter. The ques-

---

*This paper is so heavily indebted to the ideas explicated in John A. Rawls' A Theory of Justice that footnoting all the influences is hopeless. While I had considered the concept of justice in evaluation, I had no clear-cut conception of it. Of course, Rawls is not responsible for my interpretation of his work.

tions are often brought to the evaluator by people who are directly or indirectly affected by the evaluation; there are no simple answers to them, and there is no convenient placard bearing a "standard procedure" designation behind which the evaluator can hide. Whatever policy the evaluator chooses, the effects spill over into the community and the future.

"Justice in Evaluation" in Gene V. Glass (Ed.), *Evaluation Studies Review Annual* (Vol. 1). Beverly Hills, Calif.: Sage 1976.

> Justice is the first virtue of social institutions, as truth is of systems of thought.
>
> John Rawls
> *A Theory of Justice*

Evaluation is by its nature a political activity. It serves decision-makers, results in reallocations of resources, and legitimizes who gets what. . . . Evaluation should not only be true; it should also be just. Current evaluation schemes, independently of their truth value, reflect justice in quite varying degrees. And justice provides an important standard by which evaluation should be judged. . . .

Utilitarian Evaluation

. . . The student-gain-by-testing approach is based on utilitarian ethics. Utilitarian ethics, according to Rawls (1971), stipulates that a society is just when its institutions are arranged so as to achieve the greatest net balance of satisfaction as summed over all individuals. The principle of utility is to maximize that net balance of satisfaction. Utilitarianism requires that there be a common measure or index of satisfaction in order that quantitative calculations of utility can be made. In education, this common measure is almost always construed to be standardized test scores. It is the surrogate index of satisfaction. . . .

In modern economics, heavily dependent on utilitarian thought, there is a very great emphasis on the production of basic goods but little attention as to how those goods are distributed. Attention is focused on increasing total production rather than on distribution of the goods. In utilitarian evaluation the emphasis is on increasing test scores, not on how those scores are distributed. Social reforms concerned with such a distribution fail, I believe, because there is an inherent contradiction built into utilitarian evaluation.

Utilitarian justice means that total net satisfaction is maximized. If someone has greater desires and expectations than everyone else, those must be considered, desire for desire, equally with someone with fewer desires. In a sense, if one has greater expectations, one is entitled to more. It is even possible to take away satisfactions from those with less in order to appease someone who "needs" more. Similarly, in education one often hears that everyone should be educated to his potential. Implicit in this dictum is the assumption that there is a hierarchy of needs and that those with more abilities deserve more education. . . .

In education the desires (needs, objectives, etc.) are taken pretty much as given. We mount "needs assessments" to determine these needs as objectively and quantitatively as we can. In our measurement theory, based on individual differences, the needs are intrinsic and lie there waiting to be measured, prioritized, and balanced against other needs. If upper-class people have very great expectations for their children, all their desires enter in the analysis and demand satisfaction. Their fulfillment will be reflected in the common measure of achievement scores and all the basic goods and values dependent in society on those scores. Distribution across people is not nearly as important as the total sum. Maximize everywhere is the dictum. . . .

Clearly, morally, we have a problem. Since all desires are taken at face value and since expectations and desires are much higher in the upper social and economic classes, utilitarianism has a tremendous upper-class bias built into it as a system of justice. One man's desire for a Rolls Royce is just as valid a claim as another man's desire for a Ford. The greater demands of upper- and middle-class students are honored at the expense of the lower classes.

In utilitarianism it is essential that everything be conflated into one system of desires so that justice can be served. Everything must be reduced to a unitary measure so that comparisons are possible. How else can one determine the right thing to do? The basic method of comparison is the classic utilitarian "impartial spectator." By being both impartial and sympathetic to all parties, the spectator (needs assessor) can organize all desires (needs) into one coherent system of desires and gives them appropriate weight in the overall system (evaluates). An administrator or legislator (the ubiquitous decision-maker) then adjusts the limited means in order to maximize the satisfaction of those desires. The result is efficient administration with the highest possible maximum satisfaction. . . .

Pluralist-Intuitionist Evaluation

Not all evaluation is "student-gain-by-testing." A contemporary counterstream began in 1967 with the publication of Stake's "Countenance" paper (1967) and Scriven's "Methodology" paper (1967). Stake suggested the legitimacy of data other than test scores and in particular advocated using the judgments of various people connected with the program under evaluation. He also suggested that the evaluation be addressed to diverse audiences and that different audiences might want quite different information. I have called this "democratizing knowledge demands" (House, 1973). The implicit idea is one of participation, similar to the idea of pluralist politics.

These are radical ideas. Although not aimed directly at justice as such, increasing public accessibility to evaluations, both as data sources and audiences, meant that the values of diverse groups would be brought into play. At least diverse value claims could be registered in evaluation even if they could not be resolved.

In a quite different way, Scriven (1967) also deviated from the utilitarian paradigm. Although most of his classic paper suggested comparative experiments and other means of strengthening the efficiency of research methodology, Scriven suggested that the goals themselves must be evaluated—a radical idea in the utilitarian conception. Scriven also suggested that secondary and tertiary effects of programs should be examined. The utilitarian approach has a difficult time dealing with long-range effects on diverse groups.

Later these ideas developed into "goal-free" evaluation (Scriven, 1973) in which the evaluator searches for effects from the program while remaining intentionally ignorant of the program's express goals in order that he/she might better concentrate on what is happening rather than on what is supposed to happen. This prevents the dominance of predetermined goals or preselected measures of output like test scores. . . .

A third major evaluation theorist who became prominent about this time was Stufflebeam (1971). His focusing of evaluation on the concerns of decision-makers has placed him in the management school of evaluation in his early work; but in his insistence on service, data other than test scores become useful so that his formulations resulted in a broader data base. For him, decision-makers came to include not only administrators, whose concerns might be narrowly utilitarian, but also parents, the public, and most interested parties. His emphasis on the usefulness of the information expanded the classic paradigm, though tests were still a part. In later papers, Stufflebeam has gravitated towards a wider conception of evaluation and has begun employing criteria other than those directly derived from utility to decision-makers (Stufflebeam, 1975). . . .

The Illinois Gifted Program evaluation (House, Steele, Kerins, 1971) was modeled after Stake's "Countenance" model. We collected vast amounts of data, both qualitative and quantitative, but few test scores. After the evaluation the consumers were highly pleased—a good but not infallible sign of success. The legislators were happy; the overseeing advisers were happy, the state staff was happy; and even the demonstration directors, the group which had taken the most criticism, were reasonably happy.

As I went through my own mind checking on what we had done and not done, I realized that we had not investigated the possibilities of elitist attitudes developing among the students or the possible ill effects society might reap from such stratification. We had planned to investigate it, but it was so low on our priority list that we never got around to it. . . .

Later, as evaluators came to us for help, one of the first questions we learned to ask was, "Who are your audiences for the evaluation?" Much would be determined from that. In a broad evaluation, one includes all participants and audiences, faithfully reflecting their opinions and claims. Eventually, though, one senses he may be in a relativistic trap, for how is one to adjudicate conflicting claims about a program? Indeed, should one even try or should the evaluator not simply report the conflicts and be done? If not, should the evaluator do his own balancing and weighing? How does he justify that? The unease of pluralistic evaluation is well expressed by Hamilton (1974):

> *Yet, where does this lead the evaluator? By abandoning the security of objectivism for the ill-defined tenets of pluralism, have we opened the door to relativism? Shall we arrive at a position where there are no grounds for deciding the worth, truth or value of anything? Have we laid the basis for a value-free evaluation? If so, can we afford such a luxury?*

By admitting the views and consequently the criteria of diverse groups, the new evaluation has arrived at a position either of intuitionism or perhaps of relativism. The perspectives and demands of various groups must be presented without any way of ordering or choosing among them. This plurality of "first principles" Rawls calls intuitionism. There is a plurality of principles which may conflict with one another, and there are no priority rules for weighing them against each other. One strikes a balance of what's right primarily by intuition. . . .

At best, then, "new" evaluations may employ pluralistic principles to arrive at judgments which seem to be intuitively right. They are likely to do this by employing judgments and criteria of people most concerned with the project. One anticipates a feeling that judgment has been fairly and appropriately, although tacitly, arrived at. One could perhaps even describe the bases of judgments after the fact. This may be the best we can do. But it may not be. Even if the great bulk of evaluative judgments remains intuitive, is it possible to find some rough guides to socially just criteria and procedures?

Evaluation with Justice-as-Fairness

In *A Theory of Justice,* John Rawls has suggested two principles of justice by which social institutions and arrangements can be judged. Rawls calls his conception "justice-as-fairness." Justice-as-fairness is a non-teleological theory. The good is not established prior to and independent of the right, and the right is not equivalent to maximizing the good. Rather the right is established prior to the good. Each person is presumed to have non-negotiable rights which cannot be bargained away no matter how it affects the good.

Unlike utilitarianism, "justice-as-fairness" assumes that there is always a plurality of ends and a distinctness of persons so that one cannot conflate all desires into one system. An agreement by which the good can be distributed and by which disputes can be settled is arrived at first. Then, once the principles of distribution are agreed upon, individuals are free to determine their own good and to pursue it—but always in accord with the agreed-upon principles which determine what is right. . . .

The specific principles of justice for institutions are these (Rawls, pp. 302–303):

First Principle
> Each person is to have an equal right to the most extensive system of equal basic liberties compatible with a similar system of liberty for all.

Second Principle
> Social and economic inequalities are to be arranged so that they are both:
> (a) to the benefit of the least advantaged, consistent with the just savings principle, and
> (b) attached to offices and positions open to all under conditions of fair equality of opportunity.

It is clear from these principles that justice-as-fairness limits other ends. It puts boundaries around the things one may do. One does not take desires and aspirations as given. Rather, desires are restricted by the basic principles. Utilitarianism itself excludes the desires that would lead to a lesser net balance of satisfaction, and one must know many particulars to know what these are.

Justice-as-fairness specifically precludes imposing disadvantages on the few for the advantages of the many. The priority rules for the two principles of justice specify that the first principle always has priority over the second. Basic liberties are to be maximized without regard to social and economic benefits. Only then may social and economic inequalities be allowed. According to the second principle, these inequalities are allowable *only* if they benefit the *least* advantaged in the society. Inequalities are not allowable if the least advantaged are not benefited. Neither can there be any trade-offs of basic liberties for social and economic advantages.

The second principle, the "difference principle," singles out the position of the least advantaged in society to judge whether inequalities are permissible. For example, if high salaries are necessary to attract people to positions that would benefit the least advantaged, then the inequalities may be permissible. (This judgment is in contrast to the "efficiency principle" of utilitarianism. The efficiency principle allows redistributions of primary goods only to the extent that giving to one social group does not take away from another group. This puts heavy emphasis on the existing order of things.) . . .

Assuming for the moment that one accepts Rawls' elaborate and widely acclaimed theory of justice, of what import is it to evaluating, if any? Clearly, the two ungainly principles are so abstract as not to determine evaluation. On the other hand, as an important distributive mechanism, it seems reasonable that evaluation might conform to justice-as-fairness. The basic liberties protected by the first principle are political liberties, freedom of speech and assembly, liberty of conscience and freedom of thought, freedom of person and property, and so on.

In addition, the most important primary good, according to Rawls (p. 440), is self-respect. Without self-respect a person will not see that his own plan of life, whatever it is, is worth pursuing. He is cut off from a basic meaning in life. A major argument against util-itarianism is that some may be forced to give up their expectations in order to benefit the general utility. "That's progress." Having involuntarily to lower their expectations for the sake of others reduces their own basis of self-respect. This is not permissible in justice-as-fairness.

The First Principle of Justice

The first principle can be applied to evaluation in two ways: in what the evaluation looks for and in how the evaluation is conducted. The basic liberties are guaranteed by the first principle, including the right to self-esteem. For example, a major complaint of those who oppose testing in particular is that test scores lower the self-esteem of many children in school. Not only do critics claim that tests are racially and class biased, but radical economists (Bowles and Gintis, 1973) contend that tests are used precisely for the purpose of legit-imizing the hierarchical structure of the social-class system so that even the lower members of society feel they deserve to be where they are. A lowering of expectations is built in.

I will not discuss the general truth of these charges, but in justice-as-fairness these are serious concerns and the proper concern of the evaluator. Often it is easier to determine the worth of a *particular* practice, and that is closer to the evaluator's actual job. For example, sending a child home with his I.Q. score pinned to his coat, now a practice in some large cities, may be repugnant even to die-hard testers. Other practices, such as beating children to raise test scores, are usually ruled out—even if they raise test scores dramatically. There are certain things that cannot be done even in the name of the common good. . . .

The range of disagreement among experts as to the harmful effects to self-esteem resulting from tests is a good example of how indeterminate a situation can be. There is even a sense in which evaluation of any kind may be said to diminish one's self-esteem and consequent ability to pursue a life plan, a case made only too well by Glass (1975). . . .

The "new" evaluation itself opens up avenues of possible assault on self-esteem and other aspects of the first principle. The arbitrari-ness of criteria to be employed, the lack of public justification, and the disregard for conventional research methods and reporting are concerns. For example, what Stake calls the "transaction-observation" school of evaluation proceeds mainly by constructing case studies from personal observation and interview data. Whereas respondents have learned to protect themselves against questionnaires and survey techniques, they do not protect themselves as well against the new evaluation—a source of its power.

The trend in this evaluation is to become more and more per-sonalistic, which makes the evaluation extremely relevant and poten-tially explosive. I cite the responsive case-study evaluation of the PLATO Project (House and Gjerde, 1973), in which we had considerable difficulty with confidentiality, and the UNCAL evaluation now in progress at the University of East Anglia, in which at least one evaluator has been "evicted" from a field site. . . .

My current position on such problems is that I would apply the injury to self-esteem embodied in the first principle in a strong fashion. If the information is injurious to the self-respect of the person involved, it should not be included in the evaluation report—no matter how it affects the good of the project. The rights of the individual are to be protected over the good of the project. Only in the case of trading off this right for another equally important right could this principle be violated. Of course at issue in a project would be the *total system* of basic equal rights of all concerned. A despotic director infringing on the self-esteem of others would not have to be treated so gingerly. Trade-offs of basic rights are permissible. . . .

The Second Principle of Justice

After the first principal is applied fully, one turns to the second principle. That is the order of priority. The essence of the second principle is that social and economic inequities are just only when they are arranged so as to benefit the least advantaged in society. A "representative man" from the least advantaged sector must prefer his prospects with inequalities to his prospects without them. The social structure is judged from a particular social position—that of the least advantaged. The disadvantages of those lower in the social structure cannot be justified by the advantages that may accrue to the rest of the society, as would be permitted in utilitarianism. Of course, this judging must be done consistently with the first principle. One cannot trade off basic liberties for social and economic benefits.

As with the first principle, the second principle can be applied in two ways: as a criterion for the program and as a criterion for the evaluation itself. In the Illinois Gifted Evaluation, we kept in close touch with the program staff and were quite fair on the basis of the first principle. In retrospect, the major weakness was that we did not investigate possible deleterious effects from grouping talented children together. We did investigate the effects on the gifted children themselves—those lower down the hierarchy of the school system, so to speak. But we did not investigate the effects on nongifted students nor consider the broader social impact on the class system. Admittedly, these are not easy questions to resolve, partly because they have not been asked often enough. But they should have been addressed more than they were. . . .

As I have indicated elsewhere in detail, the innovation system as it now operates is a hierarchical one with teachers and students at the bottom (House, 1974). Within the educational domain, the students are the lower rung; but it is the teacher who must implement and bear the cost of any innovation. Hence, in evaluating any new innovation, an important job for the evaluator is to portray the plight of those at the bottom of the hierarchy. Within the total social scheme, the evaluator must also be concerned with the effect on the least advantaged as socially defined, i.e., the social and economically poor. . . .

The Justice of Specific Evaluation Schemes

I have suggested that many evaluation approaches rely implicitly on a utilitarian sense of justice. I would now like to examine some of the new evaluation approaches that do not—the pluralist intuitionist groups—and see what, if any, difference justice-as-fairness might make for them. I will focus primarily on the group with which I am most familiar and most sympathetic—what Stake (1974) calls the "transaction-observation" approach—which includes Stake (1973), Smith and Pohland (1974), Parlett and Hamilton (1972), and MacDonald (1974). . . .

Historically, the transaction-observation approach derives from Stake's countenance paper and from the tradition of social anthropology. The evaluators have eschewed quantitative output measures as the primary data and use a case-study methodology (or at least narrative reporting), relying heavily on interviews and observations, often quite informal, as the information base. Stake's approach has evolved into "responsive evaluation." . . . The evaluation is aimed at different audiences and indeed different value perspectives. How does one handle these sometimes conflicting situations?

> Each evaluator, in each situation, has to decide what to attend to. The evaluator has to decide. On what basis will he choose the prime questions? Will he rely on his preconceptions? Or on the formal plans and objectives of the program? Or on actual program activities? Or on the reactions of the participants? It is at this choosing that an evaluator himself is tested. (Stake, 1973).

This is a clear statement of the pluralist-intuitionist position.

One cannot choose explicitly before the fact. One does so intuitively. Actually, Stake has a strong service orientation. In attending to program activities, he is likely to be extremely attentive to the program people. This is a result of the values he carries with him, however, not an integral part of responsive evaluation. Responsive evaluation by someone else might be quite different. More recently Stake has focused on negotiations as a way of resolving value conflicts.

Generally I would criticize the case-study approach as being fair to the program participants, which I associate with the first principle, and being weaker on issues of social justice. Sometimes it is not easy to raise such nasty issues with people who are struggling to create a program and who are giving so much of themselves, especially when one has gotten to know them well through informal interviews and observation and to appreciate their points of view. Evaluators need to be sympathetic to their concerns, since the difficulty of their efforts is greatly underappreciated. On the other hand, what about the interests and concerns of those who are not represented, particularly those who often have no voice at all? The evaluator is not obligated to speak for them, but he is obligated to listen to them and to search for those viewpoints. . . .

A similar critique can be made of MacDonald's "democratic" evaluation (MacDonald, 1974; MacDonald and Walker, 1974). MacDonald has come to view evaluation increasingly as a political activity and to treat data control as a central issue. His approach is not unlike Stake's but with a few fascinating twists. "Democratic evaluation" is conceived as an "information service to the community, recognizing value pluralism, ' and responds to practitioner definitions of the program. "The criterion of success is the range of audiences served. . . . The key justificatory concept is 'the right to know.' "

Although as in responsive evaluation there is no clear way to get beyond the pluralist/intuitionist relative-value position, the value basis of "democratic evaluation," at least in rhetoric, implicitly edges close to the precepts of justice-as-fairness and democratic equality presented in this paper. One of its most radical aspects is that the people being evaluated have final say over release of the evaluation results. This enhances fairness consistent with the first principle of justice although one suspects it may cost considerably in the second. In the Rawlsian interpretation, however, participation by the least advantaged is neither sufficient nor necessary for the application of the difference principle. It is not just if the least advantaged agree to something that is not to their advantage.

Whatever the success of various specific techniques, in spirit at least, "democratic" evaluation is similar to justice-as-fairness, as is responsive evaluation, in emphasizing negotiation procedures. The evaluator negotiates with sponsor and participants. Unfortunately, the least advantaged are often not represented or considered. Justice-as-fairness is derived from a hypothetical situation in which morally equal beings negotiate how they will treat each other. The theoretical difficulty with negotiating the results of an evaluation is that people will censor what is not in their interests. In justice-as-fairness, negotiation is carried out when everyone is ignorant of his own specific interests. Nonetheless, negotiations between equals are key ideas in responsive and democratic evaluation—at least in my interpretation. . . .

Two other new promising evaluation approaches worth mentioning are goal-free evaluation (Scriven, 1973) and adversary evaluation (Owens, 1973; Levine, 1973; and Wolf, 1974). These have not been utilized enough to tell how they conform to the concept of justice-as-fairness. I would guess that goal-free evaluation will be strong on the second principle. It may respect the rights of the participants somewhat less.

The same may be true of adversary evaluation. It seems likely to raise significant social issues that other approaches do not. The adversary approach raised social issues in the TCity evaluation (Stake and Gjerde, 1974). A possible weakness is in treating the participants fairly. A trial does not always do that. Nonetheless, legal procedures have been especially invented to adjudicate claims and attain justice. This may be a promising area to look for useful techniques if not a whole approach. Wolf (1974), who most recently champions the "judicial" model of evaluation, contends that adversary procedures may have to be modified considerably to be useful.

A "Just" versus a "Good" Program

. . . A program may be good or bad simultaneously from two differ- ent viewpoints. Neither is there anything necessarily "right" about the "goodness" of something. One can have a "good" assassin (from the government's point of view) but that does not make the assassin morally right. A good program from the government's viewpoint is often not good from the viewpoint of the teacher. . . .

An aggregate single measure like gross national product or test scores is the way to indicate satisfactions. The evaluation is con- cerned with efficiency, i.e., did the program really result in the gains in achievement? Presumably these gains lead to higher social and economic pay-offs. Gains in test scores, with appropriate concern for the validity of the tests, tightness of the research design, etc., would constitute the evaluation. A conscientious utilitarian might also push for more direct affective student measure. It is assumed that raising test scores for everyone is the right thing to do regardless of other social consequences.

A pluralist-intuitionist evaluation might consist of a case study based on interviews with parents, teachers, and students and observa- tions of the classes and the school. If carefully done, the evaluation might include each of the major perspectives on the program. Repre- senting these possibly divergent views would be the task. There might or might not be specific recommendations on program improvement. The various viewpoints would not be assessed or, if they were, the assessment would be implicit and balanced after the fact. Tests and other psychometric measures probably would not be used. If they were, they would not play a significant role in the evaluation. There would be no overt adjudication of conflicting viewpoints or value systems.

How would an explicitly "just" evaluation differ? According to the first principle of justice, the basic liberties of the parents, teach- ers, and students, including self-esteem, could not be infringed upon. Any method which raised test scores at the expense of self-esteem would be judged as wrong—for any one of the concerned groups. If the self-esteem of one group depended on detracting from the self- esteem of another, that is simply not right.

By the second principle, social and economic inequalities must benefit the least advantaged in the long run. The educationally least advantaged within most settings are the children first and the teachers second. The evaluator should strive to present their views and perspectives. In addition, there are the least advantaged in the whole of society. Insofar as the educational gains are translatable into social and economic advantages to a particular group at the expense of others, the program must be justified on the contention that the inequalities are to the benefit of the least advantaged.

At least once within the priorities of the two principles as applied, the program should be regarded from the perspective of the educationally least advantaged and the socially least advantaged. In conflicting situations over inequalities, the interests of the least advantaged are to take precedence—consistent with the other principles. Excessive aspirations on the part of those higher in society are discounted in justice-as-fairness.

An evaluation procedure which was just would investigate these areas of concern. The resolution of many of these issues would depend on intuition and specific information in the context. Often there would be no resolution. By no means are intuitive judgments eliminated. They are only delimited by the moral basis of the two principles. The issues of justice would be attended to in any program and in any evaluation.

It may be that other evaluations already arrive at the same concerns. Perhaps they already employ implicit principles similar to those made explicit here. Not only do many difficult judgments remain in an evaluation consistent with justice-as-fairness but a good program and a good evaluation are still subject to other criteria that evaluators and metaevaluators often apply—insofar as the criteria can be justified. . . .

In my opinion, justice-as-fairness is clearly superior to utilitarian evaluation. It protects basic liberties and redresses the ills of those least socially and economically advantaged. I am less certain of its superiority over the pluralist/intuitionist position. In this paper I have ignored some of its inherent philosophic difficulties. For example, some critics contend that the priority of the first principle over the second means that one would never apply the difference principle On the other hand, some economists claim that even the smallest benefit to the least advantaged would justify taking nearly everything away from the advantaged.

Neither is there complete congruence between justice-as-fairness and intuitive thoughts about fairness. In my mind there is a confusion between consideration of the position of the least advantaged and their active participation in decisions. While neither consideration nor participation is required in the other two positions, in my understanding of Rawls only consideration is required. If so, I find this uncomfortably close to paternalism. Nonetheless, in spite of these reservations and others, justice-as-fairness is a prime candidate as a moral basis for evaluation and provides a standard by which evaluations can be judged for their justice.

REFERENCES

Bowles, Samuel, and Gintis, Herbert. I.Q. in the U.S. class structure. *Social Policy*, November/December 1972, January/February 1973, *3*, (4 and 5), 65–69.

516

Elliott, John. *Preparing teachers for classroom accountability.* Presented at Curriculum Development in Teacher Education Seminar, September 1975.

Ellman, Richard. Oxford in the seventies. *The American Scholar,* Autumn 1974, *43,* (4), 567-75.

Glass, Gene V. A paradox about excellence of schools and the people in them. *Educational Researcher,* March 1975, *4,* (3), 9-13.

Hamilton, David. *The end(s) of evaluation.* Presented at meeting of the British Educational Research Association, Birmingham, England, April 6, 1974.

Hampshire, Stuart. Morality and pessimism. *New York Review,* January 25, 1973.

House, Ernest R. The conscience of educational evaluation. *Teachers College Record,* February 1972, *73,* (3), 405-14. Also in Ernest R. House (Ed.), *School evaluation: the politics and process.* Berkeley: McCutchan, 1973.

House, Ernest R. *The politics of educational innovation.* Berkeley: McCutchan, 1974.

House, Ernest R. The price of productivity. *Today's Education,* September/October 1973, *62,* (6), 64-69.

House, Ernest R. Technology and evaluation. *Educational Technology,* November 1973, *13,* (11), 20-26.

House, Ernest R., and Gjerde, Craig. *PLATO comes to the community college.* Urbana: Center for Instructional Research and Curriculum Evaluation, University of Illinois, July 1973. (mimeo)

House, Ernest R., Steele, Joe M., and Kerins, Thomas. *The gifted classroom.* Urbana: Center for Instructional Research and Curriculum Evaluation, University of Illinois, 1971.

Levine, Murray. Scientific method and the adversary model: some preliminary suggestions. *Evaluation Comment,* 1973, 4, (2), 1-3.

MacDonald, Barry. Evaluation and the control of education. Norwich, England: Centre for Applied Research in Education, University of East Anglia, May 1974. (mimeo)

MacDonald, Barry, and Walker, Rob. *The social philosophy of educational research.* Norwich, England. Centre for Applied Research in Education, University of East Anglia, August 1974. (mimeo)

Owens, Thomas R. Educational evaluation by adversary proceedings. In Ernest R. House (Ed.), *School evaluation: the politics and process.* Berkeley: McCutchan, 1973.

Parlett, Malcolm, and Hamilton, David. *Evaluation as illumination: a new approach to the study of innovatory programs,* Occasional Paper 9. Edinburgh: Centre for Research in the Educational Sciences of Edinburgh, Scotland, University of Edinburgh, October 1972.

Rawls, John. *A theory of justice.* Cambridge, Massachusetts: Balknap Press, 1971.

Rosenblatt, Roger. Frederick Wiseman's "welfare." *The New Republic,* September 27, 1975, *173,* (13), Issue 3/68, 65-67.

Scriven, Michael. Goal-free evaluation. In Ernest R. House (Ed.), *School evaluation: the politics and process.* Berkeley: McCutchan, 1973.

Scriven, Michael. The methodology of evaluation. In R. E. Stake (Ed.), *Perspectives of Curriculum Evaluation,* AERA Monograph Series on Curriculum Evaluation, No. 1. Chicago: Rand McNally, 1967.

Smith, Louis M., and Pohland, Paul A. Education, technology, and the rural highlands. In R. E. Stake (Ed.), *Four evaluation examples: anthropological, economic, narrative, and portrayal,* AERA Monograph Series on Curriculum Evaluation, No. 7. Chicago: Rand McNally, 1974.

Smith, N. L. *Values in evaluation,* 1975. (mimeo)

Stake, Robert E. The countenance of educational evaluation. *Teachers College Record,* 1967, *68,* 523–40. Also in Blaine R. Worthen and James R. Sanders, *Educational evaluation: theory and practice.* Worthington, Ohio: Charles A. Jones, 1973.

Stake, Robert E. *Nine approaches to educational evaluation.* Urbana: Center for Instructional Research and Curriculum Evaluation, University of Illinois, 1974 (mimeo).

Stake, Robert E. Program evaluation, *particularly responsive evaluation.* Presented at Göteborg, Sweden, October 1973.

Stake, Robert E., and Gjerde, Craig. An evaluation of TCity, the Twin City Institute for Talented Youth. In R. E. Stake (Ed.), *Four evaluation examples: antnropological, economic, narrative, and portrayal.* AERA Monograph Series on Curriculum Evaluation no. 7. Chicago: Rand McNally, 1974.

Stufflebeam, Daniel L. *Meta-evaluation.* Occasional paper 3. Kalamazoo: The Evaluation Center, Western Michigan University, 1975.

Stufflebeam, Daniel, et al. *Educational evaluation and decision-making.* Itasca, Il.: Peacock, 1971.

Wolf, Robert L. *The application of select legal concepts to educational evaluation.* Unpublished Ph.D. dissertation, University of Illinois, 1974.

Quasi-experimental Designs

Donald T. Campbell and Julian C. Stanley

The Campbell and Stanley booklet, a classic in its field and still the most thorough catalogue of designs for data collection, is much richer in content than is suggested by our use of portions of its ideas in this chapter (see our subsection entitled "Before and After"). Here we excerpt their descriptions of four designs for data collection; but the booklet itself describes many more data-collection designs than these and includes extended discussions of the kinds of conclusions that are and are not justified on the basis of each design. For more detail on the logic of drawing conclusions from collections of data, consult Campbell and Stanley's *Experimental and Quasi-experimental Designs for Research.*

Campbell, Donald T., and Julian C. Stanley. *Experimental and Quasi-Experimental Designs for Research,* 1966 (reprinted from *Handbook of Research on Teaching,* 1963, N. L. Gage, ed.). Copyright 1963, American Educational Research Association, Washington, D.C.

. . What a check list of validity criteria can do is to make an experimenter more aware of the residual imperfections in his design so that on the relevant points he can be aware of competing interpretations of his data. He should, of course, design the very best experiment which the situation makes possible. He should deliberately seek out those artificial and natural laboratories which provide the best opportunities for control. But beyond that he should go ahead with experiment and interpretation, fully aware of the points on which the results are equivocal. While this awareness is important for exper-iments in which "full" control has been exercised, it is crucial for quasi-experimental designs.

In implementing this general goal, we shall in this portion of the chapter survey the strengths and weaknesses of a heterogeneous col-lection of quasi-experimental designs, each deemed worthy of use *where better designs are not feasible.* . . .

The Time-Series Experiment

The essence of the time-series design is the presence of a periodic measurement process on some group or individual and the intro-duction of an experimental change into this time series of measure-ments, the results of which are indicated by a discontinuity in the measurements recorded in the time series. It can be diagramed thus:

$$O_1 \quad O_2 \quad O_3 \quad O_4 \quad X \quad O_5 \quad O_6 \quad O_7 \quad O_8$$

This experimental design typified much of the classical nineteenth-century experimentation in the physical sciences and in biology. For example, if a bar of iron which has remained unchanged in weight for many months is dipped in a nitric acid bath and then removed, the inference tying together the nitric acid bath and the loss of weight by the iron bar would follow some such experimental logic. There may well have been "control groups" of iron bars remaining on the shelf that lost no weight, but the measurement and reporting of these weights would typically not be thought necessary or rele-vant. Thus it seems likely that this experimental design is frequently regarded as valid in the more successful sciences even though it rarely has accepted status in the enumerations of available experimental designs in the social sciences. . . . There are good reasons for this differential status and a careful consideration of them will provide a better understanding of the conditions under which the design might meaningfully be employed by social scientists when more thorough experimental control is impossible. The design is typical of the classic experiments of the British Industrial Fatigue Research Board upon factors affecting factory outputs. . . .

Figure 11–4 indicates some possible outcome patterns for time series into which an experimental alteration had been introduced as indicated by the vertical line X. For purposes of discussion let us assume that one will be tempted to infer that X had some effect in time series with outcomes such as A and B and possibly C, D, and E, but that one would not be tempted to infer an effect in time series such as F, G, and H, even were the jump in values from O_4 to O_5 as great and as statistically stable as were the O_4 to O_5 differ-

FIGURE 11-4 Some Possible Outcome Patterns from the Introduction of an Experimental Variable at Point $\underline{X}$ into a Time Series of Measurements, O_1–O_8

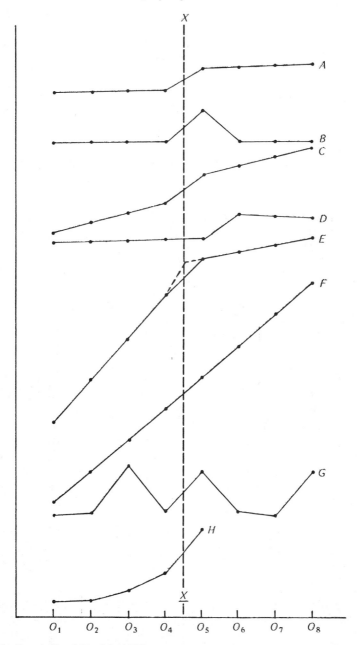

SOURCE: Campbell and Stanley (1973).

NOTE: Except for D, the O_4–O_5 gain is the same for all time series, while the legitimacy of inferring an effect varies widely, being strongest in A and B, and totally unjustified in F, G, and H.

ences in *A* and *B,* for example. While discussion of the problem of statistical tests will be postponed, . . . it is assumed that the problem of internal validity boils down to the question of plausible competing hypotheses that offer likely alternate explanations of the shift in the time series other than the effect of X. . . .

It also seems imperative that the X be specified before examining the outcome of the time series. The post hoc examination of a time series to infer what X preceded the most dramatic shift must be ruled out on the grounds that the opportunistic capitalization on chance which it allows makes any approach to testing the significance of effects difficult if not impossible.

The prevalence of this design in the more successful sciences should give us some respect for it, yet we should remember that the facts of "experimental isolation" and "constant conditions" make it more interpretable for them than for us. It should also be remembered that, in their use of it, a single experiment is never conclusive. While a control group may never be used, [this design] is repeated in many different places by various researchers before a principle is established. This, too, should be our use of it. *Where nothing better controlled is possible,* we will use it. We will organize our institutional bookkeeping to provide as many time series as possible for such evaluations and will try to examine in more detail than we have previously the effects of administrative changes and other abrupt and arbitrary events as Xs. But these will not be regarded as definitive until frequently replicated in various settings. . . .

The Equivalent Time-Samples Design

The most usual form of experimental design employs an equivalent sample of persons to provide a baseline against which to compare the effects of the experimental variable. In contrast, a recurrent form of one-group experimentation employs two equivalent samples of occasions, in one of which the experimental variable is present and in another of which it is absent. This design can be diagramed as follows (although a random rather than a regular alteration is intended):

$$X_1 O \ X_0 O \ X_1 O \ X_0 O$$

This design can be seen as a form of the time-series experiment with the repeated introduction of the experimental variable. The experiment is most obviously useful where the effect of the experimental variable is anticipated to be of transient or reversible character. While the logic of the experiment may be seen as an extension of the time-series experiment, the mode of statistical analysis is more typically similar to that of the two-group experiment in which the significance of the difference between the means of two sets of measures is employed. Usually the measurements are quite specifically paired with the presentations of the experimental variable, frequently being concomitant, as in studies of learning, work production, conditioning, physiological reaction, etc. . . .

The Separate-Sample Pretest-Posttest Design

For large populations, such as cities, factories, schools, and military units, it may often happen that although one cannot randomly segregate subgroups for differential experimental treatments, one can exercise something like full experimental control over the *when* and *to whom* of the *O*, employing random assignment procedures. Such control makes possible . . .

$$
\begin{array}{ccc}
R & O & (X) \\
R & & X & O
\end{array}
$$

In this diagram, rows represent randomly equivalent subgroups, the parenthetical *X* standing for a presentation of *X* irrelevant to the argument. One sample is measured prior to the *X*, an equivalent one subsequent to *X*. The design is not inherently a strong one. . . ..
Nevertheless, it may frequently be all that is feasible, and is often well worth doing. It has been used in social science experiments which remain the best studies extant on their topics. . . . While it has been called the "simulated before-and-after design," . . . it is well to note its superiority over the ordinary before-and-after design . . . through its control of both the main effect of testing and the interaction of testing with *X*. . . .

The Recurrent Institutional Cycle Design:
A "Patched-up" Design

. . . a strategy for field research in which one starts out with an inadequate design and then adds specific features to control for one or another of the recurrent sources of invalidity. The result is often an inelegant accumulation of precautionary checks, which lacks the intrinsic symmetry of the "true" experimental designs, but nonetheless approaches experimentation. As a part of this strategy, the experimenter must be alert to the rival interpretations (other than an effect of *X*) which the design leaves open and must look for analyses of the data, or feasible extensions of the data, which will rule these out. Another feature often characteristic of such designs is that the effect of *X* is demonstrated in several different manners. This is obviously an important feature where each specific comparison would be equivocal by itself.

The design is appropriate to those situations in which a given aspect of an institutional process is, on some cyclical schedule, continually being presented to a new group of respondents. Such situations include schools, indoctrination procedures, apprenticeships, etc. If in these situations one is interested in evaluating the effects of such a global and complex *X* as an indoctrination program, then the Recurrent Institutional Cycle Design probably offers as near an answer as is available from the designs developed thus far.

The design was originally conceptualized in the context of an investigation of the effects of one year's officer and pilot training upon the attitudes toward superiors and subordinates and leadership functions of a group of Air Force cadets in the process of completing a 14-month training cycle. . . . The restriction precluding a true experiment was the inability to control who would be exposed to the experimental variable. There was no possibility of dividing the entering class into two equated halves, one half of which would be sent through the scheduled year's program, and the other half sent back to civilian life. Even were such a true experiment feasible (and opportunistic exploitation of unpredicted budget cuts might have on several occasions made such experiments possible), the reactive effects of such experimental arrangements, the disruption in the lives of those accepted, screened, and brought to the air base and then sent home, would have made them far from an ideal control group. The difference between them and the experimental group receiving indoctrination would hardly have been an adequate base from which to generalize to the normal conditions of recruitment and training. There remained, however, the experimenter's control over the scheduling of the *when* and *to whom* of the observational procedures. This, plus the fact that the experimental variable was recurrent and was continually being presented to a new group of respondents, made possible some degree of experimental control. In that study two kinds of comparisons relevant to the effect of military experience on attitudes were available. Each was quite inadequate in terms of experimental control, but when both provided confirmatory evidence they were mutually supportive inasmuch as they both involved different weaknesses. The first involved comparisons among populations measured at the same time but varying in their length of service. The second involved measures of the same group of persons in their first week of military training and then again after some 13 months. In idealized form this design is as follows:

$$\text{Class A} \qquad X \ O_1$$

$$\overline{}$$

$$\text{Class B} \qquad O_2 \ X \ O_3$$

This design combines the "longitudinal" and "cross-sectional" approaches commonly employed in developmental research. In this it is assumed that the scheduling is such that at one and the same time a group which has been exposed to X and a group which is just about to be exposed to it can be measured; this comparison between O_1 and O_2 thus corresponds to the Static-Group Comparison. . . . Remeasuring the personnel of Class B one cycle later provides the One-Group Pretest-Posttest segment.

BIBLIOGRAPHY

Bloom, B. J.; Hastings, J. T.; and Madaus, G. F. 1971. *Handbook on formative and summative evaluation of student learning.* New York: McGraw-Hill.

This comprehensive handbook builds on earlier work by Bloom and his colleagues on the cognitive and affective objectives of school learning and can serve as a useful resource for the school OD consultant. It provides theory along with practical suggestions and solutions to the problem of assessing what students have learned. The authors view learning from a wide perspective, discussing evaluation from the points of view of different school curricula.

Brandt, R. M. 1972. *Studying behavior in natural settings.* New York: Holt, Rinehart & Winston.

Brandt's text furnishes hundreds of suggestions on how various types of institutional activity can be studied. Major emphasis is placed on observation as the primary method of naturalistic research, countering the tendency of behavioral scientists and educational researchers to depend on questionnaires and interview data.

Center for New Schools. 1972. Strengthening alternative high schools. *Harvard Educational Review* 42: 313-50.

To strengthen alternative schools, this article proposes a supportive role for research, evaluation, and feedback and emphasizes ethnographic observation and data feedback.

Festinger, L., and Katz, D., eds. 1953. *Research methods in the behavioral sciences.* New York: Dryden.

A classic in showing how to apply scientific methods to human issues, this text neatly lays out methods for both formative and summative evaluation and includes chapters on field experiments, field studies, the use of documents, interviewing, and observation.

Runkel, P. J., and McGrath, J. E. 1972. *Research on human behavior: a systematic guide to method.* New York: Holt, Rinehart & Winston.

Runkel and McGrath delineate important choices that must be made during the course of research and evaluation. At each choice-point a rationale is offered for conceiving alternatives and for the advantages and disadvantages of choosing each alternative. The book is constructed so that evaluators can use individual parts of it in tailoring their summative designs.

Selltiz, C.; Wrightsman, L.; and Cook, S. 1976. *Research methods on social relations.* 3d ed. New York: Holt, Rinehart & Winston.

This classic text shows how research can be put to use to solve social problems. Special attention is given to ethical issues in the conduct of research in social relations. Other topics of value to the organizational consultant are observation methods, questionnaires and interviews, the use of available data as source material, placing individuals on scales, data processing, and analysis and interpretation. A useful glossary is provided.

12

Institutionalizing Organization Development in School Districts

In discussing the multifarious concepts and strategies that help schools to become self-renewing organizations, this book has so far addressed itself mainly to organizational consultants who concentrate on improving interpersonal, group, and organizational processes in the local school. The present chapter departs from this emphasis in two ways. First, it raises the level of concern and analysis to that of the school district,* describing ways in which a district can provide continuing OD consultation for itself and its interdependent subsystems as well. Second, it addresses itself to specialists who are involved in OD efforts in the total district and to those who train others in OD theory and intervention strategies. The first major section describes four methods that districts can use to institutionalize OD efforts. The remaining sections describe in detail the method of establishing cadres of part-time OD specialists within districts, criteria for assessing district readiness for a cadre, means of training a cadre, and ways of maintaining viable cadres within school districts.

ESTABLISHING PERMANENT OD IN DISTRICTS

If a school district is to achieve a renewing state and sustain a favorable impact on the clients it serves, continuing attention must be

---

*We use the term *district* for convenience. In rural areas, the unit for institutionalizing OD might be the regional educational agency, such as a county office. In large urban centers, it might be a decentralized administrative unit responsible for one area of the city.

given both to the interpersonal and group skills of district employees and to the district's group and organizational processes. To achieve this requires maintaining OD training and consultation on a permanent basis by institutionalizing OD through new norms, roles, and organizational structures. Although few districts have an institutionalized capability for renewal at present, enough experimentation has been done in various parts of the country for us to describe the advantages and limitations of four modes that have evolved, each of which purports to make OD a regularized activity with defined, systematic procedures for attending to the district's functioning and efforts toward change and renewal.

Establishing New Roles. One approach to institutionalizing OD is to create within each major subsystem a new role in which one or more individuals provide continuing consultation to the subsystem of which they are a part. These persons may or may not be linked together. For example, one person may be designated the organizational specialist or school-renewal coordinator in each school; in larger schools, perhaps several persons will compose a renewal task force or planning team responsible for coordinating, planning, or providing OD consultation. The OD role may also be assumed by specially trained principals or management teams. The advantages of institutionalizing the district's capability within subsystems are that insiders have valuable insights into the subsystem's problems which others will acquire only with difficulty, that insiders are aware of subsystem resources that can be applied to problem solving, and that insiders are constantly available over a substantial period of time.

These advantages, however, are balanced by several restraints, one of which involves the power and legitimacy of the consultant role when the person or persons assigned this responsibility simultaneously hold other positions in the school. In one large senior high school, for example, a principal who had acquired special training in OD during his sabbatical achieved only moderate success as an OD consultant to his own faculty because his dual role caused his motives as a consultant to be questioned at each step of the way (Flynn 1971). In another instance, in which we trained a group of sixteen staff members of a large junior high to serve as a focal point for school renewal, members experienced extreme difficulty in establishing their legitimacy and expertise as consultants with peers who expected them to continue their old behaviors as teachers and counselors (Arends 1975).

Linking with Outsiders. A second method of institutionalizing OD is for school districts to enter into long-term contractual agreements with outside consultants, who may come from industrial organizations, from universities, from educational research centers which have special programs in OD, or from private or nonprofit firms. In this method, district personnel make contact with outside consultants to explore their concerns and to make a contract; the outsiders collect diagnostic data about the district and plan an intervention strategy;

and the outsiders, unless they are on a permanent retainer, soon conclude their work and leave. The advantages of linking with outsiders are that they have their own support systems, are highly trained and expert in the field, and have experiences with many kinds of organizations.

At the same time, however, this method of providing OD may be both expensive and difficult to obtain. First, Schmuck and Miles reported in 1971 only a small number of trained OD consultants who were interested in working in school settings; and although others have joined their ranks since then, the number is almost certainly still inadequate. Second, their "outsidedness" makes expert consultants so suspect to some groups that they may have difficulty making entry. Third, because they may have other career plans, or because the organization for which they work may transfer or reassign them, it may be impractical for a district to attempt to maintain a reliable connection with outside consultants indefinitely.

District-based OD Departments. Creating district-based OD departments—a third strategy for institutionalizing OD capabilities in school districts—has been employed in the public schools of Louisville, Kentucky, and also in York County near Toronto, Ontario. This strategy establishes full-time positions and a district-level department charged with planning and implementing organization development. Highly differentiated from other subsystems and with an identity of its own, this is the model most often employed in industrial settings.

In our view, this strategy shares many of the advantages and limitations of linking up with outsiders. If properly established, for example, an internal OD department could be given its own support system; the OD function could be differentiated from other district functions; and highly trained, experienced personnel could be obtained to exercise this function. At the same time, however, this strategy may be expensive. In addition, because in a large district the members of a central-office department can look to people in a school like outsiders, an internal department may have difficulty integrating its services with those of the rest of the district, making it suspect by potential client subsystems.

Part-time Specialists in Cadres. In our own work we have initiated and tested the design of building cadres within districts—i.e., training district members to perform OD training and consulting functions on a part-time basis for school staffs and other district work groups. Cadre members are drawn from various roles and subsystems within the district but do not consult with their own groups; their role as OD specialists is separated from their other functions. Since cadre members are not full-time, they can easily bring to the consultative work the skills and their place in the communication network that are parts of their regular jobs. The remainder of this chapter describes this strategy.

OD CADRES IN DISTRICTS

Of two cadres of OD specialists that we established in two school districts in the Pacific Northwest, one, in Kent, Washington, began operating in 1969 and disbanded in 1975; the other, in Eugene, Oregon, has been operating since 1971. Most of the generalizations, examples, and recommendations given here are based on our observation and documentation of these two projects. The Kent and Eugene cadres have also been extensively discussed in Schmuck, Runkel, and Blondino (1970); Schmuck and Runkel (1972); Wyant (1972, 1973); Arends and Phelps (1973); Runkel, Wyant, and Bell (1975); and Schmuck (1977).

After being trained by outside consultants, cadres facilitate adaptable organizational functioning in schools by making OD consultation continuingly available to a school district. They can initiate an OD effort in a district in response to requests for assistance from school staffs or other groups, or they can provide the local capacity to continue an effort already begun. Once established, a cadre is a legitimate subsystem of the district, carrying out important functions with administrative and budgetary support, with someone to coordinate its activities, and having headquarters space in which also to store its materials. It is, in short, a visible group that functions autonomously yet interdependently with other subsystems of the district.

During most of the week, part-time cadre members are full-time teachers, counselors, principals, or central-office personnel, and this dual identity gives them several advantages of insiders and outsiders alike. First, each part-time specialist becomes a channel of communication between the cadre and the subsystem in which he or she holds a regular job. Second, each specialist becomes a source of support and expertise for other cadre members who are working with a group of which the specialist is regularly a part. Third, when they consult in subsystems to which they do not regularly belong, cadre members are in effect outsiders, with the result that their perspective on the clients' situation can be relatively unbiased. Clients tend to regard specialists from outside their own staff as having an expertise and competence that warrants much the same confidence as that usually accorded to a peer or to a consultant who receives a fee.

Internally, a cadre composed of twenty or so members is organized into teams to provide consultation and training for client subsystems. Some team is responsible for monitoring the work of intervention teams and of decision making. Ad hoc teams may be created to select and train new members, prepare budgets and reports, plan self-renewal events for the total cadre, and the like. A coordinator who has major responsibility for coordinating all teams and for linking the cadre with other district subsystems is a common member of many of these teams.

Assessing Readiness for Cadres

Creating a new subsystem within an existing organizational structure is a complex process. From our experience with the Kent and Eugene cadres, plus the evidence on readiness for organization development that we have culled from other projects,* we believe that four conditions should be met before a district launches such an effort. These conditions include: (1) district readiness, (2) readiness of the trainers of specialists, (3) readiness of potential specialists, and (4) readiness to coordinate interfaces between these and the new subsystem.

District Readiness. First, like other programs or projects, establishing a cadre requires the institutional legitimacy that only top-level decision makers can provide. Although a cadre need not be initiated by top administrators—in Eugene, for example, much of the early work to establish the cadre was done by the coordinators of another district-wide project—the superintendent and other key personnel in influential positions should acknowledge its usefulness and state clearly their commitment to support the project. Emphasizing the need for such support, Runkel, Wyant, and Bell (1975) write:

> *In fact, any show of reluctance from the superintendent's office will pretty well guarantee the collapse of the project. In Kent . . . the superintendent and his cabinet participated in the first training event. The superintendent frequently stated his support of the project and when the cadre was instituted, he made a supportive announcement in the district bulletin (pp. 19–20).*

Second, top administrators must be clear about where the cadre fits into the overall organizational structure. They must know to whom the cadre will go when it needs to explain its work or to request cooperation, and they must recognize that cadre services should be equally available to all subsystems of the district if the cadre is not to be viewed as simply an extension of top administration.

Third, as Runkel, Wyant, and Bell (1975) have suggested, the cadre will require financial resources.

> *. . . It was imperative that the role [of organizational specialist] be supported with released time, a part-time coordinator, and the official blessings of the district. There were several tense moments when the teachers were negotiating for a new contract and early reports seemed to indicate that adequate money might not be available—but commitments to the project were high, and the matter was resolved with 10 days allotted to each specialist for OD work during the school year. Further, a part-time coordinator was appointed. . . . In Kent, the cadre has managed to stay alive on a budget that in most years has been about $8,000 (p. 19).*

The Kent district ended all budgetary support to the cadre in September 1974, two years after the departure of the supportive superintendent. The cadre survived the 1974/75 school year with no money but agreed, as reported by Runkel, Wyant, and Bell (1975), that it was probably impossible to continue beyond that year.

---

*See Saturen (1972); Schmuck et al. (1975); and Runkel, Wyant, and Bell (1975).

Arends and Phelps (1973) report a larger budget in Eugene. For example, in 1971-72 and 1972-73, $20,000 was allocated for cadre activities in Eugene . . . for the half-time coordinator's salary, released time for specialists, self-renewal events for the cadre, office operation and materials, outside consultants, travel expenses, and research and evaluation activities. On some occasions, the Eugene district has also provided funds to pay the salaries of building staffs that elect to work with the specialists during summer workshops just as it gives extended contracts to other district employees for other inservice (p. 44).

The Eugene cadre has a full-time coordinator and a $40,000 yearly budget at present. Thus, while establishing and maintaining a cadre need not require a major outlay of money, it cannot be done without some financial support.

Fourth, although it is not necessary for district personnel to have had extensive experience with OD, they should be aware of both its costs and benefits before attempting to establish a cadre. A new cadre will get off to a good start if schools or other district subsystems are ready to ask for consultation as soon as it is formed.

Fifth, although districts experiencing some profound or pervasive crisis are unlikely to take the long view required to launch a cadre successfully, an awareness of the need for change, coupled with confidence that crises can be averted through long-range efforts, is desirable.

Finally, the district must evidence both the skills and norms necessary to build and maintain a new subsystem. Are there people who can plan where the new subsystem will fit in relation to other departments, projects, and programs? Are they willing to allocate resources to the project? Are they receptive to the idea of part-time role holders, responsive to the interdependent needs of the new subsystem, and confident that their own resources are necessary?

In summary, district members must know and state clearly their reasons for establishing a cadre; they must obtain commitment to the effort from influential persons and groups in the district; and objectives should be clear and shared. Clear goals provide a target toward which energy can be directed, and, with shared goals, district members will perceive the effort as something wanted and valued rather than as only another program imposed on them from above.

Readiness of Trainers of Specialists. The skills and competencies that largely determine whether a cadre will develop into an effective subsystem of a district are best learned in real interventions under the tutelage of an experienced consultant who is capable of transmitting professional skills and understandings to others. Training internal specialists, improving their skills, providing for the replenishment of their ranks, as well as for the integration of their roles and functions into the district, cannot be a simple or short-term process, and those who train them should be willing and able to make a commitment of several months' duration.

We trained the specialists in Eugene and Kent, for example, only after agreeing that we were willing to engage in a long-term effort. In both districts, we provided the training at no expense in exchange for the opportunity to pursue our OD research and development goals; for their part, the districts provided released time or workshop pay for cadre members. Because our research goals have somewhat changed since then, our resources as a training team are no longer available to other districts in the way they were to Kent and Eugene. There are, however, other means by which internal specialists may be trained.

First, private consultants can sometimes be employed on a long-term basis; the names and qualifications of some of them may be obtained from the International Association of Applied Social Scientists, the National Training Laboratories Institute, or by inquiring among your colleagues. Second, the National Training Laboratories-Institute for Applied Behavioral Sciences (NTL-IABS) offers training programs for OD consultants; but as they do not help to integrate such persons into an organization, a district would have to find other means of doing this. Third, the Northwest Regional Educational Laboratory (NWREL) offers instructional systems for preparing educational training consultants. These systems (called PETC) provide workshop materials for approximately two years of training; but as they have not been designed to install and maintain specialist subsystems, a district would, again, have to assume primary responsibility for dealing with these matters.

Potential trainers of cadres need information to assess whether the project has clear objectives and goals, the support of key personnel, and other resources required to initiate and sustain a training effort. In exchange, the district's leaders will want to assess the motivation, competencies, and resources of outside consultants before contracting for training. At best, the contract should be a written document detailing the goals of the collaboration between consultant and district, the obligations of each, and a clear statement of what resources (money, prestige, logistical support) are being exchanged.

Readiness of Potential Specialists. Before a cadre can be launched, individuals who want training and a few groups ready to use the services of a cadre once it is formed should already exist in the district. When attempting to recruit volunteers for the project, it is important to inform the greatest number of people possible, giving potential members a chance to ask questions and to ascertain their commitment in advance. Two-way communication is essential at this point because many district educators will be unclear about organization development, about the purposes of cadres, and about the specialist's role. Those who view the training as an opportunity for personal growth may lack the commitment to serve as cadre members after training. Others may view the project as only another district effort to improve a specific curriculum or to implement another technical innovation.

In Kent we circulated application forms and a brief description of the project goals throughout the district. In Eugene we announced the project with a printed notice in the district's catalogue of summer staff-development workshops. Those who signed up for the workshop were invited to a meeting at which the newly chosen coordinator and a University of Oregon consultant explained organization development, outlined the project's goals, and described the functions of the proposed cadre. At the end of the meeting, interested persons filled out an application.

As potential specialists are selected for training, at least five factors should be taken into account. First, because they will take on cadre duties in addition to their regular full-time jobs in the district, applicants should demonstrate special motivation and understand the extent of the commitment required of them. Second, potential cadre members should either have some consultation competencies already or have the ability to learn them. While many of these skills can be taught in training workshops, the scope of the training task and the amount of time required to prepare the cadre will depend on the trainees' prior level of skill and understanding. Third, Macbeth (1971) has found that, in addition to skill and the ability to learn, applicants should feel optimistic that they can influence others and situations around them for change. Fourth, the applicant's past history in the district is important as well. Persons who have previously exhibited leadership abilities, who have participated in other innovative projects, who have high visibility in the district, and who have good rapport and a favorable reputation with persons in the administrative and teaching ranks should find it easier, as specialists, to help others.

Finally, the individual criteria of the selection process should be sufficiently relaxed to enable the creation of a group of fifteen to twenty-five persons representing all important role groups in the district. Role balance is particularly important if specialists are to help one another understand the district's organizational forces and problems, provide ready-made links to various groups within the district, and reduce the likelihood that they will themselves be perceived as representing the interests of any particular group. For the same reasons, districts might also pay attention to factors of sex, race, age, years of experience in the district, membership in professional organizations, or building assignment. Although expanding the group to include noncertified staff, parents, and students would increase the task of coordination, we believe that the advantages to be gained by a broader representation of interests and knowledge usually outweigh this cost.

Readiness to Coordinate Interfaces. Once the decision has been made to develop a cadre and firm agreements have been reached between the district and the outside consultants, the district must find someone to build awareness of, and support for, the cadre and to recruit potential specialists and clients. This same person should later coordinate the cadre and link the specialists with the outside consultants, with others in the district, and with one another.

In Kent and Eugene we found that this person should understand organization development, have experience as a consultant, be familiar with the working arrangements of school districts and cadres, and have skills to coordinate the efforts of diverse individuals and groups. In addition, we would seek a coordinator with leadership and administrative talents, a high tolerance for ambiguity and frustration, a high degree of trust and respect from colleagues, and demonstrated abilities in working successfully with others at difficult tasks. Skill as a trainer or consultant is important but not paramount; the critical factor is the person's ability to link the cadre with other district groups and to coordinate its efforts.

Persons with these qualities are probably rare in school districts, although many of the skills are similar to those needed in convening adult task groups. Districts may look among their own employees for someone who either has these qualifications or who could be trained to fill the position. A qualified coordinator who is found outside the district will need help in becoming settled in, and familiar with, the district.

Training the Cadre

Training, which will determine the subsequent success or failure of the new subsystem, is most often engineered by outsiders and continues over an extended period of time during which the outsiders and district personnel work together. In Kent and Eugene we used a four-phase sequence that included formal, transition, on-the-job, and follow-up training. Each phase included activities and lessons that: (1) provided specialists with interpersonal and intervention concepts and skills, (2) helped the cadre to develop subsystem norms that enabled members to work together effectively, and (3) created opportunities for them to design the structure of their new group. The first phase emphasized the first purpose; the later phases gave more attention to the second and third purposes.

Formal Training.   This phase lasts a minimum of ten days, but it is possible to spread them out over two or three months. Although additional formal training is desirable, we recognize the financial and time constraints that most districts face. Trainees should be provided with a stipend or salary if the training occurs outside the contracted year and should be provided with substitutes if it occurs during the school year. The district can usually provide workshop space at minimal extra expense. Fees for outside trainers—at least one per five or six trainees—will vary.

Activities in the first phase help cadre members to become acquainted and to learn many of the ideas and intervention techniques presented in this book. The intention is not to produce sophisticated consultants instantly but to give the neophytes a set of initial skills and the confidence to begin with clients. Runkel and Phelps (1973) listed fourteen initial skills for cadre members:

1. Paraphrasing
2. Describing behavior
3. Describing own feelings
4. Checking perceptions of another's feelings
5. Giving and receiving feedback
6. Taking a survey
7. Group problem solving
8. Methods of decision making in a group
9. Recycling goals
10. Using conflict
11. Microdesigning
12. Building the helping relationship
13. Discovering and using human resources
14. Collecting data for feedback to groups

Learning and practicing these skills is the major activity of formal training, and, as described in chapter 10, the skills are learned experientially. The following outline describes the formal training provided the Eugene cadre in the summer of 1971 (Arends and Phelps 1973).

June 14: After getting acquainted and warming up with the Who Am I? exercise, participants listened to introductions and discussed logistical concerns, then formed triads to discuss "what I hope the cadre can do for me" and heard a lecturette on paraphrasing. Forming new triads to discuss "what I hope the cadre can do for Eugene," they then listened to a lecturette outlining the clients, issues, and strategies with which organization development is concerned. Following a lecturette on behavior description, they formed cross-role groups to list their goals and concerns about the cadre. Representatives of these small groups then occupied the center of a Fishbowl to summarize what their group had discussed. After lunch they heard a lecturette on describing one's own feelings and formed small groups to build Tinkertoy models of "what this district is like." After discussing their models, they debriefed the group processes, behaviors, and feelings they had noted while working at the nonverbal task. The day ended with a lecturette on checking one's impressions of another's internal state. Participants debriefed the total day and completed the Group Expectations Survey questionnaire.

June 15: Participants warmed up by sharing their images of one another, making a name tag for a partner, and doing calisthenics. They listened to and discussed the meaning of the data feedback from the Group Expectations Survey, heard a lecturette on data-survey feedback, then practiced the process by designing and administering a questionnaire, analyzing and feeding back the data to the total group. After lunch they identified their personal goals and resources on newsprint, then milled to read the lists of others, and formed small groups to compare lists and identify resources already available to meet individual objectives. After the final debriefing of the day, participants were asked to read the chapter on goal setting in their handbook (mimeographed copies of the since-published first edition of this book by Schmuck, Runkel, Saturen, Martell, and Derr 1972).

June 16: Participants warmed up by pretending with a partner to explore a favorite place and by doing the Hand Mirroring exercise. After hearing a lecturette on constructive openness and the interpersonal gap, they formed triads to review their personal goals in terms of what they had learned from their reading homework. Following a lecturette on the importance of uncovering conflict as a means of identifying problems, participants formed groups, according to their roles in the district, to do the Imaging exercise. Stage 1 of the exercise, in which participants generate the images they have of other role groups, was completed before lunch. After lunch they completed stage 2, in which the images are shared with other groups. After the final debriefing of the day, participants were asked to read the chapter on improving meetings in their handbook.

June 17: This session began at 2:30 p.m. with a review of the phases of the Imaging exercise. In stage 3 the role groups again met separately to list examples of their behavior that might have contributed to the other groups' images of them; in stage 4 they shared these lists with the other groups. The exercise was completed with the formation of small cross-role groups in which participants identified the underlying problems which the exercise had caused to surface. The total group then discussed the strengths and limitations of the exercise and identified settings in which it could be used. After dinner they performed the Planners and Operators exercise. After the final debriefing of the day, they were asked to read the chapter on making decisions in their handbook.

June 18: During the warm-up, participants assessed their individual progress in the workshop by moving a distance from the wall that represented how far they had come. After a lecturette on the distinction between task and process inquiry in groups, they related these concepts to the chapter on making decisions. Participants next formed small groups to identify the skills they would need as cadre members, later forming two groups to identify facilitating and restraining forces related to these skills. After lunch they heard a lecturette on the function of process consultants. One group then occupied the center of a Fishbowl to reach consensus on the ten most important restraining forces, with those outside the inner circle serving as process observers; switching positions, the second group reached consensus on the ten most important restraining forces. After final debriefing they were assigned to read the chapters on organizational theory and training in their handbook.

June 21: After a lecturette on the training objectives for the second week, on general considerations of the entry phase of interventions, and on how entry works in practice, participants were given a hypothetical case study, and they formed small groups to discuss the questions they would ask to get additional information and the procedural steps they would recommend to the potential clients. Following a lecturette on general considerations about diagnosis and how it works in practice, they were given another hypothetical case and this time formed groups to list available and required data, to plan techniques for collecting them, and to plan how to tabulate and analyze them. After lunch they heard a lecturette on general considerations about planning and how it works in practice. With another hypothetical situation they planned a sequence of training events and decided who would do what in the intervention. The day concluded with a final debriefing and assignment of the chapter on designing training interventions in their handbook.

June 22: After a general lecturette about training and about the training done by the Kent cadre, participants formed four teams and were assigned an activity frequently used in training events, each group making plans to present the activity to the rest of the cadre during the afternoon. After lunch the groups took turns presenting the Five-Square puzzle, chalk murals, the Blind Walk, and a Fishbowl discussion of the strengths and limitations of the various exercises. The day concluded with a final debriefing.

June 23: After a lecturette on general considerations about assessment and evaluation at the beginning, middle, and end of interventions, and general considerations about follow-up consultation, participants were given data about prior work with a fictitious client group, and they formed teams to plan the first day of follow-up training. After lunch they heard a lecturette on the sequence of steps in organizational problem solving, formed small groups to identify organizational problems in the cadre, met as a total group to identify five problems with top priority, then formed groups again to analyze the problem of their choice by listing facilitating and restraining forces and to brainstorm ways of overcoming the most important restraining forces. The day ended with a final debriefing in these groups.

June 24: The small groups completed the problem-solving sequence by making action plans to implement the best proposals and by forecasting consequences of intended actions. The rest of the day was devoted to hearing reports from the small groups, to total group discussion, and to selecting proposals and plans to implement.

June 25: Reports, discussion, and decision making continued from the preceding day. After lunch the trainers presented a suggested reading list for the rest of the summer, and the coordinator described client groups that had requested late-summer training. Total group discussion and planning for an August workshop took up the remainder of the afternoon.

Essentially, the formal training phase serves as a springboard for considering structural issues during later phases. Trainees are not encouraged to worry about the structure of their subsystem at this point. Varying groupings are used for each activity to enable the cadre to experiment with different organizational structures and to become familiar with one another's style of operating, and the coordinator may switch back and forth almost imperceptibly from the trainer role to the participant role.

Transition Phase. The transition phase comprises at least five days following formal training and preceding actual interventions by specialists with client systems. During this period the emphasis shifts from specific intervention techniques and procedures to learning more widely applied skills associated with making entry, building contracts, diagnosing client needs, designing at both the macro- and microlevels, and evaluating intervention efforts.

Specialists are now encouraged to discuss the norms being established within their group. They ask: Are we being open with one another? Are we dealing constructively with conflict? What does it mean to learn with others? How can resources within the group best be shared? What commitments have we made or are we willing to make? In addition, the potential structural possibilities for the new subsystem become more salient for specialists during this phase. Cadre members ask: What will the coordinator's role be? What kind of governance structure will direct our actions? How can the cadre best interface with others in the district to be accepted while at the same time maintaining its independence and autonomy.

The following design was used in transition training of the Eugene cadre in the late summer of 1971 (Arends and Phelps 1973).

August 16: Reviewing agreements made in June about forming teams, participants applied these guidelines to form six teams. Each team discussed how its group composition would limit or enhance ability to work, then devoted ten minutes of discussion to each of the following topics: problem solving, communication, intervention stages, organizational issues, procedures and exercises, and survey-data feedback. The afternoon was spent planning for future work in the small teams. Group agreements were established, and process debriefings concluded the day.

August 17: The total group spent the morning making group agreements about the role of the coordinator, the role and composition of the steering committee, how decisions would be made, how group agreements would be amended or changed in the future, and how to deal with ethical matters. The teams met during the afternoon to continue planning for future work.

August 18: Team meetings continued throughout the morning. During the afternoon one team presented a prototype demonstration package that included a slide show, a design, and possible handouts. Cadre members evaluated the presentation and planned improvements, and teams met to consider using the package in forthcoming work.

August 19: Team planning continued throughout the morning. After lunch each team selected a representative for the steering committee. The total group discussed membership criteria and agreed on the steering committee's functions. The steering committee discussed future self-renewal events for the cadre and planned ways to keep records of team activities. Other participants met to evaluate the handbook and to brainstorm a list of topics for self-renewal sessions.

August 20: Teams completed their planning sessions in the morning. At an afternoon session, the total group discussed, revised, and agreed on proposals for self-renewal events generated by the steering committee. The in-service team shared its proposal for the in-service courses and described implementation plans.

On-the-job Practicum. The third phase occurs when specialists make their initial interventions with client groups. During this phase the cadre establishes norms for cadre governance, for reforming or disbanding teams, and for differentiating roles within teams and within the cadre as a whole. Agreements about ethics and about behavior toward client systems are also a focus of attention at this time. Above all, however, the trainees are now trying out their wings, with the outside trainers providing support and feedback, perhaps helping them to select client groups that exhibit a high degree of readiness and assisting them in making entry as well. Because an initial success strengthens the confidence of new specialists and gives the cadre an attractive image in the district, it is best to choose low-risk subsystems initially, saving more complex interventions until the specialists gain in confidence and skill.

Follow-up. In our own work with cadres, we substantially diminished our involvement after the initial practicum experiences. Although we continued to serve as members of some intervention teams, the specialists themselves took on increasing responsibility for their own learning, maintenance, and renewal. During this final phase, specialists acquire skills for dealing with tougher client groups, for working with varied subsystems (such as parents and students), for handling conflict, and for planning or designing their own future growth. Norms are developed for including new members and releasing retiring members. The governance team and a team for training replacement members determine retirement and formal credentialing procedures.

CADRE MAINTENANCE AND RENEWAL

If it is to provide continuing OD consultation in a district, a cadre must become a stable, adaptable, and effective subsystem in its own right. As Runkel, Wyant, and Bell (1975) observe:

> *Many new organizational arrangements and substructures fail to float when they are launched. They fail to do even the first things their designers hoped for. Of those that do stay afloat and set a course, many fall dead in the water, with sails flapping, when their original outside helpers . . . take the pilot's boat home. Some crews survive being left on their own; they manage to keep their own sails in trim. But when the original crew begins to depart and the substructure must replace them, many remain tied to the pier because recruits cannot be found or because the old crew seems somehow unable to teach the new crew the ropes. The crews of others give up and go back to the home port when their first captain leaves. Still other substructures founder on budgetary shoals. And of those that successfully negotiate all these hazards, many go under when a key administrator is changed (p. 34).*

The following sections enlarge on some of these problems.

538

Maintaining Intervention Strength

Although there is no single best way of organizing a cadre, its structure and roles should be defined and arranged clearly enough for
members to find personal fulfillment in their roles while at the same
time making progress toward the cadre's goals. To this end, members
typically work in teams, which enables them to pool their individual
skills, provide mutual support, and demonstrate to others that collaboration across district role and building lines is not only possible
but effective and enjoyable. While specialists occasionally work alone
in a differentiated role, teaming allows them to continue learning
from one another in team planning and debriefing sessions, facilitates
the mobilization of large groups of trainers when these are needed,
and provides practicum settings for new cadre members.

In Eugene, new intervention teams are formed whenever new
clients request consultation. Their criteria for composing teams include a willingness to work with others on the team, a belief that a
balanced team has been formed, and an interest in the task to be performed. Arends and Phelps (1973) describe how teams of the Eugene
and Kent cadres conducted interventions with four kinds of client
groups.

1. Building staffs. *In two years the Eugene cadre provided
   more than two days of training and consultation to 10 of
   the district's 30 elementary schools. The Kent cadre worked
   less often with total school staffs, but did train one-third of
   their district's 15 elementary schools in their first four years.*
2. District-wide groups. *Between 1971 and 1973, the Eugene
   cadre worked with the district's nurses, all junior high department chairpersons, and principals from one of four regions
   in the district. By 1973, the Kent cadre had worked with
   many district-wide groups including the superintendent's
   meetings with community groups, curriculum committees,
   and groups within their district's education association.*
3. Central office groups. *Both cadres had worked with such
   groups as the superintendent's cabinet, curriculum coordinators, and special project teams by 1973.*
4. Students and parents. *Kent specialists initiated a multi-
   ethnic camp for area high school students in September,
   1969. By May, 1971, approximately 220 students had attended camps conducted by specialists. In addition, Kent
   specialists trained PTA presidents and worked with other
   citizen groups in their community. Eugene specialists taught
   communication and problem-solving skills to classroom
   groups, student councils, and in seminars for parents in one
   elementary school attendance area. One of the largest intervention teams in the Eugene cadre was formed to work with
   the parents and faculty of an elementary school (pp. 11-15).*

A cadre also needs a structure for solving its organizational problems and making its organizational decisions. In Eugene, this struc-

ture is a steering committee composed of persons who represent intervention teams. A similar steering committee established in Kent in 1969 was replaced in 1972 by a decision-making task force composed of four cadre members elected from the membership at large. Continuity of the problem-solving–decision-making structure is ensured by having the group meet on a regular basis and by replacing a portion of the representatives at regular intervals. Members of the governance structure link other cadre members to the coordinator, prepare the budget and allocate resources, plan self-renewal events for the cadre, select clients, and plan for the selection and training of new members.

Even after the cadre is established, there must be one person responsible for most of the work of coordination. In general, the coordinator will: (1) work on intervention teams and provide demonstrations to potential client groups; (2) assist and guide the entry and contract-building processes; (3) coordinate the activities of intervention teams; (4) explain the goals, methods, and work of the cadre to interested persons in the district or community; (5) arrange for outside consultants when these are required; (6) link the cadre with district administrators by keeping the latter informed of cadre activities and budgetary requirements; and (7) link the cadre to groups outside the district, such as local universities, other cadres, state department of education and research-and-development centers, or laboratories around the country.

The Kent cadre was successively coordinated by four different persons who were paid about $750 annually on an extended-contract basis. In Eugene, the original coordinator held a half-time position and was paid on the district's administrative salary schedule; since 1974, however, Eugene has had a full-time coordinator who is likewise paid an administrator's salary. Although both cadres experienced turnover in the coordinator position—the Eugene cadre, only once; the Kent cadre, three times—these were successfully handled by a combination of forewarning and planning and by continual clarification and negotiation of the coordinator's role. Thus replacement of the coordinator need not be a precursor of failure. Runkel, Wyant, and Bell (1975) here discuss the likely causes of the Kent cadre's demise.

Apparently the greatest hindrance that happened to the cadre was the change of superintendents and the events that followed. The first event was the outspoken challenge the new superintendent issued ("prove yourselves in one year"). The cadre negotiated that successfully through its assistance to the Superintendent's Seminar and the meetings with citizenry. The next event—or lack of one—was the lack of explicit and reiterated support from the new superintendent or any of his assistants. . . . This was a strong contrast to the firm support given by the previous superintendent. The third event, of course, was the loss of all monetary support in September of 1974. We saw . . . how the budget crisis of December 1969—about

*as severe a financial loss as can be found in histories of school
districts*—did not result in the district's withdrawing funds
from the cadre. Instead, the old superintendent made use of the
cadre's services to help the district through the crisis. In contrast, when the new superintendent came up against the strong
and vocal conservative segment of the citizenry, he seemed
ambivalent about the cadre. . . . On balance . . . [we] . . . take
the view that the new superintendent came to see the cadre as
an example of the kind of radical innovation that the conservative segment of the Kent constituency would reject.*

    *In our view, the Kent cadre weathered a remarkable series
of tempests during its six-year voyage, and did so while sailing
under four different captains (pp. 35–36).*

Problems relating to time may be even greater than those relating
to money. Although cadre members with teaching assignments can
hire substitutes, this option is seldom available to counselors, central-
office staff, or building administrators. Even though the Kent and
Eugene cadres were given ten days per person per year in which to
conduct planning or interventions, many members had to return to
work that had accumulated during their absence. As Runkel, Wyant,
and Bell (1975) explain:

*Another of the Kent cadre's problems was a sheer overload of
work. Part of the overload came because the 10 percent released
time promised by the superintendent was not always honored
by the principals or other middle managers who supervised the
regular work of the cadre members. But another part came
simply because the work of the organizational consultant is
demanding during an intervention, while planning for it, and
in debriefing it—and also while conducting the self-renewing
activities necessary to maintain the capacity for everything else.
There simply was not enough understanding in enough places
in the district to make it reasonable to propose compensating
the cadre members for all the time they spent outside actual
intervention hours. In the end, being a cadre member became
a labor of love (p. 47).*

When specialists become full-time, many advantages of their
linking function are lost. It might be possible, however, to hire a full-
time coordinator and to rotate three or four half-time positions
among other specialists on a yearly basis. If this core of persons did
the demonstrations, the diagnostic interviews, and much of the
follow-up consultation that require work during regular school hours,
other specialists would be free to do major training events when they
and their clients can be released from other responsibilities. Another
solution might be to pay specialists and clients for more work in the
evening, on weekends, or during the summer.

---

*"The Kent district discovered a deficit of $1.8 million in a budget of $12 million in late
1969, during the same months that the Kent-Seattle area began a severe economic depres-
sion as Boeing took a dive" (Runkel, Wyant, and Bell 1975, p. 22).

Maintaining Differentiation-Integration

A cadre should build and maintain a group identity and cohesiveness, perform functions that no one else performs, separate its budget from those of other programs, and in so doing maintain its autonomy. This separateness is necessary if the cadre is to experiment with new ideas and behaviors and to remove itself far enough from other tasks to attend to a district's organizational processes. At the same time, however, a cadre cannot isolate itself but must maintain linkages with those who allocate financial resources, with those who work with specialists in their full-time roles, and with clients. The key to this dilemma lies in a balance of differentiation and integration. The problem is partially resolved by the role of part-time specialist and by maintaining cross-district representation, which ensures access to relevant data in the district as well as to forums in which to explain and demonstrate the cadre's functions.

Maintaining Productive Consultant-client Relationship. The following list highlights five of the most important features that cadres try to develop in consultant-client relationships.

1. *Awareness.* A cadre makes itself and its services known to potential clients in a variety of ways. Some are as informal as answering the questions of those with whom members work in their regular jobs. More formally, a cadre can prepare slide-tape presentations* and brief demonstration events that portray the goals and activities of OD training and consultation. The Eugene cadre distributed throughout the district a two-page dittoed handout which is reproduced in the appendix to this chapter.
2. *Readiness.* Because specialists believe that groups can and should be clients only when they want to be, they do not intrude on the work of groups without invitation or attempt to persuade them that they need help when they do not want it. They offer their services only in response to requests from groups that feel their work can have greater promise of success or can be done more expeditiously with outside help.
3. *Client Involvement.* In designing an intervention, specialists collaborate with clients as described in chapter 10. Specialists model interdependence, collaboration, openness, and the use of rational inquiry in their interactions with clients. They observe the client group at work and share their impressions of the processes and procedures that help or hinder the group's effectiveness, and they remain open to feedback concerning their own performance and helpfulness.
4. *Long-term Help.* Because organizational problems are a continuing part of school life, they are seldom resolved in a brief workshop but require extended consultation. Short-term efforts may lead to undesirable consequences; and, even when they are

---

*Fo examples of slide-tape presentations, see Arends et al. (1973).

initially successful, most short-term gains will quickly fade. Through demonstration and discussion, specialists reveal to potential clients the futility of quickie interventions and refuse clients who desire one-shot events except as a means of demonstrating what long-term consultation is like.

5. *Outside Stance.* No cadre member belongs to a team that provides training to his or her regular work group; more specifically, a specialist who teaches in a particular school does not join the team that works with that staff. This limitation is important for three reasons. First, a cadre member who is also a member of the client group is part of any problem or action plan that is developed and should be free to devote full energy to that task. Second, the use of specialists from other schools sets an example of interschool cooperation. Third, the failure of specialists to participate as clients in training events for their own subsystems might be perceived as a lack of faith in what OD consultation is intended to accomplish.

Supporting Specialists. Provided some released time or other compensation, specialists can take on the duties of cadre members in addition to their full-time jobs as district employees. At the same time, however, problems of role conflict can arise whenever the part-time specialist uses time from the regular position for cadre work and a supervisor wants the regular work to have top priority. If specialists maintain an open dialogue with district administrators about such possible conflicts, they need be neither frequent nor debilitating. Runkel, Wyant, and Bell (1975) elaborate.

> *Still another burden of the cadre member—though not one from which we believe we could have saved the Kent cadre or any other—is that of role conflict. Inevitably, cadre members will have to make decisions about whether to use or to disclose to other specialists diagnostic data obtained during training that could be used in making evaluations not related to the role of specialist. Or cadre members may wish to retreat from certain confrontations if they think their own status in the district could be threatened. Or they may find themselves torn between spending the next hour preparing for class or preparing for an intervention with the cadre. Or they may wonder whether their work as a cadre member or their work as a counselor or principal is the more likely to bring them a raise in salary. And so on. This is one of the hazards of the work and one of the reasons high ego strength can be an asset to a cadre member, even though it may be a liability during initial work with clients (pp. 47–48).*

The cadre will eventually have to deal with the issue of its members' commitment of time and energy. The Eugene cadre, for example, allows several categories of membership, each determined by the amount of time and energy a specialist can devote to intervention work at a particular time. "Active" specialists work on teams and participate in all meetings of the cadre; "support" specialists occasionally attend meetings or otherwise help to maintain the cadre as a district subsystem; "inactive" specialists cease all involvement for temporary periods.

Maintaining Cross-role Representation. Although a cadre of OD specialists should be representative of the various groups that are present within the district, processes of attrition and replacement may change its composition over the course of time. In Eugene and Kent, for example, we noted a decrease in the percentage of central-office administrators and a corresponding increase in the percentage of classroom teachers who were on active status as specialists. Table 12-1 indicates how cadre composition changed in Eugene and Kent from 1969 to 1973.

Such shifts do not seem to destroy the linking potential of the part-time model as long as a representative group is chosen in the first place and, as is the case in Eugene, as long as assistant superintendents take supportive roles rather than resign. While it is important to provide initial training to central-office administrators as a means of gaining their support and creating vital link-pin positions in the district, it is also important to recognize that teachers are more likely to provide services to client groups and to provide the means by which new members can become qualified to join the group when original members cease their active involvement.

Upgrading or Replacing Members. The continuing development of new technologies and strategies for OD training and consultation requires that specialists constantly improve their skills and remain receptive to new ideas that arise. Although there are a variety of ways of achieving self-renewing capability, internal OD specialists must develop plans for accomplishing it. Monthly evening sessions, summer workshops, small group seminars, or an annual retreat may help to meet this need. In addition to providing a setting in which skills can be built, each meeting can be devoted in part to goal-setting, problem-solving, or decision-making activities concerning the cadre's internal organization; at these sessions, too, the needs of intervention teams can be ascertained, roles clarified, and common concerns explored. On some occasions outside consultants can be hired to teach specialists new intervention strategies and theory or to help them improve their skills and collaborative working arrangements.

Specialists must also plan a way of ensuring that a reservoir of trained persons can be called on to replace those who resign or become inactive. In Eugene the basic strategy has been to call on those who have completed the three-term sequence of in-service courses offered by the cadre; only persons who have come to the district with comparable training and extensive experience have joined the cadre without attending these courses. By insisting that new members meet this standard and by offering assistance to applicants who do not, a cadre can avoid being labeled a clique or in-group of the

TABLE 12-1   Jobs represented in the Kent and Eugene Cadres

Kent	June 1969	January 1973
district-level administrators	4	2
coordinators or specialists	2	5
education association leaders	0	2
secondary administrators	1	3
elementary administrators	2	1
secondary counselors	4	5
secondary teachers	8	12
elementary teachers	3	8
Totals	24	38
Number of schools represented	8	12

NOTE: The 1969 data were obtained from the list of persons who participated in the initial training event held by CASEA. The 1973 data do not reflect the activity level of individuals since they were obtained from the published mailing list of members. Fourteen of 24, or 58 percent, of the original group were still active in January 1973; 24 of 38, or 63 percent, of the 1973 group were thus replacements trained by the cadre itself.

Eugene	June 1971	January 1973
assistant superintendents	3	0
coordinators and specialists	6	6
secondary administrators	3	3
elementary administrators	2	2
secondary counselors	1	0
elementary counselors	2	2
secondary teachers	4	4
elementary teachers	6	8
Totals	27	25
Number of schools represented	14	9

SOURCE: Runkel, Wyant, and Bell (1975, p. 59).

NOTE: The 1971 data were obtained from the list of persons who participated in the initial training event with CASEA. The 1973 data were obtained from a list of intervention team assignments and do not reflect accurately the extent of involvement of individuals. Twelve of 27, or 44 percent, of the original group were still on teams two years later; 13 of 25, or 52 percent, of those active or new members in 1973 were replacements trained by the Eugene cadre itself.

district—designations that might alienate it from potential client groups.

Runkel, Wyant, and Bell (1975) here describe how the self-renewal activities of the Kent cadre differed from the meetings of other groups in its school district. The same features apply to all the self-renewal meetings, retreats, and workshops of the Eugene cadre as well.

1. *The cadre initiated its own self-improvement. . . . The cadre determined its own needs, recruited its own outside consultants, and usually helped design its own training. This fact heightened commitment, readiness to learn, and the readiness of cadre members to apply their learning. . . .*
2. *The new learning was directed to group functioning, not to individual functioning. The training sessions for the cadre were always devoted to skills to be exercised in teams, not by individuals. . . .*
3. *Training sessions were not lectures, but practice. Lecturing and reading were used to illuminate practice, but practical skill was always the thing emphasized. Any consultant from outside always had to answer the demand, "All right, that sounds good. Now can you show us how to do it?"*
4. *The cadre dealt constantly with interpersonal relations among themselves. Their strong collaborative teamwork demanded high levels of trust and confidence in one another. If someone failed to do his or her part, others could not take refuge in the claim they had done their duty and leave the weaker member to be cast out by some superior. . . . The solution of the problem always . . . required airing feelings about how the stronger members acted in the team as well as how the weaker member acted.*
5. *The cadre remained alert to the desires and standards of its clients. . . . Their search for increased potential and their selection of modes of working was always responsive to the needs clients had expressed.*

A Final Note. Our experiences in Kent and Eugene have convinced us that cadres of OD specialists are strong indicators of district adaptability and are support systems for individual-school renewal as well. At the same time, however, much remains to be learned about cadres and about processes for institutionalizing them. We wonder, for example, about the future career lines of part-time specialists and about how they may link up with others for professional affiliation and recognition. We wonder, too, about the feasibility of creating student or parent cadres and about the kinds of reward structures needed to involve these persons both as specialists and as clients. For the present, we will continue to watch—we hope joined by others—the diffusion of the cadre concept and other means of making organization development a regularized activity in schools.

APPENDIX

Handout from the Eugene Cadre

List of Cadre Services.   To follow, you will find a list of our services, plus an indication of the types of interaction we feel would be
most productive and the processes we would like to follow if your
staff or group decides to request cadre assistance.

Our Bag.   Our specialty is helping you to assess your present structure, processes, and procedures; identify discrepancies between the
way things are and the way you want them to be; and initiate new
says of interacting to move closer to desired goals. Specifically, we
might help with:

- improving communication between persons and between groups
- clarifying goals and assessing progress toward them
- sharing expectations about norms and roles and forming agreements about what they should be
- dealing with conflicts that arise from miscommunication, unclear expectations, or other sources
- initiating procedures for improving meetings—setting agendas,
  assessing effectiveness, solving problems, convening groups, etc.
- clarifying influence patterns and decision-making procedures
- identifying and solving problems
- implementing innovations that require people to act in new ways
- providing a means for your staff to retrain itself, to accommodate new members, and to adapt to your changing needs in the
  future

Our Method.   Consultants are usually "hit and run" types: they
come in, observe and ask questions, make recommendations, and then
disappear. In contrast, our type of OD training involves staff members in using your own resources to make and carry out recommendations to and for yourselves. This method has several implications:

- It takes time. The "business" of a staff or unit meeting would
  be slowed up by taking time to systematically look at your processes; or a time investment would be required to take a Saturday morning or after-school session for additional training.
- It takes commitment. We can't set goals or solve problems for
  you, but we can provide opportunities and activities that help
  you set goals or find solutions that staff members really want
  and will work for.
- It takes an "experimental attitude." It involves doing things you
  don't ordinarily do, which may seem awkward or artificial at
  first (like paraphrasing, for example). It may require that you
  suspend judgment of new behaviors for some time. Experience
  has shown the value of using these procedures to focus on

specific problems and of creating situations in which the usefulness of specific processes can be demonstrated.

"Contract Building." We feel the need to do some collaborative
groundwork before you and we are committed to a specific event. We
would like to:

- be assured that a consensual decision was reached to invite us
- work with intact groups, such as the total staff, teaching unit or
  team, or other task groups
- explore goals and probable activities with members of the group
  before the event
- gather data through short interviews, questionnaires, or observation to identify the issues to be dealt with

So, we would see at least one meeting with the group (or part of it)
prior to an actual intervention to discuss goals, procedures, and problems; we would also like to get short written evaluations of our work.

Our Services. Let's say there are two basic reasons you might ask us
to do some work with you. First, there may be a specific problem or
issue to be dealt with, or people feel dissatisfied with some aspect of
the way the staff is working together. Second, you may want to improve some aspect of your work, such as expanding the ungraded
periods, sharing innovative ideas, improving meetings, dreaming about
ways to make a school a really exciting place to teach and learn, etc.
Generally, there are many kinds of things we can do.

Theory. We can convene discussion groups to talk about interpersonal relations, norms and roles, communication, etc.

Diagnosis. We can give you questionnaires or interviews to find
out how people feel about specific issues or possible alternatives.
These could simply be reported back to you, or training could
be based on the results.

Exercises. We can conduct exercises or simulations to explore
interpersonal interaction or other issues such as power, decision
making, communication, and so on.

Procedures. We can teach (mainly by giving you experience in
practicing) new ways of operating in staff or unit meetings or
in other groups.

Process Observation and Feedback. We can attend unit or staff
meetings to observe your interaction. The specialist could either
simply report his observations, or could actively step in at times
to ask the group to look at how it is working and/or to suggest
an activity or procedure to clarify what's happening or to improve group effectiveness.

Special Occasions. We could bring the total staff (or part of it)
together for special things like sharing innovations or problems,
to think about special projects you would like to get going, to
use the problem-solving sequence for a given problem, and so on.

Other. We may have omitted something, or you may think of other ways we can be of assistance to you.

What Next? We would be happy to talk with any or all of you about the things we've covered, or other ways we can help you, at unit meetings, staff meetings, or otherwise. We're looking forward to the possibility of working with you during the school year.

READINGS

The Inquiring School: Toward a Model of Organizational Self-renewal

J. N. Williamson

In this reading, Williamson argues that " . . . contemporary needs of public education cannot be met merely through changing school practice. Rather they demand a strategy for transforming the schools into centers of inquiry and self-renewal." For Williamson, this calls for problem-solving groups which he terms "inquiring teams" and describes as follows: "An inquiring team is a small, differentiated, temporary group which functions deliberately as an open system in accord with clinical processes of inquiry, with dual responsibility for self-renewal and the solution of a problem that is relevant to the social purposes of the organization." While Williamson assigns broader responsibilities to these teams than we envisage for OD cadres, the requirements for effective functioning are the same. We agree, too, with his final argument that schools and community should emerge from their separate organizational shells and engage in joint inquiry.

The Exercise of Responsibility

Clearly exercised responsibility in the activities of the team is the cornerstone that makes inquiry, in the sense that has been developed here, possible and effective. Responsibility is the vehicle through which self-renewal is initiated and the activities of the team relative to the purposes of the organization are carried out. . . .

In reference to the activities of an inquiring team, responsibility only makes sense operationally when the following conditions are satisfied:

1. the goals toward which activity is directed are clearly defined and shared;

2. the criteria by which performance is judged relative to the expressed goals are understood and accepted;

3. relative autonomy for decision-making and action with respect to the goals is given to the team and to individuals on the team;

4. the team and individuals on the team are held accountable for performance relative to their goals.

The Dual Responsibility for Renewal and the Solution of an Organizational Problem

It is possibly more convenient to think of the team's responsibility in terms of the simultaneous solution of two problems. One of these problems is associated with an operational goal, the goal to which the functioning of the team is most directly accountable. . . . For an instructional team of teachers, it might be the learning of their students in reference to some specifically prescribed outcomes; in the case of a school policy-making group, it would be effective decisions. The other problem for which the team is responsible is associated with an inquiry-goal—the continued growth and renewal of the group and of the individuals within the group. . . . These two goals may introduce tensions within the group in the immediate short term because of limited social resources. However, for the long-run viability of the organization and its overall purposes, the operations and inquiry goals must be kept in balance.

The Requirement of a Small Differentiated Group

. . . An important factor in determining the effectiveness of an inquiring team is the criterion of intimacy; all members of the group must have direct and informal communications access to all other members of the group. Consequently, the meaning of small here is relative to the purposes of the group itself, or the nature of the operations problem being addressed. . . . Here the criterion of direct communication and active personal participation in decision-making must govern the meaning of "small."

An inquiring team is differentiated according to several criteria, depending upon the nature of the problems that it addresses. Some relevant considerations here are the:

1. competencies required to solve the team's operational problems;

2. renewal and training needs of the team and the organization;

3. competencies required by the inquiry functions, such as research, training, and evaluation;

4. diversity required by the team to be able to tap the necessary variety in the environment;

5. inclusion of senior personnel in the group who are consciously able to take an objective perspective on the group's functioning and purposes, or in other words, to take the "executive" role;

6. inclusion of representatives of those groups affected by decisions made by the team.

These criteria are not equally relevant in all situations, but they do indicate that the makeup of a team will at times be very complex. For example, the criteria outlined above expose the inadequacy, from the point of view of inquiry, of basing a participatory model of policy-making in a school solely upon consideration of duly elected representatives of those groups affected by the decisions of the policy-makers. Inquiry demands that supplementary considerations be made which will ensure that competence will be brought to bear on the problems which are addressed by the policy-making group, the group will tap resources outside of themselves, and the members will be trained in the processes of representative policy-making within an environment of renewal.

The Requirement of Openness

In an earlier section on responsibility, it was argued that the degree to which members of an inquiring team could exercise responsibility and become personally involved in the work-learning environment was directly related to the team's access to an influence over relevant resources in the environment. Instructional teams must have ready access to professional literature, community resources, innovative instructional materials, and educational personnel trained in specialties such as human development, curriculum development, and research and evaluation. Students must be able to tap the abilities and interests of other students, teachers, and people in the community, and must have access to an adequate library of reference materials. In other words, their learning environment must be rich and accessible. At the level of organizational problem-solving, the school must be able to work in partnership with other community agencies, schools with similar problems, universities, and educational research and development centers. . . .

The problem of openness is complicated by the fact that it is not merely a problem internal to the organization. The environment must also be flexible and accessible to the school. It does little good for a student to be open to the resources of an inadequate library, for an instructional team to approach community resources for help that is not available, or for a school to attempt to form cooperative relationships with a university that does not wish to participate. The school and its internal and external resources must be open and accessible in a reciprocal way, and the design of effective mechanisms to bring about this reciprocity is clearly a major critical task in the effort to make schools inquiring institutions.

The Necessity of Being Temporary

A critical implication of the definition of an inquiring team is that the team is inherently a temporary structure. Since the team is an organizational unit, created, structured, and maintained to solve a particular problem, the life of the team in a fundamental sense is determined by the life of the problem. Once the problem has been solved, the team has served its purpose within the organization. How-ever, as we have seen, the team's completion of a task does not necessarily mean its total dissolution. For teams which were created to address an ongoing set of related problems, the solution of a problem may mean the conscious restructuring of the team to address the next problem.

It is important to note here the parallel relationship between our definition of an inquiring team and the notion of a project as a collaborative of diverse resources organized to solve a problem in a given amount of time. Given this similarity, our analysis of the inquiring team as the central and pervasive organizational unit of an inquiring school has added operational substance and understand-ing to the assertion of Warren Bennis and other modern organiza-tional theorists that the project as a temporary problem-solving unit will gradually replace bureaucracy as the principal organizational form of complex social organizations.

The Need to Function according to Clinical Processes of Inquiry

The preceding sections have essentially defined the requisite context or structure within which inquiry can flourish. . . . We shall now investigate the intrinsic intentional processes by which an inquiring team functions. . . .

It is the continual transference of conceptual information within an inquiring team that distinguishes its inquiry activity from mere problem-solving, and plays a critical role in the team's capacity to engage in continual renewal. The inquiring team is not only con-cerned with arriving at a viable solution to a problem, but is con-stantly probing the underlying causes, implications, and meanings of the problem itself. Inquiry requires that a continual search for under-standing, explanation, and analysis be an integral part of the routine activities of an inquiring team. The search will vary in degree and sophistication depending upon variables such as the age and experi-ence of the team members, the nature of the problem, and the time constraints imposed upon the problem. . . . A group of teachers and students attempting to help a student work through his problems of setting personal goals should also be concerned with analyzing the dynamics of the group and with communicating and understanding personal feelings expressed within the group. A teaching team should constantly be concerned not only with developing strategies by which students can reach the stated learning goals of the curriculum, but also with attempting to understand the underlying learning and development problems exhibited by their students. It is this con-tinual process of full-range questioning for understanding that is the critical component of renewal.

Decision-making, the second basic process inherent in the func-tioning of an inquiring team, is also not immediately distinctive, for decision-making is a process required of any problem-solving activity. However, as we have seen, inquiry demands that the significant decisions of the team be made as a result of active personal involvement of all members of the team. It is important to note that such a requirement does not necessarily imply that final decisions be made by team consensus or even that each member have equal influence; decisions must be made within clearly established lines of authority. . . .

Depending upon the constraints of the particular situation, ultimate authority for decision-making on an inquiring team may lie with the group as a whole or with a particular individual within the group. For example, in an inquiring school most of the significant decisions of a small instructional team probably could be made by consensus. Policy-making in the school most likely would be a shared responsibility, with certain decisions being made by the consensus of the policy-making body, others by majority vote, and still others by the principal after due advice from those affected by the decision. The critical aspect of decision-making on an inquiring team, then, is not so much the common sharing of authority in all circumstances, but rather the preservation within the decision-making process of active and intense shared involvement in the deliberations.

In a fundamental sense the final major clinical process, performance review, is what makes it possible for an inquiring team to work." . . . Inquiry requires that as a matter of course, performance be subject to continual analysis and evaluation, and that there be maintained within the team a healthy suspicion of current practice and the status quo, coupled with a drive to improve with respect to the team's values and commitments.

The Role of an Inquiring School in Its Community

The implications of inquiry as developed in operational terms in the preceding sections reach further than the internal functioning of the school itself. They suggest a radical change in perspective on the very purposes of the school in relation to the educational problems of the community. Once the school functions from a problem-solving point of view within the framework of open, inquiring teams, the whole issue of what in fact is the school and what is the community is radically altered. As we have seen, inquiry with respect to a problem requires that the makeup of the inquiring team and its resources represent the relevant areas of intervention into the problem. Although it is well known that many of the most severe learning problems that a school must address are more directly related to outside, rather than inside influences, schools continue to function as if resolutions for these problems could be found within the walls of the physical school building. Such thinking is derived from an outdated linear model of causality, which does not recognize the complex of mutual causes related to the situation. Organization by inquiring teams forces the school to dissolve its self-imposed boundaries in reference to the problems of education in the community it serves. The school must become less of a closed institution and more of a facilitator and catalyst for marshalling the community's resources, as well as a monitor for the growth and development of human learning in the community, with particular but not exclusive attention to its youth.

Here we can begin to think of the school as one educational resource and instrument among many in the community; one with certain comparative advantages and competencies as an educational institution, but also with many comparative disadvantages with respect to other resources. With respect to schooling, a fundamental implication of the inquiry point of view forwarded here is that rather than being viewed as equivalent to the community's formal educational resources, the school should be seen as the nerve center for a community's education, with responsibility not for housing the educational resources of the community, but for mustering and coordinating them. In this regard we can begin to think of the school as the hub of an inquiring community.

The ideas presented above imply a radical departure from present practice, primarily because they would have the school and the other community resources emerge from their separate organizational shells to engage in the common social purpose of fostering a self-renewing education for the community—the ultimate result of a school's functioning at the level of consciousness.

Organization Development

Richard Duffin, Arnold Falusi, and Philip Lawrence

The following reading reports the work of the Organization Development Unit of the York County Board of Education. The work of this unit confirms the premise that has guided our own cadre work—that the most significant organizational problems can be solved only from within.

R. Duffin, A. Falusi, and P. Lawrence, "Organization Development," *School Progress* (Toronto), 2-part series. Part 1, 41 (9), 1972, pp. 34-36. Part 2, 41 (10), 1972, pp. 62-64.

The functions of the OD Unit is to provide assistance for individuals or groups so that they may improve their own effectiveness. Services of the Unit are available to any employee of the board by applying to the OD office. While the Unit does report to the Board and to the Director, such reporting is couched in very general terms. The Unit reports in detail only to its clients. The need for such confidentiality would seem to be self-evident. In addition to their work in York County, the OD Unit has also worked with other Ontario school boards as well as with a community college and a university.

This article . . . will outline some outcomes of Organization Development in the York County Board over the past three years. Since the major thrust of our work has been with the administrators of the system, there are many outcomes of OD training we could have discussed. But to keep the article within manageable dimensions, we chose to deal only with a few concrete issues, mostly finan-cial and decision-making aspects of the organizational process.

We are always concerned about whether the outcomes of OD training are stable and developing patterns of behavior or temporary, rather unreal patterns which are eroded by the day-to-day pressures of life in an organization. We are also concerned to know whether the outcomes of our training are patterns of behavior which are orga-nizational-relevant and job-related or whether they are simply out-comes which make people feel good. Not that we object to people feeling good. But what we want them to feel good about is the way things are getting done in the organization and their part in the changes. All of the outcomes described are ones which have not only persisted for two years or more but ones which have grown and developed during this time.

The York County Board was formed, as were most other Ontario county boards, from a collection of smaller boards. The result was an "organization" which had all the classic behaviors and attitudes of any large-scale merger: mutual suspicion, cries for auton-omy, generalized hostility to the head office, competition for re-sources, and a collection of principals who were clustered in groups that were somewhat isolated from each other and from the total system.

In this situation, the basic problem was, "How can we create an organic entity out of this collection of discrepancies?" After careful consideration, the Board decided to employ an Organization Devel-opment strategy which would strive to change the atmosphere or "culture" of the organization so that there could be a better use of the resources of the organization, particularly the human resources. The Board decided to use part of its professional development budget for this project, on the theory that money spent on professional development should be devoted to some considerable extent to those key people who were in leadership roles and who were also, presum-ably, their most promising people. To this basic end, the OD unit was formed.

The first large-scale team building activity took place in late August, 1970, at Geneva Park, a conference centre outside of Toronto. The principals initiated a conference with the blessing of the senior administration. The OD unit was brought in because it was felt that their expertise would be helpful in making the meeting more success-ful. The organizers were careful to advise all prospective participants that attendance at this workshop was completely voluntary and con-sequently, some administrators chose not to come. Nevertheless, it is worth noting that some participants wanted nothing to do with the OD unit, and that some administrators were, at least ambivalent about the sessions. Thus, when the meetings began, the people were, in many cases, confused and somewhat resentful.

The principals' conference began with a Confrontation Meeting based upon a design developed by Richard Beckhard (Harvard Busi-ness Review; March, 1967). This particular meeting was to provide an opportunity for Sam Chapman, Director of Education, to get out into the open for the first time before the total management team the organizational problems and attitudes with which he was particularly concerned, to make clear to the total group that he was personally concerned, to collect from all and share with all the same sort of information, to arrange these items in some order or priority and to have the whole group begin to deal with these important issues and set target dates for their completion—all within a matter of hours.

Not only was this done, but the Director and his administrative council agreed to come up with answers to a number of challenging questions before the end of the conference and they even held a first meeting on these issues in the presence of their subordinates Obviously, this was, and could be, only a beginning. But it was a beginning to speak openly about the things that were being talked about furtively and, what is more important, it was a beginning to deal with these issues jointly.

By the end of the conference many of the resentments, confusions, and suspicions were alleviated, the principals had got better acquainted, a greater feeling of teamness had developed and everyone had at least a better idea of the direction in which York County was going and how they were involved in this movement. People also began to develop some differential perceptions that they, as individuals, were not the helpless victims of circumstances and powerful others and that they could each make a difference—to some degree they could influence their complex organizational world.

In addition to the conference at Geneva Park and subsequent quarterly meetings (which are only one day long, or less) the OD Unit has provided the Morton Organization Development Laboratory for all the top administrators, both business and academic, all principals and vice-principals, master teachers, attendance counselors, psychologists, and a few teachers. Attendance at the laboratory is voluntary and a few of those invited chose not to come. Their decision has been accepted without question.

The Organization Development Laboratory is a two-week residential program run one week at a time with from six weeks to six months between. The OD lab was created by Dr. Robert B. Morton, an American management psychologist, and modified for York County by Morton and the OD team. It is designed to give participants a common understanding of the realities of an organization and to provide them with a common methodology for dealing with organizational issues.

Since the participants work in functional groups of eight to ten (for example, a senior superintendent, a business officer, some of that superintendent's principals and, perhaps a staff person), the lab is designed to develop better communication channels, both vertically and horizontally within the organization. We have accumulated a good deal of data, well validated, that these large-scale interventions have had powerful consequences for good in York County.

The trustees of the Board were interested in and concerned about the OD program. Some saw OD training as a means of improving their own effectiveness. They also realized that it is very difficult to truly comprehend OD from the "outside," that is, by reading about it, talking about it, or listening to reports about it. Therefore 15 of the 18 trustees made the sacrifice of time, energy, and business and personal inconvenience to attend all or part of a Morton OD laboratory for trustees and their top administrative team.

This paper confines its attention to the consequences of OD training on financial planning and decision-making in York County. In general, there have been four major results:

1) the development of a York county identity;
2) the development of a relatively distortion-free vertical channel of communication for planning and decision-making;
3) more effective planning, problem-solving, and conflict resolution;
4) job enrichment.

By working as a team on issues that were controversial and important to all concerned, the administration has become much more of a team. We have not reached nor even approached the millennium, but prior to the OD training there was much less feeling of unity and common purpose. There was, among other things, a residual loyalty to organizations which no longer existed and an identification with their well-known practices and policies. Some individual "empires" had been lost in the shuffle, leaving their previous rulers somewhat confused and rueful. There was also quite a strong elementary-secondary split which made cooperation difficult.

Now, York County is perceived as mucn more of an entity wherein each principal better understands how the goals of his school fit in with the goals of the organization. There is now a much greater understanding of policy and other major plans because the principals have helped to shape them. For this reason the whole organization is more committed to the achievement of the plans. There is more of a feeling of "ownership" which simply was not there before. There is more resolution of conflict now by the members who share the conflict rather than kicking the problem upstairs. For example, two neighbouring high school principals met recently and resolved their conflicts over budget resources. The meeting was initiated by them, the conflicts were resolved by them, it was done quickly and amicably, and saved the area a substantial amount of money.

Prior to the OD training, the communication in York County was similar to the kind we see when visiting other organizations. Meetings were dominated by fear, by status; the boss heard what the subordinates wanted him to hear; disagreements were disguised; difficulties were denied, buried or thrown over the fence into the other fellow's yard; decisions were made on bad data, and no one disagreed with the boss even when they knew he was wrong. Also, because the groups were ineffective, agenda items sprang up in ever-proliferating profusion, and people were more than a little frustrated.

Subsequent to the training, while we still have too much of these ineffective behaviors, York County is much closer now to a situation where anyone who has the data is welcome to make an input to the discussion. Opinions are more freely expressed in a more open and supportive atmosphere. Decisions are based on better and more complete data and the quality of the decisions is much higher. Furthermore, because everyone has been involved in ways that are relevant to the issue and to his area of accountability, there is greater commitment to make the decision work. That is, the top administration can communicate to the organization in a clearer fashion and they can receive feedback from the firing line. The communication both ways is remarkably free of status distortions and other disfunctional impedimenta.

At one quarterly meeting with the principals a decision was presented to the group that had been roughed out by the total group at the previous meeting. It was accepted very quickly and has been easily implemented. Another tentative proposal was made to the meeting which the top administration thought was simple and routine. That proposal was completely altered for the better and the criticisms and recommendations were freely given and received.

One final but significant example: when the time came for the morning coffee break everyone was eager to go because it had been a busy session. When the Director finally dismissed the group they responded with considerable enthusiasm. But as they were about to leave a junior principal said, "Just a minute! I have something to say about this last item that I think is important." Without any hesitation or double takes, the entire group sat down and listened while this junior member made a highly valid point. He received support from the Director and acceptance from the whole group.

The administrative Committee of the York County Board consists essentially of the Director, the Associate Director, the Superintendent of Operations, the Superintendent of Planning & Development, the Superintendent of Business and the area superintendents. This group had become increasingly concerned and frustrated with the ineffectiveness of their meetings. About 18 months ago during a Week Two (Organizational Problem-Solving) lab they undertook to analyze this problem. After much hard and creative labor they produced their own meeting methodology. The result is that they have cut the number of items on their weekly agenda from well over 30 to no more than five. They have reduced the length of their meetings without increasing their frequency, the climate of the meetings is now much more relaxed, and much more gets done.

For several months, the group devoted the last half-hour of each meeting to the OD lab methodology of learning how to learn from experience so that their next meeting would be more effective. As they progressively refined their meeting procedures, they decided to replace the OD lab analysis for one of their own and they are working on this task at present. What is being changed here is not learning from experience but changing to a more appropriate method of learning from experience. As they have become increasingly self-sufficient, they have created their own methodologies.

The Administrative Committee has operated for months at a very high level of effectiveness. Director Sam Chapman says that this is the most effective group he has ever worked with. The changes are largely the result of the members of the committee having developed a more effective way of working and of deliberately learning from their experience as they go along. However, concurrent changes in the organization have provided the Administration Committee with much better data from the organization, which has greatly improved the quality of their decisions. This illustrates clearly how appropriate behavior in one area of an organization can powerfully reinforce appropriate behavior in another area, a sort of "snowball" effect.

The York County Board passed a formula for calculating the total number of teachers that could be hired. By applying this to predicted enrollments, there was an obvious allotment to each of the board's four geographic areas. However, before the four superintendents of the areas would agree to accept the total number of teachers to which the formula entitled them, they asked the question, "Who has special problems which might require some recognition in staff complement and what can we jointly do to help?" In this situation, one superintendent gave up a full-time specialist teacher to another area which had a greater need for these services and asked for nothing in return.

At the area level, before teachers were allotted to individual schools, the same question was asked and the principals were able to divide the available number of teachers in the way that made the most sense to the whole area. They also perceived that it made good organizational sense to leave a reserve to be used at the discretion of the superintendents so that unforeseen circumstances could be dealt with other than by crying for additional resources from the Board or by upsetting the planned structure in other schools.

Thus, staff complements are being filled on the basis of the best use of resources in terms of the needs of the whole organization. Furthermore, the decisions are increasingly being made by those who have the data. The decisions are largely being made by the principals. In one geographical area, the principals made all these decisions this year within the frames of reference defined by their superintendent. In the other areas, the principals have had a very large involvement in the decision-making process. It has not been necessary to increase the teacher-pupil ratio in York County this year despite the new budget guidelines of the department of education.

In the spring of 1969 the Director and the Superintendent of Operations examined the pupil-teacher ratios existing in the secondary schools and found that a variance from about 14.0 to just under 18 in schools that had some different problems but were still comparable. After discussion with the principals, a staff complement was established by the director which brought the pupil-teacher ratios much closer. The actual variations which existed then were greater than had been anticipated because of over-estimates in the enrollment projections made by the principals in several cases. In 1970-71, the central office did independent projections most of which were lower than the principals' estimates and some compromise was negotiated for staffing purposes. In 1971-72, the total of the principals' projections was lower by more than 300 (or about 2.2%—18 teachers—$216,000) than central office figures. This discovery did not lead them to expand their forecasts upward.

The principals' predictions have been extremely accurate despite the fact that York County has had its share of housing developments which did not develop as predicted. While the population of some parts of the County is admittedly more stable than that of a large metropolitan area, nonetheless, for the second year in a row our enrollment predictions have been highly precise. One of our area superintendents was out by a total of one pupil in a pupil population of about 11,000. And these results are largely due to the hard and smart work of the principals who have come up with prediction formulas which have been remarkably effective. Once again, the right data and the right people have provided better decisions . . .

The discovery that certain textbook titles were being ordered in one school while another school was taking the book out of service or had a surplus for some other reason led to the question of whether a more economic use of these resources could be made. The possible savings inherent in rebinding, if done on a mass scale, and in the consolidating of extra copies for possible additional enrollment seemed worth exploring.

Through a secondary school textbook inventory which identified expected enrollment, books in a usable state and books usable if rebound, a comprehensive order and distribution list for both new texts and rebound books was generated by computer.

It was expected that the data input by the schools would be poor, that principals would plan for a school reserve rather than trust the board reserve, that there would be objections about getting rebound books from another school instead of new books, and that principals would claim a budget adjustment if they supplied books to another school.

The data were inaccurate in many cases but, in spite of this, it is estimated that over $35,000 was saved in one year ($2.50 per student). None of the other concerns materialized.

Feeding back this information to all principals resulted in their decision to put in better data for 1971–72 to extend the plan to the elementary schools. Moreover, a group of principals worked through the whole operation with our system analyst and as a result developed a full understanding of the interdependence of the various people (e.g., the need to report on time), a feeling of ownership of the exercise and a part of any success that resulting savings might represent.

Although the preliminary savings in this area were well worthwhile, this is the sort of development where one might well expect a falling-off. On the contrary, the savings seem to be up considerably. It should be noted in passing that it is very difficult to assess what the savings are in such an area, because, as the organization has become more skillful in dealing with this problem, we have increasingly found surplus but useful books in one school which can be used in another. At the same time York County is providing all the schools with a wider choice of texts for a significantly smaller budget expenditure as well as freeing storage space for other uses in all the schools. We have here such a complex of interactions that it is difficult indeed to say what the word "saving" means. In York County we have made this kind of discovery, by the way, every time we have looked at the organization realistically and in detail rather than simplistically.

In conclusion, we wish to discuss two important generalizations about Organization Development.

1)   It is extremely difficult to get a good grasp of what OD is all about until you experience it. Organization Development, both in training and in practice, is experiential learning about our own (and others') behavior in work groups, and most of us are not accustomed to learning in this way. The facts (which are rarely or never about our behavior) are given to us by someone and we think about them and arrange them in some sort of cognitive pattern. We might use these cognitive packages to modify our own behavior but we think of that as something rather separate from the learning.

Essentially, what OD provides is methodology for learning how to learn from your experience (rather than some expert's experience) so that you can learn how to behave more effectively on the job. Since you want payoff from your learning to show up on the job, you do your learning in the context where the payoff is immediate. So, you have an experience, you collect your own facts about the experience, you wring from this such learning as you can and then, if possible, apply your learning to behave more effectively on the job. The learning is immediate, methodical, and behavior-centered. It is not remote, abstract nor academic.

2)   It is quite impossible to teach anybody anything of importance. The best we can do is to provide a situation in which someone may learn. And the best way to do that, in terms of organizational learning or organizational change, is to give people an opportunity to see a disparity between where they are now and where they want to be and to guarantee that they will not be punished for attempting to get to where they want to be. Under these circumstances, the potential for learning is very high and the learners will find a way to their goal that is meaningful to them, and thus, likely to be effective.

In organization terms this means it is impossible to "sell" OD as a kind of package, remedy, or aid-in-time-of-trouble, unless it makes sense to the people concerned. That is, unless they perceive a disparity between what they are doing now and what they want to do.

For example, about 18 months ago, members of the York County Administrative Council were given a set of sound and well-tested procedures for improving their meetings. They made a perfunctory attempt to use the prescription but dropped it after several time-grudging attempts to make it work. At an OD lab, as we have previously said, they produced their own set of procedures and have used them very effectively to improve their meetings. The two procedures are virtually identical but only the one produced by the group, to deal with their perceived need, was of any use.

No outsider or expert can give viable learnings or solutions to the people in an organization. There are mountains of data to support this truth and multitudes of organizations which ignore it. However, if the people on the firing line can see a meaningful disparity between where they are now and where they would like to be, and if they expect that they can deal with it, they will create their own method. *The significant problems of an organization can only be solved from the inside.*

BIBLIOGRAPHY

Arends, R. I., and Phelps, J. H. 1973. *Establishing organizational specialists within school districts.* Eugene, Ore.: Center for Educational Policy & Management.

This long report describes in detail how the cadres of organizational specialists were established, their rationale, and the success of their work. Enough information is presented for an interested district to start its own internal cadre.

Arends, R. I.; Ward, W.; Smith, M. A.; and Arends, J. H. 1976. *First time out: case studies of five neophyte consultant teams.* Portland, Ore.: Northwest Regional Educational Laboratory.

This report, which describes the problems and successes of five consulting teams as they conducted their initial OD interventions with real clients, could be used as a training tool in preparing internal OD specialists.

Murray, D. G., and Schmuck, R. A. 1972. The counselor-consultant as a specialist in organization development. *Elementary School Guidance and Counseling* 7: 99–104.

This brief article describes why and how school counselors should attempt to change their roles to act as OD consultants within schools and classrooms. Attention is also given to ways in which school counselors can become integral parts of internal OD cadres.

Preparing educational training consultants III: organization development. 1976. Portland, Ore.: Northwest Regional Educational Laboratory.

This set of instructional materials, which builds on the two sets described in the bibliography for chapter 10, aims at training educators in the concepts and skills of organization development. The strategies suggest a seventeen-day training period spread over six to eight months and can be tailored to meet local circumstances.

Runkel, P. J.; Wyant, S. H.; and Bell, W. E. 1975. *Organizational specialists in a school district: four years of innovation.* Eugene, Ore.: Center for Educational Policy & Management.

This technical research report traces the ebb and flow of a major OD effort with an entire school district over a four-year period.

The most important outcome of the consultation was the establishment of an internal cadre of OD specialists. Data indicate that the internal specialists were frequently more effective than outside consultants in facilitating school improvement.

Zand, D. E. 1974. Collateral organization: a new change strategy. *Journal of Applied Behavioral Science* 10: 63-89.

Zand suggests that one route to self-renewal is to create a collateral organization that parallels and coexists with the old organization. The collateral organization has norms differing from those usually in force and is used strategically for problem solving. In contrast to the internal cadre, the collateral organization assigns time to all members, during which all act in different ways. After training in the alternative norms, organization members act without an outside consultant.

Reference Notes

Notes to Chapter 1

Alderfer, Clayton. 1969. An empirical test of a new theory of human needs. *Organizational Behavior and Human Performance* 4:142-75.

Arends, Richard I.; Phelps, Jane H.; Harris, Martha; and Schmuck, Richard A. 1973. *Organization development: building human systems in schools.* Audio-slide presentation. Eugene, Ore.: Center for Educational Policy & Management.

Arends, Richard I.; Phelps, Jane H.; and Schmuck, Richard A. 1973. *Organization development: building human systems in schools.* Eugene, Ore.: Center for Educational Policy & Management.

Argyris, Chris. 1973. Personality and organization theory revisited. *Administrative Science Quarterly* 18:141-67.

Berlew, David. 1974. Leadership and organizational excitement. In *Organizational psychology: a book of readings,* 2d ed., ed. David A. Kolb, Irwin M. Rubin, and James M. McIntyre, pp. 265-77. Englewood Cliffs, N.J.: Prentice-Hall.

Bolman, Lee. 1974. The client as theorist: an approach to individual and organization development. In *Theory and method in organization development: an evolutionary process,* ed. John D. Adams, pp. 269-85. Arlington, Va.: NTL Institute for Applied Behavioral Science.

Buckley, Walter. 1967. *Sociology and modern systems theory.* Englewood Cliffs, N.J.: Prentice-Hall.

Campbell, J. P., and Dunnette, M. D. 1968. Effectiveness of T-group experiences in managerial training and development. *Psychology Bulletin* 70:73-104.

Friedlander, F. 1968. A comparative study of consulting processes and group development. *Journal of Applied Behavioral Science* 4:377-99.

Gardner, John. 1963. *Self-renewal: the individual and the innovative society.* New York: Harper & Row.

Harrison, R. 1970. Choosing the depth of organizational intervention. *Journal of Applied Behavioral Science* 6:181-202.

Hedberg, Bo L. T.; Nystrom, Paul C.; and Starbuck, William H. 1976. Camping on seesaws: prescriptions for a self-designing organization. *Administrative Science Quarterly* 21:41-64.

Lansky, L.; Runkel, P. J.; Croft, J.; and MacGregor, C. 1969. *The effects of human relations training on diagnosing skills and planning for change.* Eugene, Ore.: Center for Educational Policy & Management.

Lorsch, J. W., and Lawrence, P. R. 1970. *Studies in organizational design.* Homewood, Ill.: Richard D. Irwin & Dorsey Press.

Maslow, Abraham J. 1954. *Motivation and personality.* New York: Harper & Row.

McClelland, David C. 1958. Methods of measuring human motivation. In *Motives in fantasy, action, and society,* ed. John W. Atkinson, pp. 7-42. New York: Van Nostrand.

McGregor, Douglas. 1967. *The professional manager.* New York: McGraw-Hill.

Osgood, Charles E., and Suci, George J. 1955. Factor analysis of meaning. *Jour of Experimental Psychology* 50:325-38. Reprinted in 1969 in *Semantic differential technique: a sourcebook,* ed. James G. Snider and Charles E. Osgood, pp. 42-55. Chicago: Aldine.

Schmuck, Richard A. 1973. *Incorporating survey feedback in OD interventions.* Eugene, Ore.: Center for Educational Policy & Management.

Schmuck, Richard A., and Miles, Matthew B. 1971. *Organization development in schools.* Palo Alto, Calif.: National Press Books. 1976. La Jolla, Calif.: University Associates.

Schmuck, Richard A.; Murray, Donald; Smith, Mary Ann; Schwartz, Mitchell; and Runkel, Margaret. 1975. *Consultation for innovative schools: OD for multiunit structure.* Eugene, Ore.: Center for Educational Policy & Management.

Schmuck, Richard A., and Schmuck, Patricia A. 1975. *Group processes in the classroom.* 2d ed. Dubuque, Iowa: Brown.

Seiber, Sam D. 1968. Organizational influences on innovative roles. In *Knowledge production and knowledge utilization in educational administration,* ed. T. Eidell and J. Kitchell, pp. 120-42. Eugene, Ore.: Center for Educational Policy & Management.

Williamson, John N. 1974. The inquiring school: toward a model of organizational self-renewal. *Educational Forum* 38:355-71 (Part 1) and 38:393-410 (Part 2).

Wyant, Spencer H. 1974. The effects of organization development training on intrastaff communications in elementary schools. Ph.D. dissertation. University of Oregon.

Notes to Chapter 2

Arends, Jane H. 1975. Organization development for the staff, parents, and students of an urban junior high school: a case study. Ph.D. dissertation, University of Oregon.

Arends, Richard I.; Ward, William; Smith, Mary Ann; and Arends, Jane H. 1976. First time out: case studies of five neophyte consultant teams. Mimeographed. Portland, Ore.: Northwest Regional Educational Laboratory.

Brandt, Richard M. 1972. *Studying behavior in natural settings.* New York: Holt, Rinehart & Winston.

Bruyn, Severyn T. 1966. *The human perspective in sociology: the methodology of participant observation.* Englewood Cliffs, N.J.: Prentice-Hall.

Center for New Schools. 1975. A multimethod study of the development and effects of an alternative high school learning environment. Mimeographed. Chicago: Center for New Schools.

Derr, C. Brooklyn. 1972. Successful entry as a key to successful organizational development in big-city school school systems. In *The social technology of organizational development,* ed. W. W. Burke and H. A. Hornstein, pp. 41 52. Arlington, Va.: NTL Institute for Applied Behavioral Science.

Derr, C. Brooklyn, and Demb, Ada. 1974. Entry and urban school systems; the context and culture of new markets. *Education and Urban Society* 6:135-52.

Flynn, C. Wayne. 1974. Management effectiveness by organizational development. *Bulletin of the National Association of Secondary-school Principals* 58:135-41.

Fox, Robert S.; Schmuck, R. A.; Van Egmond, E.; Ritvo, M.; and Jung, C. 1973. *Diagnosing professional climate of schools.* Fairfax, Va.: NTL Learning Resources.

Fox, R.; Luszki, M.; and Schmuck, R. A. 1966. *Diagnosing classroom learning environments.* Chicago: Science Research Associates.

Guttman, Louis. 1965a. A faceted definition of intelligence. *Scripta Hierosolymitana* 14:166-81.

————. 1965b. The structure of interrelations among intelligence tests. In *Proceedings of the 1964 conference on testing problems,* ed. C. W. Harris, pp. 25-37. Princeton, N.J.: Educational Testing Service.

Hyman, Ray. 1964. *The nature of psychological inquiry.* Englewood Cliffs, N.J.: Prentice-Hall.

Kahn, Robert L., and Cannell, Charles F. 1957. *The dynamics of interviewing.* New York: Wiley.

Kaufman, Harry. 1968. *Introduction to the study of human behavior.* Philadelphia: Saunders.

Levinson, Harry. 1972. *Organizational diagnosis.* Cambridge, Mass.: Harvard University Press.

Oppenheim, A. N. 1966. *Questionnaire design and attitude measurement.* New York: Basic Books.

Phelps, Jane H., and Arends, Richard I. 1973. Helping parents and educators to solve school problems together: an application of organization development. Mimeographed. Eugene, Ore.: Center for Educational Policy & Management.

Runkel, Philip J. 1974. Bibliography on organizational change in schools: selected and annotated. Mimeographed. Eugene, Ore.: Center for Educational Policy & Management.

Runkel, Philip J., and McGrath, Joseph E. 1972. *Research on human behavior: a systematic guide to method.* New York: Holt, Rinehart & Winston.

Runkel, Philip J.; Wyant, Spencer H.; and Bell, Warren E. 1975. *Organizational specialists in a school district: four years of innovation.* Final report to

National Institute of Education from Contract no. NEC-00-3-0083, Component 1, part of the Program on Strategies of Organizational Change of the Center for Educational Policy & Management of the University of Oregon. Also available from the Educational Research Information Center (ERIC) of the U.S. government. Order no. ED 111 107, ERIC Document Reproduction Service, Post Office Box 190, Arlington, Va. 22210.

Saturen, Steven Leon. 1972. On the way to adaptability: some conditions for organizational self-renewal in elementary schools. Ph.D. dissertation, University of Oregon.

Schmuck, Richard A.; Murray, Donald; Smith, Mary Ann; Schwartz, Mitchell; and Runkel, Margaret. 1975. *Consultation for innovative schools: OD for multiunit structure.* Eugene, Ore.: Center for Educational Policy & Management.

Schmuck, Richard A., and Runkel, Philip J. 1970. *Organizational training for a school faculty.* Eugene, Ore.: Center for the Advanced Study of Educational Administration.

Scriven, Michael S. 1967. The methodology of evaluation. In *Perspectives of curriculum evaluation.* American Educational Research Association Monograph Series in Curriculum Evaluation, no. 11. Chicago: Rand McNally.

Simon, Anita, and Boyer, E. G., eds. 1967. *Mirrors for behavior.* Philadelphia: Research for Better Schools.

Simons, David L. 1974. Durability of organizational training for a school faculty. Ph.D. dissertation, University of Oregon.

Smith, Mary Ann. 1972. A comparison of two elementary schools involved in a major organizational change: or, you win a few, you lose a few. Ph.D. dissertation, University of Oregon.

Stufflebeam, Daniel L. 1971. The relevance of the CIPP evaluation model for educational accountability. Paper read at Annual Meeting of American Association of School Administrators, February 1971, in Atlantic City, New Jersey.

Stufflebeam, Daniel L.; Foley, Walter J.; Gephart, William J.; Guba, Egon G.; Hammond, Robert L.; Merriman, Howard O.; and Provus, Malcolm. 1971. *Educational evaluation and decision making.* Itasca, Ill.: Peacock.

Wacaster, C. Thompson. 1973. The life and death of differentiated staffing at Columbia High School. In *The process of planned change in the school's instructional organization,* ed. W. W. Charters, Jr., Robert B. Everhart, John E. Jones, John S. Packard, Roland J. Pellegrin, Larry J. Reynolds, and C. Thompson Wacaster, pp. 38–51. Eugene, Ore.: Center for Educational Policy & Management.

Webb, Eugene J.; Campbell, Donald T.; Schwartz, Richard D.; and Sechrest, Lee. 1966. *Unobtrusive measures: nonreactive research in the social sciences.* Chicago: Rand McNally.

Wyant, Spencer H. 1974. The effects of organization development training on intrastaff communications in elementary schools. Ph.D. dissertation, University of Oregon. For a somewhat different version by Wyant, see chapter 6 in Runkel, Wyant, and Bell (1975).

Notes to Chapter 3

Alberti, Robert E., and Emmons, Michael L. 1975. *Stand up, speak out, talk back!* New York: Pocket Books.

Allport, Gordon W., and Postman, Leo F. 1945. The basic psychology of rumor. *Transactions of the New York Academy of Sciences* (Series 2) 8:61-81.

Bales, Robert F. 1950. *Interaction process analysis: a method for the study of small groups.* Reading, Mass.: Addison-Wesley.

Bass, Bernard. 1966. *A program of exercises for management and organizational psychology.* Pittsburgh: Management Development Associates.

Bavelas, Alex. 1950. Communication patterns in task-oriented groups. *Journal of the Acoustical Society of America* 22:725-30.

Behavior Today (1974) 5:299-300.

Dyer, William G. 1969. Acceptance or change? *Human Relations Training News* 13:6-7. Washington, D.C.: NTL Institute for Applied Behavioral Science.

Gibb, Jack R. 1961. Defensive communication. *Journal of Communication* 11: 141-48.

Hale, James R., and Spanjer, R. Allen. 1972. *Systematic and objective analysis of instruction training manual.* Portland, Ore.: Northwest Regional Educational Laboratory.

Jung, Charles; Howard, Rosalie; Emory, Ruth; and Pino, Rene. 1972. *Trainer's manual: interpersonal communications.* Portland, Ore.: Northwest Regional Educational Laboratory.

Katz, Daniel, and Kahn, Robert L., Jr. 1966. *The social psychology of organizations.* New York: Wiley.

Katz, Elihu. 1957. The two-step flow of communication: an up-to-date report on an hypothesis. *Public Opinion Quarterly* 21:68-78.

Leavitt, Harold J. 1951. Some effects of certain communication patterns on group performance. *Journal of Abnormal and Social Psychology* 46:38-50.

Leavitt, Harold J., and Mueller, Ronald A. H. 1951. Some effects of feedback on communications. *Human Relations* 4:401-10.

Likert, Rensis. 1961. *New patterns of management.* New York: McGraw-Hill.

Luft, Joseph. 1969. *Of human interaction.* Palo Alto, Calif.: National Press Books.

McGregor, Douglas. 1967. *The professional manager.* New York: McGraw-Hill.

Pfeiffer, J. William, and Jones, John E., eds. 1970. *A handbook of structured experiences for human relations training.* Vol. 1. Iowa City, Iowa: University Associates Press.

Schmuck, Richard A.; Murray, Donald; Smith, Mary Ann; Schwartz, Mitchell; and Runkel, Margaret. 1975. *Consultation for innovative schools; OD for multiunit structure.* Eugene, Ore.: Center for Educational Policy & Management.

Schultz, William. 1966. *The interpersonal underworld.* Palo Alto, Calif.: Science & Behavior Books.

Wallen, John L. 1966. Group Expectations Survey: form O. Mimeographed. Portland, Ore.: Northwest Regional Educational Laboratory.

————. 1972. Emotions as problems. In *Trainer's manual,* ed. Jung, Howard, Emory, and Pino.

Notes to Chapter 4

Argyris, Chris. 1970. *Intervention theory and method: a behavioral science view.* Reading, Mass.: Addison-Wesley.

Beckhard, Richard. 1969. *Organization development: strategies and models.* Reading, Mass.: Addison-Wesley.

Derr, C. Brooklyn. 1971. Organization development and PPB for education. Mimeographed. Paper read at 1971 Convention of American Educational Research Association. Eugene, Ore.: Center for the Advanced Study of Educational Administration.

Kerlinger, Fred N. 1964. *Foundations of behavioral research.* New York: Holt, Rinehart & Winston.

Krech, David; Crutchfield, Richard S.; and Ballachey, E. L. 1962. *Individual in society.* New York: McGraw-Hill.

Mager, Robert F. 1962. *Preparing instructional objectives.* Palo Alto, Calif.: Fearon.

McElvaney, C. T., and Miles, M. B. 1971. Using survey feedback and consultation. In *Organization development in schools,* ed. Richard A. Schmuck and Matthew B. Miles, pp. 113-38. Palo Alto, Calif.: National Press Books. 1976. La Jolla, Calif.: University Associates.

Miles, Matthew B. 1965. Planned change and organizational health: figure and ground. In *Change processes in the public schools,* ed. R. O. Carlson, A. Gallagher, Jr., M. B. Miles, R. J. Pellegrin, and E. M. Rogers, pp. 11-34. Eugene, Ore.: Center for the Advanced Study of Educational Administration.

Pfeiffer, J. William, and Jones, John E., eds. 1970. *A handbook of structured experiences for human relations training.* Vol. 2. Iowa City, Iowa: University Associates Press.

Phillips, Bernard S. 1966. *Social research: strategy and tactics.* New York: Macmillan Co.

Raths, Louis E.; Harmin, M.; and Simon, S. B. 1966. *Values and teaching.* Columbus, Ohio: Merrill.

Runkel, Philip J.; Wyant, Spencer H.; and Bell, Warren E. 1975. *Organizational specialists in a school district: four years of innovation.* Eugene, Ore.: Center for Educational Policy & Management.

Schmuck, Richard A., and Miles, Matthew B. 1971. *Organization development in schools.* Palo Alto, Calif.: National Press Books. 1976. La Jolla, Calif.: University Associates.

Schmuck, Richard A.; Murray, Donald; Smith, Mary Ann; Schwartz, Mitchell; and Runkel, Margaret. 1975. *Consultation for innovative schools: OD for multiunit structure.* Eugene, Ore.: Center for Educational Policy & Management.

Schmuck, Richard A., and Runkel, Philip J. 1972. Integrating organizational specialists into school districts. In *Contemporary organization development: conceptual orientations and interventions,* ed. W. W. Burke, pp. 168-200. Fairfax, Va.: NTL Institute for Applied Behavioral Science. Also available from ERIC Document Reproduction Service, Post Office Box 190, Arlington, Va. 22210, Order no. ED 061 617.

Simon, S. B.; Howe, L. W.; and Kirschenbaum, H. 1972. *Values clarification: a handbook of practical strategies for teachers and students.* New York: Hart.

Sjoberg, Gideon, and Nett, Roger. 1968. *Methodology for social research.* New York: Harper & Row.

Smith, Maury. 1973. Values clarification. In *Annual handbook for group facilitators,* ed. J. William Pfeiffer and John E. Jones, pp. 203-12. Iowa City, Iowa: University Associates Press.

Thomson, T. M. 1972. Management by objectives. In *Annual handbook for group facilitators*, ed. Pfeiffer and Jones, pp. 130-32.

Notes to Chapter 5

Arends, Richard I., and Phelps, Jane H. 1973. Establishing organizational specialists within school districts. Mimeographed. Eugene, Ore.: Center for Educational Policy & Management.

Beckhard, Richard. 1969. *Organization development: strategies and models.* Reading, Mass.: Addison-Wesley.

Chesler, M. A., and Lohman, J. E. 1971. Changing schools through student advocacy. In *Organization development in schools*, ed. Richard A. Schmuck and Matthew B. Miles, pp. 185-212. Palo Alto, Calif.: National Press Books. 1976. La Jolla, Calif.: University Associates.

Derr, C. Brooklyn. 1971. An organizational analysis of the Boston School Department. Ph.D. dissertation, Harvard University.

————. 1970. Organizational development in one large urban school system. *Education and Urban Society* 2:403-19.

Fox, Robert S.; Schmuck, R. A.; Van Egmond, E.; Ritvo, M.; and Jung, C. 1973. *Diagnosing professional climate of schools.* Fairfax, Va.: NTL Learning Resources.

Harrison, R. 1970. Choosing the depth of organizational intervention. *Journal of Applied Behavioral Science* 6:181-202.

Lawrence, P. R., and Lorsch, J. W. 1967 *Organization and environment: managing differentiation and integration.* Boston: Harvard Business School, Division of Research.

McGrath, J. E. 1970. *Social and psychological factors in stress.* New York: Holt, Rinehart & Winston.

Runkel, Philip J.; Wyant, Spencer H.; and Bell, Warren E. 1975. *Organizational specialists in a school district: four years of innovation.* Eugene, Ore.: Center for Educational Policy & Management.

Schmuck, Richard A.; Murray, Donald; Smith, Mary Ann; Schwartz, Mitchell; and Runkel, Margaret. 1975. *Consultation for innovative schools: OD for multiunit structure.* Eugene, Ore.: Center for Educational Policy & Management.

Walton, R. E. 1969. *Interpersonal peacemaking: confrontations and third-party consultation.* Reading, Mass.: Addison-Wesley.

Notes to Chapter 6

Bales, Robert F. 1950. *Interaction process analysis: a method for the study of small groups.* Reading, Mass.: Addison-Wesley.

Fosmire, Fred, and Keutzer, Caroline. 1968. Task-directed learning: a systems approach to marital therapy. Mimeographed. Paper presented at Meeting of the Oregon Psychological Association and Western States Psychological Association, May 1968.

Fosmire, Fred; Keutzer, Caroline; and Diller, Richard. 1971. Starting up a senior high school. In *Organization development in schools*, ed. Richard A. Schmuck and Matthew B. Miles, pp. 87-112. 1976. La Jolla, Calif.: University Associates.

Hale, James R., and Spanjer, R. Allen. 1972. *Systematic and objective analysis of instruction training manual.* Portland, Ore.: Northwest Regional Educational Laboratory.

Hall, Jay. 1969. *Systems maintenance: gatekeeping and the involvement process.* Monroe, Tex.: Telometrics International.

Jackson, Philip W. 1968. *Life in classrooms.* New York: Holt, Rinehard & Winston.

Johnson, David W., and Johnson, Frank P. 1975. *Joining together: group theory and group skills.* Englewood Cliffs, N.J.: Prentice-Hall.

Lortie, Dan C. 1975. *School-teacher: a sociological study.* Chicago: University of Chicago Press.

Schein, Edgar H. 1969. *Process consultation: its role in organization development.* Reading, Mass.: Addison-Wesley.

Schindler-Rainman, Eva; Lippitt, R.; and Cole, J. 1975. *Taking your meetings out of the doldrums.* Columbus, Ohio: Association of Professional Directors.

Notes to Chapter 7

Bridges, Edwin M.; Doyle, Wayne J.; and Hahan, David J. 1970. Effects of hierarchical differentiation on group productivity, efficiency, and risk-taking. In *Learning in social settings: new readings in the social psychology of education,* ed. Matthew B. Miles and W. W. Charters, Jr., pp. 625-37. Boston: Allyn & Bacon.

Emery, F. E., and Trist, E. L. 1965. The causal texture of organizational environments. *Human Relations* 18:21-31.

Maier, Norman R. F. 1962. Leadership principles for problem-solving conferences. *Michigan Business Review* 14:8-15.

Terreberry, Shirley. 1968. The evolution of organizational environments. *Administrative Science Quarterly* 12:590-613.

Notes to Chapter 8

Alutto, Joseph, and Belasco, J. 1972. A typology for participation in organizational decision making. *Administrative Science Quarterly* 17:117-125.

Argyris, Chris. 1970. *Intervention theory and method: a behavioral science view.* Reading, Mass.: Addison-Wesley.

Bachman, J.; Smith, C.; and Slesinger, J. 1966. Control performance and satisfaction: an analysis of structural and individual effects. *Journal of Personality & Social Psychology* 42:127-36.

Belasco, James, and Alutto, J. 1972. Decisional participation and teacher satisfaction. *Educational Administrative Quarterly* 8:44-58.

Coch, L., and French, J. R. P. 1948. Overcoming resistance to change. *Human Relations* 1:512-32.

Flynn, C. Wayne. 1971. The principal as an organizational consultant to his own school. Ph.D. dissertation, University of Oregon.

Fosmire, Fred R. 1970. Some TDL-VOCOM tasks and their use in education and research. Mimeographed. Eugene, Ore.: University of Oregon.

French, John, and Raven, Burt. 1959. The bases of social power. In *Studies in social power,* ed. Darwin Cartwright, pp. 118-49. Ann Arbor, Mich.: Institute of Social Research.

Hall, Jay. 1971. Decisions, decisions, decisions. *Psychology Today* 5:51-54, 86, 88.

Hornstein, J.; Callahan, D.; Fisch, E.; and Benedict B. 1968. Influence and satisfaction in organizations: a replication. *Sociology of Education* 412:380-89.

Knutson, Andie L. 1960. Quiet and vocal groups. *Sociometry* 23:36-49.

Lafferty, J. C., and Eady, P. M. 1974. *Desert survival situation*. Plymouth, Mich.: Experiential Learning Methods.

Lewin, K. 1951. *Field theory in the social sciences*. New York: Harper & Row.

Likert, Rensis. 1961. *New patterns of management*. New York: McGraw-Hill.

————. 1967. *The human organization: its management and value*. New York: McGraw-Hill.

Maier, N. R. F. 1970. *Problem solving and creativity*. Belmont, Calif.: Brooks/Cole.

March, James, and Simon, H. 1958. *Organizations*. New York: Wiley.

Maslow, Abraham J. 1954. *Motivation and personality*. New York: Harper & Row.

McGregor, Douglas. 1967. *The professional manager*. New York: McGraw-Hill.

Mullen, David J., and Goolsby, T. M. 1974. School organizational development questionnaire. Mimeographed. Athens, Ga.: University of Georgia.

Pfeiffer, J. William, and Jones, John E., eds. 1974. *A handbook of structured experiences for human relations training*. Vol. 3. La Jolla, Calif.: University Associates.

Schein, E. H. 1965. *Organizational psychology*. Englewood Cliffs, N.J.: Prentice-Hall.

Schmidt, W., and Tannenbaum, R. 1958. How to choose a leadership pattern. *Harvard Business Review* 36:95-101.

Schmuck, Richard A.; Murray, Donald; Smith, Mary Ann; Schwartz, Mitchell; and Runkel, Margaret. 1975. *Consultation for innovative schools: OD for multiunit structure*. Eugene. Ore.: Center for Educational Policy & Management.

Simon, S. B.; Howe, L. W.; and Kirschenbaum, H. 1972. *Values clarification: a handbook of practical strategies for teachers and students*. New York: Hart.

Tannenbaum, Arnold S. 1968. *Control in organizations*. New York: McGraw-Hill.

Wallen, John L. 1970. *Charting the decision-making structure of an organization*. Portland, Ore.: Northwest Regional Educational Laboratory.

Weick, Karl E. 1976. Educational organizations as loosely coupled systems. *Administrative Science Quarterly* 21:1-19.

Wood, M. T. 1973. Power relationships and group decision making in organizations. *Psychological Bulletin* 79:280-93.

Notes to Chapter 9

Arends, Richard I.; Phelps, Jane H.; Harris, Martha; and Schmuck, Richard A. 1973. *Organization development: building human systems in schools*. Audio-slide presentation. Eugene, Ore.: Center for Educational Policy & Management.

Arends, Richard I.; Phelps, Jane H.; and Schmuck, Richard A. 1973. *Organization development: building human systems in schools*. Eugene, Ore.: Center for Educational Policy & Management.

Bigelow, Ronald C. 1971. Changing classroom interaction through organization development. In *Organization development in schools*, ed. Richard A. Schmuck and Matthew B. Miles, pp. 71-86. 1976. La Jolla, Calif.: University Associates.

Runkel, Philip J.; Wyant, Spencer H.; and Bell, Warren E. 1975. *Organizational specialists in a school district: four years of innovation*. Eugene, Ore.: Center for Educational Policy & Management.

Schmuck, Richard A. 1971. Improving classroom group processes. In *Organization development in schools*, ed. Richard Schmuck and Matthew B. Miles, pp. 29-50. 1976. La Jolla, Calif.: University Associates.

Schmuck, Richard A.; Murray, Donald; Smith, Mary Ann; Schwartz, Mitchell; and Runkel, Margaret. 1975. *Consultation for innovative schools: OD for multiunit structure*. Eugene, Ore.: Center for Educational Policy & Management.

Schmuck, Richard A., and Runkel, Philip J. 1970. *Organizational training for a school faculty*. Eugene, Ore.: Center for the Advanced Study of Educational Administration.

Schmuck, Richard A., and Schmuck, Patricia A. 1974. *A humanistic psychology of education: making the school everybody's house*. Palo Alto, Calif.: Mayfield.

―――. 1975. *Group processes in the classroom*. 2d ed. Dubuque, Iowa: Wm. C. Brown.

Notes to Chapter 10

Arends, Jane H. 1975. Organization development for the staff, parents, and students of an urban junior high school: a case study. Ph.D. dissertation, University of Oregon.

Berman, Paul, and McLaughlin, Milbrey W. 1975. *Federal programs supporting educational change, vol. 6: the findings in review*. Santa Monica, Calif.: Rand.

Crosby, Robert, and Schmuck, Richard A. 1969. Transfer and laboratory training. *Human Relations Training News* 13:3-5.

Fox, Robert S.; Schmuck, R. A.; Van Egmond, E.; Ritvo, M.; and Jung. C. 1973. *Diagnosing professional climate of schools*. Fairfax, Va.: NTL Learning Resources.

Pfeiffer, J. William, and Jones, John E., eds. 1969-74. *A handbook of structured experiences for human relations training*. 4 vols. San Diego: University Associates.

―――, eds. 1972-76. *Annual handbook for group facilitators*. San Diego: University Associates.

Phelps, Jane H., and Arends, Richard I. 1973. Helping parents and educators to solve school problems together: an application of organization development. Mimeographed. Eugene, Ore.: Center for Educational Policy & Management.

Runkel, Philip J.; Wyant, Spencer H.; and Bell, Warren E. 1975. *Organizational specialists in a school district: four years of innovation*. Eugene, Ore.: Center for Educational Policy & Management.

Schein, Edgar H. 1969. *Process consultation: its role in organization development*. Reading, Mass.: Addison-Wesley.

Schein, Edgar H., and Bennis, Warren G. 1965. *Personal and organizational change through group methods: the laboratory approach.* New York: Wiley.

Schmuck, Richard A. 1973. *Incorporating survey feedback in OD interventions.* Eugene, Ore.: Center for Educational Policy & Management.

Schmuck, Richard A.; Arends, Richard I.; and Arends, Jane H. 1974. Tailoring consultation in organization development for particular schools. *School Psychology Digest* 3:29-39.

Schmuck, Richard A.; Murray, Donald; Smith, Mary Ann; Schwartz, Mitchell; and Runkel, Margaret. 1975. *Consultation for innovative schools: OD for multiunit structure.* Eugene, Ore.: Center for Educational Policy & Management.

Walton, Richard E. 1969. *Interpersonal peacemaking: confrontations and third-party consultation.* Reading, Mass.: Addison-Wesley.

Notes to Chapter 11

In the citations that follow, ERIC refers to the Educational Research Information Center of the U.S. government. To inquire about its documents, write to ERIC Document Reproduction Service, Post Office Box 190, Arlington, Va. 22210, and include the ED order number.

Anderson, Gary J. 1973. The assessment of learning environments: a manual for the "learning environment inventory" and the "my class inventory." Mimeographed. Halifax, Nova Scotia: Atlantic Institute of Education.

Arends, Richard I., and Essig, Don M. 1972. Differentiated staffing project at Eugene, Oregon: five progress reports, January 1972. Mimeographed. ERIC order nos. ED 060 511, 060 512, 060 513, 060 514, and 060 515.

Argyris, Chris. 1973. Personality and organization theory revisited. *Administrative Science Quarterly* 18:141-67.

————. 1968. Unintended consequences of rigorous research. *Psychological Bulletin* 70:185-97.

Bigelow, Ronald C. 1971. Changing classroom interaction through organization development. In *Organization development in schools,* ed. Richard A. Schmuck and Matthew B. Miles, pp. 71-85. Palo Alto, Calif.: National Press Books. 1976. La Jolla, Calif.: University Associates.

Bowles, Samuel, and Gintis, Herbert. 1976. *Schooling in capitalist America.* New York: Basic Books.

Buckley, Walter. 1967. *Sociology and modern systems theory.* Englewood Cliffs, N.J.: Prentice-Hall.

Campbell, Donald T., and Stanley, Julian C. 1963. Experimental and quasi-experimental designs for research on teaching. In *Handbook of research on teaching,* ed. N. L. Gage, pp. 171-246. Chicago: Rand McNally. Reprinted separately by the publishers as *Experimental and quasi-experimental designs for research.*

Charters, W. W., Jr., and Jones, John E. 1973. On the risk of appraising non-events in program evaluation. *Educational Researcher* 2:5-8.

Charters, W. W., Jr.; Everhart, Robert B.; Jones, John E.; Packard, John S.; Pellegrin, Roland J.; Reynolds, Larry J.; and Wacaster, C. Thompson. 1973. *The process of planned change in the school's instructional organization.* Eugene, Ore.: Center for Educational Policy & Management.

Charters, W. W., Jr., and Pellegrin, Roland J. 1972. Barriers to the innovative process: four case studies of differentiated staffing. *Educational Administration Quarterly* 9:3-14.

Duffin, Richard; Falusi, Arnold; and Lawrence, Philip. 1972. Organization development. Part 1: What's it all about? *School Progress* (Toronto) 41:34-36. Part 2: Problems can only be solved from the inside. *School Progress* 41:62-64.

Essig, Don M. 1971. The effects of multiunit differentiated staffing organization on teachers' attitudes and instructional programs. Ph.D. dissertation, University of Oregon.

Essig, Don M., and Kennel, Paul. 1972. Learning centers: a program designed to improve the instruction of fifth and sixth grade students at Parker School. Mimeographed. Report to the Superintendent of School District 4J of Eugene, Oregon, April 1972. For information, write to Dr. Don Essig, Howard School, 700 Howard Avenue, Eugene, Oregon 97402.

Essig, Don M.; Tompkins, Russel; and Rutter, Roy. 1971. Final report on "Operation Branch": a program designed to close the communication gap between home and school. Mimeographed. Report to the Superintendent of School District 4J of Eugene, Oregon, 24 November 1971.

Favors, John. 1971. Parental involvement and its relation to student achievement. Ph.D. dissertation, University of California at Berkeley.

Flynn, C. Wayne. 1974. Management effectiveness by organizational development. *Bulletin of the National Association of Secondary-school Principals* 58:135-41.

Fox, Robert; Luszki, M.; and Schmuck, R. A. 1966. *Diagnosing classroom learning environments.* Chicago: Science Research Associates.

Fox, Robert S.; Boies, Herbert E.; Brainard, Edward; Fletcher, Edward; Huge, James S.; Logan, Cecelia J.; Maynard, William; Monasmith, James; Olivero, James; Schmuck, Richard A.; Shaheen, Thomas A.; and Stegeman, William H. 1974. *School climate improvements: a challenge to the school administrator.* Belmont, Calif.: Fearon.

Gentry, Joe E., and Watkins, J. Foster. 1974. Organizational training for improving race relations. In *Organizational development in urban school systems,* ed. C. Brooklyn Derr, pp. 138-52. Beverly Hills, Calif.: Sage.

Johnson, David W., and Johnson, Roger T. 1974. Instructional goal structure: cooperative, competitive, or individualistic. *Review of Educational Research* 44:213-40.

Jones, John E. 1973. A case study of a selected elementary school under conditions of planned change. In *The process of planned change,* ed. Charters, Jr. et al., pp. 53-65.

Kish, Leslie. 1965. *Survey sampling.* New York: Wiley.

Lansky, L.; Runkel, P. J.; Croft, J.; and MacGregor, C. 1969. *The effects of human relations training on diagnosing skills and planning for change.* Eugene, Ore.: Center for Educational Policy & Management. ERIC order no. ED 032 652.

Lighthall, F. F. 1973. Multiple realities and organizational nonsolutions: an essay on "Anatomy of educational innovation." *School Review* 81:255-93.

Murray, Donald G. 1973. Organizational development training for adopting multiunit structure: a comparative case study of two elementary schools. Ph.D. dissertation, University of Oregon.

Nelson, Jack E. 1971. Collegial supervision in multiunit schools: a study of an in-service program for primary teachers in newly formed units in schools which have received two forms of organization development training. Ph.D. dissertation, University of Oregon.

Nelson, Jack E.; Schwartz, Mitchell; and Schmuck, Richard A. 1974. *Collegial supervision: a substudy of organization development in multiunit schools.* Eugene, Ore.: Center for Educational Policy & Management.

NWREL-XICOM. 1970. *Interpersonal communication.* Tuxedo, N.Y.: Northwest Regional Educational Laboratory and Xicom.

Packard, John S. 1973. Changing to a multiunit school. In *The process of planned change*, ed. Charters, Jr. et al., pp. 105-21. Reprinted in 1975 in *Managing change in educational organizations*, ed. J. Victor Baldridge and Terrance E. Deal, pp. 393-408. Berkeley, Calif.: McCutchan.

Phelps, Jane H., and Arends, Richard I. 1973. Helping parents and educators to solve school problems together: an application of organization development. Mimeographed. Eugene, Ore.: Center for Educational Policy & Management.

Runkel, Philip J. 1975. Innovations: how long do they last? In *Organizational specialists in a school district*, ed. Philip J. Runkel, Spencer H. Wyant, and Warren E. Bell, chapter 8. Eugene, Ore.: Center for Educational Policy & Management.

—————. 1974. Personal and organizational pain. In *1974 annual handbook for group facilitators*, ed. J. William Pfeiffer and John E. Jones, pp. 148-49. San Diego: University Associates.

Runkel, Philip J., and McGrath, Joseph E. 1972. *Research on human behavior: a systematic guide to method.* New York: Holt, Rinehart & Winston.

Runkel, Philip J.; Wyant, Spencer H.; and Bell, Warren E. 1975. *Organizational specialists in a school district: four years of innovation.* Eugene, Ore.: Center for Educational Policy & Management. ERIC order no. 111 107.

Sarason, Seymour B. 1971. *The culture of the school and the problem of change.* Boston: Allyn & Bacon.

Sarason, Esther K., and Sarason, Seymour B. 1969. Some observations on the teaching of the new math. In *The Yale Psychoeducational Clinic: collected papers and studies*, ed. S. B. Sarason and F. Kaplan. Boston: State Department of Mental Health, Monograph Series.

Saturen, Steve Leon. 1972. On the way to adaptability: some conditions for organizational self-renewal in elementary schools. Ph.D. dissertation, University of Oregon.

Schmuck, Richard A.; Murray, Donald; Smith, Mary Ann; Schwartz, Mitchell; and Runkel, Margaret. 1975. *Consultation for innovative schools: OD for multiunit structure.* Eugene, Ore.: Center for Educational Policy & Management.

Schmuck, Richard A., and Runkel, Philip J. 1970. *Organizational training for a school faculty.* Eugene, Ore.: Center for the Advanced Study of Educational Administration.

Schmuck, Richard A., and Schmuck, Patricia A. 1975. *Group processes in the classroom.* 2d ed. Dubuque, Iowa: Brown.

Seeman, Alice Z., and Seeman, Melvin. 1976. Staff processes and pupil attitudes: a study of teacher participation in educational change. *Human Relations* 29:25-40.

Simon, Anita, and Boyer, E. G., eds. 1967. *Mirrors for behavior.* Philadelphia: Research for Better Schools.

Simons, David L. 1974. Durability of organizational training for a school faculty. Ph.D. dissertation, University of Oregon.

Smith, Louis M., and Keith, Pat M. 1971. *Anatomy of educational innovation: an organizational analysis of an elementary school.* New York: Wiley.

Smith, Mary Ann. 1972. A comparison of two elementary schools involved in a major organizational change: or, you win a few, you lose a few. Ph.D. dissertation, University of Oregon.

Snyder, Wadell D., and Runkel, Philip J. 1975. Can teachers be trained to change?: some effects of teacher training on teacher-student interactions as assessed by Flanders' categories. *Classroom Interaction* 10(2):19-31.

Stake, Robert E. 1973. Program evaluation, particularly responsive evaluation. Paper presented at Conference on New Trends in Evaluation at Göteberg, Sweden, October 1973. Center for Instructional Research and Curriculum Evaluation, University of Illinois at Urbana-Champaign, November 1975.

Starling, William. 1973. An unsuccessful attempt to implement an educational innovation: a case study. Ph.D. dissertation, University of Oregon.

Thomas, Terry A. 1970. Changes in elementary school principals as a result of laboratory training. Technical report no. 5. Eugene, Ore.: Center for Educational Policy & Management. ERIC order no. ED 041 368.

Tompkins, Russel; Seegerger, Joan; Winger, Jane; Dunn, Etna; Essig, Don; and Rutter, Roy. 1971. Final report on "Operation Jump": a program designed to give first-grade children a better jump on their school experiences and activities. Mimeographed. Report to the Superintendent of School District 4J of Eugene, Oregon, 29 September 1971.

Wacaster, C. Thompson. 1973. The life and death of differentiated staffing at Columbia High School. In *The process of planned change,* ed. Charters, Jr. et al., pp. 35-51.

Wyant, Spencer H. 1974. The effects of organization development training on intrastaff communications in elementary schools. Ph.D. dissertation, University of Oregon.

————. 1973. A four-year-old organizational innovation in a school district: will it survive? Mimeographed. Paper presented at a Symposium entitled "Results of Establishing a Cadre of Organizational Specialists in a School District," at the Pacific Northwest Educational Research and Evaluation Conference, May 1973, in Seattle, Washington. Also presented at the Convention of the Oregon Psychological Association, May 1973, in Bend, Oregon.

————. 1972. Organizational development from the inside: a progress report of the first cadre of organizational specialists. CASEA Technical Report no. 12. Eugene, Ore.: Center for Educational Policy & Management. ERIC order no. ED 061 596.

Notes to Chapter 12

Arends, Jane H. 1975. Organization development for the staff, parents, and students of an urban junior high school: a case study. Ph.D. dissertation, University of Oregon.

Arends, Richard I., and Phelps, Jane H. 1973. Establishing organizational specialists within school districts. Mimeographed. Eugene, Ore.: Center for Educational Policy & Management.

Arends, Richard I.; Phelps, Jane H.; Harris, Martha; and Schmuck, Richard A. 1973. *Organization development: building human systems in schools.* Audio-slide presentation. Eugene, Ore.: Center for Educational Policy & Management.

Flynn, C. Wayne. 1971. The principal as an organizational consultant to his own school. Ph.D. dissertation, University of Oregon.

Macbeth, Paul R. 1971. Preparing organizational specialists for a school district: some effects of laboratory training with an organizational development project. Ph.D. dissertation, University of Oregon.

Runkel, Philip J., and Phelps, Jane H. 1973. Description of the cadre component in the Willard Organization Development Project. Mimeographed. Eugene, Ore.: Center for Educational Policy & Management.

Runkel, Philip J.; Wyant, Spencer H.; and Bell, Warren E. 1975. *Organizational specialists in a school district: four years of innovation*. Eugene, Ore: Center for Educational Policy & Management.

Saturen, Steven Leon. 1972. On the way to adaptability: some conditions for organizational self-renewal in elementary schools. Ph.D. dissertation, University of Oregon.

Schmuck, Richard. 1977. Peer consultation for school improvement. In *Advances in experimental social processes*, ed. Cary Cooper and Clayton Alderfer, forthcoming. New York: Wiley.

Schmuck, Richard A., and Miles, Matthew B., eds. 1971. *Organization development in schools*. Palo Alto, Calif.: National Press Books. 1976. La Jolla, Calif.: University Associates.

Schmuck, Richard A.; Murray, Donald; Smith, Mary Ann; Schwartz, Mitchell; and Runkel, Margaret. 1975. *Consultation for innovative schools: OD for multiunit structure*. Eugene, Ore.: Center for Educational Policy & Management.

Schmuck, Richard A., and Runkel, Philip J. 1972. Integrating organizational specialists into school districts. In *Contemporary organization development: conceptual orientations and interventions*, ed. W. W. Burke, pp. 168–200. Washington, D.C.: NTL Institute for Applied Behavioral Science. ERIC order no. ED 061 617.

Schmuck, Richard A.; Runkel, Philip J.; and Blondino, Charles. 1970. Organizational specialists in a school district. CEPM-CASEA Technical Report no. 11. Eugene, Ore.: Center for Educational Policy & Management. ERIC order no. ED 043 973.

Schmuck, Richard A.; Runkel, Philip J.; Saturen, Steven L.; Martell, Ronald T.; and Derr, C. Brooklyn. 1972. *Handbook of organization development in schools*. Palo Alto, Calif.: National Press Books.

Wyant, Spencer H. 1973. A four-year-old organizational innovation in a school district: will it survive? Mimeographed. Paper presented at a Symposium entitled "Results of Establishing a Cadre of Organizational Specialists in a School District," at the Pacific Northwest Educational Research and Evaluation Conference, May 1973, in Seattle, Washington.

————. 1972. Organization development from the inside: a progress report on the first cadre of organizational specialists. CASEA Technical Report no. 12. Eugene, Ore.: Center for Educational Policy & Management. ERIC order no. ED 061 596.

Name Index

Subject Index

Academic achievement, evaluating, 466-471
Academic haves and have-nots, 468-471
Accountability, 163-164
Achievement, assessing satisfaction of need for, 477-478
Achievement motive, 13-14, 375-376, 427
Activity, assessing satisfaction of need for, 478
Activity motive, 13-14, 375-376
Adaptability. *See* Organizational adaptability
Adaptation, mutual, 276, 439, 440
Affiliation, assessing satisfaction of need for, 478-479
Affiliation motive, 13-14, 376-, 427-428
Agenda. *See* Meetings
Assessing changes, 20-21
Assessing designs, 61-62
Assessing progress, results, or outcomes. *See* Evaluation
Audio recording procedure, 105

Base-line data, 44
Bases of social power, 320-321

Beach ball, procedure, 263
Beckhard on goal-confrontation, conferences, 177-179
Behavior description, 95-96, 424, 430, 438-439; exercise in, 119-120
Behavioral objectives, 184-187
Billy-goat, warm-up, 251-428
Blind Walk, 423
Brainstorming, 269, 427
Buzz groups, procedure to encourage participation, 263-264

Cadres of organizational specialists, 154, 390-391, 527-548; assessing readiness for, 527-532; consultant-client relationships in, 541-542; cross-role representatives in, 543; differentiation and integration in, 541; follow-up of training, 537; in Eugene, Oregon, 527-538; in Kent, Washington, 527-548; intervention strength of, 538-540, maintenance and renewal, 537-545; membership replacement in, 543-545; on-the-job practicum for, 537; services of, 546; support, 542; training of, 532-536